SO-BCW-565

Critical Passions

POST-CONTEMPORARY INTERVENTIONS

SERIES EDITORS: STANLEY FISH AND FREDRIC JAMESON

JEAN FRANCO

Critical Passions

SELECTED ESSAYS

EDITED, AND WITH AN

INTRODUCTION BY

MARY LOUISE PRATT AND

KATHLEEN NEWMAN

Duke University Press

Durham and London

1999

© 1999 Duke University Press
All rights reserved
Printed in the United States of
America on acid-free paper ⊗
Typeset in Janson by Tseng
Information Systems, Inc.
Library of Congress Cataloging-in-
Publication Data appear on the last
printed page of this book.

CONTENTS

Acknowledgments, vii

Introduction: The Committed Critic by Mary Louise Pratt and Kathleen Newman, 1

1 FEMINISM AND THE CRITIQUE OF AUTHORITARIANISM

Killing Priests, Nuns, Women, Children (1985), 9

Gender, Death, and Resistance: Facing the Ethical Vacuum (1986), 18

"Manhattan Will Be More Exotic This Fall": The Iconization of Frida Kahlo (1991), 39

Going Public: Reinhabiting the Private (1992), 48

La Malinche: From Gift to Sexual Contract (1992), 66

The *Finezas* of Sor Juana (1993), 83

From Romance to Refractory Aesthetic (1996), 97

The Mares of the Apocalypse (1996), 109

The Gender Wars (1996), 123

2 MASS AND POPULAR CULTURE

A Not-So-Romantic Journey: British Travelers to South America, 1818–28 (1979), 133

Narrator, Author, Superstar: Latin American Narrative in the Age of Mass Culture (1981), 147

What's in a Name? Popular Culture Theories and Their Limitations (1982), 169

High-Tech Primitivism: The Representation of Tribal Societies in Feature Films (1993), 181

What's Left of the Intelligentsia? The Uncertain Future of the Printed Word (1994), 196

Globalization and the Crisis of the Popular (1996), 208

Making Differences, Shifting Boundaries (1994), 221

3 LATIN AMERICAN LITERATURE: THE BOOM AND BEYOND

Reading Vargas Llosa: Conversation Is Not Dialogue (1971), 233

Lezama Lima in the Paradise of Poetry (1974), 239

The Crisis of the Liberal Imagination and the Utopia of Writing (1976-1977), 259

From Modernization to Resistance: Latin American Literature, 1959-1976 (1978), 285

Dependent Industrialization and Onetti's *The Shipyard* (1980), 311

The Utopia of a Tired Man: Jorge Luis Borges (1981), 327

Self-Destructing Heroines (1984), 366

Satire and the Dialogues of the Dead: Diachronic Discourse in *I the Supreme* (1986), 379

Pastiche in Contemporary Latin American Literature (1990), 393

Comic Stripping: Cortázar in the Age of Mechanical Reproduction (1997), 405

4 MEXICO

Journey to the Land of the Dead: Rulfo's *Pedro Páramo* (1974), 429

Dominant Ideology and Literature: The Case of Post-Revolutionary Mexico (1976), 447

Women, Fashion, and the Moralists in Early-Nineteenth-Century Mexico (1984), 461

Waiting for a Bourgeoisie: The Formation of the Mexican Intelligentsia in the Age of Independence (1986), 476

Deluded Women (1996), 493

Afterword: The Twilight of the Vanguard and the Rise of Criticism (1994-1995), 503

Biographical Note, 517

Index, 519

ACKNOWLEDGMENTS

The editors would like to express their gratitude to Soledad Gelles, our outstanding lead editorial assistant, and the many research assistants and translators who contributed to the preparation of the manuscript: Carla Faini, Nancy Hanway, Patricia Heid, Milos Kokotovic, Carmiña Palerm, Iván Páez, and Nohemy Solórzano. We would like to express our gratitude and appreciation as well to Ken Wissoker, Richard Morrison, Jean Brady, and Amy Ruth Buchanan of Duke University Press for their support for this project.

Where bibliographic information was incomplete in the original text, the editors have attempted to correct omissions, although some variation in documentation style remains. Some minor textual corrections were made in the articles and English translations have been supplied for all articles and quotations originally in Spanish.

INTRODUCTION: THE COMMITTED CRITIC

Mary Louise Pratt and Kathleen Newman

Jean Franco is widely known in North and South America and Europe as a literary scholar, a Latin Americanist, a feminist, an interdisciplinary theorist, and an engaged scholar on the Left. Over three decades and across three continents, her career is distinguished by her politics of engagement—the engagement of a critic committed to the serious study of print texts and other cultural artifacts and practices, to the democratization of knowledge and the transformation of educational and cultural institutions, to an ongoing dialogue with a broad range of interlocutors—artists, intellectuals, activists, politicians—regarding politics and the politics of culture. Yet, Franco has never brought together in one volume her most important essays of the last quarter-century, a matter this volume proposes to remedy. To complement her five books, *The Modern Culture of Latin America* (1967), *An Introduction to Spanish American Literature* (1969), *A Literary History of Spain and Spanish American, Volume IV* (1972), *César Vallejo: The Dialectics of Poetry and Silence* (1976), *Plotting Women: Gender and Representation in Mexico* (1989), and *Marcar diferencias, cruzar fronteras* (1996), we have gathered (and, where necessary, translated) and ordered chronologically her essays on four interrelated topics: feminism and the critique of authoritarianism (part 1), mass and popular culture (part 2), Latin American literature from the "boom" onward (part 3), and Mexican literature and culture (part 4). These essays chronicle the development over some two decades of cultural studies, gender studies, and Latin American literary studies—areas of critical debate in which Franco has played a major role—and offer the trajectory of Franco's thinking, including her most recent publications of the 1990s.

Reviewing Franco's publications for this volume, it soon became evident to us that her work exhibits an impressive capacity for synthesis. Indeed, few critics share Franco's capacity to conceptualize and define the big picture without losing sight of the fact that this picture is known through its details: a text, a song, an advertisement, graffiti, a Puerto Rican funeral.

For the reader, the richness of the argument increases insofar as he or she is able to bring to bear other materials or practices, which fit, or fail to fit, into the scheme Franco proposes. This may seem obvious, but Franco's ability to tack constantly back and forth between the general and the particular is rare and highly effective both as an expository style and as a methodological commitment.

In his remarks on Franco's work at the Latin American Studies Association International Congress in Washington, D.C., in 1995, Mexican writer Carlos Monsiváis described Franco as being "sin eurocentrismo alguno" [entirely without eurocentricism] and compared Franco with the Dominican critic Pedro Henríquez Ureña, who, in the first half of the century, was one of the founders of "Latin America" as a cultural concept and a critical category. The comparison arises from Franco's three important literary histories and from her ability to trace emergent cultural problematics. Indeed, it was Franco who offered the decisive insight situating the novelist of the boom between the oral storyteller of popular culture and the star of mass media productions. These two formations, popular culture and mass media, are never absent from Franco's literary and cultural analysis, and their presence constitutes one of the most distinctive aspects of her work and of her method. Like Angel Rama, Franco seeks out the pathways where lettered, popular, and mass media cultures intersect, clash, determine, or appropriate each other. This serious and constant attention to popular culture and its participants represents a key dimension of Franco's political and cultural commitment. Elite culture in her work is conceded neither the superiority nor the autonomy that the institutions of culture seek to attribute to it.

Franco has developed, and insisted on, the ability to reflect on and judge with equal seriousness all spheres of expression, whether a subway graffiti or an avant-garde poem. One of the secrets behind this capacity is the fact that Franco is a fan of popular culture and mass media, attending to them wherever she goes or lives. Her critiques are thus never puritanical or reductive, and always valorize whatever might be the resistant or contestatory dimensions of popular and mass culture. For those of us who in the early 1980s worked with Franco on the magazine *Tabloid: A Review of Mass Culture and Everyday Life*, nothing could have been more exciting than the collective challenge of learning to reflect on popular culture, media, and the semiotics and practices of everyday life. Equally exciting were the challenges the group posed itself: first, to find humorous and ludic forms for confronting the anguishing upheavals of Reaganism and, second, to find ways to present theoretical discussion in a direct and accessible language.

In preparing this volume we also realized that these essays include something close to a full-fledged cultural history of Mexico, where Franco spent several crucial years of her life. In a series of essays on Mexico begun in the 1970s, we see Franco introduce the themes and methods of what would later be referred to as cultural studies. The British Marxists Raymond Williams and E. P. Thompson are key figures here, yet Franco goes beyond them with an aggressive and new intervention in both content and method: she introduces gender as a basic category of analysis and demonstrates the consequences. Her book *Plotting Women: Gender and Representation in Mexico* can be read as a large-scale methodological experiment whose point of entry is the referent. As its readers know, each chapter of this ground-breaking book begins with a female historical personage, and ends up proposing not simply a correction, but a reconceptualization of the historical record. Franco is waging what she herself, speaking of the *testimonio*, called a "struggle for interpretive power." It was in the context of this struggle, specifically in relation to the Latin American Studies Association, that Franco founded the Seminar on Feminism and Culture in Latin America (based at Stanford and Berkeley) in 1979, whose work continues uninterrupted today.

In her recent *Marcar diferencias, cruzar fronteras*, a collection of the set of essays she wrote in response to the intellectual and political imperative posed by the authoritarian regimes in Argentina, Chile, Uruguay, and Brazil, Franco elaborates from a feminist perspective a brilliant critique of authoritarianism and an analysis of the oppositional movements that worked in the social and semiotic openings unintentionally created by the regimes. Two key concepts in particular stand out: ethics and survival. Ethics is proposed not as a weak form of morality, but as a structure of thought and values tied to practice and capable of exerting epistemological force against the extreme instrumentality of the regimes; survival is proposed not as a minimal state, but as a powerful analytical and existential category brought into view by the clashes between authoritarianism and the gender system. Defined by common sense as a state implying the absence of culture, reflection, consciousness, and heroism, survival became the point of entry for a reconceptualization of agency. Through the gendered analysis of authoritarianism, survival acquires content as an existential, analytical, and, as Franco observes, ethical category. It becomes necessary to redefine survival in positive terms, over and against other negatives: survival versus social disintegration, versus ethnocide, versus victimization, death, passivity.

More clearly than any others, these essays on authoritarianism express the passions that drive Franco's intellectual work: an implacable critique of the depredations of capitalism, of sexual and racial hierarchy and the forms of violence that sustain them, of domination and structured inequality, of consumer society and the impoverished values it disseminates, erasing alternatives. Alongside ethics there is another category that is central to Franco's critical posture: referentiality. She insists on the right to treat representations as representations of something. For example, criticizing the mystifications of Werner Herzog, she invokes "the historical Fitzcarraldo." Reading Vargas Llosa's *El hablador* [The Storyteller], she corrects his distorted portrait of the famous Summer Institute of Linguistics. Testimony, she argues, is distinguished as a discourse by the fact that "there *is* a referent." Analyzing the figure of La Malinche, Franco insists on the importance of speculating on the historical person. Nor are Todorov and Greenblatt forgiven for the "sleight of hand by which conquest becomes mestizaje, a sleight of hand that effectively displaces attention from the mode of reproduction of colonial society to symbolic woman and, as always, helper, intermediary, intercessor and eventually . . . 'traitor' " (p. 68).

The role played by referentiality in Franco's work must be understood in relation to the ignorance of those of the metropolis whose interpretive power is such that they can authorize themselves to represent others as they please. In the essay "High-Tech Primitivism" Franco speaks of a series of films of the jungle (*Fitzcarraldo, The Mission,* and *The Emerald Forest*), condemning "this postmodern *indigenismo* [which] has developed in sublime ignorance of antecedents in Latin America where the conquest has remained such a haunting presence" (p. 190). For Franco, referentiality is still a weapon of preference against the North's ignorance and mystifications with respect to the South, against the abuses of interpretive power. Hence, her skepticism with respect to any metropolitan project that proposes to dissolve the referent in ways that legitimate this "sublime ignorance." Such versions of postmodernism generate cohesive explanations and convincing genealogies for phenomena of the most diverse character and origin, allowing the metropolis to claim and domesticate other traditions of knowledge and expression, especially contestatory or resistant traditions. If in the circle of interpretive power there is no one present to *refer* to what is *ignored*, hegemonic explanations can have the density to seem plausible and complete.

Because Franco's work does analyze, contextualize, and theorize art and politics with rigorous attention to history, she is one of the few European and U.S. scholars whose work on Latin America is considered essential reading in Latin America. In fact, her colleagues across these three decades and three continents know that Franco's presence at a conference, in a seminar, on a television program, in a workshop—whether in Buenos Aires or Havana, Bogotá or São Paulo, or London, Paris, Berlin, or Washington—is the assurance of incisive and erudite debate balanced by wit, humor, and humanity. The readers of these essays will appreciate the same qualities.

1 $\mathcal{F}$EMINISM AND THE CRITIQUE OF AUTHORITARIANISM

KILLING PRIESTS, NUNS, WOMEN, CHILDREN

The murder of three American nuns in El Salvador in December 1980, the murder of priests in Brazil and Argentina, the torture of pregnant women in Uruguay, the farming out of "terrorists'" children to military families in the Southern Cone, the admonitory raping of women in front of their families in several Latin American countries, the Mexican army's attack on unarmed male and female students in Tlatelolco in 1968, the recent kidnapping in broad daylight of a well-known writer, university teacher, and feminist, Alaíde Foppa in Guatemala, the dislodging of Indian communities from traditional lands, plus countless other incidents, all appear more and more to be the well-thought-out atrocities of a concerted offensive. It is part of a war that has pitted unequal forces against one another—on the one hand, the overarmed military who have become instruments of the latest stage of capitalist development and, on the other, not only the left but also certain traditional institutions, the Indian community, the family, and the Church (which still provides sanctuary and refuge for resistance). These institutions owe their effectiveness as refuges to historically based moral rights and traditions, rather like the immunities which (before the recent attack on the Spanish embassy in Guatemala) had accrued to diplomatic space. Homes were, of course, never immune from entry and search but until recently, it was generally males who were rounded up and taken away, often leaving women to carry on and even transmit resistance from one generation to another. Families thus inherited opposition as others inherited positions in the government and bureaucracy.

But what is now at stake is the assault on such formerly immune territories. The attack on the Cathedral in El Salvador in 1980 and the assassination of Archbishop Romero, for instance, showed how little the Church

Originally published in *On Signs*, ed. Marshall Blonsky (Baltimore: The Johns Hopkins University Press, 1985), 414–420.

could now claim to be a sanctuary. The resettlement of Indians in Guatemala, of working-class families from militant sectors of Buenos Aires, the destruction of the immunity formerly accorded to wives, mothers, children, nuns, and priests have all taken away every immune space. This assault is not as incompatible as it might at first seem with the military government's organization of its discourse around the sanctity of Church and family. Indeed these convenient abstractions, which once referred to well-defined physical spaces, have subtly shifted their range of meaning. Thus, for instance, the "saucepan" demonstrations of Chilean women during the last months of the Allende regime plainly indicated the emergence of the family as consumer in a society which, under Pinochet, was to acquire its symbolic monument—the spiral-shaped tower of the new labyrinthine shopping center. The Church, once clearly identified as the Catholic Church, and the parish as its territory, has now been replaced by a rather more flexible notion of religion. The conversion of massive sectors of the population all over Latin America to one form or another of Protestantism, the endorsement by Rios Montt, when President of Guatemala, of born-again Christianity, and the active encouragement, in other countries, of fundamentalist sects, all indicate a profound transformation which, until recently, had gone almost unnoticed. Radio and television now promote a serialized and privatized religious experience which no longer needs to be anchored in the physical reality of the parish and in the continuity of family life.

This process can be described as "deterritorialization," although I use this term in a sense rather different from that used by Deleuze and Guattari. In their view,[1] primitive society (the social machine) does not distinguish between the family and the rest of the social and political field, all of which are inscribed on the socius (that is, the social machine that distinguishes people according to status and affiliations). In the primitive tribe, the socius is the mother earth. What Deleuze and Guattari describe is a process of abstraction which takes place with the emergence of the despotic state that now inscribes people according to their residence, and in doing so "divides the earth as an object and subjects men to a new imperial inscription, in other words to the abstract unity of the State." This they call "pseudo-territoriality," and see it as the substitution of abstract signs (e.g., money) for the signs of the earth and a privatization of the earth itself (as state or private property). Advanced capitalism carries this abstraction much further, recoding persons and making repression into self-repression, exercised not only in the workplace and the streets but within the family, the one place under capitalism where desire can be coded and territorialized (as with Oedipus).

What seems unsatisfactory in Deleuze and Guattari's description of the family is that even though, reading these authors, we may recognize the family's restrictive and repressive qualities, we do not recognize the family's power as a space of refuge and shelter. What seduces us about the home (and what seduces some people about the convent) is that it is a refuge, a place for turning one's back on the world. Max Horkheimer saw (albeit in an idealized fashion) that the family could nourish subjectivities that were alien to capitalism. (Thomas Mann's *Buddenbrooks* is a good example of the subversive effects of the mother inculcating into her son all that will make him incapable of reproducing the work ethic.) In Latin America, this sense of refuge and the sacredness that attaches to certain figures like the mother, the virgin, the nun, and the priest acquire even greater significance, both because the Church and the home retained a traditional topography and traditional practices over a very long period, and also because during periods when the state was relatively weak these institutions were the only functioning social organizations. They were states within the state, or even counterstates, since there are certain parishes and certain families which have nourished traditions of resistance to the state and hold on to concepts of "moral right" (E. P. Thompson's term), which account for their opposition to "modernization" (i.e., integration into capitalism). This is not to say that the patriarchal and hierarchical family, whose priority was the reproduction of the social order, has not rooted itself in Latin American soil. But the family has been a powerful rival to the state, somehow more real, often the source of a maternal power which is by no means to be despised, particularly when, as in contemporary Latin America, the disappearance of political spaces has turned the family (and the mother, in particular) into a major institution of resistance.

It is only by recognizing the traditional power of the family and the Church and the association of this power with a particular space (the home, the Church building) that we can begin to understand the significance of recent events in Latin America. Beginning in the fifties and early sixties, "development" brought new sectors of the population, including women, into the labor force. The expansion of transnational companies into Latin America depended on the pool of cheap labor formed from the uprooted peasantry and the ever-growing sector of urban underclasses. The smooth functioning of this new industrial revolution was imperiled by the guerrilla movements and movements of national liberation which, in turn, confronted the counterinsurgency campaigns of the sixties that "modernized" the armies of Latin America, making them pioneers in the newest of torture methods and inventive masters of the art of "disappearance." It is this counterinsurgency movement which has destroyed both the notion of sacred space and the immunity which, in theory if not in practice, belonged to nuns, priests, women, and children.

Though women have never enjoyed complete immunity from state terror—indeed rape has been the casually employed resource of forces of law and order since the Conquest—the rapidity with which the new governments have been able to take immunity away from the traditional institutions of Church and family calls for explanation. Such an explanation would involve understanding not only the particular incidents mentioned at the beginning of this essay, but the profound consequences of destroying what Bachelard, in *The Poetics of Space*, called the "images of felicitous spaces," or topophilia. Bachelard's investigations "seek to determine the human value of the sorts of space that may be grasped, that may be defended against adverse forces, the space we love. For diverse reasons, and with the differences entailed by poetic shadings, this is eulogized space. Attached to its protective value, which can be a positive one, are also imagined values, which soon become dominant."[2] In this essay, I want to give these felicitous spaces a more concrete and historical existence than Bachelard's phenomenology allows, for only in this way can we understand the really extraordinary sacrilege that we are now witnessing.

Although it is impossible to separate the literary from the social, literature is a good place to begin to understand this Latin American imaginary with its clearly demarcated spaces. In common with Mediterranean countries, public space in Latin America was strictly separated from the private space of the house (brothel), home and convent, that is spaces which were clearly marked as "feminine." These spaces gave women a certain territorial but restricted power base and at the same time offered the "felicitous" spaces for the repose of the warrior. Nothing illustrates this better than the description of the return of José Arcadio Buendía's blood to its place of origin in his mother's kitchen in García Márquez's *One Hundred Years of Solitude*. The thread of blood "passed along the street of the Turks, turned a corner to the right and another to the left, made a right angle at the Buendía house, went in under the closed door, crossed through the parlor, hugging the walls so as not to stain the rugs, went on to the other living room, made a wide curve to avoid the dining-room table, went along the porch with the begonias, and passed without being seen under Amaranta's

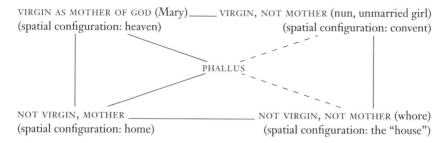

Figure 1

chair as she gave an arithmetic lesson to Aureliano José, and went through the pantry and came out in the kitchen, where Ursula was getting ready to crack thirty-six eggs to make bread."

The blood of one of the most *macho* of the Buendías thus follows the order of "feminine" domesticity, traces its path through the women's peaceful and comforting everyday activities which stand in stark opposition to the male world of physical and intellectual prowess and war (the virile or in its most recent and reduced game-cock version—the *macho*).

To view the home thus as a sanctuary obviously makes it into a male-idealized otherness (the utopia) while locking women into this pacific domesticity. House, home, and convent are undoubtedly constructions produced by a sex-gender system in which feminine categories are organized in relation to the presence/absence of the phallus, understood in this case as the source of symbolic power. The "logic" of this organization can be illustrated by a semiotic quadrangle (see figure 1).

Because there can only be one mother of God (Mary), all other women fall into one of the three remaining categories of which only one (the mother) can receive the legitimate seed that will allow the system to be reproduced. The extent to which the mother is not only sanctified by this function but is converted into the temple of the species, whose bodily configuration is identical to that of the home, is illustrated in a poem by César Vallejo. Imagining his return to the family home, his mother's body is re-entered as if it were a building:

> Your archways of astonishment expects me,
> The tonsured columns of your cares
> That have eroded life. The patio expects me
> The hallway down below with its indentures and
> its feast-day decorations. My grandfather chair expects me

> that good jowly piece of dynastic leather,
> that stands grumbling at the strapped and strapping
> behind of great great great grandchildren.

The father alone has the right to enter this temple and when he does so, it is on his knees in acknowledgment of an irreversible event.

> Between the colonnade of your bones
> That cannot be brought down even with lamentations
> And into whose side not even Destiny can
> place a single finger!

The reference in the last line is to the doubting finger of Thomas who wished to test the resurrection of Christ by touching the wound. In Vallejo's human mother/temple, no such doubt is possible, for the matrix offers the only unequivocal faith in a chaotic world.

The very structure of the Hispanic house emphasized that it was a private world, shut off from public activity. It was traditionally constructed around two or more patios, the windows onto the street being shuttered or barred. Inside, the patios with their plants and singing birds represented an oasis, a domestic replica of the perfumed garden. Respectable women only emerged from the house when accompanied and when necessary. Their lives were almost as enclosed as those of their counterparts, the brothel whore and the nun. In the fifties, I lived in such a house where windows onto the outside were felt to mark the beginning of danger as indeed, after curfew, they did. A prison yes, but one that could easily be idealized as a sanctuary given the violence of political life.

The convent was also a sanctuary of sorts, one that gathered into itself the old, the homeless, and the dedicated to God. In José Donoso's novel *The Obscene Bird of Night*, the convent has become an extended building housing the archaic, the mythic, and the hallucinating desires which are outlawed from the rest of society. It is this aspect of the Hispanic imaginary which Buñuel's films also capture. Archaic in topography, its huge, empty, decrepit rooms not only sealed it off entirely from the outside world but made it into a taboo territory, the violation of which tempted and terrorized the male imagination.

Finally there was the brothel, the house whose topography mimed that of the convent, with its small, cell-like rooms and which, as described by Mario Vargas Llosa in his novel *The Green House*, was another version of the oasis. As the convent gathered to itself the women who were no longer sexual objects, the green house offered them as the common receptacles of a male seed absolved from the strict social rules that governed reproduction.

> Blacks, mulattoes, mixtures of all kinds, drunks, somnolent or frightened half-breeds, skinny Chinese, old men, small groups of young Spaniards and Italians walking through the patios out of curiosity. They walked to and fro passing the open doors of the bedrooms, stopping to look in from time to time. The prostitutes, dressed in cotton dresses were seated at the back of the rooms on low boxes. Most of them sat with their legs apart showing their sex, the "fox" which was sometimes shaved and sometimes not.[3]

In describing these spaces, I am not describing categories of women but an imaginary topography in which the "feminine" was rigidly compartmentalized and assigned particular territories. Individual women constantly transgressed these boundaries but the territories themselves were loaded with significance and so inextricably bound to the sacred that they were often taken for spaces of immunity. With the increase in state terrorism in the sixties, mothers used this traditional immunity to protest, abandoning the shelter of homes for the public square, taking charge of the dead, the disappeared, and the prisoners whose existence no one else wished to acknowledge. With the seizure of power by the military, the dismantling of political parties and trade unions, this activity acquired a special importance. Homes became hiding places, bomb factories, escape hatches, people's prisons. From the signifier of passivity and peace, mother became a signifier of resistance. Nothing illustrates this in more dramatic fashion than an article by Rodolfo Walsh (an Argentine writer who would himself "disappear" shortly after writing this piece). His daughter, who was the mother of a small child and whose lover had already disappeared, was one of a group of *montoneros* killed in the army attack on a house, an attack which deployed 150 men, tanks, and helicopters. A soldier who had participated in this battle described the girl's final moments,

> The battle lasted more than an hour and a half. A man and woman were shooting from upstairs. The girl caught our attention because every time she fired and we dodged out of the way, she laughed. All at once there was silence. The girl let go of the machine gun, stood up on the parapet and opened her arms. We stopped firing without being ordered to and we could see her quite well. She was skinny, with short

hair and she was wearing a nightdress. She began to talk to us calmly but clearly. I don't remember everything she said, but I remember the last sentence. In fact, I could not sleep for thinking of it. "You are not killing us," she said, "we choose to die." Then she and the man put pistols to their foreheads and killed themselves in front of us.

When the army took over the house, they found a little girl sitting unharmed on the bed and five dead bodies.

The significance of such an event goes far beyond the rights and wrongs of local politics. Like the murder of the nuns in El Salvador and the kidnapping and killing of Alaíde Foppa in Guatemala, it is a cataclysmic event which makes it impossible to think of the utopian in terms of space or of the feminine in the traditional sense. Most disconcerting of all, the destruction of these utopian spaces has been conducted not by the left but by the right-wing military who have nothing left to offer but the unattainable commodity (unattainable, that is, for all but the army and the technocrats). It is true that the military of some Southern-Cone countries are now in (temporary?) eclipse, but the smell of the cadaver will not be dispelled by the commodity culture, a debt-ridden economy, and the forms of restored political democracy.

It is some time since Herbert Marcuse drew attention to the terrors of a desublimated world, one in which such spaces and sanctuaries had been wiped out. His analysis and that of Horkheimer can be seen as overburdened with nostalgia for that *gemütlich* interior of European bourgeois family life in which all the children played instruments in a string quartet. But even if we can no longer accept the now challenged Freudian language of his analysis, he undoubtedly deserves credit for monitoring the first signals from an empty space once occupied by archaic but powerful figures. Feminist criticism based on the critique of patriarchy and the traffic in women has rightly shed no tears for this liquidation of mother figures whose power was also servitude. Yet such criticism has perhaps underestimated the oppositional potentialities of these female territories whose importance as the *only* sanctuaries became obvious at the moment of their disappearance.

This is, however, an essay without a conclusion. I wrote it thinking of my old friend, Alaíde Foppa, who in 1954 provided sanctuary for those of us left behind in Guatemala and trying to get out after the Castillo Armas coup. I have a vivid memory of her reciting a poem about her five children "like the five fingers of her hand." Today there are only three children left. During the 1960s and 1970s, Alaíde became the driving force behind the feminist movement in Mexico. She was used to going back home once a year to Guatemala to visit her mother. In 1980 she did not come back. A Guatemalan newspaper reported that her whereabouts and that of her chauffeur were "unknown." To this day, Alaíde "continues disappeared" in the words of the newspaper, like many other men, women, priests, nuns, and children in Latin America who no longer occupy space but who have a place.

NOTES

1 See Gilles Deleuze and Félix Guattari, *Anti-Oedipus: Capitalism and Schizophrenia* (New York: Viking Press, 1977).
2 Gaston Bachelard, *The Poetics of Space* (New York: Orion Press, 1964), xxxiii.
3 José María Arguedas, *El zorro de arriba y el zorro de abajo* (Buenos Aires: Losada, 1971), 50. My translation.

GENDER, DEATH, AND RESISTANCE

Facing the Ethical Vacuum

O
bsession with the cadaver is everywhere in the culture of advanced capitalism. These cadavers—white punk faces, video images of putrefying flesh, film images of the living dead on shopping mall escalators, the skull underneath the cigarette advertisement, images of emaciated Africans in a world hunger rock concert, Pina Bausch dances that resemble catatonic attacks, or the jerky galvanized body of dead animals—do not indicate a real relationship with the dead, but rather one in which the dead body has become just another part of the imaginary repertoire. In the film *Under Fire* the body of the guerrilla hero can be made to seem alive by the photographer protagonist who is thus able to salvage the Sandinista revolution, which appears to depend for its success on a single charismatic figure. In a society like that in the United States, in which you mark on your driver's license the organ you are going to transplant as if anticipating the car accident that will yield your liver to another temporary recipient, death is a grisly form of exchange and not a relationship with the sacred. This fascination with the cadaver especially when it surfaces in either "primitive" or high-tech guise contributes to the apocalyptic sensation of what is now usually described as the postmodern age—postmodern being essentially the style made possible by the information explosion and technological possibilities of late capitalism.

Modernism's other has been created out of binary polarities of civilized/uncivilized, mechanical/spontaneous, intellectual/vital, modern/primitive. Postmodernism rejects these binary arrangements and has recourse to pastiche rather than opposition, celebration rather than irony.[1] It is characterized, above all, by its negation of positionality and of ethical standpoints that depend on supposedly fixed relationships of race, gender, or class. Yet "liberation" from these in advanced capitalist countries does not remove the other but rather leaves death as the ultimate other which,

Originally published in *Chicago Review* 35, no. 4 (1986): 59–79.

because of its "unrepresentability" can be shown only through these play-ful simulations of death. What Robert Jay Lifton terms "symbolic immor-tality" has gone out of style.[2] There are exceptions of course. One would like to have been present at Lacan's later seminars in which he brooded aloud on the relation between the living and the dead.[3]

The problem is that by freely using all traditions and all existing histo-ries, postmodernism seems to participate in a general process of depoliti-cization which turns even death into an aesthetic experience. Of course, we cannot appeal to "real experience" or "raw experience" as an alternative to this distancing and this refusal to evaluate, since all experience is con-structed and structured within discourses and practices. However, we can distinguish between creative acts shaped by a moral imagination. We can see that for the mothers of the disappeared in El Salvador photographing the dead is certainly not an aesthetic experience and that the action of the women who chain themselves to the railings of the Chamber of Deputies in Chile is not a mere performance.

Postmodernism's problem when confronted with death and disappear-ance can best be illustrated by Joan Didion's *Salvador*,[4] a book which scru-pulously attempts to confront terror second-hand without falling into a fruitless denunciatory prose. For Didion, who has not been tortured, who is not a Central American, and who can take a plane out of the country, terror has to be seized through its traces—in photographs, at sites where bodies once had been, as a series of surface juxtapositions of everyday life which produces horror because of its apparent normality. Perhaps the most significant passage in the book occurs during a visit to the supermarket with its cornucopia of consumer goods offered to middle-class housewives and its array of comfortingly familiar items like Camay soap and Johnson's baby powder. For Didion, it is no longer possible to extract any irony out of juxtaposition of consumer abundance and terror. "As I wrote it down," she says, "I realized that I was no longer much interested in this kind of irony, that this was a story that would not be illuminated by such details, that this was a story that would perhaps not be illuminated at all, that was perhaps even less a 'story' than a true *noche oscura*. As I waited to cross back over the Boulevard de los Héroes to the *Camino Real*, I noticed sol-diers herding a young civilian into a van, their guns at the boy's back, and I walked ahead, not wanting to see anything at all."[5]

This is an incredibly revealing passage, not only for what it says about Joan Didion but for what it says about the metropolitan relationship to the Third World in general. We go there to "see," but we cannot be illuminated because there is no longer a standpoint from which metropolitan people can see the world without being patronizing, without striking empty rhetorical poses, without pretense. It is this kind of "pudeur" which stands in the way of ethical creativity. It is this kind of ascesis, the withdrawal from moral action, which led Habermas to link postmodernism and poststructuralism to neoconservative thought and led pillars of postmodernism— Roland Barthes and Michel Foucault—to become more and more concerned with the ethical problems posed by contemporary society.

THE OTHER ETHICAL VACUUM: PEOPLE AS "RAW MATERIAL"

Postmodernism incorporates death into its imaginary repertoire as an unevaluated statement. In doing so, it offers the once-repressed face of the modern state in which death had been rendered invisible. The fact is that death happens to individuals, and the individual has long ceased to exist for the modern state, having been reduced to a series of separable functions. In a recent book, *The Year 2000*, Raymond Williams argues that this is a "logical extension of certain ways of seeing, according to which the world is regarded as a range of opportunities for their profitable exploitation."[6] He further argues that because of this people themselves have now become raw material in both capitalist and communist societies. "What is most totalitarian about the now dominant orientation is its extension beyond the basic system of an extraction of labour to a practical invasion of the whole human personality."[7]

More than an "invasion of the whole human personality," what has taken place is a splitting of any concept of identity—which accounts for the fact that all forms of secular humanism have found that the very individual on which their philosophy has depended has been dissolved. The "individual" could not survive the desacralization of the human body which, from the nineteenth century, became the object of experiment and technical control. This body was no longer a microcosm of the holy world but a machine whose parts could be separately studied and managed. The subject is now no longer an individual in the old sense, not even a ghost in the machine, but rather a kind of manager whose task is to prevent disfunction. When the manager is not efficient and the state ideological apparatuses cannot work, then society can tinker with the mind—either officially as in the many experiments in mind control carried out in the United States or semi-officially as in the death camps of Chile and Argentina.

One object of these experiments was to bypass language, that is why they aimed at wiping out "experience" or personal history; they are also indifferent to gender. The manners in which masculine and feminine are constituted are of no interest to the electrode implanters.

The use of electroshock in torture is significant insofar as it suggests the application of mind control in states of emergency. It is, however, true that electroshock torture developed logically from police methods of prisoner interrogation which seem to have been rationalized in the United States between 1930 and 1933 as the "third degree." Before electroshock, third degree used all the modern methods of torture but failed to attain "deep seated psychological zones." Proponents of this form of interrogation, therefore, first investigated the use of chemicals to change the person from within. However, in the United States, police methods came under intense scrutiny because of democratic processes (even though third-degree methods and even torture with electric prods are still used). Meanwhile, in the Soviet Union psychological methods were applied to reduce dissidents to passivity; in areas of U.S. influence, torture methods became more scientific and purposeful when the salvation of capitalism itself was at stake. In passing, it is important to note that an Amnesty International Publication, *Torture in the Eighties*, lists 67 countries in four continents in which torture is practiced.[8] This does not include the United States—and the country by country review fails to underline U.S. encouragement and responsibility for modern torture methods, nor the results which have been achieved—the traumatization of sectors of the population in El Salvador, Guatemala and the Southern Cone.

The ethical vacuum in contemporary culture is not only duplicated in modern states but helps to make them more effective since the ethical "neutrality" of technology seems to freeze any debate. In the United States, the desacralization of the body and the destruction of the "individual" (i.e., of human identity as the core of consciousness and praxis) has made secular humanism an impossible position—which explains the resurgence of religion as a means of resacralizing the body and making individual life "meaningful." The problem here has been that too often this has involved a falling back into the traditionalism of "right to life movements" and neoconservatism. The other ethical standpoints have been supplied by the feminist movement, with its critique of the "negative eros" of death and destruction and its proposal of a "positive eros" based on connectedness,[9] and by revisionary socialism.[10]

CULTURES OF FEAR

It was important to stress the ethical vacuum in metropolitan societies if only to forestall any tendency to regard the repressive regimes in Latin America and especially the Southern Cone as purely local aberrations. Joan Didion falls into this trap when she speaks of the "ineffable" quality of Salvadoran violence. It is not that the state violence in Argentina in 1976, for example, had any parallel in the United States but rather that, from the point of view of the metropolis, real Third World cadavers have fueled the "mobilized privatization" of contemporary society.[11] The Third World represents cheap and surplus labor, raw material, and political regimes which keep the costs of labor down to the minimum. The invasion of Guatemala in 1953, the overthrow of Allende in 1973, the installation of the Argentine junta in 1976, resulted in cultures of fear, because fear was the deterrant to political organization which in those countries had inhibited the effective organization of a consumer society. The attempts of Pinochet in Chile, of Martínez de la Hoz in Argentina to apply neoliberal economics came in the aftermath of brutal repression of political parties and trade unions. It is true that the towering *caracoles* or spiral-shell vertical shopping malls in Chile have come to seem more and more like monstrous symbols of a never-fulfilled cultural revolution, like the opera houses in the Amazon or the temples to Minerva in Guatemala. Nevertheless, the failure does not alter the fact that they were built, as were the economic policies of all the military regimes, on cemeteries, and the new citizens of the consumer societies browbeaten by torture and disappearance resembled the living dead rather than the upbeat Coke generation of American advertising.

What allows torture to be introduced and practiced in the supposedly enlightened modern world? Unlike mind control of metropolitan societies, torture cannot be open. It is essentially a secret practice, justified by a state of emergency. Perhaps because of this, the military sometimes combined the most barbarous torture with an element of legalism or professionalism—the presence of doctors, psychiatrists, and priests, the taking down of confessions, even the adoption of a "scientific" attitude.[12] Timerman acutely observed that though his torturers operated out of small converted basements: "they try to create a different more sophisticated image of the torture chambers. As if, in this way, they could elevate their achievements to a higher status, to a sort of high level professionalism. Their military superiors encourage this fantasy both in themselves and others, and this idea of important places, exclusive methods, original techniques, and new apparatuses, allows them to inject into their work a touch of distinction or of institutionalization." [13]

In all the Southern Cone countries, there was an element of bureaucratization (perhaps inspired by Nazi Germany) which made it easier for torturers to continue their normal relations with the outside world. They used euphemisms to communicate with one another and kept records of what they were doing.[14] In Argentina, the top ranks within the torture institutions were referred to as managers and assistant managers, as if they belonged to a corporation. In one testimony from Argentina, the victim described how the torturers outlined the "rules of the game" before using electroshock, and how they detailed the exact voltage that would be given, saying that nobody could resist that amount without talking and that the aftereffects were serious and possibly permanent.[15] In the navy secret jail in Argentina, one of the leaders was reported as justifying torture as "the only instrument suitable for obtaining the desired results," and he cited Guatemala and Algiers as precedents. This bureaucratic vocabulary has been resorted to constantly in the trials of the military in Argentina in which the accused constantly refer to "norms," "processes," etc.[16] In Chile, the torture was referred to as "work," and there was one case in which an informer asked to be transferred from the air force security force to the DINA, because he hoped for better pay and a new car.[17] A subculture developed with its own terminology of *paquetes*, i.e., packages or prisoners (Chile), *chupados*, and *trasladados*, i.e., prisoners who had been "sucked dry" of information and prisoners who were "transferred," that is to say, killed (Argentina). Further, the presence of doctors, psychiatrists, and occasionally nurses in torture sessions, as has already been noted, helped to create the notion of a routinized situation.[18]

However, because these modern methods were introduced into countries whose culture was Catholic, in which there was strong rhetorical importance given to the family, and because of the illegality of the operations, it needed more than bureaucratic language to deal with the death camps. In Hitler's Germany, Aryanism provided the ideological justification for extermination. In the Southern Cone, the situation closely resembled that described by Lifton as totalistic, that is characterized by "mystical manipulation" of its victims, by the demand for purity, the cult of confession, the "immortalizing" of certain images, and the loading of language "in ways that eliminate the ambiguity about even the most complex human problems and reduce them to definitive-sounding, thought-terminating images."

Finally, such a system puts doctrine over person "so that direct experience and past history are subsumed to (or negated by) ideology, and the individual pressed to remake himself in the doctrinal mold."[19] Lifton then goes on to argue that such a system prescribes "a single authentic avenue to immortality, so that an arbitrary line is drawn between those with a right to exist and those who possess no such right."[20] Under such circumstances, it is not surprising to find the military claiming their own immortality in religious language. Hernán Vidal, for instance, notes the yoking of technological and religious imagery in the discourse of the Chilean military (1979).[21] In Argentina, the "dirty war" was equated with a religious war. Admiral Massera, who was deeply involved with the death camps, strongly supported religion and on occasion declared that "todos obramos a parte del amor, que es el sustento de nuestra religión" [we all act in the name of love, which is the foundation of our religion].[22] There was even a case of one torturer giving a medal of our Lady to a victim and sending her, on her release, a "torturer's prayer."

> May I be faithful in war as in peace.
> May the sharp scream of bullets gladden my heart.
> Oh Lord, make my soul ready at all times for sacrifice and pain.
> Give skill to my hand so that my shot hits the target and let
> me be charitable so that it may be fired without hatred.[23]

The military's belief that they were waging a religious war helps to explain the marked anti-Semitic language of the torturers which Timerman and others have noted.

This bizarre marriage of euphemism, religious language, and modern bureaucratic language is symptomatic of the fact that torture, while purportedly extracting information, must dispense with all affective connotation. On the one hand, insult, vituperation, and threat; on the other, animal cries of pain. For the torturers, there is total control that makes them feel "like gods." The victims become death-tainted, defiled, and worse—dependent "upon the victimizing immortality system."[24]

THE MACHO RITUAL

The destruction of identity in Argentine death camps was systematic—prisoners were given numbers, forced to wear a hood (the *capucha*), which produced nausea and disorientation, were given the status of objects, deprived of any form of communication with one another so that all communication was mediated by the torturers; they were humiliated, made the butt of jokes, immobilized by being shackled to beds, made to go through the ritual of mock execution, suffered electroshock and beatings or worse; they were raped if they were women and sometimes if they were men. If they were mothers, their newly born children were seized and farmed out to military families. I enumerate these well-known facts in order to emphasize the following: (1) a certain "regularity" in the proceedings which lends credence to the fact (amply demonstrated in the Costa Gavras film *State of Seige*) that methods were taught, routinized, and exported, and data exchanged;[25] (2) the use of disappearance as a "novel" method of social control which has become prevalent in countries even like Mexico which are not under military regimes; the other aspect of disappearance being the random appearance of dead bodies in order to spread fear in the general population; (3) the mutilation, burning, and drowning of bodies in order to prevent identification which not only meant the elimination of the identity but also the impossibility of martyrdom; (4) the staging of events in order to produce effects on the general population, for instance, the attempt to demonstrate that some of the dead were killed in terrorist attacks or that the disappeared had simply left the country.

Yet this death dealing implied the incorporation in the death squads of human beings who must also have feared death. Clearly, the desacralization of the human body has to affect the torturer as well as the tortured. Here the pertinence of gender is inescapable. For only through ritualistic incorporation into the group by punishing the other could the male bonding and complicity necessary for the functioning of the torture chamber be achieved. The use of animal nicknames in Argentine—tiger, jaguar, puma, gorilla, and so on—added a totemic element to the business. There are numerous descriptions of such male initiation ceremonies. One of the most euphemistic is to be found in the Chilean *Confesiones de un agente de seguridad* [Confessions of a security agent], in which the ex-agent describes how a selected group were taken to see the prisoners held by the air force in the Academia de Guerra [military academy]. The process of incorporation was gradual—first participation in round-up of prisoners. The language in which the agent recounts his first experience of seeing torture applied is deliberately laconic, almost technical. "They applied the electric current, and she cried out. She was the fiancée of a kid from the MIR (an extreme left party). I don't remember what voltage was used. We were being tested to see who would stay in the group" (my translation).

In Argentina, those who tried to evade duty (euphemistically *tareas* or jobs) were either threatened or compromised in a manner which made it hard for them to leave the group.[26] However, the most important ritual of incorporation was the "pacto de sangre" (the pact of blood),[27] i.e., the witnessing of torture and killing, or the performance of acts such as disemboweling or mutilating in order to secure group bonding. Such practices also separated the "immortals" from the merely transient. During torture sessions, there were jokes, laughter, music, and often sadistic excitement as in the case described by Susana León Caride when a torturer irritated by the response of a prisoner began to beat a group of chained prisoners.

> It was a Dantesque incident since we were manacled and blindfolded and had no idea of the direction from which the blows would fall. We fell on top of one another, hearing cries of pain and horror. I realized that different people were beating and kicking us and lifting us up by the hair whenever we fell.[28]

There are many accounts of such moments of "exaltation," the sense of being "god" and having absolute power over people. Not only do these rituals appear primitive and archaic, but they were often described in sexual terms. Male and female prisoners were, it is true, tortured in similar ways. But male victims were often taunted about their manhood, the size of their penises, or if they were Jews, about circumcision. Electroshock was commonly applied to the testicles, vagina, breasts, and mouth. Women prisoners and sometimes men were raped.[29] Women were taunted as *putas* [whores]. Women were not only raped but also abused sexually in other ways. A Chilean woman describes how, after being tortured, she was taken back to her cell, "and individuals kept coming in, making obscene remarks, touching me, and making filthy comments."[30] Pregnant women were treated with brutality, and children born to them were farmed out to military families.

Is there something about the social construction of masculinity which accounts for the fact that torturers are usually male, or is it simply the possession of certain kinds of power (in the military and the police) which makes some of them condone and participate in these activities? The question is by no means trivial, and it is a particularly crucial one for feminists. Indeed, recent research in gender and science, gender and political philosophy, and gender and psychology underlines the intricate relationship between the construction of science as objectivity, the concept of nature (as object), the separation of the affective from the rational, and the construction of gender differentiation.

This feminist discussion has gone largely unnoticed in Latin America (with the possible exception of Brazil). It is pertinent to our present discussion, not simply because of the fact that men are generally the torturers while women have played a major role in movements of denunciation of the disappeared, but because of the way that gender differentiation has been used in this form of social control. Significantly so, since after class, race, and nation, gender is the last important category of social constructs to be "deconstructed"—that is, it is the category that persistently appears to people as natural.

This is not the place to go into the vast body of scholarship that now deals with gender differentiation. For the moment, it is sufficient to observe that the formation of masculine and feminine as social categories has been examined in relation to Freudian and post-Freudian psychology (Lacan, Juliet Mitchell, Luce Irigaray, and North American object-relations theorists such as Nancy Chodorow),[31] in relation to political philosophy (Nancy Hartsock, Jean Bethke Elshtain),[32] religion, language, and symbolic representation (Suleiman, Kristeva).[33] This is not a monolithic set of beliefs nor a unified theory but an ongoing discussion that is far from terminated. It is a discussion which, to some extent, focuses on crucial relations between signification and gender which stem from the fact that masculine/feminine are among the most stubbornly persistent of binary relationships; it is also a differentiation which underlies the formation of subjects in relation to the other. Even if we reject the Freudian/Lacanian account of the stages of separation from the primary love object, the mother, and the subject's submission to the paternal law, we cannot ignore the fact that the rituals of masculinity (whether boarding-school rites of passage, military drills, or group sexual experiences) occur at the very moment of passage to "manhood" when that separation from the feminine has to be reaffirmed (a ritual of confirmation) and feminine traits of the personality such as softness, emotional expressivity definitely abandoned. The death squad like military and police organizations build loyalty, complicity, and brutality on this differentiation, which makes the other the equivalent of the woman—passive, effeminate, silent, and all too mortal.

There are hundreds of literary accounts from all over the world of such rituals which are commonly associated with an evil "other" who must be eliminated—a tribal enemy, a ferocious animal, an effeminate schoolfellow, or a misfit in the regiment—Musil's *Young Törless*, Kipling's *Stalky and Co.*, and Vargas Llosa's *La ciudad y los perros* [The Time of the Hero], to name but three. The denigration of this other usually involves his reduction to the status of the devalued woman. These casual rituals of cruelty, which have marked the adolescence of many young men even in liberal societies are formalized, even bureaucratized in the death camps. Hernán Valdés's *Diary of a Chilean Concentration Camp*[34] is one of the most eloquent day-to-day accounts of life in a camp (terrible as it was, however, the treatment of Valdés was nothing compared with that meted out to both men and women in the Argentine camps). Hernán Vidal's discussion of this document[35] notes how the prisoner became obsessed with bodily functions such as excretion. Yet, rather than considering Valdés's obsession with body as a polar opposite to the resistance to the junta's "disembodied" declaration of principles, as Vidal argues, it would seem important to stress that Valdés like other prisoners seemed to revert to a pre-Oedipal stage the moment his masculine identity was put in doubt. Valdés's account particularly stresses the *macho* rituals and sexual language of the camp personnel. An ex-soldier describes the torture of his brother who had not been an obedient soldier. The ex-soldier commented, "He came out half crazy, the fucker, but we've all got to learn what it takes to be a man." If not, "there'd be no keeping the fuckers under control." When Valdés is taken to be tortured, one of the first questions is "Are you a queer?" There are constant sexual references during the torture both to Valdés's alleged homosexuality (associated with the fact that he is a writer) and to the supposed unbridled sexuality of his girlfriend. When Valdés emerges from the torture chamber, having been subjected to electroshock and beating he says, "My body was aching terribly. I didn't dare look at my penis. I was scared to." A prisoner who has been reduced to passivity and who was no longer dangerous was still submitted to ritual humiliation which included electric torture in the anus.[36]

In a moving account written on cigarette paper in the concentration camp in Pisagua, Chile, during the last months of 1973, the anonymous diarist records the last emotions of prisoners who know they are going to die. The pathos of this description resides in the attempt of the prisoners to assert the continuity of life even when the military tried to deny them any possibility of symbolizing death except as their total extinction and the extinction of the community to which they had belonged:

> I have seen a man condemned to death looking fixedly at his brother, I have seen him move his lips as if giving him counsel, I have seen him embrace him as if saying goodbye on the eve of a very long journey, I have seen them kissing one another on both cheeks.
>
> I have seen another condemned man rush out of the bathroom and

then rush back like a child who has to go to an examination without having learned the lesson—anxious, nervous. I have seen the condemned embracing each other and others.[37]

Graciela Susana Geuna, whose testimony is one of the most complete accounts of women's experience in the death camps, emphasizes the prisoners' regression to a pre-Oedipal stage. "We slept in a foetal position. As if we wanted to forget everything and go back to the maternal breast." [38] Though many women refused to talk, the *macho* challenge to be a man (and die) was very strong. On the other hand, the disorientation, torture, rape, and isolation of women prisoners, which induced feelings of helplessness and dependency made them particularly vulnerable to the small seductions of camp life. Their confessions of this process have not been well received, which is a pity, for it is above all through women's evidence that we begin to appreciate the importance of survival as an ethical category. They also help us to understand that, in many cases, military and militants shared a common discourse which was based on the devaluation of the unheroic feminine as other.

The polarization of masculine/feminine, active/passive which articulated the power relations within the death camps was also an intrinsic element in the discourse of the armed guerrilla. Interviews with women of the Tupamaru movement in Uruguay show that women were never completely accepted as militants, largely because their vulnerability to pregnancy was thought to undermine their ability to behave with the strength demanded of the militant. Thus, the "militant" was defined as masculine in the socially constructed sense of that word, and women "militants" were supposed to become pseudomales—only to be ridiculed as lesbians.[39] This ideology like that of the *montoneros* in Argentina left little room for tactics of survival or nuances between complete loyalty and complete treachery. People who did not talk died. The supreme irony of behaving like a man (an irony of which the military were fully conscious) was that only the military or those who were also condemned to die were able to appreciate it. Even among less militant groups, anonymous death was particularly terrible, for it deprived them of their particular form of "symbolic immortality," that is the consolation that "I live on in humankind." [40]

Those who did talk (but did not become full-fledged informants) became "abject," for they had thrown themselves out of a community, had transgressed the loyalty to friends or to a group. Many prisoners who passed through this experience or felt themselves threatened in their identity began actively to desire death. Timerman, though not in as desperate a situation as the inmates of the death camps, thought of suicide,[41] and other times he desired madness, in preference to the feeling of impotence and humiliation. Not surprisingly, he found the enemy within to be "ternura" (tenderness)—a feminine quality that threatened his survival, because it threatened his identity. Jewishness ("the mother tongue"), on the other hand, confirmed that sense of identity and community; it is a form of "behaving like a woman" without being effeminate. For an anonymous Chilean who went through the experience of torture and the random execution of cell mates, only God could provide sufficient comfort for the terror of the experience. "May the Universal Mind have received you in its breast."[42] This is not to denigrate the memory of those men and women who refused to give names and whose silence helped protect people who were still free. Given the situation, there were not many subtleties between talking and not talking.

Yet, it is also probable that, even though pain has no gender, men and women suffered their experience of the death camps in a different fashion, largely because men and women are constituted differently as individuals. The writer of the Pisagua diary describes hearing someone tortured and compares it to the pain of someone being bent over backward until he is broken. Women on the other hand, are invaded, penetrated by the enemy.

The sense of being an individual depends on a network of references and processes of recognition of the subject as a unique person. This recognition can be verbal (addressing a person by their name) or nonverbal (giving certain people precedence).[43] In Argentina and Chile, the military who ran the death camps deliberately deprived victims of individual identity by giving them numbers instead of names, by covering their faces (thus depriving them of the chief feature by which a person is recognized as such) and, in the case of Argentina, even by referring to them as "living dead" (*muertos que caminan*). This "abjection" forced male prisoners to live "as if they were 'women,' to understand, for the first time, what it meant not to be able to forget the body, to be ridiculed and battered, and to find comfort in small everyday life activities like washing clothes and talking to friends."[44] In Uruguay where prisoners were kept in solitary confinement for long periods, the dramatist Mauricio Rosencof found that the only way to survive was by imagining homely activities like walking in the park with his daughter and eating ice cream.[45]

MOTHERS AND RESISTANCE

It was important for the military government that there be no martyrs in the struggle, that there should be no historical memory, no family shrines. The reasons for this go far deeper than political expedience for it aimed at destroying any hope that death might have meaning for society at large. Young militants, executed over secret graves or thrown from airplanes, were denied their last heroic gesture. Death was to be not a form of continuity but an extirpation. In Chile prisoners were thrown into an unused furnace at Longquen and buried alive. Once a human person is reduced to a number, once nameless prisoners are thrown from airplanes, cast into anonymous graves, mutilated beyond recognition, there is a devaluation of death and hence of human identity which affects the whole of society. For, as Robert Herz wrote in "The Collective Representation of Death," "when a man dies, society loses in him much more than a unit, it is stricken in the faith it has in itself."[46] The military governments of Chile, Argentina, El Salvador, and Guatemala have dealt with their victims as Creon dealt with Polinices, casting them into oblivion and silence.

Many of those who were not killed were submitted to mock executions and made to face their own mortality. Psychologists who have dealt with torture victims in Chile have found that this is one experience for which there is no "cure."[47] Both the anonymity of deaths in the camps and the parody of death in mass execution desacralize death. This desacralization was the more terrible in that it involved the deliberate wiping out of identities. Furthermore, the dead body came to play a bizarre role in social control—since the appearance of mutilated, anonymous bodies in public places served to silence the population while "disappearance" being less explicit than death was meant to create in families and neighbors a sense of dependence on the state as the source of the truth. The *montoneros*, for their part, also used bodies in order to make a political point. Uruguay adopted a different procedure, burying their prisoners alive in solitary confinement for periods as long as ten years.[48]

As Michael Taussig has shown, the space of death (which is the space also of immortality, communal memory, of connection between generations) is particularly important as a site of struggle in the colonized areas of the world, and this struggle is of necessity ethical. It is not, however, only a struggle over the appearance and disappearance of mutilated bodies, but rather a struggle to retrieve the dead, to give them back their names and identities, and restore meaning to those lost lives. That is why the mothers of the Plaza de Mayo carry photographs of their disappeared children, why the major demonstration after the discovery of bodies in Longquen in Chile took the form of a pilgrimage and mass, why in El Salvador it is the mothers who photograph the bodies of victims and who even seek a limb or any part of a dead child that they can recognize from mass graves. In this struggle mothers have played a major role, because they are not susceptible to the threat of death.

Once a child has died, the mother (in her traditional role as mother) has nothing left to live for and can face death or worse public shame. In the words of Hebe de Bonafini when her children disappeared, she felt "tigers growing inside her."[49] The abjection of women turns into a positive value, one which can withstand behaviorist techniques, death threats, and torture. The Argentine movement began with the "odyssey" of mothers seeking their children, "visiting prisons and police stations; and finding out when one thought there was a friend among the police that they have no friends. And we began seeing the same faces over and over again. Until on the 30 of May, 1977, we first went to the Plaza de Mayo."[50]

The loss of children ejected these women from the protected circle of the home and threw them into confrontation with a state and a society which had hitherto only presented a benign aspect. A Chilean woman describes the effect of being "cast out" of normal society:

> Can anyone imagine what is to seek a loved one in an apparently "normal" society and which has suddenly become a grey, dark fortress with closed doors and officials who replied laconically "he has not been detained," "he is not on our list."
>
> Up to that day, I had lived like any other Chilean woman, member of a family which because its work and moral standard had been respectable and useful to society felt that it could have recourse to the police and justice if something happened to one of its members. I suddenly discovered that those wearing uniform were like enemies and that the judges administered justice to uphold what was called "the established order."[51]

This outcast status was especially evident during the early days of the Argentine movement when the women were commonly referred to as "las locas" [the madwomen]. Only gradually were they dignified as "las madres" [mothers]. Hebe de Bonafini would point out that "when they couldn't beat or imprison us, they chose to form an enclosure with barricades around the center of the Plaza, and we had to show our white handkerchiefs in order to be let in. Isolated from the rest of the Plaza—to avoid that 'contagion' which they fear—we walked around in a circle and then they let us leave." [52] Whereas in Chile, the Vicarí de la Solidaridad [the vicarate of solidarity] and in El Salvador, Archbishop Romero provided shelter for the activities of the families of the disappeared, in Argentina, this church support was not forthcoming. Nevertheless, it was in Argentina that the rituals and the form of protest were developed—the photographs of the children, the white headscarf, and the weekly meeting in a public place, the Plaza de Mayo, the seat of government. In "going public" in this way, the mothers overcame deep-seated taboos on "scandalous" behavior. At the same time, they showed a sure instinct in choosing such a symbolically charged public space as the Plaza de Mayo (a space associated with large public rallies, with Independence, with Peronism—in short with history). In Chile women chained themselves to the railings of the closed Congress building. In El Salvador, the mothers usually demonstrate by staging a sit-in in the cathedral. In each case, the space itself is charged with symbolic meanings that do not need to be spoken. The effort involved in overcoming both fear and shame has been described by many of the *madres*. Hebe de Bonafini describes the strength needed to return to the Plaza de Mayo on Thursdays especially after the disappearance of Azucena Villaflor de Vicenti, the first president of the organization.[53]

A Chilean woman who participated in the protest in front of the Chilean congress described how she overcame her fear:

> I was in a state of terrible nerves. I put on the chain, selected the clothes that would best hide it. As I did not have an overcoat, I wore a leather jacket and buttoned it up, though I didn't usually wear it this way, but I buttoned it up to hide the chain. As the chain was dark in color, I thought it would be less noticeable if I wore something light. I wore a light grey sweater so that the chain would show up. And I put the photograph of my loved one, which everyone carries, in my pocket book.[54]

But this resistance would not have been possible if mothers had not behaved as *mothers*. By refusing to regard their children as terrorists, by reiterating their mothering role, their particular regard for the continuation of human life, the mothers of Argentina, Chile, and El Salvador were able to interrupt the dominant discourse and resacralize the body. That also helps to account for the religious tone of these movements and the ethical dimension they give to the struggle, a dimension which emerges particularly in the struggle over meaning. Thus, the mothers' movement in Argentina has refused to accept the term *dead* as long as the military are not brought to justice and the disappeared accounted for. To speak of "death" would allow the past to be forgotten; it would have become history. Disappearance reveals a yawning gulf in the discourse of the state and points to a structural absence which, in turn, is a cover-up. In Chile, the women have elaborated their own symbolism around flowers which "symbolically show their faith in the germination of new life."[55] The mothers' movement thus brings to the fore an ethics of survival and life to counter the political use of death. However, the women who participate in these movements also stress the personal transformation that comes about with their overcoming fear. Hebe de Bonfini states, "you feel strong because you feel that you are with your children. When there were few of us at the beginning, we used to say, 'We don't feel that our numbers are small. We feel that there are many of us because each of us is accompanied by those thousands of children who are missing.'"[56] And a Chilean woman confirms the feeling of great satisfaction even though it is known the price that will have to be paid.[57]

Whereas the male bonding of the death camp torturers is based on well-established rites through which masculinity has traditionally been constituted, women's solidarity goes against the grain. It has to be achieved by a conscious effort, by overcoming fear not in the service of death but in the service of life and continuity. It also means conscious assumption of a "public self"—not a prestigious public self but a scorned and outcast public self.

The foregoing might lead us to conclude that women are not only different from, but better than men. And some recent feminist theory would certainly seem to support this. Nancy Hartsock, for instance, argues for a specifically female way of thinking, for "female construction of self in relation to others leads . . . toward opposition to dualisms of any sort, valuation of concrete, everyday life, sense of a variety of connectednesses and continuities both with other persons and with the natural world."[58] Hartsock further argues that the masculine vision not only supports a dualism that opposes active male to passive female but also "perhaps the most dramatic (though not the only) reversal of the proper order of things characteristic of the male experience is the substitution of death for life."[59]

However, a further step needs to be taken since valorizing feminine connectedness is simply an inversion of a manichean division between good and bad, strong and weak, masculine and feminine. That is why it is more useful to consider movements like those of the women of the Plaza de

Mayo as strategic movements that are called forth by a particular kind of repression, one which has, indeed, identified right and good with masculinity and masculinity with the ability to inflict death. In this light, the mothers were able to act within the same discourse, by accepting the traditional concerns of motherhood (the survival of the offspring). Yet what is remarkable particularly in the Argentine movement has been the ability of the mothers to show that the discourse on masculinity and femininity is socially constructed. For instance in a recent incident, the mothers appealed to article 259 of the Military Justice Code, which declares that "a woman whose life is publicly honest can give legal declarations in any domicile that she chose." Claiming to be "publicly honest" Zuleima Leira, one of the mothers who was asked to make a declaration before the military justices in the ongoing trials upheld her right to make the declaration at the headquarters of the Madres de la Plaza de Mayo. Hebe de Bonafini declared, "we do not recognize military justice, and that reference to publicly honest women appears totally anachronistic to us. But in any case, making them come here, looking them in the face, is like winning minor skirmishes."[60] Small though the battle was, it showed the way the mothers' movement has been able to use the symbolic power normally used against women. The incident allowed them to point out that this same military code classifies women as an "incapaz relativa" [relatively handicapped] along with invalids and those who are not familiar with Spanish. In using the position legally assigned to women while at the same time emphasizing its provisional and socially constructed nature, the mothers go beyond any essentialist definition. They expose the fact that women are considered to belong to the private sphere by bringing this out into the public. In this respect, the mothers have not only reacted to a specific situation but have introduced the possibility of transforming protest into a broader ethical position, one which is based on the ethics of life and survival and not on the ethics of good and evil.

Once the issue becomes life and survival, then a new situation arises, one in which neither the old *macho* values nor postmodernism's rejection of ethics really applies. It is at this moment that we have to recognize that, because "masculine" and "feminine" are socially constructed categories, the next move is to construct an ethics in which the value of survival no longer needs to be attached to the "weak" term in an apparently natural opposition between the masculine and the feminine. The mothers' movements in the Southern Cone and in El Salvador, though apparently articulated on a very traditional differential axis, have revealed the fictionality of the equation of public/private, masculine/feminine. They have thus opened the way toward an "emergent" ethics which is not an ethics that can be associated simply with a preordained gender, race, or class.[61] What the mothers' movement has shown is that what had been "relegated" to the feminine is in fact continuity and survival. They have, however, resisted claiming these as uniquely the concern of one particular gender and have resisted any ecumenical notion of these values which would gloss over the antagonisms in society. In this sense, the mothers' movement is not just one more movement, like the ecological movement or gay liberation. It is a movement which has its roots in the confrontation with death and which has implications far beyond its original base. For the mothers ask not simply that justice be done and the dead be remembered, but more broadly what kind of community can reestablish dialogue with its dead. Thus, speaking of their children, the mothers of the Plaza de Mayo affirm, "Their courage and the ethical meaning of life has marked the destiny of this nation, which will never again bow to those who try to oppress it."[62]

NOTES

1 The term *postmodernism* is often greeted with a certain skepticism. The best discussion of the use of the term is that of Andreas Huyssen, "Mapping the Postmodern," *New German Critique* 33 (fall 1984): 5–52. The same issue also includes articles on the postmodern by Habermas, Jameson, Foster, and others.
2 Robert Jay Lifton, *The Broken Connection: On Death and the Continuity of Life* (New York: Simon and Schuster, 1979).
3 Stuart Schneiderman, *Jacques Lacan: The Death of an Intellectual Hero* (Cambridge: Harvard University Press, 1983).
4 Joan Didion, *Salvador* (New York: Washington Square Press, 1983).
5 Ibid., 36.
6 Raymond Williams, *The Year 2000: A Radical Look at the Future and What We Can Do to Change It* (New York: Pantheon Books, 1983), 261.
7 Ibid., 262.
8 Amnesty International, *Torture in the Eighties* (London: Amnesty International Publications, 1984).
9 Nancy Hartsock, "The Feminist Standpoint: Developing the Ground for a Specifically Feminist Historical Materialism," in *Discovering Reality*, ed. Sandra Harding and Merrill B. Hintikka (Dordrecht: Reidel Publishing Company, 1983), 283–310.
10 Williams, *The Year 2000*.
11 Ibid.

12 Ximena Ortúzar, *Represión y tortura en el Cono Sur* (Mexico: Extemporáneos, 1977).

13 Jacobo Timerman, *Preso sin nombre, celda sin número* (Barcelona: El Cid Editor, 1981), 39–40. My translation.

14 Since writing this piece, this has been confirmed by the extraordinary document produced by the Archiocese of São Paulo: Joan Dassin, ed., *Torture in Brazil*, trans. Jaime Wright (New York: Vintage Books, 1986).

15 Comisión Argentina de Derechos Humanos, *Deposiciones* [mimeographed].

16 *El Diario del Juicio*, no. 1, 27 May 1985.

17 Comisión Nacional Sobre la Desaparición de Personas (Chile), *Confesiones de un agente de seguridad* (Santiago: n.p., 1984).

18 Fanny Pollarollo, *La tortura, un problema médico* (Santiago: Fundación de las Iglesias Cristianas, 1983), 12.

19 Lifton, *The Broken Connection*, 298.

20 Ibid., 298.

21 Hernán Vidal, *Dar la vida por la Vida, La Agrupación Chilena de Familiares de Detenidos Desaparecidos* (Minneapolis: Institute of Ideologies and Literatures, 1982).

22 Interview given to *Familia Cristiana* and quoted in *Clarín*, 13 May 1977.

23 Comisión Argentina de Derechos Humanos, *Deposiciones.* My translation.

24 Lifton, *The Broken Connection*, 325.

25 Cynthia Brown, *With Friends Like These: The Americas Watch Report of Human Rights and U.S. Policy in Latin America* (New York: Pantheon Books, 1985), 11.

26 *Nunca Más: Informe de la Comisión Nacional sobre la desaparición de personas* (Buenos Aires: Editorial Universitaria, 1984), 255.

27 Ibid., 254.

28 Ibid., 65.

29 Ortúzar, *Represión y tortura.*

30 Pisagua, *Pisagua: Antecedentes y testimonios e los campos de concentración* (mimeographed) (Santiago: n.p., 1983), 61.

31 Jacques Lacan, *Feminine Sexuality*, trans. Jacqueline Rose (New York: Norton, 1982); Juliet Mitchell, *Psychoanalysis and Feminism* (New York: Pantheon Books, 1974); Luce Irigaray, *Speculum of the Other Woman*, trans. Gillian C. Gill (Ithaca: Cornell University Press, 1985); Nancy Chodorow, *The Reproduction of Mothering: Psychoanalysis and the Sociology of Gender* (Berkeley: University of California Press, 1978).

32 Joan Bethke Elshtain, *Public Man, Private Woman* (Princeton: Princeton University Press, 1983).

33 Julia Kristeva, *Powers of Horror: An Essay on Abjection*, trans. Leon S. Roudiez (New York: Columbia University Press, 1982).

34 Hernán Valdez, *Diary of a Chilean Concentration Camp* (London: Victor Gollanez, 1975).

35 Hernán Vidal, "The Politics of the Body: The Chilean Junta and the Anti-Fascist Struggle," *The Social Text* vol. 1, no. 2 (1979), 104–21.

36 Hernán Valdez, *Diary of a Chilean Concentration Camp*, 138.

37 Pisagua, *Pisagua: Antecedentes y testimonios de los campos de concentración*, 36–42.

38 Graciela Susana Geuna, 21.

39 *Tupamaras*, 1980.

40 Lifton, *The Broken Connection*, 20.

41 Timerman, *Preso sin nombre, celda sin número*, 91.

42 Pisagua, *Pisagua*, 52.

43 Pierre Bourdieu, *Ce que parler veut dire: l'economie des échanges linguistiques* (Paris: Fayard, 1982).

44 Ibid., 59.

45 In conversation at Columbia University, March 1986. See also Mauricio Rosencof, "Cuando la poesía es un caballo necesario," *El Manojo* 1, no. 1 (1985).

46 Quoted in Michael Taussig, "History as Sorcery," *Representations* 7 (1984).

47 V. Arcos, M. Luna, L. Schwarz, A. Cienfuegos, and J. Monelli, *Psicoterapia y represión política* (mimeographed) (Santiago: n.p., 1982).

48 Mauricio Rosencof, "Cuando la poesía es un caballo necesario."

49 Quoted in Miguel Bonasso, "Las madres se movilizan ante el 'juicio del siglo,'" *Proceso*, no. 441 (April 15, 1985).

50 Ibid.

51 Vidal, *Dar la vida por la vida*.

52 Hebe de Bonafini, in *Historias de vida*, ed. Matilde Sánchez (Buenos Aires: Fraterna, 1985).

53 Ibid., 153.

54 Vidal, *Dar la vida por la vida*, 133.

55 Ibid.

56 Quoted in Miguel Bonasso, "Las madres se movilizan ante el 'juicio del siglo.'"

57 Vidal, *Dar la vida por la vida*.

58 Hartsock, "The Feminist Standpoint," 298.

59 Ibid., 299.

60 *La Razón*, 31 May 1985.

61 Ernesto Laclau and Chantal Mouffe, *Hegemony and Socialist Strategy: Towards a Radical Democratic Politics* (London: Verso, 1985), 176.

62 *Madres de Plaza de Mayo*, 1, no. 7 (June 1985).

"MANHATTAN WILL BE MORE EXOTIC THIS FALL"

The Iconization of Frida Kahlo

*I*n Latin America over the last decade, there has been a widespread policy of privatization of many institutions and functions formerly managed by the state. These changes have had an immense and as yet largely uncharted effect on culture and politics. In Mexico, to take one example, the film industry, television, the major publishing house (Fondo de Cultura Económica), newspapers, and museums were until recently largely supported by the state and, for better or worse, protected from the vagaries of the market. Even oppositional artists and writers worked within the dominant national culture which was largely responsible for disseminating and mapping the idea of the nation. Until the eighties, official state culture was visible in public monuments and public spaces, in the design and ideology of museums such as the Anthropological Museum, even in the hieroglyphs used to mark the subway stations in Mexico City.[1]

This national public culture was constructed around a predominantly male-centered narrative. Women were not its protagonists nor were they, for the most part, active in the public sphere. National culture tended to identify the female with territory rather than with change, with the conservative rather than with the modern. Their political activity was absorbed into the male-dominated system and there was little discussion or debate of issues specific to women.

In Mexico this version of the state is now in crisis. The myths of nationalism and national character no longer appeal to a society that recognizes class, gender, and ethnic differences more readily than its own coherence. Meanwhile, women have become actors in new social and feminist movements, campaigning against violence, and for human rights and survival issues.[2] Thus it is paradoxical that while women have become more and

Originally published in *Women: A Cultural Review* 2, no. 3 (Winter 1991): 220–227; reprinted by permission of Oxford University Press.

more actively involved as citizens, archaic versions of womanhood have been used as symbols of the new Mexico.

The new Mexican state represents itself as a break with the past, with old-fashioned anti-imperialist policies and above all with the welfare state. Instead of state intervention, market forces are the regulators of prosperity, well-being, and freedom. Privatization is widely understood to be beyond ideology; and it is associated with a pluralistic and thoroughly modern environment. However, though presented in nonideological terms, privatization *is* an ideology and a system of representation as well as effecting changes in everyday life. In particular, both on the level of representation and on the social, privatization has remapped the boundaries between the public and private spheres. What was formerly thought of as a separate affective sphere (the family, personal life) is now collapsed into this other "private" space of aggressive market forces.[3] Meanwhile the "state" and "government" have become the focus of attack. Influential Latin American intellectuals such as the Peruvian Mario Vargas Llosa and Nobel Prize–winner Octavio Paz have represented the state as monolithic and as the enemy of culture and have set state patronage in opposition to liberty.[4] Yet it can be argued that the "liberty" they promote is cosmetic, that in contemporary Latin America private enterprise has adopted an interventionist role in culture in order to promote the image of a new kind of nation-state, a nation-state that mediates rather than directs. To illustrate this, I shall focus in particular on a particular event— "Mexico as a Work of Art"—held in New York in the fall of 1990 and on the use of Woman as "mediator" and "intercessor" of the new Mexico.

Rarely has any country mounted such a large-scale publicity and cultural campaign as did Mexico in the fall of 1990. The calendar was filled with events: readings by prominent writers, concerts featuring ancient and modern Mexican music, lectures given at major museums. There was a show of Mexican painting from 1950 to 1980 at the IBM gallery; Parallel Project organized a series of exhibitions in New York's Soho district funded by Cementos Méxicanos SA; the National Academy of Design housed an exhibition of "Women painters in Mexico"; there were exhibitions of Mexican murals and prints in the Spanish Institute; graphics from the "Taller de la Gráfica Popular" in the Bronx; and "Images for Children" in the Children's Museum. And of course there was the massive and immensely successful exhibition, "Mexico: Splendors of Thirty Centuries" at the Metropolitan Museum of Art. An article published in the Mexican magazine *Nexos* described all this as "The Conquest of New York."[5]

There are many reasons why art should be so crucial to this U.S.-Mexico alliance. One of Mexico's main resources is tourism which, of course, is heavily involved with archaeological sites, churches, and museums. Yet although many who curated these exhibitions emphasized the continuity of Mexican tradition, it quickly became clear that the Mexico to which they referred was no longer revolutionary Mexico aggressively critical of gringo politics. *Forbes* business magazine proclaimed "a revolution you can invest in," assuring its readers that "the next great economic miracle will take place right on our borders." The article also congratulated President Salinas de Gortari for reducing the government's role in the economy.[6] Although the *Forbes* article was written before the opening of the exhibitions, it heralded a major change in economic relations between the United States and Mexico and, indeed, the two countries have now entered into discussions of a Free Trade Agreement similar to the Canada/U.S. agreement.

There is no doubt, however, that "Mexico: Splendors of Thirty Centuries" was the grandest show of Latin American art ever put on view in New York, one which involved a unique collaboration between state organizations such as CONACULTA, private enterprise, and U.S. organizations such as the Federal Council of the Arts and the Rockefeller and Tinker foundations. Mexican private enterprise was represented by the Fundación de Investigaciones Sociales and the Friends of the Arts of Mexico presided over by Emilio Azcárraga, head of a media empire and the privately owned television company, Televisa, and supported not only by Televisa but by most of the major liquor companies.[7]

What has all this to do with women, or, more accurately, Woman? Simply that women who, as artists, were on the margins of the major exhibitions, were at the center of the publicity for the new Mexico. It was Woman who acted as mediator between the old and the new. This was made explicit by Octavio Paz, one of the main planners of "Mexico: Splendors of Thirty Centuries" and author of the survey of Mexican art that prefaced the weighty catalog. The essay had the Nietzschean title, "Will for Form"; in it, Paz argued that Mexico forms an ideal bridge between the English-, Spanish-, and Portuguese-speaking worlds.

Written with Paz's customary brilliance, the essay explores the mysterious quality of pre-Columbian art, confronts the prevalence of human sacrifice in pre-Columbian societies (though avoiding deterring a squeamish public), describes the conquest as a cooperation between "public and private enterprise" (reminding us of the conquest of New York), and elucidates both viceregal society of "the sword, the cross and the quill," and the art of post-Independence Mexico.[8]

Paz's story is essentially one of survival and continuity. What is particularly relevant in this instance, however, is the importance Paz attaches to the Virgin as the mediator between the old religions of Mesoamerica — the dualism of eagle (day) and jaguar (night) — and the religion of the conquerors. Paz argues that coercion alone cannot account for the defeated Indians' devotion to the Virgin of Guadalupe or for their enthusiastic cooperation in decorating and building chapels. (Hence the crucial role of the Virgin as the synthesis of the Aztec goddess Tonantzín and Hispanic Christianity.) But Paz also extends this symbolism to encompass our own time and the exhibition itself:

> On the one hand, she (the Virgin) is mediation between the Old and New Worlds, between Christianity and the ancient religions. In addition, she is a bridge between the here and the beyond. She is a virgin, yet she is the mother of the Savior. She reconciles not only two aspects of reality, but the two poles of life: female and male. What better than these three figures, two of creative opposition and one of transcendent mediation, as advocates/intercessors for an exhibition of Mexican art?[9]

In his *The Labyrinth of Solitude* (1950) Paz had made Cortés's mistress, La Malinche, a central figure in the constitution of the Mexican character, a figure of betrayal, of rape and loss of identity. In the introductory essay to "Mexico: Splendors of Thirty Centuries" there is a dialectic of sorts, the creative opposition of jaguar and eagle being transcended by the Virgin. And by implication this conciliatory role also applies to the contemporary "creative opposition" between Mexico and the United States which the figure of the Virgin as symbol of peaceful coexistence transcends.

Clearly, however, the Virgin is too sectarian a symbol. It was a very different icon of womanhood that took center stage in the publicity around the exhibitions. This was Frida Kahlo's *Self-portrait with Monkeys* which appeared on every billboard and in several magazines. The painting was shown in the major exhibition at the Metropolitan Museum and proved far more seductive and reproducible than her *Henry Ford Hospital* and *Abortion* paintings that were on show at the National Academy of Design.

Self-portrait with Monkeys was said, in the Metropolitan Museum cassette, to signify "the children she could not have." In the painting Kahlo's face looks obliquely toward the spectator and is surrounded by tropical vegetation; the monkeys are twined around her neck and arms and touch her breast as if proclaiming her part of unsubdued *tropicalismo*. Advertisement supplements in the *New Yorker* reproduced that same self-portrait under the rubric, "Manhattan will be more exotic this Fall." A painting of fruit by another woman artist, Olga Costa, was similarly used to announce that "Manhattan will be fresher this Fall." In both advertisements, an insert of Manhattan skyline was shown blushing in the borrowed glow of tropical sunsets. The names of the company advertisers, "Aeromex, Bancomex and Mexicana," appeared in the bottom corner of the reproduction. In adjacent pages the Mexican tourist industry exploited this exoticism with a picture of a couple on a lonely beach that announced: "Mexico. The Magic Never Leaves You." [10]

There is nothing new in using art in advertisement. What is striking here, however, is the manner in which, to paraphrase Octavio Paz, Kahlo's portrait acts as advocate and intercessor of a new Mexico, a Mexico whose nationalist rhetoric has been tempered, a Mexico that is available as exotic and as luxuriant Nature. And the exotic and the natural, it is hardly necessary to point out, have always been terms in the unequal relationship between the center and the marginalized areas of the world.

Frida Kahlo, a woman of well-defined political convictions, one of whose last public appearances was at the demonstration protesting the U.S.-engineered invasion of Guatemala in 1954, would no doubt have been surprised to find her self-portraits used as icons of free enterprise. Painted at the height of Mexico's muralist movement, that is, a movement that espoused a public art that narrated a history of national and popular struggles for emancipation from imperialism and exploitation, Kahlo's canvases showed what was then unrepresentable in national and leftist mythology.[11] This kind of contextualization, however, was rare in the reviews and publicity surrounding the Mexican exhibitions, the one exception being the catalog for "Women in Mexico" in which the political roles of Kahlo and especially of the photographer Tina Modotti were stressed.[12] But such reminders were negligible compared to the continual replaying of the tragedy of Kahlo's physical suffering and obsessive and thwarted love. The private had not only become public, as feminists once claimed, but had become publicity.

But Kahlo's self-portrait acted as intercessor not only between the old and the new Mexico but also between high art and commercial hype. An article in the women's magazine *Mirabella*, written by Peter Schjeldahl, neatly summarized this aspect of the Kahlo cult. The heading of the article read: "She may turn out to be the greatest Mexican artist of our century—surpassing Orozco, Siqueiros, even her husband, Diego Rivera. But are we ready for Madonna to play her in the movie?"[13]

The idea of Madonna playing Kahlo was titillating. The rock star is not only a trend-setter but also a great defender of the female art of marketable seduction and erotic play. Indeed she is often represented as a modern feminist. In an article in the *New York Times* Kahlo's biographer, Hayden Herrera, explicitly addressed why Kahlo had such appeal for nineties' women, arguing that as "a Hispanic woman, bisexual, an invalid," she had "all the qualifications for a cult figure. Even Madonna is a fan."[14]

Noting the proliferation of Kahlo icons—T-shirts, fetishistic objects, reproductions, cosmetics, and jewelry—Herrera explains this fetishization by stressing that Kahlo's paintings speak directly to "us," the "we" being the privatized, tormented subject of a narcissistic society.

For a society drawn to notions of victimization and sadomasochism, Kahlo is certainly an alluring victim. For a people preoccupied with psychological health, fearful of AIDS and appalled by drug abuse, the gritty strength with which she endured her illness is salutary. Although her paintings record specific moments in her life, all who look at them feel that Frida is speaking directly to them.

She concludes that "to people numbed by poverty, violence and sorrow that confronts them in everyday life, Kahlo's paintings are restorative." In other words, the paintings are said to speak to the problems of the metropolis and to the problems of underdevelopment although it is doubtful whether those who are "numbed by poverty" ever get to see them.

Herrera's essay is particularly interesting, however, in its attempt to identify Kahlo with both Madonnas—with the rock star and the Mater Dolorosa. She makes explicit that what binds these figures to Kahlo is that they stage or make public what is usually private. Of Kahlo she writes: "When she displays her wounds, we immediately know that those wounds stand for all human suffering."

Kahlo's paintings are often described as "speaking" to us. In the in-flight article "American Way," published by American Airlines, Melissa Chessher obsessively returns to this theme: "As we approach the 21st century, it is the hurt, the grief, and the loneliness of one woman that speaks to us as individuals on the other side of the frame."[15] She also quotes art dealer Mary-Anne Martin who describes Kahlo's paintings as "intimate, pathetic and intense outpourings of personal pain and grief" that "stand like jewel-studded icons in a private chapel." This way of seeing is akin to prayer.

Art criticism, even in the press, usually obeys rather different rules, stressing the "painterly" qualities that we have been taught to notice in art appreciation classes. Not only were the rules suspended in the discussion of Kahlo's paintings but there were constant and glowing references to the market value of her life story as well as her canvases. Chessher pointed out that she was the first Latin American "to command more than $1 million for a single work . . . And pop star Madonna has purchased the rights to the artist's life-story and intends to make it into a movie." And later in the same article she returns to this miraculous event: "Collectors are paying more for a work by Frida than one by her husband."

In case anyone mistakes market success for feminism, it is important to note that Kahlo's paintings actually expose the myth of privacy, often depicting a body that was both irredeemably connected to reproduction but also invaded by science, pinned to surgical instruments with the inner organs exposed to public view. What Kahlo's paintings often put on display is the social nature of the body as well as the staged nature of representation. Even the *Self-portrait with Monkeys* is by no means an innocent view of nature but an evolution story in reverse.

The staging of Kahlo's paintings and the press reviews of her work gloss over any suggestion that the spectator is anything other than isolated and narcissistic. Rather the media presentation restores the boundary that separates the private, in order to suggest that there is some inner and authentic being that transcends the social and which accounts for the "value" of her work. At the same time, as a symbol of "Mexico as a work of art," she is able to signify feminine openness (open, that is, to the North).

There is one other aspect of the Mexican exhibitions that is worth recording. Thousands of middle-class Mexicans flew to New York on special tours in order to witness the recognition of their "high" culture. It was a middle-class event which came in the wake of decades of populism and proclaimed the existence of two Mexicos, one of which was "contemporary with the rest of the world" and had a high stake in the metropolis.

The appropriation of Kahlo is hardly surprising. In recent years the right has become adept at taking over the language and symbols of the left—Watney's revolutionaries and Reagan's freedom fighters are just two examples. But appropriation works both ways. Neighborhood organizations sprang up in Mexico in the wake of the earthquake and appropriated Superman, transforming him into the masked Superbarrio who leads demonstrations, negotiates demands, and represents the unrepresented. The performance artist, Jesusa Rodríguez, appropriates Coatlicue, the goddess of life and death, in order to ridicule the hype around the visit of the Pope. In the name of "mother Mexico" she complains that no one has ever offered her a mammarymobile or an airport reception.[16] And Frida Kahlo's self-portraits are used not only by private enterprise or the state but also by Chicano artists. It is these creative appropriations that bring recycled cultural objects into the present as tools of resistance so that marginalized groups can deploy them in their struggles for interpretive power.

NOTES

1   Nestor García Canclini has dealt exhaustively with these changes in *Culturas híbridas: Estrategias para entrar y salir de la modernidad* (Mexico: Grijalbo, 1989).

2   On women and the new social movements, see Elizabeth Jelin, ed., *Women and Social Change in Latin America*, trans. J. Ann Zammit and Marilyn Thomson (London and New Jersey: Zed Books, 1990); Jane S. Jaquette, ed., *The Women's Movements in Latin America: Feminism and the Transition to Democracy* (Boston: Unwin Hyman, 1989).

3   The separation of public and private spheres in political theory has undergone criticism even for the period of "classic capitalism" when it might have had some validity. See Nancy Fraser, *Unruly Practices: Power, Discourse and Gender in Contemporary Social Theory* (Minneapolis: University of Minnesota Press, 1989).

4   Octavio Paz, *El ogro filantrópico: Historia y política 1971–1978* (Mexico: Joaquín Mortíz, 1979). Mario Vargas Llosa, "El elefante y la cultura," *Contra viento y marea (1962–1982)* (Barcelona: Seix Barral, 1983), 444.

5   Irene Herner, "La toma de Nueva York," *Nexos* 156 (December 1990): 5–13. This is a meticulous overview of the exhibitions and their funding sources.

6   David Goldman, "A revolution you can invest in," *Forbes* (9 July 1990).

7   Herner, "La toma de Nueva York."

8   Octavio Paz, "Will for Form," introduction to "Mexico: Splendors of Thirty Centuries" (New York: The Metropolitan Museum of Art, 1990), 3-38.

9   Paz, "Will for Form."

10 Special advertising section, *The New Yorker*, October 1990.

11 See the brief discussion of Frida Kahlo's work in relation to the Mexican muralist movements in Jean Franco, *Plotting Women: Gender and Representation in Mexico* (New York: Columbia University Press, 1990).

12 Edward J. Sullivan, "Women in Mexico," in *Women in Mexico* catalog (National Academy of Design, 1990).

13 Peter Schjeldahl, "Frida Kahlo," *Mirabella* (November 1990). The same magazine has an article on another "new" Latin American phenomenon, "Brazil's Playboy President."

14 Hayden Herrera, "Why Frida Kahlo Speaks to the 90's," *The New York Times*, Sunday, 28 October 1990.

15 Melissa Chessher, "The Cult of Kahlo," *American Way* (1 December 1990): 62–68.

16 Jesusa Rodríguez, "La gira mamal de la Coatlicue," *Debate feminista*, año 1, vol. 2 (septiembre 1990): 401-03; Elena Poniatowska and Graciela Iturbide, *Juchitán de las mujeres* (Mexico: Ediciones Toledo, 1989).

GOING PUBLIC

Reinhabiting the Private

WOMEN'S MOVEMENTS AND THE SOCIAL IMAGINARY

*D*uring the last decade, Latin American women have emerged as protagonists in a number of grassroots movements—the mothers' movements of the Southern Cone, peasant movements, Catholic base communities, union movements, and local struggles around basic needs such as child nutrition, homes, soup kitchens, and water supply. These "new social movements" have given a significantly original dimension to contemporary political life,[1] precisely at a time when feminist groups have also grown rapidly in numbers and influence[2] and when an unprecedented number of women writers have emerged on the scene. If any generalized observation holds over the vast spectrum of struggles, local movements, nomadic cultures, and literary productions, it is perhaps their timeliness, their opportune emergence at a moment when the separation of the private from the public sphere—which had been the basis for the subordination of women by historic capitalism—has never seemed so arbitrary or fragile.[3] And this moment itself is, as Nancy Fraser points out, one of "emergence into visibility and contestability of problems and possibilities that cannot be solved or realized within the established framework of gendered roles and institutions."[4] One of those "problems" that could only become visible with the emergence of women's movements was the position of the intellectual. Do the new social movements represent, for the 1990s, the terrain of practice and political conscience that formerly had been occupied by the left? Between the 1920s and the 1960s, the male intelligentsia, confronting mass political and social movements (ranging from left political parties to the guerrilla movements), were again and

Originally published in *On Edge: The Crisis of Contemporary Latin American Culture*, ed. George Yúdice, Jean Franco, and Juan Flores (Minneapolis: University of Minnesota Press, 1992), 65–83.

again obliged to define their commitment, their responsibility, and art's relationship to the social. Women writers now find themselves in a similar position as they confront the reality of the new social movements. Yet they cannot simply repeat the discourse of responsibility, commitment, and representation, for literature itself no longer occupies the same position in the cultural spectrum as it did in the past.

THE NEW SOCIAL MOVEMENTS

In Latin America two factors contributed to women's participation in the new social movements—the authoritarian regimes of the 1970s and the extreme hardship caused by debt crisis and neoconservative policies that have been put into effect without the protective shield of the welfare state. Despite "redemocratization," the threat of authoritarianism and its consequences still cast shadows on national politics; and despite promises of economic miracles, the majority of Latin Americans have no access to the consumer society that is celebrated daily on television screens and billboards. Furthermore, as states become less and less inclined to take responsibility for the breakdown and collapse of services, people are often cast on their own resources, as was evident in Mexico after the earthquake disaster.[5] It is in these situations that women have increasingly acted as citizens, a position that had been difficult for them to assume as long as the public sphere was assumed to be a masculine domain.

Although it is easy to see that both military governments and redemocratization under the aegis of free-market capitalism alter the relation of the citizen to the state, it should also be emphasized that even in "welfare" states (Chile, Uruguay, and Mexico in the 1960s), the social contract rode on the inequalities of the sexual contract, which subordinated women to a reproductive rather than a citizen's role. Though women's participation in politics was not impossible, existing social arrangements did not encourage participation.[6] Under military regimes, this situation worsened since political activity in the public sphere was banned. Thus, in Argentina between 1976 and 1982 only those who unquestioningly supported the military regime were defined as citizens, and large sectors of the population found themselves in the shadowy realm of the subversive.

Yet, although the culture of fear—the use of torture, disappearance, and death-camp executions—was intended not only to deter the militant opposition but also to freeze all public activity, it was ineffective as a deterrent against the mothers of disappeared children. These women, known

as the Mothers of Plaza de Mayo, not only gathered together in a public place but used their marginalized position to reclaim the *polis*. They
created an Antigone space in which the rights (and rites) of kinship were
given precedence over the discourse of the state. For though the military
were secretly torturing and killing women and children, as well as male
militants, in their public rhetoric they represented themselves as protec-
tors of the family of the nation and ridiculed the demonstrating mothers
as "locas" [madwomen] who were outside the family of the nation. A few
old women raving about their children in the name of motherhood hardly
seemed much of a threat.[7]

Many scholars, particularly outside Latin America, have essentialized
the mothers' movements, arguing that the women exemplified "maternal thinking" by acting within their traditional roles.[8] Others regard the
mothers' movements as purely conjunctural and unable to generate a more
lasting political movement.[9] But such arguments overlook the fact that
the mothers did not merely act within a traditional role but substantially
altered tradition by casting themselves as a new kind of citizen and also
by appealing beyond the state to international organizations. Their use of
symbols was particularly eloquent and effective. They wore white kerchiefs
and silently carried blown-up snapshots of their children, often taken at
family gatherings. In this way, "private life"—as an image frozen in time—
was represented publicly as a contrast to the present, highlighting the destruction of that very family life that the military publicly professed to
protect. The women turned the city into a theater in which the entire
population was obliged to become spectators,[10] making public both their
children's disappearance and the disappearance of the public sphere itself.
In doing so, they drew attention to the very anomaly of women's presence
in the symbolic center of the nation, Plaza de Mayo.

The Chilean feminist Julieta Kirkwood argued that paradoxical as it
seemed, authoritarian governments often forced women to make connections between state repression and oppression in the home: "People have
begun to say that the family is authoritarian; that the socialization of children is authoritarian and rigid in its assignment of gender roles; that education, factory work, social organizations, and political parties have been
constituted in an authoritarian manner."[11]

Certainly, authoritarian regimes had the effect of enhancing the ethical
value of private life, religion, literature, and art as regions of refuge from
the brutal reality of an oppressive state. The church, especially in Chile,
courageously sheltered and defended human-rights movements. Yet as the

case of Sandinista Nicaragua would show, the church could also prove to be a barrier that prevented women from debating sensitive issues such as reproductive rights.[12] This is why, despite Julieta Kirkwood's belief that authoritarian governments awakened women to the domestic oppression, human-rights movements, particularly those dominated by the church, did not necessarily induct women into feminism.

Survival movements are a different matter. These movements come into being when the state can no longer deal with the day-to-day survival of its citizens. Women who must feed their families, find shelter, and protect their children in areas where policing is nonexistent, ineffective, or in the hands of drug lords, have been forced to take matters into their own hands, organizing soup kitchens and glass-of-milk programs, and occupying land for housing. It is in these movements that awareness of women's oppression has strengthened, although their activists often repudiate the label of feminism, which has been tainted by associations with man-hating puritans or with middle-class women whose interests do not coincide with those of the subaltern classes.[13] Nevertheless, some grassroots movements, especially in Brazil and Mexico, have had an extraordinary political impact, forcing governments to respond to issues such as housing and violence against women. In Mexico, for example, women participated actively in the neighborhood groups formed to help in the work of reconstruction after the 1985 earthquake, sometimes because they were heads of households, sometimes because their men were away or working.

The power of such grassroots movements has had an impact on the feminist movement in which, more and more, their presence, their questioning, and their politics have become an issue.[14] In any event, these social movements cannot be ignored. They exist all over the continent; they have produced their own organic intellectuals. And in many ways, as I shall now go on to argue, they have a direct and an indirect impact on culture.

WOMEN INTELLECTUALS BETWEEN COMMERCIALIZATION AND GRASSROOTS MOVEMENTS

Is there any connection between the new social movements and the emergence of a substantial corpus of writing by women? The answer seems to be a qualified no, qualified because there is a literature and art that springs directly from disappearance, poverty, and survival.[15] This exception merely underscores the deep-rooted class privilege that had traditionally been associated with literature.[16] At the same time, it is no coincidence that women's writing and new social movements have emerged at a time when the nation has ceased to be the necessary framework either of political action or of writing and when a dominant ideology of pluralism seems to undermine oppositional stances that rest on marginality.

One of the ironies of pluralism is that even commitment becomes marketable. There is now an unprecedented demand for literary works by women, particularly works that, in some way or other, seem to reflect women's "experience." Traditional genres such as lyric poetry and the novel compete with biographies, autobiographies, testimonials, and chronicles. Similarly, nearly all styles now appear equally valid. Women write bestsellers and hermetic avant-garde fiction. They are realists, magical realists, writers of fantasy, defenders of aesthetic space, destroyers of the aesthetic. Women's writing is neither a school nor a style. Indeed, the genre and mode in which women write constitute their positionality within a debate whose terms are seldom explicitly articulated. The separation of the intellectual from the popular classes, the gulf between different class positions on sexuality, are transposed into questions of narrative voice, genre, and style.

The class privilege of the intelligentsia has always posed a problem for Latin Americans, but in women's writing it becomes particularly acute since women writers are privileged and marginalized at one and the same time. Further, on questions of sexuality there is a considerable cultural gap between the middle classes and working classes. This may explain why some women writers feel obliged to separate the political from the aesthetic. Consider, for example, the case of the Chilean writer Diamela Eltit. She actively collaborated with the *Por la vida* [For Life] movement, which stages demonstrations to publicize disappearance; she wrote novels that are so hermetic they seem to baffle critics, and she staged public performances such as kissing a homeless man or reading her novel in a brothel in a poor sector of Santiago. In this one author, we find a tangle of conflicting intentions: to act against the authoritarian state, to take literature symbolically into the most marginal of spaces, to work against the easy readability of the commercial text, to foreground the woman's body as a site of contention, to increase or exaggerate the marginality of art, and to juxtapose literature's marginality to that of prostitutes, vagabonds, and the homeless. Or consider the very different example of Elena Poniatowska, whose chronicles and testimonials "give voice" to the subordinate classes and set the everyday language of survival against official history but who also writes an autobiographical novel, *La "Flor de lis,"* in which she powerfully affirms her identity with her snobbish and aristocratic mother from whom she cannot separate herself, except by transposing her desire onto the heterogeneous "mother country," Mexico, which her biological mother had always rejected. It is not that we should see these writers as contradictory but, rather, that they both confront the problem of class stratification, which can no longer be overcome simply by proclaiming oneself the voice of the subaltern.[17] It is the very intractability of this situation, the impossibility of the grand maternalist or avant-garde gesture, that accounts for the importance of testimonial literature, a genre that seems to cross the breach of class and racial stratification.

APPROPRIATING THE PUBLIC SPHERE

The testimonial is a life story usually related by a member of the subaltern classes to a transcriber who is a member of the intelligentsia. It is this genre that uses the "referential" to authenticate the collective memory of the uprooted, the homeless, and the tortured, and that most clearly registers the emergence of a new class of participants in the public sphere. The testimonial covers a spectrum between autobiography and oral history, but the word *testimony* has both legal and religious connotations and implies a subject as witness to and participant in public events. Clearly, it is not exclusively a women's genre, although it lends itself effectively to the story of conversion and *conscientización* that occurs once women transgress the boundaries of domestic space. The momentous nature of this move can only be appreciated when we recall that, within the traditional left, a woman knew "that she could never take power which is the workers' and peasants' prerogative. It was recognized, though, that she possessed another kind of power, power within the home, affective power, emotional blackmail (as queen, angel, or demon of the home) either because of her biological nature or because of the fact that she took pleasure in submission. And being so well trained in the private sphere, she abhors the public sphere."[18] Many testimonials by women thus bear witness to the breaking of the taboo on "going public" and their initial fears. A Mexican woman, for instance, states, "Of course I was afraid. Many of us were confronting something new, others had some experience from before the foundation of the Union of Neighborhoods. Now we understand that the Union is a political and civic education, a link between Mexican women and their own reality."[19]

But if these women acquire a political education through their activities, they do not necessarily subscribe to a feminist agenda or at least to a feminist agenda that separates women's problems from those of society as a whole. As a Mexican woman from a neighborhood organization states, "If we understand our own problems to be rape, abortion, violence, our aim should not be to make our men the prime enemy but to situate these as social problems that affect both men and women and make these demands those of the entire social movement."[20]

Because of its exemplary nature, testimonial literature has become an important genre for empowering subaltern women. It is important, however, to stress that the term *testimonial* embraces a corpus of texts that range from fragments embedded in other texts to full-length life stories like those of the Guatemalan Indian woman Rigoberta Menchú and the Bolivian Domitila Barrios de Chungara. The common feature of these stories is generally an abnormal event that activates the subject, the appropriation of public space, and the successful acquisition of a new public identity. In the most powerful of these narratives, for instance, that of Rigoberta Menchú, the narrator is able to exercise some control over the information, thus constituting her own subaltern narrative.[21]

On the other hand, for the woman intellectual who records and edits the testimony the process is of an altogether different nature. For very often the intellectual virtually disappears from the text in order to let "the subaltern speak," thus raising the question of her relationship to the political struggles she records. Is it that of a bystander? An impartial observer? Is she creating on the basis of somebody else's raw material? Or is it possible by means of double-voicing to bridge the gulf between the intelligentsia and the popular classes?

The chronicles and testimonial novels of Elena Poniatowska, though not simply focused on women, are interesting in this respect. Poniatowska has consistently amplified the testimonial genre by converting it into fiction and by incorporating many testimonials into a chronicle of a single event. This corresponds to a recurrent theme of "popular agency," that is, the potentiality of ordinary people (the young people of *La noche de Tlatelolco* [The Night of Tlatelolco], the earthquake survivors of *Nada, nadie* [Nothing, Nobody]) to act on their own behalf. Lurking under the surface is a certain utopian belief in popular power that becomes quite explicit in her essay "The Women of Juchitán," which in the guise of a description of a collection of photographs celebrates the eroticization of the social.

"The Women of Juchitán" was written as an introduction to a book of photographs by Graciela Iturbide. Juchitán is the rebellious town in the province of Oaxaca, which has been the scene of a running war against the central government and the domination of its party, the PRI (Partido Revolucionario Institucional). "The Women of Juchitán" is, indeed, frankly utopian and even contrasts with other more sober chronicles of Juchitán, notably those of Carlos Monsiváis.[22] But the essay is not to be judged as a piece of exposé journalism; rather, it is an imaginative vision of a society structured around women's sexuality. She describes the Juchitec women thus:

> You should see them arriving like walking towers, their window open, their hearts like windows, their ample breadth a moonlit night. You should see them come, they are already the government, they, the people, guardians of men, givers of food, their children riding their hips or swinging in the hammock of their breasts, the wind in their skirts, flowery vessels, the honeycomb of their sex overflowing with men. Here they come, bellies swaying, their machos in tow, their machos who, in contrast, are wearing colorless pants, shirts, leather sandals, and straw hats which they lift high into the air as they shout, "Long live the women of Juchitán."[23]

This celebration of excess is an antidote to the sober and often pedestrian accounts of women's movements that prevail in academic literature. Poniatowska's view is not that of the participant observer of a single event but a lyrical essay on the possibilities of nonpatriarchal sexuality and politics. In the writing of Poniatowska (and perhaps that of Rosario Ferré), we find the utopian dimension of women's writing in the fusion of sexual and political liberation. At the same time, this particular bridging of class difference is not common. For most women writers, it is the family romance itself that first must be undermined from within.

REINHABITING THE PRIVATE

The international marketing of Latin American literature under the brand name of "magic realism"; the seductive example of television, where melodrama and romance reach vast audiences; and the unabashed marketing of writers such as García Márquez and Vargas Llosa have given commercialization a good name, at least in certain circles. There is no reason to begrudge Isabel Allende the same translation rights as García Márquez or those of progressive writers such as Ariel Dorfman and Eduardo Galeano. The proliferation of women's studies courses and the incorporation of

Third World women writers into the curriculum have suddenly provided them with the kind of international readership that the writers of the "boom" have long enjoyed. Why then do I, unreasonably and with the temerity of an outsider, want something *more* than the merely marketable? Perhaps because the global reach of a novelist like Allende seems to put "quality" writing too readily at the service of the formulas that have always acted as female pacifiers—heterosexual romance combined with seigneurial goodwill toward the subaltern classes. The texts that most interest me are neither those in which the subaltern speaks while hiding the intellectual agent of that speech, nor those that refuse to acknowledge the privilege on which the "lettered city" has always depended. Yet in order to challenge that privilege women writers have been forced to re-examine that hidden sphere of the public/private dichotomy—the private itself, which traditionally has been so closely linked to the subjective and to the aesthetic.

The *private* is, in fact, a slippery term, used by economists to define private enterprise as opposed to the state and by social scientists to refer to the family or the household. But it also refers to the individual and the particular as opposed to the social. Even for male writers, however, the private was necessarily riddled with conflict; while seemingly the space for freedom and creativity, insofar as it was the space of the individual, the private revealed the limitation of death and mortality. In Vallejo's *Trilce* and Neruda's *Residencia en la tierra* [Residence on Earth], the private is the space of death, of futility, and redemption is only achieved through a new configuration of the social. In other writers, the limitations of male individuation can only be overcome by some incorporation or union with the feminine—in the poetry of Octavio Paz, for example, or the compensatory fictions of Puig and Rulfo—though this feminine is an ideal construct with little relationship to women's bodily experience.

The "ideology of the aesthetic" which, as Terry Eagleton claims, came into being with the bourgeois state's separation of the ethical, the political, and the aesthetic, bridged the frontiers between private and public.[24] Yet this aesthetic was also coded in a way that excluded the domestic, the banal, and the routine—in other words, those aspects of private life that were thought of as "feminine" and that reflected its colonization by the state.[25] The aesthetic allowed men to have their cake and eat it too, to separate the private from the (masculine) public sphere of citizenship so that eventually it could serve as a negative dialectic, while at the same time they relegated women to domestic space that was too crudely material to enter into the aesthetic. The contribution of French feminism, beginning with Simone de Beauvoir, was precisely to signal that scandalous move which had sublimated male sexuality while erasing the body and particularly the female body from consideration.[26]

Like French feminists, many Latin American women writers understand their position to be not so much one of confronting a dominant patriarchy with a new feminine position but rather one of unsettling the stance that supports gender power/knowledge as masculine. This "unsettling" is accomplished in a variety of ways, through parody and pastiche, by mixing genres, and by constituting subversive mythologies. The writing of Rosario Ferré, Luisa Valenzuela, Cristina Peri Rossi, Griselda Gambaro, Reina Roffé, Ana Lydia Vega, Albalucía Angel, Carmen Boullosa, and Isabel Allende — for example — corresponds to this project of displacing the male-centered national allegory and exposes the dubious stereotyping that was always inherent in the epics of nationhood that constitute the Latin American canon.[27] But there is also a reverse strategy, for if the sexual contract excluded women from the public sphere it also allowed middle-class women a particularly privileged and leisured existence, thanks to the class division between mistress and servant. The ambiguous overlapping of privilege and the aesthetic was indeed the central concern of Latin America's leading woman modernist, Clarice Lispector.

Known outside Brazil, thanks in part to the writings of the French feminist Hélène Cixous, Lispector seems a modernist *par excellence*, one of the few women to have gained acceptance in that exclusive male club.[28] The scandal of Lispector's writing, however, is not so much her "mastering" of modernist aesthetics as the inescapable and often quite naked intrusion of class difference and gender subordination that only serves to highlight the ugly scaffolding on which the temple of beauty has been erected. In her novels and short stories, sheltered women who have accepted the "sexual contract" without difficulty suddenly find themselves exposed by a simple breakdown of everyday life — the chauffeur hasn't turned up or the maid has just left. In one of her short stories, "Beauty and the Beast; or, The Wound That Was Too Big," a woman emerges from a beauty salon to find that her chauffeur has mistaken the time and there is no way to get home. She has money with her, but the bill is of such a large denomination that no taxi driver would take it. In the midst of this farcical dilemma, she is confronted by a wounded beggar who asks her for money. Lispector turns this raw encounter into an implacable demonstration of all the ethical, political, and aesthetic discourses that render dialogue between these two marginalized members of society impossible. The two are incommensurable. "Do you speak English?" the woman absurdly asks the beggar who, believing her to be mad or deaf, shouts at the top of his voice, "FALO" (a word play on "I speak" and phallus). Is the wounded beggar, whose name she forgets to ask, necessary for beauty, for conspicuous consumption, for the aesthetic? Lispector's writing is always on the edge of this disturbing possibility. Lispector's last novel, *The Hour of the Star*, is a powerful exploration not only of subaltern silence, but of authorial power. A plain, poor, and not very intelligent girl from the Northeast becomes the subject of the narrative written by a sophisticated male writer who, of course, appears to have absolute control over the material. The story is deliberately banal. The girl finds a boyfriend who leaves her for someone else. A fortune teller promises that she will meet her true love, and as she rushes across the street in happy anticipation she is run down by a speeding car. Despite the narrator's condescending attitude toward his material, the novel raises the disturbing question of whether aesthetic pleasure is in any way superior to or different from the poor girl's self-deception. In one of her most powerful novels, *The Passion According to G. H.*, a woman tidying up the room of a maid who has just left her service finds a cockroach (metonymically linked to the servant class), tries to kill it, and then when it is dying, she is driven to ingest the liquid it exudes in a parody of Christian communion. In all these texts, the idea that all forms of life are equal shockingly foregrounds arbitrary inequalities.

The epiphany that critics inevitably underscore in Lispector's writing is achieved in full awareness of the savage heart that gives life to the aesthetic; that savagery is represented not by the cockroach or the beggar or the working girl, but by those who occupy the center thanks to the marginalization of the Other.[29] While it is true that Othering is a feature of modernist writing, Lispector, epiphany and all, allows the roughness and the violence of the operation to surface.

Lispector's position has been an isolated one, however. Her modernist aesthetic was seen as apolitical, especially in the 1960s when literary and political commitment found their ideal representations in the guerrilla fighter. The guerrilla movement became not only the logical extension of cultural politics, but also a test of heroism. It was precisely in the aftermath of guerrilla politics that women's writing acquires special significance since it is precisely women's marginalization that seems to provide a critical standpoint, especially for those women who were caught in the contradictions of a vanguard movement that allowed them equality only in death.

The generation of women formed in the oppositional politics of the 1970s and 1980s is understandably engaged with problems of exile, marginality, and the nomadic—problems, in other words, that emerged with full force at the end of the 1970s.[30] The genres at their disposal, however—poetry and narrative—come to them loaded with the freight of history. Poetry, once widely practiced and appreciated, has receded in importance: "committed poetry" is more likely to be transmitted through the lyrics of popular songs than in published collections. And narrative, too, is far more widely diffused through television genres than through the printed word. In consequence, to write poetry or narrative that refuses to fall into the category of romance inevitably means addressing a restricted public, although this is not necessarily a disadvantage, as I hope to show in my discussion of two writers, the Peruvian Carmen Ollé and the Argentine Tununa Mercado.

Noches de Adrenalina [Nights of Adrenaline][31] by Carmen Ollé can be regarded as a form of "testimonial." The poems in the collection monitor her long march through the political movements of the 1960s to self-exile in Paris. The poetic subject thus repeats the itinerary of a famous predecessor, César Vallejo, for whom the body was simultaneously the source of individuation and its negation. For Ollé, there is no escaping the body:

> fat / small / beardless / hairy / transparent /
> rickety / big ass / dark circles under her eyes (p. 9).

Yet she is not simply determined by this destiny, for the body in all its gross and universal materiality is both the support and the object of sexual fantasy that seeks satisfaction in guilty adolescent masturbation, painful and pleasurable orgasm, adult narcissism. She pictures the women of her generation sobbing in front of the bathroom mirror, "before *The Death of the Family* caught up with us" (p. 10). At San Marcos, the heroes are the militant leftists: "By day they interrupted our metaphysics classes with rage / and we would applaud that sweaty black hair on / their backs" (p. 10). Her very identity is, at this stage of her life, mediated by the male orgasm. "I opt for nudity. / I can't contemplate it but for the mirror or in his eyes / in his aroused look that marks a curve / veering from the waist toward the butt / and erect loin and I am she who turns on his axis / while the reflection he offers me doesn't belong to me / he authors the instant in which my body is his pleasure / and barely lit up by the lamp this is nudity of nothing / other than desire" (p. 36). As in the poetry of César Vallejo, the harsh and sometimes pleasurable bodily sensations form a sort of babble that constantly disturbs the more sedate progress of intellectual history—Marxism, existentialism, the counterculture. The poet-narrator is constantly on the alert, monitoring the emissions of the body—pissing, menstruation, lubrication—as well as its gradual degeneration, from the lost tooth to the last period. And yet the poems chart not only the body's aging and the intellect's disillusionment, but a process of transformation. This does not involve, as in the testimonial, an appropriation of the public sphere, but a transcendence of the social limitations imposed by gender division.

> I love her
> as I would a fickle woman
> and not knowing how to love her makes me sick
> our desire is rigid and hardly
> fired by a feminine body
> maturity has obstructed what in adolescence
> was transparent
> he/she (p. 54)

Given Ollé's subsequent development,[32] *Nights of Adrenaline* can perhaps be considered a kind of exorcism of Leiris and Bataille, holding out the possibility of self-love that the devaluation of the feminine has obstructed. But more than this, it suggests that there can be no "public sphere of debate" that does not include the hitherto "private" body.

Exile with its politically charged pathos has, perhaps predictably, provided many women writers with a correlative for their own marginality. In Tununa Mercado's novel *En estado de memoria* [In a State of Memory],[33] the narrator is a nomad who wanders between Mexico, Europe, and Argentina. But this novel is less a description of exile than a series of off-center meditations that allow the author to question "literature," the politics of exile (and of marginality), the seduction of memory, and the possibility of the aesthetic.

What is original about Mercado's text is indeed its questioning of marginality. The position of Mercado's narrator is essentially one of vicariousness. She is employed as a ghostwriter and editor, someone who has never pursued writing as a vocation and yet earns her living as a writer; but vicariousness is also the condition of her entire life down to the clothes that she wears, which are castoffs that had belonged to other people, and her different "homes," which never seem to belong to her and where "everything was provisional." The narrator's political activity is also vicarious. In Mexico, she demonstrates outside the Argentine embassy to protest events that have happened to people far away, knowing that the demonstration is only a shadow of "real" politics elsewhere. On a visit to Spain she offers to visit the native soil of one of her friends, a Spanish exile, thus vicariously searching for somebody else's past. In Mexico, she spends her weekends visiting the house of another exile—Leon Trotsky—and obsessively going over the last days of his life. On a visit to Argentina, she finds herself one day walking into her old primary school and trying to recapture, as an adult, the sensations of childhood. But such experiences are not of recovery, but rather of loss and absence, of death and disappearance. Returning home definitively to "redemocratized" Argentina, she still feels homeless. Even the Thursday ritual of the mothers in the Plaza de Mayo cannot give her any sense of belonging since, after the first euphoria of return, after the expressions of solidarity, she recognizes that the energy of the anti-authoritarian movement has drained away in the new pluralistic yet strangely depoliticized environment.

Mercado's novel thus confronts one of the major issues of our time—the issue of a pluralism that permits and even encourages difference. The narrator's obsession with a tramp, a "linyera" she meets in the park, may, in fact, reflect a certain nostalgia for a marginality that has, however, no longer any possible social significance. For the marginal is merely an individual rebellion while, on the other hand, the social text has become unreadable except individually.

This dilemma is illustrated by the experience of an exile reading group in which the narrator participates. The reading group embarks on a thirty-year reading of Hegel's *Phenomenology of Mind*. This experience does not open up universal knowledge for the narrator and her friends, but rather becomes a teasing process in which the readers are sometimes absorbed by the reading, sometimes completely baffled, but never in control of it. What the reading produces is a revelation, a feeling, and a cooperation, but not knowledge/power. This "distracted" relation to a text, chosen almost at random, is matched by her attitude to writing, which she never accepts as a life project or in a spirit of professionalism. The narrator compares writing to weaving, though the two processes are not exactly analogous. Absorbed in weaving, she can attain a felicitous state of self-forgetfulness. Writing, on the other hand, is essentially a negative revelation: "not knowing, not being able to fill the vacuum, not comprehending the universal."

Who better, then, than such a narrator to register the irrevocable absences; the sense of loss, of time wasted; the fragility of justifications that sum up the purely negative state of exile? In its refusal of rhetorical and institutional certainties, the novel confronts the reader with an aesthetic that is also ascetic, an absolute state of nonpossession, an anarchy. At the novel's end, the narrator is writing on a wall that gradually slips out of view, "like paper through a crack." When the wall of gender difference comes down, it is not simply the center that is destroyed but also marginal positions, including that of "woman" and "woman writing as woman." The "writing on the wall" both heralds a destruction and performs that destruction.

The imperative for Latin American women is thus not only the occupation and transformation of public space, the seizure of citizenship, but also the recognition that speaking as a woman within a pluralistic society may actually reinstitute, in a disguised form, the same relationship of privilege that has separated the intelligentsia from the subaltern classes. The woman intellectual must witness not only the destruction of the wall, but that of her own anonymous inscription on that very wall.

In the documentary film *Double Day*, an Argentine schoolteacher was asked why girls lined up on one side of the classroom and boys on another. "Because this is the girl's side and that's the boy's side," the teacher replied without even the slightest inkling that his answer might seem absurd. This is the natural (and the ideological), the way things seemed to be. But the ways things seem to be now are not the way they were when the film was made. Girls sit on the boys' side. Women have broadened the public sphere of debate, not only as members of social movements but as intellectuals. In Mexico, for example, women act both as intellectuals in MUSIAL, "Mujeres por la soberanía y la integración de América Latina" [Women in support of Latin American sovereignty and integration] and also as mediators for marginalized women.[34] The woman intellectual cannot claim unproblematically to represent women and be their voice, but she can broaden the terms of political debate by redefining sovereignty and by using privilege to destroy privilege. I have myself shamelessly privileged a few texts that unsettle the idea that women now occupy unproblematically "their" space, for this is one way of striking a path through the forest of pluralism.

NOTES

1 See Jane S. Jaquette, ed., *The Women's Movements in Latin America: Feminism and the Transition to Democracy* (Boston: Unwin Hyman, 1989). See also "The Homeless Organize," *Nacla Report on the Americas* 23 (Nov.–Dec. 1989); Ilse Scherer-Warren and Paulo J. Krischke, eds., *Uma revolucão no cotidiano? Os novos movimentos sociais na America do Sul* (São Paulo: Editora Brasiliense, 1987); and

Elizabeth Jelin, ed., *Women and Social Change in Latin America*, trans. J. Ann Zammit and Marilyn Thomson (London: Zed Books, 1990). See also Giovanni Arrighi, Terence K. Hopkins, and Immanuel Wallerstein, *Antisystemic Movements* (London: Verso, 1989).

2 Nancy Saporta Sternbach, Marysa Navarro Aranguren, Patricia Chuchryk, and Sonia Alvarez, in "Feminisms in Latin America" (unpublished essay), have given a detailed analysis of the various "encuentros de mujeres" [women's gatherings].

3 We have to distinguish between the critique of theories that are based on the notion of the public sphere (for instance, those of Habermas) and the real effect of this imaginary separation. For a critique, see Nancy Fraser, *Unruly Practices: Power, Discourse, and Gender in Contemporary Social Theory* (Minneapolis: University of Minnesota Press, 1989).

4 Fraser, *Unruly Practices*, 134.

5 Alejandra Massolo and Martha Schteingart, eds., "Participación social, reconstrucción y mujer: El sismo de 1985," *Documentos de trabajo* 1 (UNICEF, Colegio de México). On women and the new social movements, see Elizabeth Jelin, "Citizenship and Identity: Final Reflections," which is the concluding essay in Jelin, *Women and Social Change in Latin America*, 187.

6 One of the best discussions is found in Carole Pateman, *The Sexual Contract* (Oxford: Basil Blackwell, 1988).

7 See, for instance, J. P. Bousquet, *Los locas de la Plaza de Mayo* (Buenos Aires: El Cid, 1983); and Elizabeth Jelin, ed., *Ciudadanía y participación.*

8 See, for example, Sara Ruddick, "Maternal Peace Politics and Women's Resistance: The Example of Argentina and Chile," *The Barnard Occasional Papers on Women's Issues* 4 (winter 1989): 34–55.

9 For instance, María del Carmen Feijóo, "The Challenge of Constructing Civilian Peace: Women and Democracy in Argentina," in Jaquette, *Women's Movements in Latin America*, 72–94, recognizes the contribution of the mothers' movements but also sees possible limitations.

10 For instance, they circulated money with messages written on the notes, thus implicating random members of the public in the struggle. See Hebe Bonafini, *Historias de vida* (Buenos Aires: Fraterna, 1985), 162.

11 Julieta Kirkwood, *Ser política en Chile: las feministas y los partidos* (Santiago: FLASCO, 1986), 180.

12 Maxine Molyneux, "Mobilization without Emancipation? Women's Interests, the State and Revolution in Nicaragua," *Feminist Studies* 11 (1985). See also Joel Kovacs, *In Nicaragua* (London: Free Association Books, 1988), which has some interesting things to say about everyday life in Nicaragua and the relations between women. See esp. chap. 4, "La mujer."

13 See, for instance the testimonies in Massolo and Schteingart, "Participación social, reconstrucción y mujer."

14 For a detailed discussion of some of the tensions, see Saporta Sternbach et al., "Feminisms in Latin America." On Brazil, see Sonia Alvarez, "Brazil"; and

for Chile, Patricia M. Chuchryk, "Feminist Anti-Authoritarian Politics: The Role of Women's Organizations in the Chilean Transition to Democracy." Both articles are included in Jaquette, *Women's Movements in Latin America.*

15 See, for example, Ruth Molina de Cuevas, *Y me vistieron de luto* (San José, Costa Rica: Editorial Universitaria Centroamericana, 1990). The poems are dedicated to her sons who disappeared and "to the mothers who like myself are waiting."

16 Angel Rama, *La ciudad letrada* (Hanover, N.H.: Ediciones del Norte, 1984).

17 Eltit discusses her performances on the BBC film "Love and Power," which was part of the series *Made in Latin America.* It must be remembered, however, that highly codified avant-garde writing and performance have been particular features of literature under authoritarian regimes. For Elena Poniatowska, see *La "Flor de Lis"* (Mexico: Era, 1988).

18 Julieta Kirkwood, *Ser política*, 191.

19 Massolo and Schteingart, "Participación social, reconstrucción y mujer," 76.

20 Ibid., 78.

21 Elizabeth Burgos-Debray, ed., *I . . . Rigoberta Menchú: An Indian Woman in Guatemala*, trans. Ann Wright (London: Verso, 1984). There have many articles on Rigoberta Menchú. See, for example, George Yúdice, "Marginality and the Ethics of Survival," in Andrew Ross, ed., *Universal Abandon?: The Politics of Postmodernism* (Minneapolis: University of Minnesota Press, 1988). See also Moema Viezzer, ed., *"Si me permiten hablar": Testimonio de Domitila, Una mujer de las minas de Bolivia* (Mexico: Siglo XXI, 1977). See also David Acebey, ed., *Aquí también Domitila* (Mexico: Siglo XXI, 1985).

22 Carlos Monsiváis, *Entrada libre: Crónicas de una sociedad que se organiza* (Mexico: Era, 1987).

23 Graciela Iturbide and Elena Poniatowska, *Juchitán de las mujeres* (Mexico, D.F.: Ediciones Toledo, 1989), 13–14. See also Poniatowska's chronicle of the 1985 earthquake, *Nada, nadie: Las voces del temblor* (Mexico: Era, 1988).

24 Terry Eagleton, *The Ideology of the Aesthetic* (Oxford: Basil Blackwell, 1990).

25 As Nancy Fraser points out, in *Unruly Practices*, even in classic capitalism the family was never totally private.

26 For a discussion of French feminism in relation to Hispanic culture, see Paul Julian Smith, *The Body Hispanic* (Oxford: Oxford University Press, 1989).

27 Among writers whose work has been translated, we might mention Rosario Ferré's *Sweet Diamond Dust* (New York: Ballantine, 1988); Isabel Allende's first novel, *The House of the Spirits*, trans. Magda Bogin (New York: Knopf, 1985); and Luisa Valenzuela, *The Lizard's Tail*, trans. Gregory Rabassa (New York: Farrar, Straus & Giroux, 1983). Some interesting attempts to change the "subject" include Cristina Peri Rossi, *La nave de los locos* (Barcelona: Seix Barral, 1984), and *El campo*, by Griselda Gambaro, a theater piece that acts out the savagery of the death camp and male-female relationships. Albalucía del Angel, in *Estaba la pájara pinta sentada en el verde limón* (Barcelona: Argos Vergara, 1984), rewrites the story of Colombian *violencia.*

28 See Hélène Cixous, *Reading with Clarice Lispector*, trans. Verena Andermatt Conley (Minneapolis: University of Minnesota Press, 1990). For a critique of Lispector as exemplary woman writer, see Daphne Patai, "El esencialismo de Clarice Lispector," *Nuevo Texto Crítico* 3 (1990): 21–35.

29 "A Bela e a Fera ou a ferida grande demais" [Beauty and the Beast; or, The Wound That Was Too Big] is included in Benedito Nunes, ed., *Paixão Segundo G.H.* (Campus Universitário, Trinidad; Florianópolis SC, Brazil: UNESCO, Coleção Arquivos, 1988), 151–57. The novel has been translated as *The Passion According to G.H.*, trans. Ronald W. Sousa (Minneapolis: University of Minnesota Press, 1988). Also translated by Giovanni Pontiero is *The Hour of the Star* (New York: Carcaner, 1986).

30 In general, the left position has been that socialism will bring about women's liberation. See, for example, Latin American and Caribbean Women's Collective, *Slaves of Slaves: The Challenge of Latin American Women*, trans. Michael Pallis (London: Zed Press, 1977); Isabel Larguía and John Dumoulin, *Hacia una ciencia de la liberación de la mujer* (Caracas: Universidad Central de Venezuela, 1975); Heleieth Saffioti, *Women in Class Society*, trans. Michael Vale (New York and London: Monthly Review Press, 1978).

31 Carmen Ollé, *Noches de Adrenalina* (Lima: Cuadernos de Hipocampo, 1981). Translations by Ann Archer.

32 She has since published in a nonconfessional mode, *Todo orgullo humea la noche* (Lima: Lluvia, 1988).

33 Tununa Mercado, *En estado de memoria* (Buenos Aires: Ada Korn, 1990). For these last paragraphs—especially the questioning of "marginality"—I wish to express my debt to Josefina Ludmer, especially in the light of her recent work on delinquency, the state, and the counterstate. For a different but powerful discussion of marginality, see also Diamela Eltit's conversations with the man known as "El Padre Mío," Diamela Eltit, *El Padre Mío* (Santiago: Francisco Zegers, 1989).

34 MUSIAL, which includes some of Mexico's most prominent women intellectuals, began as a discussion group. The women now issue declarations as women and intellectuals on particular problems concerned with sovereignty—on Panama and Nicaragua, for example.

LA MALINCHE

From Gift to Sexual Contract

*I*n his book, *The Labyrinth of Solitude*, published in 1950 when post-revolutionary Mexican nationalism was at its height, Octavio Paz commented on the "strange persistence" of Cortés and his mistress and interpreter, La Malinche, in the imagination and sensibility of Mexicans, arguing that the persistence of such myths revealed a still unresolved identity conflict.[1] In the decades since the publication of the essay, the concept of national identity has come to seem anachronistic and the *pachuco* [urban Mexican Americans] whom Paz took as a grotesque hybrid, neither authentically Mexican nor North American, is now increasingly seen as the vanguard of a new transnational culture while La Malinche, no longer victim or traitress, has become the transfigured symbol of fragmented identity and multiculturalism.[2]

Nowhere is this reevaluation of La Malinche more striking than in certain revisionary accounts of the discovery and conquest, especially Tzvetan Todorov's *La Conquête d'Amérique* and Stephen Greenblatt's *Marvelous Possessions*.[3] Both of these books reflect the contemporary preoccupation with alterity, representation, and hybridity. They thus highlight an aspect of the conquest that nineteenth- and twentieth-century heroic narratives had tended to dismiss. Although the positivist Justo Sierra once described La Malinche as "el verbo de la conquista" [the word of the conquest],[4] generally speaking her representation in the heroic narrative is a less flattering one. William Prescott's *Conquest of Mexico* published in the 1840s attributes La Malinche's linguistic ability to the fact that Castilian "was to her the language of love."[5] In the 1920s, when William Carlos Williams wrote *In the American Grain*, a classic statement of pan-American identity, his account of the tragic fall of Tenochtitlán centered on a confrontation between Moctezuma and Cortés in which the crucial role of the *lengua*

Originally published in *Beeld en Verbeelding van Amerika*, ed. Wil Pansters and Jan Weerdenburg (Utrecht: Bureau Studium Generale, Universiteit Utrecht, 1992), 71–88.

or interpreter is altogether ignored.[6] As Teresa de Lauretis points out,[7] in heroic narratives, woman is a helper or land to be conquered. In the dramatic narrative in which rivals war to the death, woman is simply irrelevant. But there is something obtrusive in the figuration of La Malinche especially in Bernal Díaz del Castillo's account of the history of the conquest, which lends credence to both Todorov and Greenblatt's foregrounding of the "go-between," translator, and interpreter.

For contemporary critics the conquest and discovery are paradigmatic events whose repercussions extend into the present. For Todorov, "C'est bien la conquête de l'Amérique qui annonce et fond notre identité présente" [It is the conquest of America that presages and founds our present identity] (p. 14). For both of them, La Malinche occupies a crucial position as interpreter and intermediary. Without her, Todorov believes, the conquest of Mexico would have been impossible. Echoing generations of Mexican historians, he states that "she is the first example and for the same reason the symbol of the mixing of cultures: she announced therefore the modern State of Mexico and beyond that, our present state because although we are not all bilingual, we are bi- or tri-cultural" (p. 107, my translation). The slippage in this passage is from "she" to some universal "we," and thus it elides both discontinuities and the unique nature of Spanish colonialism. To cite La Malinche as the "first example" and the "symbol" of the merging of cultures (and modern multiculturalism) is to glide too rapidly over the epistemic and real violence that this symbolization implies.

Although Greenblatt's account of the discovery and conquest is somewhat different from Todorov's,[8] he too places an emphasis on interpreters and go-betweens. Cannibalism and idolatry, he argues, constituted a blockage for Spaniards in their dealings with the Aztecs and made necessary the exclusion of the Aztecs from civilized intercourse. "Nonetheless communication had to take place so that some human bridge was needed for information to pass between the invaders and the defenders and it was Doña Marina who fulfilled this role." She is, according to Greenblatt, "object of exchange, model of conversion, the only figure who appears to understand the two cultures, the only person in whom they meet" (p. 143). And he further notes that "for virtually everyone in Bernal Díaz's history—Indians and Spaniards alike—the site of the strategic symbolic oscillation between self and other is the body of this woman" (p. 143).

Noting that "in 1492, in the introduction to his *Gramática*, the first grammar of a modern European tongue, Antonio de Nebrija wrote that language has always been the partner [*compañera*] of empire, he claims that

Cortés had found in Doña Marina his *compañera*" (p. 145). This slippage
between metaphor and metonymy is a significant one for it conceals a crucial element, the fact that there could be no bridge, encounter or *compañera*
without a prior act of violence which symbolic appropriation conveniently
veils. Both Todorov and Greenblatt essentially overlook the significance of
the sleight of hand by which conquest becomes *mestizaje*, a sleight of hand
that effectively displaces attention from the mode of reproduction of colonial society to symbolic woman as (and as always) helper, intermediary,
intercessor, and eventually (in nationalist discourse) traitor.

It is generally believed that La Malinche's indigenous name was Malinalli, the name of a day in the Aztec calendar which was represented by a
twisted reed. Malinalli is the sign not only of a day but also refers to the
helicoid symbol that binds the two opposing forces of the cosmos in constant movement, which makes the forces of the lower world rise and those
of the heavens descend. The indigenous referred to her as Malintzin.[9] To
the Christians, she was known by her baptismal name of Doña Marina.

Cortés first encountered her when she was given to him by one of the
chiefs of Tabasco, as a gift along with nineteen other women, and miscellaneous items that included lizards, diadems, and dogs. Cortés, who had
initially passed her on to his captain Puertocarrero, quickly discovered that
she was bilingual. Because Jerónimo de Aguilar, a Spaniard who had been
held captive in Cozumel knew the Maya language, he was able to translate from Spanish to Maya and Marina from Maya to Nahuatl. As Bernal
Díaz del Castillo noted, Doña Marina knew the language of Guatzacualco
"which is that of Mexico and knew that of Tabasco; as Jerónimo de Aguilar knew that of Yucatan and Tabasco which is all one, they understood
each other very well; and Aguilar declared it in Castellano to Cortés."[10]
The two of them very quickly formed an efficient team, certainly efficient
enough to enable Cortés to grasp the complex political intrigues and unrest
among the various tribes who were subject to Aztec domination. Cortés's
encounter with the enslaved and bilingual Marina was thus both fortu-
itous and fortunate especially as she was also good-looking and apparently
happy to become his mistress and native informant.[11] Of course she didn't
have to be a woman to serve as *lengua* and informant but it was precisely
gender, as I shall argue, that accounts for her overdetermined position in
the "encounter."

Since Cortés refers to her only briefly in the *Cartas de relación*, what we
know of Doña Marina comes primarily from the historians and chroni-
clers of the conquest, particularly Francisco López de Gomara's *History*

of the Conquest of Mexico and Bernal Díaz del Castillo's *True History*, and from the "probanza" or testimony drawn up to provide proof of her service to the Spanish crown. There are also the indigenous chronicles and codices in which she is represented in her role of interpreter, as well as some popular traditions some of them extant to the present, which associate La Malinche with the Virgin and with the mythical Llorona.[12]

López de Gomara's history, though written by a man who had never set a foot in New Spain, almost certainly reflects the view of Cortés himself and those of the conquistadores from whom he was able to gather eyewitness accounts. Not surprisingly he makes Cortés the central protagonist, the creator of strategy, and the intellectual as well as the practical author of the conquest. López de Gomara describes La Malinche as a slave who was offered freedom by Cortés in exchange for becoming his *faraute* (derived from the French, herault or herald) and secretary. Cortés's official historian thus insists on the fact that she was a slave, in contrast, as we shall see to Bernal Díaz del Castillo's insistence on her noble origins. And although López de Gomara cannot avoid mentioning Cortés's carnal relationship with her, he does so almost as an aside when he reports that Cortés was criticized for marrying her off to Juan Jaramillo, who was drunk at the time, because he himself had offspring by her (p. 270). At the end of the history, listing Cortés's children, López de Gomara says only that there was a Martín Cortés (in addition to Cortés's son, Martín, by his Spanish wife, Juana de Zuñiga) "who was born of an Indian" (p. 374). Here Doña Marina is simply the *unnamed* mother of one of the first *mestizos*, the bastard son whom Cortés legitimized by papal decree. It is important to emphasize this silence around Marina's role in reproduction. The fact that Marina bore a son some time during the arduous fighting of the conquest, was married by Cortés to one of his lieutenants Juan Jaramillo, and then, once again pregnant (this time by Jaramillo), accompanied Cortés on the even more arduous march south to Honduras, giving birth to a daughter, María, on board the boat that brought the expedition back to Veracruz is, of course, too much the natural state of things to merit the historian's attention.[13]

In contrast, Bernal Díaz del Castillo elevates Doña Marina to a position that was, in many ways, almost equal to that of Cortés and certainly in his view she was the most powerful member of the indigenous population after Moctezuma. Writing in order to correct López de Gomara's account and to show that the conquest was not simply the work of one man but of many, Bernal Díaz del Castillo, had every reason to stress that the conquest was a team effort and one in which a woman played a major role.

Doña Marina, he records, "had virile strength even though every day she heard that they might kill and eat our flesh and even though she had been beseiged in past battles and though now all of us were wounded and suffering we never saw any weakness in her but only a strength greater than that of woman" (p. 1:242).

Though in this passage, Bernal Díaz del Castillo raises Doña Marina to the status of honorary male, he also implies that she was far more than a ventriloquist, for she inflects Cortés's speech with emotions of friendship or anger. For example:

> When Cortés spoke to them amicably through Doña Marina, they brought much maize and poultry and pointed out the road we had to follow (p. 2:268).

> Cortés asked Doña Marina and Jerónimo de Aguilar, our lenguas, why the chiefs were so agitated after the arrival of those Indians [i.e. Moctezuma's tribute collectors] and who were these people. And Doña Marina, who understood very well told him what was happening (p. 1:185).

> Moctezuma bade him welcome and our Cortés replied through Doña Marina wishing him very good health. And it seems to me that Cortés, through Doña Marina offered him his right hand (p. 1:314).

> Then Cortés embraced Moctezuma twice and Moctezuma also embraced Cortés and Doña Marina who was very sagacious, said to him artfully that he was pretending sadness at our departure (p. 1:410).

The coquetry she practices in this last interchange suggests that she felt that she had a certain amount of freedom to perform within the permitted code. More than this, her skill in the art of persuasion was an essential element in winning over the indigenous population. Violence, it is true, preceded hegemony but hegemony could not be established without securing some willing allies and participants as Cortés well knew.[14] The indigenous historian, Alva Ixtlilxochitl, writing long after the conquest would even acknowledge that "the *lengua* Marina was charged with preaching the Christian faith and at the same time speaking of the King of Spain. In a few days she learned the Spanish tongue which saved Cortés a great deal of work and seems to have been almost miraculous and very important for the conversion of the indigenous and the foundation of our holy Catholic faith."[15] In the *probanza* of her services to the conquest, one witness, Gonzalo Rodríguez de Ocaña, stated that "because of Doña Marina's work, many Indians became Christians and submitted to the rule of your Majesty." [16] Here we clearly see the identification of the feminine with the constitution of hegemony, a hegemony that after the violence will be secured by loving words (*palabras amorosas*). Marina is not only interpreter and translator, but the paradigm figure in the conversion of conquest into empire.

The episode for which she is best known is also the one which would later turn the translator into *tradditora*, that is, her denunciation of the Cholulan conspiracy. It was in Cholula that Moctezuma made his most determined effort to stop the Spanish advance by ambushing the invaders at night. The conspiracy was revealed to Doña Marina by an old woman who, "seeing her young and wealthy," wished to save her life and marry her off to her son. In Bernal Díaz del Castillo's account, it also happens to be the one episode in which she speaks in her own voice.[17] "Oh mother," she replies, "how grateful I am for what you have told me. I would leave now if it wasn't for the fact that I have no-one to bring me my clothes and jewels which are plentiful. On your life, mother, only wait with your son for a little while and tonight we will depart; for now those lords are awake and will hear us" (pp. 1:290-94). By means of this ruse, Marina learns all the details of the plot and promptly warns Cortés. With Marina at his side as interpreter, Cortés surrounds the Indians and warns them of the cost of treason, after which, according to Bernal Díaz del Castillo, "we killed many of them and others were burned alive." It is in this episode that Marina proved the strength of her loyalty to Cortés. It seems deplorable to many modern readers that the quite extraordinary political intelligence and calculation that Marina displayed in this episode should only have benefited the Spaniards. However, her situation neatly illustrates the thoroughly gendered inflection of terms such as *loyalty* and *treachery*. The conquerors were constantly demanding loyalty to their "just" cause and though they were apparently bonded by common religion and nationality, in reality their loyalties were generally temporary and opportunistic, especially as the justification for their mission was invented and mythologized as they went along.[18] On the other hand, it is difficult for women in patriarchal societies to bond with other women, since their loyalty is transferred on marriage or concubinage from the natural family to the new owner.

What is more difficult to understand is the fact that this exogamous system operated so efficiently despite the cultural gap between Spaniards and the indigenous. As far as the exchange of women was concerned, the "otherness" of the indigenous seems to have been unimportant. Women were passed around freely between the indigenous and the Spaniards and between Spaniards and Spaniards, though of course no Spanish women were presented to indigenous allies.

It is in this context that Bernal Díaz's account of Marina's early life is particularly significant, especially as it occurs as a lengthy digression that precedes the account of the conquest itself and includes information which he could only have acquired at a much later date when the conquest was almost complete. It is an artful narrative device whose purpose is both to emphasize La Malinche's status as a princess and to account for her loyalty to the Spanish cause.

She was, he writes:

> the daughter of the chief or Principal of Painala, a powerful lord who had several districts subject to him, eight leagues from Guazacoalcos. He dying while this lady was an infant, his widow married another chief, a young man, by whom they had a son whom they determined to place in succession after them. They therefore gave the girl to certain Indians of Xicalango, to carry off secretly and caused it to be rumoured that she was dead: which report was corroborated by taking advantage of the death of a child of her age, the daughter of a slave. The people of Xicalango gave her to those of Tabasco, and the latter to Cortés, by whom she was presented to a cavalier named Alonzo Hernández Puertocarrero. When he went to Old Castille, Cortés took her to himself, and had by her a son who was named Don Martín Cortés and who was a commander of the order of San Tiago. She afterwards on an expedition to Higueras married a cavalier named Juan Jaramillo.
>
> Doña Marina had by her birth an universal influence and consequence through these countries; she was of a fine figure, frank manners, prompt genius and intrepid spirit; and an excellent linguist, and of most essential service to Cortés whom she always accompanied. I was acquainted with her mother and half brother who was at the time I knew him grown up; they governed their territory conjointly, the second husband also being dead. They were afterwards baptised, the mother by the name of Marta, the son by the name of Lazarus; this I know, for in the expedition to Higueras when Cortés passed through Guatzacoalacos, he summoned all the neighboring chiefs to meet him in that settlement; and amongst many others came the mother and half brother of the lady. She had told me before that she was of that province, and in truth she much resembled her mother who immediately

recognized her. Both the old lady and her son were terrified, thinking that they were sent for to be put to death, and cried bitterly, but Doña Marina dried their tears, saying that she forgave them, that at the time they sent her from them they were ignorant of what they did; and then she thanked God who had taken her from the worship of idols to the true church and was happier in having a son by her lord and master Cortés and in being married to a cavalier like her husband than if she had been sovereign of all the provinces of new Spain. This story brings to my mind that of Joseph in Egypt when his brothers were in power (pp. 155–56).[19]

Bernal Díaz del Castillo finishes this account by swearing to its accuracy, an indication that he was concerned that it should be accepted as a true history.

But was it? The story itself could only have come from Doña Marina and not only does it conflict with López de Gomara's suggestion that she was sold into slavery,[20] but it has suspicious parallels with other popular narratives. Bernal Díaz himself is struck by its similarity to the story of Joseph. Other critics have pointed out that it resembles the chivalresque romance, Amadís de Gaula. It is a theme that is also found in the Mixtec story of the insulted princess.[21] There are also, as I shall point out later, significant similarities to the Oedipus myth. Did Doña Marina mistranslate her own story or simply skillfully adapt it to the requirements of the conquest narrative?

There is no way of ascertaining the truth but what we do know is that the account of the girl's violent separation from a cruel mother fits very neatly into the story of the conquest, for it confirmed both the cruelty of the indigenous and Marina's extraordinary fairy tale elevation from slave to princess.

But though the story "fits in," she herself stands out partly because of the enthusiasm with which she fulfilled her role as interpreter, an enthusiasm that could be attributed to female mimicry. Indeed, Luce Irigaray has asserted that mimicry is the "only path" available to women within patriarchal discourse.

> To play with mimesis is . . . for a woman, to try to recover the place of her exploitation by discourse, without allowing herself to be simply reduced to it. It means to resubmit herself to . . . "ideas," in particular to ideas about herself, that are elaborated in/by masculine logic, but so as to make visible by an effect of playful repetition, what was sup-

posed to remain invisible; the cover-up of a possible operation of the feminine in language.[22]

In the context of conquest, however, this "playfulness" simply serves the master plot more effectively. Thus the irony of the fact that when in Bernal Díaz del Castillo's chronicle, she acquires her own voice it is to enable the conquest and the march towards Tenochtitlán to go on.

For the indigenous who represented her in their painted books she was clearly "alone of all her sex," often depicted in the meetings between Cortés and Moctezuma standing between the two men or actively gesturing as if to emphasize that she as much as Cortés is in charge.[23] She often stands in a position of power occupying the same plane as Cortés and Moctezuma, from whom she does not avert her eyes. Indeed, the curious metonymy by which Cortés was known as Malinche and addressed as such by the Aztecs suggests that they regarded her as the incorporation of conquest. Yet, to paraphrase Homi Bhabha, she was "the same but not quite."[24] The fact that Doña Marina wears indigenous dress in these codices emphasizes her racial difference from the Spaniards and her gender difference from the men who surrounded her, even while she is metonymically associated with the conquerors. But might not this suggest that the place of the conquered was that of the "feminine"? Homi Bhabha's colonial mimicry, in the Latin American case, is feminized. For the integration of the indigenous into a system that was both pluralistic and hierarchical, they had to become like women or children (*in-fans*—without speech).

Ironically, therefore, the "gift" of Doña Marina to the Spaniards was the beginning of the end of the gift economy. That is why it is important to note the transition from gift exchange to contract exchange. In her comprehensive book on La Malinche in Mexican literature, Sandra Messinger Cypess seems to conflate the two, observing, "The practice of exchange of women was common among the Indians and acceptable, too, among the Spaniards; neither side saw the transfer of women as an unusual custom. It would be expected, then, that Marina would already have been conditioned by her socialization as a slave among the Amerindians to obey the commands of her new masters."[25] Although this is one way to make sense of La Malinche's loyalty to Cortés, the explanation does not indicate the extent of real and epistemic violence that this exchange involved. The problem is the word *socialization*, which, like its mirror word *internalization*, rests on a clumsy separation of "inner" from "outer" and does nothing to account for the formation of subjects in specific social formations.

Furthermore *exchange* is itself an inexact word. Marina was either given or sold by her mother into slavery, a condition which, though not permanent for the Aztecs, had physical as well as psychological consequences. Because the slave was no longer a member of the social body or *capulli*, he or she became a kind of commodity, that could be given away, sold for sacrifice or other purposes. This change in status was thought to bring about a change in the very physical makeup of the person, since for the Aztecs the body was inseparable from society and the world.[26] Doña Marina's elevation from slave to faraute was thus more than a liberation, for it implied a radical transformation of her person. Not surprisingly, she would vehemently assert on her return to Coatzacoalcos that she would rather be the mother of Cortés's son and wife of Jaramillo than a princess of the Aztec empire.

Cortés's behavior in this deal was perfectly pragmatic although it went right against any ideology of *limpieza de sangre*, which the Spaniards evoked in their dealings with Jews and Moors. The reconquest of Spain and the expulsion of foreign elements runs counter to the deliberate policy of *mestizaje* which was encouraged by the Spanish crown and by Cortés himself. The traffic in women was not only accepted by the Spaniards as natural but provided them with necessary services, both sexual and practical. Cortés knew the importance of peopling the New World with a new kind of inhabitant, one who had ties of blood with both conqueror and the indigenous, for he had his son by Marina legitimized by the papacy. Thus while Cortés would lecture Moctezuma on monogamy, the traffic and exchange of women of which Marina was simply the best-known example was used by Cortés to great effect in sealing alliances and creating a *mestizo* population. Not only in Tabasco but along the route into the interior, Cortés received presents of Indian women, some of whom were distributed among his men. The prettiest of the eight girls given to Cortés by the fat chief of Cempoala was baptized Doña Francisca and, like Marina, handed over to Puertocarrero; the Tlaxcalans gave Cortés 300 women, who were baptized and handed over to the soldiers. Bernal Díaz del Castillo mentions at one point that he had four *naborías* who presumably helped carry his kit, cook, and serve him in other ways. The names of most of these women who gave birth to the new population of *mestizos* were unrecorded.

Roger Bartra notes, however, that when Malintzín and the nineteen other women were offered to Cortés, he gave an image of the Virgin to the Tabascans in exchange.[27] "No doubt the women given as gifts quickly lost their virginity, but the same could be said of the image which the indigenous peoples received."

But let us not be deceived as to the nature of this exchange in which real women were given in return for a symbolic woman—the gift is not exchanged for real women but for an imaginary ideal in comparison to which all women would feel their lack and inadequacy, an essential condition for their acceptance of a sexual contract.

Earlier I observed that the story of La Malinche resembled that of Oedipus. Both Oedipus and La Malinche were abandoned by a parent in the expectation that they would die or disappear, both return with devastating consequences to their mothers. In the Oedipus myth, this involves the violation of the taboo against marrying the mother. In La Malinche it involves a rather different change of fortunes—she returns not to become a social outcast but to demonstrate the superiority of the voluntary sexual contract that now replaces the exchange of women as gifts. The story of a woman's brutal separation from her mother, her enslavement, and salvation by a stranger is not simply to be explained in the same terms as "traffic in women" in tribal societies but is a qualitatively different narrative in which the *gift* has been transformed into the *contract*. Thus in La Malinche, we have the exemplary history of a transition from exogamy and gift to sexual contract, a contract that is, however pacted on the prior condition of violence.[28] Cortés had, after all, defeated the Tabascan chief who presented him with Doña Marina. In the Freudian system, male adulthood is achieved through suppression and sublimation, the assumption of the name of the father. But Freud's preoccupation with the European family prevented him from seeing that the "dark continent" was not only woman but conquered populations who would either be excluded from civilized intercourse or would become involved in a vaster game of colonial mimicry.

The importance of this *mestizaje* can scarcely be overestimated. It is *mestizaje* that separates Latin America from all other colonial ventures. It helps to explain why theories of postcolonialism never seem to approximate to the reality of the continent and why the politics of race has always been so blatantly based on constructed rather than essential categories.

It is this which perhaps helps to explain La Malinche's fall from grace during the national period in the late nineteenth and early twentieth centuries. The premium on originality, the tendency to offer racial explanations for economic underdevelopment and "backwardness" obviously made *mestizaje* a delicate problem and turned La Malinche into a scapegoat, the "most detested woman of the Americas" according to Georges

Baudot.[29] The literature on Mexican nationalist ideology is too vast to re-view in brief, but two particular aspects of La Malinche's incorporation into the national narrative are too important to be overlooked. The Cho-lula incident made it easy for her to be transformed into the treacherous origins of the Mexican nation, but how did she become La Chingada, the violated woman of Octavio Paz's *Labyrinth of Solitude*?

Paz was writing at a time when *malinchismo* had passed into popular journalistic language. Four decades after this classic essay was published, it is not easy to reconstruct the now forgotten texts to which it was a re-sponse. If we understand *malinchismo* to be a code word for the Communist left, then we read Paz's essay as an attempt to sublimate the very specific ideological struggle into a national psychodrama of masculine aggression and the victimization not only of woman but of the feminine in all of us.

Paz would associate La Malinche with La Chingada, *chingar* being the unutterable taboo word, "fuck." She is the raped woman, the raped land, the wound that was opened with the conquest. In these terms, the Mexican nation is itself, as Paz would point out, the product of "violation, seizure and mockery." Paz acknowledges that the historical Doña Marina, "gives herself of her own free will to the Conqueror but he, as soon as her useful-ness has been exhausted, forgets her. Doña Marina has become a figure that represents Indian women, fascinated, raped or seduced by Spaniards. And just as a child cannot forgive the mother who abandons him to look for the father, the Mexican nation cannot forgive the treachery of La Malinche."[30]

Although Paz is critical of *malinchismo*, which he interprets as fear of the feminine, his notion of the feminine is more closely linked to Modern-ist aesthetics than to colonial oppression, marking what Andreas Huyssens has termed "imaginary male femininity."[31] To refer to La Malinche as La Chingada restores the violence of the conquest, which seems to fade into the background for Todorov and Greenblatt whilst at the same time reaffirming the identification of woman with territory, or with passive vic-timization. By transforming her into La Chingada, Paz hides the fact that she collaborated. It is not oppression that has to be accounted for but La Malinche's passage from the oppression of slavery to the apparent free acceptance of the sexual contract which, of course, also excluded women from true citizenship.

It is this difficult problem of *malinchismo* that has special significance for both Mexican and Mexican American women writers. Although this is too large a subject to enter into at this point, it is worth emphasizing this continued "persistence" of La Malinche within contemporary writing by women. In her essay, "Daughters of La Malinche," Margo Glantz observes the extent to which modern Mexican authors such as Rosario Castellanos, Elena Garro, and Elena Poniatowska have been haunted by the ghost of La Malinche.[32] It is not only their position in the national narrative that is at stake, however, but the imperative to conquer by seduction which results in women's self-hatred and serialization. In Rosario Castellanos's poem, "La Malinche," for example, the mother contemplates her image in her daughter, and hates her, and then destroys the mirror and with it any possibility of female solidarity. According to Margo Glantz, many women feel themselves to be aliens within the nation and attempt to become incorporated into the indigenous *madre patria* [mother land] which is personified in the *nana* of Rosario Castellanos's novels, in the maids of Poniatowska's autobiography, and the peasants of Elena Garro's fiction.[33] At the end of her autobiographical novel, *La "Flor de Lis"* (1988) which relates a child's intense relationship with an upper-class mother who keeps herself aloof from the society in which she lives, Elena Poniatowska describes the painful and precarious separation from the mother and her discovery of a new family — the heterogeneous population she meets on the streets and buses. Thus, the modern writer relives the Malinche story of separation from natural parents this time in order to empower herself as a writer.

It is perhaps not surprising that it is among the Mexican American population of the United States that La Malinche has become a major focus of contention. The Chicano movement of the 1960s was an assertion of nationalism in the face of discrimination, an assertion of self-worth like the black power movement. It was a moment of male self-definition. La Malinche, who had betrayed the Indian cause with which the Chicano movement identified itself, was thus once again the symbol of shame. Cherríe Moraga wrote forcibly, "Upon her shoulders rests the full blame for the 'bastardization' of the indigenous people of Mexico to put it in its most base terms; Malintizín, also called Malinche, fucked the white man who conquered the Indian peoples of Mexico and destroyed their culture. Ever since, brown men have been accusing her of betraying her race, and over the centuries continue to blame her entire sex for this 'transgression.'" Moraga saw the La Malinche myth as inhibiting the sexuality of the Chicana, not to mention eliminating lesbianism as a possibility.[34] On the other hand, for Adelaida R. del Castillo she is seen as an exemplary humanistic mediator.[35] In a survey of the corpus of literature by Chicanas that refers directly or indirectly to their identification with La Malinche, the critic

Norma Alarcón describes her as just as problematic when she becomes exemplary token as when she becomes the symbol of self-loathing.[36]

Although it would seem that the figuration of La Malinche is confined to colonialist or nationalist discourse, there are signs that she has "persisted" in postmodernity. In a witty performance, Jesusa Rodríguez has her literally turn into "media." As anchorwoman for the new global communication network in the great city of Tecnocratitlán, La Malinche presides over an Americanized consumer society. But by now, she no longer even needs to be imagined as a real person, for everyone knows she is only a simulation.[37] And this, of course, is the final irony.

NOTES

1 Octavio Paz, "Los hijos de la Malinche." In *El laberinto de la soledad*. (Mexico: Fondo de Cultura Económica, 1967), 59–80, esp. 78.

2 For a discussion of these reinterpretations, see Norma Alarcón, "Chicana's Feminist Literature: A Re-vision through Malintzín/or Malintizín: Putting Flesh Back on the Object," in Gloria Anzaldúa and Cherríe Moraga (eds.) *This Bridge Called my Back: Writings by Radical Women of Color* (New York: Kitchen Table Press, 1983), 182–90. For La Malinche and modern Mexican literature by women, see Margo Glantz, "Las hijas de la Malinche," in Karl Kohut, ed., *Literatura mexicana hoy. Del 68 al ocaso de la revolución* (Frankfurt am Main: Verfuert Verlag, 1991), 121–29.

3 Tzvetan Todorov, *La conquête de l'Amérique. La question de l'autre* (Paris: Le Seuil, 1982); Stephen Gleenblatt, *Marvellous Possessions. The Wonder of the New World* (Chicago: University of Chicago Press, 1991).

4 Justo Sierra, "Evolución política del pueblo mexicano," in *Obras completas xii* (Mexico: UNAM, 1977), 49. There is an exhaustive discussion of the literature on La Malinche in Sandra Messinger Cypess, *La Malinche in Mexican Literature. From History to Myth* (Austin: University of Texas Press, 1991).

5 William Prescott, *The Conquest of Mexico* (Philadelphia: Lippincott and Co., 1863), 1:295.

6 William Carlos Williams, "The Destruction of Tenochtitlan," in *In the American Grain* (New York: New Directions, 1956), 27–38. For a discussion of the *lenguas* and in particular of La Malinche, see Margo Glantz, "Lengua y conquista," *Revista de la Universidad de Mexico* (October 1989). Doña Marina's skill as a translator seems to have been in stark contrast to Cortés's inability to pronounce or transcribe names in nahuatl. See George Baudot, *Utopie et histoire au méxique. Les premiers chroniqueurs de la civilisation méxicaine (1520–1569).* (Toulouse: Privat, 1977).

7 Teresa de Lauretis, *Alice Doesn't. Feminism, Semiotics, Cinema.* (Bloomington: Indiana University Press, 1984).

8 Greenblatt stresses what he calls mimetic exchange and particularly the rhetoric employment of the "marvellous" to justify possession.

9 For a discussion of the names of Doña Marina, see Hernán Cortés, *Letters from Mexico*, trans. Anthony Pagden (New Haven, Conn.: Yale University Press, 1986, 464.

10 Bernal Díaz del Castillo, *Historia verdadera de la conquista de la Nueva España*, ed. Miguel León Portilla, two vols. (Madrid: Historia, 1984), 159. Unless otherwise stated, translations are mine.

11 The main contemporary and near contemporary sources, apart from Bernal Díaz del Castillo are Francisco López de Gomara, *Historia de la conquista de México* (Caracas: Biblioteca Ayacucho, 1979), vol. 65; Hernán Cortés, *Letters from Mexico*, trans. and ed. Anthony Pagden (New Haven, Conn.: Yale University Press, 1986). See also John H. Elliott, "The Mental World of Hernán Cortés," in *Transactions of the Royal Historical Society*, Fifth Series, 17 (1967), and John H. Elliot, "The Spanish Conquest and Settlement of America," in Leslie Bethell, ed., *The Cambridge History of Latin America* (Cambridge: Cambridge University Press, 1984), vol. 1; Hernán Cortés, *Escritos sueltos de Hernán Cortés* (Mexico: Biblioteca Histórica de la Iberia, 1871), vol. 12.

12 There is as yet no thorough study of either the popular image of La Malinche nor of her portrayal in the codices. Although these clearly indicate her importance and suggest why Cortés and others associated with her should have been addressed as Malinche, a detailed study of the significance of her dress and gestures has yet to be made. In "A la Chingada" in *La Jaula de la melancolía. Identidad y metamorfosis del mexicano* (Mexico: Grijalbo, 1987), Roger Bartra sees La Malinche as the mirror image of the Virgin of Guadalupe. In a biography, *Doña Marina, "La Malinche"* (Mexico: Somonte, 1969), 159–63, Mariano G. Somonte describes how La Llorona myth (the myth of a woman lamenting her lost child) derives from the lament of the sacrified goddess, "Cihuacoatl," but is the basis of modern "superstitions" which link La Malinche and La Llorona.

13 Gayatri Chakravorty Spivak's discussion and translation of Mahasweta Devi's "The Breast-Giver" is exemplary in its emphasis on the subaltern body as productive and not simply reproductive. Her essay also shows the trap of "interpreting" such instances in terms of first-world feminism. See Gayatri Chakravorty Spivak, "A Literary Representation of the Subaltern," in *In Other Worlds. Essays in Cultural Politics* (New York: Methuen, 1987), 241–268.

14 "Cortés always attracted the chiefs with good words," according to Bernal Díaz del Castillo in *Historia verdadera*, 155.

15 My translation. The quotation is included in the appendix to Somonte, *Doña Marina*.

16 My translation. *Probanza de buenos servicios y fidelidad con que sirvió en la conquista de Nueva España la famosa Doña Marina*. Patronato 56, no. 3, Ramo 4. Archivo General de Indias, Sevilla, España.

17 This key incident is given prominence in many of the chronicles and is included

in the record of services of Doña Marina used by her grandson, don Fernando Cortés in his appeal for a pension. See Somonte, *Doña Marina*, 174. There is also a vivid version in Antonio de Solís, *Historia de la conquista de Mexico* (Madrid: Cano, 1798).

18 Beatriz Pastor, *Discursos narrativos de la conquista: mitificación y emergencia* (Hanover: Ediciones del Norte, 1983).

19 This quotation is taken from a translation by Maurice Keating (London, 1800).

20 Several versions of the conquest prefer that Doña Marina be born of slaves. For instance Francisco Cervantes de Salazar, *Crónica de la Nueva España* (Mexico: Porrúa, 1985), 134 gives two versions of her birth, one of which records her as having been born of slaves and the other "truer version" that she was the daughter of a lord and a slave woman.

21 See for instance, "La princesa guerrillera" from the *Mixtec codice*, Selden I. Bodleyan Library, Oxford. The story is summarized in Maria Sten, *Las extraordinarías historias de los códices mexicanos* (Mexico: Joaquin Mortiz, 1972). According to this tale, a princess whose brothers have been killed decides to avenge their death. On the journey she undertakes for this purpose, she meets and marries a prince but when she is taken to her husband's country, she is insulted and takes revenge on her enemies, thereafter living happily ever after with her husband. In her article, "Bernal Díaz del Castillo frente al otro: Doña Marina, espejo de princesas y damas," included in Augustin Redondo, ed., *Les representations de l'Autre dans l'espace ibérique et ibero-américain* (Paris: Presses de La Sorbonne Nouvelle, 1991), 77–85, Sonia Rose-Fuggle emphasizes the Biblical parallels in this life story.

22 Luce Irigaray, *This Sex which is not One*, trans. Catherine Porter (Ithaca, NY: Cornell University Press, 1977), 76.

23 See Somonte, *Doña Marina*, for reproductions of the *lienzos* in which Marina is shown interpreting for Cortés. He also includes reproductions of a coat of arms of Tabasco on which Doña Marina's portrait appears and reproductions of the Codice de Cuautlancingo in one of which she is portrayed without the Spaniards, accompanied by another Indian woman, and followed by a group of musicians.

24 Homi Bhabha's concept of colonial mimicry is, of course, extremely suggestive for a study of Doña Marina. See "Of Mimicry and Man; The ambivalence of Colonial Discourse" *October* 28 (1984): 125–33. The "ambivalence" consists of the fact that the colonizer wants to create a colonized in his own image only to produce someone who is "not quite/not white." Doña Marina is not only "not white" but not male.

25 *La Malinche*, Cypess, 33.

26 Alfredo López Austín, *Cuerpo humano e ideología. Las concepciones de los antiguos nahuas* (Mexico: UN, 1984), 2 vols. See esp. 1:226–51. This point about the relationship of the body to "self" is also made by Serge Gruzinski, in *Man-Gods in the Mexican Highlands. Indian Power and Colonial Society, 1520–1800*, trans. Eileen Corrigan (Stanford, Calif.: Stanford University Press, 1989), 20.

27   Bartra, "A la Chingada," 207. Bartra is referring to the transformation of the Virgin into the "dark-skinned" Virgin of Guadalupe.

28   Carole Pateman, *The Sexual Contract* (Cambridge: Polity Press, 1988).

29   George Baudot, "Malintzín, L'Irrégulière," in Claire Pailler, ed., *Femmes d'Amérique* (Le Mirail, University de Toulouse, 1986). The term *malinchismo* became current in the twentieth century but the equivalence between La Malinche and the nation was already made explicit by Ignacio Ramírez in the nineteenth century. For nineteenth-century literature featuring La Malinche see Cypess, *La Malinche*. In the late forties and fifties, there is an abundant literature defending her, much of it imaginative rather than scholarly. See, for example, Federico Gómez de Orozco, *Doña Marina. La dama de la conquista.* (Mexico: Ediciones Xochitl, 1942); Somonte, *Doña Marina;* and J. Jesus Figueroa Torres, *Doña Marina. Una india ejemplar* (Mexico: Costa-Amic, 1975).

30   Paz, *The Labyrinth of Solitude*, 77–78.

31   Andreas Huyssens, "Mass Culture as Woman," in *Beyond the Great Divide* (Bloomington: Indiana University Press, 1986).

32   Glantz, "Las hijas de la Malinche."

33   Ibid. See also Jean Franco, *Plotting Women. Gender and Representation in Mexico* (New York: Columbia University Press, 1989).

34   Cherríe Moraga, "From a Long Line of Vendidas: Chicanas and Feminism," in Teresa de Lauretis, ed., *Feminist Studies. Critical Studies.* (Madison: University of Wisconsin Press, 1985), 173–90.

35   Adelaida R. del Castillo, "Malintzín Tenepal: A Preliminary Look into a New Perspective," in Rosaura Sánchez and Rosa Martínez Cruz, eds., *Essays on la mujer* (Los Angeles: University of California Chicano Studies Center Publications, 1977), 124–49.

36   Alarcón, "Chicana's Feminist Literature."

37   Jesusa Rodríguez, "La Malinche en Dios T.V.," in *Debate feminista*, no. 3:308–31.

THE *FINEZAS* OF SOR JUANA

he Spanish word *fineza* has always struck me as rather strange, perhaps because the definitions of it which one finds in the dictionary do not correspond to the importance this concept acquires in the work of Sor Juana. I am not only referring to the *Carta Atenagórica* [Athenagoric Letter], but also the "secular" texts, especially her play *Los empeños de una casa* [The Trials of a Noble House]. Certainly the definition Sor Juana gives for the word could not be any clearer: in the *Carta Atenagórica* she says that "those outward indications and actions performed by a lover, motivated to do them by his love, that is a 'fineza'" (ll. 474–76).[1] However, it is difficult to find a synonym for this word in English. The English word *finesse* does not exactly translate the connotations of *fineza*, which, in the Hispanic societies of the seventeenth century, had to with the "norms for courtly behavior" (*leyes de urbano*)[2] and, above all, with the etiquette of love. In the first dramatic interlude, which follows the first act of *Los empeños de una casa*, Sor Juana includes "Fineza" among the imaginary beings gathered at the palace; together with Attentiveness, Love, and Respect, Fineza competes for the ladies' scorn and disregard. Fineza bases her own aspirations on the following (vv. 82–86):

> En lo fino, lo atento,
> en lo humilde, en lo obsequioso,
> en el cuidado, el desvelo,
> y en amar por sólo amar.
>
> [On what is courteous, attentive,
> On what is humble, and obsequious,

Originally published as "Las finezas de Sor Juana" in *Y diversa de mí misma entre vuestras plumas ando; Homenaje internacional a Sor Juana Inés de la Cruz*, ed. Sara Poot Herrera (Mexico: Colegio de México, 1993), 247–56. Translated by Patricia Heid.

On solicitude, on watchfulness,
And on loving for the sake of loving.]

The judge, however, disqualifies her from the game, pointing out that (vv. 100–12):

y el amante verdadero
ha de tener de lo amado
tan soberano concepto
que ha de pensar que no alcanza
su amor el merecimiento
de la beldad a quien sirve;
y aunque la ame con extremo,
ha de pensar siempre que es
su amor, menor que el objeto,
y confesar que no paga
con todos los rendimientos;
que lo fino del amor
está en no mostrar el serlo.

[and the true lover
has to have such a sovereign
concept of his beloved
that he believes his love
can never come to deserve
the beauty of the one he loves;
and although he may love her to the utmost,
he must always keep in mind that
his love is worth less than its object,
and admit that his love cannot possibly compensate,
even with all of its benefits;
because the purest aspect of love
lies in its not revealing itself as love.]

As Octavio Paz has shown, basing his observation on a note by Alberto G. Salceda, the courtly pastimes, the "gallantries of the palace," and the tradition of courtly love, which had its beginnings in the tributary societies of the Middle Ages, persisted in a stylized form in the seventeenth century among the noble class.[3] The dances of the period with their bows of reverence and flirtations mimicked this game of intimacy and distance. In *Amor es más laberinto* [Love is the Greater Labyrinth] (the second act, written by

Juan de Guevara), the women come on stage dressed up in costumes, wearing masks and hats with feathers because, as Ariadna says (vv. 381–84):

Ceremonia es, más que adorno,
este disfraz tan usado,
vinculado a los festines
cortesanos de Palacio.

[It is ceremony, rather than decoration,
this practice of masquerading,
which is part of the courtly
entertainments of the Palace.]

And the king that presides over the ball emphasizes that these are "permissible gallantries" (vv. 511–14):

A las aras del respeto
llega el deseo tan sagrado,
que en veneración del culto
humos gasta el holocausto.

[To the altars of respect
comes such sacred desire,
that in her veneration of the cult
her offering goes up in smoke.]

Respect and courtesy (*fineza*) were, therefore, modes of behavior between the sexes that did not have anything to do with the religious ethic; rather, they dealt with the implicit rules that determined distances and intimacies among a group of persons of the same social rank. These rules did not permit the exercise of power which occurred in the relationship between a confessor and his faithful followers. As we are well aware from the exemplary tales of pious nuns and the *Respuesta a Sor Filotea de la Cruz* [Response to Sor Filotea de la Cruz], the confessor felt obliged to intervene, demand, and prohibit.[4] The confessor commanded and the nun obeyed. One gave orders, humiliated, and even insulted; the other accepted, humbled herself, and said nothing. In the gallantries of the palace, on the other hand, it was the women who held the power, even if it was only the power of disregarding and rejecting.

The aristocratic rules for behavior were called *manners* in English, and *civilité* in French. These were not so much expressions of intimacy, but rather affirmations of the distance and respect necessary for maintaining social relations. Manners and *civilité* prohibited the spontaneity that was considered to be a characteristic of the lower class. In *The History of Manners*, Norbert Elias[5] comments that the French bourgeoisie employed the concept of "civilization" in the eighteenth century to universalize their aspirations, and to combat the culture of *civilité*—Rousseau's *Confessions* obviously played a key role in this struggle. For Sor Juana, who lived in a society in which the Church had established itself as the official watchdog of all manners and customs, the imaginary beings gathered at the palace allowed her to explore idealized forms of behavior that had nothing to do with dogma or an imbalance of power, although, as we will see further on, she does not accept these rules of conduct without critical examination. In *Los empeños de una casa* and in the secular and religious poetry, one encounters forms of social behavior that do not depend on arbitrary or despotic use of power, nor on the anachronistic and phallocentric code of honor. The playful aspect of the gallantries opens up a space in which it is no longer necessary to negate the other person in order to assert one's own identity. As Teseo confirms in *Amor es más laberinto*, it is possible "ser fino con la que quiere, / sin ser grosero con otra" [to be attentive to the one you love, / without being rude to another lady] (vv. 539–40). And one's command of one's emotions is not governed by logic. Mutual attraction between lovers is a rare occurrence, and there does not exist one "correct" solution for the woman who must choose between, say, a Silvio and a Fabio. This kind of decision always involves making a leap outside of all logic, a leap which implies putting oneself at risk. Neither religious dogma nor tradition offer clear rules for surviving in the "real world." These normative systems cannot help a woman to choose between lovers or make a decision, the consequences of which will last a lifetime,[6] just as logic cannot help one to choose between the inductive and deductive methods of reasoning. Therefore, there is always an inherent factor of arbitrariness in the conduct of love, as well as in orderly, methodological procedures.

And this is precisely the problem when we begin to read the secular work of Sor Juana. How are these signs of courtly life and behavior, which acquire so much importance in her work, represented? And how are we to read and interpret them? What I want to suggest in this essay, basing my analysis primarily on *Los empeños de una casa*, is that Sor Juana does not simply reproduce the gallantries of the palace, but that she also proposes an alternative code of conduct. The conventions of the honor play, which are by this time depleted of meaning, are used by Sor Juana to explore new criteria of conduct. And by modifying the gallantries of the palace, she demonstrates that it is not necessary to negate another person in order to assert one's own identity—that one can treat another person (whether man or woman) with respect, while at the same time recognizing the mutual differences between them. Moreover, although this utopian situation seems to apply only to those of the noble class, in her dramatic works the lower classes enjoy a freedom of expression that is prohibited to the aristocracy. The modes of behavior of the upper classes do not permit them to express themselves openly, nor do they allow them hope, which, according to the first dramatic interlude, is considered to be a "country girl" that does not belong in the palace.

How can we explain the fact that a nun who had renounced all worldly concerns took so much interest in the problems of her world? I do not believe that these issues interested Sor Juana only as abstract problems. On the contrary, one can read *Los empeños de una casa* and the courtly love poetry not only as belated genres and conventions but as a response to a concrete problem of the period.

According to Patricia Seed, at the end of the seventeenth century a change occurred in the relationship between parents and children and, above all, in the power exercised by parents over children in their decision to marry.[7] Before this period, the Church had often protected children when their parents, in self-interest, attempted to marry them against their will. For their part, the children often blatantly ignored parental power by getting married on their own or by getting engaged to someone, which would later be authorized by the Church, even if it was against their parents' wishes. The Church's stance in this issue resulted from its misgivings about materialistic attitudes in society, in which the social status of a person did not necessarily correspond to his or her wealth. Seed cites several interesting cases, among them one of particular interest, which occurred in Mexico City in 1644.

Pedro de Agüero, the son of a wealthy family from Mexico City, gave his promise of marriage to a certain woman against his father's will. His fiancée's family was at that time living in a large house, which they shared with other families. In order to prevent the marriage, a man who was working for Pedro's father forced his way into the fiancée's house, where Pedro was at the time, and attacked him, creating a public outrage. In order to avoid further trouble, Church officials secretly married the couple, and, in addition, several witnesses swore on behalf of the fiancée's virtue.

Incidents like this one were fairly common, from which we gather that the entangled situation of the lovers in *Los empeños de una casa* was not simply a product of Sor Juana's imagination, but that it responded to the new situation that was beginning to take shape at the end of the seventeenth century. In the period in which Sor Juana was writing, the Church was not getting involved as frequently in defending young lovers and, correspondingly, the self-interest of parents was beginning to prevail. According to Seed, this change resulted from the new values established by the mercantile class, which necessarily had as its priority the consolidation and concentration of wealth. This argument is not only plausible but it also suggests a different way of approaching *Los empeños de una casa*. Without disregarding other valuable readings, this approach emphasizes the importance of one of Sor Juana's constant preoccupations—her emphasis on those modes of behavior which are based on merit and respect and not on self-interest or an imbalance of power.[8]

In *Los empeños de una casa*, Pedro is a wealthy man who, at the end, is left without a mate, and Don Rodrigo is a father who does not succeed in marrying off his daughter for personal gain. It is significant, however, that the happy ending comes about primarily due to the servant, Castaño, and not because of the Church's intervention. The play not only takes a position on a very common problem of the period, but it also facilitates the process of transforming the honor play (just as Lope de Vega did with his play *El perro del hortelano* [The Gardener's Dog]) into the "comedy of manners." This transformation is far from trivial. Sor Juana equates the code of honor with paternal self-interest, and she challenges patriarchal conventions with the values of love and mutual respect. Her theme is not the guarding of honor but rather the honorable behavior of the two lovers, in contrast to the manipulative behavior of the other characters, such as the jealous Doña Ana, the violent Don Juan, and the wealthy Don Pedro. Her theme is based on the conflict between self-interest and free will, between the problems caused by jealousy and the true respect one feels for another person.

At the beginning of the play, Leonor flees from the house of her father, Don Rodrigo, in order to avoid having to marry Pedro de Arellano, and to arrange her own marriage to Carlos de Olmedo. The plan is foiled by Pedro, who, taking advantage of the commotion caused by Leonor's flight, kidnaps her and takes her to his own house, where he lives with his sister Ana. By coincidence, Carlos, who is also loved by Ana, takes refuge in this same house. And it is here, also, where Don Juan, Ana's rejected lover, shows up as well. Pedro and Ana, the hosts, try to take advantage of this situation in order to achieve their own objectives—they transform the house into a labyrinth in chiaroscuro where, as in the forest in *A Midsummer Night's Dream*, the lovers get lost, mistake each other's identities, and in the end, meet again.

How can one impose order in this house/labyrinth, given that it is a space in limbo where neither paternal commands nor religious ethics carry any weight? In this space there are only wills in conflict, wills that seem equal, and yet are also different. Listening to a song about love and jealousy, the lovers (hidden from one another) respond differently to the words: one takes issue with them, the other agrees with them. Each character interprets the lyrics, "la pena más severa que puede dar el amor" [the most severe punishment that love can give],[9] according to his or her own situation. For Don Pedro, this punishment is the lack of favor from his beloved; for Doña Ana, it is a jealous passion; and for Leonor, it is being without the person she loves. How can we balance these different interests, particularly when an unpredictable element, such as "chance," intervenes?

It is worth noting that here Sor Juana is touching on a subject that could not be approached by either the Church or the code of honor, since it did not involve a sin or the social status of any of the persons involved. There was no religious or social rule that could have successfully resolved this conflict of wills or offered a "correct" solution to this dilemma.

This problematic space (the labyrinth), which today is inhabited by psychology and all kinds of experts in "human relationships," was governed in the seventeenth century (at least insofar as the nobility was concerned) by the code of behavior (the "manners") established by the aristocracy —a code that encompassed rules for excluding everyone and everything socially "below" the upper class. Although Sor Juana seems to preserve this separation between the elite and the lower class, it is worth noting that the servants in *Los empeños de una casa* play a significant role in the dénouement of the play. It is the servants who turn the lights on and off; it is Castaño who, disguising himself as Leonor, frustrates Don Pedro's aspirations as a lover; it is Celia who lets Carlos out of the house, and so on. Moreover, the servants have the ability to distinguish what is real from what is not real— an ability the noble characters lack. Since the servants cannot even aspire to courtly ideals, they do not mistake external behavior for the truth.

The title of the play, *Los empeños de una casa*, possesses a certain ambiguity. "Dejar en prenda" [leaving something as collateral] originally had to do with paying a debt or keeping a promise. The problem is that the "empeños" [obligations] of the play leave a lot of room for misunderstanding, especially when verbal contracts are not honored. Doña Leonor believes that she is married to Don Carlos because he has given her his word; at the same time her father is in the process of arranging her marriage to Don Pedro. For his part, Don Juan believes that Doña Ana is engaged to him, because in Madrid she had listened to his declarations of love without displeasure. Indeed, Doña Ana admits responding to Don Juan's advances; but because "love is blind," she then falls in love with Don Carlos, a love which turns to jealousy when she finds out that Leonor also loves him. Verbal assent or tacit consent no longer suffices in these situations.

Don Pedro and Don Juan think it is sufficient to respect your beloved and to show her gestures of love (*fineza*); when these external signs of love no longer work, they resort to violence. In the case of Don Juan, respect had enabled him to keep his "flames" (*olas*) of passion contained; but when he thinks he has Doña Ana in his power (in reality, he is mistaken; he really has Leonor), he loses all respect for her (vv. 791–94):

¡ . . . que forzada me has de oír
si no quieres voluntaria,
y ha de escucharme grosero
quien de lo atento se cansa!

[and you must listen
to my rudeness
having tired
of my politeness!]

When Don Juan finds Don Carlos (whom he believes to be Doña Ana's lover) hidden in the same house with him, he scorns all respect—he now considers it "a tyrannical law" that prevents him from taking revenge on his cheating lover.

In a similar fashion, Don Pedro emphasizes his gestures of love (*fineza*). With Doña Leonor sequestered in his house in order to "soften her up," he brags about his gestures of love [*su fineza*], assuring her that ". . . el desdén / más mi fineza acrisola, / que es muy garboso desaire / el ser fino a toda costa" [. . . your contempt / only purifies my attentions (*fineza*) more, / since to be attentive at all costs / is a very genteel form of rejection] (vv. 275–78). He does not understand the reason for Leonor's disdain, but he mistakes it for a courtesy (*fineza*):

Mas sin duda mi fineza
es quien el premio me estorba,
que es quien la merece menos

quien siempre la dicha logra;
mas si yo os he de adorar
eternamente, ¿qué importa
que vos me neguéis el premio,
pues es fuerza que conozca
que me concedéis de fino
lo que os negáis de piadosa?

[It must be my attentiveness
that keeps me from my prize,
for it is the one who least deserves it
who gets what he hopes for;
besides, if I have no choice but to adore you
for all time, what does it matter
that you hold back my prize?
since you must know that
what you hold back in pity,
you bestow in finesse.]

Like Don Juan's "respect," Don Pedro's "courtesies" are based on power and violence. On several occasions, Castaño hits on the perfect word for this situation—it is a form of "rape" (*tarquinada*)—a violation of the woman thinly disguised by the man's gallantry. It is for this reason that Pedro becomes the target of a very cruel practical joke: Castaño, disguised as a woman (Leonor), promises to marry him, without concealing "her" true motives for doing so (vv. 537-40):

no os muráis,
por amor de Dios, siquiera
hasta dejarme un muchacho
para que herede la hacienda.

[don't you go dying on me,
for the love of God, at least
until you give me a son
that can inherit your estate.]

Although Pedro recognizes that this false Leonor does not speak to him with the courtesy (*fineza*) that is due to someone with his social rank and upbringing, he ends up falling for the trick, blinded as he is by his own desire.

As for Don Rodrigo, the key word for him is "honor," but honor that is based on material interests. The true nature of his honor is revealed when Don Carlos gives him over to a woman who is supposedly Doña Ana (but in reality, Doña Leonor). Don Rodrigo has incurred "an obligation" (*un empeño*), which he can now exchange for something else. His own "honor" (the marriage of Doña Leonor and Don Pedro) is achieved by means of blackmail. As he tells Don Pedro (vv. 862–64):

> que habiendo de ser mi yerno,
> el quereros ver honrado
> resultará en mi provecho.

> [because now that you will be my son-in-law,
> my desire to see your honor untarnished
> will also be to my advantage.]

Don Rodrigo's honor becomes too flexible. In theory, a stain on his honor should lead to revenge unto death (p. 152). Yet, when Don Rodrigo does not follow through with this, despite the compromising situations of Doña Leonor and Doña Ana, he shows how outdated this code really is. Fearing that Pedro may take revenge on Don Carlos, Don Rodrigo argues "It is the task of cleverness / to dress up necessity / in the guise of kindness" (vv. 948–50). It is not in the best interests of Don Carlos and Don Pedro to fight a duel unto death. When the honor of another person is involved, Don Rodrigo acts in a pragmatic way, although this ultimately results in a marriage lacking mutual affection.

Carlos and Leonor obviously represent idealized types. Leonor is distinguished by her beauty and erudition but, as Stephanie Merrim has pointed out, she plays a somewhat passive role in the play.[10] Carlos, although he is definitely "manly," possesses all of the virtues most appreciated by Sor Juana herself (vv. 449–60):

> tan humilde en los afectos,
> tan tierno en los agasajos,
> tan fino en las persuasiones,
> tan apacible en el trato
> y en todo, en fin, tan perfecto,
> que ostentaba cortesano
> despojos de lo rendido,
> por galas de lo alentado.

En los desdenes sufrido,
en los favores callado,
en los peligros resuelto,
y prudente en los acasos.

[so humble in his affections,
so tender in his attentions,
so smooth in his persuasions,
so easy-going in his manner
and in everything, finally, so perfect,
that he would show off in a courtly manner
the evidence of his defeat,
as if it were a prize to encourage him.
    Rarely saying a negative word,
never bragging about his favors,
unswerving in danger,
and prudent in taking chances.]

Here we have an index of everything that is desirable in a man—sensitivity but also firmness, and above all, the quality of free will, so appreciated by Sor Juana that she constantly reiterates its importance, with the verses "no halla en lo obligatorio / lugar lo fino" [there is no room in obligation / for gestures of love] (vv. 193-94). While the role of Leonor in the play is to resist male attentions she neither seeks nor desires, the role of Carlos is to represent a code of behavior superior to that of the rest of men. This is why he does not act in a rash way when he encounters Leonor in Don Pedro's house. Instead, he looks for arguments which might justify her presence, rather than judging her prematurely.

In comparison with *Los empeños de una casa*, *Amor es más laberinto* seems a more abstract work because of its classical theme. I am not going to enter into a detailed discussion of this work, the second act of which (about the ball) was written by Don Juan de Guevara. But it does deserve some attention because of the many detailed speeches it contains about loving behavior. For example, Fedra cannot demonstrate her love for Teseo, because etiquette does not permit the woman to declare her love first (vv. 627-30):

ha menester una dama,
aun cuando amante se nombra,
dar a entender que se vence,
mas no mostrar que se postra.

[a lady needs,
even when a lover declares himself,
to let him know that she has been conquered,
but not to show that she is vanquished.]

Neither play successfully pairs up all of its lovers. There is always one
man who is left out of the game (Pedro, Lidoro), and there is always one
woman (Ana, Ariadna) who gets married out of obligation rather than for
love. What is most significant in *Amor es más laberinto* is that the loving gestures (*la fineza*) of Ariadna, who saves Teseo's life, are not sufficient to earn
his love. Once again, gestures of love (*la fineza*) motivated by self-interest
are not truly loving gestures. Teseo, for his part, wins Fedra because of his
personal "merit," because of the victory he obtained in the war. In a long
speech at the beginning of the play, Teseo describes his heroic deeds and
he argues that one's actions are more important than his social rank (vv.
478-80):

con decir que los primeros
que impusieron en el mundo
dominio, fueron los hechos.

[by reminding you that the first ones
to exercise their power in the world
were deeds and actions.]

This is a strange argument given that, according to Teseo, deeds also produce inequality between men. Nevertheless, his speech emphasizes once
more a utopian vision of society, in which merit and selflessness would be
valued above all else.

In *Las trampas de la fe* [The Traps of Faith], Octavio Paz indicates that
the argument over what constitutes the greatest benefit conferred by God
—an argument developed in the *Carta Atenagórica*—is "a divine version of
Sor Juana's conception of the highest love as love that does not need to be
reciprocated" (p. 517). Sor Juana's dramatic works modify this argument
slightly, as they represent love that has indeed been reciprocated. What
Sor Juana will not accept, however, is obligation, indebtedness, or blackmail. It is precisely for this reason that when gestures of love (*la fineza*) are
made, they are shown to be ambiguous, because they could possibly cause
the other person to feel obligation or indebtedness, thereby inhibiting his
or her free will. Paz thinks that Sor Juana's "deliberations about 'negative
gestures of love' reflect the ongoing debates of her time about grace and

free will" (p. 518), and that Sor Juana was attacking "a person and a group" (p. 518). The theatrical works enable us to see another element that comes into play in this argument: the privileging of action and merit over loving favors and other external demonstrations of love.

   Sor Juana creates a utopian space that does not depend on the debts and the financial obligations of a tributary society, nor on the transactions and rates of interest of a mercantile society.

NOTES

1 I quote the *Obras completas de Sor Juana Inés de la Cruz*, ed. A Méndez Plancarte (vols. 1, 2, and 3), and A. G. Salceda (vol. 4) México: F.C.E., 1951–57). The *Carta Atenagórica* appears in vol. 4, pp. 412–39.

2 *Amor es más laberinto*, v. 1204. The speech occurs in the first act, which was written by Sor Juana; the second act is the work of Juan de Guevara.

3 See Octavio Paz, *Sor Juana Inés de la Cruz, o Las trampas de la fe*, 2nd ed. (México: F.C.E., 1983), and A. G. Salceda, *Introducción* to vol. 4 of the *Obras completas*, pp. xxiv–xxvi.

4 See, for example, my book *Plotting Women. Gender and Representation in Mexico* (New York: Columbia University Press, 1989), which describes the relationships between confessors and nuns who were mystics.

5 See Norbert Elias, *The Civilizing Process*, vol. 1: *The History of Manners*, trans. E. Jephcott (New York: Pantheon Books, 1978).

6 For example, Sor Juana's ballad "Supuesto, discurso mío" [Of course, speech of mine] (p. 1: 20), where she writes: "Más hago yo, pues no hay duda / que hace finezas mayores, / que el que voluntario ruega, / quien violenta corresponde. / Porque aquél sigue obediente / de su Estrella el curso dócil, / y ésta contra la corriente / de su destino se opone" [I accomplish more, there is no doubt, / for she who responds to her lover with passion / makes a greater gesture of love / than he who pleads for her love in the first place. / For he is docile, / simply following the path of his Fate, / whereas she goes against the tide, / and rebels against her allotted destiny] (vv. 93–100). There are also several sonnets on the same theme—"que no me quiera Fabio . . ." [I hope Fabio doesn't love me . . .] (p. 288), "Feliciano me adora y le aborrezco . . ." [Feliciano adores me and I abhor him   ] (pp. 288 89), "Al que ingrato me deja . . ." [The ungrateful one that leaves me . . .] (p. 289)—and almost all are categorized as poems of "Love and Discretion" by Plancarte in the *Obras completas*. The sonnet, "Si los riesgos del mar considerara" [If I were to consider the risks of the sea] (p. 279), discusses the need to put oneself at risk in order to achieve life's most worthy goals.

7 See Patricia Seed, *To Love, Honor, and Obey in Colonial Mexico. Conflicts over Marriage Choice, 1574–1821* (Stanford: Stanford University Press, 1988).

8 See, for example, the excellent readings of S. Merrim, "*Mores geometricae:* The

'Womanscript' in the Theater of Sor Juana Inés de la Cruz," in *Feminist Perspectives on Sor Juana Inés de la Cruz*, ed. S. Merrim (Detroit: Wayne State University Press, 1991), 94–123; and R. Chang Rodríguez, "Relectura de *Los empeños de una casa*," *Revista Iberoamericana* 44 (1978): 409–19.

9 Rodríguez highlights these multiple interests in her essay cited in n. 8, above.

10 See Merrim, "*Mores geometricae*," 106.

FROM ROMANCE TO REFRACTORY AESTHETIC

*I*t is always significant when a foreign loan word appears in a language because it suggests some product or area for which there is as yet no indigenous expression. In recent months, I have frequently come across the English word *light* in journals and newspapers in Latin America. The fashion for *light* seems to have its origin in *El hombre light* [The Light Man], a book published in Spain. It was intended as a contrast to "el hombre masa," the mass man made famous by Ortega y Gasset. But it is now used all over Latin America as a kind of index for the postmodern sensibility. In Mexico, it refers to easily readable literature, what might in the past have been described as middle-brow writing. "Literatura light" [light literature] is most often written by women—Laura Esquivel, Angeles Mastretta, Sara Sefchovich, and Isabel Allende—some of whom are best-selling authors, the sales of whose books are rivaled only by those of García Márquez. At a different end of the political spectrum, women writers figure prominently in what is sometimes called the neo-avant-garde and have nothing but scorn for "literatura light."

The differences between these groups of women writers—and of course there are also men whose work is considered "light," and men in the neo-avant-garde—are significant for two reasons. They reflect divergent attitudes to mass-mediatized society and different versions of what constitutes feminism in contemporary Latin America.

It is perhaps not surprising that the term *light* should be in vogue just at a moment when women dominate the mass market. They enter this market on terms very different from the novelists of the boom period when Latin American writers revolutionized the form and the language of the novel. One of the aims of the new novelists of the sixties was not only to address a new readership but also to encourage critical reading, for ex-

Originally published in *Latin American Women's Writing: Feminist Readings in Theory and Crisis*, ed. Anny Brooksbank Jones and Catherine Davies (Oxford: Oxford University Press, 1996).

ample, the "lector cómplice" [accomplice reader] of Cortázar, the good buddy who was invited to share the adventure of innovation in contrast to the "lector hembra" [female reader] incapable of anything but a routinized reading. "Accomplice readers" were expected to be agile enough to respond to literary allusions, complex punning, experiments with fictional time, and dense language. The reader of *Rayuela* [Hopscotch], *Tres tristes tigres* [Three Trapped Tigers], *Conversación en la Catedral* [Conversation in the Cathedral], *Terra Nostra* and *Yo el Supremo* [I the Supreme] were therefore in possession of what Pierre Bourdieu calls cultural capital, a reserve of knowledge of literature, history, and philosophy. In short, they were preferably cultivated university graduates. Women in these same novels were frequently represented as ignorant, unsophisticated, naïve, prejudiced, inflexible, or archaic, and so on. The patriarchal narrative portrayed men as the protagonists of national liberation and Enlightenment through progress so that, not surprisingly, male writers also set the agenda for what counted as literature. Women used the tactics of the weak to mimic, modify, and parody such narratives. Nevertheless, what strikes one about the literature written by women before the seventies, with one or two notable exceptions such as Clarice Lispector, is how rarely their writing was considered innovative or avant-garde. Think for example of Silvina Ocampo or Beatriz Guido as compared to Borges, or Armonía Sommers compared to Onetti. It is only in contemporary readings that these women have begun to be recognized as something more than secondary players.

But a new paradigm came into effect in the postdictatorial societies of the Southern Cone and the modernized neoliberalism of other countries, a paradigm of pluralism and multiculturalism which has favored women's writing. It is a cliché of postmodernism to say that with the end of the master narratives of historical progress and Enlightenment, women and ethnic minorities have been given a voice. This seemed to be born out by the book fair in Santiago, Chile, this December, in which women writers were featured—Isabel Allende's latest novel *Paula*, Angeles Mastretta's *Arráncame la vida* [Mexican Bolero], Cristina García's *Dreaming in Cuban*, Laura Esquivel's *Like Water for Chocolate*. But it is significant that these featured writers all write what I will term art romance. If the fair had been held in Mexico, it would no doubt have included Sara Sefchovich's novels *Demasiado amor* [Too Much Love] and *La señora de los sueños* [The Lady of Dreams] as well: novels which Mexican critics have designated as "light" but which had a big national readership. In addition to art romance women's biographies are also best-sellers, at least in Mexico—for instance,

Tinísima by Elena Poniatowska, *Nahui Olin: La mujer del sol* [Nahui Olin: The Woman of the Sun] by Adriana Malvido, not to mention Hayden Herrera's *Frida* and Martha Zamora's *Frida, el pincel de la angustia* [Frida, the Brush of Anguish].

Indeed, a parallel can be drawn between women's writing in England and the United States in the last century, especially when mass literature was coming into being, and this contemporary emergence of best-selling writing by Latin American women authors. All of you will no doubt remember Miss Prism in Oscar Wilde's *The Importance of Being Earnest*, who was the author of an unpublished three-decker novel which absorbed her attention so much that she placed it in her perambulator and left the baby in the unclaimed luggage at Victoria Station. Wilde was writing at a time when women were being accused of flooding the market with cheap romance, forcing "serious" writers like Henry James and Thomas Hardy to revise their craft, and witty writers like Wilde to ridicule them. In his article "Mass Culture as Woman," Andreas Huyssen has shown how women and mass culture were discussed in analogous terms by modernist writers whose work was often felt deeply threatened by popular literature and its women practitioners.

In Latin America, however, there was little popular written literature in the nineteenth century. Popular culture was predominantly oral. The literate public was small. And this literate public tended to favor foreign best-sellers. One of Rubén Darío's poems mentions Paul de Kock, a now forgotten but popular novelist who epitomized "light" literature for the Modernists. In the first part of the century, light literature was primarily written by men—Vargas Vila, Luis Spota of Mexico, Hugo Wast in Argentina, catered to the middle- and upper-class readership who were not prepared to spend their energies on so-called serious writing.

It was not until a new wave of mass culture—in the form of "telenovelas" [soap operas], photonovels, comic strip novels—began to be produced in the fifties and sixties that popular literature became an issue. People began to take notice of the runaway success not only of *telenovelas* but also the romances of Corín Tellado. It is perhaps no coincidence that publishing itself was also undergoing radical changes from small artisan-type publishers like Joaquín Mortíz, who was a personal friend of many of his authors, to huge intercontinental organizations like the Spanish-based Planeta. Planeta organizes important literary prizes that are reminiscent of the Miss America contest, in Santiago, Buenos Aires, and Mexico. The considerable monetary prize generally goes to "readable" authors rather than to avant-garde or experimental texts. The idea of a writing that may be too avant-garde to be commercially viable became more and more difficult to put into practice. It is in this context that the art romance often written by women has emerged.

There is an additional factor. Latin American literature always sought international recognition. Nowadays that recognition is in the form of measurable sales, and in this respect women writers are scoring points. A recent article published in *Confluencias* notes the runaway success in Germany of Isabel Allende's *La casa de los espíritus* [House of Spirits] and Angeles Mastretta's *Arráncame la vida* [Mexican Bolero], both of which were on the best-seller lists for weeks. Laura Esquivel's *Like Water for Chocolate* may now be better known than *Cien años de soledad* [One Hundred Years of Solitude]. Judging by the book blurbs, the main appeal of this abroad is still the exotic, which explains why "magic realism" has turned into such a sales cliché.

Interestingly, the successful women writers I have mentioned believe that they are writing with a feminist inflection or, for instance, in the case of Angeles Mastretta, that they are depicting a form of women's power in defiance of stereotypes. They thus represent a version of feminism, whether it is by portraying women's liberation from victimization or by creating strong women characters such as Alba in *La casa de los espíritus*, Catalina in *Arráncame la vida*, or Jesusa in *Hasta no verte Jesús mío* [Until I See You, Jesus] by Elena Poniatowska, who take power into their own hands. Sara Sefchovich, in whose novels protagonists are empowered by powerful female erotic fantasies which lift them out of their humdrum lives, describes herself as "a militant feminist, wife and mother, and a voracious reader." However, in her novel *La señora de los sueños*, women only find sexual liberation, intellectual knowledge, political activism, or religious enlightenment through dreams inspired by their reading.

It is interesting that many of the novels I have mentioned fall into the category of romance. Romance has strong defenders, among them Fredric Jameson who, in *The Political Unconscious*, invented the category of "art romance" to describe novels such as *Le Grand Meaulnes* of Alain Fournier or Stendhal's *La chartreuse de Parme*. The back cover blurb of Angeles Mastretta's *Arráncame la vida* evokes Stendhal's passionate women, thus associating her novel with this particular canon.

Commenting on Northrop Frye's discussion of romance, Jameson observes that "he insists on the essential marginality of the most characteristic protagonists of romance, slaves or women, who, by their necessary recourse to fraud or guile rather than to sheer physical power, are more closely related to the Trickster than to the Solar Hero."[1] We should keep in mind that what seduces is the trickster's guile, is his or her use of the system rather than any desire to desestabilize or overturn the status quo.

Popular romance, that is Harlequin romances as opposed to art romance, also has its defenders (for instance, Janice Radway) who claim that, contrary to elitist criticism, the readers of Harlequins are not simply passively seduced by the form but rather enjoy and play with its conventions. The game in the Harlequin is limited to the single goal of trapping a man higher in social rank and wealth. Seduction is thus not only the theme of the romance but also describes the relation of writer to reader.

In art romance, the trickster role of woman has a different outcome. In Angeles Mastretta's *Arráncame la vida*, for example, Catalina's marriage to Andrés Ascensio, who eventually rises to the position of Governor of Puebla and right-hand man of the President of the Republic, begins the story of a long struggle in which Catalina gradually uncovers the vast system of greed, brutality, and corruption which constitute local and national politics. She is finally liberated by the death of Andrés. Mastretta's narrative inverts the structure of popular romance; like other art romances, however, the story evolves chronologically over time and culminates in a personal liberation which, however, leaves the system intact. Although women's oppression is equated with political repression, what beguiles us in the novel is Catalina's wiles both as seductress and as deflator of macho pretentions.

But for the neo-avant-garde, this traditional structure is itself a problem. Writing in postdictatorship Argentina, Tununa Mercado observes that literature largely reverted to traditional realist structures. She concludes, "One might imagine that in a time of fragmentation when certainties disappear, that there might be a correlative in exploratory artistic forms; that dismemberment might repeat its trauma in language, in the construction of language, in the structure of communication. But this has not happened at all."[2] The neo-avant-garde would thus argue that to leave the "house in order" (a phrase which was uttered by Alfonsín at the end of the military regime and which is taken up by Tununa Mercado) is to evade the urgent task of constituting a new aesthetic to challenge the narrative of seduction of the commodity. Mercado comments on the irony of her own surname—"mercado," market, "the unavoidable new sign of Menemist Argentina which corrodes urban life, and clouds and obliterates consciousness." She goes on to criticize the pluralism of neoliberal societies, which practice a formal rather than a participatory democracy. Pluralism makes ideas, divergencies, anger, and confrontation disappear merely by invoking (the threat to) economic stability. Women's literature that relies on the seduction of traditional narrative despite its "feminism" thus becomes a literature of accommodation.

The requirement of the new aesthetic is that it should undermine the values of the marketplace and open new areas of inquiry. In her book *Masculino/Femenino* [Masculine/Feminine], Nelly Richard, who belongs as a critic to the neo-avant-garde, shifts the meaning of "feminine" rather drastically so that it is no longer associated with the limited feminist goal of equality. Rather, the feminine includes everything—transvestite performance, certain artistic practices, some by male artists—all that destabilizes the discursive structures of media-dominated societies whose discourse she describes as monumental, pluralist, and massive. By monumental she means the obliteration of ambiguities; by massivity she means the substitution of quantitative criteria (for example, sales or polling); and by pluralism she means diversity of opinion without acknowledgment of real differences. Like several other contemporary writers and critics, Richard is concerned with the inequalities between center and periphery, but for her, center and periphery are not necessarily geographic areas, since there is a periphery in the United States and a center in Chile. Rather, they are used to distinguish a hegemonic discursive formation which constantly reproduces market criteria of evaluation from the margins where the validity of this discourse breaks down.

Now this may seem reminiscent of the avant-garde of the twenties, except that she is writing in a radically different environment, one in which revolution is no longer a possibility, in which neoliberalism is triumphant and the exclusion of vast sectors of the population from education and from health and adequate living states has become evermore flagrant. Yet there can be no return to a committed literature such as that practiced by the left for two reasons. Firstly, the left is no longer viable as an opposition to neoliberalism and secondly, the literary intelligentsia has become marginalized—forced either to capitulate to the market or to write on the margins.

Although poetry is the most marginalized form of writing at the present time, for the purposes of this essay I shall concentrate on narrative precisely because narrative is a point of contention, linked in its realist form to the market. Because it is impossible to describe writing adequately in an essay, I shall limit my discussion to two women writers—Tununa Mercado from Argentina and Diamela Eltit from Chile.

Perhaps a word is necessary about the context in which they are writing. During the military government, Mercado, a native of Córdoba, Argentina, lived in exile in Mexico. Diamela Eltit began to write during the Pinochet regime in Chile and formed part of an activist vanguardist group, CADA (Colectivo de Acciones de Arte), which took part in unconventional acts of protest against the dictatorship. With redemocratization in both Argentina and Chile, the postdictatorship state declared a "punto final [full stop]" to investigations of repression, inaugurating a deliberate policy of putting the past behind and obliterating memory.

Memory thus became an important topic particularly in women's fiction. One thinks of Luisa Valenzuela's story "Cambio de armas" [Other Weapons], in which a woman tries to recover her memory obliterated by torture; or Matilde Sánchez's *El dock* [Dock], in which the protagonist attempts to explore the death of a friend in a guerrilla shoot-out which she first sees on television. But what particularly interests me in Mercado's and Eltit's writing is their radical rethinking of writing itself and, in particular, their hostility to what one might term the story, by which I mean a plot structure, characters. For Mercado, writing is different from literature and occurs "in that much maligned place—the ivory tower which is so far from literature and so near to writing." Now this may seem surprising and even shocking at first glance until we realize that the tower is a place that women have had to occupy and conquer. Elsewhere I termed this "reinhabiting the private," pointing out the way the term "private" covers so many contradictory meanings—in classical political thinking, it refers the feminine space of reproduction as against the masculine space of production, it refers to private life as the space of the self as against social space, to private enterprise against the state, domesticity as against action in the world, a household or private space as against the public sphere.

What characterizes Mercado and Eltit is that they reorganize these meanings on new lines. Mercado disassociates the private sphere from the family. Both disassociate affect from family romance, body from self. Mercado's theory of the minimal and Eltit's marginality are awkward, not easily categorizable concepts. What both authors attempt is to make "the private" a kind of reserve energy from which the so-called public sphere can be destabilized allowing an "eros" that is not simply tied to romantic love to emerge.

In her critical writings, Tununa Mercado deliberately blurs the compartmentalization of the aesthetic as if it only applied to art, music, and literature. There is no discontinuity for her between perception in the service of literature and perception in the service of everyday life. "Just as contemporary feminist theory linked the private and the political, thus clearing away the dichotomy that had been detrimental to women, so the political dimension can no longer be considered a supplement." She describes her project as nothing less than a politics for the end of the century. Both Mercado and Eltit's work could only be written out of experiences of marginality and disorientation of exile and dictatorship, experiences which are then brought to bear with great force on redemocratized societies.

These are large claims. In Mercado's case they are made for what the terms "la letra de lo mínimo," a minimalist concept of value that goes against the grain of media practices. Mercado declares that she has never been able to interest herself in character, plot, all the normal rules of novel-writing, and that her writing does not easily fit into conventional genre categories. In a talk she titled "La casa en orden" [The Tidy House], she pointed out that the metaphor of the tidy house, cleaned up after the dictatorship, epitomized the euphemism that persisted even after redemocratization and which, for the returning exile, was particularly alienating. Mercado's one novel, *En estado de memoria* [In a State of Memory], consists of a series of meditations and evocative images of incidents randomly brought together in the memories and observations of a first-person narrator during exile in Mexico and after her return to Argentina. What is striking is that for this narrator most experiences are second-hand or vicarious. She wears second-hand clothes, buys second-hand furniture, and has a number of second-hand experiences. For instance, she visits the birthplace of a friend in Spain reliving his nostalgia; she visits Trotsky's house in Mexico reliving a political experience that was never hers. In one very telling incident, she joins a reading group which is embarking on a thirty-year reading of a cult book of the exiles, Hegel's *The Phenomenology of Mind*, a philosophical inquiry into mind which ignores the body completely. The experience of reading Hegel does not open up a universal knowledge for the narrator and her friends but becomes a teasing and fragmentary process. This "distracted" reading of a text, chosen almost at random, is matched by the narrator's attitude to writing which she never accepts as a life project or in the spirit of professionalism. Thus what she seems to suggest is not that writing and life should be conflated as did the historic avant garde, but rather that eros underwrites both "escritura" [writing] and everyday life. The domestic is not an inferior compartment of existence but a tactile, sensuous relationship with things. One of the stories in *Cánon de alcoba* [Canon of the Boudoir], which were widely described as "erotic" texts, describes a housewife going about her daily tasks caught up in this eros of materiality.

The problem of exile is thus the experience of disassociation on many levels. Alberto Moreiras has described postdictatorship societies as suffering from melancholia and the sense of loss. In Mercado's case, the violence of the separation of past and present produces a melancholy which is exacerbated by the loss of community and affect.

In its refusal of rhetorical and institutional certainties, the novel confronts the reader with an aesthetic that is also an ascetic, an absolute state of nonpossession and anarchy. On her return from exile, the protagonist seizes on the one constant in her life—a "linyera" [homeless man] who sleeps on a bench in the park, his head resting on a copy of *The Life of Perón*. The *linyera* is of course an outsider, an outcast. He is also the male intellectual who still inhabits public space if only as a derelict. Mercado's protagonist recognizes a fragile and tenuous fraternity. At the end of the novel, she has begun to write in a room whose view is barred by a wall. As she writes, the wall begins to crumble and slips out of view, "like paper through a crack." It is as if the barriers between self and other, inner and outer, private and public, are paper barriers which it is the work of writing to destroy.

Diamela Eltit has also overturned the relations between public and private, disassociating family and nation, self from body. She has by this time a considerable literary production beginning with the novel *Lumpérica* (1983), which must surely be regarded as one of the great works on the military regime. In *Lumpérica*, a woman sits on a park bench under an illuminated sign in the center of Santiago. The entire novel is about the different attitudes of this body which is under the vigilance of an illuminated advertisement. What this novel achieves is the disassociation of self from body, which is the experience of torture. However, Eltit is never referential or overtly allegorical. To read one of her novels—*Por la patria* [For the Fatherland] (1986), *El cuarto mundo* [The Fourth World] (1988), *Vaca sagrada* [Sacred Cow] (1992), *Los vigilantes* [The Vigilantes] (1994)—is to share in this radical experience of disassociation. As it would be impossible to discuss any of these novels in detail, I shall refer to Eltit's essay on her own writing, "Errante, errática" [Errant, Erratic] (1993) and two projects —*El padre mío* [My Father] (1989) and *El infarto del alma* [Soul Attack] (1994)—which in a certain way illuminate her attitude to narrative. Eltit's first four novels were written under the dictatorship, an experience which she describes as "pasional y personal" [passional and personal], as a gesture of survival. She states that it is in the structures of her writing where marginality resides. Like Mercado, she rejects the story. "For me, ambiguities are more important."[3] Her aim is to work, she says, "with fragments of materials, with scraps of voices," (p. 20) to explore nomadically, with the experience of the nomad (actually "a la manera vagabunda" [the vagabond way]), "genres, masks, simulacros and verbalized emotion" (p. 20). Again, like Mercado, she sees the limits of public discourse and attitudes which "structure the conditioning of behavior which, when not stereotyped, is repressive" (p. 21). "I think of literature more as a disjunctive than as an area of responses that leave readers happy and content. The (ideal) reader to whom I address myself is more problematic, with vacancies, doubts, a reader traversed by uncertainties. And there the margin, the multiple possible margins mark, among other things, pleasure and happiness and also turbulence and crisis" (p. 21).

For Eltit, the danger of thinking in terms of women's writing or feminist writing is that it ghettoizes. "A novel that declares itself as feminist or feminine or by a woman, would not be subversive merely because it referred to real dilemmas. . . . The space of the romance is not the only possible one for woman, nor are unlimited sacrifice, nor anecdotal references to sexual liberation (the only themes). More important, it seems to me, is to reveal the constellation of deliberate thinking which connects the individual to the public, the subjective to the social" (pp. 23–24). Julio Ortega describes her work as "putting into crisis the masculine and the feminine as biological destiny, social roles, discursive economies, fables of identity and verification of power."[4]

It is easy to see how the military dictatorship with its control of language, the social, and private body, should have inspired a series of novels which seek to construe marginalized subjectivities without making them characters in the usual sense. Eltit's writing after the dictatorship includes a "testimonio" of a schizophrenic vagabond, *El padre mío*, a novel, *Los vigilantes*, and an essay which accompanies a book of photographs of mentally ill in the sanitarium of Putaendo, *El infarto del alma*, which paradoxically is a book about love, about the patients who have formed loving relationships in a former tuberculosis clinic now converted into a home for the mentally sick. Although this is a collaborative work, I believe it also forms an interesting introduction to her narrative. This essay takes up the matter of her novels in another form. Indeed, their radical strangeness resides in the absence of deictic markers that situate the characters in a recognizable time and place, or markers of characters and fixed attributions of gender.

The mental home is a former tuberculosis asylum in a remote countryside on the edge of the Andes. With the end of the tuberculosis threat it was converted into a mental home. Commenting on this change, she writes, "the withdrawal of the tubercular body from the productive scene, if accompanied by an insatiable insistence on the productive body, on regulated feelings and the completely sedentary notion of desire . . . The sanitarium changes meaning with the violence of all territorial wars. From sanitarium into asylum. The poverty of lungs was replaced by mental poverty. . . . the liberatory loving romantic dream by the strait jacket to restrain this forbidden, unintelligible delirium."[5] The patients are outsiders, deprived of citizenship yet still hungry for love.

Many of the patients photographed are old, many ugly, and all of them have been diagnosed as "mad." Paz Errázuriz's photographs, however, focus not on the solitude of madness or the freakishness, but on the loving relationships that have been formed in the asylum. These are photographs of couples evidently from the lower classes—the faces are of the "huaso" or lowest rung in that class-conscious society—but always photographed in pairs. Eltit's text is part commentary, but the book mixes genres and in-includes a pastiche of the lover's speech, an inquiry into love, sickness, and marginalization, an interview of one of the patients recorded by Errázuriz, the account of her journey, and first impressions of the asylum. Most of all, it is a meditation on that intense form of affect which has been likened to madness because of the loss of the sense of self and in which the imaginary plays so intense a role. *El infarto del alma*, it goes without saying, is not a sociological tract, but rather a stripping away of the "social" to arrive at the most elemental form of affect.

I conclude by saying that I have placed Eltit and Mercado in a totally artificial juxtaposition in order to emphasize the vastly different project of art romance and this other space which attempts to resist market values. A century ago, the starving artist, the misunderstood poet, were figures for an authenticity which could not be bought nor understood by the bourgeoisie. Mercado and Eltit are not trying to strike this particular pose. Perhaps their aesthetic can be best described by revealing its difference from the great Latin American epic of national identity. Underlying that epic was an unexamined notion of subjectivity that often took gender for granted and made nation or community the love object. What these women writers point out is that "nation" and "community" will mean nothing without a new understanding of what has always remained marginal.

NOTES

1 Fredric Jameson, *The Political Unconscious. Narrative as a Socially Symbolic Act* (Ithaca, NY: Cornell University Press, 1981), 105.
2 Tununa Mercado, "La casa en orden" [The Tidy House], unpublished lecture given at Duke University, 1994.
3 Diamela Eltit, "Errante, errática," in *Una poética de literatura menor: La narrativa de Diamela Eltit*, ed. Juan Carlos Lértora (Santiago: Editorial Cuarto Propio, 1993), 20.
4 Julio Ortega, "Diamela Eltit y el imaginario de la virtualidad," in *Una poética de literatura menor*, 55.
5 Diamela Eltit and Paz Errázuriz, *El infarto del alma* (Santiago: Francisco Zegers, 1994), 59-61.

THE MARES OF THE APOCALYPSE

A friend of mine who belongs to a group of two men called "Las Yeguas del Apocalípsis" [The Mares of the Apocalypse] came to New York from Chile on the weekend of June 26, 1994 for the Stonewall Anniversary celebrations. With him he brought photographs of several of Las Yeguas's performances in Santiago, where they have staged a number of activities in drag or naked on the street, often combining performance with installation or using public events (e.g., the Communist Party Congress) for their staging.[1]

In one of the photos, Las Yeguas appear as *The Two Fridas*. In this photo they are shown posing as the Mexican painter Frida Kahlo, who in recent years has become both a cult and kitsch figure. In *The Two Fridas*, Kahlo creates a double image of herself, showing one side costumed in Victorian dress, cutting the arteries of her heart with surgical scissors, and the other side showing her image wearing a Mexican dress, holding a miniature portrait of Diego Rivera. In the United States the painting became an icon inspiring all kinds of interpretations around themes of suffering womanhood, the pain of divorce from Rivera, and the aesthetics of self-representation and self-fashioning. As I have pointed out elsewhere, the tacit rules of art criticism which excise biographical reference are almost always overlooked in discussions of Kahlo's paintings.[2] Her personal story has also inspired a Mexican publishing boom, not only in biographies of Kahlo but also biographies of other suffering women—for example, Elena Poniatowska's *Tinísima* and Adriana Malvido's *Nahuiolin: La mujer del sol* [Nahuiolin: The Woman of the Sun] (Nahuiolin was, like Tina Modotti, a sex cult figure of the bohemian twenties).[3] These books are titillating portraits of women whose political militancy is upstaged by their suffering and who are usually depicted as abject.

Originally published as "Desde los márgenes al centro: Tendencias recientes en la teoría feminista" in *Marcar diferencias, cruzar fronteras* (Santiago: Cuarto Propio, 1996), 117–134.

In contrast, Las Yeguas, the Chilean performance artists, represented Kahlo's painting as a pastiche, a living copy transported into a different cultural environment and "performed" by two gay men. Bare to the waist, the two performers wear long Mexican and Victorian skirts like the Kahlo self-portraits, but clothed only from the waist down. Instead of the same person in different guises, there are two different faces, both of them dark *mestizo* faces.

There are, of course, many ways to read the Chilean performance, but in these "plague years" it suggests the fate of gay affect brutalized not by infidelity but by the threat of AIDS. At the same time, the pose of the artists brings out the proud and defiant in Kahlo's portrait rather than the abject. One of the performers, Pedro Lemebel, who also writes "chronicles of the city" for Santiago newspapers, said of the AIDS crisis: "It would seem that societies need these pandemias in order to stratify the borders that subvert them: the procedure gets rid of several birds with a single shot of the syringe. It reduces the demographic explosion, regulates contagion, punishes minorities and turns the erotic into a sepia postcard of family life."[4]

The dual portrait/performance lifts individual suffering onto the political plane defined by the pandemia. The name the performers gave themselves — "the mares" (rather than the horses) of the Apocalypse — employs a slang term for gay men, "yeguas," an alternative to the more common "locas" (madwomen). By cross-dressing, the gay males lay claim to (feminine) affect. The portrait can thus be understood in terms of Judith Butler's theory about "queerness," which she sees as "a specific reworking of abjection into political agency." "The public assertion of queerness," she writes, "enacts performativity as citationality for the purposes of resignifying the abjection of homosexuality into defiance and legitimacy."[5] Especially for those critics with a stake in psychoanalysis, transvestism also constitutes a disruption of the oedipal story. It is easy to see why this should be so since Freud categorized lesbianism as perverse. Transvestism seems to highlight the masquerading that Joan Riviere in the twenties described as the ruse of the oppressed female.[6] The transvestite performance, in the case of the Frida Kahlo imitation, fakes an identity that is already a fake. Interestingly, the Spanish *travesti* also translates the English word *travesty*, a patently clumsy copy of an original. Thus the performance of the Kahlo painting is a travesty, a staging of an original that is already staged. Performance, pose, masquerade — all refer to the slippage in which the precarious nature of gender identity is exposed by a performance, whether a performance in keeping with society's norms or a deliberately exaggerated performance, a parody or pastiche. Of course there is nothing new in this. Marjorie Garber's influential *Vested Interests*, which studied transvestism over a long historical period, demonstrated how cross-dressing has continually surfaced on the margins of society.[7] But in recent times, the politicization of both U.S. and Latin American gay culture during the AIDS crisis has given new meaning to public performance and parody, because one way that gay men and women acquire visibility in the public sphere is by foregrounding and parodying stereotypical identities.

The uses of the body, the foregrounding of the precariousness of gender identity, and the emphasis on performance are very much part of contemporary sensibility. Even though cross-dressing is not in itself "subversive" and is often encouraged on certain ritual occasions such as carnaval, the attention given to it in recent criticism marks a movement of the margin to the center that occurred first of all in gay criticism and more recently in lesbian writing.[8] This attention has focused primarily on new readings of texts in which homoerotic elements had previously been ignored, and on gay and lesbian writing that often identifies the gay and the lesbian as the vanguard.

For instance, in her well-known book *Borderlands/La frontera*, Gloria Anzaldúa makes both the ethnically "other" and the homosexual bearers of a new sensibility:

> Being the supreme crossers of cultures, homosexuals have strong bonds with the queer white, Black, Asian, Native American, Latino and with the queer in Italy, Australia and the rest of the planet. We come from all colors, all classes, all races, all time periods. Our role is to link people with each other—the Blacks with Jews with Indians with Asians with whites with extraterrestrials. It is to transfer ideas and information from one culture to another. Colored homosexuals have more knowledge of other cultures; have always been at the forefront (although sometimes in the closet) of all liberation struggles in this country; have suffered more injustices and have survived them despite all odds. Chicanos need to acknowledge the political and artistic contributions of their queer.[9]

Anzaldúa's own experience as a Chicana lesbian who as a Chicana suffered the racism of Anglo society and as a lesbian could not fall back on any idealized notion of the Mexican family, led her to privilege a third space, the space of the in-between, of those who did not fit into Anglo society—the "atravesados" [crossovers].

Although they have since gone different ways, Anzaldúa and Cherríe

Moraga, coeditors of *A Bridge Called My Back*, introduced into what was then predominantly Anglo feminism the disruptive voice of minorities struggling from a position of marginality within their own communities. The importance of this debate has recently been recognized in Mexico where a special issue of *Debate feminista* (titled "Fronteras, límites, negociaciones") included an interview with Anzaldúa in which she explicitly privileges lesbian-Chicanas as an avant-garde who are developing new ideas, in alliance with those heterosexual women "who are writing the latest and most incisive theory in the United States" among Chicana artists.[10] Moraga's recent work in theater has become the focus of important theoretical discussions on lesbian sexuality.[11]

Why should transvestism, lesbianism, and gay writing become so important to gender theory? At first glance it may seem that, like early feminism, there is a need to bring these questions out into the open. But there is more to it than just the need to reveal the issues. Transvestism undermines the idea of socially constructed gender constituted on the basis of "natural" sexual difference and thus questions the separation of sex from gender that is at the heart of much feminist thinking. The notion of sex as natural and gender as socially constructed is a key distinction in the arguments between "essentialists" and "constructionists." While essentialists tend to attribute male and female roles to biological differences, constructionists tend to posit sex as prior to social constructions of gender categories. While this idea liberated "woman" from nature, it also all too often led to a functionalist account of women's oppression that ignored the nonheterosexual.

In a brief account of the history of the term *gender* in feminist theory Donna Haraway notes that "the tactical usefulness of the sex/gender distinction in life and social sciences has had dire consequences for much feminist theory, tying it to a liberal and functionalist paradigm despite repeated efforts to transcend those limits in a fully politicized and historical concept of gender."[12]

Judith Butler, in her influential book *Gender Trouble*, states that compulsory heterosexuality "requires that certain kinds of identities cannot exist—that is, those in which gender does not follow from sex and those in which practices of desire do not follow from either sex or gender" (p. 17). In a second book, *Bodies that Matter*, Butler elaborates on the argument that sex is a materialization of regulatory norms that are in part those of heterosexual hegemony. These norms are secured through citation and repetition and "the limits of constructivism are exposed at those boundaries of bodily life where abjected or delegitimated bodies fail to count as bodies." [13] I want to stress this point because clearly it moves the marginalized transvestite to the very center of both agency and theory.

What is striking in Butler's argument is that it often sounds like a transposition into gender of Marxist class consciousness, except that it is performance rather than praxis that does the trick. By performance, Butler means not only staging but also the performative in speech act theory — "A performative is that discursive practice that enacts or produces that which it names" (*Bodies that Matter*, p. 13). The hegemonic speech act can be delegitimized through parody while the public staging of the abjected is intended to bring about a paradigm shift that affects conceptions of identity. This transformation of staging into agency is crucial to Butler's argument and is achieved by sliding from performance to performativity. The critique of the hegemonic constitution of gender comes about "through the contentious practices of 'queerness' as a specific reworking of abjection into political agency. . . . It is the politicization of abjection in an effort to rewrite the history of the term, and to force it into a demanding resignification" (*Gender Trouble*, p. 21).

Butler's emphasis on performance and parody accounts for the fact that transvestism plays such a crucial role in her arguments because the transvestite is a performer whose identity is always fashioned. In *Bodies that Matter* she pays particular attention to the film *Paris Is Burning*, directed by the white, Jewish lesbian Jenny Livingstone, who filmed black transvestites performing identities to which they could not realistically aspire — the corporate yuppie, mother and child, and so on. For bell hooks, the film reproduces the white ethnographic gaze by turning the camera on black voguing; for Butler, it opens the possibility of a resignification of terms which have always excluded gays, for instance *mother* and *home* (p. 137).

What Butler finally seems to be arguing for is a broadening of "cultural intelligibility" and the acceptance into active citizenship for the "queer." In this sense her books respond to the politics of identity as practiced in the United States where, as George Yúdice has pointed out,

> Identity became a practice, a performance, a deployment across the institutionalized terrain of the social formation because performing identity was the means to appropriate by reaccentuating or reconfiguring the genres available for social participation, forms for negotiating all aspects of life from health, education, and housing to consumption, aesthetics and sexuality. Moreover not only identity but the very

understanding of "needs" and "satisfactions" are open to interpret-ability and performativity. Such an authoring process goes beyond the limits of the term constructionism, which emphasizes the pressures on institutions and economy; the new or reinvented identity groups author and perform their identities contingently.[14]

Globalization has speeded up the circulation of symbols and cultural repertoires, including feminism and gay culture, so that it is not surprising to find Latin Americans participating in these debates. In Nicaragua, for instance, the death of Rock Hudson from AIDS opened up public discus-sion of the disease and a debate on homosexuality took place in the press.[15] Even in Cuba homosexuality can now be discussed rather than merely stig-matized as was evident in the film *Strawberry and Chocolate.* Television talk shows like "Cristina" (based in Miami but shown in Latin America) are public confessions of what had formerly been hidden or private and are rapidly shifting the limits of the permissible. Everywhere there is appar-ently greater pluralism, a liberalization of morals, and more permissive-ness. Yet abortion in many countries is still illegal and takes many lives. Women's bodies are still defined according to Catholic morality and every-day life is marked by the stresses of consumer culture that has given rise to pauperization on a vast scale.

Not surprisingly, then, it is the migrant Latin American academic or the Latin Americanist who is opening up space for "queer theory." At recent MLA and Latin American Studies Association conferences it was the gay panels, not the feminist or "political" panels, that drew overflow crowds, and there is a growing interest in gay Latin American writing that is re-flected in many recent publications.[16]

Yet historical and regional differences give both homosexuality and transvestism different inflections within Latin America, where a tradition of paternalism secured by male bonding traditionally linked the social, the economic, and the sexual hierarchies. One of the best accounts of this tra-dition is Roger Lancaster's *Life Is Hard*, in which he argues that in Nica-ragua, a certain class of passive homosexuals known as "cochones" affirm rather than contest machismo.[17] In a chapter of the book entitled "Subject Honor: Object Shame," Lancaster argues that the "cochón" is essential to the self-definition of the macho in a society where homosexuality is iden-tified with anal penetration. For Lancaster the "cochón" exemplifies the cultural difference between north and south. "Nicaraguan cochones are *ontologically* different from Anglo-American homosexuals. Both are clearly stigmatized, but they are stigmatized in different ways, according to different rules. . . . An altogether different word [than homophobia] is necessary to identify the praxis implicit in machismo whereby men may simultaneously desire to use, fear being used by, and stigmatize other men" (p. 269; emphasis mine).

Although I prefer to think that the difference between U.S. gay rights and the example of the Nicaraguan "cochones" has more to do with the political matrix than with any ontological difference, the argument that homosexuality under certain circumstances reinforces the existing power structure is valid. What interests me, however, is the transformation now taking place between this traditional situation and the new situation of democratic pluralism, overseen by neoliberalism.

Nowhere is this change more apparent than in Chile, where first repression and then the "economic miracle" produced a strong critique, mostly in literary circles, not only of patriarchy in the past but of the mass-mediatized permissiveness of contemporary society. The mechanisms of the older regime (which were similar to those described by Roger Lancaster) were brilliantly exposed in José Donoso's novel, *El lugar sin límites* [Hell Has No Limits], published in 1966.[18] The protagonist of this novel, Manuela, represents the forbidden and yet seductive limits of the paternalistic order, offering an apparent transgression of gender boundaries by dressing and performing as a flamenco dancer. Homoeroticism was permissible in this society as long as it was disguised, marginalized in the brothel, and controlled. At the same time, male pleasure derived from the very ambiguity of the transvestite performance because the macho could treat the transvestite performer as a woman and therefore as abject. When, as a crude joke, Manuela is forced by his patron to act like a man and to make love to the brothel owner La Japonesa (and thereby apparently fathering a daughter), the "travesty" becomes quite blatant. A not-quite-man acts as a man while wanting to masquerade as a not-quite-woman. This could only happen in a society where the social attributes of masculinity and femininity are rigidly governed by a hierarchy of power defined as masculine and where woman possesses only the power of seduction and masquerade. Donoso's novel links the transvestite to a society in which virility, economic power, and political power sustain hierarchical relations that are also actualized in the class and power differences between the macho and the passive homosexual.

Set in a historical period of transition and modernization, *El lugar sin límites* is the tragedy of anachronism, both the anachronism of a town doomed to death and decay because it is bypassed by the railroad, and the anachronism of Manuela herself whose devotion to her "art" allows the men to indulge in the fantasy of homoeroticism without appearing to succumb to it. The brothel acts as a kind of heterotopia—an alternative space within the system. However, it proves to be a fragile space. Modernization brings about the end of patriarchal protectionism and the male fantasies it encouraged. The aging Manuela can no longer sustain the illusion. Beaten, left to the dogs, s/he becomes redundant.

The marginalization of prostitutes and transvestites in brothels was essential to the patriarchal landowning order in which power was secured through filiation and male bonding, usually in opposition to the abject. In Chile, this relative tolerance came to an end (although without any essential change of the social structure) with the military government of Pinochet, which violently disciplined society to make way for the economic miracle. It was not only Communists and socialists who were stigmatized as subversive, but also gay men and transvestites. The Chilean case was not unlike that of Nazi Germany in which the homosexual tendencies in the army were violently repressed. In both societies the idea of discipline was paramount and the fear of sexual disorder correspondingly intense.[19]

This moment of increased repression is caught in *La manzana de Adán* [Adam's Apple], a collaborative photoessay by the photographer Paz Errázuriz and the writer Claudia Donoso, which can be read as a postscript to *El lugar sin límites*.[20] The two authors lived with the transvestites in a Talca brothel called, appropriately, "La Jaula" [The Cage], whose inhabitants were as secluded from society as if they were in a convent. Although the book was published after redemocratization, the material was gathered during the military regime at the beginning of which transvestites were taken to a ship anchored offshore, where they were tortured and sometimes killed. Those who survived the torture risked imprisonment and persecution. Yet they took the risk not for political reasons (indeed some of them were quite right-wing) but rather because of love and their carefully nourished illusions of being "artists" and performers. Like Manuela, they believe that it is the ability to perform the illusion of womanhood that is important. "My show was so convincing that they all thought I was a woman," one of them says, "but at the end of the show I used to remove my wig so they could see I was a *travesti*" (p. 121).

What made it impossible for the military government to tolerate this was the fear of ceding to the "pacifist, cowardly, immoral, lowly, base and demoralizing."[21] The "originality" of the Chilean experiment, if it can be so described, is that the employment of shock tactics and the destruction of these undisciplined or insubordinate elements ushered in the "free market" whose ultimate consequence was "deterritorialization," the abstraction of affect and the opening up of new possibilities of desiring production. Once the military embraced the marketplace, it was impossible to stop the flow across borders of "undisciplined" rock music and television programs portraying permissive lifestyles. Redemocratization—with its staging of electoral democracy, free choice, and pluralism—was not so much a consequence of this as a solution to the tension between control and commodification. The policing of the shopping malls and the ghettoization of the poor have ensured that the marginalized remain relatively invisible.

Whereas social scientists tend pragmatically to work within this situation and engage in struggles over violence against women, citizenship, and rights, a number of artists, writers, and cultural critics have become concerned with exposing the unfreedom of capitalism freedom, a project which for them includes theorizing the feminine and the transvestite as figures for marginalization. Under the military regime in Chile, a "neo-avant-garde" developed new forms of political art designed to overcome the "forgetting" of the past. This group, whose work has been documented by Nelly Richard, also transgressed the rigid disciplinary lines—including those of gender—established by the government, and focused on questions of exclusion, marginality, and the abject rather than defining themselves in terms of left or right.[22] As Julia Kristeva has pointed out, it "is not lack of cleanliness or health that causes abjection but what disturbs identity, system, order. What does not respect borders, positions, rules. The in-between, the ambiguous, the composite."[23]

With the ending of the military regime, the political art of the neo-avant-garde took on a new turn, demonstrating how deeply the social imaginary continued to be implicated in gender stereotypes. This was powerfully illustrated by an incident in Venezuela, where the Chilean artist Juan Dávila exhibited a postcard depicting a berouged Simón Bolívar with female genitalia. The postcard was initially shown at London's Hayward Gallery in the "Unbound" exhibition, where it apparently caused no surprise; however, when exhibited in Venezuela it was taken as a national affront.[24] In Dávila's work, Bolívar, the "father" of Latin American independence, is strangely transmogrified. Although shown on horseback in a traditional "virile" and martial pose, he is clothed in a halter top that reveals women's breasts, his trousers are open to show both a vagina and testicles, and he wears an earring and lipstick. Dávila's "Bolívar" thus interrogates the past in a particularly disturbing way by exposing the hero not only as public man but also as public woman. As Michael Taussig has shown, America has traditionally been figured by a woman, and Bolívar is shown in one of his portraits embracing a diminutive female allegory of the continent.[25] When Bolívar's sex is radically altered, however, the male gendered heroic version of the emancipation narrative is disarticulated and the complicity between official history and the marginalization of the feminine becomes evident. But while the stereotype of heroism is constituted as male, the feminine side of Bolívar seems to suggest prostitution and degeneracy. The two stereotypes coexist like twins in the postcard, which makes it all the more disturbing. The precarious and never sutured separation of gender and identity becomes, in this case, the place of fantasy and the utopian, and this in turn is what permits a new "madre/patria" [mother/land] to be imagined.

What distinguished the neo-avant-garde from the traditional left during and after the military regime was precisely its focus on the need to disrupt the gender categories that supported both the old authoritarianism and the new. Starting from a position similar to that of French feminism, in which the feminine is essentially that which is dispersed, marginal, incoherent, the major theorist Nelly Richard makes the peripheral and the feminine the privileged site of insubordination. In a collection of essays, *Masculino/femenino*, [Masculine/Feminine] she argues that the feminine (but not necessarily woman) is always on the side of destabilization. Like Judith Butler, she tends to privilege the transvestite for highlighting the precarious nature of gender boundaries, but, unlike Butler, she yokes this to the insubordination at the periphery. She writes that the berouged transvestite exaggerates and thus unmasks the Latin American practice of "retoque" [touching up, enhancing].

> Seen from the center the peripheral copy is the degenerate (rebajado) double, the devalued imitation of an original which has acquired surplus value because it has originated in the metropolis. But seen from its own point of view, that copy is also a postcolonial satire of the way that first world fetishism projects as its Latin American image false representations of originality and authenticity (primitivist nostalgia for a virgin continent) that Latin America then falsifies in a caricature of itself as Other in order to satisfy the demand of the other. . . . The feminized overacting, posing as what was/is not (neither feminine nor original) resignifies both the copy and its mechanisms of doubling

and simulation as a criticism from the periphery of the Eurocentric (paternal) dogma of the sacredness of the founding, single and true model i.e. metropolitan signification.[26]

The language here is dense and at times unorthodox (for instance the use of the term "surplus value" applied to the symbolic realm); however, what should be emphasized is the mode in which the transvestite stands not only for the "hyperallegorization" (Richard's word) of the feminine, but also for Latin American subversion of rules of cultural intelligibility that emanate from the West. Thus the transvestite becomes not simply the figure for the instability of gender categories but for the parody of the Western episteme itself.

A remarkable series of novels by Diamela Eltit take the implications of this idea to the limit.[27] These novels, *Lumpérica* (1983), *Por la patria* [For the Fatherland] (1986), *Vaca sagrada* [Sacred Cow] (1991), and *El cuarto mundo* [The Fourth World] (1988), along with her early performance of self-mutilation, her testimonial recording of a schizophrenic in *El padre mío* [My Father] (1989), and her collaboration on a photoessay on love among the lunatics of Putaendo,[28] obsessively hold up the distorting mirror of the marginal to reflect the monstrous and fragmented image of the classical center. In order to draw together the threads of my argument, I shall briefly consider the novel *El cuarto mundo*, which figures a fourth world of virtuality out of the fragments of family romance as it is displaced from the center onto the peripheral Third World.[29]

Eltit's novel begins in the period of repression recording the victory of the "most powerful nation in the world," by which she may mean transnational capital. However, to represent the novel as an allegory of Pinochet's economic miracle would be a misrepresentation. Rather, the effects of discipline, repression, shame, and marginalization constitute bodies and subjects that are wounded, emaciated, "beautiful," suffering, feverish, and marked by plague and violence. A fragmented underclass with no stable identity engages in an intense play of affects dominated by desire, rejection, jealousy, loss, and guilt. These *sudaca* [lumpen] bodies and subjects imperfectly live a version of the family romance that never conforms properly to the oedipal paradigm. Indeed, the very fact that the novel is narrated first by a twin brother who seeks his identity in difference from his sister, and then by the sister, indicates the wound (of gender difference) that the novel seeks to bring into crisis. The father acts as the surrogate of the state. The mother is by turns libidinous, faithless, a masquerader, abject.

But masculine and feminine characteristics are not necessarily distributed along traditional gender lines. A younger sister is "more like the father," the twin brother is feminized and is given the name Maria Chipia. He also commits incest with the sister, who eventually gives birth to a *niña sudaca* who is then identified as diamela eltit's child (lowercase in the original) "who will go on sale" (in other words the novel itself as it enters into the circuit of exchange).

The novel opens with the conception of the twins and closes with a birth that defies the incest taboo and foundational heterosexuality and endogamy. The "fourth world" of the novel is the accumulation of fragmented identities and affects of those who constitute the "prey" of "the most powerful nation in the world"; their weapon against marginalization and eventual extinction is the utopian fantasy of a "*sudaca* fraternity" that sutures gender division. The novel can thus be described as a "travesty" of the oedipal story as well as the story of the "privatization" of the periphery, which, in the hegemonic view, has no public sphere and no history. For Eltit the virtuality of fiction is what allows the unnameable to be named. It also allows her to contest a terrain hitherto occupied only by male homosexual writers such as Severo Sarduy and Ramos Otero, for whom transvestism is bound up with the activity of writing.[30]

What I have tried to show in this essay is the way in which the transvestite has come to figure in recent theoretical writing in the United States and in Chile, and within the framework of apparently liberal societies in which the gay and the lesbian are no longer silent citizens. My intention has not been to review gay and lesbian literature, but rather to track the metaphorization of transvestism in relation both to gender theory and avantgarde writing. What has fascinated me, in both cultures, is the way that new articulations of the utopian have been made possible by moving to the center of theory those bodies that were formerly marginalized as perverse; whereas in the United States the emphasis is on empowerment, in Latin America both transvestism and Diamela Eltit's depiction of the crisis of gender are addressed to the larger problem of "Western" hegemony itself.[31]

NOTES

1   Since writing this paper, "Las Yeguas" have split up. Both men are writers. Pedro Lemebel publishes "Crónicas de la ciudad" [Chronicles of the City] in newspapers. These are to be published by Editorial Cuarto Propio this year. Francisco Casas is a poet.

2 Jean Franco, "Manhattan Will Be More Exotic this Fall: The Iconization of Frida Kahlo," *Woman: A Cultural Review* 2, no. 3 (winter 1991), and this volume, p. 39.

3 Elena Poniatowska, *Tinísima* (Mexico: Era, 1992); Adriana Malvido, *Nahuiolin: La mujer del sol* (Mexico: Diana, 1993).

4 Included in the edition of "Crónicas" to be published by Editorial Cuarto Propio in Chile.

5 Judith Butler, *Bodies that Matter: On the Discursive Limits of "Sex"* (New York: Routledge, 1993), 21. In her earlier *Gender Trouble: Feminism and the Subversion of Identity* (New York: Routledge, 1990), she tended to insist on the parodic.

6 Joan Riviere, "Womanliness as a Masquerade," in Victor Burgin, James Donald, and Cora Kaplan, eds., *Formations of Fantasy* (London: Methuen, 1986).

7 Marjorie Garber, *Vested Interests: Cross-Dressing and Cultural Anxiety* (London: Penguin Books, 1992).

8 See David William Foster, *Latin American Writers on Gay and Lesbian Themes: A Bio-Critical Sourcebook* (Westport, Conn.: Greenwood Press, 1994).

9 Gloria Anzaldúa, *Borderlands/La Frontera: The New Mestiza* (San Francisco: Aunt Lute Books, 1987), 84–85.

10 Gloria Anzaldúa, "Ya se me quitó la vergüenza y la cobardía," Conversation with Claire Joysmith, *Debate feminista*, 8 (September 1993): 16.

11 See, for example, Teresa de Lauretis, *The Practice of Love: Lesbian Sexuality and Perverse Desire* (Bloomington: Indiana University Press, 1994), esp. the discussion of Moraga's play *Giving up the Ghost*, 205–15.

12 Donna Haraway, *Simians, Cyborgs, and Women: The Reinvention of Nature* (New York: Routledge, 1991), 136.

13 Butler, *Bodies that Matter*, 15.

14 George Yúdice, *We Are Not the World* (Durham, N.C.: Duke University Press, 1999).

15 Roger Lancaster, *Life Is Hard: Machismo, Danger and the Intimacy of Power in Nicaragua* (Berkeley: University of California Press, 1992), 256.

16 See, for example, David William Foster, *Gay and Lesbian Themes in Latin American Writing* (Austin: University of Texas Press, 1991), and Foster, *Latin American Writers*.

17 Lancaster, *Life Is Hard*, 235–78.

18 José Donoso, *El lugar sin límites* [Hell Has No Limits] (1966; Barcelona: Seix Barral, 1987).

19 Klaus Theweleit, *Male Fantasies: Women, Floods, Bodies, History* (Minneapolis: University of Minnesota Press, 1987).

20 Paz Errázuriz and Claudia Donoso, *La manzana de Adán* (Santiago: Zona, 1990).

21 The quotation is from Theweleit, *Male Fantasies*, 387.

22 Most recently in her book, *La insubordinación de los signos (Cambio político, transformaciones culturales y poéticas de la crisis)* (Santiago: Editorial Cuarto Propio, 1994).

23 Julia Kristeva, *Powers of Horror: An Essay on Abjection* (New York: Columbia University Press, 1982), 4.

24 I am grateful to Marcial Godoy for allowing me to see a copy of the postcard and for his related work on the deterritorialization of the body.

25 Michael Taussig, "America as Woman: The Magic of Western Gear," in *Mimesis and Alterity: A Particular History of the Senses* (London: Routledge, 1993), 176–92. I wrote this article before the publication of an issue of *Revista de Crítica Cultural* (Nov 1994): 9 devoted to the Dávila affair.

26 Nelly Richard, *Masculino/Femenino: Prácticas de la diferencia y cultural democrática* (Santiago: Francisco Zegers Editor, 1989), 68. The translation is mine.

27 For a more extensive discussion of Eltit's writing, see Juan Carlos Lértora, ed., *Una poética de literatura menor: La narrativa de Diamela Eltit* (Santiago: Editorial Cuarto Propio, 1993).

28 The testimonial of the schizophrenic is *El padre mío* (Santiago: Francisco Zegers Editor, 1989). See also *El infarto del alma* (with Paz Errázuriz) (Santiago: Francisco Zegers Editor, 1994).

29 Julio Ortega, "Diamela Eltit y el imaginario de la virtualidad," in Lértora, ed., *Una poética de literatura menor,* 79.

30 Severo Sarduy, *Escrito sobre un cuerpo* [Written on a Body] (Buenos Aires: Sudamericana, 1969); Manuel Ramos Otero, *Cuentos de buena tinta* (San Juan: Instituto de Estudios Puertorriqueños, 1992), esp. "Inventario mitológico del cuento," 155–66.

31 In concentrating on Chile, I have inevitably passed over the important theoretical and literary contributions of Manuel Puig of Argentina, Severo Sarduy of Cuba, Manuel Ramos Otero of Puerto Rico, José Joaquín Blanco of Mexico, and many others. This is explicable since my interest here is the alliance of feminist theory and theories of marginality rather than in gay literature as such.

THE GENDER WARS

In July of last year, several members of the Argentine planning committee that had drawn up the guidelines for a national curriculum resigned when they discovered that changes to their proposal had been made, apparently by the Minister of Education under pressure from the Catholic Church. Mention of Darwin and Lamarck had been eliminated, references to sex education had been erased, and the word "gender" had been replaced by "sex."

The Auxiliary Bishop of Buenos Aires, Hector Aguer, defended the removal of the word "gender," arguing that its use "intended to provoke an ideological shift and to generate a new conception of the human person, of subjectivity, marriage, the family and society. In short, what is proposed is a *cultural revolution*." Using the word *gender* as a purely cultural construct, detached from the biological," he warned, "makes us into *fellow travelers* of radical feminism." Bishop Aguer went on to quote well-known U.S. feminist Shulamit Firestone's *The Dialectic of Sex* to highlight the "dangers" of feminism. Firestone applied Marxist dialectics to the male/female relationship, said Aguer, "in order to reach the conclusion that Marx had not dared to make: namely to modify the sexual condition of women to liberate her from maternity and her dependence on the family."

While it may be amusing to think of the Catholic Church hierarchy wading through feminist theory, its attempts to demonize feminism by associating it with communism should not be taken lightly. The fact that the debate over gender has surfaced simultaneously in recent months in many different Latin American countries suggests that this concern for semantics masks a surreptitious campaign against women's and gay rights.

Originally published in *NACLA Report on the Americas* 29, no. 4 (1996): 6–9. Copyright by the North American Congress on Latin America, 475 Riverside Drive, no. 454, New York, NY 10115. The author wishes to thank Marta Lamas, Tununa Mercado, Rosa María Fort, and Kemy Oyarzún for providing materials for this article.

For post-1960s feminism, gender refers to socially constituted differences between masculine and feminine. This definition of gender is considered a dangerously destabilizing concept in Latin American circles close to the Catholic Church, one that undermines the natural relations of marriage and reproduction. According to critics of "gender," once people accept that differences between men and women are socially constructed and hence modifiable, then the road is open for legalized abortion, the acceptance of homosexuality, the recognition of "irregular" families, and the collapse of family values.

The touchiness of the Church on this matter can be read as a reaction to the growing number and influence of feminist and women's groups. While only a handful of feminist organizations existed in Latin America two decades ago, now hundreds of women's organizations throughout the region define themselves as "feminist." Women have also become prominent actors in grassroots social movements. While these two sectors of the Latin American women's movement have their differences, there is an ongoing effort by many groups to bridge the divide. In fact, some sectors within the grassroots women's movement have become increasingly receptive to feminist political goals, including the championing of reproductive rights. The Church views this trend with alarm. By challenging the word *gender* and alternative definitions of family, the Church hopes to strike a blow at the very foundations of feminism.

The Catholic Church's position appears to be out of touch with public opinion. For example, it continues to oppose birth control, even though most Latin American women favor the use of some form of artificial contraception. A poll taken in Lima after President Alberto Fujimori's recent decision to make contraception available to poor families is a case in point. The poll showed that 95 percent of the population believed in God, yet 80 percent also said that Peruvians agreed with using contraceptives. Likewise, the Church considers abortion a "grave sin," yet it is widely practiced in the region. Given the difficulties of access to contraceptive methods, abortion has become a major form of birth control in Latin America. In Chile, there are an estimated 170,000 abortions a year. One out of every two pregnancies in Mexico and one out of every three in Peru ends in abortion. Since abortions are performed clandestinely and often in less than optimal conditions, this is also a pressing health issue for Latin American women. Abortion is the fourth most common cause of maternity deaths and the third most common cause of hospitalization in Mexico. In Colombia, 74.5 percent of maternal deaths are the result of botched abortions.

"Family" is the other sensitive issue, not only because of gay and lesbian households but also because the Church's ideal of a married couple as the pillar of society is unrealistic for many Latin American women. In the poorest sectors of society, women often bring up children on their own. In Chile, for example, 40 percent of all families are not headed by a married couple. Of every seven babies born in that country, one is the child of an adolescent, and in 61 percent of those cases, the baby is the offspring of an unmarried mother.

Instead of recognizing these realities, the Vatican is trying to discredit feminism. In order to do this, the Church uses trendy-sounding rhetoric which equates feminist platforms with imperialism. The bishopric of Argentina recently argued that abortion is a form of "modern biological colonialism inspired by powerful nations that impose their decisions on those of weaker peoples who cannot make themselves heard." He urged the faithful to stand up against this "colonialism." The Catholic Church's defense of the poor — especially in these neoliberal times — is a praiseworthy goal, and the argument that the North is imposing population policies on the South is not without some validity. But for many women in the hemisphere, abortion is not an absolute good — it is, rather, a desperate remedy.

Precisely because its position is so rigid (*neither* abortion *nor* contraception) and has such little relation to reality, the Vatican must woo women by other means. In a clear fence-mending move prior to the Fourth World Conference on Women in Beijing, Pope John Paul II addressed a *Letter to Women* in which he thanks them for their devotion, and praises their mission as mothers, wives, daughters, workers, and nuns.

In his letter, the pope recognizes that women have frequently been marginalized and even reduced to slavery, and he expresses regret that certain "sons of the Church" might have contributed to women's oppression. He refrains, however, from exploring the reasons for this situation on the grounds that "it would not be easy to attribute precise responsibility considering the strength of cultural sedimentations that, through the centuries, have formed people's mentalities." What the pope does not seem to realize is that, when he refers to the obstacles that impede women's full incorporation into social, political, and economic life, he needs the word *gender* in order to explain the "cultural sedimentations" that account for inequalities.

It is in the world conferences organized by the United Nations that the Vatican is most active in its campaign against feminism and reproductive rights. The Vatican's observer status at the United Nations gives it the right to participate in these U.N. conferences—a right not accorded to any other religious group. As Cecilia Olivares of the Free Choice Information Group (GIRE) in Mexico points out, "Despite its status as observer, the Vatican—a state that includes neither women nor children in its territory and whose members don't have sex and do not reproduce since they have made a vow of chastity—places obstacles in the way of decisions on the sexual and reproductive lives of millions of people on the planet."

In the planning stages of the Rio de Janeiro Conference on Environment and Development (1992), the Cairo Conference on Population and Development (1994), and the Fourth World Conference on Women in Beijing (1995), the Vatican was vocal on questions of family, marriage, divorce, and reproductive health. For example, the Church put pressure on Latin American governments to send anti-abortion delegates to the Cairo conference. Argentine President Carlos Menem was recruited to the cause, and tried to get a declaration affirming the sacredness of life from the moment of conception included in the Presidential Summit Meeting of Latin American leaders held in Cartagena just before the Cairo conference. Once that conference got under way, the Vatican allied itself with Islamic fundamentalists in an attempt to scuttle documents favoring reproductive rights. When it was unsuccessful in its bid to erase certain clauses from the final documents, the Vatican resorted to insisting on bracketing phrases it considered controversial, including *family group* and *gender.*

Harshly criticized for its heavy-handed approach in Cairo, the Church shifted gears in the preparations for the Beijing conference, initiating an all-out ideological war against the concept of gender. A key battlesite was the "Draft Platform for Action," a preparatory document for the Beijing conference. The platform is a complex document that deals with a vast number of women's issues—from population to the feminization of poverty to violence against women. One objection raised by Vatican spokesman Joaquín Navarro-Vals was that the word *gender* was used more frequently than the word *mother.* Archbishop of Tegucigalpa and president of the Latin American Episcopal Conference, Oscar Rodríguez, asserted that the aim of the Beijing conference was "to force society to accept five types of gender: masculine, feminine, lesbian, homosexual and transsexual." The preparatory document gives no evidence to support such a claim. "The differences between women's and men's achievements and activities," the draft platform states, "are still not recognized as the consequences of socially constructed gender roles rather than immutable biological differences." But, of course, this was precisely the definition of gender that the Vatican found perturbing.

The news that the word *gender* was unacceptable quickly surfaced in Latin American discussions prior to Beijing. In Chile, it began even before Josefina Bilbao, minister of the National Women's Service (SERNAM), had published the government position paper on Beijing. In an interview with *Política y Sociedad*, she tried to wiggle out of the controversy by defining *gender* according to the *Dictionary of the Royal Academy* as "a group of beings who have one or various characteristics in common."

Once the position paper was published and being debated in the Senate, Bilbao attempted to sidestep the issue of gender altogether, focusing instead on the conference themes of poverty, education, and political participation, as she would do in the paper she later presented at the Beijing conference. A group of conservative senators, however, challenged the position paper, centering their attack on the use of the word *gender*. The senators complained that "many people use the word without further clarification, claiming that masculine and feminine respond merely to cultural and sociological constructions and not to biological conditions that constitute the psychology of woman and man. According to this conception, the difference between the sexes does not have a natural origin, a view that has consequences for the individual, for the family, and for society." These "ambiguous ideas" were declared unacceptable.

The alternative position paper that the senators came up with, although eventually defeated, is illustrative of what lies behind the struggle over the meaning of gender. Every Chilean, said the dissident senators, had the constitutional duty to preserve "the essential values of Chilean tradition." They claimed to be defending that tradition against "value-oriented totalitarianism" (code for feminism), which they argued would allow all kinds of unnatural practices. These senators defined the family as the stable union of men and women within marriage, and they deemed inadmissible any term or action that threatened the family or "admitted that persons of the same sex might constitute a family." Senator Hernán Larraín Fernández reminded Bilbao that she herself had declared that homosexual families were not "part of Chilean reality." Larraín also argued that reproductive rights implied a view of reproduction in a "purely animal context, dehumanized the concept of sex, and opened the door to the argument in favor of abortion." These rights were described as "highly inconvenient and dangerous." Clearly, the senators' position is an argument for the exclusion of gay men and women from citizenship and the criminalization of abortion.

The Catholic Church has also found itself pitted against multilateral lending institutions over population-control policies. The World Bank and the Inter-American Development Bank see these policies as a way to reduce poverty and facilitate women's participation in the wage-labor force. Latin American governments are caught in a bind between this imperative to "modernize" and opposition to birth control and abortion coming from the Church and other conservative groups. Peru illustrates the hard choices that neoliberal governments face on this issue. In his inaugural address to the nation on July 28, 1995, President Fujimori unexpectedly broke ranks with other Latin American countries on the issue of birth control, announcing that the state would facilitate access to family planning for poor families. "We have been and shall continue to be a pragmatic government, without taboos or 'sacred cows,'" he said, in a pointed reference to the Church. "Peruvian women must be in control of their own destinies."

Fujimori was playing the modernization card, appealing to multilateral lending institutions by promising that by the year 2000 poverty would be reduced by 50 percent and that 50 percent of social spending would be targeted for women. A government document drawn up in 1993 and obtained by the Peruvian journal *Oiga* revealed exactly how large the population problem loomed in the government's scheme of things. The document forecasted that, at its current growth rate, within four decades Peru would have to support "a population of eight million hungry uneducated and unemployed people in a climate of absolute poverty and deeply inured delinquency." For those belonging to this "social surplus," the document recommended vasectomies for men and tubal ligation for women. Not surprisingly, this language led to comparisons between Fujimori's population control and the Nazi's "final solution." Church leaders denounced it as a proposal "for the 'mutilation' of men and women by the power of darkness."

Fujimori answered his critics in a speech at Beijing, where he characterized himself as "a blue-jeans President" in touch with contemporary problems. He announced that a "social miracle," which would boost women from mere survival into productive development, would follow his "economic miracle." However, this claim to be protecting women rings hollow given that Fujimori has demolished workers' rights, including health and safety regulations for women in the workplace.

Meanwhile, the Catholic Church continues its virulent opposition to reproductive rights. The gender debate that it has prompted in Latin America is clearly a smoke screen for a vicious attack on women's rights. Not only is the Church fighting a losing battle, but more seriously, its campaign has obscured the real issues. The Beijing conference, if it achieved nothing else, registered the fact that "women's issues"—including their human rights—have moved to the fore of the world's political agendas. Both multilateral lending institutions and feminist groups are in favor of promoting sex education, making contraception widely available to women, and decriminalizing abortion. It seems clear, however, that these common stances rest on fundamentally different assumptions. While Latin American feminists see these issues as essentially about the rights of women to control their own lives, the World Bank and the Inter-American Development Bank are primarily interested in population control. Illegal abortion, perhaps the most inflammatory issue, is a significant threat to women's health in Latin America, and criminalization only serves to perpetuate the problem. On the other hand, emphasis on birth control and abortion rights to the exclusion of women's education, development, and changing role in society is just as questionable. It is *these* debates that should have been foregrounded and not the struggle over the use of the word *gender.*

2 Mass and Popular Culture

A NOT-SO-ROMANTIC JOURNEY

British Travelers to South America, 1818–28

What is wanted here is law, good faith, order, security. Anyone can declaim about these things, but I pin my faith to material interests. Only let the material interests once get a firm footing and they are bound to impose the conditions on which alone they can continue to exist.—JOSEPH CONRAD, *Nostromo*

I never wore gold buckles or anything else made of gold. Begging your pardon, Excellency, but everyone saw you and described you as looking like that, in that attire. Don Juan Robertson, for example, painted that image of Your Eminence. That's why I ordered you to burn the grotesque portrait painted by the Englishman in which he showed me in a very strange guise, a confused mixture of a monkey and a sulky girl, sucking on the immense sipper of a maté vessel that wasn't at all Paraguayan and worse still, against a background representing a Hindustan or Tibetan landscape that in no way resembled our open countryside.
—AUGUSTO ROA BASTOS, *I the Supreme*

There is no home-coming for the man who draws near them unawares and hears the Sirens' voices.—HOMER, *The Odyssey*

Given the mystery that surrounded the Spanish Empire and the gothic shudders the Catholic Church inspired in good Protestants, it is no wonder that the British approached the possibility of travel to postindependence Latin America with a sense of moral purpose. They were in fact missionaries of capitalism whose aim was nothing less than the informal colonization of the continent.[1] And although in the course of their travels they produced some of the first and best descriptions of the

Originally published as "Un viaje poco romántico: Viajeros británicos hacia Sudamérica" in *Escritura* 4, no. 7 (January–June 1979): 129–42. Translated by Mary Louise Pratt.

pampa and its inhabitants, their accounts never lose sight of the ultimate goal, integrating South America into the world market and transforming its inhabitants into consumers.

At the outset the British, who sent an expeditionary force to take Buenos Aires in 1806, envisioned the conquest of the entire continent. But the failure of the expedition quickly turned their attention to the tempting possibilities of informal colonization. The newly independent states needed industries, settlements, and technicians, and some of the new governments, notably that of President Bernardino Rivadavia in Argentina, took measures to attract them. The result was a new wave of British travelers, many of whom wrote travel books which also served as guides, histories, and cautionary tales. These books exemplify the signifying practices of nascent imperialism.[2]

Who were these travelers? Frances Bond Head, an ex-captain of the army, was representing the Rio Plata Mining Association when he arrived in Argentina in 1825, armed with a concession from President Rivadavia to work several mines using Cornish miners whom he had brought with him. Known as the "Galloping Head," he made four trips across the pampa, on one occasion traveling from Mendoza to Buenos Aires in only eight days. Head's report on the poverty of the mines abandoned by the Spanish and the difficulties in exploiting them became an influential document.[3] Joseph Andrews, a mining engineer, army captain, and representative of the Chilean and Peruvian Mining Company, made a similar trip across the pampa in 1825 and published his *Journey from Buenos Aires* in 1827.[4]

Though more optimistic than Head with regard to the investment possibilities of Latin America, Andrews lost "two of the best years" of his life on the expedition, and in return received only criticism for his work.[5] In 1828 a third traveler, John Miers, published *Travels in Chile and La Plata*, an account of his trip from Buenos Aires to Santiago where he hoped to establish a copper processing plant. He was accompanied by his pregnant wife, who gave birth prematurely at the foot of the Andes. Leaving his wife and child in Mendoza, Miers proceeded to Chile to encounter nothing but misfortunes and frustrations, including the loss of his capital. J. A. B. Beaumont published his *Travels in Buenos Aires and the adjacent provinces of the Rio de la Plata* in 1828,[6] reporting the failure of two British settlements, one in San Pedro in the province of Buenos Aires and the other in Entre Ríos. These had been established by the Rio de la Plata Agricultural Association, founded by Beaumont's father under the sponsorship of Rivadavia, who became president in 1825. Beaumont found both settlements to be in trouble, one having been sacked during the war between Argentina and Brazil, the other having lost most of its inhabitants. Alongside these travel books, J. P. and W. P. Robertson's *Letters on Paraguay*,[7] whose authors had tried to negotiate a business deal with the formidable Doctor Francia, offer an enterpreneurial perspective on this period.

These travel books seem to adopt the simplest form of narrative, in which an unproblematic subject embodies the mobility of a mercantile age. In contrast with the novel, whose characters act in an imaginary space, thus opening the text to different points of view, and in contrast with the lyric poem in which the connotative value of language cuts through the linearity of reading, travel books introduced heterogeneity only to explain it away. The traveler (our vicarious self) is exposed to alienation and estrangement, but he will always return to the motherland (which, in fact, he has never left in spirit). Though they were contemporaries of the Romantics and members of a culture which in the eighteenth century had produced the cult of nature, these early nineteenth-century British travelers felt a need to distance their writings from the emotional response to nature or aesthetic contemplation. Beaumont objected to the possibility that his book might be considered beautiful, believing that austerity of presentation ensured the correct mental attitude in the reader. He explained that his book was primarily an attempt to provide useful information for those wishing to immigrate or invest. Hence he was not going to indulge in useless expense—large print, wide margins, fine paper, showy illustrations. In the introduction to his travels, Joseph Andrews adopts a blunter instrument. He refers to himself in the third person though, like the putative author of Cortázar's story "Blow-Up," he occasionally forgets himself and switches to the first. Nevertheless, the third person narration alerts the reader to the fact that the book is utilitarian rather than subjective or aesthetic.

But what marks the difference between these English travelers to Latin America and Romantic wanderers is their manner of observing landscape. For the eighteenth-century aesthete, landscape evoked the experience of the "sublime," a mixture of beauty and terror. Landscapes were viewed as if they were paintings, that is, as ordered arrangements of tones and contrasts. When, with Arthur Young, a new type of traveler appeared on the scene who stressed observation more than emotive response, description was restructured from a pictorial perspective.[8] With Rousseau and the Romantics, the pictorial perspective opened onto an oracular reading of nature, and landscape became an allegory of self-alienation and return to the unity of death.[9]

Given these powerful aesthetic traditions and the attraction of the exotic, it was obviously important for these missionaries of capitalism, committed as they were to productivity, to demonstrate that the Argentine landscape was not one that inspired aesthetic pleasure or sublime emotions. The pampa, with its monotonous flatness and a vegetation that in some seasons consisted mainly of giant thistles, certainly could not be compared with the Alps or the English lakes, as Beaumont pointed out. Beaumont found that there was nothing to inspire the imagination of the writer in the landscape. Neither beauty nor the sublime. There was not even anything to remind him of past glories. In his view, landscape could inspire aesthetic contemplation, moral reflection, or, failing these, display its potential for economic development. That is why the traveler to Latin America is constantly reminded of the ugliness and emptiness of nature in order to emphasize that it is above all a place for development.

J. P. Robertson parodies travel books in order to demonstrate the underdeveloped and miserable state of the pampa:

> After I had left Luxan I *saw* two miserable villages called Areco and Arrecife; I *saw* three small towns, called San Pedro, San Nicolas, and the Rosario, containing each from 500 to 800 inhabitants: I saw one convent called San Lorenzo, containing about twenty monks; and I saw also the posthouse huts. I *saw* thistles higher than the horse with the rider on his back, etc. (pp. 194–95; italics mine).

John Miers deprives even the Andes of all sublimity, finding the mountains too mountain-like:

> We look in vain for those varied outlines, the beautiful perspectives, the endless retrocession of distant objects — those charming picturesque views, which at every step call forth our admiration in the Alpine scenery of Europe (preface).

These unpopulated regions did, however, have their charms. Here instead of contemplating the sublime, the traveler can abandon himself to the fantasies of class privilege. Robertson mentally covered the shores of the Paraná with "immense herds of gently lowing cattle" enclosed in fields and looked forward to "the foundation of a city and a village, peopled with artisans and merchants."

Captain Andrews, who tended to see the pampa as an unkempt garden regrettably inhabited by a lazy and uncultured people, projected his vision of an industrial utopia onto the Andes themselves, imagining these marvels of creation "submitted to the miner's tools:"

> Gazing on the nearest chain and its towering summits, Don Thomas and myself erected airy castles on their huge sides. We excavated rich veins of ore, we erected furnaces for smelting, we saw in imagination a crowd of workmen moving like busy insects along the eminencies, and fancied the wild and vast region peopled by the energies of Britons from a distance of nine or ten thousand miles (pp. 1: 214–15).

It is worth noting in passing that this wealth will be produced by workers resembling insects, a prospect accepted with complacency, in contrast with Head's brief but horrified recognition of the brutality of Chilean mining life. But Captain Andrews has no similar doubts about his mission. Though the mountains inspire a line or two of verse, he is rapidly reminded of the horrors faced by the mariners of Coleridge and Camoes. "Who knows but it was designed as a warning to us not to make doggerel verses but to keep a good look out, and mind the helm." In other words, poetry distracted from the instrumental task of exploiting the earth.

The ideology of Captain Andrews is of course exceptionally transparent, but it is nevertheless interesting to note, in this comparatively early stage of capitalist expansion, so clear an awareness of goals. Even on the few occasions when he comes across memories of the past or the presence of history Andrews thinks only of their exchange value. For instance, arriving at a marvelous grove of huge trees, "patriarchs of the forest," mossy with age, covered with creepers, splattered with parasites like stars on their trunks and branches. "They seemed coeval with old time, and supplied associations of age, which the castled ruin inspires in Europe, but which would be vainly looked for here" (p. 1: 224). Asking the trees to reveal the mystery of creation, Captain Andrews seems more interested in his own thoughts than in their replies.

> Whatever they might have answered, they must have trembled, had they known my thoughts and found that their end was well nigh come, for Don Thomas and myself were calculating, that a few years of a company's employment of capital, would make desperate havoc among them (p. 1: 224).

If nature is there to be transformed, what remains of Spanish colonial civilization is seen as a ruin. A Jesuit establishment, now in ruins, is viewed as a relic

> of the most artful and comprehensive system, which the ingenuity of man has devised for subverting the best principles of our common nature, and reducing the human intellect to barbarous dependence on the wills of demising men and soul degrading dogmas, for the profit of a few (p. 1: 103).

This scene was genuinely picturesque, for the ruins of the Jesuit buildings were half-covered with ivy. Nevertheless, for Captain Andrews nostalgia for the past is not permitted in Argentina. He pointedly observes that in Europe such ruins would have been "converted into something more useful or honorable, for example, a cotton factory or a Lancaster school."

Letters on Paraguay by the Robertson brothers illustrates the way these travelers felt obliged to deny any moment of aesthetic pleasure by means of what can only be described as an alienation effect. As J. P. Robertson approaches the city of Rio de Janeiro feeling a magical apprehension, the mist through which he was passing clears and there is an enchanting vision of movement and beauty. But the enchantment depends on distance: "All this, however, we saw in perspective. When we came to a closer inspection of the component parts of the scene, the aspect which nature had worn remained the same; but that which art had assumed was changed indeed" (p. 1: 139).

The conscious rejection of the romantic vision is just as impressively illustrated in Beaumont's account of an encounter with a "morenita linda," [pretty brown girl]. This object of desire is quickly deprived of any idealized quality when the traveler sees her in the grotesque setting of the famed *Matadero*, or slaughterhouse, making *morcilla*, her hands and arms covered with pig's blood and flesh as she stuffed the entrails. This scene at first diminished the girl's attraction although he reacts positively when she begins to explain that she is making the *morcilla* for sale in a neighboring village. The entrepreneurial spirit seems to overcome his distaste. It is perhaps not too much to see here a micromodel of these travel books: the discourse distances itself from romantic idealization and initiates an overtly purposeful action which justifies and sublimates the sordid infrastructure.

The scene of the "morenita linda" has a certain element of the grotesque which becomes even more apparent when Beaumont describes the crude table manners of the *gauchos*. In this use of the grotesque, he and the other travelers are heirs of the Romantics, and at the same time, the grotesque becomes a useful way of incorporating unfamiliar and heterogeneous elements as implicitly or explicitly in violation of an aesthetic norm. Consider Captain Andrews's description of an African he meets on the banks of a flooding river and who immediately reminds him of Shakespeare's Caliban:

> The African rode on a mule, stark naked. His eyes were black and fierce, covered by eyebrows of frightful shagginess, and, from ardent spirits which he had been swallowing, they literally flamed in their sockets. His expanded nostrils, which seemed to constitute all the nose he possessed, were well night inhumed in the backward curl of his upper lip. His mouth was enormously large, and the expression of his features demonical (p. 1: 31).

Far from being the savage beast Captain Andrews depicts, the reader learns that this man is a well-known local figure, a bullfighter married to a "respectable young woman." And in fact, it is thanks to his help that the travelers are able to ford their wagon across the river. Though the description is a caricature, in fact he was trying to help them: "at first it was difficult to understand what he wanted." However, this could not altogether mollify the captain, especially as "the negro attempted to amuse us with a variety of antics, singular and disgusting enough" (p. 1: 33).

The scene between Captain Andrews and the African is interesting for another reason as well, for the traveler's refusal to hear and understand. In this respect the traveler is an heir of Ulysses's crew, who are unmoved by the song of a siren which they cannot hear. That is why these travelers generally describe religion as gibberish, and why the erotic (river baths, the body, dances) must be observed from a decorous and blurred distance and accompanied by the appropriate moral homilies. This distance is guaranteed by the speaker, who always presents himself as a unified subject, and whose unity and purpose can only be maintained by suppressing the discourse of the other.

The extreme example is John Miers's *Travels in Chile and La Plata*. Traveling with his wife, he had embarked "on a merchant bergantine called 'Little Sally' with some 70 tons of machinery, tools and baggage, and with various skilled workers, engineers, millwrights and refiners." [10] Miers turns himself into the least problematic subject of his collective adventures. His wife, the workers, and the engineers appear as a collective mind whose voice is invariably that of Miers himself. What the reader never hears is the discourse of anyone else, whether Miers's own party or the people surrounding them. Miers always refers indirectly to others' discourse and protects his own Protestant purity by not hearing (for example, "after dinner, one of the slaves pronounced a long *unintelligible* blessing").

It is particularly important to emphasize the unintelligibility to these travelers of Catholicism with its vulgar customs, for religion was a tangible obstacle to the integration of these countries into the international market. Joseph Andrews, heir to centuries of Protestant propaganda, sees priests and monks as if they were reincarnations of the Marquis de Sade:

> All that could pander their own sensual appetite in the aboriginal manners they suffered the natives to retain, and where the glimmering light of nature had infused a consciousness of right and wrong — a conduct open and candid, they laboured to obliterate every trace of manly virtues by enveloping the mind in the net of hideous superstition (p. 1: 150).

For the Robertson brothers, who were merchants, the obstacle to progress is rather the austerity imposed on people by the clergy. They perhaps felt more acutely than Captain Andrews the need to instill the appropriate spirit of consumerism in a people accustomed to fasting for religious purposes. But it is perhaps Miers who makes the most explicit connection between Catholicism and obstacles to progress, for religion in his account produces *a delay in the journey itself* and is thus incorporated into the narrative as an obstacle to his orderly progress. After spending a day in a posthouse for want of available horses, Miers comments on the "savagery" of the inhabitants, and of the fact that "there appeared among them no idea of religion nor even sign of devotion." Yet despite this absence, religion is blamed for the delay which Miers attributes to "some superstitions I cannot discover. It was Easter Sunday, and it probably had to do with some related circumstance" (p. 1: 46).

Miers's travel book is particularly interesting because the string of delays and digressions he suffers are not only virtual allegories of obstacles to progress, but they also impede the very flow of the narration (while at the same time they are its indispensable features). These obstacles are of the most diverse nature but perhaps the most important is pleasure. Just as poetry was hostile to the instrumental prose of Captain Andrews, any pleasant diversion must be rejected by John Miers. At the same time his book displays a positively compulsive attitude toward time, revealing Miers as a true son of the industrial age.

> I rose at half past four, and called up our peons, determined, if possible, to accomplish two long stages this day; but I perceived among them a preconcerted disposition to delay. By stopping, under various pretenses, upon the road, they made it a *journey of pleasure*. Notwithstanding my utmost entreaties, I could not get the preparation completed till six o'clock. One obstacle after another was opposed, so that we did not set off till ten minutes before seven (pp. 1: 114–15; italics mine).

The most devastating digression in Miers's journey and in his account occurs when he encounters the physical obstacle of the Andes, at the same time his wife is about to give birth. Miers is not just delayed, but forced to turn back in order to leave his wife, now suffering from puerperal fever, and the child in Mendoza. The wife has become, literally, baggage.

"Galloping Head," despite his fundamentally different attitude toward landscape (to which I return below) likewise displays a compulsive attitude toward time. This is reflected in the very style of his book in which notes often replace full sentences: "Galloped on with no stopping, but merely to change horses until five o'clock in the evening—very tired indeed, but on coming to posthut, saw the horses in the corral, and resolved to push on" (p. 45).

Given that these travelers embody progress so explicitly, it is important that their superiority appear natural.[11] Obviously, the *gauchos* surpass them in activities specific to the pampa, but the traveler easily claims the advantage when it comes to manners, since it is he who establishes the norm against which the "barbarians" are judged. Moreover, he has the advantage of being the observer, a position he must not abandon too quickly in favor of becoming a participant. Perhaps for this reason, John Miers liked to separate himself physically from the other travelers and his hosts. As representative of an individualist culture, he rejected with particular vehemence the communal sipping of *mate:* "These people never hesitate to receive into their mouths the tube which but an instant before was in the mouth of another. In the most polished society, the same tube will pass around in the same manner from one to another (p. 1: 44).

The inferior nature of the inhabitants of the pampa is further underscored by another trait, their absence of curiosity. Among them the authentic task of the traveler—to observe—becomes not only the sign of a superior intelligence, but also an attribute of a progressive mentality. Miers, who seems completely unaware that curiosity can take different forms in different parts of the world, and who in any case could not hear what people were saying, observes, "It is probable that a carriage with four horses has never before been seen in this untravelled part of the country; this and our ridiculous troop of horsemen in any other place would have brought everyone to their doorstep" (pp. 1: 32–33).

Such remarks would be no more than obvious instances of an ideological reading of the pampa if it weren't for an interesting and illuminating exception. I refer to the *Rough Notes* of Frances Bond Head, in which pleasure, active enjoyment, and aesthetic contemplation make way for a harsh critique of the values of industrial society. The *Rough Notes* also clarify why Captain Andrews and John Miers maintained such careful control of their narration, so this otherness would not enter it. Paradoxically, in many ways what Head calls for is a preindustrial ideology that is much more traditional. From his point of view, societies follow cycles and begin to degenerate when austerity is replaced by the practice of luxury. The expansion of British commerce and industry pointed to degeneration, which is why Head could see the Indians of the pampa as a potential force for the future. Beaumont thought they could be integrated into civilization as soldiers and artisans, but for Head they represented the seeds of a projected future when they would "proclaim the guilty conscience of our civilized world, brought to the moment of retribution; that the signs of the father are visited on the sons, that the descendants of the Europeans are, in turn, trapped beneath the feet of the naked Indians, in agony and torture begging them in vain for mercy" (p. 73).

Though Head is simply drawing on the *topos* of the perils of luxury which he has inherited from the eighteenth century, he also has an acute appreciation of the freedom of pampa life in contrast with the rigid exploitation that characterized the lives of the working classes in most "civilized" communities. But what sets this narrative apart from those of other travelers is the highly developed aesthetic sense it displays. Head finds the Andes "magnificent and sublime" (p. 96); the mountains "can only be viewed with admiration and astonishment" (p. 86). The air is cool and refreshing and "the spectacle is genuinely magnificent." Of all these travelers, Head is the only one for whom such scenes are not digressions or obstacles but a source of sensuous pleasure:

> As I lay on the ground upon my back, the objects around me gradually became obscure, while the sun, which had long ago set to us, still gilded the summits of the highest mountains, and gave a sparkling brightness to the snow which faded with the light of day. The scene

underwent a thousand of beautiful changes; but when it was all lost in utter darkness, save the bold outlines which rested against the sky, it appeared more beautiful than ever (p. 86).

It is also significant that when, like the other travelers, Head permitted himself a vision of the future, he saw not industry but rather something like a pastoral city-state in which "people have nothing to do but take their herds to graze, and with no preparation, cultivate any amount of land they might desire" (p. 6).

But Head finds his greatest pleasure in promoting himself, something he enjoys for its own sake. Thus for him the gaucho is not an object to be observed with curiosity but a travel companion whose skills produce admiration. In contrast with Miers, who always sets himself apart to keep a distance from contaminating lifeways, Head's instinct is to come closer:

> I moved my saddle and poncho very near the party, and as soon as I had eaten some meat I again lay down, as the delightful fresh air blew over my face, I dropped off to sleep just as the *niñas* were singing very prettily one of the *tristes* of Peru, accompanied by a guitar (p. 86).

Head finds sources of aesthetic pleasure in an immense variety of experiences. One of these recalls Beaumont's encounter with the "morenita linda," though the young beauty Head meets is husking corn a few steps away from a woman who is skinning a cow. Like Beaumont, Head is enchanted by the simplicity of the scene, but what enchants him is not the possibility of comparing beauty with productivity, but the fact that there are no mirrors in the house. " 'What, then you have never seen your own face?' 'No sir' she replied lowering her eyes to the corn." Not only does Head permit the girl to speak (in contrast with the other travelers who almost always speak for others), but he is impressed by her simple beauty in and of itself, so he does not have to take note of it to recall it. The aesthetic impression has priority and is more endurable for Head than instrumental considerations. And while other travelers view themselves as epitomes of the advance of civilization in an empty, backward region, Head regards the wild liberty of the gaucho as an allegory of the independence and nobility of the simple life. The country itself "had an air of unrestricted liberty." The inhabitant of the region, the gaucho, values the "unrestricted liberty" of his life and "free of submissions of any kind, his mind often fills itself with sentiments of liberty as noble as they are harmless, though of course, he participates in the savage habits of his life" (p. 14).

Head's appreciation of *gaucho* life is certainly conditioned by a focus on the people as noble savages, and his critical attitude toward a facile cultural superiority. Thus, he sees a moral virtue in austerity since luxury only breeds discontent. For him the *gaucho* exists without desires and his life has more nobility than that of the enslaved workers. On the other hand, his references to industrial society are frequently negative. A plague of locusts he witnesses reminds him of people in the city of London, and the emaciated Chilean miners in the Andes evoke pity and the reflection that only avarice could explain the transportation of miners to work in such a place. Head asks himself naïvely how, seeing the liberty of the *gaucho*, anyone in the region would voluntarily choose industrial slavery.

One could speculate that the devastating report with which Head closes his book, declaring the impossibility of working the mines profitably, has its roots in his growing awareness of what industrialization would mean in the context of dependency. Nevertheless, as for many nineteenth-century writers critical of the goals of industrialization, his opposition seems based on attitudes that are traditionally aristocratic. What is perhaps more interesting is the possibility of the negative critique which his account allows because it allows pleasure and aesthetic contemplation to interrupt the purpose-filled flow of the narrative. In this respect his writings anticipate those of Hudston and Robert Cunninghame Graham. But Head's values have their own source in an education based on the classics and in particular on a preference for the sober republican virtues over the degeneration of empire (implicit in his vision of the pastoral city-state, of the *gaucho* as a noble savage, and in his call for austerity). We should not forget that Gibbons's *Decline and Fall of the Roman Empire* had a special exemplary force for the nineteenth-century British. The energetic utilitarianism of Captain Andrews and John Miers is of a rather different order, however. Judging the inhabitants and the country by their own productive norms, they find it lacking everything except obstacles to progress, and these are better overcome not by converting the inhabitants but by introducing new immigrants. For them, the people are by nature incapable of integration into a productive society.

Of all these travelers, it is perhaps the Robertson brothers who see most clearly that as missionaries of capitalism, their task is not to convert Latin America to productive habits but rather to stimulate consumption. What must be created are new desires and needs. Thus the Catholic Church is criticized not for its laxity but for the austerity it imposes, a critique that anticipates Western capitalism's condemnation of socialist austerity, and whose echo is felt in the opening of Echeverría's *El matadero* [The Slaughterhouse].

Yet this is the same Robertson who finds it shocking that a mother would raise medical topics at the table in front of her daughters (p. 3: 144–45). The inconsistency between promoting transgression (by means of transgression) and appropriating a puritan taboo is only apparent, for it suggests the displacement of desire and of attitudes toward the body in the direction of the commodity fetishism that characterizes the capitalist economy.[12]

These travel books were written long before British imperialism consolidated itself as such, and they introduced ideal forms for the discourse of this "new spirit." The unified subject (except in the case of Head) is mobile, progressive, and yet unchanging. The diversity it encounters can be accommodated within the predominantly linear narrative form only insofar as the teleology remains undisputed. When, as in the case of Head, disturbing moral and aesthetic values are allowed to traverse the discourse, then the way is opened for a critique of the imperialist enterprise.

NOTES

1 The term is used by Eric J. Hobsbawm, *Industry and Empire* (London: Weidenfeld and Nicholson, 1968), 121.

2 Julia Kristeva, "Quatre practiques signifiantes," in *La révolution du langage poétique* (Paris: Du Seuil, 1977), 86–100.

3 Frances Bond Head, *Rough Notes Taken During Some Rapid Journeys Across the Pampas and Among the Andes* (London, 1826). I used the edition published under the title *Journeys Across the Pampas and Among the Andes*, ed. C. Harvey Gardiner (Carbondale: Southern Illinois University Press, 1967). The *Reports Relating to the Failure of the Rio Plata Mining Association* appeared in 1827.

4 The original edition was published as "Captain Andrews, Late Commander of H. C. S. Windham." *Journey From Buenos Aires through the Provinces of Cordoba, Tucuman and Salta, to Potosi, thence by the Deserts of Caranja to Arica, and subsequently, to Santiago de Chile and Coquimbo, undertaken on behalf of the Chilian and Peruvian Mining Association, in the years 1825–6*, 2 vols. (London: John Murray, 1827).

5 Ibid., 275.

6 John Miers, *Travel in Chile and La Plata, including accounts respecting Geography, Geology, Statistics, Government, Finances, Agriculture, Manners and Customs, and the Mining Operations in Chile. Collected during a Residence of Several Years in These Countries*, 2 vols. (London, 1826).

7 J. P. Robertson and W. P. Robertson, *Letters on Paraguay containing an Account of*

a Four Years' Residence in that Republic, under the Government of the Dictator Francia, 2 vols. (London, 1838–1839).

8 Samuel H. Monk, *The Sublime. A Study of Critical Theories in XVII-century* (Ann Arbor: University of Michigan Press, 1960), 221.

9 M. H. Abrams, *Natural Supernaturalism: Tradition and Revolution in Romantic Literature* (New York: W. W. Norton, 1971).

10 In English, *baggage* is a colloquial term for a woman and also means "loose woman," but rarely has the term been applied more literally than in this instance.

11 Here and in what follows I am using Louis Althusser's definition of ideology as a representation of the imaginary relation of individuals with their real conditions of existence, from which it follows that ideology is inscribed in material practices: "these practices exist in the material actions of a subject acting in full consciousness in accord with his beliefs." See Louis Althusser, *Lenin and Philosophy and Other Essays* (New York: Monthly Review Press, 1971), 170.

12 By fetishization Marx means those goods consumed independently from those who produce them (*Capital* [New York: International Publishers], 71–83).

NARRATOR, AUTHOR, SUPERSTAR

Latin American Narrative in the Age of Mass Culture

Ahora es la hora de recostar un taburete a la puerta de la calle y empezar a contar desde el principio los pormenores de esta conmoción nacional, antes de que
tengan tiempo de llegar los historiadores. [Now is the time to lean a stool against
the front door and relate from the beginning the details of this national commotion, before the historians have a chance to get at it.]

—GABRIEL GARCÍA MÁRQUEZ, "Los funerales de la Mamá Grande" [Big Mama's Funeral]

What has taken place in the New World up to the present time is only an echo of
the Old World—the expression of a foreign life—and as a land of the Future, it
has no interest for us here, for as regards History our present concerns must be
that which has been and that which is.—HEGEL, *The Philosophy of Right*

The Latin American novel of the late fifties and early sixties, while
privileging the author as originator and founding father, sets the
author against two other paradigmatic figures—the chronicler/story-
teller, whose skills derive from orally transmitted culture, and the superstar of mass culture production. These three figures—author, narrator, and
superstar correspond to radically different technologies of narrative, which
are closely related to memory, history, and repetition as modes of inscrib-
ing individual and social life with more than ephemeral significance. These
categories, however, are not to be taken as ideal. The singularity of Latin
American uneven development allowed the persistence of orally transmitted culture in rural and marginalized urban areas of Latin America, determined the limitations of print culture and literacy, and, more recently,
permitted the access of millions of hitherto tradition-bound people to

Originally published as "Narrador, autor, superestrella: La narrativa latinoamericana en la
época de cultura de masas" in *Revista Iberoamericana* 47, nos. 115 and 116 (January–June 1981):
129–148, and in *La cultura moderna de América Latina* (Mexico: Grijalbo, 1986).

"modernization" through the example of the media, especially film, radio, television, and photonovels. It was precisely the rapidity of this leap from communal memory to the serialized experience of the media, but also the continuing dynamism of orally transmitted culture and literature as cultures of resistance, that accounts for the peculiarly powerful interplay of memory, history, and repetition in the novel of the late fifties and early sixties.[1] Moreover, I shall also argue in this essay that the chronicler, the author, and the superstar not only generate certain texts but also serve as social allegories.

Of these figures, the chronicler or storyteller belongs to what is most archaic in the culture, evoking a time when power was exercised through speech. As the unofficial historian of a predominantly oral/aural culture, the storyteller and singer of tales derive authority from knowledge of tradition, from inventive skills deployed within ritualistic forms, and also from the close coordination between the individual memory of the storyteller and the collective memory of the listeners.[2] It is not simply, as Walter Benjamin suggests, that "the storyteller takes what he tells from experience—his own or that reported by others. And he, in turn, makes it the experience of those who are listening to his tale," but also that the story that is told reinforces communal values and teaches useful forms of behavior.[3] That is why oral culture is both powerfully conservative and also (as long as the community persists) powerfully resistant to the disembodied authority of writing. It is also dependent on the art of memory and hence on the lived contact between generations. Plato's warning that writing undermines memory and serves merely to recall is still relevant in Macondo when memory fails with insomnia and writing has to replace it. In Latin America, oral culture was excluded from the canon of what constituted culture during the colonial period; it was stigmatized as barbaric in the nineteenth and early twentieth centuries, dignified as folklore or used as an index of the popular and therefore of the authentic in many realist novels of the twenties, thirties, and forties.

With print culture, collective and individual memory split apart. History records public events and makes individual memory personal and irrelevant to posterity. But orally transmitted culture survived with its genealogical authority and its ritualistic modes, especially among the lower classes and marginalized groups and races, providing them with fragile links with the past. Literature, on the other hand, became sharply divided from history, and the two took on different functions: as Sansón Carrasco remarked in *Don Quixote*, "it is one thing to write as a poet, another as a historian: the poet can tell or sing of things not as they were but as they should have been, while the historian must write of them not as they should have been but as they were, without adding anything or taking away from the truth." Furthermore, print offered a new kind of immortality, the immortality of survival long after the disappearance of the empirical person who had once born a name. So Shakespeare would promise that "His beauty shall in these black lines be seen / And they shall live, and he in them still green."

For the dependent and colonized parts of the world, the separation of history and literature was to have vast consequences because history constituted what Foucault called "a discourse of power," whose rules of exclusion and selection were organized by the metropolis as essential to its cultural hegemony. Thus Latin Americans were assigned the role of children who would never mature by eighteenth-century philosophers, of barbarians by the nineteenth century, and their continent as a land of the future was relegated by Hegel to silence. It is no exaggeration to say that much Latin American literature was spun off by this problem of anachronism, which was particularly acute because Latin American intellectuals until recently had to "think what others had done," and also because intellectual emancipation and the power to generate their own discourse was essential in the struggle for liberation. As late as 1967, in his essay on "La nueva novela hispanoamericana" [The New Latin American Novel], Carlos Fuentes still speaks of a cultural lag between the universal aspirations of the writer and a national reality "que ofrecían como actualidad los temas ya tratados por Balzac, Zola, Tolstoi, Howells o Dreiser, y ello exponía al escritor a un provincianismo de fondo y a un anacronismo de forma" [which offered as contemporary the topics already treated by Balzac, Zola, Tolstoi, Howells or Dreiser. This exposed the writer to provincialism in content and anachronism in form].[4] And even more recently, a story by José Revueltas, "Hegel y yo" [Hegel and I], confronts a member of the *lumpenproletariat* on whom the Universal Spirit had never rested with "Hegel" (in the person of a legless student)—"Hegel con toda su filosofía de la historia y su Espíritu Absoluto. . . . Forrado en piel, una piel de cochino bien curtida, reluciente, olorosa" [Hegel, with all his philosophy of history and his Universal Spirit. . . . Bound in leather, a fine pigskin, shiny and fragrant].[5]

It is not surprising, therefore, that authorship becomes the remedy of anachronism. By this I do not refer merely to authoring in the restricted sense given by Foucault when he speaks of the "person to whom the production of a text, a book, or a work can be legitimately attributed,"[6] but also to the author as originator or founding father of a new state, which can create its own discourse. I wish to show that in the novel of the sixties, authorship is duplicated, for there is not only the authoring of a novel but also the novel itself becomes a model in which the utopian project of founding a new society on the margins of the old is projected.

This concept of authorship, depending as it does on original creation and the power of the individual to support it, was confronted by a quite different technology in the mid-sixties — that of a mass culture instrumental in integrating masses of people into a consumer-oriented culture. The production of this mass culture is vastly different from either orally transmitted culture or writing. Because it is standardized, the author or authors are unimportant and originality of form is of little value. It is repetition which causes the mass culture product to be recognized and a slight variation in content is enough to make it appear that it is not merely a repetition. This helps to explain why the star (or at least the person who performs in the soap opera or photonovel) takes on such importance, for it is the star that has now become memorable. Daniel Boorstin remarks in his book, *The Image:*

> What the entertainment trade sells is not a talent, but a name. The quest for celebrity, the pressure for well-knownness, everywhere makes the worker overshadow the work. And in some cases, if what there is to become well-known is attractive enough, there need be no work at all. For example, the Gabor sisters in the fifties became "film personalities" even though they had made almost no film at all. How thoroughly appropriate, too, that one of them should have become "author" of a best-selling "book." [7]

But there is another reason for the importance of the star in mass culture and that is as a focus of apparent unification in an increasingly serialized and atomized society.

> The agent of the spectacle, put on stage as a star, is the opposite of the individual; he is the enemy of the individual in himself as obviously as in others. Passing into the spectacle as a model for identification, the agent has renounced all autonomous qualities in order to identify himself with the general law of obedience to the course of things. [8]

At the very peak of its achievement the Latin American novel thus faced a powerful rival — an international pop culture which appealed to young people as a force of liberation from the oppression of the family. Mass cul-

ture (especially film and the detective story) had early on exercised a fascination over Borges for whom the problem of "repetition" is central. None
of the novelists of the boom could escape it. García Márquez, Roa Bastos,
Vargas Llosa, Cabrera Infante, and Fuentes all wrote film scripts, perhaps
not understanding that *auteur* and *author* are not quite the same. Fuentes's
novel *Cambio de piel* [A Change of Skin] was dedicated to Shirley MacLaine
and interspersed with pictures of movie stars; Manuel Puig parodies popular literature and the movies; Cabrera Infante and Luis Rafael Sánchez
parody popular songs; Vargas Llosa parodies soap opera in *La tía Julia y el
escribidor* [Aunt Julia and the Scriptwriter]; and Cortázar took over Fantomas.

In the rest of this essay, I shall develop some aspects of the interplay between storyteller, founding father, and star and between memory, history,
and repetition in the novels of the boom.[9]

STORYTELLER INTO AUTHOR

When Don Segundo Sombra rode away from the *gaucho,* he symbolically
enacted the disappearance of a tradition of learning from experience and
oral transmission and its replacement by book learning. It is interesting to
measure the distance between Guiraldes's ideal synthesis of experience and
the book with an allegory of the sixties—García Márquez's "Big Mama's
Funeral"—in which the disappearing world of oral culture can only be
treated in terms of the marvelous and the grotesque. The chronicler who
undertakes to describe Big Mama's funeral before the historians can take
over is dedicated to the task of rescuing what he knows the audience would
wish to remember, not causes or public speeches but the sheer magnificence of the ceremonial. Rather than accuracy, he is concerned with the
importance and wealth of the event and the listing of the participants
not as individuals but as representatives—"la reina de la ahuyama verde,
la reina del guineo manzano, la reina de la yuca harinosa etc" [the soy-
bean queen, the banana queen, the meal yucca queen].[10] What dies with
Big Mama, however, is not simply a culture but also a form of power—the
power that flows from the body (and by extension) from the territory of
the supreme person. What replaces her is the less visible power of a president: "calvo y rechoncho, el anciano y enfermo presidente de la república
desfiló frente a los ojos atónitos de las muchedumbres que lo habían in-
vestido sin conocerlo y que solo ahora podían dar un testimonio verídico
de su existencia" [Bald and chubby, the old and ailing president of the

Republic paraded before the astonished eyes of the crowds who had seen him inaugurated without knowing who he was and who only now could give a true account of his existence] (p. 168). What has to be recorded by the chronicler is not this unimpressive and remote president but what he replaces—the whole carnavalesque world dedicated to the production of the useless, the grotesque, and the spectacular. For García Márquez's chronicler, this perishable scene has to be rescued and recorded before it is relegated to oblivion by the standardized discourse of reason. This salvaging of what has neither use nor exchange value is also the economy on which *Cien años de soledad* [One Hundred Years of Solitude] is founded. Macondo is a society posited on the negation of the capitalist work ethic and the encouragement of the free play of human faculties and idiosyncrasies outside the realm of alienated labor. The separation of play from work corresponds to the separation of the reality from the pleasure principle and the real from the imaginary. However, because Macondo is a utopia of play, it cannot aspire to the apotheosis of history which, in any case, is written elsewhere; therefore its lives must go unrecorded except in the coded text that is outside the system of use values and exchange. Macondo comes to occupy an ideal space in which the individual virtues of heroism and intellectual daring flourish without the constraints of the bourgeois state and virtually without the contamination of actual power and instrumentality. Thus *One Hundred Years of Solitude* enacts the process of founding a new kind of society unknown to Western culture, traces its pathos, and shows its ultimate impossibility. The limits of Macondo trace a social allegory, showing that the energies which are frustrated in the reality of Latin America can be released in fiction and that fiction can stave off the taboos on which society is founded. But it is fiction of a peculiar kind. Just as alchemy fused science and religion, theory and practice, before their separation in the modern age, so *One Hundred Years of Solitude* seeks to revive the chronicler for whom things as they are and things as they might be are not yet distinct. Anachronism is thus made to function positively and to generate the utopia in which the originality of America can be displayed.

The analogy between the founding father of Macondo and authorship has another dimension, however. For the story is not only told but chronicled, and the chronicler stands between the stage of oral transmission and authorship. Melquíades lives apart but shares the life of the family. He acts as their memory, but the moment when his chronicle can be read and deciphered by a reader is also the moment when a new relationship appears, one which destroys the very anachronism on which the novel was based. Behind the chronicler, the author has made his appearance.[11]

AUTHOR AND FOUNDER

At its height, the European novel set out to be the history of the individual in society. In contrast, the Latin American novel of the late fifties and early sixties placed the individual as inventor or founder at the margin of the society and even outside it altogether. If we take Onetti's *Juntacadáveres* [Body Snatcher] and *El astillero* [The Shipyard], Vargas Llosa's *La casa verde* [The Green House], Carpentier's *Los pasos perdidos* [The Lost Steps], García Márquez's *One Hundred Years of Solitude*, and Carlos Fuentes's *La muerte de Artemio Cruz* [The Death of Artemio Cruz], and even certain allusions and sections of Cortázar's *Rayuela* [Hopscotch], we discover a persistent *topos*, that of the foundation of a society (even if it is only the Club de Serpientes) that appears to its founder to be unprecedented—outside the system of exchange, hierarchy, and power which condemned Latin American countries to anachronism and to the status of dependency. In order to illustrate this *topos*, I shall refer in some detail to the Fushía's island episodes of *The Green House* and, incidentally, to novels by Onetti and Fuentes.

The Fushía episodes of *The Green House* are interlaced with others and are set within the framing situation of a boat ride to a leper colony where Fushía ends his days. Since the temporal structure and narrative deployments have been described by numerous critics, I shall simply comment on what I take to be its allegorical significance as a founding moment. Composing his novel out of achronological fragments, and using a technique by means of which the present constantly dialogues with and comments on the past, Vargas Llosa is able to illuminate Fushía's rise and fall through the ironic light of the reader's foreknowledge. And there is not only foreknowledge; the novel depends also on preconceptions because Fushía's island is loaded with allusions to other islands, especially to Robinson Crusoe's island, and to utopia itself. Just as Crusoe's island is a distorted model of European production since he is supplied with tools from the shipwreck, so Fushía's island represents a distorted model of Latin American enterprise, since Fushía cannot break into the "legitimate" system of exchange organized by Julio Reátegui and is forced to make his way by theft from the Indian communities. In other words, he is a pirate and parasite and not an entrepreneur.

Fushía's island is presented as both evil and blessed; it is an earthly paradise abundant in birds and game yet guarded by the sinister *lupuna* trees which mark it as a place of taboo for the Indians. The passage from untamed nature to culture takes place in a matter of hours. Fushía kills the undergrowth by burning it down, slaughters the birds, and provides the Indians and "Christians" with their first cooked food.

> El fuego iba limpiando la isla y despoblándole: de entre la humareda salían bandadas de pájaros y en las orillas aparecían maquisapas, frailecillos, shimbillos, pelejos que chillando saltaban a los troncos y ramas flotantes: los huambisas entraban al agua, los cogían a montones, les abrían la cabeza a machetazos y el banquete se están dando, Lalita, ya se les pasó la furia y ella yo también quiero comer, aunque sea carne de mono, tengo hambre (p. 218).

> [The fire was cleaning and depopulating the island: from out of the smoke there came flocks of birds, and monkeys appeared on the bank, maquisapas, frailecillos, shimbillos, pelejos, who were shrieking as they jumped onto floating logs and branches; the Huambisas went into the water, caught a lot of them, split their skulls with their machetes, and he what a banquet they would have, Lalita, they're over being mad now, and she I want something to eat too, even if it is monkey meat, I'm hungry] (p. 200).[12]

The taboo which had made the Indians fear the destruction of the *lupunas* and Lalita's repugnance at the diet disappear in a matter of seconds. A new community has been founded with the destruction of nature and the cooking of food. The island that had been full of birds takes the first step toward settlement and colonization. The next stage is the building of the house, which is marked by the appearance of the *paucar*—a bird that signifies sociability. The vertiginous rapidity with which Fushía's island develops and declines is, however, in direct contrast to Crusoe's enterprise. Crusoe kept careful account of time and knew how to postpone immediate satisfaction by investing labor in such a way that he would reap future rewards. His "indefatigable pains and industry" are evaluated in months and years and he names his black slave "Friday" in perfect consonance with metropolitan time. Crusoe's island is perfectly synchronized to the metropolis. Fushía, in contrast, is discordant. Because of his impatience, he cannot found a permanent community. The island is a transit point, a step to a future. He attributes no value to labor and the attempt by the *huambisas* to grow yucca is "pura mierda" [a crock of shit (p. 218)]. Value is determined, then, not by labor but by exchange. His white mistress, Lalita, is prized, the *chunchas* [Amazonian indigenous women] are without value, rubber is valued, yucca devalued. Thus Fushía's foundation, which appeared to be outside the system, turns out to be subject to exchange values imposed by the system.

Within the structure of the novel the fall of Fushía's empire almost immediately follows its founding, and the degeneration of the island precedes its discovery. When Fushía abandons it and embarks on the trip to the leper colony, it reverts to nature in a matter of weeks.

> Solo encontraron residuos de objetos herrumbosos, convertidos en aposentos de arañas y las maderas apolilladas minadas por las termitas. Salieron de las cabañas, recorrieron la isla y aquí y allá se inclinaban sobre leños carbonizados, latas oxidadas, añicos de cántaros.

> [All they found were the remains of rusty objects, converted into spider nests, and the worm-eaten boards, chewed up by termites, would sink under their feet and slowly give way. The men came out of the huts, they covered the island, and here and there they would come across charred pieces of wood, rusty cans, pieces of crockery] (p. 239).

The trees colonize, devour, and imprison in a way that is roughly analogous to Fushía's occupation of the island.

Fushía's enterprise cannot be compared to that of the early entrepreneur capitalists because he demands immediate satisfaction. He is more of a consumer than a producer and he demands satisfaction in the present, thus sacrificing permanence. His effectiveness declines with his virility. Nor can he organize a real community out of the marginalized remnants of society—the drugged *sierra* Indians, Lalita, a deserter, and the Indians. Except for the Indians, the characters will filter back into a society in which communal life and memory have broken down. Fushía's leprosy and the decline of the island colony are moral punishments meted out by the real author to a character who represents the desire of the bourgeoisie without the ability to postpone immediate enjoyment.

This "natural" closure which conceals an ideological message is common in narrative of the early sixties and calls for comment. We can find parallels in the "failure" and physical degeneration of Artemio Cruz and in Larsen's final enterprise in the shipyard. In the latter, Larsen is reduced to cannibalizing the remains of a once flourishing enterprise and observing its slow reversion to nature. Witnessing the machine tools "pierced by the rancorous shoots of the nettles," he sees nature as purposeful and destructive of human endeavor—symbolized by the tools whose "eyes" recall the human purpose for which they were invented. In contrast to the passive, littered, and abandoned industrial landscape, nature is full of energy. In his tour of the shipyard, Larsen sits down on an abandoned life raft whose wood is "rot proof," although the manufactured rubber is full of holes. All around, he sees the unequal battle, "las costras de orín, toneladas de hierro, la *ceguera* de los yuyos creciendo y enredándose" [the layers of rust, the tons of metal, and the weeds *blindly* growing around everything] (p. 34). And in both versions of his end, Larsen's last conscious impressions are of the secret growth of moss and the implacable continuous life in which the human is irrelevant.

> 1. Sorda al estrépito de la embarcación, su colgante oreja pudo discernir aun el susurro del musgo creciendo en los montones de ladrillos y él del orín devorando el hierro.

> 2. Pudo imaginar en detalle la destrucción del edificio del astillero, escuchar el siseo de la ruina y del abatimiento. Pero lo más difícil de sufrir debe haber sido el inconfundible aire caprichoso de setiembre, el primer adelgazado olor de la primavera que se deslizaba incontenible por las fisuras del invierno decrépito.

> [Deaf to the din of the boat, his eager ear could still make out the whisper of moss growing among the piles of bricks and that of rust devouring metal] (p. 189).

> [he was able to imagine in detail the destruction of the building in the shipyard, to listen to the hissing of its ruin and extinction. But the hardest thing for him to bear must have been the unmistakable, capricious September air, the first attenuated perfume of spring, which came slipping irresistibly through the cracks of decrepit winter] (p. 190).

Fredric Jameson has applied the term *strategies of containment* to those moments when, in the realist novel, the internal dynamics fail to incorporate totality in "any adequate narrative way."[13] The dilemma of the novels of the early sixties is that they project a model of enterprise which is limited to the individual and his lifespan (the masculine possessive adjective is also significant). The novelist comes along to rescue from oblivion not "real" people but energies, desires, and dreams which have been swept aside in the backwash of history. But they are energies, desires, and dreams which still accrue to individuals. In this sense, it is an ideology of individual enterprise which is put into play even though the novels are not coextensive with ideology. However, there are also ideological contradictions inherent in making the individual the source of all enterprise and creation. Thus in *The Green House*, individual identity is undermined by the shiftings and migrations of the characters (made necessary by the totalizing project), which cause them to take on new roles and positions—yet enterprise can only be depicted in individual terms. In those novels where a community is created outside the system, as is the case with Macondo and Fushía's island, it is "fathered" as an individual male enterprise with the female and the older communal ways of life of the Indians being undervalued. These older communal ways of life exist in many of the novels as traces, like Anselmo's harp in *The Green House*, which is the last tenuous link with the community from which he had come, or like the hitching post in *The Shipyard*, which is the last reminder of the *gaucho* life. Thus the individual project, essentially discontinuous and fragmented, emerges out of the vacuum left both by the failures of dependent capitalism and by the disappearance of older communities whose traces still persist in the popular culture and imagination in contrast to the rationalized life for which the model is still the metropolis. At the same time, the very notion of individual "character" seems to founder as long as the novelist tries to maintain any degree of verisimilitude within the framework of a dependent society: what characterizes Larsen, Artemio Cruz, and Fushía is the radical discontinuity between the past and the present and even the splitting of the personality altogether. We can account for this in part by the fact that the novel's totalizing project cannot encompass the history of Latin America as a continuous development of which the individual character is a microcosm.[14]

Those characters who represent the entrepreneurial energies are not as representative as, say, the Buddenbrooks were of the national bourgeoisie. It is Petrus not Larsen, Reátegui not Fushía who are part of the system. Larsen and Fushía suggest an absence—the absence in the reality of Latin America of a dynamic, self-determining class. Indeed, Carlos Fuentes states as much when he accuses the Mexican bourgeoisie of being "totalmente ajena a cualquier idea de grandeza histórica, desconoce las maneras de consagrarse públicamente y posee una buena conciencia infinita que le hace considerar sus pequeños valores como eternos y perfectos" [totally alien to any concept of historical grandeur. It ignores the ways of becoming publicly consecrated and it possesses an infinite good conscience which causes it to deem its little values eternal and perfect].[15] Fuentes's own character, Artemio Cruz is split between the autonomous energy which should have led to an independent nation and the dependent bourgeoisie who have compromised with the system.

The novelist's "desacuerdo con el mundo" [disagreement with the world], to use Vargas Llosa's term, thus seems to be less with the notion of individual enterprise as such than with its frustration in a dependent society. Marginalized by history, the novelist challenges the universality of metropolitan ideology by showing where it breaks down. Characters take hold of their destinies only on death beds, amid ruins, or in the comparatively empty space of the jungle.

The authors of these novels, therefore, stand at the gates of oblivion. Not for nothing does García Márquez choose as his epigraph for his first novel Creon's command that Polinices be unmourned and buried without a sign to perpetuate his name. The mark that generations failed to leave in the book of history is now inscribed not as chronicle but as a dream of self-fulfillment which can only be accomplished in the sphere of art. And as with Deleuze and Guattari's despotic territory, everything flows from the body of the author to whom alone immortality accrues. Thus, the culmination of this cycle of novels is, fittingly, Augusto Roa Bastos's *Yo el Supremo* [I the Supreme] which, ten years after *One Hundred Years of Solitude*, comments sardonically on this supreme I. Echoing the epigraph of *La hojarasca* [Leaf Storm], Dr. Francia, who vainly tried to author a new kind of state, replies that putrefaction will attack not only those buried outside the city "without any cross or any sign to perpetuate their names" but also those who lie "beneath fatuous mounds and those more fatuous still who command pyramid mausoleums to be built in which to house their carrion-like treasure." Though this novel lies out of the scope of the present discussion, it needs to be mentioned because it questions the very analogy on which the previous novels are based. Francia, though a "Supreme I," is never able to found a discourse and the dictator's "I" never coincided with the "he" of historical record. Commenting on his own novel, Roa Bastos describes the *Supremo* [Supreme] in the following terms: "busca y ensaya la instauración de la Escritura del Poder, desconfiando del poder de la escritura" [he seeks and tries to establish the Writing of Power, suspicious of the power of writing]. Rebelling against the concept of authorship of these novels of the sixties, Roa Bastos creates a "compiler" who no longer pretends to be the unique originator but uses the already given, in order to "poner en cuestión el concepto de la propiedad individual de los bienes intelectuales y artísticos" [question the concept of the individual property of intellectual and artistic goods].

I the Supreme closes one cycle, only to open another. But this novel is not typical of what happened in the case of the boom writers I have been discussing. Writers like Vargas Llosa, García Márquez, and Fuentes, who had cared about reaching a public in the early sixties, soon confronted the phenomenon of a new culture, a mass culture which appropriated the forms and genres of traditional narrative—romance, detective novels, gothics, drama. Many novels written after the mid-sixties thus try to incorporate mass culture as a theme and parody its language and genres—the novels of Vicente Leñero, Manuel Puig, and Cabrera Infante, but also later works by Fuentes and Vargas Llosa, illustrate this new reality.

FROM AUTHOR TO SUPERSTAR

European writers faced the problems occasioned by the rise of mass culture in the late nineteenth century, when the avant-garde in France fastidiously separated itself from market literature and parodied its products. In England, Hardy and Conrad in the 1890s were already struggling with the fact that mass literature had taken over plot and had stereotyped character and mimed the "impersonal" narrative voice which had allowed the writer to immolate himself in the work. Henceforth no self-respecting writer can *not* be self-conscious. In James Joyce's *Ulysses*, Bloom canvasses advertisements and Molly Bloom is already a star in embryo; the irony is not that they perpetuate the myth of Ulysses but their distance from it. Yet Joyce's recourse to myth is significant. For myth is called up to organize on a higher plane the chaos of trivial impressions and automatized responses which add up to daily life. Modern mass culture, as Fredric Jameson has shown, is characterized by repetition. And modernism's striving for the new is, in reality, an effort "to produce something which resists and breaks through the force of gravity of repetition as a universal feature of commodity equivalence."[16] In contrast, the mass culture "text," whether music, photonovel, or film, is always a repeat, there being no original.

To posit, thus, a bonding between modernism and mass culture helps to situate a writer like Cortázar, whose entire work is a struggle against the choking effects of the automatic gesture and banal speech. However, here I am going to confine my remarks to writers like Fuentes and Vargas Llosa (and marginally to Manuel Puig) because their response to mass culture is far more ambiguous. Both these writers also hark back again and again to an ideal — Balzac for Fuentes, Balzac and Flaubert for Vargas Llosa. As the latter states in his book on Flaubert,

> Pienso que el trastorno que significó para la cultura en general y para la literatura en particular el nacimiento de la sociedad industrial, el desarrollo veloz de la alta y media burguesía, es tan importante para explicar el anacoretismo de Flaubert como su situación familiar. En todo caso, es evidente que las condiciones estaban dadas para que, a partir de esta actitud de desesperado individualismo ante la vocación, lúcidamente asumida como una ciudadela contra el mundo, surgiera una estética de la incomunicabilidad o del suicidio de la novela.

> [I think the upheaval that the birth of industrial society (and along with it the rapid development of the upper and middle bourgeoisie) represented for culture in general, and for literature in particular, should be given as great weight in explaining Flaubert's hermetism as his family situation. In any event, it is evident conditions were such that the result of this desperate, stubborn single-mindedness with regard to his vocation, lucidly chosen as a citadel against the world, might well have been an aesthetic of incommunicability or of the suicide of the novel].[17]

But, argues Vargas Llosa, Flaubert solved the problem by producing a novel which is both critical and read. "Sin renunciar a su pesimismo y desesperación, convirtiéndoles más bien en materia y estímulo de su arte, y llevando el culto de lo estético a un límite de rigor así sobrehumano, Flaubert escribió una novela capaz de congeniar la originalidad y la comunicación, la sociabilidad y la calidad" [Without renouncing his pessimism and his despair, transforming them, rather, into material and impetus for his art, and carrying the cult of the aesthetic to an almost superhuman degree of rigor, Flaubert wrote a novel capable of conjoining originality and communication, social value and quality] (240). Balzac offers a similar touchstone for Fuentes. Both writers react to mass culture not by adopting a modernist aesthetic (despite Fuentes's trendy experiments) but rather by straining older forms of narrative to accommodate the displacement of significance from author to star. Mario Vargas Llosa's attempt is the most halfhearted. In *Aunt Julia and the Scriptwriter* he sets a projection of himself "Mario" as an aspiring writer against the "Balzac" of soap operas, a writer who pins a map of Lima on his wall to guide him in this modern *Comédie Humaine*. The problem is that in soap opera it is not the author who is idolized by the masses but the star who incarnates the role so that the novel rings false from the start. The *escribidor*'s [scribbler, or scribe] inventiveness is eventually defeated by the system which is insatiable in its desire for the increasingly violent material that is needed in order to overcome the formulaic plot which must always culminate in an enigma strong enough to make the listener turn on the next episode. In order to meet that demand, the *escribidor* deals with more and more dangerous subjects from incest to cannibalism, and eventually defies the ultimate taboo by involuntarily confusing characters. Despite the constant violation of traditional morals by the radio soap opera, Mario's own attempt to marry his aunt comes up with the traditional difficulties. The soap opera, thus, has no direct effect on societal morals. As parody, however, *Aunt Julia* falls down precisely because it misses the mark. In reality, the soap opera's adoption of traditional narrative codes, especially the enigma, allows it to raise so-called taboo subjects and problems while at the same time providing for their regular defusing. What is at stake in this novel is the issue of creativity in the age of mass culture, but it is a creativity still conceived in terms of Balzacian authorship, now reproduced in parodied form for the "masses."

In contrast, Carlos Fuentes has been, from the early sixties, very much aware of the appearance of the star as a threat to the "author." Indeed, his *Zona sagrada* [Holy Place] can be seen as an allegory of the distorting effect of stardom on authorship—as the film star Claudia continuously exclaims to her son (Mito, the narrator) who, unlike the star, cannot withstand time, "Yo duro" [I endure]. But Claudia is, in fact, another version of the author. She is both Circe and Penelope and her son aspires to unite with her. From his holy place, the space of the narrator, Mito contemplates the ever changing, ever enduring face of the star, the "idea platónica del ser humano" [platonic idea of the human being]. His story is the attempt to possess this image symbolically and fetishistically. In one of the final chapters, Mito dresses in his mother's clothes in order to be her, only to find that this pantomime converts him into an impostor—a dog—who vows the destruction of the "witch." Like the troglodyte to whom the narrator gives the name of Argos (Ulysses's dog) in Borges's *El inmortal* [The Immortal], the narrator/dog of *Holy Place* is also Homeric, being a reincarnation of the mythic "Telemachus." The mythological references in the story, along with the fact that *Holy Place* seems to refer to María Felix and that the Claudia of the novel claims to have succeeded Pancho Villa as the symbol of Mexico, have tended to obscure the allegorical force of this confrontation between narrator and star. The problem is that Fuentes remains locked within the sphere of the star, in opposition to whom the narrator can only fall into attitudes of contemplation, narcissism, and self-immolation.

There is a further telltale link with mass culture. If the era of mechanical reproduction involves the phenomenon of repetition, it is because both memory and history no longer serve as indexes of individual and public destiny. Repetition fixes a pattern or habit in the mind of the consumer and thus enables new material to be absorbed while reinforcing the original position. Repetition in modern society serves to channel desires and needs within narrow boundaries and hence contain them. Thus it is somewhat different from ritual in traditional societies whose function was, as Lévi-Strauss pointed out, to "conjoin"—to bring together. The repetition of mass culture, especially in radio and television where the public may sit alone, is that it is addressed to the isolated individual and emphasizes the separation by attaching his or her desires to the specular image or object. What Fuentes tries to do in *Holy Place* is to rescue the repetition which is the only form of immortality that mass culture offers and elevate it to the plane of "myth" by forcing Claudia and her son successively into the roles of Penelope/Telemachus, Circe/the beasts, and so on. While an avant-garde aesthetic (like that of Cortázar) tries to shock or break out of automatized repetition, Fuentes tries to dignify it.

This essential ambiguity toward mass culture can be illustrated from a rather more complex novel, *A Change of Skin*. The narrator of the novel, Freddy Lambert, "portador de la palabra posible y los personajes portadores de las palabras devenido imposible" [bearer of the possible word and the characters bearers of words, turned impossible][18] really belongs anachronistically to an earlier version of the novel, *El sueño* [The Dream]. It was almost as an afterthought that Fuentes himself incorporated *A Change of Skin* into a McLuhanesque framework. "Hay algo más en *Cambio de piel*, algo que solo ahora entiendo, al leer a Marshal McLuhan y es una cierta participación en el nuevo mundo circular, o de integraciones simultáneas y explosivas que ha venido a sustituir al mundo lineal, individual, del punto de vista y las motivaciones" [There is something else in *A Change of Skin*, something that I understand only now, reading Marshal McLuhan. It is a certain kind of participation in the new circular world, or the world of simultaneous and explosive integrations that has come to replace the linear, individual world-of-the-point-of-view and the motivations].[19] The global village is a reality which demands a new kind of narrator and a new kind of a novel which (as he explained on another occasion) demanded that the novelist himself be sacrificed. Thus, because the bourgeois novel of

Mexico is no longer possible, because the totalizing vision cannot encompass all the images of a consumer age and because the age of technology only knows stars not heroes and repetition and not history, the old form of novel is displaced by a "happening." The Beatles rather than Balzac become the model. The novel that Fuentes had originally conceived around the year 1965 as *The Dream* had still included existential characters with personal memories and family histories. Only in the course of writing did such histories come to seem irrelevant for, as he explained,

> vivimos en sociedades modernas maltratadas, inundadas de objetos, de mitos y aspiraciones de plástico, aluminio, y tenemos que encontrar los procedimientos, las respuestas, al nivel de esa realidad; tenemos que encontrar las nuevas tensiones, los nuevos símbolos, la nueva imaginación, a partir del Chicle Wrigleys y la telenovela y el frug y el bolero y los muchachos de antes no usaban gomina. Antes que en la cultura, el mexicano o el bonaerense o el limeño actuales somos contemporáneos de todos los hombres *en las mercancías y las modas.*

> [we live in mistreated modern societies, overflown/saturated by objects, myths, and plastic and aluminum aspirations; so we have to find the procedures, the answers, that correspond to that particular reality. We have to find the new tensions, the new symbols, the new imagination that stem from Wrigley's chewing gum, and TV, and frug, and the *bolero*, and *Los muchachos de antes no usaban gomina.* The Mexican—as well as the guy from Buenos Aires, or the guy from Lima—from today are contemporaries with every person *in commodities and in fashion*, rather than in culture] (italics mine).[20]

Thus while grasping some of the features of the "society of the spectacle," Fuentes also succumbs to the attraction of its stellar universalism. This explains why in *A Change of Skin*, originally an existential novel with four characters, is overlaid with an allegory of its own destruction. It also helps to explain the somewhat gratuitous use of photographs—the little Jewish boy rounded up by the Nazis, stills from the *Cabinet of Dr. Caligari*, and photographs of the film stars of the thirties. We may note in passing, too, how often Fuentes has himself photographed with film stars and how he likes to dedicate his books to them.[21] But we should also ask why the photographs in *A Change of Skin* exist—except as a gesture to the image whose importance Fuentes grasps without knowing how to incorporate it in fiction. But this is not quite correct. For at the end of the novel when the collapse of the pyramid in Cholula has crushed the older characters, leaving the narrator with a carnavelesque group, the *monjes*, the narrator reveals the contents of his trunk, including a series of photographs that show all the places the characters in the novel have visited. There is also a number of old movies—*El Golem, Nosferatu, El ángel azul, Vampyr, Das Rheingold*, and *Caligari*—the very movies, in fact, that are mentioned in Kracauer's *From Caligari to Hitler*, which studies the relation of film and totalitarianism. *A Change of Skin*'s narrator is called Freddy Lambert and, at the end of the novel, is found, like Caligari, to be in a lunatic asylum. Readers will have little difficulty, however, in recognizing in Freddy a late reincarnation of a Balzacian hero, Lucien Lambert, who went mad after intensive immersion in "irrational" philosophies. We are expected, therefore, to appreciate the "irrational"—represented by the youth culture, the happening, guiltless eroticism, and so on—against the rationalizing mission of modern society by which the older generation in the novel is contaminated. Because the "change of skin" of the title is not only a description of the novel but of radical changes in Fuentes's own view of literature, the last part has an extraneous quality as if it belonged to some other work. But it is also as if the Cholula pyramid that comes down on some of the characters is also meant to cut off the older features of the novel—the plot that hinges on a journey, the characters whose past dominates the present—and to liberate energies from this very destruction. But if this is the case, Fuentes reflects rather than subverts what is taking place in corporate society—namely, the release of people from the determinations of their past in order to organize desires and energies more effectively around consumption. It is significant that in all of Fuentes's later novels—*A Change of Skin, Terra Nostra*, and *The Hydra Head*—there is an author/narrator who is mad, marginalized, or transformed. In *The Hydra Head*, the manipulated protagonist becomes Diego Velázquez and he, in turn, has been "authored" by Timon of Athens. It would thus seem that Fuentes can conceive of the author in modern society only by identifying him with an anachronistic figure or by making him a manipulator.

Apart from the mandarin response—the attempt to abstract the novel from the world altogether in a reaction similar to that of the "pure poetry" movement of an earlier generation—the age of mass culture invites a hybrid amalgam of earlier forms of narration, such as oral histories and biographies or parody. Yet it is also worth mentioning briefly the possibilities offered by two other writers—Cortázar and Manuel Puig—who attempt to aestheticize the commodity.

I shall confine my remarks on Cortázar, for the sake of brevity, to a few points. First, I refer to his attempt in the key novella, *El Perseguidor* [The Pursuer], to transfer creativity from the narrator to the performer. Jazz performance, we should note in passing, becomes one of the key terms for conveying the utopian unification of what has always been separated in bourgeois culture — spectator and performer, reader and author, oppressed and rulers. In addition, for Cortázar, ready-made objects and mass culture can themselves always be rearranged so that they lose their character as commodities. With Cortázar's politicization in the sixties, this sphere of creative activity includes not only art but also politics. Yet despite this politicization of the aesthetic of the avant-garde, particularly in *Libro de Manuel* [A Manual for Manuel] the significance of Cortázar's confrontation with mass culture is that he chooses only superceded forms. That is why he picks Fantomas, a hero already consecrated by the surrealists to combat the "vampiros multinacionales" [multinational vampires] rather than some more contemporary figure like James Bond. *Fantomas* is subtitled *Una Utopía realizable* [A Realistic Utopia]. In this comic-strip tale of a plot by the CIA to destroy the world's libraries, the authors are far from dead. They are alive and named Octavio Paz, Alberto Moravia, Susan Sontag, and so on. But as a hero of the age of individualism, Fantomas can no longer be useful in the fight against corporations, and hence must rely not only on the support of writers but also ultimately on the masses whose myriad voices communicate their adhesion to the human cause. The utopian thus consists of this ideal communication between Fantomas, the anonymous masses, and the writers, yet, significantly, whereas the latter are *named*, the masses are only represented as accents "una voz argentina" [an Argentine voice], and the hierarchy of elite, mass, and mass culture is perpetuated.

All the writers I have mentioned retain an allegorical dimension either by duplicating "authorship" through characters or, as in the case of Fuentes and Cortázar, by setting the "narrator" off against the star. The originality of Manuel Puig in *La traición de Rita Hayworth* [Betrayed by Rita Hayworth], is that he dispenses with allegory and captures the seriality of mass culture, which speaks to people in isolation and not as groups. Puig achieves this effect by compiling the novel out of fragments of spoken and inscribed discourses — interior monologue, letters, diaries, commonplace books, conversations, and school essays. Film (like religion) not only provides ideas of good and bad, beautiful and ugly, and right and wrong to many of the people in the novel but also provides a common reference point—for instance, for Toto and his father or Toto and his mother. Film thus begins to edge out religion. The film star provides an ideal type from whom Toto derives his ideas of mortality and immortality, and from whom women derive their ideas of desirable males and men their idea of desirable females. Thus a whole lore is created which affects language, modes of behavior, and belief. All this is set in a provincial town and at a specific historical period—from 1933 to the early years of the Perón period, when Eva Perón's glamour became a form of political control. She became the ideal not only because she possessed what others desired but also because she was the source of largesse. In the novel Peronism is incidental rather than central. The historical moment of the novel is, however, of some importance because it was also a crucial moment in the history of the cinema, the moment when Rockefeller effectively sabotaged the national industry by starving it of celluloid. It is the Hollywood cinema which fulfills the needs of Toto and his mother, a cinema in which spectacle predominates. Racism, snobbery, bullying, and the machismo of daily life mark the miserable inadequacy that the cinema obliterates, not by action but by encouraging narcissistic contemplation.

Unlike avant-garde texts which try to salvage language and forms from the automatic reactions encouraged by mass culture, *Betrayed by Rita Hayworth* encourages contemplation by aestheticizing the banal, by endowing it with a certain nostalgia. In a sense the novel remains within the limitations of the class it describes, the petty bourgeoisie who are the most serialized and whose expectations are limited to individual upward mobility and integration.

What I have tried to show in this essay is not a progression or development but a moment of change. Before the fifties, it was common for novels to portray an intellectual hero who embodied the ideal in the attempt to dominate brute reality. In the novels I have mentioned, however, the novelist and the implied narrator separate themselves from the represented social enterprise whose frustration and failure is in direct contrast to the novelist's own achievement as author of an original text, as creator of "another reality." The narrator's abandonment of the attempt to rediscover the jungle colony at the end of Carpentier's *The Lost Steps* clearly allegorizes the separation that allows the artist to step out of the anachronism to which his country had been condemned. For reasons which are extremely complex and relate to the destruction of certain relatively stable novelistic devices such as character and the increasing focus on the free creativity of the reader, as well as the breakdown of certain hitherto durable social formations in Latin America itself, the totalizing project by which the novelist constructed the "alternative reality" seems to have become impossible in the late sixties. Novelists not only faced the era of mass culture which destroyed any notion of an original national culture but also were sometimes themselves converted into stars. The effect of the spread of mass culture in Latin America was thus not only the attempt by the more entrenched avant-garde writers to produce the unconsumable text but also the confrontation of authors of the boom with the irresistible glamour of the superstar and the predominance of the image. What happens to the novel in the period when the image has increasingly become the bearer of ideology and meaning is, however, still not clear.

NOTES

1 For the link between narrative technologies and social formation, see Jean Franco, "La literatura, la crítica literaria y la teoría de la dependencia," *Siempre* 720 (November 1975).

2 For a discussion of memory in oral/aural culture see Walter Ong, *The Presence of the Word* (New Haven: Yale University Press, 1967).

3 Walter Benjamin, "The Storyteller," in *Illuminations* (London: Jonathan Cape, 1970), 83–109.

4 Carlos Fuentes, *La nueva novela hispanoamericana* (Mexico: Joaquín Mortiz, 1969), 23.

5 Included in *Material de sueños* (Mexico: Era, 1974).

6 Daniel Bouchard, ed., *Language, Counter-Memory, Practice: Selected Essays and Interviews* (Ithaca: Cornell University Press, 1977).

7 Daniel J. Boorstin, *The Image: A Guide to Pseudo-Events in America* (New York: Atheneum, 1973), 168.

8 Guy Debord, *Society of the Spectacle* (Detroit: Black and Red, 1970), 61.

9 This essay is part of a longer study, part of which has been published as separate articles, e.g., "Ideología dominante y literatura: el caso de Mexico posrevolucionario," in Carlos Blanco et. al., eds., *Cultura y dependencia* (Guadalajara: Bellas Artes, 1976); "The Limits of the Liberal Imagination," *Punto de contacto* I, dic. 1975; "Conversations and Confessions. Self and Character in *The Fall* and *Conversation in The Cathedral*," *Texas Studies in Literature and Language* vol. 19, no. 4 (winter 1977); "The Crisis of the Liberal Imagination and the Utopia of Writing," *Ideologies and Literature* 1 (Dec. 1976–Jan. 1977).

10 Translation from *No One Writes to the Colonel and Other Stories*, trans. J. S. Bernstein (New York: Harper and Row, 1962), 168.

11 Josefina Ludmer, *Cien años de soledad: una interpretación* (Buenos Aires: Editorial Tiempo Contemporáneo, 1972).

12   Original Spanish from Mario Vargas Llosa, *La casa verde* (Barcelona: Editorial Seix Barral, S.A., 1968). English translations are from Mario Vargas Llosa, *The Green House*, trans. Gregory Rabassa (New York: Harper and Row, 1968).

13   Fredric Jameson, "Reification and Utopia in Mass Culture," *Social Text* (Winter 1979): 130–48.

14   For some reflections on *personaje* see Noe Jitrik, "Jugar su papel dentro del sistema," *Hispamérica* 1, no. 1 (July 1972): 17–29.

15   Carlos Fuentes, "Radiografía de una década: 1953–63," in *Tiempo Mexicano* (Mexico: Joaquín Mortiz, 1971), 78–79.

16   Jameson, "Reification and Utopia in Mass Culture."

17   Mario Vargas Llosa, *La orgía perpetua: Flaubert y "Madame Bovary"* [The Perpetual Orgy: Flaubert and Madame Bovary] (Barcelona: Barral, 1975), 272–73.

18   Interview with Alberto Díaz Lastra, "La cultura en Mexico," *Siempre* 718 (29 March 1967).

19   Ibid.

20   Interview with Emir Rodríguez Monegal, included in Helmy F. Giacoman, ed., *Homenaje a Carlos Fuentes* (New York: Las Americas, 1971), 47–48.

21   This is carried to the extreme in an interview with James R. Fortson, in *Perspectivas mexicanas desde París* (Mexico City: Corporación Editorial, 1973), first published in the Mexican playbody *El*, for this converts Mario Vargas Llosa into a male pin-up and has a section headed "Kant y los detergentes."

WHAT'S IN A NAME?

Popular Culture Theories and Their Limitations

*O*ne of the risks that any scholar faces when writing on or teaching popular culture in the United States is that the field is regarded as an amorphous, ill-defined, and even dubious area by the academic establishment. Women's studies, black and Chicano studies have, for years, confronted their marginalization either by becoming defiantly "other" or by adopting the protective covering of rigor, discipline, and science. The burden of proof of respectability is upon the newcomer. At the same time, academic respectability may be hard to attain when, as Pierre Bourdieu has shown, the cultural hierarchies set up by academe are closely related to class stratifications and differentiations.[1] To engage in a study of popular culture, however modestly, is an act of defiance against the hierarchization of cultural values and the subordination of the popular.

A further risk is involved in inaugurating the study of Latin American popular culture in the United States where the overwhelming tendency to pursue empirical research has isolated scholars from theoretical debates on this subject in both Europe and Latin America. U.S. academics may, in fact, be surprised to learn that the term *popular culture* is not accepted uncritically and that, indeed, the broader category of "everyday life" is increasingly the focus of investigation.

In discussing popular culture theory, therefore, there can be no better place to begin than with the multitude of terms used to categorize the uncanonized and signifying practices which lie outside the control of institutions such as schools and universities. In fact the area in which we are interested covers all that is not institutionalized as "high culture" and includes that which has been variously described as "mass culture," "popular culture," "folk culture," "entertainment," "media," "communications," or "culture industry." These terms, which are seldom clearly defined and which describe overlapping phenomena, frame the field of study in a cer-

Originally published in *Studies in Latin American Popular Culture* 1 (1982): 5–14.

tain way and imply a certain program. For instance, the term *folklore* has
its origins in German Romanticism, in Herder's notion that the true spirit
of the race or nationality resides in the people (the folk) of rural areas as
yet unaffected by modernization. The term *lore* introduces a distinction
between the elaborated knowledge which society has institutionalized (as
literature, history, religion, medicine, and law) and the unwritten practices of "ingenuous" peoples. At the other end of the scale, *mass culture,
culture industry,* and *consumer culture* designate the mass-produced culture
of industrial society. Unlike *folk culture, mass culture* generally implies distaste on the part of the user for the product, yet both terms imply a similar
attitude toward industrial society.[2] The term *mass* came into use about the
time of the French Revolution as a term of contempt.[3] Twentieth-century
thinkers such as Ortega y Gasset, F. R. Leavis in England, Dwight McDonald in the United States, Adorno and Horkheimer in Germany inherited
this dismissive use of the term *mass* and began to define mass culture
against an implicit model of individualized, original, structurally complex
high culture. According to these thinkers, high culture alone is capable of
moving people, developing their critical consciousness, and providing rich
aesthetic experience. Mass culture, on the other hand, preconditions the
responses of its audience and educates them as consumers rather than as
active participants.[4]

The term *popular culture* at first sight seems less restricted and yet upon
inspection, it proves to be equally programmatic. *Popular* is, to begin with,
ambiguous, referring both to what belongs to and what comes from the
people. It also refers to inferior kinds of practices as in "popular press" and
"popular taste." Nowadays *popular culture* is used in contradictory ways.
On the one hand, the *Journal of Popular Culture* tends to adopt the criterion
of popularity as defined by the market—a simplistic approach which hin-
ders any theoretical enquiry—and on the other hand, European and Latin
American critics have tended to define popular culture as emancipatory
and revolutionary in contrast to oppressive mass culture. Michèle Mattelart, for instance, describes popular culture as a "qualitatively different
practice, the end of pre-history, as Marx would say, carried out by other
social actors. Between mass culture and popular culture is the distance that
separates the system whose legitimacy is founded upon the subjugation
of conscience and a system in which the 'masses' cease to be the submis-
sive spectators of a representation contrary to their interests and become
the active subject of cultural experience linked to their own project of liberation."[5] This definition is perhaps too utopian to be serviceable at the

present time. It factors out of popular culture the richly problematic area which the dominant culture attempts but cannot completely control. This approach tends to oversimplify mass culture as the expression of a dominant ideology.

Finally even apparently neutral terms such as *media* and *communication* are not without problems. Scholars who use these terms tend to elide culture and information. Umberto Eco, for instance, claims that when there exist three conditions—namely, a homogenous industrial society, channels of communication directing messages to an indeterminate mass audience, and productive groups who work out and send messages by industrial means—"the difference in nature and effect between the various means of communication (movies, television or comic strips) fade into the background compared with the emergence of common structures and effects."[6] This is not to say that critics such as Eco have not contributed to theory but rather that the term *communications* bestows a spurious air of unity on a very diverse field. Its apparent neutrality, on the other hand, does not prevent Eco from making the same assumptions about the difference between high and popular culture (now transposed into the difference between open and closed texts) as more traditional critics.[7]

Not only have these taxonomies found their way into Latin American criticism but they have also been supplemented by many other categories. It is interesting to observe, in this respect, that just as *mass* and *folk* imply attitudes to industrial society, so the categories formulated in Latin America imply responses to modernization or, in plainer terms, to the implementation of capitalism. Thus the study of popular culture became integrated into the conflict between civilization and barbarism, between cosmopolitanism and cultural nationalism, or was part of the program of movements such as *costumbrismo, indigenismo,* or of resistance to cultural imperialism. These programmatic terms make it clear that popular culture has usually been regarded either as a phenomenon to be recorded before its inevitable disappearance or as a force of resistance to capitalist modernization. Nineteenth-century *costumbristas,* for instance, who were responsible for the collection and preservation of much material, were activated by this sense of imminent loss even when they also resigned themselves to its inevitability. The Mexican geographer García Cubas thus felt compelled to describe Mexican customs in order to provide a balance sheet and make "la justa comparación con lo que al presente se desarrolla, lo que la sociedad ha perdido y lo que ha ganado. Ha perdido casi en su totalidad, su genuina y nacional fisonomía—trocada por la de caracteres extraños de servil imitación" [The exact comparison with what is currently being developed, with what society has gained and lost. It has almost totally lost its authentic national character—bartered away in exchange for the strange characters of servile imitation].[8] The attitude of the *costumbrista* was therefore that of a passive spectator of an inevitable process in which what had seemed most typical and original in national culture was doomed to destruction. In contrast, the cultural nationalists deployed elements of popular culture not as resistance to capitalism but rather as myths of social cohesion to shore up the potentially disintegrating effects of modernization. As Carlos Monsiváis put it, speaking of Mexico: "As regional and local ties disintegrated, urban popular culture became the cohesive elements of the recently constituted national society."[9] Cultural nationalism usually relied on a stereotyped and static view of popular culture and thus masked the process of transformation which was eliminating the very basis of this culture in rural communities. It was in this context that a new and militant brand of folklore studies emerged, promoted by a group of intellectuals whose stake was in the establishment of a counterhegemony in opposition to capitalism. José María Arguedas in Peru,[10] Roa Bastos in Paraguay,[11] Zapata Olivella in Colombia,[12] Miguel Barnet in Cuba,[13] and Américo Paredes in the United States.[14] All went beyond the simple collection and preservation of folklore to document cultures of resistance.

In the fifties, the massive migration of rural people into the cities and a further stage of industrialization brought a new element into the picture. Up to this point, the manner in which Latin America had been articulated into the world economy had allowed many rural communities to retain traditional customs and views of the world. When the community on which it is based remains intact, orally transmitted culture is highly resistant to capitalism and highly creative in its response to new pressures. Latin America offers some impressive examples of the tenacity and cohesion of traditional communities such as those of the *sierra* Indians and of the black communities of the Caribbean. The preservation of *yoruba* and African religions in Cuba and Brazil, and the tenacity of traditional ballad themes are but a few examples of this vital aspect of Latin American culture. One feature of this orally transmitted culture, however, deserves emphasis—that is, the vital link that it constituted with the past and which could always be reactivated through ritual and performance. In traditional communities, participants thus have access to the past and to the totality of experience in a way that is impossible once the community loses its cohesion and its members are dispersed. Further, the introduction of script and print culture also alters people's relations with the past since the knowledge repertoire of any individual is greatly increased once knowledge can be stored. However, this very increase of information means that no individual can have access to the whole of his or her community's experience as is possible in traditional communities. Further, the accumulation of "cultural capital" becomes possible with the introduction of print and this sharply differentiates those who have a broad repertoire from those whose repertoire is restricted.[15] Even though in Latin America, print culture never attained the complete dominance that it acquired in Europe and the United States, it nevertheless widened the gulf between urban and rural cultures, between the "culturally competent" according to metropolitan standards and the "uneducated." At the same time, the very conservatism of rural communities which made them living links with the past also meant that they became an important source for high culture in its search for the expression of Latin American originality. It was this configuration of the cultural field that industrialization in the fifties and sixties (import substitution and agrobusiness) broke down. As communities were affected by massive migration to the cities, the old forms of orally transmitted culture were lost. Traditional storytellers, singers and musicians, weavers, and painters began to disappear or found themselves integrated into the commercial circuit. There were radical changes in artisan products which began to be made for the tourist trade and airport display.[16] Folk music was incorporated into commercial forms as well as into the "nueva canción" [new song]; oral narrative became market literature or was replaced by the soap opera and the photonovel. The transformation has been all the more far-reaching because of the instrumental use of the new media in the process of "modernization" for which cinema provided an early model. Cinema introduced a new and powerful realism which no longer depended on the word and it also implied an enormous technical distance between the individual receiver and the technically qualified production team. Radio and television provided yet more powerful forms of mobilization and control. To begin with, as Raymond Williams has shown, by being introduced into the home, they both contributed to the privatization of life under capitalism and affected the family itself.[17] Television, in particular, also involves a different structuring of time as an uninterrupted flow and a perpetual anticipation. Whereas orally transmitted culture is often engaged in the reactivation of the past, the electronic media constantly appeal to the future, while at the same time emphasizing the sense of the actual, of people speaking in the present.

What has been so distinctive about the introduction of the electronic media in Latin America is that they were widely regarded, particularly by proponents of modernization, as instruments of change. Indeed, as Armand Mattelart has shown, the study of the new media in Latin America was initiated as part of the drive for "modernization" and thus focused on satellite education, transmission of birth control, and agricultural information.[18] At the same time, early studies of urban popular culture of the *barriadas* [lower-class neighborhoods] were motivated by the apparent problem of why poor people did not move up the social ladder. Oscar Lewis's "culture of poverty" studies, for instance, focused on urban popular culture only insofar as it explained the transmission from generation to generation of fatalistic and feckless attitudes.[19] The optimistic view of the media as the instruments of modernization was not widely shared in Latin America where U.S. domination of media technology became known as "cultural imperialism." Not surprisingly the first studies of cultural imperialism came from Venezuela, which was heavily saturated with American radio and television programs and commercials.[20] At this stage of the investigation, critics tended to focus on the penetration of the multinational corporations into Latin America and their integration of new sectors of the population into the consumer culture through advertising and the media.[21] Following on the studies of Herbert Schiller in the United States,[22] much criticism of cultural imperialism concentrated on corporate control of the media and the ramifications of the corporate structures,[23] but the problem quickly acquired a new dimension when the "war of the media" in Allende's Chile revealed their potentiality as a hidden weapon of destabilization. The Belgian sociologist Armand Mattelart identified the role of the media in new forms of right-wing mobilization and showed how, at the same time, they broke down older forms of solidarity. With Ariel Dorfman, he undertook "readings" of television programs and comic books (Donald Duck, Superman, Sesame Street) to uncover their ideological message and, at the same time, he attempted to devise counterstrategies. Mattelart argued that the media not only attempted to manipulate and influence the viewer or observer and induce him or her to support and reproduce individualism and competitiveness, but that they actively destroyed other forms of culture and even history itself. "Media attempts to deprive people of their memory. While giving the illusion of relying upon and assuming a patrimony of myths, this culture actually standardizes, serializes and appropriates history which it mutilates and reduces to a series of miscellaneous news items."[24] While certainly responsive to the gravity of the situation, however, Mattelart's theory, like all theories of cultural imperialism, introduces new problems by considering the media as uncontradictory expressions of the dominant ideology. This tendency is evident in an even more exaggerated form in the writing of Antonio Pasquali, who argued that the very fact that television relied upon the image rather than on the word produced a passive audience:

> Creemos firmemente que la intencionalidad de nuestra conciencia ante el signo verbal y visual no es estructuralmente la misma . . . la información de tipo audiovisual es, en propiedad, la más irracional e irracionalizadora de cuantas producen una masificación del contexto social en que actúan, que es tanto como decir, el medio masificador más operante de todo, ya que no se dirige al receptor come ente racional y por eso diversificado sino al receptor masa y a sus aglutinantes: lo instintivo, lo irracional, lo inconsciente colectivo.

> [We firmly believe that the intentionality of our conscience facing the verbal and visual sign is not structurally the same . . . audiovisual information is, properly speaking, the most irrational and irrationalizing of the many (kinds of information) that produce a massification of their social context. This is equivalent to saying that it is the most massifying medium of all since it is not directed to a rational and thus diversified audience but to a mass audience and that which binds it: instinct, irrationality, and the collective unconsciousness.] [25]

In media criticism, we have to guard against this natural bias of the intellectual in favor of print culture. By attributing rationality exclusively to the verbal sign, Pasquali excludes the mass of the people from the rational. He thus fails to take into account contemporary evidence on the logics of nonliterate cultures which do not necessarily depend on the verbal sign and yet display their own kind of rationality. In addition, he ignores the potentiality and complexity of the image. In other analyses of this period, a blatant class distinction was sometimes drawn between the culturally competent who were, supposedly, able to exercise judgment and the naive viewer. What is perhaps most surprising is that these culture critics tend to speak of the transformations brought about by television as if it were something happening to other people when in fact the new media has affected all forms of culture.

Thus far, I have tried to show that traditional and new forms of popular culture have been organized under a series of programmatic rubrics and that the newest media, especially television, are almost universally regarded as mere instruments of manipulation. This, in turn, has given rise to a whole series of assumptions which, to my mind, need revising:

1. The assumption that contemporary mass culture is the contradictory and direct expression of the ideology of the dominant class. Thus the only resistance to this dominant ideology has to be found in an uncontaminated "authentic" popular culture.
2. The assumption (made by many high culture critics) that the only true culture is that which involves the intense focusing of attention and that "distracted" viewing is invalid.
3. The assumption that the effect of mass culture on the public is that which is intended by the emitter of the message.
4. The assumption that mass culture is identifiable through its "products" or "artifacts."

In order to counter these assumptions, it will be necessary to reject the reified dichotomy between popular and mass culture and to consider the whole spectrum of Latin American culture from the lore and legends of the backlands, the graffiti on city walls, television soap operas, photo-novels, *salsa*, and hundreds of other manifestations, not as artifacts with fixed values but rather as a manifold of changing signifying practices. The only problem with considering mass culture in this way is that the terms then seem to dissolve into a myriad of practices out of which it is difficult to fashion a theory. The trick is to move from a static to a dynamic perspective, to place these signifying practices within a historical process, which, in the last decades, has involved the violent incorporation of Latin America into a new stage of capitalism and which has therefore led to a series of cultural breaks and discontinuities. One of the most important of these has been the transition from traditional rural economies to wage labor and from communally based cultural practices to privatized forms of culture. It is a process which can be observed in many different stages. Thus Michael Taussig in *The Devil and Commodity Fetishism* has documented one particular moment of transition—the proletarianization of the peasants of the Cauca valley.[27] Instead of taking the static view of the folklorist, he urges us to regard devil beliefs as "collective representations of a way of life losing its life" and to view them instead "as intrinsic manifestations that are permeated with historical meaning that register in the symbols of that history, what it means to lose control over the means of production and to be controlled by them." But in considering this response of popular culture to these transitions, it is also important to take into account the particular technology of knowledge (oral transmission, script, electronic media) which dominates in a given society and how this helps to structure reality. In the case of the devil beliefs, it is not simply that the peasants see reality in a certain way but that their worldview is limited and yet given its peculiar potentiality by the fact that their culture is an oral culture. As I have indicated, these technologies are not the sole determinants of culture but they do affect it in important ways; for instance in their very different structuring of time which, in turn, affects the way people relate to the past. Moreover, these technologies acquire different significance in particular social formations. Print was the dominant form of ideological control during the nineteenth century, though its place has now been taken by the electronic media. The dominant technology tends to be the most closely controlled which is the reason why, at the present time, the strict censorship by authoritarian regimes of print and television leaves a space for resistance filled by the spoken word in the form of rumor, jokes, clandestine readings, and dramatic representations.

This brings us to another crucial distinction—that between authoritarian societies and those in which hegemony is exercised within civil society. In the former, the public space for cultural creativity has all but disappeared.[27] Outside the area of propaganda, there is mass culture. It is this reduction of public space which is intended to prevent the development of any counterhegemony and to control and strictly limit signifying practices.[28] Thus it is not possible to consider the photonovel or the soap opera (for example) as being identical phenomena in an authoritarian society and in countries such as Venezuela and Mexico in which there exists a civil society in all its complexity. In an authoritarian society such as Argentina, strict guidelines control radio and television. They are made to show respect for heroes and institutions, stress the importance of family ties, and exalt family transcendence as the basic tenet of Christian society.

In contrast, in societies such as Venezuela and Mexico, dominant groups establish hegemony through a variety of institutions and practices but this hegemony is never unopposed and does not have to be enforced by unadulterated propaganda. Rather, as Gramsci[29] has shown, hegemony is a constant process of transaction and struggle. Photonovels, comics, soap operas, popular fiction, cinema, dance, music festivals, fashions, and everyday life may represent attempts at control but they also have to meet the real desires and needs of people. Above all, they have to entertain. There are thus often contradictory thrusts within the texts themselves. To take one obvious example, a news program such as Zabludovsky's *24 horas* [24 Hours] often has cameramen who film a different story from the one being related by the voiceover. A recent segment on El Salvador, for instance, showed a woman scavenging in trash cans for food while the voiceover related the official view of the junta reform program. This dislocation between text and image opens up a critical space.

This brings us to the question of reception which is now increasingly engaging the attention of Latin American critics. Michèle Mattelart and Mabel Piccini at the time of the Allende regime in Chile had already attempted to document audience reaction to television by conducting a study of a *campamento* [shanty town] audience.[30] More recent studies have tended to shift from surveys of audiences to investigating the manner in which texts align their readers so that texts can be decoded.[31] Eco shows how the "common frames" (our prior knowledge and inferences about the world) and "intertextual frames" (our prior knowledge and inferences about conventions and genres) interfere with the uncontradictory reception of the text. Ideological biases of readers also account for the fact that texts are read in ways in which the author never intended. Stuart Hall makes distinctions between dominant decodings from the hegemonic viewpoint (which "carries with it the stamp of legitimacy and defines within its terms the mental horizon, the universe of possible meanings of a whole sector of relations in a society or culture") and the negotiated reading. The latter "contains a mixture of adaptive and oppositional elements; it acknowledges the legitimacy of the hegemonic definitions to make the grand significations . . . while, at a more restricted situational (situated) level, it makes its own ground rules—it operates with exceptions to the rule. It accords the privileged position to the dominant definition of events while reserving the right to make a more negotiated application to 'local conditions,' to its own more *corporate* positions." One example given by Hall is that of a decision to strike made by workers who apparently accept government arguments about wage restraint in the national interest. In addition, Hall argues that where readers have an alternative frame of reference to the hegemonic frame, they may read or view according to an oppositional decoding.[32]

Reception theory is one way of avoiding the notion of the mass culture text as merely manipulative. Semiotic studies, on the other hand, have mostly remained within the limited framework of demonstrating the ideological positioning of the reader or viewer. Recent Freudian readings similarly tend to reintroduce manipulation as "strategies of containment."[33]

Clearly, as David Morley has shown, studies of how readers are aligned or "interpellated" now need to be complemented not only by studies of possible aberrant decodings but also by the limits of the discursive space itself, "which in turn has a determinate effect on the practice of readings at the level of particular text-reader encounters."[34]

To summarize, *popular culture* is at best an ambiguous term. My own preferred definition would be the broadest possible and would include a spectrum of signifying practices and pleasurable activities most of which fall outside the controlling discipline of official schooling. It is the area described by Bourdieu[35] which is traversed by class stratifications and subtle subcultural distinctions acquired largely in a noninstitutional setting. Popular culture would thus encompass an area of increasing interest to Latin American scholars, the area of "everyday life" in which new policies of control and discipline have been exercised[36] and which has now become crucial as an arena of struggle and resistance.

NOTES

1 Pierre Bourdieu, *La distinction* (Paris: Les Editions de Minuit, 1979).

2 Jean Franco and Julianne Burton, introduction to special issue on "Culture and Imperialism," *Latin American Perspectives* 5 (winter 1978): 2–12.

3 Raymond Williams, *Keywords: A Vocabulary of Culture and Society* (New York: Fontana, 1976).

4 Franco and Burton, "Introduction," 1978.

5 Armand Mattelart and Seth Siegelaub, *Communication and Class Struggle I* (New York: International General, 1979).

6 Umberto Eco, *A Theory of Semiotics* (Bloomington: Indiana University Press, 1979), 13.

7 Umberto Eco, *The Role of the Reader: Exploration in the Semiotics of Texts* (Bloomington: Indiana University Press, 1979).

8 Antonio García Cubas, *El libro de mis recuerdos* (Mexico: n.p., 1904), 144.

9 Carlos Monsiváis, "Las etapas históricas," *Textos* 9–10 (1975).

10 José María Arguedas, *Formación de una cultura nacional indoamericana* (Mexico: Siglo XXI, 1975).

11 Augusto Roa Bastos, *Las culturas condenadas* (Mexico: Siglo XXI, 1978).

12 Manuel Zapata Olivella, *Cuentos de muerte y libertad* (Bogotá: Narradores Colombianos de Hoy, 1961).

13 Miguel Barnet, *Cimarrón* (La Habana: Gente Nueva, 1967).

14 Américo Paredes, "El folklore de los grupos de origen mexicano en Estados Unidos," *Folklore Americano* (1964): 146–63.

15 Bourdieu, *La distinction*.

16 Nestor García Canclini, *Arte popular y sociedad en América Latina* (Mexico: Grijalbo, 1977).

17 Raymond Williams, *Television* (New York: Schoeken Books, 1975).

18 Mattelart and Siegelaub, *Communication and Class Struggle*, 9.

19 Oscar Lewis, "The Culture of Poverty," in *Anthropological Essays* (New York: Random House, 1970).

20 Antonio Pasquali, *Comunicación y cultura de masas* (Caracas: Ediciones de la Universidad, 1964); Ludovico Silva, *La plusvalía ideológica* (Mexico: Nuestro Tiempo, 1971).

21 Evelina Dagnino, "Cultural and Ideological Dependence: Building a Theoretical Framework," in *Structures and Dependency*, ed. Frank Bonilla and Robert Girling (Stanford, Calif.: Stanford University Press, 1973), 127–48.

22 Herbert Schiller, *Mass Communication and the American Empire* (Boston: Beacon Press, 1971).

23 Armand Mattelart, *La cultura como empresa multinacional* (Mexico: Era, 1976).

24 Mattelart and Siegelaub, *Communication and Class Struggle*, 45.

25 Pasquali, *Comunicación y cultura de masas*, 54.

26 Michael Taussig, *The Devil and the Commodity Fetishism* (Chapel Hill: University of North Carolina Press, 1980).

27 José Joaquín Brunner, *La estructuración autoritaria del espacio creativo* (Santiago: FLASCO, 1979).

28 José Joaquín Brunner, *Ideología, legitimación y disciplinamiento en la sociedad autoritaria* (Santiago: FLASCO, 1980).

29 Antonio Gramsci, "The Modern Prince," in *Selections from the Prison Notebooks*, ed. and trans. Quintin Noare and Geoffrey Nowell Smith (London: Lawrence and Wishart, 1971), 125–205.

30 Michèle Mattelart and Mabel Piccini, "La televisión y los sectores populares," *Comunicación y cultura* 2 (1974): 3–75.

31 Eco, *The Role of the Reader*; Stuart Hall, "Encoding/Decoding," *Culture, Media, Language* (London: Hutchinson, 1980), 128–38.

32 Hall, "Encoding/Decoding," 134.

33 Fredric Jameson, "Reification and Utopia," *Social Text* (1979).

34 David Morley, "Texts, Readers, Subjects," *Culture, Media, Language* (London: Hutchinson, 1980), 178.

35 Bourdieu, *La distinction.*

36 Brunner, *Ideología, legitimación y disciplinamiento.*

HIGH-TECH PRIMITIVISM

The Representation of Tribal Societies in Feature Films

Maybe man will kill the beast and look into the eyes of the other as his equal.

—MILTON NASCIMENTO, *Yahuarete* [1]

*D*uring the five hundred years since the conquest of America, the representation of the indigenous has been essential both to the imperial venture and to the formation of the new Latin American nations. The cannibal and the noble savage stood on the other side of the boundary that defined civilization, signifying both "otherness" and origins.[2] At the present time, as tribal societies turn into "endangered species," as interminable hours of television documentary inform us that we are watching the last remnants of tribal culture, a marked change can be detected which transforms the indigenous from being "others" and converts them into multicolored strands in a pluralistic weave. The 1984 MOMA exhibition, " 'Primitivism' in Twentieth-century Art: Affinity of the Tribal and the Modern," can serve as one "benevolent" example of this *neo-indigenismo*; it juxtaposed "anonymously" created *artifacts* of non-Western culture with some of the most famous paintings of Picasso, Braque, and Matisse.[3] By arranging its exhibits under innocuous headings such as "affinities" and "concepts" the exhibit managed to ignore the wars and the colonization which brought the African mask into the orbit of the "collectible."[4]

A similar innocence marked the exhibit of South American cultures in New York's Natural History Museum, where a diorama of painted warriors has the caption, "There is no such thing as art for art's sake among the Amazonian Indians"—thus suggesting that "difference" is largely a matter of aesthetics.

Originally published in *Mediating Two Worlds: Cinematic Encounters in the Americas*, ed. John King, Ana López, and Manuel Alvarado (London: BFI Publishing, 1993), 81-94.

Neo-indigenismo has, however, acquired another facet because of the global angst over the environment and the destruction of the rain forests. All of a sudden, the tribal "other" has become a model of survival, a natural ecologist. The worldwide attention given to the murder of Chico Mendes (the rubber-tapper whose union had formed alliances with the forest tribes) and the struggle among film companies in Hollywood for movie rights over the Chico Mendes story, and the 1989 space voyage of the Discovery, part of whose mission was to study the erosion of the rain forest, are symptomatic of a shift which has made hitherto remote struggles over land rights in Amazonia central to planetary survival.[5] The difficulty here is that "ecology" all too often conceals a complexity of political and economic factors, not the least important of which is capitalist development. Nothing illustrates better the difficulty of separating the mode of production from the ethnical intent than a series of feature films, all of which in one way or another depict critically the Western conquest of untamed nature and tribal societies, yet end up by reproducing oppressive acculturation.

NEO-INDIGENISMO WITH AN ALL-STAR CAST

Films such as *The Mission, Fitzcarraldo,* and *The Emerald Forest* were intended to be something more than entertainment; they were made by directors with reputations for making "serious" films and they are explicit in their critique of Western ideas of progress. Roland Joffe (*The Mission*) had directed *The Killing Fields,* Werner Herzog (*Fitzcarraldo*) had already filmed the much acclaimed *Aguirre: The Wrath of God* in South America and would go on to shoot *Where the Green Ants Dream* in Australia, and John Boorman (*The Emerald Forest*), an expatriate Briton, had directed *Deliverance.*[6]

What is astonishing about these films is their ghostly recapitulation of the history of Amazonia itself; thus, even though *The Mission* takes place on the borders of modern Paraguay and Brazil far south of Amazonia, the material on which it draws reflects the history of the Catholic missions and their long march over the centuries into the remotest areas of the rain forest. *Fitzcarraldo* records the history of a later period, that of the rubber boom at the end of the nineteenth century; and *The Emerald Forest* brings us into the present and the construction of the Trans-Amazon highway and dams as part of contemporary Brazil's economic expansion. It is, however, this last stage of Amazonian expansion which is really at issue in the films even though they transpose their concerns into the past or into fantasy. It is important to bear in mind, however, that modern development in the Amazon dates from the military government that came into power in the sixties, although U.S. experts were advocating the exploitation of the rain forests long before.[7] The military's "national integration" policy promoted a "land frenzy" in an area where the frontier law of the survival of the strongest prevailed, and encouraged destruction and even genocide whose net result is now predicted by some to be global disaster. The "holocaust" of the Amazonian forest would in this case be an event that would rival "the massive extinctions of dinosaurs and other species in the Cretacious Period, which changed for ever the world and the path of evolution."[8]

There are obvious reasons why feature films which depend on capitalist modes of production should encounter difficulties in representing ecological concerns whose solution depends on global change. *The Mission* and *Fitzcarraldo* transpose the problem into the historical past, thus avoiding the complexity and messiness of contemporary struggles. Yet the appropriation of historical narrative undermines their objective, and serves to freeze real problems in an anachronistic mode. Furthermore, the demands of narrative structures that belong to the continuing saga of the white man's search for identity make it difficult for the films to avoid underpinning the already secure foundations of paternalism. The inevitable dislocation between stated intent and narrative logic is obvious in all three films, for each film begins or ends with extradiegetic explanatory captions whose connection to the narrative is tenuous. The caption is, in fact, a kind of tag that indicates the contemporary problem that the narrative evades.

Our knowledge of tribal societies in South America comes in the main from missionaries, explorers, and ethnographers. The Jesuit missionaries who (long before Rousseau) propagated the myth of the noble savage regarded America as a utopia, as a territory that had not yet felt the corrupting winds of Europe. Their mission was both to bring the indigenous into the harmonious choir of the Christian world and to preserve their innocence. In Jesuit mythology, music soars over differences of culture and brings about an almost magical understanding:

> The priests were unable to penetrate the forest on foot: there were too few of them and, in any case, the Indians persisted in fleeing in fear from the white man. But the Fathers noticed that when they sang melodies from their canoes, the Guaraní crept to the river banks and surreptitiously watched them pass.[9]

Chateaubriand retells this tale in his *Spirit of Christianity*, but it remains a potent myth down to the present. "Indians," according to one historian, "came into the settlements drawn by the magnificence of divine worship."[10] The myth, of course, represses mention of the many skirmishes that accompanied the founding of the missions or their political importance as frontier posts in as yet uncolonized areas.

The Mission draws heavily on this Jesuit mythology. Father Gabriel (Jeremy Irons) plays his recorder in an apparently empty forest out of which the Indians begin to emerge to listen to the music. This indigenous music is used to accompany "sublime" scenes of the rushing Iguaçú waterfalls. The choral singing of the *Ave Maria* and the *Agnus Dei* reinforce the Jesuit vision of a missionary utopia in which all voices sing in harmony. The utopian is also suggested by scenes of naked children playing in the river, shots of flourishing crops, and sweeping panoramas of unspoiled nature. The utopia is, however, threatened by *realpolitik*, for the film is set in 1750, seven years before the Jesuits were expelled from Latin America by the Spanish crown and at a moment when some of the mission territories were about to pass from Spanish to Portuguese control. The issue is whether the Jesuit fathers will allow the missions (and the Indians) to fall to the Portuguese. Two opposing strategies of resistance are represented in the clashing personalities of the aggressive, guilt-ridden Father Rodrigo (Robert de Niro) and the passive resister, Father Gabriel. Both oppose the reasons of state which ordain the transference of Indian territories to the slave-owning Portuguese; Father Rodrigo resorts to armed struggle to resist the closure and is killed; Father Gabriel is an advocate of passive resistance and is also killed. Thus neither armed resistance (read guerrilla warfare) nor passive resistance (read liberation theology) prevail against reasons of state. Joffe himself explicitly saw the film as reflecting a contemporary dilemma and likened the opposing tactics of the two Jesuits to modern discussions within the left.[11] The point is, however, that resistance fails and the Indians are either slaughtered or flee back into the jungle. At the end of the film, a naked girl comes into the ruins of the mission and picks up a broken violin from the water. Armed with this fragment of civilization, she gets into a canoe with a group of children and they paddle upriver, fleeing from the army and the slave-traders. The film is framed by a narrative voice, that of Father Luis Altamirano, a representative of the state, who was historically a major enemy of the missions. It is he who improbably voices a pious lament for the bloodshed just before the final caption, which reads:

The Indians of South America are still engaged in the struggle to define their land and culture. Many of the priests who, inspired by faith and love, continue to support the rights of the Indians for justice, do so with their lives. "The light shines in the darkness; the darkness has not overcome it." (from John 1:5)

The words sound particularly strange when they are put beside other kinds of calculation—for instance, the violent death of 100,000 Guatemalans, mostly Indians, in the past ten years. How many Indians does it take to make one Jesuit martyr? Is the Church the only force defending the Indians? By bringing the audience into the present, in the final caption, the film reveals only too clearly its own limitations, and especially the fact that the drama is played out not by the indigenous community but by different and conflicting branches of the imperial power. What history teaches, in the film, is the inevitable triumph of *realpolitik*. Resistance takes the form of martyrdom.

In its opening caption the film claims the authority of historical truth. This "truth," however, is from the first unable to stand up to the demands of dramatic narrative. For instance, one of the missions is headed by a Guaraní Indian (played by a Cambodian actor), although the indigenous were excluded from the Jesuit Order. The spectacular opening sequence in which a Jesuit martyr is tied to a cross and sent tumbling down the Iguaçú falls achieves its shock effect at the expense of historical accuracy. There is no record of any Jesuit being martyred in this particular way, but from a narrative point of view the scene serves to identify the Indians with those who crucified Christ and thus positions itself in the same relation to Indian culture as did the Church in the colonial period. In other words, the Indians are too childlike to understand the significance of what they are doing.

The Indians in the film were not Guaraní but Colombian Indians, brought in by air to Santa Marta and Cartagena, where most of *The Mission* was filmed. Does it matter? After all, *Lawrence of Arabia* was filmed in Spain. What makes *The Mission* different is its claim to be representing the truth of history, this is not to mention the paradox of uprooting tribes in order to make a film whose explicit message is ostensibly to show how Indians were enslaved and forced to abandon their tribal lands.

This contradiction clearly concerned Daniel Berrigan, the antiwar activist and Jesuit who was one of five Jesuits brought in as advisors and as actors for the film. In his published diary of the filming (see note 6), Berrigan is unable to reconcile his need to defend Jesuit heroism and his scepticism of the film industry. Shaken by his confrontation with a colossal dream machine which not only re-presents but *is* a mode of production whose embryonic forms were already embedded in colonial society, he unsuccessfully attempts to justify the transportation of "unspoiled" Onani Indians 350 miles by air to inhabit a film village by suggesting that the Indians have "chosen" to be in the film.

> In consenting to travel to Santa Marta, the Indians have landed in the world for the first time. A truly awesome thought. They have arrived in our world, which goes by the presumptive name of the real world. One can only glance at the radiant faces and breathe a prayer. God help them.
>
> They also entered the economy when they came here, perhaps that says it all, "real" and "world" and more. The arrangement is that the families will be paid two-thirds of the stipulated salary; the remaining third goes into a communal fund for education and medical needs (p. 64).

Again and again in his diary, Berrigan reveals himself to be conscious of being a participant in the colonization he condemns, of being a cog in a machine oiled by the same colonial fantasies (the civilizing mission) that had haunted the eighteenth-century Spaniards and Portuguese.

Yet Berrigan's diary is situated within the same labyrinth of mirrors as the film. Although he sees the irony of reproducing an eighteenth-century struggle in a zone of Colombia where army units in camouflage fatigues are engaged in counterinsurgency against guerrillas and where one of the stars in the film, De Niro, had to have armed guards to protect him from kidnappers, he also believes that in portraying the Jesuits the film will be able to capture "a spontaneous generation occurring in Western culture itself" (p. 34). But this is precisely the problem of a historical film which is too faithful to history, for it cannot represent what has gone unrepresented.

Fitzcarraldo is an even more thoroughgoing attempt to repeat history than *The Mission*. As Les Blank (whose documentary *Burden of Dreams* is a critical commentary on the filming of *Fitzcarraldo*) said, "It's damned weird to have people risking their lives to fulfill a mad Bavarian's impossible fantasies."

Those fantasies are, however, not just individual but collective, and have their origins in German Romanticism. The opening caption reads: "The Cuhuari Yaku, the jungle Indians, call this the land where God did not finish creation. Only after man has disappeared, they think, will he return to finish his work." This is Herzog's version of the myth of the return of the culture hero; but it also sounds like an echo of late Romanticism.[12]

Though nature is a necessary element of Herzog's particular version of the sublime [13] his outburst during the filming, recorded in Les Blank's film, seems to come right out of Hugo's *La Légende des Siècles:*

> I see fornication and asphyxiation and choking and fighting for survival growing and just rotting away . . . the trees are in misery, the birds are in misery. . . . They screech in pain. . . . It's an unfinished country. It's prehistorical. The only thing missing is the dinosaur. It's cursed . . . even the stars look like a mess.

Had he listened to the Machiguenga Indians he had brought into his camp he might have told another story.

The historical Fitzcarraldo was a rubber baron and Indian hunter who did in fact take a boat across the land between two Amazon tributaries— though he sensibly did so by breaking the boat into pieces before carrying it across land.[14] Herzog tried the same feat by using bulldozers and winching the entire boat over a forty-degree incline, a feat which put the lives of workers at risk. The Brazilian engineer withdrew from the project. The actor Klaus Kinski, who replaced Jason Robards after the latter contracted amoebic dysentery, risked drowning in the rapids. There was an air crash in which people died. The actors spent months trapped in the rain forest. Herzog in his interviews with Les Blank seems obsessed with the awesome logistics of his film, but just as *The Mission* created the illusion of the eighteenth-century real only to become trapped in colonialism, so Herzog is trapped in the glories and miseries of entrepreneurial capitalism of which the film is a product. Music, in this case the opera that Fitzcarraldo will bring to Iquitos, expresses the will to power in nondestructive form. The Jesuit myth of conquest through music is recycled once again when Fitzcarraldo puts a record of Caruso on the phonograph when his boat is stopped by warlike Jíbaros. The Jíbaro drums cease as Caruso's voice soars across the forest and the tribe is then peacefully recruited to execute Fitzcarraldo's mad dream—which they also sabotage by loosening the boat from its moorings in the belief that it must be sacrificed.

Les Blank's film and book *The Burden of Dreams* is far more of a deconstructive enterprise than Berrigan's diary partly because, unlike Berrigan, he is not a participant in the film project. However, he is not a detached observer, either. *Burden of Dreams* positions itself precisely as an ironic entrepreneurship which is linked to the destruction of the rain forest and the Amazon basin. What *Burden of Dreams* reveals is what it means to shoot a film about old-style capitalist enterprise in a zone that is on the verge of devastation because of that enterprise and where ecological issues are deeply implicated in local politics.

Blank's film shows the indigenous to be anything but silent actors in the process. For instance, Herzog had originally intended to make the film in Ecuador, apparently unaware of the tense politics of a border zone which was rapidly being colonized by new settlers, explored by oil interests, and overrun by the Ecuadorian and Peruvian armies. He originally contracted Aguaruna Indians as extras, but a newly formed Aguaruna Council objected to the filming. The Aguaruna Council, who knew quite well what the historical Fitzcarraldo had represented, believed that Herzog was intending to do a film on the exploitation of rubber workers at the turn of the century and they objected to this on the grounds that it did not represent indigenous culture in the present. In other words, they did not want to be represented either as victims or as living in some timeless world. They were conscious of belonging to a political movement and knew how to defend their right to control their own representation. In 1979, they surrounded Herzog's camp and the film crew were forced to flee downriver. Fourteen months later, Herzog had managed to recruit Indians, mostly from the Campa and Machiguenga tribes (traditionally enemies). The Indians had been promised land rights—though at the end of the film these had not been acquired. In any case, Herzog does not seem to have known that land rights in the Amazon are something of a myth unless they can be protected by force. In Les Blank's film, Herzog says he does not want the Indians to be contaminated with Western civilization and speaks of the tragedy of their disappearance—the loss of "cultures, languages and mythologies." Yet he makes a film which is an intervention in the process he deplores. As in *The Mission*, the director's understanding of historical truth stands in the way of any ironies—this is left to Les Blank's "extra-diegetic" material. In both films, the mode of production is a continuation of the colonization they purport to describe and there is no way, within the realist convention, that critical distance can be achieved.

John Boorman's *The Emerald Forest* is an attempt to escape these contradictions worthy of Eratostratus, the man who won fame by burning down the temple. Boorman is clearly conscious of the problems posed by a film such as *Fitzcarraldo* and even alludes to Herzog by including a fanatical Italian photographer in the film who is so intent on photographing "the Fierce People" that he does not realize that they are about to club him to death. Boorman uses nonindigenous actors and gives the tribes fictitious names—"the Fierce People," "the Invisible People," "the Bat People." Yet his attempt to represent tribal culture from an ecological perspective is, if anything, even more problematic than the other two films.

The Emerald Forest is, however, more like Crocodile Dundee than The Mission or Fitzcarraldo. It belongs to a class of films described by Meaghan Morris as "fables of survival in a global context."[15] It is the story of an American dam builder working in the Brazilian Amazon whose son, Tommy, is kidnapped by the Invisible People. After twelve years of searching the father finds him, but Tommy now remembers his civilized life only as a dream. A neighboring tribe, the Fierce People, have been armed by Brazilians who are recruiting Indian girls for a jungle brothel, one of the inmates being Tommy's young bride. Tommy enlists his father's technological knowledge (and gun) as an ally in their struggle against the Brazilians and the Fierce People, and the brothel is destroyed. Tommy's father now realizes that the dam he is building threatens the survival of his son's tribe. While Tommy uses shamanistic knowledge to produce a downpour, the father sabotages the dam, thus saving his son but presumably destroying his "self." The paradox of the film is that it tries to suggest the possibility of an ethic within capitalism by showing that we can learn ecology from the "good" primitive and halt the unbridled conquest of nature—but only if we are prepared to destroy the products of our own technology. This sounds bolder than it really is. To begin with, the film remains within a masculinist ideology of the oedipal narrative; secondly, the tribal peoples are simply a backcloth against which the father/son drama is played out. Thus The Emerald Forest can be read as the story of how capitalism (the father) can survive and save its own children. This is the significance of making a captive white boy its hero. What the white boy learns is not how to overcome nature but to survive. It marks the moment when there is no more nature to conquer so that the white male saga has to be recycled. Thus Boorman, like Joffe and Herzog, is trapped in his own story which turns opposition to capitalist development into the inner struggle of the failing hegemonic power which now needs to appropriate shamanistic knowledge for its own survival.

The Emerald Forest seems to illustrate Trinh T. Minh-ha's comment that "the part of the Savior has to be filled as long as the belief in the problem of 'endangered species' lasts."[16] The father of the film not only plays the part of Savior but the explicit message that closes the film speaks on behalf of people who from the Western point of view are, indeed, "invisible": "The rain forests of the Amazon basin are disappearing at the rate of 5,000 acres a day. Four million Indians lived here; 120,000 remain. A few tribes have never been in contact with the outside world. They still know what we have forgotten." The last phrase suggests that the film is in a position to understand what has been lost. Yet Boorman's own knowledge of tribal cultures can only come from Western discourse itself—for instance, an episode in which the boy is covered with stinging ants as an initiation ordeal is lifted straight out of Alain Gheerbrant's *Journey to the Far Amazon*.[17] Nevertheless, there is a certain irony in Boorman's admission in his diary *Money Into Light*[18] that the father who built the dam must now destroy his own labor, an irony that is missing from *The Mission* and *Fitzcarraldo*.

WHAT CAN THE "OTHER" SEE?

This postmodern *indigenismo* has developed in sublime ignorance of antecedents in Latin America where the conquest has remained such a haunting presence. Indeed, the fragments of indigenous civilization which are everywhere to be seen[19] were embedded in the walls of buildings, frozen in sculpture, and stereotyped as actor in the constant recapitulation of the process of enslavement. In popular belief, the "evil wind" of the conquest still blows, still infects society.[20]

The encounter of Western civilization with the New World tribal societies was without precedent; the mythic narrative of that encounter is as compelling as the myths of Moses, Oedipus, Antigone, or Don Juan and, like these myths, it seems to have to be recast with each shift in history. The indigenous figured both in the Spanish Empire's self-legitimation as a universal monarchy and in the period of national formation in the nineteenth century as the mythic origin of nations. *Indigenismo* was a literary mode that was closely connected to the consolidation of the state. It was not so much a confrontation with the "other" as an argument about national identity and the problem of whether the Indian could be integrated into the nation. National institutions such as the Instituto Nacional Indigenista founded after the revolution of 1910–17 in Mexico were central to this project of acculturation. By the sixties, however, most Latin American writers were resisting any association with the primitive. Alejo Carpentier's *Los pasos perdidos* [The Lost Steps], which is indebted both to Lévi-Strauss's *Tristes tropiques* and Gheerbrant's *Journey to the Far Amazon*, narrates a musicologist's journey (music, once again) into the primitive in order to reject its validity. The modern artist's task is not to retrace the passage from primitive to modern. His only place is in the contemporary world. Yet Carpentier exemplifies the modernism of writers such as Carlos Fuentes or Julio Cortázar, some of whose work is, nevertheless, strongly marked by the fantasy of a return of the primitive.

Just as in Europe, the "discovery" of primitive art encouraged among some members of the avant garde a mystical, reverential attitude to "otherness," a desire for those shamanistic powers that had been excluded from Western science in Latin America, and inspired a reevaluation of the indigenous civilizations.[21] Writers and poets such as José María Arguedas, Miguel Angel Asturias, and Ernesto Cardenal turned to Maya and Inca civilizations as sources of cultural renewal and originality. This ethnographic *indigenismo* drew on a greatly increased repertoire of knowledge of indigenous cultures, including transcriptions of the orally transmitted literature of the Americas. The search for an authentic culture embodied in the indigenous was, however, questioned by many, particularly the Brazilian avant garde who celebrated appropriation ("cannibalism") rather than originality and who recognized that, to paraphrase Meaghan Morris, "predation" was "the universal rule of cultural exchange."[22] This "cannibalism" would eventually find its expression in film, most explicitly in Nelson Pereira dos Santos's *How Tasty Was My Little Frenchman*, which amusingly turned the tables on colonial myth by making a Frenchman who believes that he has found the treasures of El Dorado the unwitting victim of Tupinamba cannibalism.[23]

Appropriation is a characteristic of all levels of Latin American culture from *salsa* to the soap opera. The point I wish to make, however, is that appropriation always assumes the existence of a prior text to be used and "cannibalized"—as Pereira dos Santos cannibalized the chronicles of discovery. This also permits the kind of ironic distancing that was absent from *The Mission* and *Fitzcarraldo*.

The intertextual irony acquires particular force when the prior text is central to the construction of hegemonic discourse. For instance, when he was in Mexico, the Spanish director Luis Buñuel made *Adventures of Robinson Crusoe;* this film turns the entrepreneurial Robinson of Defoe into a creature whom solitude makes mad. He is reduced to speaking to his own echo and libidinous women haunt his dreams. He is only saved by the arrival of another human being, Friday. For a time, the two of them live as equals and together repel marauders who attempt to capture the island.

Yet by the end of the film, Crusoe is dressed in the garments of a dead sea captain while Friday wears the clothes of a seaman, thus suggesting that the racial hierarchy will be restored.[24]

Appropriation thus takes on a different meaning when it is directed against the master discourse which has tended to be narcissistic. A recent catalog for an exhibition of a group of Venezuelan painters and artists who undertook the "reverse journey" to Europe comments on this narcissism: "The seeker of dreams arrives finally at the gates of his [sic] city of desire, a fantastic city that has been revealed to him as a promised destiny. He discovers it and finds to his surprise that in place of the unknown gaze, is his own image, his own history."[25]

One member of this group, Diego Rísquez, made a series of films, one of which he called *Amerika Terra Incógnita*. This film is not merely a "reverse journey" but a displacement of the ethnocentricity of Western discourse not only in the past but in the present.

The film opens with a citation from the now familiar repertoire of the sublime, a shot of virgin forest. A small group of Spaniards are loading treasure onto a boat. In a rustic cage they have trapped a handsome young Indian warrior whom they are taking back as part of the plunder. The Indian is taken to the Spanish court where Velázquez is painting *Las Meninas*. Because the Indian is represented but has no voice within the dominant order, the film is without dialogue except for the words, *Tierra, tierra* [Land, land], spoken when the Spaniards reach their own land on their return from the "tierra incógnita."

In Rísquez's film, the Indian peers through an aperture in the wall precisely as Velázquez prepares to paint *Las Meninas*, but the representation is thrown into disarray by this anomalous figure. In similar fashion, taking considerable poetic license, Vivaldi, who is conducting at court, finds his music is disrupted by the calls of jungle animals and birds. Rísquez thus offers a countermyth to that of the Jesuit conversion through harmony by showing that the New World introduced disharmony into the classical scheme of representation. What Rísquez suggests is that the scene of representation — the court and its painter and musician — perform for a spectator whose presence they cannot acknowledge, the subjugated Indian.

But though films like that of Rísquez foreground the problem of representation, they cannot themselves create an alternative discourse. Nor are they part of what Michel de Certeau calls "the long march of the Indian peoples" who are concerned neither with irony nor inversion but rather, as de Certeau points out, with a *political* third way. In this third way:

their specificity is no longer defined by a given, by their past, by a system of representations, an *object* of knowledge (and/or of exploitation) but finds its affirmation in a set of procedures—*a way of doing things* exercised within an encompassing economic situation which creates among the oppressed the foundations for revolutionary alliances. "Cultural specificity" thus adopts the form of a *style of action* which can be deployed within the situations created by capitalist imperialism.[26]

Depredation has forced mobility on to once settled peoples, obliging them to resist and adapt in new ways. This is illustrated by Rigoberta Menchú's description of the resistance of Guatemalan Indians:

> In the jungle, the people are absolutely hidden beneath the mountains. They do not have specific spots to flee from and return to. Their huts are for fifteen days, for a month, for two months, depending on the climate, on the rain, on many things. The problem is that if they spend as much as two months in a community, because they travel to and fro to move their things, to collect their products, their trails begin to get big. When they get big it is easier for the army to follow them and attack a community. So the people are constantly mobile.[27]

Thus their problem is not simply "preserving their culture," as we are often given to understand, but rather a political problem of how to achieve a social system that will permit their own—and our—survival.

NOTES

1 Columbia Records, 1988.
2 I deliberately do not use the term *Third World*. For work on representation of the indigenous in the colonial period, see Peter Hulme, *Colonial Encounters: Europe and the Native Caribbean, 1492–1792* (London and New York: Methuen, 1986). See also vol. I of Francis Baker et al., eds., *Europe and its Others* (Colchester: University of Essex, 1984).
3 William Rubin, ed., *"Primitivism" in 20th-century Art: Affinity of the Tribal and the Modern*, 2 vols. (New York: The Museum of Modern Art, 1984).
4 James Clifford, "Histories of the Tribal and the Modern," *The Predicament of Culture: Twentieth-century Ethnography, Literature, and Art* (Cambridge, Mass.: Harvard University Press, 1988), 196–97.
5 Susanna Hecht, "Chico Mendes: Chronicle of a Death Foretold," *New Left Review*, no. 173 (January/February 1989): 57–68.
6 Two of these films, *The Mission* and *Fitzcarraldo*, generated a number of spin-offs. The filming of *The Mission* is recorded in Daniel Berrigan, SJ, *The Mission:*

A Film Journal (New York: Harper and Row, 1986). The filming of *Fitzcarraldo* was recorded in Les Blank and J. Bogan, eds., *Burden of Dreams: Screenplay, Journals, Photographs* (Berkeley: North Atlantic, 1984), as well as in the film, *Burden of Dreams*. See also the script *Fitzcarraldo*, trans. Martje Herzog and Alan Greenberg (San Francisco: Fjord Press, 1982), which differs considerably from the finished movie. *The Mission* also ran into trouble with the Indian extras who threatened to strike over nonfulfillment of the contract.

7 In the forties, for instance, a well-known Latin Americanist, Carleton Beals, saw the Amazon as a "storehouse for a super civilization" and described in utopian terms a future of "great air-cooled cities" that would arise "on the banks of the Amazon and its tributaries." See Carleton Beals, "Future of the Amazon," in *Survey Graphic—Magazine of Social Interpretation*, 30, no. 3 (March 1941).

8 Alexander Cockburn, "Trees, Cows and Cocaine: an Interview with Susanna Hecht," *New Left Review*, no. 173 (January/February 1989): 33.

9 Quoted by Philip Caraman, *The Lost Paradise: an Account of the Jesuits in Paraguay, 1607–1768* (London: Sidgewick and Jackson), 213.

10 Ibid.

11 *Cahiers du Cinéma*, no. 66 (1986): 36.

12 Count Hermann Keyserling, *South American Meditations* (London: Jonathan Cape, 1932).

13 Alan Singer, "Comprehending Appearances: Werner Herzog's Ironic Sublime," in Timothy Corrigan, ed., *The Films of Werner Herzog: Between Mirage and History* (New York and London: Methuen, 1986), 183–205.

14 See, for instance, the appendix (13) on Fitzcarraldo in P. Dionisio Ortiz, OFM, *El Pachitea y el alto Ucayali: Visión histórica de dos importantes regiones de la selva peruana*, vol. 2 (Lima: Imprenta San Antonio, 1974), 894-96. According to this account, Fitzcarraldo's father was North American, his mother Peruvian. The empire he built from rubber was destroyed by Indians when he died.

15 Meaghan Morris, "Tooth and Claw: Tales of Survival and *Crocodile Dundee*," in *The Pirate's Fiancée: Feminism, Reading, Postmodernism* (London: Verso, 1988), 241–69.

16 Trinh T. Minh-ha, "Difference: A Special Third World Woman Issue," *Discourse*, vol. 8 (fall-winter 1986-7): 11–37.

17 Alain Gheerbrant, *Journey to the Far Amazon: An Expedition into Unknown Territory*, trans. Edward Fitzgerald (New York: Simon and Schuster, 1954).

18 John Boorman, *Money into Light—"The Emerald Forest:" A Diary* (London: Faber and Faber, 1985).

19 Oskar Negt and Alexander Kluge, "The Public Sphere and Experience: Selections," *October* 46 (fall 1988): 60-82.

20 Michael Taussig, *Shamanism, Colonialism, and the Wild Man: A Study in Terror and Healing* (Chicago: University of Chicago Press, 1987).

21 See, for instance, Antoine Artaud, "Concerning a Journey to the Land of the

Tarahumaras," in Jack Hirschman, ed., *Antoine Artaud Anthology* (San Francisco: City Lights Books, 1965), 69–83.

22 Morris, *The Pirate's Fiancée*, 267.

23 Richard Peña, "How Tasty was my Little Frenchman," in Randal Johnson and Robert Stam, eds., *Brazilian Cinema* (Cranbury, N.J.: Associated University Presses, 1982), 191–99.

24 The film was made in Mexico and released in 1952 and was Buñuel's first color film. See Francisco Aranda, *Luis Buñuel: A Critical Biography* (New York: Da Capo, 1976), 156–59.

25 Flyer published by Museo de Arte Contemporáneo, Caracas, October 1984.

26 Michel de Certeau, "The Politics of Silence. The Long March of the Indians," *Heterologies: Discourse on the Other*, trans. Brian Massumi (Minneapolis: University of Minnesota Press, 1985), 225–33.

27 "Rigoberta Menchú on the state of the opposition in Guatemala," *Central American Bulletin* 8, no. 1 (December 1988): 8.

WHAT'S LEFT OF THE INTELLIGENTSIA?

The Uncertain Future of the Printed Word

*I*mmanuel Wallerstein recently argued that we are now entering the black period "which can be said to have begun symbolically in 1989 . . . and will go on for at least 25 to 50 years." A characteristic of this period is that there is no longer a common social discourse so that, in the immediate future, people "will be acting somewhat blindly."[1] Wallerstein is by no means unique in finding the present confusing and the future impossible to predict. In Latin America, "sin futuro" [without a future] is inscribed on the T-shirts of marginalized youth, and it could just as well be the slogan of the intelligentsia, many of whom are still mourning the end of utopia. If the angst is particularly acute in the region, it is perhaps because, from the colonial period onward, Latin America has been a chosen site for the practical realization of utopian projects—the foundation of Vera Paz by the Dominicans in the sixteenth century, the Tolstoyan back-to-the-land utopias of those who rejected European industrialization early in this century, and the political utopias of guerrilla movements in more recent years. The utopian vision of the future, however, has now vanished. If the future is imagined at all, it is as a city in ruins as in Peruvian novelist Mario Vargas Llosa's *The True Story of Alejandro Mayta*, or at best in the modest social-democratic terms of Mexican political scientist Jorge Castañeda's *Utopia Unarmed*.[2]

The utopian vision was sustained in large part by a literary intelligentsia whose medium was print culture. It was this intelligentsia who shaped the identity of nations. It was they who acted as the critical consciousness of society, as the voice of the oppressed, as the teachers of future generations. They were held—and held themselves—in high regard. Indeed, Cuban independence hero José Martí is still referred to as "the apostle,"

Originally published in *NACLA Report on the Americas* 28, no. 2 (September–October 1994): 16–21. Copyright 1997 by the North American Congress on Latin America, 475 Riverside Drive, no. 454, New York, NY 10115.

the Mexican José Vasconcelos compared himself to Moses, and for Nicaraguan poet Rubén Darío, poets were "towers of God." This prestige has to be understood in the context of societies with high levels of illiteracy. The intelligentsia were not only major actors in the public sphere, but also—at least in public perception—mediators for the popular classes and advocates of social change.

The Cuban revolution was an event of cultural as well as political significance for the Latin American intelligentsia. Carlos Fuentes, Gabriel García Márquez, Julio Cortázar, and Mario Vargas Llosa were among its earliest supporters. For over a decade, Cuba helped set the cultural politics of the hemisphere. By the late sixties, however, the definition of what constituted revolutionary writing had become more rigorous. With Cuba's persecution of homosexuals, and the reprimand and later the imprisonment of the poet Heberto Padilla, writers became deeply divided between those, like García Márquez, who continued to support the revolution, and those, like Vargas Llosa, who became its critics.

Disillusionment with socialism, the electoral defeat of the Sandinistas, and the collapse of Communism do not, however, wholly account for the prevailing angst. Present-day writers in the Southern Cone and Central America have also inherited the traumatic aftermath of repressive military governments and civil war, followed by a new era of modernization under the aegis of neoliberalism that has mixed extreme poverty with rapid technological development. This modernization is nowhere more evident than in the dramatic changes in the shape of the city itself. The once familiar cityscapes—with their cafés, centrally located theaters, and public spaces—have turned into urban nightmares. Cultural landmarks have been obliterated, and video viewing in the home is considered safer and more practical than journeys from the suburbs into dangerous city centers for evening entertainment.

Everywhere in contemporary Latin America, there is a sense of the literary intelligentsia's diminishing importance and displacement from public discourse. This displacement is exacerbated by the growing privatization of culture. Increasingly, cultural institutions—galleries, music, and television channels—are managed by private enterprise. Even national universities, traditionally the focus of political activism, now compete with thousands of private universities, many of which are geared to business rather than culture. In Mexico, where state patronage of culture has traditionally been strong, Emilio Azcárraga, the television magnate who markets soap operas as far afield as Russia and China, has become one of the leading actors in the art world. He was responsible for organizing "the Friends of the Arts of Mexico" (the sponsors of the Museum of Metropolitan Art exhibition, "Mexico: Splendors of 30 Centuries," in New York) and for staging, in Mexico's Museum of Modern Art, one of the most important exhibitions of Chinese art ever shown in the West.[3]

The shift in patronage is particularly striking in Mexico because of a tradition of cultural nationalism that dates back to the revolution. The recent national award of generous lifetime fellowships to Carlos Fuentes, Octavio Paz, Carlos Monsiváis, and Elena Poniatowska (to name only a few of the recipients) follows a tradition of protecting national culture. In the present context, however, it can be seen as a calculated effort to re-assert the state's support of high culture, at a time when mass culture is a growth industry and publishing is dominated by multinational concerns such as the Spanish-based publishing company Planeta, which now pub-lishes in Mexico and Argentina.

The new technologies of communication have created a class of tech-nocrats and new audiences for whom print culture has lost its luster and now competes with—and is often superseded by—visual and aural culture. This has been accompanied by the industrialization of "popular" arts, such as artisan products and regional music, and the growth of a massive cul-ture industry, especially television. The Argentine critic Nestor García Canclini describes this remapping of the cultural field as "reconversion."[4] At the simplest level, reconversion refers to the retooling of culture in the age of high tech, so that a high level of literacy is no longer the inevitable stepladder to modernity. Music and the television image, rather than the printed word, have become the privileged vehicles for the exploration of Latin American identity and the nature of modernity.

Mexican critic Elena Poniatowska's lament for the lost golden age of folk art in a recent issue of the magazine *Nexos* thus sounds anachronistic. "Nowadays they mass produce San Martín de Porras, all of them coming out of the same mold," she writes. "The brush in his hand cannot sweep the vulgarity from our imagination. The Child Jesuses which are dressed by congregations, the little Babes, the Holy Child of Atocha—which used to have their own personalities—now all wear the same hat and sandals, and carry the same gourd and basket. Popular religious art is evil. Moder-nity is not creative."[5]

Although this fear of homogenization and massification has been a leitmotif of writers since the nineteenth century, nowadays postmodern culture critics are telling us to forget authenticity. The postmodernists contend that television, mass marketing, and new technologies have democratized culture, breaking down the boundaries between "high" and "low," and making possible hybrid combinations (*salsa*, for example) that enrich Latin American culture. Latin American culture, they argue, has always been heterogeneous and has always drawn on all kinds of repertoires, and can thus claim to be postmodern *avant-la-lettre*. Far from implying the death of local cultures, García Canclini argues, the market has stimulated the invention of new artisan designs, allowed culture to reach new publics, and forced people to invent a new political symbolism and new forms of social action. As an example of the latter, he cites the masked Superbarrio in Mexico City who dresses in a costume reminiscent both of Superman and the kitsch outfits of wrestlers, and negotiates on behalf of the marginalized sectors of the population. Equally promising, the video camera, electronic mail, and tape recorders have made the absolute control of information increasingly difficult. One of the significant features of the Chiapas uprising was the way the rebels appropriated modern technology—particularly email, fax, and video-recorded messages—to transmit their demands.

Thus even though technology and information overwhelmingly flow from north to south, many critics now stress the fact that certain characteristics of postmodern culture—pastiche, citation, parody—have always been features of Latin American culture. What was once designated "cultural imperialism"—according to which Latin America was the passive recipient of Hollywood movies, Disney cartoons, and television serials— is now considered inventive cultural bricolage, whereby imported technologies and fashions are used to create new cultures. Nineteenth-century modernization, which drew a racially heterogeneous population into the big cities, not only stimulated modernism in the arts but helped to produce what are now considered to be distinctively "Latin" styles out of the melange of African, European, and indigenous influences. *Tango, bolero*, and *samba* were invented in urban barrios, but were later appropriated by high culture as the epitome of "Latinity."[6] Novels such as the Argentine Manuel Puig's *Heartbreak Tango* and the Puerto Rican Luis Rafael Sánchez's *The Importance of Being Daniel Santos*, the essays of Carlos Monsiváis on Agustín Lara in *Lost Love*, and films such as the Mexican Mara Novaro's *Danzón* and the Argentine Fernando Solanas's *Tangos: The Exile of Gardel* explore the ways that popular lyrics, dance, and rhythms constitute a common "Latin" or regional language, cementing social groups and individual relations.

Rock music offers a striking example of this transculturation. Despite the fact that it emanated from the hegemonic centers of power and was part of a transnational music industry, rock became a kind of vanguard of resistance to rigid moral and family codes. An early aficionado, the Mexican novelist José Agustín claimed that, for young people of his generation, rock represented an emancipation from the stuffy discipline of a middle-class childhood. "Without any intellectualism," he writes, "rock gave me indescribable pleasures—I have had orgasms, experienced the undescribable sensation of coming out of nowhere, contortions, upturned whites of the eyes and the certainty of finding myself in regions where time no longer exists."[7]

The military governments of the Southern Cone turned rock into resistance when they suppressed music magazines and arrested young people wearing the wrong style of clothes. All over Latin America, rock music threw into relief the authoritarianism of the older generation as well as the idealistic nostalgia of the Left. Yet as in the case of *tango* or *samba*, rock lends itself to many different kinds of appropriation. The very term *rock nacional*, used in Argentina, represented an attempt to rid the music of its "satanic" origins in the United States.[8] Yet, during the Malvinas-Falklands war, the military government tried to court young people's support by holding a rock concert for National Solidarity. Likewise President Fernando Collor de Mello organized a massive rock concert to celebrate his neoliberal victory in Brazil. At the other extreme, punk and funk were appropriated by the most marginalized sectors of Latin American society.[9]

Popularity has close links to populism in Latin America. When Dominican Juan Luis Guerra sang in Lima, his concert was compared both to a soccer match and a visit by the pope.[10] Like *salsa* singer Rubén Blades, Guerra has used his popularity to draw attention to poverty and other social ills. The titles of some of his songs speak for themselves: "El costo de la vida" [The Cost of Living], "Si saliera petróleo" [If They Strike Oil], and "Ojalá que llueva café" [I Hope That It Rains Coffee]. He describes *merengue* as a rhythm for the feet and a message for the head, and claims that his lyrics speak of the suffering of the continent. Significantly, not only a writer like the neoliberal Vargas Llosa runs for president, but also the progressive musician Blades.

It is Cuban-American *salsa* singer Celia Cruz—not Rodó or Bolívar—who is the contemporary apostle of Latinity. In "Pasaporte latinoamericano" [Latin American passport] she sings of "a single Latin American people" who communicate in the common language of *samba*, *guaracha*, and *salsa*, a people who are driven by the work ethic and self-help: "Si no lo hacemos nosotros, entonces quién va a ayudarnos?" [If we don't do it ourselves, who will help us?] It is celebrity singers like Rubén Blades, Brazilian Caetano Veloso, and Juan Luis Guerra who take up the cause of social justice and—in the case of Veloso—explore the relations between consumer culture and "authenticity."[11]

Music illustrates the fact that clearcut distinctions between tradition and modernity, native purity, and degraded imports have become tenuous. Music is integral to consumer culture, yet focuses desires and aspirations in unpredictable ways, ways that are not necessarily communicable by the literary intelligentsia. Observing the marginalized punk aficionados in Mexico City as symptomatic of the society of the spectacle, Carlos Monsiváis notes that they are indifferent to his applause or attention.[12] In this environment, the intellectual may feel estranged. Attending the funeral of the *plena* musician Cortijo, the Puerto Rican novelist Edgardo Rodríguez Juliá describes his trip into the housing project where the musician was lying in state as if it were a journey to another planet, one whose strange language was "the measure of an unbridgable distance between my condition and theirs."[13] Juan Flores's witty account of the dismay expressed by the Puerto Rican intelligentsia when it was proposed that the Fine Arts Institute of Puerto Rico be named after Cortijo demonstrates that in some circles at least there is a stake in maintaining high culture primarily because of its exclusionary elitism.[14]

The other powerful rival of print culture is, of course, television, which reaches audiences far larger than any book or periodical. Thus it is not surprising that many well-known writers—Vargas Llosa, Octavio Paz, and Juan José Arreola, among others—have hosted television programs with mixed success. In Chile, the playwright and novelist Antonio Skármeta "popularizes" literature through television. By virtue of numerous television appearances, Carlos Fuentes has become a spokesperson for Latin America within the United States.

The best-selling author in Latin America, García Márquez, is acutely conscious of the fact that the average *telenovela* [soap opera] reaches a public much vaster than the combined readership of all his novels. "In a single night, one television episode in Colombia alone can reach 10 or 15 million people," he claims. "I still haven't sold 10 or 15 million of all my books, so it's natural that someone who wants to reach people will find soap operas attractive. . . . The medium is an invitation to the true mass dissemination of one's ideas, and it has to be used. I'm absolutely sure that in a *telenovela* I can command the same signs as I command in literature, and as I'm trying to command in film."[15] Brazilian producers often adapt novels for television. And melodrama, the mainstay of popular theater, has now been recycled, producing a type of television soap opera which outdoes U.S. products in the global market.[16]

Whereas print culture was once associated with modernity and the formation of national consciousness, television has now become the index of contemporary globalized culture. As the Argentine political scientist Oscar Landi acknowledges, television has an ambiguous effect on the culture. It "colonizes and destroys our previous way of life," but also "puts us in contact with the world and stimulates us to look for that which, without TV, we would never know about." What used to be claimed for literature—that it offered insights into the deep undercurrents of history and into the nature of language—is now the province of television. According to Landi, "television could help us to live with the limitations of reason because it could constantly show us the conventional, ambiguous, and slippery nature of language whatever its form—oral, written, printed, or combined with the screen and with the everyday objects which some of us have in our homes."[17]

But television is too closely linked to its use by authoritarian and military governments in the recent past, and in some countries, too ideologically linked to the state for the literary intelligentsia to feel optimistic about its pedagogical potential. The Mexican performance artist Jesusa Rodríguez calls television a virus and a powerful—because unrecognized— form of censorship.[18] In a discussion between Carlos Monsiváis and the Chilean writer Diamela Eltit, organized by the Mexican journal *Debate feminista*, both writers tried to grapple with the fact that, in apparently free societies, there was still much that could not be expressed.[19]

Argentine critic Beatriz Sarlo observes that the public space once dominated by the intelligentsia has now been occupied by the media. Parameters of social debate in mass-mediatized society are limited by all kinds of implicit, rather than explicit rules. The Chilean critic Nelly Richard, who was involved with groups of oppositional artists during the Pinochet regime, has argued that with redemocratization, the culture of fear has been replaced by a culture of massification (the quantitative evaluation of popularity), monumentality (which does away with ambiguity), and pluralism (a range of viewpoints that are never allowed to come into conflict).[20]

Worse still, literature itself is now mass-mediatized. With the globalization of the book industry and the publication of translations and best-sellers, the stake in popularity and translatability has grown. The market is not tolerant of writing that is too experimental or "untranslatable." Some writers now court rather than reject commercialism. For instance, there is little doubt that Mexican novelist Laura Esquivel's *Like Water for Chocolate* was written to appeal to a broad market.[21] Even the older generation is not indifferent to marketability. It is interesting to compare, in this respect, Vargas Llosa's gossipy *A Fish in the Water* (1993) with his deeply layered political novel, *Conversation in the Cathedral* (1969); or the plain narrative style adopted by García Márquez in *The General in His Labyrinth* (1989) with the baroque and labyrinthine *Autumn of the Patriarch* (1975). It is little wonder that prize ceremonies organized by the Planeta publishing house resemble the Miss Universe contest and are designed to promote best-sellers. Experimental writing, which used to be encouraged by small publishing houses such as Joaquín Mortiz and Sudamericana, has fallen by the wayside.

Despite all this, literature—on the surface, at least—is flourishing. There is a plethora of new novelists, young poets, and performers writing in every conceivable style and on every conceivable topic. Literary representation is still thought indispensable among those formerly excluded from citizenship in what Angel Rama called "the lettered city"—the indigenous, the black and mulatto populations, women, and gays. Literature still confronts official versions of history, explores the meaning of exile and memory, and disrupts the taboos that have been placed on female sexuality and what Luisa Valenzuela calls "dirty words."[22]

At a time when the boundaries between genres and the differences between high and low, fiction and reality, are blurred, what is more difficult to defend is the specificity of literature's oppositional clout. In a last-ditch defense, Octavio Paz recently argued that poetry "has become an art on the margins of society. It is the other voice. It lives in the catacombs, but it won't disappear." For Paz, this marginal status allows "clandestine poetry" to act as a "critique of consumer society."[23] It is ironic that Paz, whose respect for abstract freedom often puts him in the ranks of conservative libertarians, thus finds himself aligned with some younger critics in opposition to the culture industry and the marketplace. The lack of popular appeal, however, does not necessarily translate into a subversive language powerful enough to rock the capitalist boat.

What had, in the past, given literature its special claim to be resistant to consumer society had to do with the nature of reading. Avant-garde and modernist literature drew attention to language, invited slow and careful reading, and demanded the ability to decipher the code, to read between the lines. This was seen as a crucial counterforce to the clichés and fetishization of cultural artifacts in mass society. Avant-garde art and literature tried to stem commodification by focusing attention on means rather than ends, on language rather than plot or overt message. It was the "autonomy" of the literary text, its rejection of vulgar popularity, that gave credibility to the notion that it could stand in opposition to social conventions. In the sixties, it was still plausible to claim that literature was revolutionary and that the writer fought guerrilla battles with his pen.

What renders this problematic for contemporary writers is not simply the lure of popularity but the rapid appropriation and conversion of the formerly shocking or innovative into fashion or style. "Magical realism," once taken as the index of Latin American originality, is now little more than a brand name for exoticism. No wonder that for critics on the left the explicitly political and ethical aspects of literature seem to have emigrated elsewhere, for example, into the "testimonial."[24]

Perhaps the problem that most troubles critics, however, is that of value. In contemporary culture, discrimination between good and bad art seems to have flown the coop. In a discussion of art that could also be applied to literature, Beatriz Sarlo puts some of the blame for the prevalence of what she terms "cultural populism" on sociological criticism because it reduces all art to function. Thus, "in the name of the relativism of values and in the absence of other criteria of difference," Sarlo writes, "the market is taken to be the ideal space of pluralism. Yet instead of remaining neutral, it could be argued that the market exercises powerful forms of intervention over the public and over artists. The market holds absolute sway, especially over those artistic productions connected to the culture industry and thus displaces the hierarchical authority of experts of the traditional type." Overthrowing hierarchies is one thing but refusing to discriminate at all is, according to Sarlo, even worse since the failure to discuss values leads to passive collaboration with neoliberal democracy and wrests any oppositional function from art.[25]

It is no accident, then, that the appeal for a reassertion of the value of the aesthetic has been raised in the context of a redemocratization which has stratified social classes more than ever before and in ways that, for better or worse, bypass the lettered city. Mass culture and neoliberalism dilute the oppositional value of the aesthetic. On the other hand, Sarlo's defense of aesthetic value cannot be disentangled as easily as she would wish from the exclusionary and elitist culture of modernism.

For literary practitioners, as distinct from critics, the problem seems not so much discrimination, but rather the difficulty of disrupting the seductions of consumerism. Diamela Eltit, for example, who began writing during the Pinochet dictatorship, says that her task as a novelist is to "put into writing something that is refractory to commodities, to comfortable signs."[26] This might sound like a rerun of the avant-garde program were it not for the fact that Eltit undertakes, in her novels, nothing less than the total restructuring of gender and sexuality—something which the avant garde tended to take for granted. Like many of her contemporaries, Eltit works within a traditional genre—in this case the novel—while radically altering its syntax.[27]

Interestingly, one literary genre that captures the mood of the times without being subservient to it is the "chronicle," which seems to be able to duck and dart through the neoliberal net. Carlos Monsiváis, Edgardo Rodríguez Juliá, and the Chilean Pedro Lemebel are among its most devastating practitioners. The essay too has changed its ways, springing loose from its pedantic moorings to encompass the fantastic. For example, in his book *The Repeating Island*, Cuban author Antonio Benítez Rojo uses chaos theory to make sense of the Caribbean, and in *The Cage of Melancholy*, Mexican anthropologist Roger Bartra playfully revises the whole discussion of Mexican national character in terms of the mysterious evolutionary freak, the axolotl.[28]

What these examples have in common is their refusal to respect boundaries of genre or the clear distinction between the fictional and the factual. At the same time, they stress performance as the central metaphor both for the artist and for the way that everyday life is lived. For Antonio Benítez Rojo, the Caribbean is less a fixed place than a mobile galaxy of the gestures and rhythms of its inhabitants who are inflections rather than stereotypes. Performance also exposes to parody and critique any notion of original essence—whether of nation, gender, or ethnicity. Thus performance artists such as Jesusa Rodríguez in Mexico and Las Yeguas del Apocalípsis in Chile offer some of the most searching exposures of national myths and socially defined sex-gender norms.[29]

These are, of course, random examples, but they signal the tectonic shift from apostlehood to the nomadic margins—which is certainly appropriate in the era of Benetton internationalism and email universalism. The conclusion is not as paradoxical as it seems. In the age of global flows and networks, the small scale and the local are the places of greatest intensity.

NOTES

1 Immanuel Wallerstein, "The Agonies of Liberalism: What Hopes of Progress?," *New Left Review* 204 (March/April, 1994).

2 Jorge Castañeda, *Utopia Unarmed: The Latin American Left After the Cold War* (New York: Alfred A. Knopf, 1993).

3 *Mexico: Splendors of Thirty Centuries* (New York: Metropolitan Museum of Art and Bullfinch Press, 1991), p. ix. On the global reach of Televisa, see Fernando Mejía Barquera, "Ecos de los medios en 1993," *Revista Mexicana de Comunicación* 33 (January–March, 1994).

4 Nestor García Canclini, *Culturas híbridas: Estrategias para entrar y salir de la modernidad* (Mexico City: Era, 1989).

5 Elena Poniatowska, "El otro gran arte," *Nexos* 183 (March 1993): 37.

6 For a fuller discussion of literature and mass culture, see William Rowe and Vivian Schelling, *Memory and Modernity: Popular Culture in Latin America* (London: Verso, 1991).

7 José Agustín, *Contra la corriente* (Mexico: Diana, 1991).

8 Alfredo Beltrán Fuentes, *La ideología antiautoritaria del rock nacional* (Buenos Aires: Centro Editor de América Latina, 1989).

9 John Beverley, "Postmodern Music and Left Politics," in *Against Literature* (Minneapolis: University of Minnesota Press, 1993), 124–41.

10 Juan Luis Guerra, "Sentir al son del pueblo," *La tortuga* 47 (1992): 57–60.

11 Veloso's music has gone through many phases. See Charles A. Perrone, *Masters of the Contemporary Brazilian Song MPB 1965–1985* (Austin: University of Texas Press, 1989). In a television interview for *The Americas* series, Veloso said that he walks a tightrope between folk tradition and the international music industry.

12 Carlos Monsiváis, *Escenas de pudor y liviandad* (Mexico: Grijalbo, 1981), 299.

13 Edgardo Rodríguez Juliá, *El entierro de Cortijo* (Rio Piedras, Huracan, 1983).

14 Juan Flores, "Cortijo's Revenge: New Mappings of Puerto Rican Culture," in *Divided Borders: Essays on Puerto Rican Identity* (Houston: Arte Publico Press, 1993), 92–107.

15 "Of love and levitation," interview with Patricia Castaño and Holly Aylett, *Times Literary Supplement*, no. 4516 (20–26 October 1989): 1152.

16 Jesus Martín-Barbero, *De los medios a las mediaciones: Comunicación, cultura y hegemonía* (Barcelona: Ediciones G. Gili, 1987). For Brazil, see Renato Ortíz et al., *Telenovela: História e Produção* (São Paulo: Editora Brasiliense, 1989).

17 Oscar Landi, *Devórame otra vez: Qué hizo la televisión con la gente. Qué hace la gente con la televisión* (Buenos Aires: Planta, 1992), 192.

18 "A Touch of Evil: Jesusa Rodríguez's Subversive Church," interview with Jean Franco, *T.D.R.* 36, no. 2 (summer 1992).

19 Diamela Eltit and Carlos Monsiváis, "Un diálogo (ó dos monólogos?) sobre la censura," *Debate feminista* 9 (March 1994).

20 Nelly Richard, *Masculino/femenino: Prácticas de la diferencia y cultura democrática* (Santiago: Francisco Zeghers, 1993), 13–14.

21 See Antonio Marquet, "¿Como escribir un best-seller? La receta de Laura Esquivel," *Plural* 237 (June 1991): 58–67.

22 Examples of historical novels are too numerous to mention but an exception should be made for Roa Bastos whose *Yo el supremo* (1974) explores the nature of historical writing, national consciousness, and subjectivity.

23 Quoted in *The New York Times*, 11 June 1994.

24 Beverley, *Against Literature*, 22.

25 Beatriz Sarlo, "El relativismo absoluto o como el mercado y la sociología reflexionan sobre estética," *Punto de vista* 48 (April 1994).

26 Diamela Eltit, "Errante, errática," in Juan Carlos Letora, ed., *Una poética de literatura menor: La narrativa de Diamela Eltit* (Santiago: Editorial Cuarto Propio), 21.

27 Diamela Eltit's novels are not yet translated but it is worth mentioning the staging of gender and marginality in her first novel, *Lumpérica* (Santiago: Ediciones del Ornitorrinco, 1983) and the exploration of socially constituted sex and gender in *El cuarto mundo* (Santiago: Planeta, 1988).

28 Antonio Benítez Rojo, *The Repeating Island: The Caribbean and the Postmodern Perspective* (Durham: Duke University Press, 1992). Roger Bartra, *La jaula de la melancolía: Identidad y metamorfosis del mexicano* (Mexico: Grijalbo, 1987).

29 Performances are difficult to discuss because of their particularly ephemeral nature. Jesusa Rodríguez, however, contributes regularly to *Debate feminista*, published in Mexico, and Pedro Lemebel is about to publish his chronicles of Santiago, *La esquina es mi corazón*, with the Cuarto Propio publishing house.

GLOBALIZATION AND THE CRISIS

OF THE POPULAR

*S*ocial scientists in Latin America increasingly insist that there is a "crisis of the popular."[1] This statement seems to refer both to a political crisis of agency and to the theoretical problem of identifying the popular within the heterogeneous pluralism that characterizes postmodernity.[2] Culture is no longer securely located in a place of origin or in a stable community and is constantly reinvented by people on the move, as Homi Bhabha shows in his book, *The Location of Culture*.[3]

The "hybridity" of this culture that develops out of displacement, juxtaposition, or the sheer speed of its transmission has produced a new set of problems for the analyst as well as new cultural configurations. In this essay, I shall discuss two of the latter concepts—the resurfacing of the popular as nostalgia in new representations of Latinity, and the replacement of the hybrid and the subaltern for the popular in discussions of agency. Finally, I want to suggest that the disruptive potential sometimes attributed to the popular is perhaps best grasped in those moments when at the margins and on the periphery Enlightenment discourse loses its explanatory force.

It is obvious by now that the cultural transformations of the last decade have produced more disarray than understanding. These transformations raise questions that range from methodology to political strategy, as García Canclini recognizes when he asks "How does one study the millions of indigenous peoples and peasants who migrate to major cities or the workers who are incorporated into the industrial organization of work and consumption? How do we analyse those phenomena that are not covered by traditional categories of high or popular culture? How to build societies with democratic projects shared by everybody without making everyone the same?"[4] The questions clearly relate to two apparently diverse prob-

Originally published in *The Legacy of the Disinherited: Popular Culture in Latin America: Modernity, Globalization, Hybridity and Authenticity*, ed. Ton Salman (Amsterdam: CEDLA [Centrum Voor Studie en Documentatie van Latijns Amerika], 1996).

lems—that of fragmentation and hybridity and that of the growing homo-geneity of places drained of any local or national particularity—urban cen-ters, airports, shopping malls. Both homogeneity and hybridity challenge older definitions of national identity and community.

Alberto Moreiras argues,

> Si el capitalismo transnacional fundamenta su dominación global en la constitución de una red simbólica que reduce al extremo toda posibili-dad de un Afuera, si lo real se retira hasta el punto de que la naturaleza y el inconsciente no son ya más que en la medida en que la industria cultural los produce como simulacros, si estamos reducidos a la indi-gencia de tener que pensar la historia a partir de la ausencia de historia ¿cuál es entonces el sentido que pueden guardar las diferencias locales? ¿Qué hace el Brasil diferente de Francia o a Uruguay de España?

> [If transnational capital bases its global domination on the constitu-tion of a symbolic network that reduces to the extreme every possi-bility of an Outside, if the real has receded to the point where nature and the unconscious no longer exist except insofar as the culture indus-try produces them as simulacra, if we are reduced to thinking history as the absence of history, what is then the meaning of local differences? What makes Brazil different from France or Uruguay from Spain?][5]

Thus when critics refer to the "crisis of the popular," they are not only referring to the impossibility of appealing to some strata of folk culture personified in the abstract "gaucho," "Indian" or whatever, but also to their own dilemma faced with these global cultural symbols and with the local and infinitely varied products of hybridity which neither correspond to older representations of "the national popular" or of populism, nor amount to transculturation in the traditional sense.

"The popular" was formerly an index of Latin American difference, a difference that was measured by *distance* from the metropolis by the class who were closest to the metropolis and as the foundation for nationhood (the independent *gaucho*, the "authentic" rural population). But, equally, popular culture served as an index of "underdevelopment" (it was pre-Enlightenment, preliterate)—of tradition as opposed to progress, back-wardness as opposed to modernity—"malandragem" [trickery], "choteo" [mockery], "relajo" [lack of discipline] as opposed to a work ethic.

What has also changed over the last decades is not only the dualistic way of understanding culture as "high" or "low," "avant-garde" or "traditional" but also a change of values so that hybridity is now seen as creative and enriching while purity unhappily evokes ethnic cleansing. Migrations, the mixing of high-tech and "primitive," of mass-mediated and oral culture, the scrambling of languages as they cross borders, the scrambling of social classes that can no longer be securely stratified except through taste—all this has seriously compromised any notion of an undiluted popular culture "made by the people themselves" (to use Raymond Williams's phrase).[6]

For not only are people on the move as never before but their cultural repertoire is no longer limited by place, tradition, and actual cultural contact. Gilles Deleuze and Félix Guattari describe this as "deterritorialization," by which they mean the abstraction of value on the levels of the affective, the social, and the economic. Deterritorialization accounts not only for the physical uprooting of people from a place of their own, but also for a "liberation" from cultural rootedness and filiation. Affect, for example, is released from family ties and circulates through abstract identifications and affiliations—for example, the generic "Latinos" in the United States.[7] New, volatile cultural identities are formed out of "in-betweeness";[8] and differences are not necessarily between nations, ethnic, and linguistic groups but rather are stylistic, the self-fashioning of subgroups and individuals who place their own inflection onto the generic international media culture.[9]

This transformation from stable groups whose characteristics have been elaborated over time and, in particular, locations into transient and ephemeral constellations was vividly captured by Edgardo Rodríguez Juliá in his essay, "El entierro de Cortijo" [Cortijo's Funeral].[10] This essay, which describes the funeral of a popular musician held in a Puerto Rican housing project built during the Operation Bootstrap period, also charts the impossibility for the intellectual of finding some essence of Puertoricanness in a crowd whose only common characteristic is its chaotic diversity. The "Mayorquan" onlooker (Rodríguez Juliá) finds himself in a heterogeneous, multiracial mob of compatriots whose language—a drug-culture slang— is unintelligible to him. Observing "them," the chronicler (described as myopic) cannot adopt some privileged position as observer for whom the crowd is an object of analysis because he is aware that "they" are reading him: "también ellos son capaces de leerme, ya me tienen leído: ese tiene cara de mamao" [They too are capable of reading me, they have already read me: this one looks like a drunk]. The realization that "they" can read "us" spreads like glaucoma over the once confident imperial eye. The chronicler is caught between his position as outside observer and his fear of imminent submersion into the crowd, whose clothing styles and bodies tell not one but multiple and often contradictory life stories—for instance, the worker whose tight tropical shirt with palm trees and a sunset (evoking a tourist paradise) is stretched over a muscular body that betrays a history of hard manual labor. What strikes Rodríguez Juliá is not simply the hybridity of culture but the fact that its multifaceted and evanescent surface can be read as so many personal and fragmented histories that it defies categorization.

During the musician's funeral, the Church and political parties attempt and fail to use Cortijo's popularity to mobilize the crowd around their particular agendas. But how can they represent this mass brought together not by a common nation or a common religion but by the serialized experience of mass culture that has as many different inflections as there are people? Rodríguez Juliá can only find a tenuous sense of continuity and community nostalgically evoked by a few chords of guitar music played by some young people after the crowd has left (trampling disrespectfully over the graves).

What Rodríguez Juliá's chronicle also illustrates is that the ideal of community persists among the intelligentsia in the form of nostalgia. This nostalgia, moreover, is often evoked by music, especially the tango, the *danzón*, and the *bolero* in many recent novels, for instance in Manuel Puig's *Boquitas pintadas* [Heartbreak Tango] and Luis Rafael Sánchez's aptly named *La importancia de llamarse Daniel Santos* [The Importance of Being Daniel Santos] (which celebrates the "Latinity" of the *bolero* singer of the title), as well as in films such as *Danzón* and *Tango argentino* [Argentine Tango]. However effective as art, their reliance on nostalgia suggests that Latinity is like the Cheshire cat: only the grin remains. Benítez-Rojo's *The Repeating Island*—a persuasive attempt to define Caribbean difference—finds commonality in "walking, dancing, playing an instrument, singing, or writing in a certain kind of way" which displace "participants toward a poetic territory marked by an aesthetic of pleasure, or better, an aesthetic whose desire is nonviolence." Acknowledging that this in itself is not exclusive to any human group, he adds, "what *is* characteristic of the Caribbean peoples is that, in a fundamental respect, their aesthetic experience occurs within the framework of rituals and representations of a collective, ahistorical and improvisatory nature." [11] It is only on this abstract level, rather than in brute reality, that any claim for community can be made.

Art as well as literature uses popular culture to express nostalgia for a lost community. Latino artists who are born or living in the United States—Pepón Osorio, Amalia Mesa Bains, and Carmen Lomas Garza, and the Puerto Rican artist Antonio Martorell, for example—use everyday objects such as the matrimonial bed or mosquito netting, domestic altars, and ex-*votos* to evoke memories of family and home. The recent "Recovering the Popular" exhibition (1994) at the Museo de Barrio in New York City, in which Latino artists (including Cubans, Bolivians, Puerto Ricans, and Chicanas) participated, illustrated the depth of this nostalgia—for instance, one installation consists of a careful reconstruction of an old-time *bodega*. Many artists who contributed to the catalog mentioned the importance of recuperating memories of the homeland past. Side by side with this recuperation, mass culture was reenchanted (for instance, in a portrait of Celia Cruz).[12]

I was at the opening of this exhibition when Celia Cruz herself put in an appearance, followed by an entourage of television cameras and lights. It was an amusing and yet telling instance of the failed attempt to revive the aura of the work of art in the age of mechanical reproduction since all those present were jostling for the attention of the media star and turning their backs on the paintings, which certainly could no longer be contemplated in the conventional way.[13] Certainly the displacement of old-style popular culture (the *bodega*, the saints) by the transnational superstar who, at the same time, represented Latinity-within-globalization was dramatically evident.[14] Indeed, the painter of her portrait, Mary Kent, wrote in the catalog, "Afro-Antillean music has been the single most unifying element of the Hispanic culture . . . Popular culture has transcended its low status and has entered the world of high art" (p. 24).

It is curious, though hardly surprising, that celebrity singers are at the forefront of this crossover between high and popular art and of these redefinitions of Latinity. Juan Luis Guerra, Ruben Blades, Celia Cruz, and Caetano Veloso are global celebrities credited with propagating Latinity throughout the world. When Juan Luis Guerra sang in Lima, his concert was compared both to a football match and to a visit by the pope; thanks to him, one commentator said, "the world is being flooded from end to end with merengue and bilirubina."[15]

These global celebrities tend to transmit messages that range from protection of the environment to attacks on poverty, and they are fully conscious of their role as cultural mediators. Indeed, they often express their "responsibility to the people" in ways which recall the writers of the sixties. Guerra describes *merengue* as a rhythm for the feet and a message for the head, and claims that his lyrics address the suffering of the continent. The titles of his songs are self-explanatory: "El costo de la vida" [The Cost of Living], "Si saliera petróleo" [If We Only Had Oil], and "Ojalá que llueva café" [May It Rain Coffee]. It used to be writers who claimed to be spokesmen for the people; now Ruben Blades as well as Vargas Llosa runs for president and it is Celia Cruz and not Rodó or Bolívar who defines Latinity. In "Pasaporte latinoamericano" [Latin American Passport], Cruz sings of a single Latin people, who communicate in the common language of *samba*, *guaracha*, and *salsa*, a public that is powered by the work ethic and self-help, "Si no lo hacemos nosotros, entonces, ¿quién va a ayudarnos?" [If we don't do it ourselves, who is going to help us?]. Singers like Caetano Veloso express their concern about the authenticity of regional music as it becomes appropriated by the global music industry and transformed into "world music" while contributing precisely to this transformation; rappers like the *gauchesque* singers use rhyming skills to score points against rivals and enemies. Such celebrities "represent" popular sentiments and demands but within market permissibility.

Despite gestures toward political intervention, these singers' use of the leverage supplied by "popularity" is limited. Their "protest" remains within the parameters of what is culturally intelligible in free-market capitalism, where quantity rules over complexity.

Given this shifting cultural map, cultural theory has increasingly questioned the structure of a discourse that separates popular from high culture on the grounds of value. García Canclini, for instance, argues that the differentiation of art and artisan products is a form of social distinction. He also argues that global culture and tourism do not inevitably bring about the degeneration of artisan products but contribute to their enrichment and expansion.[16] In somewhat similar fashion, Jesús Martín Barbero considers media and older forms of popular culture to be interdependent (for instance, the soap opera takes over where melodrama left off, and, conversely, orally transmitted culture uses mass culture icons). Soap operas, in fact, can be compared to scripts which are always open to inventive use and interpretation.

Furthermore, according to these critics, it is nonsense to characterize Latin America as a mere consumer of the mass culture that originated in the north, for not only has Latin America developed a thriving culture industry of its own, but Latin Americans are adept at turning metropolitan technology to creative use. Indeed, their originality is less a matter of inventing the new as of improvising with whatever is at hand. Martín Barbero argues that "The sense of freeplay" (my inadequate translation of *desmadre*) and "the capacity for improvisation are the secret of a communitarian creativity which basically consists of revitalizing the new through the old." [17] María Celeste Olalquiaga argues that recycling, cultural trans-vestism, and bricolage "indicate not only the ability of Latin American cul-ture to deal with the complexities of postindustrialism, but also how such humorous reversals (as for instance the juxtaposition of technology and primitivism in samba parades) can promote an awareness of these issues at a popular level and, in the final instance, show them within a broader con-text than their First World counterparts ever do." [18] What had formerly been the sign of underdevelopment has become avant-garde and popular taste, and what formerly was denigrated as kitsch can no longer be subor-dinated to high culture norms.

So far I have been discussing the relation of popularity to questions of identity. But there is a quite different sense in which *popular* is used to de-scribe the counterhegemonic. The source is, of course, Gramsci, whose concept of the "national popular" is still used by some of the Latin Ameri-can left. [19] Yet even here one can speak of the crisis of the popular since many of those whose stake is in resistance to capitalism or in struggles for justice have shifted ground, abandoning the term *popular* for *citizen-ship* or *civil society*, and thus emphasizing forms of social organization that are outside traditional party structures. For instance, in his book *Entrada Libre: Crónicas de una sociedad que se organiza* [Free Entry: Chronicles of a Society in the Process of Organizing], Carlos Monsiváis examines grass-roots movements in which people take power into their own hands, often in defiance of the government. [20] But these groups can no longer be described as the "popular classes" in the old sense, because the movements include intellectuals, workers, schoolteachers, housewives, and doctors. It is "civil society" in which Carlos Monsiváis lodges his utopian hope of true partici-patory democracy. [21] From representation of the popular or popular repre-sentation, the emphasis shifts to new forms of mobilization and agency.

The crisis that makes critics avoid the use of *popular* is linked to the emphasis on democratic and grassroots participation. Here, too, however, there are struggles over interpretation between those who endorse the agenda of redemocratization under capitalism and those who resist this and look to the periphery or the margins for the destabilization of mean-ings produced by the center. Not surprisingly, it is in Chile, and among writers and culture critics, where this radical stance has been theorized—especially in the work of artists such as Juan Dávila, Eugenio Dittborn, and Paz Errázuriz, in the writings of Diamela Eltit, and in the criticism of Nelly Richard. For all these writers and critics, it is at the margins that the meaning generated by the center loses substance and sense. Thus resistance no longer resides in what might traditionally have been termed *the popular*, but rather in those marginalized groups who are culturally unintelligible within the Western episteme. This is somewhat close, though not exactly equivalent, to the "subaltern" in the writing of Gayatri Spivak.[22]

Are *popular, publics*, and *subalterns* simply interchangeable terms? Not if we take seriously Johannes Fabian's remarks that the "popular" may reveal the cracks in the system.[23] Indeed what I want to suggest in the remainder of this essay is that perhaps the cracks are in the incompatibility between the discourse generated by the center and the scrambling of that discourse at the margins. Given the international division of labor, there are now sectors of the world's population who do not experience capitalism as democracy or change as progress, who are without access to the information network, and who are not incorporated into the Western episteme. We should thus examine carefully those moments when the Enlightenment narrative no longer has universal explanatory power, when a fundamental division appears between the metropolitan worldview and its resignification along the periphery, when the project of the center (which is, of course, no longer geographically located) is misrecognized along the periphery. I use the terms *center* and *periphery* in full knowledge of the fact that they are associated with dependency theory, although, currently, like the term *Third World*, they are seen as strategically useful in cultural analysis.[24]

This misrecognition is perhaps most clearly registered in the discipline of anthropology, especially when the self-conscious and self-reflective metropolitan anthropologist comes up against that which is found to be culturally unintelligible. Nowhere has the dilemma been more frankly expressed than in Nancy Scheper-Hughes's recent book *Death Without Weeping: The Violence of Everyday Life in Brazil*.[25] In the course of her fieldwork, the author came up against attitudes toward the death of children in an endemically hungry society that were at odds with her feminist belief in women's caring and nurturing roles. She also encountered a subaltern understanding of the power structure that countered her own faith in betterment through enlightenment. In her book, incompatible narratives are revealed in her own personal struggle to understand why mothers let starving children die.

Death Without Weeping is a six-hundred-page book that wrestles not only with the author's humbling lessons but also, more profoundly, with the epistemological and ethical problems of what constitutes knowledge and with the definition of ethical behavior in a society that suffers chronic starvation. In the community that she calls the Alto, mothers practice triage to

ensure that the fittest survive. Faced with a practice that goes against Western pieties about mothering (according to which mothers would do anything to prevent the death of a child), Scheper-Hughes concludes, "Among
the women of the Alto [the concept] to let go . . . implies a metaphysical
stance of calm and reasonable resignation to events that cannot easily be
changed or overcome. . . . And so a good part of learning how to mother
on the Alto includes knowing when to let go of a child who shows that he
wants to die" (p. 364).

But it is not only the thesis of the book that I want to discuss here,
but also the particular conflict which the author frankly acknowledges between her own intervention as a "good American" into people's lives and
the stubborn knowledge of the reality that she encounters but cannot altogether accept. This is not just a question of national character nor even
of imperialism. In the United States, there is the deeply ingrained belief in
redemption through healthy diet, correct family behavior, and education,
all of which are seen as universal values. Twice, Scheper-Hughes tries to
save starving children. In one case, she is successful in saving a boy who
grows into a reasonably healthy teenager only to be killed in a gang fight.
On another occasion, she attempts to force a starving child into a taxi to
take her to the hospital, only to find that she can't budge the screaming
child, who is convinced that if she goes to the hospital her organs will
be taken and exported for transplant operations: "No amount of coaxing
could convince Mercea that her tormented little body was not going to be
sold to the ghoulish doctors" (p. 234). U.S. optimism based on middle-
class expectations and good living comes up against a kind of knowledge
that speaks in a different language.

What constitutes this knowledge is, of course, a repetitive history that
goes back at least as far as the conquest, when it was rumored that the Spaniards were extracting fat from the bodies of the Indians. Perhaps something
like Bourdieu's "habitus" is useful here to describe the complex of disposi-
tions that are formed through family, education, peer groups, cultures, and
collective memory.[26] The rumor about extracting body parts, however, fits
into a very ancient narrative, as Hughes herself acknowledges.

> The body-snatching rumors were so widespread in the favelas and poor
> neighborhoods of Pernambuco that local journalists soon picked up
> the story and went to great lengths to expose the credulity of the popu-
> lation, sometimes cruelly satirizing people's fears as bogeymen stories
> . . . As the people of the Alto see it, the ring of organ exchange proceeds

from the bodies of the young, the poor, and the beautiful to the bodies of the old, the rich, and the ugly and from Brazilians in the southern Hemisphere to North Americans, Germans and Japanese. (p. 235)[27]

Body-part rumors are thus not just metaphors or symbols; they also add a modern inflection to the Peruvian *pishtaco* stories (still current in the Andes), according to which *ladinos* kidnapped Indians and extracted grease from their bodies, sometimes for medicinal purposes but also to grease guns or sugar mills or machines. In this story, what is interesting is not the abstraction of surplus value from labor but the use of the body to keep conquest and industry going. As one researcher has observed in modern versions of the story, the grease is always exported and even is rumored to have been used in space rockets. Nor are such stories confined to Latin America—although in the United States body exploitation is most often attributed to visitors from outer space.[28]

Such rumors mark the body as the direct object of exploitation, liable to be cannibalized for energy, blood, or spare parts. In the *pishtaco*, the grease makes the colonial and the capitalist war machine function and requires the death of the donor. Both the body-parts rumors and the Andean stories demonstrate the local within the global. The body is no longer for reproduction within the family structure but rather a tradable commodity that can be exported to keep the global elite going.[29]

The body-parts rumors are closely related to adoption stories, since it is widely believed that blonde women visiting Latin America intend to kidnap children. Many are accused of using the adopted children for body parts. Reproduction, which ensures the permanence of a community, thus becomes a token of the subaltern's loss of control over the body.[30] What is being narrated draws on a social imaginary that is produced and reproduced by the failure of progress and the certainty of exploitation. It is at this point that the Enlightenment narrative becomes dysfunctional in places where it has never functioned in the first place.

What I have argued here is that the "crisis of the popular" can be understood in different ways. On the one hand there is a crisis of terminology when older senses of the word *popular* no longer correspond to any stable group, and the idea of "a culture made by a people themselves" is no longer viable. This has resulted in attempts to describe local, regional, national, or "Latin" difference in terms of hybridity or nostalgia. On the other hand, the crisis of the popular can also be understood as a problem of agency within neoliberal societies in which social stratification is understood in terms of consumption and where social movements may be constituted across class lines. But there is also another sense in which the popular (defined by marginality within the world system) "brings into crisis" the Enlightenment discourse of improvement through self-help, education, and upward mobility. The traditional pedagogical stance of the center toward the periphery is reversed because the periphery has something to teach us.

But destabilization cannot simply be left to the periphery. It is also crucial that intellectuals at the center should begin the process of dismantling their own position of privilege.[31] And a good place to begin might well be with questioning their stake in "the popular" especially when the popular, in their representation, inhabits those places where they themselves are privileged visitors.

NOTES

1 As has often been pointed out the term *popular* has contradictory meanings ranging from "the culture actually made by themselves" (Raymond Williams) to the common denominator of taste as in "pop culture." Underlying the use of *popular*, there is an appeal to the people, either as the founding principle of the constitution as in "we the people" or as the collective hero of nationhood. The people are also appealed to both as the dynamo of change and the repository of communitarianism. For ambiguities around the term, see Geneviève Bollème, *El pueblo por escrito: Significados culturales de lo "popular"* (Mexico: Grijalbo, 1986).

2 García Canclini's reference to the "crisis of the popular" occurs in an unpublished manuscript on consumption. There is an interesting analysis of transnation identities by Xavier Albó, "Our Identity Starting from Pluralism in the Base," in John Beverley and José Oviedo, eds., *The Postmodern Debate in Latin America*, special issue of *boundary 2* 20, no. 3 (fall 1993): 18–33.

3 Homi K. Bhabha, *The Location of Culture* (London and New York: Routledge, 1994).

4 Néstor García Canclini, *Culturas híbridas: Estrategias para entrar y salir de la modernidad* (Mexico: Grijalbo, 1989). English translation, University of Minnesota Press, 1994.

5 Alberto Moreiras, "Postdictadura y reforma del pensamiento," *Revista de crítica cultural* 7 (November de 1993): 26–35.

6 Raymond Williams, *Keywords: A Vocabulary of Culture and Society* (Glasgow: Fontana, 1976), 198–99. On fin-de-siècle popular culture in Mexico, see "Cultura popular del fin de siglo," *Memoria de papel* 4, no. 11 (September 1994).

7 Gilles Deleuze and Félix Guattari, *Anti-Oedipus: Capitalism and Schizophrenia* (New York: Viking Press, 1972).

8 Renato Ortiz, "Una cultura internacional-popular," Editora Brasiliense (1994): 105–45; Bhabha, *The Location of Culture*.

9   Jesús Martín Barbero, *De los medios a las mediaciones. Comunicación, cultura y hegemonía* (Mexico: G. Gili, 1987), 218-19.

10 Eduardo Rodríguez Juliá, "El entierro de Cortijo" (Río Piedras: Huracán, 1983).

11 Antonio Benítez-Rojo, *The Repeating Island: The Caribbean and the Postmodern Perspective*, trans. James E. Maraniss (Durham, N.C.: Duke University Press, 1992).

12 "Recovering Popular Culture/Recobrando la cultura popular," El Museo del Barrio's Twenty-fifth Anniversary Exhibition, September 9-October 30, 1994, New York, El Museo del Barrio, 1994.

13 This is an allusion, of course, to Walter Benjamin's well-known essay, "The Work of Art in the Age of Mechanical Reproduction," in *Illuminations* (London: Jonathan Cape, 1970), 219-53.

14 Jean Franco, "What's Left of the Intelligentsia: The Uncertain Future of the Printed Word," NACLA *Report on the Americas* 28, no. 2 (Sept/Oct 1994): 105-45.

15 "Sentir al son del pueblo," interview with Armida Testino, *La Tortuga*, no. 47 (1992): 57-60.

16 Néstor García Canclini, *Las culturas populares en el capitalismo* (Havana: Casa de las Americas, 1981). More recently, García Canclini writes of *culturas híbridas* [hybrid cultures] and in some recent collaborative work of "publics" (Néstor García Canclini, et al., *Públicos de Arte y Política Cultural. Un estudio del II Festival de la Ciudad de México* [Mexico: Universidad Autónoma Metropolitana, 1991]).

17 Barbero, *De los medios a las medicaciones,* 218-29.

18 María Celeste Olalquiaga, *Megalopolis: Contemporary Cultural Sensibilities* (Minneapolis: University of Minnesota Press, 1992), 85-86.

19 Nelly Richard, in *La insubordinación de los signos (cambio político, transformaciones culturales y poéticas de la crisis)* (Santiago: Editorial Cuarto Propio, 1994), criticizes this concept as irrelevant to modern culture.

20 Carlos Monsivais, *Entrada libre: Crónicas de una sociedad que se organiza* (Mexico: Era, 1987). However the relative optimism of these essays could not last given the political climate of Mexico in 1994, in which the Zapatista uprising has paradoxically strengthened the PRI, at least among the electorate who fear violence.

21 The Zapatista rebellion in Chiapas obviously reintroduces class and ethnicity as mobilizing forces although (despite some expressions of solidarity from outside Chiapas) the military have effectively contained the rebellion.

22 Subaltern studies was initiated in India as a questioning of the assumptions that had underpinned the historical study of the Indian peasantry. See Ranajit Guha and Gayatri Spivak, eds., *Selected Subaltern Studies* (New York: Oxford University Press, 1988). In Spivak's work, the subaltern is a point of interruption of Western discourse; see "Can the Subaltern Speak?" in Cary Nelson and Lawrence Grossberg, eds., *Marxism and the Interpretation of Culture* (Urbana: University of Illinois Press, 1988), 271-313. For the Chilean situation, see Richard, *La insubordinación de los signos.* The founding of the Latin American Subaltern Studies group in the United States, at least according to the founding statement, seems to correspond to the need of metropolitan intellectuals to have access to

the subaltern—a position that Spivak specifically critiques in the article mentioned above. For the founding statement see Beverly and Oviedo, *The Postmodern Debate in Latin America.*

23 "Opening Remarks" at the Conference on Popular Culture in Latin America: Legacy of the Disinherited, Amsterdam 1996.

24 See Spivak's discussion of essentialism in the interview included in *Outside/In the Teaching Machine* (New York and London: Routledge, 1993), 1–23.

25 Nancy Scheper-Hughes, *Death Without Weeping: The Violence of Everyday Life in Brazil* (Berkeley: University of California Press, 1992).

26 Pierre Bourdieu, *The Field of Cultural Production. Essays on Art and Literature* (New York: Columbia University Press, 1993), 64.

27 On the world's black market, "a heart can go for about $20,000. A liver is worth up to $150,000 a slice. Lungs sell for $25,000." James Hogshire *Sell Yourself for Science*, quoted by Eric P. Mash, "What's Life Worth?" *New York Times* (Sunday magazine section), 14 August 1994, pp. 34.

28 For stories of abduction by aliens, see John E. Mack, *Abduction: Human Encounters with Aliens* (New York: Charles Scribner's, 1994). The television series *Twilight Zone* often deals with abduction.

29 Peter Gose, "Sacrifice and the Commodity Form in the Andes," *Man. The Journal of the Royal Anthropological Institute* 21, no. 2 (June 1986).

30 Rumors have also been spread for political reasons, such as the antivaccination rumors reported in *Siempre*, January 1975.

31 Richard, *La insubordinación de los signos.* I also recommend the "testimonial" of a schizophrenic tramp recorded by Diamela Eltit in *El Padre Mío* (Santiago: Zegers, 1989), which reveals the impossibility of information retrieval.

*I*n 1968, a utopian year if ever there was one, Stanley Kubrick released *2001: A Space Odyssey.* It was just a year after the first landing of men on the moon—a Motown hit, sung in *The French Connection* was "Everybody's Going to the Moon." The film not only made Richard Strauss's *Thus Spake Zarathustra* a muzak hit heard in every elevator, but also encapsulated, in one stunning shot, the history of technology from the first weapon to the space ship. An anthropoid discovers a heavy bone which he uses, not as a tool for labor as Marx would have it, but as an arm to strike an opponent. Thrown into the air, it becomes the space ship of *2001.* The film is obsessed with the boundlessness of space and with the release from gravity, and the spaceship is represented as a rhythmic machine rotating to the accompaniment of Johann Strauss's "Blue Danube" waltz. Although the movie was made at the height of the cold war, the only enemy the astronauts face, apart from boredom, is a rebellious computer called HAL who unplugs the life-support system of three hibernating scientists and sends one astronaut whirling in emptiness. The camera dwells on this figure rotating helplessly, weightlessly in the atmosphere until it resembles the bone thrown in the air by primitive man or a satellite spaceship. In the final sequence, "Beyond Infinity," the spaceship advances into a magma of color: the camera gazes into the face of the last surviving astronaut as speed dissolves it into particles. It is there that we reach the point described by Paul Virilio as "(el) olvido final de la materia y de nuestra presencia en el mundo, mas alla de la barrera del sonido y mas alla de la barrera de la luz" [The final forgetting of matter and our presence in the world, beyond the sound barrier and the speed of light], in other words, speed produces indifference.[1]

The end of the film, however, draws back from this dissolution. The surviving astronaut lands in a room that might be on Jupiter but could be

Originally published as "Marcar diferencias, cruzar fronteras" in *Las culturas de fin de siglo,* ed. Josefina Ludmer (Buenos Aires: Beatriz Viterbo, 1994): 34–43.

in Kansas. He walks into a postmodern apartment in which there are re-productions of Watteau paintings on the walls, as if to remind us of the artificial pastorals of the Enlightenment. Here in a single-sex and "time-less" finale he watches his older self eating a meal, then an even older self lying in bed pointing to a mystic pillar and a newborn child. The opti-mistic view of the technological conquest of this final frontier is capped by a curiously shrunken and narcissistic ending in which privatized man is reduced to a meaningless life cycle salvaged only by the promise of yet another mystery beyond infinity.[2]

This future world beyond ideology, politics, and history could only be a fantasy conceived as a "center" as yet uncontaminated by the alien bodies of women or peoples of color, a center that believes itself to have reached the end of history.

Watching *2001: A Space Odyssey* in the nineties is an interesting experi-ence because it conveys both the lost-in-space feeling of the end of the millennium as well as the end-of-Enlightenment-man narrative, a story which had equated history with the advance of technology; the exclusion from Kubrick's spaceship of any but white males and their male-gendered computer is one of the more notorious aspects of the film. As we near 2001, that exclusive center no longer holds and is replaced by a dispersed center flowing in and out of cyberspace; the territories of former metropolitan nations have been invaded, their boundaries crossed, border fences are full of holes, and the male body can no longer stand in as the inviolate recep-tacle of an identity or the human being. The hard-on of male integrity gives way to (amniotic) fluidity. The metaphor of flow increasingly domi-nates over framework and fixed location,[3] speed alters the very notion of space: "space is no longer in geography—it's in electronics. Unity is in the terminals. It's in the instantaneous time of command posts, multinational headquarters, control towers, etc. Politics is less in physical space than in the time systems administered by various technologies, from telecommu-nications to airplanes. There is a movement from geo- to chrono-politics: the distribution of territory becomes the distribution of time."[4]

Although "flow"—as one of the dominant concept metaphors in this speeded-up chronopolitics—gives rise to celebrations of multiple position-alities, intersections, cross-roads, margins, excess, and chaos, it also pro-duces angst. For abstraction has reached a new level, and cruising in this hyperspace transcends "the capacities of the human body to locate itself."[5] If body still matters at all, it is only insofar as it is no longer "the" body and no longer securely bonds a self.

The sense of sublime produced by global flow and motion is a startling contrast to older political metaphors of alternative oppositional space. Whether actually liberated territories or personal space outside consumer society, the occupation of alternative territories seemed necessary in order to organize foci of resistance. During the sixties in the United States, personal utopias were described in terms of space exploration—the trip, the high, being spaced-out, "Lucy in the sky with diamonds." In Latin America, utopias were more often geographical territories claimed for a project outside capitalism—Solentiname, Marquitaria, the liberated territories of El Salvador, and, of course, Cuba. But in both cases, resistance was thought to depend on claiming a place "outside" the system.

The global flow, however, has no outside, only interstices occupied by new space invaders—women, gay writers, the indigenous, the marginal who have displaced the traditional boundary setters. This has produced a particularly acute sense of crisis in Latin America where the intelligentsia had traditionally occupied or monopolized public space and, even in some formulations, constituted public space. Certain texts capture this invasion and displacement in a particularly vivid fashion. Consider, for instance, Edgardo Rodríguez Juliá's graphic description in *El entierro de Cortijo* [Cortijo's Burial] of crowd suffocation, of finding himself immersed in a heterogenous and unclassifiable mass who have gathered to pay a last farewell to the musician.[6] But there are other ways of being lost in the present. The Chilean poet Raúl Zurita journeys into the Atacama desert and inscribes the words, "Ni pena ni miedo" [Neither regret nor fear] in forty-foot letters on the mountainside. Without any transitive verb that might orient desire or rejection, "Ni pena ni miedo" aspires to the longevity of the ruin or the rune, rather than the transient tagging of graffiti. At the same time, it is a monumental gravestone commemorating, perhaps, the death of the author. "Se trata," said Zurita in an interview with *El Mercurio*, "de un momento que sobrepasa una simple persona, una generación o un momento" [It's about the moment that surpasses a simple person, a generation or a moment.] "Es un testimonio colectivo, aunque la idea sea de uno en particular" [It's a collective testimony, although the idea might come from one person in particular].[7] Like the lines traced by the Nazcas in the deserts of Peru, the words are described as "huellas que se van a confundir con las demás marcas o geoglifos del desierto" [footprints that blend with the other marks and hieroglyphs of the desert]. Zurita's monument is lost in time as well as space. "Tengo la sensación de que empezamos recién una travesía donde de pronto no te queda otro que dar vueltas en círculos concéntricos; corres el riesgo de morirte de sed, pero no hay salida tampoco" [I have the feeling that we have just begun a journey in which suddenly all you can do is go around in concentric circles; you take the risk of dying of thirst, but there is no exit]. For Zurita, there is no possibility of poets being "torres de dios, profetas" [towers of God, prophets], apostles, or even "escritores comprometidos y responsables" [committed and responsible writers], because the future is now unpredictable.

Beatriz Sarlo attributes this bewilderment to the loss of agency of the intelligentsia in a public sphere that is increasingly occupied by the mass media.[8] The period of uninterrupted flow, she says, is not coincidentally one of symbolic poverty in which the intelligentsia is forced to accept a more humble and more egalitarian position which often involves their integration into a program that they have not designed and in which they no longer represent an avant-garde. Her analysis, however, seems to depend on the identification of the public sphere *only* with the nation-state.

In orthodox political terms this may be true but it does not account for the new types of state and nation that have lately emerged. Xavier Albó suggests that in present-day terms the public sphere is no longer solely constituted by the nation-state; speeded-up flows of money, peoples, information across national boundaries which undermine the principle of the union of the state, and the nation which had underpinned political thinking in Latin America also produces new state formations—for example, the nation-under-the-state, i.e., the multinational state, in which formerly autonomous nation-states are dominated by meta-state policies.[9] An example would be the map made by the World Bank which charts flows that ignore national boundaries. Cristal Bartolovich quotes a document in which the Bank self-consciously disclaims the implications of this overcoding of the nation-state, saying that their map does "not imply the expression of any opinion whatsoever on the part of the World Bank or its affiliates concerning the legal status of any country, territory, city or area, or concerning the delimitations of its boundaries or natural affiliation."[10]

Albó's other category is the nation-over-the-state (or trans-state nation), which would embrace the definition of *nation* by indigenous peoples in Latin America as they demand recognition of territories irrespective of national boundaries and claim "certain margins of autonomy." Sandinista Nicaragua's problem with the Mosquito Indians certainly illustrates the conflict between this indigenous "nation-over-the-state," which crossed national boundaries between Nicaragua and Honduras and the invaded national territory defended by the Sandinista government.

Thus it is not so much, as Sarlo suggests, that the intelligentsia pragmatically compromises with the nation-state, but that there is a global redefinition of the state which has forced the intelligentsia to reconsider their position so that they are variously described as cognitive mappers (Jameson), nomads (Deleuze and Guattari), borderland shamans (Anzaldúa), cyborgs (Haraway), or as the irreducible margin in the center (Spivak).[11] Margins, borders, and frontiers have also been refunctionalized not necessarily as boundaries of actual territories but rather as boundaries of neoterritories that mark not only geographical but also psychological space. Gloria Anzaldúa, for instance, argues that "the borderlands are physically present whenever two or more cultures edge each other, where people of different races occupy the same territory, where under, lower middle and upper classes touch, where the space between two individuals shrinks with intimacy."[12]

Although Anzaldúa describes the border as "una herida abierta" [an open wound], and a "thin edge of barbed wire"—thus affirming, at least on one level, its material existence—she argues that "living on borders and margins, keeping one's shifting and multiple identity and integrity is like trying to swim in a new element, an 'alien' element." The border for her is both existential and geographical, a place of abjection and excess.

In Martin Hopenhayn's collections of aphorisms, *Escritos sin futuro* [Writings Without a Future], the title of which resonates with the *sin futuro* on the T-shirts of the *desechables* [disposables], there is rather a different charting of a loss of self-centered agency.

> Sensación de que el poder - filoso - de las armas y el romo - poder del mercado han grabado sus marcas en nuestra piel, nos dibujan señales en el rostro para distinguirnos o mezclarnos a distancia, nos poblaron brazos y piernas con un alfabeto que no entendemos o no compartimos, pero que sigue alli, desenroscado sobre nuestra propia linea de fuego. Sensación de que somos de agua, y como tales nuestra combinacion es fluir y derramarnos, salpicar y ser navegados, mojar y ser bebidos, ahogar y saciar la sed de los demas, transitar entre recipientes al acecho de una residencia que insiste en postergarse.

> [A sensation that the sharp-edged power of arms and the blunt power of the market have carved their marks into our skin, drawing signs on our faces to distinguish us or merge us at a distance, have peopled our arms and legs with an alphabet that we do not understand or share, but which remains there untwisted across our own line of fire. Sensation

that we are made of water and our fate is to flow and spill, to splatter and be sailed upon, to drench or be swallowed, to drown and sate the thirst of others, to flow from one receptacle to another seeking an abode that continually postpones itself.][13]

Hopenhayn extends the notion of flow to the self, to the subject marked by power and the market; some of his aphorisms are written "against this power" and others "for an individual politics." He finds an ethics not in resistance but in "going with the flow": "Etica para la crisis: apostar por el flujo entre la unidad y la diferencia, por el desgarro de lo uno en lo diverso, por la contorsión de lo múltiple en lo único. Asumir la propia plasticidad como única forma de ser incondicional a si mismo" [Ethic for the crisis: bet on the flow between unity and difference, on the breach of the one within the many, on the contortion of the multiple in the singular. To assume one's own plasticity as the only means of belonging unconditionally to oneself] (p. 93). There is perhaps no need to emphasize this flux had constituted the feminine for the modernists. We might also think of this "going with the flow" (to use the words of the pastor of the drive-in church) as a form of deterritorialization. This term, which has now entered common usage, is associated with the work of Deleuze and Guattari whose *Anti-Oedipus* was described by one critic as a "great river of a book" (the flow once more).[14] Their coauthored books *Anti-Oedipus* and *A Thousand Plateaus* undertook both to break the dialectic and to remap the social, the economic, and the affective according to the universal energy of desiring production released by capitalism.[15] If I mention *Anti-Oedipus* and *A Thousand Plateaus*, it is because, more than Jameson and David Harvey,[16] Deleuze and Guattari think of space and mapping as perpetual movement like today's video maps. Not surprisingly, they compare capitalism's decoding with a trip to the moon. "One sometimes has the impression," they write, "that the flows of capital would willingly dispatch themselves to the moon if the capitalist State were not there to bring them back to earth" (*Anti-Oedipus*, p. 258). They describe capitalism as a gravityless drift into more and more abstract spheres. These abstractions are not only realized on the level of money and exchange as in Marx, but also on the level of the social and the affective. Deleuze and Guattari thus significantly extend Marx's insight that capitalism displays "a cosmopolitan, universal energy which overthrows every restriction and bond" to every facet of life. As Lyotard remarks, "Capitalism deculturalizes peoples, dehistoricizes their inscriptions, repeats them anywhere at all as long as they are marketable, recognizes no code marked by the libido but only exchange value: you can produce and consume every-thing, exchange, work or inscribe anything any way you want if it comes through, if it flows, if it is metamorphozable. The *only* untouchable axiom bears on the condition of metamorphosis and transfer: exchange value." [17]

Individual bodies and groups "become maps traversed by lines, meridi-ans, geodesics, tropics and zones marching to different beats and differing in nature" (*A Thousand Plateaus*, p. 202). The complexity of this process, which they carefully distinguish from "tracing," also allows for escape lines into the real. Reterritorializations involve the production of new and more abstract neoterritories like Disneyland, territories composed of new eth-nicities, Bosnian Serbs, Croat Muslims, or archaic neoterritories like gang turf marked only by tags—graffiti which can be overpowered by the tag-ging of a rival gang, or even a book. And they advocate not opposition to this process of fragmentation but rather intensification to the point where the whole edifice becomes destabilized—literature and art being one of the places where this intensification is often played out, and the "mythic" South as another.

Deleuze and Guattari's account of capitalism thus not only obliges us to rethink both the fetishism of the commodity and the oedipal, but it also allows for nonstate forms of reterritorializations such as gangs, neo-ethnicities (for example, *mestizaje* and Latinity) as well as new identities constituted around difference and hybridity. One example of this would be Celia Cruz's reinvention of *Arielismo*, which embraces both economic integration into the metropolis and Latin difference:

> Miles de caras y almas buscando paz y progreso
> Tenemos los mismos sueños, ves cuánto nos parecemos
> Pasaporte latinoamerico
> Nicaragua y Puerto Rico, mexicanos y cubanos
> Queriendo echar pa' delante con esfuerzo y trabajo.
>
> [Thousands of faces and souls searching from peace and progress
> We have the same dreams, see how alike we are
> Latin American passport
> Nicaragua and Puerto Rico, Mexicans and Cubans
> Wanting to get ahead with energy and hard work.] [18]

Celia Cruz salvages difference on a cultural plane while identifying Latin Americans with the Protestant ethic of work and progress. At the other extreme, writers and critics, especially those savvy enough to have caught on to Deleuze and Guattari's mythical exaltation of the nomadic and minorities, perhaps perversely, practice forms of strategic reterritorialization by identifying themselves with the potent force of peripheries, borders, and checkpoints.[19]

For Deleuze and Guattari reterritorialization is not to be confused with place or location. This has left an opening for Latin Americans to resignify "periphery," "border," and even "Latin America" as *places* of flux, unserviceability, and excess. Both the U.S.-Mexican border and the Caribbean can thus be celebrated as mobile, inbetween spaces. I am here referring not only to Gloria Anzaldúa's positing of the border as a third place, but also Emily Hicks's notion of border cyberspace, and Nelly Richard's periphery.[20] One of the most eloquent examples of this "strategic reterritorialization" is, however, Antonio Benítez-Rojo's *The Repeating Island*, in which he reconjugates Deleuze and Guattari with chaos theory and turns the Caribbean into a starry constellation:[21]

> If some one needed a visual explanation, a graphic picture of what the Caribbean is, I would refer him to the spiral chaos of the Milky Way, the unpredictable flux of transformative plasma that spins calmly in our globe's firmament, that sketches in an "other" shape that keeps changing, with some objects born to light while others disappear into the womb of darkness: change, transit, return, fluxes of sideral matter (p. 4).

Benítez-Rojo describes his project as analyzing "certain aspects of the Caribbean while under the influence of this attitude, whose end is not to find results, but processes, dynamics, and rhythms that show themselves within the marginal, the regional, the incoherent, the heterogeneous, or, if you like, the unpredictable that coexists with us in our everyday world" (p. 3).

Fin de siglo [End of the century] does not apply here because there is no end. There is no apocalypse in the Caribbean, says Benítez-Rojo, only chaos that "looks toward everything that repeats, reproduces, grows, decays, unfolds, flows, spins, vibrates, seethes" (p. 3). Contrast this with another fin de siècle writer, Rubén Darío, who is driven by a different kind of flow—"ondas atávicas" [atavic waves], which draw him, nostalgically, to the Mediterranean past and beyond the reach of "la ciencia comercial (que) lo acapara todo" [commercial science (which) engulfs all].

To be sure, Darío's "Epístola a Madame Lugones" was written not at the end of the nineteenth century but rather in 1916. Yet, even though the two writers seem to move in different directions, the underlying motor in both is commerce. Darío attempts to recapture its pristine moment of innocence when commerce meant connection. In Benítez-Rojo, it is a war machine.

The tendency to consider globalization either in terms of homogenization or as productive of indiscriminate heterogeneity has, in some quarters at least, undermined any possibility of an aesthetic or of Latin American difference. The selective appropriation of Deleuze and Guattari allows Latin American critics to maneuver in global space while retaining the privilege of minority location. It may be that this is the one way of enabling an aesthetic and even some tenuous notion of identity in the gravityless flux of this fin de siècle.

NOTES

1 Paul Virilio, *Estética de la desaparición* (Barcelona: Anagrama, 1988), 128.

2 Although the film is based on Arthur Clarke's novel, which has a sequel, Kubrick chooses to end his film on a religious note—the worship of the universal and apparently eternal mystery of male birthing.

3 Manuel Castells, *The Urban Question: A Marxist Approach*, trans. Alan Sheridan (London: E. Arnold, 1977).

4 Paul Virilio, *Speed and Politics* (Columbia: Sémiotexte, 1986).

5 Fredric Jameson, *Postmodernism, or, The Cultural Logic of Late Capitalism* (Durham, N.C.: Duke University Press, 1991), 44.

6 Eduardo Rodríguez Juliá, *El entierro de Cortijo* (Río Piedras, Puerto Rico: Ediciones Huracán, 1985).

7 Interview with Ana María Lara, *El Mercurio* (Chile), 22 August 1993.

8 Beatriz Sarlo, "El relativismo absoluto o cómo el mercado y la sociología reflexionan sobre estética," *Punto de vista*, no. 48 (April 1994): 27–31.

9 Xavier Albó, "Our Identity Starting from Pluralism in the Base," *boundary 2* 20, no. 3 (fall 1993): 18–33.

10 Crystal Bartolovich, "Boundary Disputes: Textuality and the Flows of Transnational Capital," *Mediations* 17, no. 1 (December 1982): 24.

11 With the reservation that none of these authors refers specifically to a traditional intelligentsia but rather to a new breed of organic intellectuals. See Gilles Deleuze and Félix Guattari, *A Thousand Plateaus, Capitalism and Schizophrenia* (Minneapolis: University of Minnesota Press, 1987); Donna Haraway, "Cyborg Manifesto: Science, Technology and Socialist-Feminism in the Late Twentieth Century," in *Simians, Cyborgs, and Women: The Reinvention of Nature* (New York: Routledge, 1990), 149–81; Fredric Jameson, *Postmodernism*; Gloria Anzaldúa, *Borderlands/La frontera. The New Mestiza* (San Francisco: Aunt Lute Books,

1987); Gayatri Chakravorty Spivak, *Outside/In the Teaching Machine* (New York: Routledge, 1994).

12 Anzaldúa, *Borderlands*, preface.

13 Martín Hopenhayn, *Escritos sin futuro* (Santiago: Editorial, Contrapunto, 1990), 8.

14 Jean François Lyotard, "Energumen Capitalism," *Sémiotexte* 2, no. 3 (1977): 16.

15 Gilles Deleuze and Félix Guattari, *Anti-Oedipus: Capitalism and Schizophrenia* (New York: Viking Press, 1972), esp. p. 337. See also *A Thousand Plateaus*.

16 David Harvey, *The Condition of Postmodernity* (Oxford: Blackwell, 1989); Jameson, *Postmodernism*.

17 Lyotard, "Energumen Capitalism," 20.

18 Celia Cruz, "Pasaporte latinoamericano." Thanks to Lawrence La Fontaine-Stoke for providing the song lyrics.

19 A salient example is Mexican performance artist Guillermo Gómez Peña. See the collection of his performance texts, *Warriors for Gringostroika* (St. Paul, Minn.: Graywolf Press, 1993).

20 Emily Hicks, *Border Writing* (Minneapolis: University of Minnesota Press, 1991); Nelly Richard, *Masculino/Femenino* (Santiago: Francisco Zegers Editor, 1989).

21 Antonio Benítez-Rojo, *The Repeating Island. The Caribbean and the Postmodern Perspective*, trans. James Maranis (Durham, N.C.: Duke University Press, 1992).

3 Latin American Literature:
THE BOOM AND BEYOND

READING VARGAS LLOSA

Conversation Is Not Dialogue

*I*n the European novel, the home is the fortress and symbol of the bourgeois family, the material proof of its ideals and moral values. Inside it, private lives unfold, and outside there is the public world, business—and threatening elements. The café, the bar, the house of prostitution are the negations of domestic virtues, of thrift and hard work; these are places in which the deep contradictions of society reveal themselves. It is not surprising, therefore, that the novel, in its criticism of bourgeois society, so often takes us outside the home to the bar, the "sacred temple" where middle-class man confesses his errors and reveals his human tragedy. Thus, in Camus's *The Fall*, one of the most important novels of the modern period, the bar "Mexico City" is the place where the repentant judge "preaches," and where he invites "all good people to submit to authority." In *The Fall*, as in *Conversation in the Cathedral*,[1] man can stumble and fall, but he can never escape.

Although the structure of *Conversation in the Cathedral* is similar to that of *The Fall*, its content is far more varied and complicated. Instead of a repentant judge, there are two protagonists: the reporter Santiago Zavala, son of an industrialist, Don Fermín, who had supported President Odría; and "el sambo" [black] Ambrosio, formerly the chauffeur for both Cayo Bermúdez, the right-hand man of Odría, and for Fermín Zavala—he is now working part-time for the dog pound in Lima. Separated by the café table between them, the two protagonists represent two irreconcilable aspects of Peru—irreconcilable because of race, language, and social class. Santiago is a failure of a man, a mature man who, to Ambrosio, will always be a spoiled child. To Santiago, Ambrosio is black, and "todos los negros se parecen" [all black people look alike]. (Ana, Santiago's wife, would call

Originally published as "Lectura de Conversación en la Catedral de Mario Vargas Llosa" in *Revista Iberoamericana* 37 nos. 76–77 (July–December 1971): 763-68. Translated by Patricia Heid.

him "un negro asqueroso" [a disgusting black man].) Amalia, the servant in the home of Santiago's family and later Ambrosio's wife, is the "cholita" [little half-breed] or the "huachafa" [broad, chick]. The novel is full of terms that divide and separate—"bourgeois," "know-it-all," "Trotskyite," "gay," but the fundamental class difference separating Ambrosio and Santiago is the one which determines and actually generates the novel. The novel is, in the words of Sartre, "the thread of Ariadne that takes us to different ways of grouping human beings"—with the one difference that, in Peru, in order to have a comprehensive vision one needs to have two, not one, of Ariadne's threads.

But *Conversation in the Cathedral* also poses a question—"¿En qué momento se había jodido el Perú?" [Exactly when did Peru get so fucked up?] and the answer, "No hay solución" [There is no way out of this mess], is given in the first paragraph. The novel, therefore, poses a question to us that is impossible to answer, just like the riddle of the sphinx. The riddle is understood as soon as the taboo is broken; the novel is understood when we can rise above the deep-rooted divisions and attain a totalizing vision of the whole. The novel is, therefore, a model which allows us to criticize Peru and, at the same time, it facilitates and paves the way for us to overcome and rise above this criticism. The reader has a broader perspective than the protagonists, who only understand one particular aspect of reality and only tell those parts of their past which are agreeable to hear. Santiago tells the story of his first love and his marriage to Ana; Ambrosio tells about his lovers, his getting married to the servant, Amalia, and his brief encounter with his father, Trifulcio. Each one tells what the other can understand, but all the dirty and terrible details of their lives remain buried beneath the surface of the conversation, and they appear to the reader only in the form of phantasmagoric dialogues, lost conversations that are woven into the real dialogue between Ambrosio and Santiago. This method of representation is extraordinarily rich in possibilities, and it allows for the development of various shades of irony. Thus, when Ambrosio confesses to Santiago his ambition to become rich, a flash of memory carries him back to the beginning of his life, to the time when he first set out for Lima to make his fortune with Cayo Bermúdez.

"So, kid, you want to know, what would I have liked to be in life?" says Ambrosio. "Filthy rich, of course."

"So tomorrow you're leaving for Lima," said Trifulcio. "And what are you going for?"

In just a few words, the author conflates the retrospective vision of the grown man who is a failure and the youthful vision of a young man who has his whole future in front of him. The past is a ghost which haunts the communion feast, a ghost viewed by each person through different eyes. Freed from the constraints of chronological sequence, each one of these past moments breaks from its original circumstance, combines with different events, and suggests daring comparisons. The interrogation and the torturing of a man, an *aprista*,[2] in prison is linked, by means of this new ordering, to a dialogue with Senator Landa about schemes for winning votes. The dialogues of different people at different moments resonate in strange ways with other people at other times. Trifulcio asks his son, Ambrosio, for money, and it is the ironic voice of Cayo Bermúdez which answers, talking about the hardships and the rewards of family life. The rhetoric of Bermúdez is doubly empty because it is linked in the text with a scene of true violence between a father and his son, a scene in which Trifulcio pulls a knife on Ambrosio in order to rob him.

> "I bet you think I'm a real scum, one that even steals from his son, one that even takes money from his son," said Trifulcio. "I swear to you, this is only a loan."
>
> "I feel a little jealous hearing about this, Mr. Zavala," Bermúdez said. "In spite of the headaches, there must be real rewards to being a father."

There is so much irony in these final words! Cayo Bermúdez is the right-hand man of Odría, the "father" of the nation and the center of the system of *compensación*—benefits received in exchange for loyalty and service. The nation, like the family, is a system of both sacrifice and benefits, both based on real violence. Trifulcio has to sustain his authority as a father by using a knife, just as Odría has to maintain his authority through oppression. The dialogue thus represents a small-scale model of society under Odría. Moreover, Trifulcio's action is later reflected in the action of his son, Ambrosio, who uses a knife to kill Hortensia, the ex-lover of Cayo Bermúdez. After the fall of Bermúdez, Hortensia has to live on what she can make by blackmailing Santiago's father, Don Fermín, who has homosexual relations with Ambrosio. In order to defend his protector (and substitute father), Ambrosio kills her. Thus, the father's behavior is repeated in the actions of his surrogate son.

Trapped like flies in a tangled web of circumstances, neither Santiago nor Ambrosio come to see more than one aspect of reality, and for this reason they never successfully come to understand each other. Ambrosio lies to Santiago. Santiago, for his part, makes his true confession to his friend, the journalist Carlos. After four hours of conversation, Ambrosio and Santiago separate, insulting each other: "Sépase que no se merecía el padre que tuvo, sépaselo. Váyase a la mierda, niño" [Just know this, you didn't deserve the father you had, just know that. Go to hell, kid], says Ambrosio. The dividing line between two worlds, two attitudes, two languages seems impossible to overcome.

If from its very first pages the novel develops from the premise that there is no way out of the mess, the bar, *La Catedral*, is the symbol of futility. It is worthwhile to examine carefully this *topos*, which is a microstructure of a society focused on consumption. It is a bar, restaurant, house of prostitution, and meeting place for all the various races of Peru:

> Beneath the zinc roof, crowded together on benches at rough-hewn tables is a buzzing and hungry mass of people. Two Chinese men in undershirts carefully watch the coppery faces from their place behind the counter, the angular features that chew and drink, while a lost little mountain boy in a tattered and soiled apron hands out steaming bowls of soup, bottles, bowls of rice. A lot of affection, a lot of love, that is what is coming out of a multicolor phonograph, and in the back, behind all the smoke and noise, the unmistakable smell of food cooking and liquor, behind the dancing swarms of flies, there is a wall full of holes—stone, huts, a thread of the river, the leaden sky—, and a broad woman, bathed in sweat, deftly handles pots and frying pans surrounded by the hissing of the stove.

In this picture of so much energy and activity, the city—"piedras, chozas, un hilo del río" [stone, huts, a thread of the river]—and the love song barely heard on the phonograph remain in the background. In the foreground, there is a vision of voracious consumption. Everything is focused on the immediate activity of "masticar" [chewing], "beber" [drinking], "distribuir" [handing out], "manipular" [handling]. In the table is carved out a reference to love—"se distingue un corazón flechado, un nombre de mujer: Saturnina" [one can see a heart with an arrow through it, the name of a woman: Saturnina]. Saturnina reminds us of Saturn, because in this cathedral the true religion is that of ephemeral pleasure, and the true god is the god of time. Moreover, Saturn, the god who eats his own children, is a powerful symbol of a society that absorbs all rebellion, that converts its children into failures or conformists. The very structure of the novel confirms its "saturnine" nature. Divided into four sections, each section has a unifying theme that articulates conversations, time periods, characters. In the first part, for example, there are various cases of breaking with one's family. Santiago breaks off with his father; Ambrosio and Cayo Bermúdez leave the country and head for Lima. The second section is dominated by relationships based on self-created interests or on sexual perversion, both of which reflect the values of a society dedicated to consumption and not to production and creation. The home of Hortensia, Cayo Bermúdez's lover, is not only the setting for lesbian orgies, but, at the same time, a cornucopia of goods:

> There was a little of everything: platters, place settings, piles of table-clothes, tea settings, large glasses, small glasses, long ones and short ones and flat-bottomed ones, wine glasses . . . You could find everything in the pantry: cookies, raisins, potato chips, canned goods packed in water, cartons of beer, whisky, and mineral water.

This accumulation, destined for consumption, does not have anything to do with production or creation. On the contrary, it is based on theft. Like the cathedral and the dog pound, it is the symbol of an economy based on immediate gratification. This economy appropriates a product by means of cunning, theft, or deceipt—never by means of productive work. And just as there is no true production, the economy is reduced to two kinds of activity—eating and evacuating. The only product is excrement. There is a good reason why the nickname for Cayo Bermúdez is Cayo Mierda [Cayo the Shit]; and there is a good reason why there is an abundance of scatalogical references, even in the descriptions of the city of Lima, which is described as being "color de caca" [the color of shit]. If the product of a consumer society is excrement, its center is money, and its sexual relations are a reflection of sterility and perversion. Hortensia and the prostitute Queta perform sadistic lesbian scenes for Cayo Bermúdez and his friends. The policeman who tortures the *aprista* Trinidad is a homosexual. Don Fermín takes Ambrosio into his service because he needs a homosexual relationship. The children slip drugs to the servant, Amalia, in order to seduce her. But the symbol of the political regime in all its baseness is Cayo Bermúdez, worrying about the cleanliness of the country, just as the prostitutes worry about the cleanliness of their bodies. His sexual perversion—he prefers to look and not participate—is the mirror of a government that uses weakness and perversion to manipulate the people. Ariadne's thread, which starts out from Ambrosio and Santiago, carries us to the most honorable and the most corrupt people of society, all of them equally manipulated and perverted by a political regime that is based on corruption.

There is no dialectic process which would provide "a way out of this mess." The regime and those in power are constantly threatened by treason and blackmail, but revolution never breaks out. Saturn goes on eating his children. Things appear in different forms, but there is never any real change. In the third section of the novel, there occurs a series of scandals that seemingly threaten the stability of the political regime—Hortensia's death, a journalistic investigation, the conspiracy between Senator Landa and General Espina, the insurrection of Arequipa. But the result is always the same. The scandal is suppressed, the public is deceived, and the stability of the dominant class remains intact. In the final section, Saturn is truly the one who triumphs. The changes that are produced—Santiago's marriage, the death of Don Fermín, the fall of Bermúdez—are, in reality, changes resulting from the passage of time, rather than from a transformation of man or society.

Within a totally corrupt atmosphere, individual success has no meaning. Ambrosio, who always wanted to work on his own, fails in his attempt to start a business in Pucallpa. He ends up working in the dog pound, stealing dogs in order to survive. Santiago rebels against his father and enlists in a communist organization in San Marcos. In the end, he succeeds in partially freeing himself from failure by working as a journalist. Ambrosio sums up the human tragedy in the words which end the novel: "He would work a little here and there; if he was lucky, a rabies epidemic would break out for a time and they would call him up again, and then, a little work here, a little work there, and then, well, then he would die, right, kid?"

NOTES

1 Mario Vargas Llosa, *Conversación en la Catedral*, 2 vols. (Barcelona: Seix Barral, 1969).
2 Member of the APRA Party, the Alianza Popular Revolucionaria Americana [American Popular Revolutionary Alliance] founded by Víctor Raúl Haya de la Torre in the 1920s.

LEZAMA LIMA IN THE PARADISE OF POETRY

*F*or José Lezama Lima, poetry is paradise.[1] The theme of his novel *Paradiso* (1966) is the poet's search for the "invisible" world that is beyond the tangible. The novel frequently refers to general ideas —glory, love, nobility, dignity in the face of death, stoicism—in other words, to a series of values that don't belong to any particular social class, nor to any group in prerevolutionary Cuba, values that had become part of an empty rhetoric. Therefore, Lezama Lima has to give them meaning.

Lezama Lima considers man "a being-for-the-resurrection." Life and poetry have a profound religious sense for him; this ideal meets its opposite in prerevolutionary Cuba, a society in which life lacked transcendence and whose values were grotesquely displayed in the air-conditioned mausoleums that still exist in Havana's cemetery. I mention these mausoleums because they are a reproduction in miniature of a society's tastes, and the tastes of Havana point to a consumer society. Dedicated to the acquisition of riches, Havana seemed to be a version, although an even more degraded one, of Miami, a consumer society superimposed on a colonial city. Havana was a center of prostitution, of the mafia, and of gambling, and its odyssey can be found in the novel that is a compendium of the spoken and written language of prerevolutionary Cuba, *Tres tristes tigres* [Three Trapped Tigers] by Guillermo Cabrera Infante.[2] The "hero" of the novel is a disc jockey whose adventures chronicle the destruction of a language and a culture. When Cabrera Infante's characters hear Bach on the radio, it is a Bach who has been deformed by the waves of the Atlantic. Shakespeare becomes Shakeprick; Castilian becomes malleable, recast in the *mulatas*' mouths. *Three Trapped Tigers* is the anti-utopian odyssey of neocolonialist degradation.

Originally published as "Lezama Lima en el paraíso de la poesía" in *Vórtice* 1, no. 1 (spring 1974): 30–48. Translated by Carla Faini.

While Cabrera Infante captures a Cuba that is only a parody or a bad imitation, Lezama Lima evokes a world that has been lost or that never existed, a world in which individual lives had form and style and where art suggested the eternal realms. It would be difficult to conceive of two writers who were more different and at the same time so complementary.

Paradiso belongs to a Latin American tradition that was initiated by modernism and German Romanticism in Europe. It is the tradition that considers poetry to be a privileged genre, where language flees from utilitarian daily discourse. Lezama Lima takes this hypostatization of poetry beyond symbolism. Art is not just a vision of beauty or just a religion, rather it is the very essence of being. By combining neo-Platonism with Orphic and Pythagorean symbolism, the author arrives at a theory of an ascent toward God by means of poetry that also facilitates continuity and gives shape to history. Lezama Lima considers class wars to be the domain of nature and relegates them to the "surface," although they are commonly seen as the foundation of human civilization; he believes that it is poetry that links generations through the mysterious path of images. The poet is not only the high priest; he is also the bearer of the sacred flame.[3] His acutely developed senses detect the nuances of this invisible world which can only be made visible with words:

> A troubled ghost of conjectural nothings, the one who is born into poetry feels the weight of his unreality, his other continuous reality. His testimony of not being, his witnessing of the innocent act of birth leaps from embarcation to a conception of the world as image. The image as an absolute, the image that knows itself to be an image, the image as the last of possible histories.[4]

Lezama Lima views the physical world as an imperfect reflection of the noumenal world, and images (which are different from rhetorical figures, such as metaphors, that are used in order to translate an image into words) are the mirrors of the noumenal world.

> I believe that the miracle of the poem is that it manages to create body, a resistant substance that is fixed between metaphor which creates infinite connections as it goes along, and a final image that secures the survival of that substance, that *poiesis*.[5]

In this manner poetry provides the real continuity, and it is through poetry that man becomes a "being-for-the-resurrection."

I acquired that point of view from which I confront Heidegger's theory of a being for death, raising the concept of poetry as bringing about the prodigious causality of a being for resurrection, the being who conquers death and all that is on the side of Saturn.[6]

Thus, Lezama Lima's structures contrast with Marxist views, given that what he considers to be foundational the Marxists consider to be superstructure. For Lezama Lima social and economic life change, but there is something beyond change: poetry which defies and conquers time.

It is not my aim to examine in detail what Lezama Lima says about poetry. In brief, he reorganizes, in his own way, all of the theories that exalt the poet and lets the theories about the historic evolution of words and concepts fall by the wayside. Given this ahistoric vision, it is interesting that he chooses the genre of the novel for his best work and that he distances himself from all the modern trends that define literature as a form of subjective expression "that does not lead to general conclusions."[7] On the other hand, Lezama Lima's theory on poetry and art in general seems to belong to another era, when one could still talk about a totality, when literature did not reject abstraction. Because of this, it would be useless to place *Paradiso* in the same category as the modern novels which are based on the specificity of experience; perhaps it should be classified with Montemayor's *Diana* or Bunyan's *Pilgrim's Progress*.

The theme of *Paradiso* is an ascent toward poetry by way of the material world, which is represented by family, friendship, and schools. Lezama Lima himself describes the early stages of the search, which begins in the "family placenta" of José Cemí. (The name is derived from *sema* or sign. As I later learned, it is also a pre-Columbian reference.) In the second stage, Cemí leaves his family to experience "the opening of an exterior world, the time of friendship;" finally he ascends through an oneiric and symbolic landscape toward his encounter with poetic destiny.[8]

This ideal plan locates the novel outside historic time in such a manner that even when it discusses social groups—the family, students, and so on—it presents them in terms of archetypal relationships. In contrast, everything that constitutes texture in the realist novel—descriptions of the workplace, political and social forces, café society, bordellos, factories—is excluded or minimized. Yet, Lezama Lima wrote *Paradiso* in a historical moment in which the oppressive politics of the fifties weighed heavily on Cuba, when it was impossible to ignore the corruption and degeneration of the island. But rather than use the novel as a mirror of society, he constructs an ideal world and an idealized society which features the best of Hispanic and creole life. Although the events from the end of the nineteenth century and the beginning of Machado's dictatorship take place during the time frame of the novel, Lezama Lima eliminates almost everything of historical significance in order to focus on what seems stable and lasting to him—in other words, archetypes. Even when some passages could be seen as tableaux of local customs, they have a symbolic purpose within the book. For example, Cemí's parents' marriage brings together Basque stoicism with the Rialta family's "creole high spirits," a contrast which, nevertheless, does not demonstrate a nationalist tendency on the part of the author. Rather it serves as a metaphor of the clash of disparate elements which produces a poetic revelation.

Lezama Lima's preoccupation with a "higher plane" causes him to ig-nore not only historical material but also novelistic standards. Many critics have commented on the arbitrariness of his methods, the abrupt changes of time and place, the digressions, the introduction of long dialogues using artificial language, and so on. One of his most ardent admirers, Julio Cortá-zar, has pointed out that when Lezama Lima wants to resume the narration of a character who has been abruptly jettisoned, he does so using clumsy transitions such as "What was young Ricardo Fronesis doing while the story of his ancestors was being told?"[9] In the same manner, he divides the text into chapters, not to separate topics or indicate the passage of time, but rather as arbitrary breaks in the narration. As a result of this capriciousness, many critics regard Lezama Lima as if he were Rousseau's gatekeeper for the Hispanic continent, an "innocent saint." Even Cortázar speaks of an "ingenuous American innocence which opens its eyes in an Orphic manner on the very beginning of creation," and he adds, "Lezama before the fall, Lezama Noah who, as represented in certain Flemish paint-ings, patiently attends to the embarcation of the animals."[10]

For Mario Vargas Llosa, Lezama Lima is a primitive in a state of per-petual wonder before the brilliant objects that he has found in Western culture. He uses erudite references, myths, and readings as:

> simple "themes," objects that dazzle him because in his own imagina-tion he has surrounded them with virtues and values that have little to do with their use, but which he utilizes as propulsion for the thick river of metaphors, playing with them with the greatest freedom and even unscrupulousness.[11]

What Vargas Llosa appreciates is the imagination and inventiveness of an author who doesn't need to rely on "facts" or his observations of life. He seems to state, along with Vallejo, "It is important to smell like a madman, arguing how hot is the snow, how swift the tortoise." The critic and poet Armando Alvarez Bravo even goes so far as to say that the best passages of *Paradiso* are the ones containing the least empirical and autobiographical material. "For me, the imaginary elements in the text have more value than the real because of their energy, an energy that, paradoxically, manages to transform them in certain moments into reality." [12]

This point of view concurs with a contemporary school of thought that rejects reality as something inferior to the imagination or "creation." We could cite, for example, some of Cortázar's essays on the novel, or Mario Vargas Llosa's book on García Márquez, in which he states that the novelist is "God's replacement." Nevertheless, in Lezama Lima's case, this theory might overlook certain aspects of his work, perhaps even the most fundamental one. Because, as we have seen, *Paradiso* is an allegory, a genre that by definition relies on a system of references exterior to the novel itself. In Lezama Lima's novel, the allegorical nature is not evident in the first few chapters, but beginning with chapter 12, it is quite obvious. I am referring to various episodes whose symbolism is derived from Pythagorean theories or from an amalgam of theories about poetry. If we look at the incidents in chapter 12, for example: a child playing a game with his grandmother, who shows him a Danish vase; the history of a Roman legion; a dreamlike trip through the city; and the story of a music critic who survives for decades in a cataleptic state. Although these incidents appear unrelated, there is a common thread that runs through them all: that thread is resurrection, even though it appears to have taken the wrong road (earthly glory, prolonging the life of the body, and so on). In chapter 13, Cemí reappears traveling on a bus where he meets up with his spiritual mentor, Oppiano Licario, the man who accompanied his father on his death bed. The bus, which bears no resemblance to ordinary buses, takes the reader to an atemporal zone, as Lezama Lima explains to us:

> This encounter was outside time in an almost oneiric dimension on a bus propelled by the bull's head which turned the gears of a bus. This bus does not refer to the usual Aristotelian causation but rather is a bus like those vehicles, those Mediaeval embarcations which brought together two worlds.[13]

Dream and vision become the portals to the "other" world, the invisible world. We will set this grotesque vehicle aside for the moment and continue following Lezama Lima's allegory.

In the final chapter, Cemí undertakes a mystical journey through a passageway in Oppiano Licario's house, in which he discovers relics of the Holy Grail and which eventually leads him to the illuminated center where Licario's cadaver is placed. Licario's sister serves as his guide during this final stage of the search; she gives Cemí Oppiano's message about the resurrection and the defiance of time. The novel ends where poetry begins—"hesicastical rhythm: we can begin."

There is no doubt that Lezama Lima had allegorical intentions. He has even explained some of the hermetic allusions on several occasions. We must also remember that, by its very nature, allegory leans toward hermeticism. In the Middle Ages and the Renaissance, it meant "an obscure intention," something hidden from the masses, only accesible to those who dedicated themselves to reading. It is impossible that Lezama Lima was unaware of this tradition. Widely read, he is a pathfinder along the forgotten trailways of literature. Besides, literature doesn't have a past for Lezama Lima; it is always in the present tense, in such a manner that allegory is built from a widely varied collection of material taken from poetic theory, Pythagoreanism, Orphianism, and neo-Platonic theories. One can read *Paradiso* without knowing all of this, but the chapters that the critics believe demonstrate the most "imagination" are precisely the ones that rely the most on allegorical interpretation. The very names of the characters point toward a hidden intention: Cemí means "sign"; Oppiano, the name of a Latin poet, refers to poetic aspirations given that Licario follows Icaro. Fronesis is a name taken from a Platonic dialogue. This plan seems to me to be the opposite of the type of symbolism that allows the reader freedom by the multivalence of allusions.

Nevertheless, this same intention to hypostasize poetry leads to unexpected results. Writing an allegory in the twentieth century is not the same as writing an allegory in the sixteenth century. Currently, there is no one common culture for all educated people. Speaking about Persephone in the sixteenth century touched on a common code; in the twentieth century it sounds odd because it no longer belongs to a common symbolic system used by everyone. Thus, when he makes mythological allusions, Lezama Lima highlights the impossibility of comparing the modern world with the Greek world. The effect of this lack of congruency can be seen clearly in the following description of a bull (or minotaur) whose head is on a Cuban *guagua* [bus]:

> To the right of the steering wheel, a circle of burnished steel spun its pinions led by the decapitated head of a bull. The head went round when the bus was going at top speed, its horns shined like phosphorus beginning to glow. Suddenly the head sketched a red note, exhaustion brought up the tip of its tongue and the excited phosphorus of the horns began to dim. The bus was abandoning itself to sluggishness.[14]

The first impression is that the author is sticking out his tongue at us. The pompous, "cultured" nature of the description—*testa* for head, for example—instead of highlighting the solemnity of the search, produces a comic or, more succinctly, grotesque effect. The grotesque, always produced when incompatible elements are mixed together,[15] is characterized by the simultaneous presence of the ridiculous and the monstrous. In times past, fighting with the minotaur meant battling death; thus our bewilderment when faced with this comic bull.

Instead of the harmony that was so prized by Renaissance men, or the "measured" tone that characterized traditional allegory, Lezama Lima presents us with the opposite: a world in reverse, a lack of equilibrium, a world that is ruled by King Momo. Consider another example, a description of a grandmother whose memory leaps over the years to bring the remote past closer to the present.

> Her ninety-four years were like wands in the hands of Cagliostro's gnomes. Just as in some painters objects move in front of their spatial accommodation, time had escaped from its succession to situate itself on favorite, tyrannical planes, as if Persephone and the polis of the present seemed to have such domestic cordiality that they hid the asymmetries of their extraction, the laments of their vanished wanderings (p. 112).

On reading this passage, one forgets about the grandmother because the images are strung out in such an exaggerated manner that they command center stage: the little canes in elves' hands; the deformed perspective of the painting; the association of "Persephone" and the "polis of the present." Each element seems to spring to life of its own accord, and lead us far away from the original referent. Thus, the effect of estrangement, very common in modern poetry, is produced, but it goes much further than a mere linguistic effect. There is a fundamental discord between Persephone and the polis of the present—in other words, between a mythology that was viable in Europe until the eighteenth century and the remote, alienated Cuban society. The Greek aristocratic values, which would also be those of the aristocracy during the Renaissance, had already lost their meaning in bourgeois society and even more so in a dependent society like prerevolutionary Cuba, where there was an additional degree of remove. To speak of Cuba in language appropriate to Greek society does not bring the two cultures closer together, rather it highlights the distance between them. This distance is revealed at the beginning of the novel by the mix of naturalism and the fantastic:

> Baldovina's hand separated the edges of the mosquito netting and felt around, squeezing softly as if a sponge were there and not a five-year-old boy. She opened the boy's nightshirt and examined his chest covered with welts, brightly colored furrows, inflating and contracting in a great effort to achieve a natural rhythm. Then she unfastened the flap of his nightshirt and looked at his thighs, his small testicles full of welts growing larger, and as she moved her hands down she felt his cold and trembling legs. Just then, at the stroke of midnight, the lights went out in the houses on the military post and went on in the sentry boxes. The lanterns of the patrolling sentries created a flickering monster that rose up out of the puddles, scaring the black-beetled shadows.
>
> Baldovina was desperate, disheveled. She needed help now: each time she drew back the mosquito netting, she saw the body lying there and the welts on it more prominent. To assuage her terrified urge to run away, she pretended to search for the servant coupe at the other end of the house. She looked like the royal wet nurse in charge of the little prince, retreating room by room through the burning castle, obedient to the orders of her fleeing master and mistress (p. 3).

The lexicon used in this description comes from two different codes: first, that of diagnostic naturalism and, second, that of literature of the fantastic and fairy tales. Verbs such as *hurgó* [squeezed], *separó* [she separated], *abrió* [opened] suggest a diagnosis since they refer to the body and its infirmities (testicles covered with welts). They belong to practical, daily life, like the humble sponge and the servant. But at the magical hour of midnight, everything is transformed, just like in a fairy tale. The lantern outside resembles a *monstruo errante* [flickering monster]. Baldovina becomes a stewardess and the house a castle. The parents of the sick child are absent, leaving him exposed to all the dark forces of sickness and nightmares. And according to tradition in the narrative of the grotesque, the reader is at the same time conscious of two very different levels: the daily world and the nightmare. From now on, the house is transformed into a dream land-scape; even the welts on the child's body "seem" to be animals capable of jumping out of bed and "moving of their own accord." The two servants who come to help Baldovina are transformed into strangers—one seems to be a "secular clergyman from Ivan the Terrible's era." The servant, Trini-dad, is compared to the Holy Spirit, and her husband is compared to Saint Christopher. But we are not really dealing with a comparison, because you can only compare things that have some aspect in common.

It is characteristic of Lezama Lima's style that the word *parece* [re-sembles] introduces a term that is totally dissimilar. Some critics attribute this disparity to "poetic license," and claim it demonstrates Lezama Lima's creative abilities. For Julio Ortega, however, the strange comparisons fre-quently refer to the hidden symbolism of the novel. The scene with the servants, for example, marks the first appearance of a triangle (also of the name Trinity) which is one of the recurring symbols in the novel.[16] Never-theless, Ortega seems to overlook the grotesque aspect of the scene.

Perhaps one could find a precedent in Góngora's poetry and in the con-ceptualism of the Golden Age, which also used metaphor to link disparate elements. But the aim of the Golden Age writer was to impress and to show off his inventive powers, not to introduce a comic or absurd aspect in a work whose tone was serious or tragic. Julio Ramón Ribeyro approaches a more exact description of Lezama Lima's style when he states, "This system of cultural references which are without relevance in our time, be-cause of this very fact—like those objects of everyday use which acquire artistic value with time—take on in Lezama Lima's prose an ornamental value."[17]

Furthermore, Ribeyro emphasizes the ironic impact of this translation of yesterday's cultural references to the contemporary world. But we must ask ourselves the motivation behind this ironic effect, because the gro-tesque and the ironic are not the same thing. For now, we will limit the term *grotesque* to descriptions such as that of the bus or Baldovina rescu-ing the child from the burning castle, both of which separate themselves from the original term of the comparison in order to transform themselves into autonomous images. The irony is transparent in the episode in which Rialta speaks about prisoners who come to do yardwork:

"You understand, orders from on high," they said savagely, and the soursops began to bleed milk, their flesh showed a smile of the milk of human kindness. Somehow these lines from Shakespeare came to mind, and the flash of the pomegranates brought to mind a line from Mallarmé. Bald and girded with zebra skins as they were, they exchanged cigarettes with their guards. I doubt that the powers of persuasion of Shakespeare's secrets, or Mallarmé's, would have stopped those canailles from invading the marine honeycomb of the soursops and strawberries (p. 125).

"Culture" comes face to face with barbarism here, although it is an ineffective confrontation. The *canailles* destroy the fruit in the garden and invade the orchard; Rialta's eloquence and cultured irony are powerless to stop them. Her protests are made with an irony that is too subtle for the prisoners to understand. Lezama Lima's ideal of a cultured, aristocratic society that tends its garden is clearly outlined here—an ideal that must be reached (if it can be reached) in a society with no shared culture and that doesn't understand. Barbarism is present within the garden itself, waging acts of destruction and preventing the development of an aristocratic culture.

In addition to the grotesque and the ironic, there is another prominent style in this book. I am referring to what is called "mock heroic" in English—in other words, a burlesque imitation of what is heroic. It is important to distinguish here between the parody of a style and the burlesque or carnavalesque imitation of certain actions, given that the English term encompasses both of these intentions. In *Paradiso*, the two are complementary, because many times words translate the burlesque meaning of actions. In fact, *Paradiso*'s tone is rooted not only in the carnavalesque but also in the traditional Cuban figure of the *negro catedrático* [black professor],[18] an Afro-Cuban person who uses cultured, erudite words when more common words would be appropriate. This is the linguistic equivalent of the carnaval rite in which a slave wears the master's clothes in order to make fun of him.

Several literary antecedents are also worth noting, such as Valle-Inclán's *Sonatas* [The Sonatas], where we find "heroic" language and acts that come close to parody. The tone in Valle-Inclán's last novels is definitely that of parody and nonsense, while that of *Sonatas* is ambiguous and borders on the grotesque and the mock heroic. In *Sonatas*, nostalgia for the heroic lingers in spite of the mockery. The same thing happens in *Paradiso*, where, alongside the absurd, ridiculous, or trivial nature of the events that take place, a noble, generous, heroic lifestyle can also be intuited.

Like *Sonatas*, *Paradiso* does not represent future possibilities, rather it is a comparison between a glorious past and a degraded present: the father of Cemí, just like the Marqués de Bradomín, is a heroic man who lacks a heroic context. Another masterpiece in the mock heroic style is *The Dunciad* of Alexander Pope, a work that attacks contemporary literature (while parody normally destroys that of the past), demonstrating the impossible abyss between the literature and society of the Golden Age and that of the eighteenth century. What destroys the possibility for a truly heroic literature for Pope is the trivial nature of life and the meanness of contemporary men compared to men of the past. Heroic gestures are empty and meaningless in eighteenth-century England, and, in a reciprocal manner, trivial events are elevated and given significance through the use of pompous language.

It seems to me that *Paradiso* draws on the tradition of the *negro catedrático* as heavily as if it were a literary tradition, or at least a common vision with writers like Pope or Valle-Inclán for whom the epic serves as a model, despite the impossibility of resurrecting yesterday's heroes. Epic and mythic references abound. For example, an old servant of the colonel's goes on a mission to save her son's life. In contrast to an epic poem, however, the incident is based on a simple error: her son is not in danger. Nevertheless, the author highlights the similarity between Mamita's gesture and the missions of times past: "In spite of its briefness the scene had something of antique grandeur, garbed in Cuban dress" (p. 30).

On other occasions the characters repeat the feats of ancient heroes. For example, the Danish doctor, Selmo Copek, who is visiting Kingston with the colonel, suddenly finds himself enveloped in a cloud that emanates from beneath the arm of a traffic policeman, which the author compares to "a concentrated cloud of dense steel-blue, like those that enveloped Hera or Athena when they moved among the Trojan or Achaen combattants" (p. 30).

If this scene causes laughter, how will the reader respond when presented with the following: a student from the countryside, who habitually masturbates in class, is caught by the teacher:

> The roll of dice thrown by the gods out of boredom that morning
> was to be completely adverse for the violent arrogance of the powerful
> rustic. The last of the teacher's explanatory syllables resounded like a

funeral rattle on the island of Cyprus. Leaving at the end of class, the students had the look of people waiting to be disciplined, waiting for the Druid priest to perform the sacrifice (p. 199).

Not only are the references to Cyprus and Druids jumbled but the solemn and portentous tone is applied to a vulgar and trivial incident. The text literally speaks out of tune, and the discord allows us to perceive the absence of the enchantment that in ages past accompanied the most minute details of life. The fact that Lezama Lima is not careful about the appropriateness of the comparison is another proof that he is more interested in pointing out the absence of the heroic than in looking for similarities. Frequently, as in the following description, the mythological comparison is grotesquely exaggerated. Here Adonis is surprised in a homosexual embrace, and succumbs only metaphorically.

> The great athlete showed all the perfection of his body, made iridescent by the retrocopulative eon. The Adonis was succumbing in ecstasy to the fang of the bristly creature. The two wretches, standing at first, now shot through with the tension of electricity that inundated them, began to relax, curving down the descending parabola of pleasure. Then the Adonis, with the expiration of the process, bit the wooden bedstead. The cry of the defeated gladiator, who once before had bitten a pole on the field of tourney, was heard again when he rendered to the fang of the young boar, the triumphant novice (p. 244).

Lezama Lima plays freely with mythological references — the legend of Adonis really serves as a pretext for creating an "epic" or "heroic" atmosphere for a banal, and perhaps even embarassing, act. The *lidia* [battle] has become a homosexual act, the triumph of male pleasure. In almost all of the episodes that have been mentioned, the effect is comical, with carnavalesque overtones. Perhaps the humorous tone also comes from the sexual theme. This may be seen clearly in the adventures of Farraluque who has sex with the servants, boys, and even the cook when they are locked up together on Sunday afternoons. In this episode, the cup and lance of the Grail are transformed into a bucket and a paintbrush, and the boy finds a world in reverse (like carnaval), which means total liberty.

In many other scenes, even against a background of violence or tragedy, the element of parody does not entirely disappear. For example, a battle between students and the police is presented as a fight between the forces of light and the forces of darkness. The leader of the students is compared to Apollo and the struggle is converted into a holy war. The violence of the scene is diluted by the picturesque. For example, a soldier mounted on a black horse wounds a student in the cheek. Instead of violence, the reader seems to attend a chivalric joust. At the same time, brutal reality sometimes erupts: "They turned their faces away, and then real terror overcame them when they saw in the distance the haunches of the black horses and the vengeful look that was being cast on them, now that blood had been shed" (p. 222).

For a moment, the reader sees a Cuba in which students are jailed, tortured, and killed, but the view changes quickly. In the next moment, we return to the mythological battle.[19] This example shows the fundamentally ahistoric focus of the text which converts the students into archetypal symbols of culture (light, Apollo, and so on) and the soldiers into archetypes of combat and war. It is the old battle of the pen and the sword.

I do not wish to imply that violence is relegated to a secondary plane, however, because it is introduced in a manner that does not require concrete references to historical events. Perhaps more directly than it addresses violence, the book addresses the frustration and desperation of people like the colonel or Rialta, who do not have any opportunities to explore their options. The colonel is a soldier without a war, a man whose talents can only be employed in military exercises, and who dies ignominiously of the flu during the epidemic of 1919. Rialta spends her childhood in exile, where she loses a brother in an accident and enjoys only a few years of happiness before losing her husband, then her brother Alberto. Nevertheless, neither the colonel nor Rialta are really tragic characters because the context prohibits tragedy. We see why this is the case by examining two scenes—the moment that Cemí's sister, Violante, is almost drowned, and the occasion on which Rialta, his mother, undergoes surgery to remove a tumor. The first occurs at a swimming pool where the father has taken his children to make them stronger and healthier:

> José Cemí could see his sister, with the pineapple-leaf hair of a tiny gorgon, glassed in at the bottom of the pool. Two aides ran to the frightening submersion with long poles ending in curved tridents for cleaning the bottom of the pool, and began the extraction with magical opportuneness. Straddling the fork, Violante ascended to the kingdom of the living like a little Eurydice. Blood and leaves covered her

legs, the leaves of damp ivy that appeared when the water receded and the calcified walls turned purple straining to receive the welcome air (p. 129).

The ornamental language effectively turns Violante into a figure that is more symbolic than real. Even her suffering is glossed over, because when she returns to life her pain is diluted by a complex comparison with the walls of the swimming pool: "the calcified walls turned purple straining to receive the welcome air." Lezama Lima wants to keep the reader at a distance, and perhaps this corresponds to his vision of death as the threshold of another life rather than an end point. As with the description of Adonis, the comparison between Violante and Eurydice is not accurate given that the latter remained in the realm of Pluto. This is another method of reducing the impact of death and preventing tragedy in the text.

The passage that describes Alberto's death provides another example of how Lezama Lima diminishes the impact of a scene involving death. At first, the author appears to ascribe great solemnity to José Cemí's uncle's death, because, before dying, he hears some mysterious predictions from a Mexican musician. The guitar music that the Mexican plays triggers a series of fantastic visions for Alberto, who sees Chinese gardeners resting on the backs of tortoises who are chewing lettuce. Without exploring all the potential meanings of these visions, we can see that they are related to the esoteric theme of the book and, more precisely, they refer to the Tao. Unlike Violante and Rialta, however, Alberto really dies. Nevertheless, despite all the foreshadowing, his death is not a solemn event; rather, it happens casually:

> The driver, carried away by the singing in the dawn breeze, had failed to see the gate that had dropped to cut off traffic, and a locomotive, refusing to stain the neatness of the morning with a whistle, pulled its last car into the vehicle's path. The driver felt his chest cave in; Alberto, in the quick stop, shot forward against the windshield, was cut on the face, and as the blood began to flow, a second lurch snapped his neck, and he fell lifeless (p. 195).

Death is reduced to a cliché ("he fell lifeless") whose banality seems to erase the expectations built up by the Mexican's song and Alberto's defiant attitude. It is as if Caesar, leaving the forum, died run over by a horse instead of stabbed to death by his enemies. Lezama Lima eliminates the tragedy of death in a deliberate, calculated manner. On the other hand, the

death of the colonel, also accidental, is described with a certain element of
pathos, above all in an episode in which he converses with the only Cuban
in the hospital, Oppiano Licario:

> Tears filled the Colonel's face. When he heard what Oppiano was say-
> ing, he smiled with deep joy. He made an effort to breathe again and
> turned his head. He was dead. Beside him, the friend whom he'd met
> that morning. His joy had ended in the absolute solitude of hospital
> and death (p. 154).

The deaths of Alberto and the colonel lack transcendent tragedy: first,
because there is no collective memory to remember them, and, second, because the circumstances of their lives impede the possibility of a death that
is congruent with their lives. Alberto does not die as a bohemian, nor the
colonel as a soldier. Although Lezama Lima tries to bring them as close
to lofty, noble antecedents as possible, he cannot achieve a tragic effect. It
is not Cuban reality that betrays him. The example of Martí and the attack on the Moncada had demonstrated that heroism was a possibility in
twentieth-century Cuba. If it does not enter into Lezama Lima's vision, it
is because the world is a book for this writer and everything must be written into a book before it can achieve greatness. This focus is linked to the
artist's position in countries like Cuba, which is that of acting as a channel or transmitter of Western culture, which is absorbed through its best
works, without awareness of the fact that these are made up of language,
ideological themes, and motifs elaborated by a dialectic between imagination and reality.

A writer like Lezama Lima can easily reconstruct his own version of the
myth of the creator using fragments of the Western tradition, while maintaining his belief that the ordinary deaths of his father and his uncle will
finally achieve transcendence by their inclusion in his book. But even when
we believe that Lezama Lima has inverted true values (as I believe that he
has), it does not diminish the importance of *Paradiso*, which shows, like no
other book of this century, the impossibility of absolute or universal values,
and their true condition of "relative norms." The colonel's stoicism, for
example, not only appears to be a useless virtue but also becomes dangerous and counterproductive. It is clear that Lezama Lima always tries to
salvage something from the degradation, even if it is something as unmen-
tionable as Rialta's tumor, which he describes in a picturesque tone as if it
were an exotic object:

Inside a transparent vessel, a kind of crystal pot, was the fibrome, the size of a large ham. In the part of the vessel where it was resting, the tissue was turning purple with the more rapid detention of blood there. The rest of the fibrome still showed bright red tissue, weakened into pink or growing into an oven red. Some blue strips stood out from the rest of that excess flesh, collecting the white-capped coloration of a rainbow surrounded by still ominous clouds. The tissues through which the scalpel had slipped appeared more polished, as if it had been caressed by the steel in its most elaborated delicacy of penetration. In its visible fragment it resembled a peninsula cut out of a map, with its eruptive traces, strange lava flows, its orographic arrogances and its traces of hydrographic slides. Those unfeeling fibers inside the glass jar looked like a dragon run through by a lance, by a ray of light, by a thread of energy capable of destroying those mines of cardboard and carbon, extending through its galleries like a hand that goes along opening, until it left undecipherable inscriptions on oscillating walls, as if its base were advised by the advances and retreats of the waters of coral penetration, dreamy, which reach hillocks that stand out from the tamped-down surface of the damp and metallic night. The fibrome still looked like a coral living in its subterranean arborescence (p. 322).

This is a good example of how Lezama Lima tries to elevate a banal, daily topic and give it a loftier meaning. Despite a few common phrases ("a large ham," for example), despite the clinical references to a scalpel, the reader soon forgets the first level as she enters the true geography of subterranean caverns, coral reefs, and landscapes that are populated by mythological figures (St. George and the Dragon). This descriptive orgy can even be justified because it relates this passage to the larger theme of the novel. The tumor on the mother's womb takes on a symbolic meaning given that it signifies Cemí's separation from his family in order to continue his search with two friends, Fronesis and Foción. The tumor alienates him from his mother, just as madness will later distance him from Foción. Nevertheless, this symbolism (and here we can mention Lukács)[20] seems superimposed, as opposed to developing from the internal logic of the text. The tumor's colors suggest the golden hues of the *Book of Hours*, and the water in which it is preserved "has something of 'theion Hudor,' of divine water." We might think, on reading these sentences and linking them with the references to mother and dragon (in other words, the terms from alchemy that signify the philosophical rock), that we have the key to the hidden meanings and the novel is analogous to the purifying process which alchemists must conduct. In this interpretation, the tumor symbolizes the artist's creation, which is not engendered as one conceives children but rather is the result of a deformation of nature.

This interpretation is not implausible, given that the text refers constantly to archetypes and flees from the concrete materiality of life. This is clearly seen in many of the erotic episodes, which almost always involve three, not two, people. Love between a couple, between a man and a woman, even when it seems happy, never achieves any type of transcendence. In the case of Celia and Nicolás, the parents of Foción, for example, erotic life turns into a type of daily routine. They close the windows "when passion is more forceful than the breeze, and at midnight they open the doors and windows so that the breeze can blow over spent passion." The introduction of a third person, the "one who eternally waits, Juliano," transforms the situation, and turns routine into tragedy. The third person is a constant in the erotic scenes. He frequently observes from a distance, which increases passion; Farraluque's amorous adventures, for example, always include a couple and someone who observes. In New York, Foción falls in love with a brother and a sister. Godofredo spies on Fileba and Eufrasio through a crack in the wall. These scenes of love and passion provoke a mixture of laughter and disgust, repulsion and attraction. The participants themselves sometimes have conflicting feelings. Simply reading the description of Eufrasio and Fileba's love is enough to convince the reader that the author wanted to achieve a grotesque effect. Eufrasio ties his testicles together with a rope "in order to achieve the most passion and the furthest distance from his lover;" meanwhile, Fileba's eyes display "a glance like a halcyon's dead in the stormy coldness, drifting into eternity wide-eyed" (p. 218).

The scenes involving Juliano's lovers (he dies during an orgasm), recall a similar incident from Valle-Inclán's "Sonata de Otoño" [Autumn Sonata] that also triggers contradictory responses. When Lucía meets up with Fronesis at the movie theater, the pair are not only spied on by Cemí and Foción, but they also watch the love story of Tristan and Isolde on the screen, retold in a grotesque manner:

> The projector was now passing through a tempestuous darkness. Isolde runs to the seashore; the bird flies off with the golden hair from her locks, wheeling once round the braids knotted tightly on top of her head. She lies down onto the sand, dozing off. A crab, unable to hide

his surprise, cannot penetrate the circle that surrounds her, where even the waves in a prolongation of voluptuous dissatisfaction lap and recede (p. 273).

The abbreviated images on the screen mirror Foción and Cemí's feelings as they watch Fronesis, whom they could see when the screen was bright. Mystery and dissatisfaction, which are the principals of wisdom, are heightened by distance and ignorance. Not knowing causes and effects reduces the observer to an ignorant child's level, but at the same time gives him a child's vision, free of adult constraints. As we have seen, the aim of allegory is not to clarify but rather to hide; in the same manner the grotesque and the carnavalesque are forms of mixing, bringing together that which is normally kept apart. Confusion is the opposite of clarification. Lezama Lima's goal is not a deeper understanding. Rather he seeks to return the reader to a prelogical state, and, at the same time, to surround the most banal events and characters with mystery and suggestions of divinity.

The naturalist writer tries to bring the reader so close to characters that they lose all mystery and are completely exposed. Lezama Lima, on the other hand, tries to preserve banality and suggest divine presence. For this reason he rarely presents characters directly; he prefers to evoke or suggest them, as in this scene in which Cemí's father looks at Rialta's house through the blinds:

> The blinds' play converted the domicile of the new neighbors into a polyhedron whose lights converged on the momentary edge of the blinds. For him the newcomers became fragments of chance and mystery, sparks surrounding the blinds with a plane of massaged and divided light, his vision retaining fragments which he could not reconstruct in the totality of a body or a situation, so that they continued their caress with an undefined and floating voluptuousness (p. 72).

Surrounding people with mystery is the first step. It is necessary to break with convention, to fragment the everyday vision in order to perceive the hidden wholeness, the wholeness that is the poet's goal. At the end of the novel when Cemí arrives at the room where Oppiano Licario's corpse lies, it is in order to receive the poet's inheritance; Oppiano "in a silence that was as prolonged as the tide, gave him the key and the mirror" (pp. 615–16). But at this point the novel appears to the reader to be a contradictory project. The reader must wait at the door; he or she cannot follow Cemí and enter poetry's paradise unless he or she is a poet. The novel has to suggest "the invisible world, without revealing it; it has to re-introduce mystery into a world that is too obvious and too easily explained, but without offering us the key." Hence the need for allegory, hermetic symbolism, and the grotesque.

Today, when taking the historical situation into account, *Paradiso* appears to be a negative work. From independence until 1959, Cuba's history offers a spectacle of degradation, lies, and subordination to the sugar-growing monopolies, which leaves us with very few real examples of human dignity. Lezama Lima tries to erase reality, to look for something timeless and dignified; he finds it in the concepts of "culture" and "poetry" as expressions of purity and altruism. *Paradiso* represents a formidable struggle against the contingency in which everything that is unnatural is used to fight against nature in order to overcome it. Nevertheless, it is an unequal battle.

What *Paradiso* demonstrates is the relativity of culture and the impossibility of looking at Cuban society through the lens of archetypes, since the comparisons turn out to be false and repetitions end in deformations. As in carnaval, dressing as the king only serves to proclaim one's real condition of slavery. When Lezama Lima seizes upon Greek mythology, esoteric books, and all of the Western tradition that exalts the writer, he does not produce a tribute but rather a parody that allows us to see the limitations of this culture and its impotence. The colonel and Alberto cannot live important, heroic lives because this is not an option for them. Colonial society does not achieve dignity and autonomy. This impossibility is passed into the style of the book, in the mismatches, the lack of harmony, and the grotesque. Far from diminishing the value of *Paradiso*, this impossibility demonstrates that the novel has reached a deep level of truth.

Until 1959, the writer's profession separated him from the rest of society, and gave him more lofty values than those of the society which surrounded him. But this separation is dangerous, for the writer is often left behind by historical events. What is interesting about *Paradiso* is that it shows the impossibility of this project, since even when the writer wants to express heroism or tragedy he must resort to irony and parody. The colonized man cannot totally liberate his imagination from the conditions which limit him.

NOTES

1 José Lezama Lima, *Orbita de Lezama Lima*, ed. Armando Alvarez Bravo (Havana: Unión Nacional de Escritores y Artistas de Cuba, 1966) 42–44.

2 Guillermo Cabrera Infante, *Tres tristes tigres* (Barcelona: Editorial Seix Barral, 1965).

3 Lezama Lima's ideas about poetry can be found in his editorials for the magazine *Orígenes* as well as in various books of essays: *Introducción a los vasos órficos* (Barcelona: Barral Editores, 1971); *Sierpe de don Luis de Góngora* (Barcelona: Tusquets Editor, 1970); "Mitos y cansancio clásico," in *La expresión americana* (Madrid: Alianza Editorial, 1969).

4 José Lezama Lima, "Las imágenes posibles," in *Introducción a los vasos órficos*, 23.

5 Lezama Lima, *Orbita*, 31.

6 Ibid., 35.

7 Rosemary Tuve, *Elizabethan and Metaphysical Imagery* (Chicago: University of Chicago Press, 1947), 394.

8 A description of the "theme" of the novel was published in an interview with Armando Alvarez Bravo that was included in *Recopilación de textos sobre José Lezama Lima: Valorización múltiple* (Havana: Casa de las Américas, 1970) which, unfortunately, is missing from my shelves.

9 Julio Cortázar, "Para llegar a Lezama Lima," in *La vuelta al día en ochenta mundos* (Mexico: Siglo Veintiuno Editores, 1967), 137–155.

10 Ibid., 140.

11 Mario Vargas Llosa, "*Paradiso* de José Lezama Lima," in *Amaru I* (1967), 75.

12 From the interview with Alvarez Bravo in *Valorización multiple*.

13 Lezama Lima, *Orbita*, 25–26.

14 This and future citations from *Paradiso* are taken from José Lezama Lima, *Paradiso*, trans. Gregory Rabassa (New York: Farrar, Straus and Giroux, 1974), 406.

15 Philip Thomson, *The Grotesque* (London: Methuen 1972).

16 Julio Ortega, "Paradiso," in *La contemplación y la fiesta* (Caracas: Biblioteca Ayacucho, 1969), 77–116.

17 This citation is taken from an essay by Ribeyro which was originally published in *Eco* (Bogotá), and subsequently included in *Lezama Lima: Valorización múltiple* (Havana: Casa de las Américas, 1972).

18 I became aware of this thanks to a conversation with J. Portuondo.

19 Mario Vargas Llosa comments on this scene in which action seems to be subordinated to "plastic values" in his essay "*Paradiso* de José Lezama Lima."

20 There is an excellent discussion of Lukács's critique of symbolism in Fredric Jameson, *Marxism and Form* (Princeton, N.J.: Princeton University Press, 1972) 196–202.

THE CRISIS OF THE LIBERAL IMAGINATION
AND THE UTOPIA OF WRITING

It is as old a component of bourgeois ideology that each individual, in his particular interest, considers himself better than all others, as that he values the others, as the community of all customers, more highly than himself. Since the demise of the old bourgeois class, both ideas have led an after-life in the minds of intellectuals, who are at once the last enemies of the bourgeois and the last bourgeois. In still permitting themselves to think at all in the face of the naked reproduction of existence, they act as a privileged group; in letting matters rest there, they declare the nullity of their privilege. —ADORNO, *Minima Moralia*

I

*A*n ideological distinction is often made in contemporary criticism between literature in the established sense and *écriture*, between the text that reflects and the text that acts, between the mimetic and the nonmimetic, between the "readerly" and the "writerly."[1] These taxonomies are symptomatic of a crisis of the narrative in which the radical, and indeed revolutionary new criticism, challenges the very assumptions on which liberal humanistic criticism was based. The latter, now on the wane, though once dominant in Anglo-American criticism, had held literature to be a moral endeavor and the novel a genre to which "the emotions of understanding and forgiveness were indigenous, as if by the definition of the form itself"[2] In this vein, Lionel Trilling lamented in *The Liberal Imagination* (1950) the contemporary novel's loss of power and energy. "No connection exists," he declared, "between our liberal educated class and the best of the literary minds of our time." And this is to say that there is no connection between the political ideas of our educated class and the

Originally published in *Ideologies and Literatures* 1, no. 1 (December 1976–January 1977): 5–24.

deep places of the imagination.[3] The breakdown of connections between the social and the literary systems which the liberal humanist regarded as an apocalyptic prophesy of coming disaster was enthusiastically fostered by the avant-garde in its campaign against the reactionary canons of the past. The French new novelists, Structuralists, post-Structuralists, and others deconstructed the novel, finding that its codes, the concept of character, and even the tense in which it was generally written have been so many devices which "naturalized" the bourgeois order and thus reproduced its ideology.[4] Character, for instance, reflected a concept of human nature, "essential to the ideological domination and smooth economic running of society." Hence it was urgent to produce a new writing which could constitute a kind of practice that could not be reduced to reproduction and could therefore stave off and avoid recuperation by bourgeois society.[5] *Écriture* thus became a modal concept, distinct from literature in the old sense, and used to designate a variety of subversive practices—activity over passive receptivity, play over productive labor, the open as against the closed text. Between the new and the old writing, there was, it was claimed, a fundamental cleavage which was more than a revolt of the new against outworn conventions. Indeed the claim was made that *écriture* constituted a revolutionary practice.[6]

Turning to Latin America, we find a similar war between the ancient and the modern. The new novelists of the late fifties and early sixties attacked the traditional Latin American novel as "primitive" and "provincial" and promoted the new novel both as technically advanced and as a universal form of writing. However, the way that some of these new novelists distinguish their writing from the social novel which had predominated in the thirties and forties is revealing. For they stress the individual diversity and the subjectivity of the new novel as against the socially constructed view of reality which informs the primitive novel and gives it a certain sameness. The new novelists according to Mario Vargas Llosa "no se esfuerzan por expresar 'una' realidad, sino visiones y obsesiones personales: 'su' realidad" [do not try to express one universal reality, but rather personal visions and obsessions: "their" reality].[7] The primitive novel, he implies, is simple and invariable because its raw material is presented in an unsophisticated manner while the new novel employs complex techniques and is diversified. There is no need to stress that a model of production underlies this criticism so that the description of the difference between the new and the old novel seems to be precisely that which differentiated the recently modernized economies of Latin America from the monoculture which had predominated in the past. Such a comparison might appear mechanistic, were it not for the fact that it is explicit in criticism itself. Mario Vargas Llosa, for example, asserts that the "novela de creación" [creationist novel] (his term for the new novel) has not completely obliterated the primitive novel but that the two continue to coexist in the same culture, "como los rasca-cielos y las tribus, la miseria y la opulencia" [like skyscrapers and tribes, misery and opulence].[8] There could be no more patent association of the new novel with the ideology of modernization, with its outward manifes-tations in the skyscrapers and the conspicuous consumption of the middle classes; and the primitive novel which has its parallel in the backwardness of the marginalized sectors of the population. Just as, on the economic level, import substitution had diversified the economy, so in the novel, primitive production had been superseded by diversified and more com-plex techniques. "A diferencia de lo que pasaba con los primitivos, no hay un denominador común ni de asuntos ni de estilos ni de procedimientos entre los nuevos novelistas: su semejanza es su diversidad" [Unlike what happened with the primitive novelists, there is no common denominator either of subjects or style or method among the new novelists: their simi-larity is their diversity].[9]

   This concept of diversification lends a spurious unity to writers who shared in the euphoria of the "boom." In effect, however, there were funda-mental ideological differences between those liberal-existentialist writers who clung to a romantic conception of expressing their personal rebellion through their work; "revolutionary" writers who in the wake of Surreal-ism strove to bring about an alteration in the readers' perception of reality; and, on the extreme left (so to speak) those writers who believe that the old concepts of literature must be completely destroyed and a radically different practice which would eliminate the separation of reader from au-thor and critic constituted. For the latter, the cultural revolution was to be inaugurated in writing itself. Such fundamental ideological differences scarcely surfaced openly during the sixties, perhaps because, in the im-mediate aftermath of the Cuban Revolution, there was a certain group solidarity, in fact, almost a syndicalist spirit. This sense of solidarity (at any rate, up to the Padilla affair in 1968) tended to overlay the very con-siderable differences between the new novelists. Further, the success of the new novel tended to conceal the fact that there was a crisis in the market-place since the novel reached new sectors of the population only to lose a potential readership to the newer mass media. These crises and contra-dictions are most clearly manifested in a number of texts which reflect on writing itself. For this reason, I shall concentrate, in the present discussion, on three such narratives—*Aura* by Carlos Fuentes, "Las babas del diablo" [Blow-up] from the collection, *Las armas secretas* [Secret Weapons] by Cortázar, and *Cobra* by Severo Sarduy. Though written at different periods, and though they are quite diverse they share a common problem—that of producing a text which transgresses bourgeois society. I shall argue that in each of them a utopian space is suggested and determined by a negation of what they consider to be bourgeois but that in each case, such a concept is based on a now archaic stereotype—that of the individual enslaved by the ethic of work and production. And because the stage of bourgeois society to which they stand in opposition is outmoded, the textual revolution they promote may in fact be a reproduction of the mobility, freedom, metamorphosis (in other words the dance of the signifier)—which is the essence of technological society itself.

II

Notwithstanding his obsession with the modern and indeed with the modish, Carlos Fuentes is the most traditional of the three writers under discussion. Because his tendency is accumulative rather than dialectical, he piles new theoretical acquisitions onto old without laying bare or even recognizing the contradictions between them so that his initially mimetic view of the narrative has become overlaid by nonmimetic theories. "Myth," "imagination," "language," each in turn and sometimes together, are taken to be the positive dynamics of the new novel which sometimes is said to subvert society and sometimes is described as if it were a prediction or its shadow. These inconsistencies are particularly apparent in *La nueva novela hispanoamericana* [The New Spanish American Novel] (1969) part of which was written as early as 1964.[10] Thus at one point, he has the contemporary novel of Europe and North America embodying the myths and prophesies of a new era characterized by the "end of ideology" and the brave new world of technology. The capitalist-socialist dichotomy, he declares, is not now the predominant factor; "sino una suma de hechos—fríos, maravillosos, contradictorios, ineluctables, nuevamente libertarios, nuevamente enajenantes—que realmente están transformando la vida en las sociedades industriales: automatización, electrónica, uso pacífico de la energía atómica" [rather a sum of facts: cold, marvelous, contradictory, irresistible, newly liberating, newly alienating—that are really transforming life in the industrial societies: automation, electronics, the peaceful use of atomic energy].[11] It is not so much that the novel no longer reflects society but that it no longer reflects a "superseded" stage of the class struggle. When he turns to Latin America, however, Fuentes is concerned with modernity in another sense. As in the case of Mario Vargas Llosa, what is stressed as "modernity"—namely diversification and individualism—are the very qualities promoted by the technological-industrial era of dependency. He describes the new novel as "diversificada, crítica y ambigua" [diversified, critical and ambiguous], showing that, since the forties, it has progressed from "la tipicidad a la personalidad" [stereotyping to character], from "las disyuntivas épicas a la complejidad del aislamiento frente a la comunidad" [epic dilemmas to the complexity of isolation from the community] (pp. 26-27). This, it need hardly be stressed, is an individualistic vision with an emphasis on personality and on the isolation of the writer. It is therefore not surprising that, on the political plane, it should be translated into a plea for democratic pluralism and a belief that the monolithic Mexican political system would eventually be transformed by a more diversified economy. Thus he writes, "La diversificación económica, social y cultural de México acabará por imponer métodos y soluciones nuevas. El país no puede tener una sustancia moderna y una práctica anacrónica" [The economic, social and cultural diversity of Mexico will eventually impose new methods and solutions. The country cannot sustain a modern substance and an anachronic practice].[12] It is indeed curious that Fuentes, for all his modernity, should embrace beliefs that are not too different from the positivism of Herbert Spencer, who had been convinced that with industrialization and trade, all countries would inevitably progress toward democratic pluralism.

Behind such statements, there lies some kind of theory of reflection which would make politics and culture the mirrors of a stage of production. Yet Fuentes would also have literature released from this reflective role, so that it becomes the "pure contrast" to bourgeois society. This explains why he describes Borges as the pioneer of the new narrative since he identified freedom with the imagination and "con ambas constituye un nuevo lenguaje latinoamericano, que, por puro contraste, revela la mentira, la sumisión y la falsedad de lo que tradicionalmente pasaba por 'lenguaje' entre nosotros" [both of them constitute a new Latin American language, which, by pure contrast, reveals the lie, the submission and the falsity of what has traditionally passed for "language" among us] (p. 26). In the same essay he declares:

nuestra literatura es verdaderamente revolucionaria en cuanto le niega al orden establecido el léxico que éste quisiera y le opone el lenguaje de la alarma, la renovación, el desorden y el humor. El lenguaje, en suma, de la ambigüedad, de la pluralidad de significados, de la constelación de alusiones: de la apertura.

[our literature is truly revolutionary in that it denies the lexicon that the established order desires and instead opposes it with the language of warning, of renovation, of disorder and of humor. In sum, the language of ambiguity, plurality of signifiers, of a constellation of allusions: of an opening] (p. 32).

This statement is extremely significant since it touches the description of the "subversive" language of the new novel in terms which reflect the politics of the Echeverría *sexenio* [presidency], namely *pluralidad* [plurality] and *apertura* [opening]. What is represented as revolutionary is both a liberation from overt commitment and a value-free, open text which is freed from any possible anachronism of content. What had distinguished the old novel was its regional and social provincialism.

Form and technique are universal and therefore permit the writer to transcend, culturally at least, the "backwardness" of his native country. "Nuestra universalidad," he states, "nacerá de esta tensión entre el hacer cultural y el deber tecnológico, de esta insoportable tensión entre las formas de nuestra literatura, nuestro arte, nuestro pensamiento, inseparables de la totalidad, y las de-formas de nuestra economía, nuestra dependencia, separables, fragmentadas" [Our universality will be born out of this tension between cultural power and technological responsibilities, from this insufferable tension between the forms of our literature, our art, our thought, inseparable from the totality, and the de-formation of our economy, our divisible, fragmented dependence] (p. 35). The clear implication here is that culture is one and indivisible while the economy is not. In fact, the reverse seems to be true. The economy is part of a global system in which countries like Mexico are dependent precisely because other countries are developed. Culture like technology seems universal but it is a mistake to believe that because writers or technocrats can acquire universal skills and even develop them creatively that they are acting in a neutral or unmotivated context.

In May 1968, Fuentes was in Paris during the student demonstrations. It happened that 1968 was also an important date in Mexico and that the difference between May 1968 in France and October 1968 in Mexico was

to be instructive. In France one student was killed and the creative potential of the movement rapidly evaporated. In Mexico, hundreds of students
were killed and imprisoned for demanding the most basic human rights.
However, October 1968 produced a cultural response, in the writings of
José Revueltas, Elena Poniatowska, and many others. Yet it is May 1968 in
France which Fuentes celebrates as the vision of a utopia, with the artist as
the ideal type in the postrevolutionary society:

> 'L'Imagination au Pouvoir! . . . Los estudiantes de Francia le dieron
> un contenido grave e inmediato a las palabras visionarias y rebeldes
> de los artistas: el hombre, cada hombre, es capaz de definir su propio
> destino como un artista define, creándola, su propia obra. Y como una
> obra de arte y responsabilidad individual es la instancia suprema de la
> responsabilidad colectiva y, simultáneamente, lo es ésta de aquella.

> [Power to the imagination! . . . The French students gave serious and
> immediate substance to the visionary and rebellious artists' words:
> man, each man, is capable of defining his own destiny as an artist de-
> fines it by creating his own work. And just as a work of art and indi-
> vidual responsibility are the supreme examples of collective responsi-
> bility, so the reverse is also true.] [13]

This vision in which life becomes art and art life is not one that in Fuentes's
novels, at least, emerges from a social movement or has any social outcome. On the contrary his literary utopia turns out not to be in the future
but in the past.

To find a more detailed discussion of what constitutes revolutionary art,
we must turn to Cortázar who, in 1970 published his essay, "Literatura en
la revolución y revolución en la literatura" [Literature in the revolution
and revolution in the literature] in reply to the Colombian critic, Oscar
Collazos.[14] The position he defines here is the same as that of a much earlier
essay, "Situación de la novela" [Situation of the novel], written in 1954.[15]
Published when the influence of existentialism was at its height, this early
essay explains why Cortázar rejected the protest novel and socialist realism,
which, he argues, are motivated by conscious design and therefore do not
constitute explorations of the new. The realist novel reproduces language,
feeling and passions "por medio de un cuidado método racional" [by means
of a careful, rational method] while the new (existential) novel incorporates "su propia teoría, de alguna medida la crea y la anula a la vez porque
sus intenciones son su acción y presentación puras" [its own theory, in a

way creating it and negating it at the same time, because its intentions are its action and its pure presentation]. Between 1954 and 1970, in both his critical and literary texts, he was to emphasize the superiority of the open work and of the novel as a form of cognition and self-exploration. "Literatura en la revolución y revolución" [Literature in the Revolution] is, therefore, the coherent development of a theory of writing as self-discovery and of the writer as exemplary. In 1970, he explicitly states that the writer himself, in order to create great literature, must have reached a high stage of development since it is this achievement alone which allows him to address those who have not yet embarked on the journey, "incitando con las armas que le son propias a acceder a esa libertad profunda que sólo puede nacer de la realización de los más altos valores de cada individuo" [inciting them with his own weapons to accept this profound liberty that can only be born of the realization of the highest values of each individual].

By its very nature, Cortázar's path of liberation is only open to the few; and this minority, as he wrote in 1954, could not be incorporated in public life: "no estarán instalados en el poder, ni dictarán desde la cátedra las fórmulas de la salvación. Serán tan sólo individuos que mostrarán sin docencia alguna una libertad humana alcanzada en la batalla personal" [they will not hold positions of power, nor will they teach the formulas of salvation from the university]. In 1970, his earlier elitism has been modified but the literary revolucion—"la revolución total y profunda en todos los planos de la materia y de la psiquis" [the total and profound revolution of all material and psychic levels]—is more than ever necessary if the material and social revolution is to be completed. Nor surprisingly, the truly revolutionary writer devotes himself, not simply to protest but to the creation of "una literatura de fermento y contenido revolucionarios" [a literature of revolutionary ferment and content]. Cortázar thus privileges literature beyond all other forms of human activity although his ultimate vision like that of many utopian socialists is the fusion of art and life.

An even more extreme view of the revolutionary nature of writing has however, been suggested by another generation of writers[16] who, in the age of the mass media, see the supreme danger of making literature into something consumable. The most theoretical of these younger writers is Severo Sarduy, a Cuban living in Paris and associated with Roland Barthes, Phillipe Sollers, and other contemporary French critics. His work, however, is not simply a translation of French critical theory but is profoundly marked by the influence of Bataille and Paz and by his own personal obsessions.

Sarduy adopts a view that bourgeois society is supported by a system of writing which, because it has structured people's whole perception of themselves and the world consolidates the status quo and ensures that even literature that is revolutionary in intention reproduces its subliminal order. Thus he declares:

> I believe contrary to what many of my friends think that the real support of the bourgeoisie is not an economic system, that is, not solely an economic system. I'd like to propose the following thesis: the support of the petit bourgeoisie, is a pseudo-natural system of writing. Every regime rests on writing. A revolution that doesn't invent its own writing has failed. The role of the writer is so important that I would even ask: what can be more than a writer? What's the point of all those acts of "confrontation" except for writing, because writing is a force that demythologizes, corrupts, mines, cracks the foundation of any regime. The epistemological breakthrough that everyone talks about so much has not happened and cannot happen—we know that after all of *Tel Quel*'s efforts among others—unless it begins with and is nurtured in a piece of writing.[17]

It is hardly necessary to comment on the idealistic nature of this statement which inverts the Marxist relationship between base and superstructure, nor to stress that, like Fuentes and Cortázar, Sarduy makes the writer into the modern hero. Yet he is more specific than they in suggesting that the transgression of bourgeois society is achieved by a self-referential form of writing:

> Lo único que la burguesía no soporta, lo que la "saca de juicio" es la idea de que *el pensamiento pueda pensar sobre el pensamiento*, de que *el lenguaje pueda hablar del lenguaje*, de que *un autor no escriba sobre algo, sino escriba algo*. Frente a esta transgresión, que era para Bataille el sentido del *despertar*, se encuentran repentina y definitivamente de acuerdo, creyentes y ateos, capitalistas y comunistas, aristócratas y proletarios, lectores de Mauriac y Sartre.

> [The only thing that the bourgeoisie will not tolerate, that "drives it crazy," is the idea that *thought can think about thought*, that *language can talk about* language, that *an author doesn't write about something, but rather he writes something*. Faced with this transgression, which for Bataille was *awakening*, believers and atheists, capitalists and communists, aristocrats and proletarians, readers of Mauriac and Sartre sud-

denly and definitively found themselves to be in agreement with each other.] [18]

What separates different members of society from the enlightened is here neither class nor religious or political convictions but the revolution of self-referentiality; only when thought and writing reflect on their own practices, and are therefore no longer instruments *for* something can the "awakening" take place. The question that now arises is whether self-referentiality can be regarded as a transgression or merely an activity which registers withdrawal and disapproval like the Medieval friars' vow of poverty. It also behooves us to enquire whether that bourgeois whose prejudices are transgressed is not a mythic creation, or at least a phantom of a repressive order whose character has, since the nineteenth century, radically changed. For in present-day society, it is not a *bourgeois individual* who counts, but rather a global system which is kept stable by repressive tolerance in the metropolis and by direct violence in the periphery, especially where the dominant order has been directly challenged by political action.

The answer to this and to other questions raised by these writers can however best be answered by an examination of their creative writing. Fuentes's "pure contrast" to bourgeois society, Cortázar's "revolution in literature," and Sarduy's "transgression," after all, are theories which have emerged from the practice of writing itself.

III

Carlos Fuentes's writing is of two distinct kinds; on the one hand, there are a number of tightly constructed allegorical narratives such as *Aura*, *Zona sagrada* [Holy Place], and *Cumpleaños* [Birthday]; which are relatively brief and whose action is spatially confined. On the other hand, there are those novels which cover a historical span and move in broader spaces in an attempt to totalize the historical experience of Mexico. On further inspection, however, the novels of this second kind also tend toward enclosure. What had appeared to be historical development turns out to be a journey of life which is brought to a halt in the cell-like space of a bedroom, a pyramid, or a tent where the subject confronts his own mortality. Artemio Cruz's journey from Hermosilla ends in a hospital room: the protagonists of *Cambio de piel* [A Change of Skin] end not in Veracruz but beneath the pyramid. In this respect, *Aura*, with its setting of the dark house on the

Calle Donceles is the analogue of the Fuentes narrative, a micromodel of the basic and obsessive configuration of all his creative writing.

Aura crosses the threshold between reality and imagination to offer an allegory of art. Its form departs very little from that of the traditional narrative, except for the authorial voice which addresses the protagonist, Felipe Montero, as "tú" [you (informal)] throughout the course of the story. This was a device which had been used by Michel Butor in some of his novels and was employed by Fuentes himself in sections of *La muerte de Artemio Cruz* [The Death of Artemio Cruz] which belongs to the same period as *Aura*.[19] The use of future tense in much of the narrative is also unusual. When the anonymous narrative voice warns, the protagonist, "Vivirás ese día, idéntico a los demás, ya no volverás a recordarlo sino el día siguiente" [You will live this day, identical to all the others, you will not even remember it until the next day], it situates the narrator in the position of Red Scharlach in Borges's "La muerte y la brújula" [Death and the compass] as the one who anticipates the protagonist's every move, and *who therefore has the power.* The journey that Felipe Montero takes from being a routine-bound petit bourgeois to becoming the willing prisoner of the darker forces is one that has already been traversed by the writer whose voice speaks through the text.

Far from taking the reader onto a voyage into the unknown, however, *Aura* discloses the familiar paraphernalia of the Gothic novel, a bricolage of romantic remnants and old Vincent Price movies. Descriptions insistently allude to the Gothic: "Todos los muros del salón están recubiertos de una madera oscura, labrada al estilo gótico, con ojivas y rosetones calados" [The four walls are paneled in dark wood, carved in Gothic style, with fretwork arches and large rosettes].[20] The back of Aura's chair is made of "madera de la silla gótica" (p. 26) [Aura sits in a wooden gothic chair][21] and Consuelo is described as "delgada como una escultura medieval, emaciada" (p. 27) [she's thin, even emaciated, like a medieval sculpture].[22] It would be a dull reader who failed to pick up and construe the clues of howling cats, drug-inducing plants that flourish in darkness, green-eyed women, and sacrificed goats. And the very obtrusiveness of these clues suggests an allegorical reading.

The protagonist of *Aura*, Felipe Montero, initially leaves the "real" world and enters the magic house on the Calle Donceles because of a contractual agreement he makes with the widow of General Llorente to edit the General's memoirs. Montero belongs, by right, to the routine world

of the petty bourgeois. He is "ordenado" [neat], "escrupuloso" [conscien-
tious],[23] a man for whom one day is the same as the other for he is caught
in the repetitive cycle of bourgeois society. By profession he is a historian
"cargado de datos inútiles, acostumbrado a exhumar papeles amarillentos,
profesor auxiliar en escuelas particulares, novecientos pesos mensuales"
[full of useless facts, accustomed to digging among yellowed documents,
part-time teacher in private schools, nine hundred pesos a month].[24] The
contract with society offers him the barest survival; his contract with Consuelo (the name is surely significant) offers him more than this for it gives
him time to work on his own personal project, the description of which
bears a strange resemblance to Fuentes's future novel, *Terra Nostra:*

> Si logras ahorrar por lo menos doce mil pesos, podrías pasar cerca
> de un año dedicado a tu propia obra, aplazada, casi olvidada. Tu gran
> obra de conjunto sobre los descubrimientos y conquistas españolas en
> América. Una obra que resume todas las crónicas dispersas, las haga
> inteligibles, encuentre las correspondencias entre todas las empresas
> y aventuras del siglo de oro, entre los prototipos humanos y el hecho
> mayor del Renacimiento.

> [If you can manage to save at least twelve thousand pesos, you can
> spend a year on nothing but your own work, which you've postponed
> and almost forgotten. Your great, inclusive work on the Spanish dis-
> coveries and conquests in the New World. A work that sums up all the
> scattered chronicles, makes them intelligible, and discovers the resem-
> blances among all the undertakings and adventures of Spain's Golden
> Age, and all the human prototypes and major accomplishments of the
> Renaissance.][25]

But the contract he makes in the house of Donceles Street has also brought
him into the realm of imagination and desire which will use him as their
instrument.

This allegorical reading is accentuated as I have pointed out, by the use
of well-worn allusions and literary conventions. The very name of the desired woman, Aura, is a pun on a bird of prey and a gentle breeze and the
use of pun for this all-important character draws attention to the device
itself and ultimately to the ambiguity of desire. As allegory, *Aura* refers
to the liberation of the petit bourgeois from the everyday world through
his coupling with the darker forces of creation. The aged Consuelo uses

Montero to recreate her own youth; their deathly nuptials involve him in a confrontation with mortality and the immolation of self:

> apartarás tus labios de los labios sin carne que has estado besando, de las encías sin dientes que se abren ante ti: verás bajo la luz de la luna el cuerpo desnudo de la vieja, de la señora Consuelo, flojo, rasgado, pequeño, y antiguo, temblando ligeramente porque tú lo tocas, tú lo amas, tú has regresado también.

> [You stop kissing those fleshless lips, those toothless gums: the ray of moonlight shows you the naked body of the old lady, of Señora Consuelo, limp, spent, tiny, ancient, trembling because you touch her. You love her, you too have come back.] [26]

What does this *también* [you too] signify if it is not the "author" situated where Eros and Thanatos are united? The witchcraft and the drugs bring about the alchemy of art and immolate Montero's ego in the work.

The division between the world of work and the world of desire and imagination corresponds, as is clear from the epigraph, to the division between male and female:

> El hombre caza y lucha, la mujer intriga y sueña; es la madre de la fantasía, de los dioses. Posee la segunda visión, las alas que le permiten volar hacia el infinito del deseo y de la imaginación . . . Los dioses como los hombres nacen y mueren sobre el cuerpo de una mujer . . . (Jules Michelet)

> [Man hunts and struggles. Woman intrigues and dreams; she is the mother of fantasy, the mother of the gods. She has second sight, the wings that enable her to fly to the infinite of desire and the imagination . . . The gods are like men: they are born and they die on a woman's breast . . . (Jules Michelet).] [27]

The force represented by woman is atavistic, directed toward the past not to change. She is the instrument of darker forces, akin to the animal world, and yet removed from it. Her goal is not change but the reincarnation of General Llorente, Consuelo's dead husband.

It follows from this that Fuentes's view of the imagination is, like Plato's, associated with the past and not with the future. At the deepest level, therefore, he allegorizes art as *re*-production rather than an exploration of the unknown. Nor surprising, the next novel he wrote would be given the title

Cambio de piel [Change of Skin] and the constitutive image would be that of the snake sloughing off its old skin.[28] *Aura* indeed reveals the contradictions in Fuentes's writing; for this author who is obsessed by the modern cannot really conceive of a future that is not the reincarnation of the past. Unlike Cortázar's leap into space, Fuentes's allegory of art makes it a reliving of what others have done. And interestingly, this is the analogue (but not a critique or an overturning) of dependency itself.

IV

Cortázar's "Las babas del diablo" [Devil's Spittle; retitled "Blow-up"] is a satirical confrontation with the absurdities of creation, yet is altogether different in tone from his story, "El perseguidor" [The Pursuer], which appeared in the same collection, *Las armas secretas* [Secret Weapons] (1959), and which he believed to be a turning point in his writing.[29]

The protagonist (or comic scapegoat) of "Las babas del diablo"[30] is Robert Michel, a photographer, writer, translator, and complete bourgeois who though part Chilean lives and works in Paris. In his quest for something to be photographed, he stumbles inadvertently onto the very problem of attempting to turn reality into art and discovers that, like the cloud formations which can be called either "Las babas del diablo" or "Los hilos de la Virgen" [The Virgin's Threads] (and which have nothing to do with good or evil), there is nothing behind the text beyond its own transient and insubstantial configuration. In the course of the story, Michel tries both to take a photograph and to tell the story of how he took the photograph. Photography is, in fact, a key metaphor since, of all the arts, it seems the most able to register momentary reality. As Michel soon discovers, however, all art mediates and invents more than it translates. There are thus constant cross-references between photography and writing, both of which require a primal decision which is also a point of view. Thus the very choice of narrative voice involves Michel in an initial dilemma: "Nunca se sabrá cómo hay que contar eso, si en primera persona o en segunda, usando la tercera del plural o inventando continuamente formas que no servirán de nada" [It'll never be known how this has to be told, in the first person or in the second, using the third person plural or continually inventing modes that are useless].[31] In fact, Michel never decisively makes the initial choice without which traditional narrative cannot begin. Though committed to the realist illusion, he constantly demonstrates its conventionality by slipping from first- to third-person narration and then back again.

Language and the camera, more than the artist or the subject, determine the configuration of the completed work. In "Las babas del diablo," elements which literary discourse had ordinarily concealed from the reader and those aspects of art normally hidden from the viewer jump to the foreground. When Michel confesses that he does not know how he is going to end the sentence he has just begun, it is grammar itself which resolves the problem rather than Michel. In fact, "Las babas del diablo" allows no device to appear as natural. For instance, when Michel uses the present tense to refer to events in the past, the reader is immediately aware that the present-of-the-writer is excluded. The birds and clouds which pass the window in front of which he is writing are not "present" in the text. Even translation (where there is an original text-to-be-translated) can never be faithful to an original.

"Las babas del diablo," then, opens up a gulf between the phenomenal and the conventional. When literature tries to translate reality, it simply deforms it. Thus when Michel describes a woman in the park as "delgada y esbelta" [thin and svelte], he is, at once, aware that these are not *mots justes*. On the other hand, when he inadvertently slips into the past tense and allows invention freer rein, he creates an original text. To write "sus ojos que caían sobre las cosas como dos águilas, dos saltos al vacío, dos ráfagas de fango verde" ["her eyes fell on things like two eagles, two leaps into nothingness, two puffs of green slime"][32] is to make that leap into space which is the function of art.

"Las babas del diablo" is, however, also a meditation on the instrumentality of art in capitalist society. For, on the one hand, Michel believes in the utopian innocence of art, and art that is, as little as possible, different from life itself. Yet his own motives are far from pure. When he tries to take a photograph of a woman meeting an adolescent in the park, he not only reads his own moral judgments into the event but believes that he can alter reality and not simply reflect it by the mere act of photographing. Michel is thus able to rationalize his interference as a moral action which saves the innocence of adolescence from the schemes of a corrupt woman:

> De puro entrometido le había dado oportunidad de aprovechar al fin su miedo para algo útil; ahora estaría arrepentido, menoscabado, sintiéndose poco hombre . . . Mejor era eso que la compañía de una mujer capaz de mirar como lo miraba en la isla: *Michel es puritano a ratos, cree que no se debe corromper por la fuerza.* En el fondo, aquella foto había sido una buena acción.

[Out of plain meddling, I had given him the opportunity finally to take advantage of his fright to do something useful; now he would be regretting it, feeling his honor impaired, his manhood diminished. That was better than the attention of a woman capable of looking as she had looked at him on that island. *Michel is something of a puritan at times, he believes that one should not seduce someone from a position of strength.* In the last analysis, taking that photo had been a good act.] (italics mine)[33]

The "entrometido" [intruder] is, of course, not only Michel but Cortázar himself whose comments on Michel mirror Michel's judgments of the woman. The reader is thus put on guard against moral judgments passed off as art. Similarly the boy's flight with which Michel identifies himself is analogous to Michel's own flight when the woman and a "third-person" (a clownlike man sitting in a car out of camera focus) abruptly turn on him. The boy saves his innocence through the flight, Michel saves his photograph and Cortázar in turn uses both to create "Las babas del diablo." The act of liberation is thus turned into a commodity.

But his is by no means the final outcome. As Michel enlarges the photograph and produces the blown-up print, a new element comes into play, namely the reading of the text (whether photograph or story). For the second time Michel is forced to interfere for when the photograph comes to life, the boy is once again menaced by the woman and by a new actor—the man who he had originally excluded from the camera eye and who now becomes the real mover of events. It is this man who grows in importance until he begins not only to blot out the subject but also to erase the author himself. This pimp, clown, or death's head whose face has holes in place of eyes like a photographic negative is, in fact, negation itself, the "nothing" behind "las babas del diablo." The second salvation of the adolescent not only obliterates the author, however, but also the subject of the photograph leaving only a space, like a windowframe, looking out onto the passing clouds and the birds:

a veces, en cambio todo se pone gris, todo es una enorme nube y de pronto restallan las salpicaduras de la lluvia, largo rato se ve llover sobre la imagen, como un llanto al revés, y poco a poco el cuadro se aclara, quizá sale el sol, y otra vez entran las nubes, de a dos, de a tres. Y las palomas, a veces, uno que otro gorrión.

[and for a change sometimes, everything gets grey, all one enormous cloud, and suddenly the splotches of rain cracking down, for a long spell you can see it raining over the picture, like a spell of weeping reversed, and little by little, the frame becomes clear, perhaps the sun comes out, and again the clouds begin to come, two at a time, three at a time. And the pigeons once in a while, and a sparrow or two.][34]

This is the final paradoxical innocence of art, to become indistinguishable from nature. Cortázar's irony and self-criticism ensure, however, that this is not seen as a utopian possibility, but rather as a project fraught with contradiction. What the story does is to destroy the support on which an older form of literature has been based but it does not yet envisage anything to replace this.

Though "Las babas del diablo" is only a minor work, it can be considered representative of Cortázar's early problematic. To put the practice of writing into a critical perspective as Cortázar does, to show the conventionality of what appears natural creates a healthy disrespect for bourgeois society. On the other hand to set up this critical distance while making the reader aware of the way art "naturalizes" its conventions may not necessarily result in a revolutionary change or in the creation of the new man. In fact, at this stage of his writing, Cortázar can only conceive change on an individual basis. In "Situación de la novela," he wrote:

> No en vano el mejor individualismo de nuestro tiempo entraña una aguda conciencia de los restantes individualismos, y se quiere libre de todo egoísmo y de toda insularidad. René Daumann escribió esta frase maravillosa: "Sólos, después de acabar con la ilusión de no estar sólos, no somos los únicos que estamos sólos" (pp. 242–43).

> [It is not in vain that the best individualism of our time contains within it an acute consciousness of the remaining individualisms, and wants to be free from all egoism and all insularity. René Daumann wrote this marvelous sentence: "Alone, after ending the illusion of not being alone, we are not the only ones who are alone."]

Cortázar's explorations did not, of course, stop at this point. He went on to write *Rayuela* [Hopscotch] and *Libro de Manuel* [A Manual for Manuel][35] in which there are structural incompatibilities between individual exploration and the oppressive social order. Even so, revolutionary action is still conceived on an individual basis. The "club de serpientes" of *Rayuela* and the guerrilla group of *Libro de Manuel* are individuals bound by friendship not by the social practice of the workplace; and revolution is the combination of a series of individual decisions. The very fact, however, that in these later works Cortázar increasingly has to include the raw data of political and sociological information—the testimony of torture victims and data of U.S. military missions in *Libro de Manuel*, data from the Russell Tribunal in *Fantomas contra los vampiros multinacionales* [Fantomás against the Multinational Vampires] (1975) seems to suggest that the concept of the novel as an individual exploration of being has its limits since society has long since left behind the stage of the liberal summer (to use George Steiner's expression) when, at least, there was a certain space for individuals to work for the realization of utopia. But in the sixties even the liberal facade of governments like those of Britain and France had been torn away to reveal state-condoned repression and torture. Cortázar's aesthetic demands as its precondition a liberal society which no longer exists.

v

Of the three works under discussion, Severo Sarduy's *Cobra* represents the most extreme break with traditional fiction. Indeed, it has been hailed both as a quite new kind of writing as well as a destruction of the concept of authorship itself. The translator of the English version declares:

> he . . . creates *Cobra* on the basis of mutilated quotations from *Cobra*, again and again breaking down the old discourse, the old concept of authorship and of fidelity to authorship, erasing the difference between the original and the plagiarized, to indicate perhaps that all texts are one: *l'écriture*. Writing that is never finished: a book that is incessantly written.[36]

Roland Barthes, on the other hand, is not so much interested in *Cobra* as a destruction of the concept of authorship so much as the realization of the utopia of the "rapture text." Indeed he puts *Cobra* outside any possibility of recuperation by institutionalized language and criticism, exclaiming:

> encore, encore, encore plus! encore un autre mot, encore une autre fête. La langue se reconstruit *ailleurs* par le flux pressé de tous les plaisirs de langage. Où, ailleurs? au paradis des mots. C'est là, veritablemente une texte paradisiaque, utopique (sans lieu), une hétéroglogie par plénitude: tous signifiants son là et chacun fait mouche: l'auteur (le lecteur) semble leur dire: je vous aime tous (mots, tours, phrases, adjectifs, ruptures) pêle-mêle: les signes et les mirages d'objets qu'ils représentent: une sorte de franciscanisme appelle tous les mots à se

poser, à se presser, à repartir; texte jasé, chiné, nous sommes comblés par le langage tels de jeunes enfants à qui rien ne serait jamais refusé, reproché, ou, pire encore, "permis." C'est la gageure d'une jubilation continue, le moment où par son excès les plaisir verbal suffoque et buscule dans la jouissance.

[more, more, still more! one more word, one more celebration. Language reconstructs itself elsewhere under the teeming flux of every kind of linguistic pleasure. Where is this elsewhere? In the paradise of words. *Cobra* is in fact a paradisiac text, utopian (without a location), a heterology by plenitude: all the signifiers are here and each scores a bull's eye; the author (the reader) seems to say to them: I love you all (words, phrases, sentences, adjectives, discontinuities: pell-mell: signs and mirages of objects which they represent); a kind of Franciscanism invites all words to perch, to flock, to fly off again: a marbled, iridescent text; we are gorged with language, like children who are never refused anything or scolded for anything or, even worse, "permitted" anything. *Cobra* is the pledge of continuous jubilation, the moment when by its very excess verbal pleasure chokes and reels into bliss.][37]

Here I shall merely note in passing that the utopia which Barthes reads in *Cobra* is a plenitude in which there is never determination or selection; in which one choice does not cancel another. In a similarly rapturous accolade, Hélène Cixous writes:

Impossible to hold it still—what? where?, which way?—this text is on the run, slipping out the back way, swerving out of line with any conceivable edge of text, of land, or of water—impossible to catch hold of any thread in this flying carpet slip—stitched in gold zig-zag.

What hand, what memory, what master, what law would dare boast of being able to regulate its course for an instant? *Cobra* forgets herself somewhere at the outer limits objectively and subjectively, with the unrestrained boldness of beings to come.[38]

Cobra is here placed outside the scope of criticism because of its futuristic mobility. The reader is in utopia and must not ask how he got there.

One of Sarduy's models for the revolutionary text is, in fact, the baroque: "Barroco que recusa toda instauración, que metaforiza el orden discutido, al dios juzgado, a la ley transgredida. Barroco de la Revolución" [Baroque that declines any restoration, that metaphorizes the order in question, that judges god, that transgresses the law. Baroque of the

Revolution].[39] In its break with denotation (or the referential), baroque is analogue to the erotic:

> Como la retórica barroca, el erotismo se presenta como la ruptura total del nivel denotativo, directo y natural del lenguaje-somático-, como la perversión que implica toda metáfora, toda figura.

> [Like Baroque rhetoric, eroticism presents itself as a total rupture with the denotative level, direct and natural from somatic-language, like the perversion that all metaphors imply, all figures.][40]

Thus the erotic like the language of the baroque seeks nothing beyond pleasure. The way in which the writer might break away from denotative language is best illustrated through poetry. Writing of the Surrealists, Sarduy speaks of producing a *secousse:*

> A través de ese sacudimiento del signo que lo vacía de significado el poeta restituye el mundo a su puro espectáculo, lo convierte en un catálogo de significantes.

> [By means of this shaking of the sign that empties it of significance, the poet restores the world to pure spectacle, he converts it into a catalogue of significations.][41]

We recognize both in Severo Sarduy's own version of *écriture* and in the reception of *Cobra,* a recurrent contemporary obsession with mobility, metamorphosis, play, and enjoyment as against the supposedly bourgeois values of organization, work, and deferment of pleasure. However, it is possible that those values which appeared revolutionary in contrast to the nineteenth-century bourgeois are, in fact, reflections of a new stage of capitalism itself. For the moment, however, I wish to leave this problem aside and address myself to the manner in which mobility and metamorphosis are embodied in the text. For in one respect (and notwithstanding the supposed destruction of the concept of authorship), there is a curious and quite distinctive feature of Sarduy's style which deserves notice. *Cobra* is for the most part, written in a series of simple sentences with a minimum of subordinate clauses. For example:

> Pactaron no pensar en la cita. Escondidas tomaban librium. Para que durmiera todo el día en el caldo, le dieron a Pup una pastilla. Tejían. Hablaban de las inclemencias del tiempo. Confesaron desgano. A las seis de la tarde Cobra empezó a pintarse. A las ocho, frente al espejo,

aguardaba en el camarín. A las diez sonó el timbre para el primer espectáculo.

[They agreed not to think about the date. They drank Librium in secret. In order for him to sleep all day in the broth, they gave Pup a pill. They sewed. They talked about bad weather. They confessed their disgust. At six in the afternoon, Cobra began to paint her/himself. At eight, in front of the mirror, s/he waited in the dressing room. At ten, the bell rang for the first show.]

The staccato effect of the short sentences produces the impression of constant but unrelated and discontinuous activities. The metamorphosis is suggested primarily by word play, particularly punning, paronomasia, and anagrams. The title of the book itself is an anagram of Copenhagen, Brussels, and Amsterdam. Cobra is also the third person of the present indicative of *cobrar* [to recover, to collect, to charge], and is replete with anagrammatic formations—*obrar, boca, barroco* [to work, to build, to perform; mouth; Baroque], some of which refer to an Octavio Paz poem "La boca habla" [The mouth speaks] which Sarduy quotes. This kind of textual production eschews the referential in order to display the power of words to create new configurations. It was a procedure much favored by the Surrealists and is common in Latin American poetry. In *Cobra*, this verbal play is used to create characters and situations. Cobra is a transvestite from the Lyric Theatre of the Dolls who under the aegis of a Señora/Buscona (mediator) prepares for a role as "queen;" but she is also a woman with a strangely marked face seen on the streets of Paris and in a reduced form is a dwarf castrated by Dr. Katzbob. The "white dwarf" is also an astronomical term for a dead star. Characters are, then, not separate identities but signifiers. For instance, a group of motorcyclists are also hippies or Tibetan lamas. Thus character, like the verbal pun becomes a kind of splitting *apart* of an apparent identity to show the disparate possibilities of the signified.

It might be argued that, by removing language from denotation and instrumentality, Sarduy creates a text that stands in opposition to the rigidity of institutionalized speech and the preconceived habits of the bourgeois order. Indeed, as critics have pointed out, the text parodies traditional narrative, reveals the syntactic model of textual production, and, in general, criticizes its own practice. Moreover it constantly draws attention to fictionality. The basic set of contrasts around which *Cobra* gyrates is the East/West polarity. We are never allowed to believe, however, that we are dealing with a real opposition but rather with a *bricolage* of rituals, beliefs, landscapes, and representations, including the mistaken Indies of Columbus's log book. At this point, we begin to wonder what is served by this continual foregrounding of the "arbitrary" nature of the sign since the supression of history, the visual pun, and the abstraction of signs from their original context are precisely the features that also characterize the mass media.

Before dealing with this problem, however, it is useful to remind ourselves of the close relations between the East/West polarity in *Cobra* and Octavio Paz's *Conjunciones y disyunciones* [Conjunctions and Disjunctions]. The Spanish edition of *Cobra* indeed has, on its jacket, the very picture of the *yogin* whose body is a *mandala* which had also appeared in Paz's book. This latter is a learned disquisition on the contrast between Eastern and Western notions of the body, particularly as seen in the extremes of Western puritanism and Tantric orgy. Paz abstracts these beliefs from any historical context to present them as a pure opposition between a civilization which sublimates the excremental and represses the body; and a civilization which worships the body and indeed, reads it as a kind of writing. In the West, the repressed body, "martirizada por el sentimiento de culpa y la ironía" [tortured by the feeling of guilt and irony] took refuge in art. The supreme task of the modern artists is to recover the physicality of experience: "el poeta y el novelista construyen objetos simbólicos, organismos que emiten imágenes. Hacen lo que hace el salvaje, convierten el lenguaje en cuerpo. Las palabras ya no son cosas y, sin cesar de ser signos, se animan, *cobran* cuerpo" [the poet and the novelist construct symbolic objects, organisms that emit images. They do what the savage does; they convert language into a body. Words are no longer things and, without ceasing to be signs, they become animated, they are embodied] (italics mine).[42] The healing of the breach between words and the body may be said to represent the utopian aspect of *Cobra*.

Is *Cobra* an unmotivated text, a freeplay of the sign? The important East/West dichotomy suggests motivation; and there are, in fact, a number of situations which support this view. I refer here to the preparation of Cobra for the transvestite festival in which she is to become queen of the dolls; the "reduction" of Cobra who is also Pup, the dwarf, whose name, in turn, suggests *poupée* [doll] and the pupae of insect metamorphosis. In another "situation," Pup is castrated by Dr. Katzbob (to bob means to cut). There are also allusions to a journey through Spain (Córdoba-Cobra), and to Tangier. Now Tangier is a place that pioneered sex-change operations and one of the "transgressions" committed by the text is that against the institutionalization of sex roles in Western society.

Of course it can be effectively argued that this is simply one of many possible readings of the text but it is a reading encouraged by the word-play, by names and situations. In fact, the central metaphor of *Cobra* is the body as sign but a body that can be converted into spectacle. What Hélène Cixous describes as the movement of the text is, in reality, a dance of signs, the constant metamorphoses which allow no fixed point of reference and which invite enjoyment and not use.

Now although this may transgress the rigidity and institutionalization of older forms of society, this is also very much akin to that "empty-ing of reality" which Barthes called "myth." To be sure, he is talking of representation not language, a representation in which things "appear to mean something by themselves."[43] But this is what Sarduy attempts with language. Further, the promotion of gratuitousness in opposition to the instrumentality of bourgeois society is not in itself revolutionary. It is per-haps utopian but, as is evident, private utopias are permissible within the world system. What is now taboo is social action.

VI

The problem that Sarduy, Cortázar, and Fuentes share is that of converting individual statement into social practice. The realist novel had an appear-ance of being a reflection of society. The avant garde exposed its rhetoric and showed that even when an author appeared to be holding society up to criticism, the very structures of the narrative reproduced its assump-tions. In the attempt, however, to find new and unrecuperable forms, the new novelists value the mobile, the gratuitousness, the infinitely change-able, which are the very values promoted by a new stage of capitalism. In the case of contemporary Latin American writers, this is particularly strik-ing and particularly contradictory. As we have seen, one of the ideals of both Fuentes and Cortázar is to create a space for individualism and im-plicitly Sarduy also glimpses the utopia of this private world. The novel, once the privileged place for the exploration of the individual is, however, increasingly irrelevant on the social level. It is, in fact, the global sys-tem which has changed character leaving the avant-garde novelist tilting at the windmills of an old bourgeois stereotype who institutionalized litera-ture and converted language into his instrument, who deferred pleasure and embraced the work ethic. To attack such an individual is anachronistic at the present time when the global system has taken on quite different characteristics. The dominant ideology is now reproduced in every facet of daily life, in the very pursuit of pleasure. It encourages the setting up of private worlds but sets taboos around politics, compartmentalizes information, and, in general, flourishes on the suppression of history. Thus Fuentes, Sarduy, and Cortázar embrace a dangerous kind of modernity. In the case of *Aura*, this is particularly fascinating because as an allegory for art it clearly reveals the conversion of Montero's *social* vision (his project to synthesize the history of the Renaissance) into a private dream which is a *reproduction*. In *Cobra*, the attempt is made both to attack convention and to produce a pure, unmotivated pleasure text and again this reproduces rather than revolutionizes the values of mobility and metamorphosis while placing a taboo on the political and the historical. Of the three writers only Cortázar attempts to convert the individual exploration into a social one, though not in "Las babas del diablo" which is a devastating *reductio ad absurdum* of art's pretense to reflect reality. Not until his latest writing would he face the incongruity of a utopian vision of life converted into art and art into life when set beside the information produced by tribunals on torture and repression. This dichotomy in Cortázar's later writing is indeed a significant symptom, showing as it does the difficulties of converting the individual lifestyle into a revolutionary movement or even into a significant transgression of the present system.[44]

NOTES

A version of this paper was presented at a conference on Ideology and Literature sponsored by the Department of Spanish and Portuguese, University of Minnesota; the Joint Committee on Latin American Studies (Social Science Research Council); and the American Council of Learned Societies, February 1976.

1 I refer particularly to Roland Barthes, *S/Z* (Paris: Editions du Seuil, 1970); Julia Kristeva, *La révolution du language poétique* (Paris: Editions du Seuil, 1974). See also Jonathan Culler, *Structuralist Poetics* (Ithaca, N.Y.: Cornell University Press, 1975).

2 Lionel Trilling, "Manners, Morals and the Novel," in *The Liberal Imagination* (New York: Anchor Books, 1953), 215.

3 Trilling, "The Function of the Little Magazine," *The Liberal Imagination*, 94–95.

4 For a discussion of "naturalization" see Jonathan Culler, *Structuralist Poetics*, 134–60.

5 Jean-Louis Baudry, "Ecriture, Fiction, Idéologie," in *Théorie d'ensemble* (Paris: Editions du Seuil, 1968), 127–47.

6 This is the claim made by Philippe Sollers, *Logiques* (Paris: Editions du Seuil, 1968) and Kristeva in *La révolution du language poétique*.

7 Mario Vargas Llosa, "Novela primitiva y novela de creación en América Latina," *Revista de la Universidad de México* 23, no. 10 (June, 1969): 31.

8 Ibid., 31.

9 Ibid., 31.

10 The first chapter of Fuentes's *La nueva narrativa latinoamericana* (later revised), was originally published as an article: "La nueva novela latinoamericana" in *Siempre* 579 (29 July 1965).

11 Carlos Fuentes, *La nueva novela hispanoamericana* (Mexico: Editorial J. Mortiz, 1969), 18.

12 Alberto Díaz Lastra, "La Definición Literaria, Política y Moral de Carlos Fuentes," *Siempre* 718 (29 March 1967).

13 Fuentes, *La nueva novela hispanoamericana*, 90–91.

14 Julio Cortázar, "Literatura en la Revolución y Revolución en la Literatura: Algunos Malentendidos a Liquidar," *Marcha* (9–16 January 1970) and in Oscar Collazos and Julio Cortázar y Mario Vargas Llosa, *Literatura en la revolución y revolución en la literatura* (Mexico: Siglo Veintiuno Editores, 1970).

15 Julio Cortázar, "Situación de la novela," *Cuadernos Americanos* 3, no. 4 (July–August, 1950): 294–97.

16 I refer particularly to Salvador Elizondo (Mexico), Néstor Sánchez (Argentina), and Severo Sarduy (Cuba).

17 Interview with Jean Michel Fossey, "From Boom to Big Bang," in *Review* 74 (winter 1974): 12.

18 Severo Sarduy, "Del Yin al Yang (Sobre Sade, Bataille, Marmori, Cortázar y Elizondo)," *Mundo Nuevo* 13 (Julio 1967): 8.

19 Richard M. Reeve, "Carlos Fuentes y el desarrollo del narrador en segunda persona: un ensayo exploratorio," in *Homenaje a Carlos Fuentes* (New York: Las Americas, 1971), 77–87. Butor's *Degrés* (1960), however, used the first-person narrator with the narrator addressing himself to a "tú" who is his own nephew and a student in his class at the *lycée*.

20 This citation (and all future citations from *Aura*) is from the following bilingual edition: Carlos Fuentes, *Aura*, trans. Lysander Kemp (New York: Farrar, Straus and Giroux, 1975), 39.

21 Ibid., 43.

22 Ibid., 47.

23 Ibid., 3.

24 Ibid., 5.

25 Ibid., 65.

26 Ibid., 145.

27 Ibid., epigraph.

28   The novel was originally given the title *El sueño* (*Siempre* [29 september, 1965]).

29   Luis Harss, *Los nuestros*, 5th ed. (Buenos Aires: Editorial Sudamericana, 1973), 273. For a discussion of "El perseguidor," see Saul Sosnowski, "Conocimiento poético y aprehensión racional de la realidad," A study of "El perseguidor" by Julio Cortázar, in *Homenaje a Julio Cortázar* (Long Island City, N.Y.: Las Americas, 1972), 429–444.

30   For a discussion of the scapegoat character in Cortázar's work, see Alfred Mac-Adam, *El individuo y el otro (Crítica a los cuentos de Julio Cortázar)* (Buenos Aires: Ediciones La Librería, 1971).

31   Julio Cortazar, *Blow-up and Other Stories*, trans. Paul Blackburn (New York: Collier Books, 1974), 100.

32   Ibid., 105.

33   Ibid., 112.

34   Ibid., 115.

35   I omit *62 modelo para armar*, which he himself described as a "laboratorio" [laboratory] in his reply to Oscar Collazos.

36   Suzanne Jill Levine, "Discourse as Bricolage," *Review* 74 (Winter 1974): 35.

37   Roland Barthes, *The Pleasure of the Text* (New York: Hill and Wang, 1975), 8.

38   Hélène Cixous, " 'Ocobrabaroco.' A Text-Twister," *Review* 74 (Winter 1974): 26.

39   Severo Sarduy, "El barroco y el neobarroco," *America Latina en su literatura*, 2nd ed. (Mexico: Unesco, 1974), 184.

40   Ibid., 182.

41   Dialogue with Tomás Segovia and Emir Rodríguez Monegal, "Nuestro Rubén Dario," *Mundo Nuevo* (7 January 1967): 36.

42   Octavio Paz, *Conjunciones y disyunciones* (Mexico: Editorial J. Mortiz, 1969), 84.

43   Roland Barthes, "Myth Today," *Mythologies*, trans. Annetee Lavers (New York: Hill and Wang, 1972), 143.

44   A detailed study of Cortázar's later work is outside the scope of this article. I am at present at work on a more extended discussion of the point I make here. For a historical survey of theories of revolutionary literature which envisage a utopia in which art becomes life, see Robert C. Elliott, "The Costs of Utopia," *Studies on Voltaire and the Eighteenth Century*, CLI-CLV (1976).

FROM MODERNIZATION TO RESISTANCE

Latin American Literature, 1959–1976

*N*ow that the excitement that surrounded the "boom" of Latin American writing in the sixties has dissipated, it is clear that literature itself was in crisis and that certain canons and assumptions that had long given support to writers and critics had become questionable. The symptoms could be identified in certain novels which were unable to reconcile conflicting intentions (*Cambio de piel* [Change of Skin] by Carlos Fuentes, for instance[1]) or were blocked by the impossibility of completion as was José María Arguedas's *El zorro de arriba y el zorro de abajo* [The Fox Above and the Fox Below][2]; at other times, there were marked changes between an author's earlier and later works, as in the case of Cortázar and Vargas Llosa[3] or radical revisions were made of earlier theoretical positions like those made between the first and second editions of Octavio Paz's *El arco y la lira* [The Bow and the Lyre] or between the final version of Carlos Fuentes's *La nueva novela hispanoamericana* [The New Spanish American Novel][4] and the articles on which it was based. If this crisis was felt most acutely in the novel, it was because certain of its integral features—its linearity, the mimetic (i.e., its claim to represent a moral or historical truth), the concept of character and even the tense in which it was written—had come to seem problematic. These characteristic features were criticized as so many devices which "naturalized" the bourgeois order and thus reproduced its ideology,[5] while writing that activated the reader's perceptions was assumed to transgress bourgeois ideology. Terms like *modernism* (in the Anglo-American sense),[6] avant-garde, or the more recent *écriture*[7] are signposts of this break between the older reflectionist aesthetics[8] and new writing which, however, had contradictory aspects. On the one hand, this new writing appears to be on the side of revolution and is directed toward changing people and society by breaking down rationalization and preconceived ideas (in Surrealism); or by disturbing the apparently natural

Originally published in *Latin American Perspectives* 5, no. 1 (winter 1978): 77–97.

order of things which is in fact an ideological order (écriture); or, as in the Brechtian technique of estrangement, laying bare the social structure which determines daily life. Despite the considerable differences between these groups, movements, and individuals, they share the assumption that a revolutionary poetics must involve a revolutionary change of form and language. Another aspect of the new poetics is associated with the changes in perception which have already taken place with urbanization and industrialization. It was Walter Benjamin[9] who first suggested a relationship between shock devices and the urban experience and described the profound changes in the social significance of art in the age of mechanical reproduction. Is it possible that the devices of shock, simultaneity, the juxtaposition of disparate elements, all of which activate perception, may not always or necessarily be "revolutionary" but may indeed be methods for breaking down deep-rooted attitudes which stand in the way of full acceptance of consumer society? Is there a difference between a revolutionary poetics and a poetics of modernization?

The debate between realism and modernism is scarcely new; what marks the contemporary discussion, however, is the virtual disappearance of the argument for realism. Yet having discounted realism, critics on the Left cannot but be aware that the "revolutionary" tactics of surprise, the substitution of the freeplay of signs for a dialectics of text and the break with the authority of the past constitute the grammar of advanced capitalism. Hence the need to distinguish between the project of an "empty" avant-garde which turns technology into an object of contemplation and the active relationship between art and society theorized (for example) by Brecht.[10] What follows is an attempt to discriminate between these different aesthetic projects over the last two decades.

HISTORY AND THE REALISTS

One of the crucial issues that separated the iconoclastic new novelists in the early sixties from those who still defended realism and traditional forms of narrative was the former's rejection of "referentiality," that is literature's obedience to or validation of an extraliterary order and more especially of an already codified version of history. In rejecting such extraliterary concerns in order to affirm the autonomy of art, these new novelists set themselves not so much against official art which they regarded as nonexistent or beneath contempt but rather against a dogmatically defined realism on the one hand and provincialism on the other, both of which, they believed, condemned them to cultural anachronism. "Technique" and "innovation" were the keys to their liberation from this backwardness. The new novel, said Mario Vargas Llosa, "is no longer 'Latin American'; it is freed from that servitude. It no longer serves reality, it now uses reality" (my translation).[11] For Carlos Fuentes, the novelist's freedom to appropriate techniques developed in the metropolis implied his liberation from the anachronism to which Latin American dependency condemned him.[12] Even more radical claims would be made by Severo Sarduy and Octavio Paz for whom the self-referentiality of art and not its reflection of reality constituted a transgression of the limits of bourgeois society.[13]

Such a general embarrassment with the referential (also common to European and North American modernism) is not confined to the more militant iconoclasts among the new novelists but invades realist texts of the period. Traditionally, realism (whether critical realism or a socialist realism that subordinated events and characters to a transcendental goal) had been the privileged mode of left-wing writing. The realist was the mediator between historical forces and their incarnation in characters and situations. José Revueltas aptly summarized the process thus: "Aesthetics does not constitute a closed system of values (the Beautiful, the Sublime, the Noble, etc.) but constitutes the historically and socially changing reflection in the human brain of the objective sentiments and emotions contained in external reality."[14]

For the critical realist, not only does literature truthfully reflect history through the mediation of the writer but, by revealing connections and continuities which would otherwise remain hidden, it enables the reader to take a critical, conscious, and dialectical distance from events. Realist writing is cognitive in intention and speaks directly and rationally to the conscious awareness of the reader. However, as recent Marxist criticism has increasingly shown, even the best-made realist works often constitute coherent totalities in appearance only, and it is through gaps, inconsistencies, and dislocations in the text that the work not only reveals its production but also its incompleteness and silences.[15] Thus for example, a work like Neruda's *Canto General* [General Song] strikes us as an organic totality precisely because of its sustained poetic tour de force. Though the coherence and unity of the poem are attributed to nature and history, the very fact that their continuity and purposiveness has to be communicated through the *poet* seems to throw into relief the subjectivity Neruda wishes to overcome. Such incompatibilities remain latent, nevertheless, for they are subordinated to the unifying and totalizing intention of the poet. However,

in the writings of José María Arguedas, Augusto Roa Bastos, and José Revueltas, whose central concern with the objective representation of reality
separated them radically from the liberal-existential writers of the 1960s
"boom," it was no longer possible to evade the fact that history had become
not a stable structure but a problematic area. For all these writers history
had been grasped initially as a continuous progressive development, moving through predictable stages in revolutionary change, but it eventually
came to present itself as a shifting panorama, a text subject to revision
and rereading. Understanding history was no longer a matter of listening
to the oracles of the land and the people but rather involved attempting
to discern the rationality of the text of history that had been distorted
and partially erased by the dominant class. As I shall go on to show, the
structural problems that beset José María Arguedas's *The Fox Above and the
Fox Below* (1971) and José Revueltas's increasing apprehension of irrational
forces behind society's rational facade make it impossible for them to accept the linear historical progress they had assumed in their early writing.

The way in which the changing problematic of history comes to constitute a stress within the novelistic text can be grasped quite clearly by
examining *The Fox Above and the Fox Below* in which Arguedas can no longer
deploy the opposition between coastal capitalism and sierra feudalism as
he had done in *Todas las sangres* [All the Bloods] (1964)[16] in order to articulate characters and situations. The urban immigration, the flight from the
land, and the breakdown of the traditional sierra community were emotionally devastating to Arguedas because a certain set of values that derived
from roots were threatened by change and were already being replaced by
the modern values of mobility, adaptability, and professionalism, as rural
peoples found their way to the slums of Lima and the coastal ports. Arguedas was aware that what was needed in his novels was more than a new
theme or different types of characters, but he was unable to define this new
quality by anything more precise than "city," by which he meant sophis-
tication. His novel in consequence is split by his uncertainty. Having envisioned a socialist state developing out of the Indian commune, he now
witnessed the erosion of this organic community and is left without his
fictional scaffolding. As a result, there is a division in the novel between a
personal diary in which he faces both the problem of writing and his own
projected suicide and a realist narrative whose ending he could not foresee. He attributes the failure to his own weakness and inadequacy, his lack
of professionalism and "technique." "I fear that to follow the thread of the
'foxes,' that I have to learn something or much more from the cortazars,

but that means not only having learned the 'technique' which they dominate but also having lived somewhat as they have lived." Yet he is also aware that techniques may be a trap—"a false short cut to solve certain difficulties, especially for those who seek the order of things in the manner of ordinary people and not in the manner of the city or the newly constituted city; for those also who seek it in the manner of the lark rather than of the jet plane." [17] Arguedas, so often regarded as ingenuous or provincial in literary matters, voices a problem that the more sophisticated would have difficulty in solving, the problem that technique or device alone does not necessarily make a text revolutionary.

With Revueltas we approach the problem of referentiality from a different perspective. As a lifelong militant on the Left, the main problem that concerns him in his writing is how humanity can reach a higher stage of consciousness and how the rigid dogmatism of the revolutionary vanguard can be replaced by creative and liberating attitudes. Yet there is a structural problem in much of his writing which stems directly from his realism, for he tends to adopt a third-person narrative and therefore an apparently objective form which privileges the writer as a hidden god who has set a universe in motion and controls the reader's responses. The reader is involved only insofar as he or she identifies with the characters and the characters are nearly always imprisoned (literally or metaphorically). The reader can only identify with an arrested form of consciousness and there is no "otherness" which would allow dialectic development. This is most clearly observed in the novel *El apando* [The Womb] (1969),[18] which was written in prison after the 1968 Tlatelolco massacre. The title of this novel can refer to solitary confinement, to drugs (since these are a form of imprisonment in the cycle of need and satisfaction of need), and the womb in which the fetus is enclosed before birth. On the literal level, the novel relates the efforts and the failure of a group of convicts to outwit prison guards and smuggle drugs (which represent a spurious form of liberation) into prison. The drugs are concealed in the uterus of a woman visitor, the mother of the most wretched of the criminals. Analogies are thus set up between the uterus, the drug, and the prison, all of which represent repetitive cyclical activity rather than dialectical liberation. Yet the limitation of Revueltas's text lies as much in the restriction of the form itself as in the theme, for unwittingly it is always the omniscient writer outside the text who appears to have the privileged overview and who supplies the rational ordered consciousness unavailable to the entrapped victim. The third-person narration helps to increase the distance between this higher stage of rationality, implied by the hidden presence of the author, and the characters caught in the tread-mill of repetition. The manifest problem of the text is the failure to liberate consciousness; the latent problem in which Revueltas himself is trapped is the separation of the rational (the mind) from the physical (and desire). Interestingly, this latent drama becomes the theme of the story, "Hegel y yo" which Revueltas published just before he died and which he evidently intended as a fragment of a longer work.[19] In it, "Hegel" is a crippled stu-dent imprisoned in the same cell as a guilt-ridden murderer whose chief diversion is kicking him around in his wheelchair. It is an almost allegorical confrontation of crippled reason with the nightmares of desire. By impli-cation the dialectical process is blocked in this confrontation.

In both Revueltas's and Arguedas's later writing, the unresolved prob-lem is that of the author's relation to the text which realism tends to mask. In fact, their struggle with realism is precisely what makes their narrative more interesting than that of many writers who simply sloughed off the problem, asserting the superiority of their subjective fantasies. However, it was also precisely because realism had become problematic that people looked to Cuba for a new, revolutionary aesthetic.

THE CUBAN REVOLUTION: PRAXIS

Cuba was thus expected to provide a new cultural as well as political van-guard in the early sixties although, for reasons which I will outline briefly, the emphasis shifted very rapidly from the substance and form of art to the question of praxis.[20] The most specific statement on cultural questions were initially made by Che Guevara who was particularly interested in lit-erature. Further, he was conscious of the fact that form itself constituted an ideological question, that socialist realism, for example, was rooted in nineteenth-century alienation of the writer in capitalist societies. He real-ized that the Cuban revolution must affect the forms of art and not merely introduce new themes.[21] Yet because he felt that these forms could only be produced by new men and women, he tended to suggest that the new art was still only a utopian possibility. In the present, the revolutionary writer's first loyalty was to the struggle itself, and the highest form of struggle was at the battle front. As he wrote in his Bolivian diary: "This kind of struggle gives us the chance to become revolutionaries, the high-est level of the human species, but it also allows us to become men: those who cannot attain one or another of these states ought to say so and leave the fight."[22] In this hierarchy of revolutionary values, the other kinds of praxis open to intellectuals were seldom specifically defined and tended to be subordinated to the armed struggle, as is clear from the declaration of the Congreso Cultural de la Habana:

> The intellectual can serve the revolutionary struggle from different fronts: ideological, political, military. . . . The activity of the intellectual may follow different paths: he/she may provide the ideology of the revolutionary classes, may participate in the ideological struggle; may conquer nature on behalf of the people by means of science and technology or by creating and popularizing artistic and literary works, and where the occasion reasons, he or she may commit themselves directly in the armed struggle.[23]

Not surprisingly, this produced a nagging consciousness that the intellectual's real revolutionary responsibility was with the *foco* [cell].[24] Given the fact that armed insurrection had taken place in many Latin American countries at this time, it is not surprising that many young writers should have regarded this as their priority. Some of them—Javier Heraud (Peru), Otto René Castillo (Guatemala), Roque Dalton (San Salvador), Francisco Urondo (Argentina)—would die participating in rural or urban guerrilla warfare. Guerrilla warfare also became thematically important in the literature of the sixties—for example in *País Portátil* [Portable Country] (1969) by Adriano González de León, in *Los fundadores del alba* [The Founders of Dawn] (1969) by Renato Prado Oropeza, and in *Libro de Manuel* [A Manual for Manuel] (1973) by Julio Cortázar.[25] More important, the very loftiness of the guerrilla example tended to suggest the superiority of the man of action over the intellectual and writer. This is clear in many of the poems written on the death of Che. The sense that guerrilla and intellectual represent irreconcilable destinies clearly surfaces in a poem by Antonio Cisneros which describes his reunion with an old friend who has become a Maoist:

> And he spoke of the Long March along the Blue River of turbulent
> waters,
> Along the Yellow River of cold currents. And we saw ourselves
> Strengthening our bodies, jumping and racing along the shore,
> Deprived of the music of flutes, without wine and
> With no other wisdom than that of the eyes.
> And the young stallions were lost behind the walls
> And he went back that night to Sommerard street

Thus it was.
Slow difficult gods, trained to gnaw at my liver each morning
Their faces are dark, ignorant of revelation.[26]

The Cultural Congress in 1968 would devote many sessions to discussing the role of the intellectual, stressing the need to heal the breach between the cultural avant-garde and the revolutionary vanguard. Conclusions were seldom more specific than Mario Benedetti's neat dichotomy of functions according to which "In the dynamic aspect of the revolution the man of action should be a vanguard for the intellectual, and in the sphere of art, thought, and scientific investigation, the intellectual should be a vanguard for the man of action.[27] When later in 1968, Heberto Padilla's prize-winning collection of poems, *Fuera del juego* [Out of the Game][28] was criticized for its "ambiguity" and because of a detachment contrary to "the active engagement which characterizes revolutionaries," it was the logical outcome of a position which defined revolutionary praxis primarily as participation in the armed struggle or on the economic front in Cuba itself. Works which were innovatory in form and language like Reinaldo Arenas's *El mundo alucinante* [Hallucinations] (1966); Lezama Lima's *Paradiso* [Paradise] (1966); and Alejo Carpentier's *El siglo de las luces* [Explosion in the Cathedral] (1962)[29] in fact spring from the writers' sense of their own special mission rather than from any revolutionary praxis.

Partly as an aftermath of the Cultural Congress of 1968, there developed a broader and more ecumenical theory of intellectual commitment of which the paradigmatic work is Fernández Retamar's *Calibán* (1971).[30] In this essay, the genealogy of culture is reconstituted in such a way that all Third World writers who can be said in some way to have liberated themselves from the deformed image imposed by the metropolis come to belong to the Third World revolution. Thus thinkers such as Alfonso Reyes or Rodó can be recuperated as precursors of this tradition.

This ecumenical approach was not without problems for the question of class did not enter into it, and it implied a nationalist (without internal class contradiction) outlook within the fraternity of Third World nations. Further, it tended to become vulgarized into the conviction that Third World peoples were pure and revolutionary as against the corrupt and unrevolutionary "First World," a conviction that was encouraged by some members of the European Left. Sartre, for instance, would humbly beg the Cultural Congress to be allowed to join the dazzling ("relampagueante") Third World revolutionary vanguard[31] and another delegate confessed to the "sickness of the west" and stated "Desconfía de mis palabras. . . . Estoy enfermo y contagioso" [Mistrust my words. . . . I'm sick and contagious].[32] A rather absurd aftermath was the criticism of those Latin American writers who exposed themselves to the dangerous air of the metropolitan nations. Neruda, for instance, was criticized for attending a Pen Club meeting in New York and when in 1971, Heberto Padilla was imprisoned and released after a confession (which led to an international protest), the National Congress of Education and Culture would condemn writers who made a reputation in Latin America only to settle in "the rotten and decadent societies of Western Europe and the United States in order to become agents of the imperialist metropolitan culture" (my translation).[33] On the political level, this obfuscated the revolutionary struggle, fostering the false notion of a quiescent metropolitan working class which fully consented to the policy of their leaders; on the cultural level, it substituted *ad hominem* polemic for criticism. An attempt by the Colombian novelist Oscar Collazos to evaluate texts on the grounds of the writers' closeness to Latin American experience in an essay, "La encrucijada del lenguaje" [The Crossroads of Language], was largely unsuccessful and brought immediate replies from Cortázar and Vargas Llosa.[34] Indeed, it is significant that, to explain why *Cien años de soledad* [One Hundred Years of Solitude] [35] should be more "authentic" than Carlos Fuentes's *Cambio de piel* [Change of Skin], Collazos has to resort to the old romantic notion that the writer is somehow "impregnated" before "giving birth" to a work of art:

> The work of a writer originates in a series of individual experiences which mark him, which leave him in a heavy, alienated and pregnant state and which each author owes to a specific social and cultural reality. . . . Creation is in the manner of a birth, an act of liberation, and the exercise of our own de-alienation.[36]

An explanation which depends on an analogy between childbirth and literary production must be inadequate. It substitutes a natural process for a theory. But more than this it glosses over the fact that the work of art does not simply come into being but is produced, using language and structures which inevitably include ideological traces.

Another possible explanation of why these Cuban (or Cuban-related) attempts to provide a universal theory did not work out was that there were fundamental differences between the situation within the island itself and in the rest of Latin America—all the difference, in fact, between a country struggling in the initial stages of its liberation from global capitalism and experiencing social change, and countries which were being forcibly integrated into advanced capitalism. The major problem of Cuba, as formulated after 1969, was that of building a literate labor force dedicated to long-term social goals and able to make responsible decisions. This was clearly not a possibility in the rest of Latin America where the gradual elimination of *focos* [cells] of armed insurrection represented one more stage in securing the domination of the multinational corporations. In the integration of new sectors of the population into capitalist economy, the dominant ideology took the form not only of the overt promotion of development but also of the subliminal messages which inculcated the desirability of modernization through media representation and lifestyles. Speed, mobility, and change were signifiers of the modern. It was precisely this ideology which writers outside Cuba confronted or incorporated into new aesthetic tendencies.

THE BOOM OF THE NOVEL AND
THE LIBERAL IMAGINATION

In the early sixties, many writers who supported Cuba and the struggles of national liberation believed that new techniques "revolutionized" literature. In this, they were the heirs of the European avant garde in its restless conquest of "new" areas of experience. Yet in Latin American context, the claims of the new novelists often took on a strange lexical similarity to the language of economic modernists and developmentalists. The Uruguayan novelist Juan Carlos Onetti would speak of the importation of technique from the metropolis: "we should import from there what we lack—technique, professionalism, seriousness—but only these. We should apply these qualities to our reality and trust that the rest will be given to us in addition."[37] For his part, Carlos Fuentes would contrast the universality of culture with the backwardness of Latin American technology while claiming, "our universality will come from this tension between cultural credit and technological debit (my translation).[38] In Mario Vargas Llosa's view, the new novel differed from the "primitive" novel precisely because of diversification of technique. He specifically compares the primitive and the creative stages in the development of the novel with the unequal stages of economic development in Latin America where "skyscrapers and Indian tribes, misery and opulence" coexist (my translation).[39] This lexicon—of *técnica* [technique] of accounting terms like *haber cultural* [cultural patrimony] and *deber technológico* [technological duty], of diversity and unequal development—suggests the subliminal structures of an economy of literary production. Yet it would be a mistake to believe that the novels of these authors simply express modernity. On the contrary, their interest lies precisely in the fact that by introducing the "autonomous character" of the metropolitan novel into Latin American environment, they set in motion the contradictions of individualism within a dependency context. These contradictions are, in turn, related to their individualistic view of cultural production and their utopian concept of writing itself as an unalienated form of production practiced as yet only by the chosen few. The writer himself or herself becomes the vanguard example of the new man and woman; and Carlos Fuentes would greet May 1968 in the following words:

> Power to the Imagination! The French students gave a serious and immediate content to the visionary and rebellious words of artists: man, each man is capable of defining his own destiny as an artist defines his work in the act of creation. And like a work of art, individual responsibility is the supreme instance of collective responsibility, and vice versa.[40]

Vargas Llosa's *García Márquez: Historia de un deicidio* [History of a Deicide][41] with its depiction of the artist as Lucifer rebelling against reality and all societies in order to create his own reality exemplifies another view of the writer-hero. Yet in the liberal-existentialist novels these writers produced in the early sixties, there is an interesting disparity between the highly individualized characters and the deterministic network of events and structures in which they are caught. I refer here to Onetti's *El astillero* [The Shipyard] (1961), Fuentes's *La muerte de Artemio Cruz* [The Death of Artemio Cruz] (1962), Vargas Llosa's *La casa verde* [The Green House] (1966), and *La ciudad de los perros* [The Time of the Hero] (1963), García Márquez's *El coronel no tiene quien le escriba* [No One Writes to the Colonel], and *One Hundred Years of Solitude* (1967) and (less directly, perhaps) Cortázar's *Rayuela* [Hopscotch] (1963).[42] In these novels the individual, that motor-force of early bourgeois society, becomes a phantasmagoric hero or a grotesque, superfluous excrescence whose talents and ingenuity are out of all proportion to the limitations of the environment. Larsen, Artemio Cruz, Fushía, Aureliano Buendía are entrepreneurs who will never build a capitalist society and who are, in fact, deprived of that essential element of the entrepreneur—an investment in the future. Indeed, though Vargas Llosa would stress the diversity of the new novels, they are remarkably analogous in situating their characters in a kind of impasse

in which the only freedom open to them is that of being able to reconstruct the past. (*The Time of the Hero* is an exception because its characters
are adolescents, though their future is already determined.) For characters
like Larsen (*The Shipyard*), who lives off the debris of a deserted shipyard,
Fushía (*The Green House*), who pirates the rubber in a jungle already controlled by a network of entrenched interests, Artemio Cruz who develops
his personal fortune out of property expropriated by the Mexican revolution, free enterprise means adapting to a situation whose basic features are
already given and their only area of choice and free activity becomes the
past which they reconstruct and reinterpret in a *post hoc* endeavor which is
analogous to that of the novelist. Creation and imagination have by implication no future dimension. The articulation of the novel around the
individual, "autonomous" character reaches its supreme expression in *One
Hundred Years of Solitude*, a novel which exaggerates the individuality, indeed the idiosyncrasies of the Buendías while constantly nullifying the
transcendence of their actions. The very concept of "autonomous character" is made visible in this way, the tragedy being that there is no real space
in which individuals can fully realize their aspirations.

It is not surprising that to the young generation which followed the
"boom," it would be "character" itself which now appeared as an outworn
convention or at best problematic. This subsequent generation (for instance, Hector Libertella of Argentina, José Agustín and Gustavo Sainz in
Mexico) would textualize modernity by adopting the language of the international youth style. The urban environment of their novels, the references
to pop culture, drugs, and sexual liberation codified the modern as against
the "folkloric," and as against traditional family mores and the family itself.
Language, especially the acquisition of a youth dialect, marked the gulf
between the old and the new. Groups like *El Techo de la Ballena* [The
Whale's Roof] (Venezuela), which held an "homage to necrophilia," were
able to provoke predictable scandals. Interestingly, however, what began as
the sign of the modern sometimes turned into political protest precisely
because the youth rebellion demanded the same freedoms which existed
in advanced industrial countries. Thus in Mexico, we have the paradox of
Tlatelolco, 1968, where young people were massacred to make the country
peaceful for the multinational sport of the Olympic games though, in fact,
it was these young people who sat in the Vips, drank Coke, and promoted
the international style and thus acted as the vanguard of modernization
itself. The weakness of the youth rebellion was precisely its anarchistic
individualism which, as Chile would show, could in some instances be used

in a reactionary cause. For right-wing students also wore long hair and listened to pop music.

MANDARIN PRAXIS

It is a characteristic of our (historical) contradiction that significance (bliss) has taken refuge in an excessive alternative: either in a mandarin praxis (result of an extenuation of bourgeois culture), or else in an utopian idea.[43]

According to the ideology of multinational corporatism, it was technology and not the class struggle which was changing the world. *The Rockefeller Report on Latin America*[44] attributed some of the sweeping changes to the new communications systems and the increased awareness among the disadvantaged of what they were missing. The gulf between rich and poor, it declared, is "made to seem all the worse by the facility of modern communications."[45] Yet the fundamental change was not the appearance of television sets or supermarkets or a growing middle class but rather the international division of labor on which the Rockefeller Report also insisted. The blatant intention of incorporating masses of Third World workers into a cheap labor pool accounts for the ferocity with which the guerrilla movements had to be suppressed, as well as the undermining of nationalist movements. Yet considering the obvious changes brought about by industrialization and mass communications, it was not hard to persuade Latin Americans that they were now like the "rest of the world" even if only in its alienation. Carlos Fuentes would write: "we are up to the neck in the rat-race: just like any gringo or Frenchman, we are dominated by the world of neon lights and Sears Roebuck and washing machines and James Bond films and Campbell soup tins."[46]

The argument that Latin America was "like the rest of the world" had been advanced by Octavio Paz as early as the 1950s. In the 1960s, he developed a far more sophisticated argument to show that technology had drastically changed perceptions in the industrial nations. It was an argument based on the fact that technology had destroyed previous images of the world—whether Christian or secular—fundamentally changing language itself: "Technology comes between us and the world, closes off every perspective to the glance: beyond its iron, glass or aluminum geometries, there is strictly nothing, except the unknown, the region of the formless which is not yet transformed by man"[47] (Paz, 1971:316).

Under these circumstances, the "referential" disappears, giving way to the free play of the sign in empty space. Instead of a more or less fixed set of codes there is a "repertory of signs invested with temporary and variable meanings, a universal vocabulary of activity, applied to the transformation of reality and which becomes organized in one way or another according to the different resistances it meets."[48] Instead of a tradition and a continuous development toward a recognizable future, technology offers a blank space to be filled and a play of signs which, by virtue of their indeterminate context, are constantly susceptible to new configurations. Technology thus potentially becomes a force of liberation which "liberates imagination from every mythology and confronts it with the unknown" (my translation).[49] On the other hand, Marxism is seen by Paz as an archaic theory, limited by its superseded historicism and out of touch with contemporary developments. His hope is for a "politics of the now," analogous to modern poetics as he conceives them.

By making poetry the highest example of human creativity, Paz eliminates daily life, popular culture, and the mass media from consideration. He is almost exclusively concerned with high culture (or, at best, high-quality artisan culture) and tends to deploy his poetics not so much as a revolutionary theory but rather as a refutation of historicism, putting himself beyond both bourgeois and Marxist thought since both these ignore poetry, the body, and the erotic and hence are blind to significant areas of experience. Stating that the age of revolution and of utopian politics has ended (but how?), Paz makes his own "poetics of the now" into the model for all activity in postindustrial society, but in order to do this, he must suppress difference and change in favor of a high degree of abstraction. The more general the categories employed, the more they subsume, and this very generality makes his and all such archetypal theories ultimately unsatisfactory. Yet the greatest inconsistency in Paz's work—and one which characterizes much contemporary writing—is that while attempting to reconcile the involvement of the reader in the text and the renunciation of the privileged status of the author as the sole creator of the work, it continues to idealize "literature" and to address a highly specialized and competent readership.

Paz is thus a good example of modern poetics used to counteract the historical. However, it is perhaps more enlightening to consider a different example—for instance, that of Carlos Fuentes since here we have a writer whose thinking shifted dramatically in the course of the sixties and who ended by rejecting the mimetic, the representational and the very historical structure on which his early writing was posited. By the time Fuentes

came to write *The New Spanish American Novel* in 1969, he had already confined the capitalist/socialist dichotomy to the status of an archaic myth,
superseded by "a sum of facts—cold, marvelous, contradictory, ineluct-
able, once again liberating, once again alienating—which are really transforming life in industrial societies: automation, electronics, the peaceful
use of atomic energy."[50] A new aesthetic must now replace the older realism: "Just as the traditional economic formulae of industrialism cannot
solve the problems of the technological revolution, bourgeois realism . . .
cannot provide the ultimate questions and answers of contemporary man,"
and this in turn means the adoption of a language "de la ambiguedad, de la
pluralidad de significados, de la constelación de alusiones, de la apertura"
[of ambiguity, of plural meanings, of a constellation of allusions, of open-
ing].[51] At this point, it is interesting to note that a necessary relationship is
established between "apertura" (that is openness to creative solutions and
opportunities) and "ambiguity" (which may sometimes be synonymous
with confusion or with euphemism). What is more striking however, is the
fact that *apertura* and *pluralidad* are also political terms and, indeed, are
used by Fuentes himself in his political essays.[52]

Fuentes adopted a new aesthetics in the very process of writing his appropriately named novel *A Change of Skin*. Originally having written and
completed it under the title *El sueño* [The Dream] as early as 1965, he
finally published the revised *A Change of Skin* in 1967. The final version
was a text which, he declared, "paralyzed history." "There is no historical
progress—this is what the novel is saying: there is no eschatology; there
is pure perpetual present. There is the repetition of a series of ceremonial acts" (my translation).[53] Thus the alternative to a bourgeois idea of
progress or to Christian eschatology becomes the suppression of change.
It is not surprising that the novel ends with an enactment of Fuentes's own
"change of skin" in which a narrative which had centered on character and
on existential choice is destroyed and replaced by a "happening" produced
by the mad narrator, Freddy Lambert, in a lunatic asylum. The protagonists of the happening are no longer "characters" but transformable figures
who are freed from the burden of identity and hence from responsibility
and ethical choice. They are signifiers for which the signified is "modernity" itself. And Freddy Lambert's name, an obvious reference to Balzac's
Lucien Lambert who was driven mad attempting to converse with angels is
meant to signify the final alienation of the author. Thus more than a happening, *A Change of Skin* is an allegory of Fuentes's own transition from
the author who had once attempted to write Mexico's Balzacian novel to

the author whose destruction of "mimesis" is potentially self-destruction. It is significant that in his more recent *Terra Nostra* (1975)[54] there is a full-scale rearrangement of the past according to the author's whim so that Philip the Second marries Elizabeth of England. History thus becomes converted into a kind of science fiction in which the author projects his own ideological fancies under the guise of "imagination."

The attack on character is symptomatic; it implies the end of mimesis and representation, a shift from the creation of recognizable identities to the concept of a permutable role, or a "figure," from situations which are analogous to daily life to narratives which lay bare their own process of production. I refer here to the Mexican Salvador Elizondo's *Faraboeuf* (1965) and *El hipogeo secreto* [The Secret Hypogeum], Cortázar's *62 Modelo para armar* [62 A Model Kit] (1968), the exiled Cuban writer, Severo Sarduy's *Cobra* (1972) and the novels of Argentina's Néstor Sánchez, among others.[55] What these writers have in common is a refusal to narrate a "something" and a recourse to certain privileged techniques and figures—the pun, the polyvalent event, metamorphosis, etc. These texts invite a different kind of reading which preempts criticism while drawing the reader into the creative process. Their claim to be revolutionary rests on two arguments: firstly, that by showing the process of signification, they penetrate beneath the "natural" appearance of linguistic and literary structures. Secondly, by producing unconsumable texts, by breaking down the barriers between criticism and writing and attending more to pleasure than to the reality principle, they block society's attempt to institutionalize writing's subversive potential. Such texts are playful and, like the erotic, they represent the ultimate transgression of bourgeois society in that supposedly they can neither be reproduced nor exchanged (reproduced in the sense that every reading is a different reading. Since the texts are self-referential, they do not constitute use-values). Under the name of *écriture* (*escritura*), first elaborated by Roland Barthes (1967) and the Paris journal *Tel Quel*, such a theory underlies much of the best contemporary Latin American criticism and some of the texts to which I have already referred. The most extravagant claims for its revolutionary potential were made by the exiled Cuban writer Severo Sarduy who, for some years, has lived in Paris. He has declared that the self-referential text alone transgresses bourgeois society and further that, since every regime is based on a kind of writing,

> a revolution that doesn't invent its own writing has failed. The role
> of the writer is so important that I would ask: what can be more than

a writer? What's the point of all those acts of "confrontation" except for writing, because writing is a force that demythologizes, corrupts, mines, cracks the foundation of any regime. The epistemological breakthrough that everyone talks about so much has not happened and cannot happen—we know that after all of *Tel Quel*'s efforts among others—unless it begins with and is nurtured in a piece of writing.[56]

Even if we accept Sarduy's premise here it is hard to see how such a subversion could occur unless it were generalized throughout large sectors of society, something which his texts with their heavy reliance on readership competence exclude.

Even if we set aside the elitist nature of texts which are addressed to readers already schooled in certain literary antecedents (especially Octavio Paz and contemporary French critics), their subversive potential rests on disputable premises. Firstly, these are said to reveal their own production process and hence to show the underlying ideological structure of traditional narrative. Secondly, because they constitute closed systems, they are said to defy a society which is bent on reducing everything to signs and messages and which institutionalizes art. Yet if the texts merely reveal their own self-constitution, they become little more than technical tours de force and their authors "move into the proximity of industrial technocrats."[57] Further, far from being irrecuperable by society, their very "neutrality" makes them eminently suitable for recuperation by university departments of literature, since established literary criticism has long defended the autonomy of art. And, as the case of Borges shows, authors of self-referential texts may even be useful cult figures in the service of reactionary governments.

However, writers such as Sarduy and Elizondo do not simply display technical virtuosity, for their novels are also attempts to short-circuit the social connotations of language which they link directly to desire. The body and the text become analogous and writing becomes a corporal act. In this way, their texts aim to overcome the old dichotomies of subjectivity and objectivity, mind and body, thought and feeling. However, they do so by reducing the social aspects of language and behavior to mere automatism. At the same time, the body/text analogy tends to produce a literary hedonism, a private zone of enjoyment which can be quite comfortably contained and protected within societies characterized by repressive tolerance.

A writer like Cortázar is particularly interesting because he attempts to overcome some of the contradictions and limitations of avant-garde writing, though only after he himself had passed through periods of militant hostility to committed writing.[58] In his early stories (e.g., *Las armas secretas* [Secret Weapons], 1959), he had often parodied naïve realist assumptions and he had warned readers against reductionist interpretations which validated his work by reference to reality. For Cortázar creative writing is not a reflection of reality but an exploration of "otherness" (what is not within subjectivity); hence, for a long time, he tended to separate nonreferential fictional works from texts which commented directly on society, culture, and daily life.[59] Even though he incorporated newspaper cuttings into his novel *Hopscotch* (1963) these were not intended to be read as references to a reality outside the text but were intended to reinforce the invasion of reality by the absurd. His *A Manual for Manuel* (1973), however, marks a break with previous practice:

> Though for years I have written texts linked to Latin American problems, along with novels and stories from which these problems were absent or in which they appeared only tangentially, here and now the waters have come together and their reconciliation has not been easy as perhaps is evident from the confused and agonized trajectory of a certain character.[60]

A Manual for Manuel, in fact, combines referential texts (newspaper clippings) with a fictional story of a group of urban guerrillas who plan and carry out a kidnapping operation in Paris as a kind of avant-garde political action. It is, therefore, an overtly political novel whose opposition to the status quo was explained by the author in the following terms:

> What is narrated, what I have tried to relate is the affirmative rigor as against the escalation of contempt and fear, and this affirmation has to be the most solar and vital in man, his erotic and ludic thirst, his liberation from taboos, his demand for a shared dignity in a world that is free from the daily horizon of jaws and dollars.[61]

This utopian element in the novel is represented above all by the group of young people brought together by love, personal contact, and friendship. They stand against the organized state apparatus whose ideology is represented in the newspaper cuttings. Because the newspapers refer to actual events of the early seventies referentiality is once again built into the text, the "fictional" elements serving to offset the repressive anonymous language of advanced capitalism by constructing and suggesting new kinds of relationships. However, the text is as interesting for what it omits as for what it includes. Historical experience has no place in the utopian community. Cortázar's classless guerrilla group is without a past, without a basis in the workplace, with no connection to other organizations, and there is no learning from experience. Truth is in the action itself. Behind *A Manual for Manuel* is still the structure of the avant-garde and the belief that a few creative people can wreck the machine.

The avant-garde group is the central figure of many of Cortázar's novels —for instance El club de Serpientes [The Serpent Club] in Hopscotch— though its implications only explicitly surface in one of his most recent texts, *Fantomás contra los vampiros multinacionales* [Fantomas and the Multinational Vampires].[62] In this fable, a group of writers—Cortázar himself, Alberto Moravia, Octavio Paz, Susan Sontag—alarmed at the destruction of books by the multinational corporations and intelligence agencies, are helped first by Fantomas (the hero of pulp literature and early French cinema) and then by thousands of anonymous voices on the telephone. An inhuman international system is pitted against "humanity" (but only the writers have names). The fable is, in turn, framed by a referential text for it begins with Cortázar's attendance at the Russell Tribunal on torture and ends with the report of the tribunal. The fable is thus intended to represent the utopian dimension of the work, yet its very disposition reveals its ideology. For Fantomas is obviously intended to represent an older form of mass culture (he precludes the multinational comics and was a cult figure among the surrealists) though in fact, he embodies the myth of extreme individualism. Thus we have an opposition consisting of named writers, Fantomas (popular mythic hero) and the anonymous voices of the masses. The implicit hierarchic structure which privileges the writer as an exemplary figure was made explicit in Cortázar's reply to Oscar Collazos when he stated:

> The sign of all great creation is that it comes from a creator who, in some way, has already broken these barriers and who writes from a different point of view, calling out to those who, for multiple and obvious reasons have not been able to cross the boundary, encouraging them with appropriate weapons, to accept that profound liberty

which can only come from the realization of the highest values of each individual.[63]

BREAKING OUT OF THE CULTURAL GHETTO

Despite declarations to the contrary, the avant-garde text still privileges the writer hero though at the cost of abandoning a sense of history and place. This space came to be occupied by another kind of text which narrated the unofficial history of Latin America. I refer here to essays such as Rodolfo Walsh's *Operación masacre* [Operation Massacre] (1964), García Márquez's *Historia de un náufrago* [Story of a Shipwreck] (1970, written 1965), Elena Poniatowska's *La noche de Tlatelolco* [The Night of Tlatelolco] (1971)[64] which went into 25 editions by 1975, Carlos Monsiváis's *Días de guardar* [Holidays], and Guillermo Thorndyke's *No, mi general* [No Sir General].[65] One might also include in this category, oral histories and tape-recorded memoirs of hitherto marginalized sectors (of which Miguel Barnet's *Biografía de un cimarrón* [Biography of a Runaway Slave][66] is an example). Yet, however interesting, such texts cannot replace literature which, by virtue of its very fictionality, produces distancing and displacements within discourse that allow critical understanding of processes and ideologies which might otherwise be accepted as natural. However, it is also crucially important, at the present juncture, for literature to break out of the cultural ghetto of the avant-garde where it has been reduced to technique or hedonism. This is by no means easy for in the age of the mass media, the gulf between literature and mass culture has widened. Even in situations such as that which prevailed in Chile during the Unidad Popular (UP) government when the social function of art and literature could be openly debated, older aesthetic ideologies were retained even by some writers on the left. One radical solution, suggested just before the UP government took power was the radical seizure of culture from the hands of the elite to restore it to the people.[67] The writer, it was suggested, would have to be proletarianized. There were also embryonic attempts at this time to link cultural activities to mass mobilization through popular song, commando group art, and street theater. Such efforts were not, of course, confined to Chile. A pioneer of a new kind of "teatro jornal" in Brazil, Augusto Boal had long affirmed that theater "can be practised by anyone."[68] Such efforts, however, were closely bound to specific forms of struggle and they depended on the minimum of democratic structures so that they have not survived repression.

There remains the Brechtian alternative, that of building into literature not only the force of experience but also the knowledge that will allow critical judgment. Brecht stated, "the great and complicated things that go on in the world cannot be adequately recognized by people who do not use every possible aid to understanding."[69] Such a recommendation has particular force at the present time since both information and historical experience are repressed or devirtualized by the mass media which make a radical separation between information and historical experience. On the other hand, literature can restore some of this essential information as two symptomatic texts show: these are *Homenaje a los indios americanos* [Homage to the American Indians] (1972) by Ernesto Cardenal and Roa Bastos's *Yo el supremo* [I the Supreme] (1974).[70]

Cardenal's poems deploy quotations from pre-Columbian texts, from travelers' log books and historical records in order to convey the history of the genocide practiced on the Indians. One of the most interesting features of this collection of poems, however, is the demystification of poetic language by the virtual elimination of traditional poetic figures such as simile and metaphor. The result of this is that the reader is made to confront discourse of and about the American Indian with as little mediation by the poet as possible. Cardenal no longer draws attention to himself as sole producer of the poem but arranges different kinds of discourse in such a way that the reader's attention is drawn to its ideological import.

Similarly in *I the Supreme*, the compiler claims that all that he has done is to copy faithfully what has been said by others so that much of the novel is drawn from historical records and travel accounts relating to Paraguay during Dr. Francia's dictatorship and which are set against many other kinds of discourse, including a private diary in which the dictator struggles with self-expression. The text provides the reader with historical knowledge in such a way that the complexity cannot be reduced to simplistic judgments. Rather than merely reflecting history, it restores the concrete individual which historical discourse omits and at the same time reveals history as something which is produced and not a given or an eternal truth. At the same time, such texts are not simply rearrangements of history according to some countercultural subjective fantasy and hence they go beyond Reinaldo Arenas's *Hallucinations* and Carlos Fuentes's *Terra Nostra*. On the other hand, both Gabriel García Márquez's *El otoño del patriarca* [The Autumn of the Patriarch] (1975) and Alejo Carpentier's *El Recurso del método* [Reasons of State] (1974) could be included among these "information" texts which by supplying knowledge about the past also focus a critical light on the relation between power and dependency in the present.

Plainly the very status of literature has changed in the last decades and with it, the potential readership of both novels and poetry. The change can best be measured by contrasting the implicit appeal to the "pueblo" in Neruda's *General Song* with the contemporary erudite text which is plainly directed to a public of students and university-trained people. Though literary critics often scoff at references to the writer's public as vulgarly sociological, all texts have built-in codes which indicate their virtual audience. Neruda's poetry, for instance, uses the devices of oral tradition so that even though his language is complex, it does not need an academic listener to be understood. The contemporary "erudite" texts suppose competent readers and makes the writer either a culture hero or a member of a phalanstery of taste.[71] It is against the elitism of this position and against the paternalistic populism of certain realistic texts that Roa Bastos's novel stands. It opens up the possibility of literature, film, television programming which does not simply separate the reader/observer from identification with characters or situations in a text (most modern literature goes this far) but allows active participation in a process of political learning. It is along lines such as these that radical writing and criticism can begin to separate itself both from the passive model implied by realism and the vacuity of the modernizing avant garde.

NOTES

1   Carlos Fuentes, *Cambio de piel* (Mexico City: Joaquín Mortíz, 1968).
2   José María Arguedas, *El zorro de arriba y el zorro de abajo* (Buenos Aires: Losada, 1971).
3   Cortázar's transition to more directly political literature is discussed later in the article. Mario Vargas Llosa's farce, *Pantaleón y las visitadoras* (Barcelona: Seix Barral, 1973) constitutes a major change from his serious treatment of politics which reached a peak in *Conversation in the Cathedral*, trans. Gregory Rabassa (New York: Harper Row, 1970).
4   Carlos Fuentes, *La nueva novela latinoamericana* (Mexico City: Joaquín Mortíz, 1969).
5   Roland Barthes, *Writing Degree Zero*, trans. Annette Lavers and Colin Smith (London: Cape, 1967).

6 Modernism in Spanish American criticism refers to a group of poets writing between 1880 and 1918. In Anglo-American criticism, it is used in a more general sense to refer to widespread rejection of a view of poetry as the "expression" of autobiographical revelations and feelings.

7 *Écriture* was first used by the French critic Roland Barthes (*Writing Degree Zero; The Pleasure of the Text*, trans. Richard Miller [New York: Hill and Wang, 1975]) to supplant the term *style* but later came to differentiate a particular type of writing from "literature" as institutionalized in the educational system. The term *avant-garde* came to be used at the end of the nineteenth century to indicate newness and originality in artistic creation. *Écriture*, though difficult to define exactly, indicates a radical break from theories which hold literature to be either a "reflection" of reality or an expression of the author's feeling. *Écriture* instead makes literature an activity which produces or constitutes meaning.

8 *Reflectionist* refers to theories based on the metaphor of the mirror which hold literature to reflect, through its forms or content, social formations and historical movements. See Georg Lukács, "Introduction to a Monograph on Esthetics," In *Marxism and Art*, Maynard Solomon (New York: Knopf, 1973), 409–19.

9 Walter Benjamin, "The Work of Art in the Age of Mechanical Reproduction," in *Illuminations* (London: Jonathan Cape, 1970), 219–53.

10 Bertolt Brecht, "Theatre for Pleasure or Theatre for Instruction," in *Marxists on Literature*, ed. David Craig (London: Pelican Books, 1975), 412–20.

11 Mario Vargas Llosa, "Novela primitiva y novela de creación en América latina," *Revista de la Universidad de México* 22 (June 1969): 31.

12 Fuentes, *La nueva novela latinoamericana*, 35.

13 Severo Sarduy, "From Boom to Big Bang," *Review* 74 (winter 1974); Octavio Paz, "El signo y el garabato," in *El signo y el garabato* (Mexico: Joaquín Mortíz, 1973).

14 José Revueltas, *El conocimiento cinematográfico y sus problemas* (Mexico City: UNAM, 1965), 5.

15 Much contemporary Marxist film and literary criticism is now concerned with texts which dislocate the tendency of the spectator/reader to identify with characters and situations and further face readers with contradictions in their own situation. In new texts this is done not by hiding the manner in which it is constructed but rather by making this process visible. For criticism along these lines, see Louis Althusser, "The Piccolo Teatro's Bertoluzzi and Brecht: Notes on a Materialist Theater," in *For Marx* (New York: Vintage Books, 1970); Terry Eagleton, *Criticism and Ideology* (London: New Left Books, 1977); and Pierre Macherey, *Pour une théorie de la production littéraire* (Paris: Maspero, 1966).

16 José María Arguedas, *Todas las sangres* (Buenos Aires: Losada, 1964).

17 Arguedas, *El zorro de arriba y el zorro de abajo*, 211.

18 José Revueltas, *El apando* (Mexico City: Era, 1969).

19 José Revueltas, "Hegel y yo," in *Material de sueños* (Mexico City: Era, 1974).

20 In this article I am not primarily concerned with culture within Cuba, since changes in infrastructure make this a different case from the rest of the conti-

nent. Most existing commentaries start from the unacceptable premise that literature is a privileged form of cultural production and can be considered in isolation as the standard by which revolutionary culture is to be judged. They then go on to judge Cuba literary production by normative "international" standards. For an example of this, see *Revista Iberoamericana* 92–93 (July–December 1975). My own article, "Contexts of Cuban Writing," *Cambridge Review* 91 (20 February 1970): 104-7, now needs bringing up to date.

21 Ernesto Guevara, *El socialismo y el hombre en Cuba* (Havana: Ediciones de la Revolución, 1965).

22 Ernesto Guevara, *El diario del Che en Bolivia* (Buenos Aires: Editora América Latina, 1968): 275.

23 Declaraciones del Primer Congreso Nacional de Educación y Cultura, *Casa de las Américas* 65-66 (1971).

24 Carlos María Gutiérrez, "Mala conciencia para intelectuales," *Marcha* 1386 (12 January 1968).

25 Adriano de León González, *País portátil* (Barcelona: Seix Barral, 1969); Renato Prado Oropeza, *Los fundadores del alba* (Havana: Casa de las Américas, 1969); Julio Cortázar, *Libro de Manuel* (Buenos Aires: Sudamericana, 1963).

26 Antonio Cisneros, *Canto ceremonial contra un oso hormiguero* (Havana: Casa de las Américas, 1968).

27 Mario Benedetti, "Relaciones entre el hombre de acción y el intelectual," *Casa de las Américas* 7 (March–April 1968): 116-20; "Las prioridades del escritor," *Marcha* 1546 (4 June 1971).

28 Heberto Padilla, *Fuera del juego* (Havana: Casa de las Américas, 1968).

29 Reinaldo Arenas, *El mundo alucinante.* (Mexico City: Diógenes, 1996) (*Hallucinations*, trans. Gordon Brotherston [Penguin Books, 1976]); José Lezama Lima, *Paradiso* (Mexico City: Era, 1968) (*Paradiso*, trans. Gregory Rabassa [London: Secker and Warburg, 1974]); Alejo Carpentier, *El siglo de las luces* (Mexico City: Ediapsa, 1962) (*Explosion in a Cathedral*, trans. John Sturrock [Boston: Little, Brown, 1963]).

30 Roberto Fernández Retamar, *Calibán* (Mexico City: Diógenes, 1971).

31 María Gutiérrez, "Mala conciencia para intelectuales."

32 Declaraciones del Primer Congreso Nacional de Educación y Cultura, 18.

33 Ibid.

34 Oscar Collazos, et al., *Literatura en la revolución y revolución en la literatura* (Mexico City: Siglo XXI, 1970).

35 Gabriel García Márquez, *Cien años de soledad* (Buenos Aires: Sudamericana, 1967).

36 Collazos, *Literatura en la revolución y revolución en la literatura*, 35.

37 Juan Carlos Onetti, cited in Angel Rama, in *Marcha* 1220 (28 August 1964).

38 Fuentes, *La nueva novela latinoamericana*, 31.

39 Vargas Llosa, "Novela primitiva y novela de creación en América latina," 35.

40 Fuentes, *La nueva novela latinoamericana*, 90.

41 Mario Vargas Llosa, *García Márquez: Historia de un deicidio* (Barcelona: Barral Editores, 1971).

42 Juan Carlos Onetti, *El astillero* (Buenos Aires: Fabril, 1961); Carlos Fuentes, *La muerte de Artemio Cruz* (Mexico City: Fondo de Cultura Económico, 1962); Mario Vargas Llosa, *La casa verde* (Barcelona: Seix Barral, 1966) and *La ciudad y los perros* (Barcelona: Seix Barral, 1963); Gabriel García Márquez, *El coronel no tiene quien le escriba* (Medellín: Editorial Aguirre, 1961); Julio Cortázar, *Rayuela* (Buenos Aires: Sudamericana, 1963).

43 Barthes, *The Pleasure of the Text*, 38–39.

44 Rockefeller Report, *Rockefeller Report on the Americas* (New York: Quadrangle Books, 1969).

45 Ibid., 1.

46 Carlos Fuentes, "Entrevista con Emir Rodríguez Monegal," in *Homenaje a Carlos Fuentes*, ed. Helmy F. Giacoman (New York: Las Américas, 1971), 47.

47 Octavio Paz, *Los signos en rotación y otros ensayos* (Madrid: Alianza Editorial, 1971).

48 Ibid., 317–18.

49 Ibid., 318.

50 Fuentes, *La nueva novela hispanoamericana*, 18.

51 Ibid., 32.

52 Carlos Fuentes, *Tiempo mexicano* (Mexico City: Joaquín Moritz, 1971).

53 Carlos Fuentes, "Situación del escritor en América latina," *Mundo Nuevo* 1 (1966): 11. My translation.

54 Carlos Fuentes, *Terra Nostra* (Mexico City: Joaquín Mortíz, 1975).

55 Salvador Elizondo, *Faraboeuf* (Mexico City: Joaquín Mortíz, 1965); Julio Cortázar, *62 Modelo para armar* (Buenos Aires: Sudamericana, 1968); Salvador Elizondo, *El hipogeo secreto* (Mexico: Editorial J. Mortíz, 1968); Severo Sarduy, *Cobra* (Buenos Aires: Sudamericana, 1972).

56 Sarduy, "From Boom to Big Bang," *Review* 74 (winter 1974).

57 Hans Magnus Enzensberger, "Commonplace on the Newest Literature," in *The Consciousness Industry*, trans. Michael Roloff (New York: Seabury Press, 1974).

58 Julio Cortázar, "Situación de la novela," *Cuadernos Americanos*, 52 (July–August 1950); *Las armas secretas* (Buenos Aires: Sudamericana, 1959).

59 Julio Cortázar, *La vuelta al día en ochenta mundos* (Mexico City: Siglo XXI, 1967); *Ultimo Round* (Mexico City: Siglo XXI, 1969).

60 Cortázar, *Libro de Manuel*, 7.

61 Ibid., 8.

62 Julio Cortázar, *Fantomas contra los vampiros multinacionales* (Mexico City: Excelsior, 1975).

63 Cortázar quoted in Collazos, *Literatura en la revolución y revolución en la literatura*, 64.

64 Rodolfo J. Walsh, *Operación masacre* (Buenos Aires: Continental Service, 1964);

Gabriel García Márquez, *Relato de un náufrago* (Barcelona: Tusquets, 1970); Elena Poniatowska, *La noche de Tlatelolco* (Mexico City: Joaquín Moritz, 1971).

65 Carlos Monsiváis, *Días de guardar* (Mexico City: Joaquín Moritz, 1971); Guillermo Thorndyke, *No, mi general* (Lima: Mosca Azul, 1976).

66 Miguel Barnet, *The Autobiography of a Runaway Slave*, trans. Jocasta Innes (New York: Panther, 1968).

67 Armand Mattelart, *La comunicación masiva en el proceso de la liberación* (Mexico City: Siglo XXI, 1971).

68 Augusto Boal, "La impotencia de Superman y la potencia del teatro," *Marcha* 1571 (26 November 1971).

69 Bertolt Brecht, "Brecht Event" [Transcript of a discussion on Brecht held at the Edinburgh Festival], *Screen* 16, no. 4 (1975–1976): 17.

70 Ernesto Cardenal, *Homenaje a los indios americanos* (Buenos Aires: Cuadernos Latinoamericanos, 1971); Augusto Roa Bastos, *Yo el supremo* (Mexico City: Siglo XXI, 1974).

71 Barthes, *The Pleasure of the Text*.

DEPENDENT INDUSTRIALIZATION AND

ONETTI'S *THE SHIPYARD*

The kind of mirage . . . reminds me personally of certain primitive borderline areas in the Tropics. Junk of all kinds, the bones of dead sawmills, mattresses, house-coats, shattered sculptures, carcass of the motorcar, mastheads, stranded skins or sails on the river front. I know that sort of splintered world—neither capitalist nor communist.—WILSON HARRIS, *Palace of the Peacocks*

The port of *El astillero* [The Shipyard] is neither haven nor a starting point for adventure but a purgatory inhabited by "ánimas en pena" [condemned souls], a place of waiting, futility, decay, emptiness. Critics have often compared Onetti's writing to that of another inventor of an emptied world, William Faulkner. I prefer a different comparison or contrast, one with a world that is replete, surfeited with things, like that of *Buddenbrooks* or that of many of Balzac's novels. The contrast with *Buddenbrooks* is particularly instructive, for here, despite the charting of a decline, the solidity of their environment and its substantiality are never in doubt. "They had dark red damask wall-paper, a heavy round table upon which the samovar was steaming, a massive sideboard, and chairs of carved nut-wood with rush seats" (pp. 246–47). The goods the Buddenbrooks buy and the money they invest, form a solid reality that is, at the same time, a true indicator of their worth, for reward comes in proportion to their dedication, as payment for "thirst for action, for power and success," for the aggressive energy which makes Thomas long "to force fortune to her knees," Failure when it comes is genetic failure, and with it there is the introduction of other values that strike at the heart of puritan effort. Yet substance is still there even at the end, at the sad dinner party that closes the book, when the family consists only of the old survivors. Sesami Wiechbrocht raps on the

Originally published as "La máquina rota" in *Texto crítico* 6 nos. 18–19 (July–December 1980): 33–46. Translated by Carla Faini.

table with a gesture of defiance which is not an empty gesture, for though the Buddenbrook empire has collapsed the rest of the world has not. The objects they own have changed hands but they persist, are durable. The Buddenbrooks may have disappeared but civilization has not broken down.

In contrast to this is *The Shipyard*, in which the scaffolding of enterprise exists but in which the flesh has melted away. Here people inhabit the ghosts of objects whose worth is mere fantasy. It is a world of pure forms without entelechy, of abstraction without substance, of matter which has never been observed to grow or come into being, only to decay and to go to waste. The society which inhabits *The Shipyard* is an aged society, never seen in the time of its youth and energy. Even the chronologically young (the hotel employee whom Larsen talks to at the end of the novel) are as cynical as old men. Angélica Inés, the Juliet to Larsen's Romeo, is young only in appearance, in the "restos de infancia" [traces of her childhood], which persist "en los ojos claros que entornaba para mirar . . . un poco en el pecho liso, en la camisa de hombre y el pequeño lazo de terciopelo en el cuello" [in her blue eyes as she turned them to look around her . . . her flat chest, the man's shirt she was wearing and the little velvet bow at her neck.] (p. 15).[1] Angélica Inés is never more than a "convincing imitation" of a youth, and her presence has the mustiness of things preserved. If her hair appears to be "sin edad" [ageless], on her face there are "arrugas recientes" [recently acquired wrinkles] (p. 16). Her strange laugh resonates a note of dissonance among the cobwebs of the shop, but it is the dissonance of madness, not of youth. So she is ambiguity itself, neither completely woman (since she has no experience) nor completely young, neither untouched by time nor mature, possessed of a past that has not really made a mark on her, wasted but without having gone through the essential experiences of womanhood. The incidents of her life have happened to her, like the rain which falls at her meeting with Larsen, like the flood that is her first traumatic remembrance. Angélica Inés embodies the tension which repeats itself throughout the novel: the tension between the experience which corrupts and the emptiness of a life lived without experience, expressed in her empty motiveless laughter.[2]

This empty emotional relationship is paralleled by empty work relationships. The shipyard is a place whose only function is that of work—without work it is meaningless. The ship is almost a clichéd symbol for life, and the port where the ship is harbored, safe from the storms of experience, is also the shipyard where vessels are made fit for journey. The whole topography of *The Shipyard* is thus redolent of a symbolism of faith, strife, and progress toward an end. But the journey and the port are ambivalent in their implications. The port is salvation from the stormy sea of life but it is also the gateway to progress. We recall in *Moby-Dick* that the *Pequod* left the harbor in what one critic has called "a vengeful and aggressive drive which is analogous to the progress of 'advanced civilization.'" In Melville's novel, man's relation to nature is technological, the ship is the "mobile replica of an advanced technological society," but it is also a cathedral, a church dedicated to this insane faith in progress, the obsession with the white whale of the unknowable.[3] In *The Shipyard*, both the Christian and the "progressive" symbolism are equally inapplicable to the present.

It is precisely this ambiguity which gives the novel its density, for the reader is always being referred to two great myths—the Christian myth and the myth of progress—from the standpoint of a present in which they have ceased to act as cohesive forces. The standpoint is thus from disintegration in which man (a pattern-forming animal) can only assemble patterns he knows to be ephemeral. One device for showing this is in the motif of the shipyard itself, that business which has not business yet preserves all the apparatus of work. Using the empty forms, Larsen can pose problems which appear to be meaningful:

> This affair of the *Tiba*, and the gringo Chadwick & Son. When these things happen, when they come to our knowledge . . . Do we confine ourselves to sending a letter or do we rely on an agent in El Rosario? I say El Rosario, but I mean any port within our sphere of influence (pp. 47–48).

The whole trick here is to make the matter of the *Tiba* sound as if it referred to a reality, when patently it does nothing of the kind. (Let us note in passing that Larsen's *Tiba* stands in relation to the real *Tiba* as the novel to "reality"). What is absent from the *Tiba* is actuality, existence.

The Shipyard is, then, a question of patterns and models without any signified. The passing of time has eaten away at the substance leaving only the empty forms.[4] The shipyard is an "industry" without industry and Larsen appears as "saviour" in this empty world without having any power to resurrect or create life. He has all the attributes of God, but is not God:

> He was *watchful, uneasy, implacable and paternal*, covertly *majestic*, determined to lavish promotions and dismissals, needing to believe that all this belonged to him and needing to surrender himself unreservedly to all this, with the sole purpose of giving it a meaning, a meaning

which could be transferred to the years he had left to live, and therefore to his whole life (p. 35).

Larsen is a "god" who needs a creation in order to be assured of his own
meaningful existence. Yet plainly he is unable to create a universal order.
He can only marshal what is given into a pattern of individual meaning. To
differentiate himself from chaos and death is difficult and his project (or
his personality) is continually under threat so that although he is given the
attributes of God, these seem to float free of an eternal and infinite being
in relation to which they might make sense. Applied to a finite and defeated creature, they can only be ironic. Beneath Larsen's feet as he walks
in the shipyard is an emptiness which connotes a spiritual as well as physical void: "He descended the steps awkwardly, feeling unsafe and exposed,
trembling excessively when, as he reached the second flight, the walls came
to an abrupt end, and the rattling iron steps spiraled down into the void"
(33). The Spinozan universe in which God or nature as well as individual
man form part of a totality, in which all things strive to persist in their
own being, has been undermined. Suddenly man finds himself alone, gesturing over the void, not even sure of his own identity.[5]

The landscape is always one of fragments, of heterogeneous elements
piled together. Outside Gálvez's cabin, Larsen finds a "timonera ladeada"
(the distorted rudder of life's journey), weeds, "el esqueleto herrumbreado
del camión, la baja muralla de despojos, cadenas, anclas, mástiles" [the
rusty skeleton of the truck, the low wall of debris, chains, anchors and
masts] (p. 64). Inside the shipyard, the motionless machine is even more
in evidence. Larsen considers them as "paralizadas tal vez para siempre"
[paralyzed probably forever] (p. 35). The sheds are filled with "cadáveres de
herramientas" [the corpses of tools] (p. 35); an eternity, an infinity of dead
machines stretches "más allá del último peldaño de toda escalera imaginable" [higher than the topmost step of any imaginable stairway] (p. 35).
Instead of a great chain of being envisaged by the eighteenth-century philosophers, Onetti presents us with a great chain of deadness. There is no
staircase leading to a technological heaven. The shipyard has never in itself
represented a functioning whole, for it was a place where ships were re-
paired, not produced. When Larsen envisions it working, he reconstructs
a center of communication rather than a place of *production*:

> There had been glass panes in the window; twenty or thirty men had
> bent over the desks; each pair of torn wires had once plugged into a
> telephone; a girl unerringly plugged in and pulled out the jacks on the

switchboard ("Petrus Limited, good morning"); other girls walked alluringly to the metal filing cabinets. And the old man made the women wear gray overalls. Perhaps they thought that it was he who forced them to remain unmarried and not give rise to scandal. Three hundred letters a day, at least, were sent off by the boys in the dispatch section. And there at the back, invisible, almost legendary, as old as he was today, confident and tiny, the old man (p. 28).

The office turns into a parody of the church which is seen as an immense system of communication leading finally to God and demanding the absolute dedication of its members. Even Larsen's inductive reconstruction of a whole from the evidence of broken windows and cables which leads him to his vision of "el viejo" [the old man] resembles a neo-Platonic induction of God's existence from the imperfect forms. But the analogy between the office and the church, like the analogy between the shipyard and a religious order, only serves to cast doubt on all systems of belief by revealing them to be based on common forms which man fleshes out with significance. When Gálvez writes to Larsen, for instance, his letter is taken to be a "miracle" because it testifies to the "presence and truth of a God whom he, Kunz, had blasphemed." The language is not, however, intended to deceive the reader into believing it to be a miracle, rather it is meant only to draw attention to the parallel between the way God's presence has been revealed to men and Larsen's relation with the other employees. What the reader measures is the distance between a divinely ordered universe and a Larsen-centered universe.

In this respect, the novel and Larsen's project are analogous. The reader may suspend belief and enter into a dialogue with the writer, but Onetti asks him to be more sophisticated than this, to balance within his or her mind the possibility of belief and coherence and at the same time of skepticism and disintegration. Like Larsen, he wants us to walk on a tightrope over the void. This is why the "plot" of the novel—the projected marriage of Larsen with Angélica Inés, Gálvez's denunciation of Petrus, the embezzlement has verisimilitude and, at the same time, is shown to be a "plot," that is, a *fictional* device. In *The Shipyard*, the return to chaos, the tendency to formlessness prevails over form and organization. Hence, when Larsen first visits the shipyard, the decay seems to him a vision of eternity: "Right from the very beginning and for all eternity, there was nothing more than the steeply pitched roof, the layers of rust, the tons of metal, and the weeds blindly growing and twining around everything"

(p. 34). Despite the appearance of life and growth in the "yuyos" [weeds] (to which we shall return later), eternity is clearly associated with fragmentation, loss of function, and disorder. The "tonelada de hierro" [tons of metal] represent mere accumulation rather than a teleology. Thus Larsen's role as "god" or "saviour" is limited to that of monitoring decay:

> deliberately taking upon himself the bitterness and the skepticism of defeat, drawing these from the metal spare parts in their tombs, the corpulent machines in their mausoleums, the cenotaphs of weed, mud and shadows, lurking-places arranged *without a plan*, which had contained, five or ten years ago, the proud and stupid willfulness of a workman or the coarseness of a foreman (p. 35).

The deliberate contrast with a preestablished harmony is expressed in the words "sin concierto" [without a plan]. Without purpose, there is only a pile of useless artifacts, "mud and shade," a cemetery of machines. Larsen cannot save it not only because belief in God has been lost but also because there is no longer any belief in man or man's confident harnessing of nature to the wheels of progress.[6] The "voluntad estúpida y orgullosa de un obrero" [the proud and stupid willfulness of a workman] and "la grosería de un capataz" [the coarseness of a foreman] objectively may have been as absurd as belief in miracles, but they had nevertheless been the motor forces of production. However, there has been no transformation of this class-divided production system into a new social order. Instead, outside factors have brought about decay and left littered fragments of a material order, just as religion left institutional fragments (marriage) of a spiritual order. Just as concepts like "salvation" and "faith" survive from the divinely ordered world, so do concepts such as "value" survive from the sphere of production and labor. Evaluation is extremely important to Larsen, although the values he attaches to objects represent neither exchange nor use value, being mere fragments from the past. Despite the inapplicability of prices fixed many years ago, he goes on "hablando del precio por metro de la pintura de un casco de barco en el año 47 o sugiriendo tretas infantiles para ganar mucho más dinero con el carenaje de buques fantasmas que nunca remontarían el río" [discussing the price per yard of painting the hull of a ship in the year 1947 or suggesting childish tricks for earning much more money for the careening of phantom ships which would never come up the river again] (p. 48). Again, these ghostly "values" allow Larsen to structure and order his world, just as religious values and institutions sustain him even in his skepticism. So a life raft is valued at "mil pesos" [one thousand pesos], and the shipyard at "treinta millones" [thirty million].

> And that figure does not include the enormous appreciation of some of the goods in the last few years; nor does it include many others which can still be salvaged, such as miles of roads which can partly be reconverted to salable land, and the first section of the railway (p. 26).

Yet even as Larsen attaches value to them, the objects are slipping back into valueless chaos. He is forced to recognize that his evaluations are pure fantasy. The rusty truck which might have been worth "más de cincuenta mil si lo hubieran cuidado, con sólo meterlo bajo techo" [more than fifty thousand if they had taken care of it, just by putting it under cover] (p. 33), testifies to the illusory nature of the prices. The "if" measures a vast abyss between what lies before the eyes and what might have been. The objects in the shipyard are valueless because they are no longer part of a production/consumption system, and even when cannibalized for their spare parts the buyers hardly covet them enough to offer more than a token amount.

> The men from the truck would take one or two steps forward to look at it, would frown and would show each other, mutely, almost pitifully, the ravages of rust, the anachronistic details, the differences existing between what they were looking for and what they were being offered. (121)

Again, we have only to contrast the Buddenbrooks, at the moment in the novel when Tom's father tells him:

> "We are arranging the rye sale I told you about with Van Hankdom and Company."
> "What is he giving?" Tom asked with interest, ceasing to tickle Tony.
> "Sixty thalers for a thousand kilos—not bad, eh?"
> "That's very good. Tom knew this was excellent business."

The Buddenbrooks function within a market economy which also provides an objective gauge, their skill at judging the situation being matched by their power and prestige within society. In *The Shipyard*, it is not only belief in Christianity and belief in progress that have failed, but also the social consequences of communal belief. Thus when Larsen bargains with the two men in the shipyard, the skepticism of the buyers shows that they

do not share Larsen's system of values. Similarly his relations with Angélica Inés betray the same lack of a common system—the games that Larsen
plays in the *glorieta* [summerhouse] are not shared by the woman. He sees
the *glorieta* as always the same "escena fallida" [failed scene] and she sees it
as a place of deception.

We return to the empty forms; the pattern of progress and salvation, the
glorieta, the money values. Their emptiness allows for multiplicity of function, but this means that their cohesive and universal attributes disappear.

But how has this stage been reached? A historical process is vaguely
suggested in the novel in the career of the dying Petrus. An immigrant
capitalist, he had tried and failed to buy a house belonging to the aristocratic Latorre, a house on an island. There is, therefore, a skeleton of
a historical or social allegory. The Latorre house to which Petrus aspires
cannot be taken over and becomes a museum, suggesting that in that area
(perhaps the Plate Region, perhaps Latin America), the historical development from land-owning aristocracy to capitalist society has somehow
been frustrated. The *astillero* [shipyard] remains an enclave and its owner
never takes control of society, although Díaz Grey imagines at one point
a Petrus who had realized his ambition:

> Petrus, our master, watching over us, our needs and our wages, from
> the cylindrical tower of the palace. It is possible that Petrus might have
> given it a finishing touch by having a lighthouse built; or we might
> have found it enough, to embellish and enliven our submission, to con-
> template from the promenade along the beach, on fine evenings, the
> lighted windows like stars, behind which Jeremías Petrus was keeping
> vigil and governing us (p. 111).

But, in fact, the house of Petrus is never allowed to become a dynasty. The
daughter, Angélica Inés, is a madwoman; the house on the island never
became his. And the house he finally builds on stilts as protection from
floods is doomed to inner destruction.

There are remnants of other social orders within the novel. The bar,
Chamamé, harks back to a period before the Latorres, before Petrus, to
a time when there had been *gauchos* and knife fights and trading in skins.
The bar belongs to a period when the horse, the knife, and cattle were all
parts of a pastoral production system. But this era has also passed. Like
the shipyard, it is now a mere conglomeration of meaningless survivals like
the "viejo aindiado" [old man with Indian features] who now waits tables:

a few tables, chairs and bottles, another lantern in the corner formerly occupied by the hides and which now held a platform for the musicians. And on a vertical joist, another notice: "It is forbidden to use or carry weapons"—grandiloquent, unnecessary, displayed there as a sop to authority which took the form of a militiaman with corporal's chevrons who tied his horse to the little tree on the corner every evening (p. 136).

This scene epitomizes the degeneration of a whole *gaucho* ethic and the corresponding social order. Only the rhetoric is left (the notice on the wall) and this is now absurdly inapplicable in a society in which a "milico" [militiaman] can keep order. To Larsen, the Chamamé represents "el infierno que le tenía destinado desde el principio del tiempo, o que él se había ido ganando, según se mire" [the hell to which he had been destined since the beginning of time, or which he had gradually been earning for himself, depending on how one looks at it] (p. 138). But patently Larsen thinks this not because he associates himself with the reminiscences of a pastoral era but simply because it is yet one more example of a ghostly survival.

But we have passed too quickly over one fundamental aspect, for Petrus is also an immigrant. In some basic way, he fails to take over the country, to belong to it (he often travels to Europe). Whereas in Europe the progress of society could be seen as a continuous process beginning with mastery of nature, institutionalized in organizations and belief systems which acted as common ground for individuals, Puerto Astillero is a place where one way of life (the *gaucho*) is dead and the other (capitalism) has only briefly taken hold before collapsing because of outside forces. There is, therefore, the suggestion of social and political reasons for the emptiness. In the Latin American settings, neither Christianity nor progress seem to have attained the solid institutionalization or have become the motor forces that they did in European society. The superficial nature of their hold on the continent is emphasized by the deliberate suggestion of a theatrical stage in the descriptions of the shipyard, the *casilla* [shack], and the house that are often presented as if they were the proscenium of an Elizabethan stage where the label "wood" or "palace" served to indicate the kind of action that might take place there. So Larsen sees the *casilla* as "part of the game; that they had built it and were living in it with the sole purpose of enacting those scenes which could not be performed in the shipyard" (p. 75). The shipyard is the place where he acts out work relationships, Santa María the place for social relationships, the *glorieta* is the place of courtship, the *casilla* the place for human companionship outside the institutions. But all of these places seem to have the provisional or temporary quality of the political and social context "the rootless continent" and of the *moradas* [abodes] which the individual occupies in his journey through life. Larsen's continuous use of the words *farce* and *game* are significant. The novel is somber enough to suggest tragedy, yet tragedy would suggest that human action was important. This is plainly not the case because Larsen cannot aspire to individual dignity in the face of extinction, only to a much more humble relationship with the cosmos. All around there is "indifference" [*indiferencia*], the undifferentiated chaos. There is no real struggle possible with this adversary so that, at most, Larsen can attain a stoical resolution, a determination "not to be discouraged by the solitude, the uselessly limited space, the eyes of the tools pierced by the rancorous shoots of the nettles." Space is "uselessly limited" because underneath any order there is always the threat of chaos and disintegration, and these will inevitably prevail. Purpose and consciousness are symbolized by the eyes of the instruments, although, significantly, these are pierced (i.e., blinded) by the weeds in their struggle for life. In the course of the novel, *weeds* and *river* come to signify the grim forces of existence against which Larsen's struggle becomes increasingly ludicrous. The forces are purposive, active, and energetic in a passive and littered industrial landscape. In his tour of the shipyard and its surroundings, Larsen sits down on an abandoned life raft in which the wood is "rot-proof" but the man-made rubber is full of holes. All around he sees the unequal battle, "las costras de orín, toneladas de hierro, la *ceguera* de los yuyos, creciendo y enredándose" [the layers of rust, the tons of metal, and the weeds *blindly* growing around everything] (p. 34). As the novel progresses, these forces of destruction seem to increase triumphantly so that Larsen's last conscious impression is of the secret growth of moss. "Deaf to the din of the boat, his eager ear could still make out the whisper of moss growing among the piles of bricks and that of rust devouring metal" (p. 189). In the second version of his "end," a new element enters:

> [he] was able to imagine in detail the destruction of the building in the shipyard, to listen to the hissing of its ruin and extinction. But the hardest thing for him to bear must have been the unmistakable, capricious September air, the first attenuated perfume of spring, which came slipping irresistibly through the cracks of decrepit winter (p. 190).

What collapses is the collective and the individual project: what continues to grow is nature. There is entropy and evolution but nature is blind, a mere force whose project is undifferentiated survival. The only flourishing nature in *The Shipyard* consists of weeds and thistles, the trees and flowers of cultivated nature being virtually absent except from "el mundo difícil de la glorieta" [the difficult world of the summerhouse], that halfway stage between nature and human achievement (the house). But even this territory is invaded by "yuyos" [weeds]. "Beyond the lozenge-shaped holes in the summerhouse, distant yet ever present, the lower part of her cut off by the weeds, Josefina was scolding the dog and fixing the stakes for the roses" (p. 22). This passage is doubly ironic. The weeds are triumphant, yet Josefina continues behaving as if she is controlling nature (the dog, the roses). The men and women of the novel are separated from nature but also unable to control its blind advance. This is particularly obvious in the case of Angélica Inés, who does not even fulfill her biological role as a woman, being too repressed. Her dream of a horse she had loved,[7] her fear of floods, the incident in which she emerges from Larsen's office with torn clothes offer glimpses of this repressed side of her personality. A madwoman, she represents an extreme of alienation without consciousness, and she stands in direct contrast to Gálvez's pregnant wife.[8] Careless of her appearance, surrounded by dogs, and always within earshot of the river, Gálvez's wife does not evade time as Angélica Inés appears to do but rather obeys the rhythm of nature. The woman's fulfillment is, however, not a truly human fulfillment, but simply like the blind procreation of the *yuyos* is an act of the species. That is why Larsen describes her as *concluída* [finished]. She is "lista, quemada y seca como un campo después de un incendio de verano, más muerta que mi abuela" [finished, burnt, and arid as a field after a summer fire, deader than my grandmother] (p. 133). She has simply become a channel of procreation, a body "con un feto avanzando allí" [with a fetus growing there] (p. 134). *Concluída* [finished] therefore becomes synonymous with *preñada* [pregnant] and with *muerta* [dead]. Critics have often pointed out that Onetti associates biological maturity with the onset of corruption.[9] In the story "La cara de la desgracia" [The face of disgrace], Ana María dies at the moment of sexual maturity. In *Juntacadáveres* [Body Snatcher], a novel which explores an earlier stage in Larsen's life, experience and corruption go together. In this novel, Onetti has declared that far from being a symbol of degeneration, Larsen "was a man who suffered for his art. His art consisted in attaining the perfect prostitution. And he sacrificed himself for this. I think he died because of this."[10] Onetti talks with his tongue in his cheek, yet there is also the suggestion that the demonic is the real. Life evolves according to the bio-

logical plan, fulfilling the drive of the species, but any attempt to base a
life project on this would be self-deceiving since the extent of human life
does not usually coincide with biological maturation. There is the paradox
that life projects are often conceived when human beings are already past
the procreation stage and when, biologically, there is no more reason left
for living, when they have reached "los años muertos" [the dead years].
Hence, for Larsen to dedicate himself to "la prostitución perfecta" [the
perfect prostitution] is paradoxically a form of authenticity (that is, recognition of the true nature of things).

Although *The Shipyard* was written before *Body Snatcher* it represents a
more advanced stage in Larsen's awareness and also a more complex situation, in which the question of biological fulfillment (Gálvez's wife) or sterility (Angélica Inés) are simply strands in a larger pattern. In this earlier
novel, the clock is turned back to natural time with man's cultural and
technological achievements diminished, rendered empty and useless. Design belongs to the weeds or to the fetus advancing in the body of Gálvez's
wife; all else is dead.

There is more than a hint here of the "blind unconscious striving of
the will" described by Schopenhauer. Indeed, the novel is Schopenhauer-
ian in its entire outlook, in its presentation of life as only a "constantly
prevented dying, an ever-postponed death." As Schopenhauer puts it: "We
pursue our life, however, with great interest and much solicitude as long
as possible, as we blow out a soap-bubble as long and as large as possible,
although we know perfectly well that it will burst." And Schopenhauer,
too, has an analogy between sea and life:

> Life itself is a sea, full of rocks and whirlpools, which man avoids with
> the greatest care and solicitude, although he knows that even if he suc-
> ceeds in getting through with all his efforts and skill, he yet by doing
> so comes nearer at every step to the greatest, the total, inevitable, and
> irremediable shipwreck, death; nay, even steers right upon it.

In this sea of life, actuated by a will that serves the species, man is both
universe and alone: "every individual, though vanishing altogether and diminished to nothing in the boundless world, yet makes itself the center of
the world, has regard for its own existence and well-being before everything else." Only by seeing through the *principium individuationis* does man
attain effacement and a certain measure of serenity.

There are, therefore, many analogies between Schopenhauer's philosophy and Larsen's trajectory, not only in Larsen's gradual disillusionment

but also in the presentation of the objective world as a series of forms, as merely phenomena. Onetti also appears to share Schopenhauer's distaste for procreation, which is proof of complete servitude to the species. Thus the ultimate disillusionment for Larsen comes when he sees Gálvez's wife in the throes of giving birth, and turns away in disgust.

> He saw the woman on the bed, half naked, bleeding, struggling, clutching her head which she was turning from side to side in anguish. He saw her incredibly round belly, her glassy eyes blinking rapidly, and her clenched teeth. Only gradually did he understand and fully absorb the nature of the trap. Trembling with fear and disgust, he left the window and set off for the coast (p. 188).

Larsen's viewpoint in the scene (separated from the woman by the windowpane and her own intense absorption in the act), indicates his distance from the event. Traditionally, birth symbolizes man's hope in resurrection, but for Larsen it is a "trap," the trap by which the species continues its senseless course. In his return to Puerto Astillero from Santa María he had already experienced a vision of nature's permanence. Gálvez's wife gives birth alone, for nature does not need human intervention. The pathetic fallacy does not work and even dawn can no longer arouse hope. So Larsen

> blinked and turned his smarting eyes on the day which had just dawned, blind and irrepressible, the same day which had slipped its light over the scaly backs of gigantic beasts sunk in stupor, and would again slide, with the same unexpected precision, over the herds of other animals born from *a renewed absence of man* (p. 107).

Nature's precision, nature's stature is so much greater than that of man, whose defeat is assured. Animals will continue to populate the earth but Christianity and progress, man's presence having failed, are superfluous. Larsen says goodbye to any hope of the human ordering of the cosmos during his last meeting with Petrus, when he sees him not as "el viejo" [the old man] who had built a functioning order but rather as a sick old man whose approaching death parodies the death of God. Larsen is reminded, at the sight of him, of stagnation of empty forms, of breakdown, "algún charco, un agujero en forma de ventana, alguna bisagra destornillada y colgante" [a puddle, a hole in the shape of a window, an unscrewed hinge hanging loose] (p. 96). In a strange, Gethsemane-like scene (perhaps also a *memento mori*), Larsen kisses the yellow, skull-like head, thinking "si despierta y mira lo escupo" [if he wakes and sees me, I'll spit at him] (p. 101).

The kiss is a recognition of the common involvement of man in a journey toward old age and death, but it also marks Larsen's moment of betrayal. He can no longer believe in any kind of meaning and order, and from this point onward his journey becomes a spiritual journey, and his task is that of monitoring the chaos which is also "reality."

> This body, my legs, my arms, my sexual organs, my guts, everything which puts me on friendly terms with people and things; my head, which is me and for that reason does not exist for me; but there is the hollow part of the chest, no longer hollow but full of remains, wood-shavings, filings, dust, the débris of everything I once cared for, everything which in the other world made me either happy or miserable. And it was so pleasant and I was always ready for anything, if I had only let myself stay there, or if I had been able to stay (p. 107).

He refers to the world of illusion in which he could have believed in either Christ, or God, or Petrus. By renouncing that world, he somehow renounces the body. Instead of ascending from chaos's hell toward God, he descends from God in order to sacrifice himself in chaos, in a kind of parody of Dante. Everything turns into dust, junk, and fragments which can never be part of a totality or harmony.

The question as to why this vision is attributed to Larsen and not to an intellectual protagonist suggests another interesting contrast with *Buddenbrooks*. In Mann's novels, as in many other novels of that time, the capitalist project is completely opposed to the disinterestedness of art. This conflict between alienated work within a system of exploitation and the nonalienated work of the artist has been widely explored in Marcuse's work, for example. In contrast to this, the work of art for Onetti is analogous to Larsen's project: to the project of putting the shipyard to work and to the "perfect prostitution" that had been in place in the past. Larsen's significance lies in the fact that he is a replacement; he is a substitute whose ambition is to occupy Petrus's place. He does not want to, or is not able to, repeat the act of creation. In contrast to Europe, where capitalist industry and the modern novel originated, Puerto Astillero represents the already given; here Larsen enters without the conviction of the creator of the system. He does not control either origin or destiny; he makes a living from selling degenerated materials that others have produced. Also, he is not able to produce an ideology or a system of values valid for others. Extending the analogy again to the novel, one reaches the conclusion that it can only be part of an individual project to counteract death and destruction, although it is not able to produce social values. Like *Cien años de soledad* [One Hundred Years of Solitude] by García Márquez, like *Conversación en la Catedral* [Conversation in the Cathedral] by Vargas Llosa, the realm of fiction allows the writer to abstract individual values from social values. In this way the novel turns into "consolation," into a bitter game around a "tomb without a name." [11]

NOTES

1   The first edition is from 1961 (Buenos Aires). A second edition was published in Montevideo in 1967. I used the edition included in Juan Carlos Onetti, *Obras completas* (Mexico: Aguilar, 1970), 1049-1201. A bibliography, biographical data, and some critical essays on *The Shipyard* and other novels can be found in Jorge Ruffinelli, ed., *Onetti* (Montevideo: Biblioteca Marche, 1973). The numbers after the English translations come from Juan Carlos Onetti. *The Shipyard*, trans. Rachel Caffyn (New York: Charles Scribner's Sons, 1968).

2   John Deredita, "El lenguaje de la desintegración: Notas sobre *El astillero*," in Ruffinelli, *Onetti*, 220-37, comments in a similar manner. He highlights the relationship between entropy and the concept of character, and he points out that Díaz Grey's point of view, which the novel also reflects, is very similar to Larsen's. Deredita is critical of that hesitation in regard to the point of view.

3   Leo Marx, *The Machine in the Garden* (New York: Oxford University Press, 1964).

4   See Yvonne Perier Jones, *The Formal Expression of Meaning in Juan Carlos Onetti's Narrative*, Cuaderno No. 59 (Cuernavaca, Mexico: CIDOC, 1971).

5   For a discussion of a mythical Santa María, see Luis Alfonso Diez, "La novia," a short story by Juan Carlos Onetti, in *Nueva narrativa hispanoamericana* 1, no. 2 (Sept. 1971): 185-95.

6   See Jaime Concha, who makes a similar comment when he discusses Onetti's first novels in "Sobre *Tierra de nadie*," in Ruffinelli, *Onetti*, 139-40.

7   In an interview with Emir Rodríguez Monegal, Onetti denies the allegorical intention. See Emir Rodríguez Monegal, "Conversación con Juan Carlos Onetti," in Ruffinelli, *Onetti*, 257. I will come back to this issue at the end of this essay.

8   For a discussion of madness as a form of escape in Onetti's work, see Fernando Aínsa, *Las trampas de Onetti* (Montevideo: Editorial Alfa, 1970), 88-91.

9   Angel Rama, "Origen de un novelista y de una generación literaria," in Juan Carlos Onetti, *Recopilación de textos sobre Onetti: Valoración múltiple* (Havana: Casa de las Américas, 1969).

10 Onetti states twice that Larsen is an artist: in an interview with María Ester Gilio, "Un monstruo sagrado y su cara de bondad," in Onetti, *Valoración múltiple*, 16; and in the interview with Monegal, "Conversación con Juan Carlos Onetti," 251.

11 *The Shipyard* can be considered allegorical in Paul de Man's sense, *Allegories of Reading* (New Haven, Conn: Yale University Press, 1979). For a study of the narrative organization in a novel by Onetti see Josefina Ludmer, *Para una tumba sin nombre* (Buenos Aires: Edhasa, 1978). For allegory as a social concept, see Agustín Martínez A.'s study on Walter Benjamin, "Reificación y Alegoría," *Escritura* 7 (Jan./June, 1979): 47–68.

THE UTOPIA OF A TIRED MAN

Jorge Luis Borges

ABSTRACTION

$\mathcal{J}$t is hardly possible to open a book of criticism these days without encountering a reference to Borges. The name magically transports writers from the drier labors of analysis and explanation to the oasis of parable. His "fictions" have the force of a demonstration while remaining eminently *disponibles*, which possibly explains why they appeal to the avant-garde left like Michel Foucault and Gilles Deleuze, to the quietist skeptic in the university profession as well as to those who take the unequal balance of power between metropolis and periphery as part of the natural order of things. In effect, the graph of Borges's reputation outside the Argentine began to rise rapidly after 1961 when he was corecipient with Samuel Beckett of the Formentor Prize. This was precisely the time when Gérard Genette, Foucault, Barthes, Derrida, the *Tel Quel* group, and others had begun to challenge the procedures of discourse and the assumption on which traditional narrative, history, metaphysics, science, and anthropology based their authority. The fictions opportunely became the exemplary texts. The laughter provoked by reading Borges's imaginary Chinese taxonomy[1] shattered, according to Foucault "all the familiar landmarks of my thought, *our* thought, the thought that bears the stamp of our age and our geography."[2] Everyone would surely want to join this particular revolution which involved no bloodshed. Borges's fictions could be claimed as examples of *écriture*, as religious, metaphysical, or skeptical demonstrations, as existential searches, as demonstrations of stoical quietism, and, more modestly, as proof that Latin America was indeed in the avant-garde.[3] On the other hand, Borges's works also hold comfort for conservatives. They do not shatter the peace and order of military governments. They confirm metropolitan critics in their belief that Latin

Originally published in *Social Text* 4 (fall 1981): 52–78.

America, and Argentina in particular, do not deserve the civilized pleasure the fictions provide. According to one critic, it is only Borges's "triumphant overflow of civility and intelligence that salvages the entire continent of brutality and stupidity." In all that barbarism, he is held up as the exception that proves the rule.[4]

What is surprising is not that the fictions are read in these different ways nor that they become arguments both for the right and for the left, but rather the critical consensus: everyone agrees that what the fictions display is mastery. There is no argument about the fact that they mime other kinds of writing—narrative, literary criticism, encyclopedic writing, learned disputation, philosophy, and religious exegesis—in order to open up the whole bag of tricks; that they reveal how the disparate fragments of culture, how linguistic rules, deictics, and narrative strategies combine to suggest the illusion of an order and a direction; that like Nietzschean genealogy, they suggest the magnitude of mental constructs which seem to have a life of their own, so magnificently have they been able to conceal their origins in human power and gullibility; that what is offered in the canonical fictions *El Aleph* [The Aleph] (1949) and *Ficciones* [Fictions] (1944) is usually an enigma, fragments, arguments designed to frustrate interpretation. As the reader is drawn into the game of interpretation, it gradually becomes clear that what seemed to be a solid path is actually a stage set which can be rearranged for quite a different play or performance. It is this control on the very edge of chaos that constitutes the mastery. The fictions conceal nothing. As in tightrope walking the skill is visible to all. Any reader (any reader with "competence") can pick up some of the clues, for they are meant to be deciphered. Much Borges criticism, for this reason, tends to become a second-level demonstration of the skill and mastery of the fictions. The few hostile critics, mostly on the left, have been forced to attack on the ungrateful terrain of *ad hominem* argument. They assail his conservative political opinions and actions, his oligarchic alliances, and his snobbery.[5] At best, left criticism has only been capable of appealing for an approach to Borges which will put the textual strategies back into a "context." The disadvantage of this is that it denies the very capability—the abstraction from concrete situations—which gives the fictions their power. Yet it is precisely mastery, and the abstraction mastery is based on, that demand analysis. If Borges's fictions are machines that reveal the interests behind both empirical and hermeneutic knowledge the better to detach the reader from the knowledge effects, they properly participate in a widespread contemporary tendency to regard science, technology, and the interpretative sciences as ideological (Habermas) or as discourses of power (Foucault). In effect, the Borges fiction deploys the agonistic struggle (or dialectics in the traditional sense), the search for meaning, archaeological reconstruction, and narrativity in all its forms, as epistemological paradigms. The fact that two or more paradigms often appear in a single story undoubtedly subverts their claim to represent truth. It is not surprising, therefore, that Pierre Macherey finds in the Borges fiction the ideal model for "literary production" by means of which ideology is made visible. Yet the fictions are not only subversions of epistemological paradigms: they destroy in order to instruct in a new kind of reading activity and as such they are didactic. The fictions can, indeed, be compared to a spiritual exercise in which the world must be read skeptically in order to provide the motor force for spiritual withdrawal and privatized intensity.

COMMUNITY

The most powerful motors of knowledge-production in Borges's fictions are rivalry and enigma: these stand in analogy to two different cognitive processes—disputation and hermeneutics. Only when combat is exhausted, when one of the protagonists is defeated or dies, or when the search is completed, does the possibility of withdrawal and self-knowledge arise. The *askesis*[6] which results from these sequences—struggle/victory (or defeat)/revelation; or, search/discovery (or frustration)/revelation— functions on two levels: both as the outcome of plot and as a readerly activity. The implied reader of the Borges text is thus often the allegorical shadow of its protagonists and vice versa. Both, however, undergo conversion, the privileged place for which is a limit or frontier.

The spatialization of conversion is well illustrated by the story, "The Theologians" (*The Aleph*) in which two medieval scholars, Aureliano of Aquilea and John of Panonia, are called on to refute the beliefs of the "monotonous sect" who hold that every event is destined to be repeated. John's refutation is direct and literal, so that his rival Aureliano must strategically adopt a different mode, that of allusion and reliance on the words of others. Thus the need to differentiate himself from his rival is the productive principle of an indirect style. Years later, John is himself considered to be heretical since the arguments he had used against the "monotonous sect" become suspect in the context of a new struggle—the one now waged against the heresy of the "histrionics" who believe that no two moments are ever the same. Aureliano, whose arguments were veiled, escapes criticism and, indeed, denounces his rival, who is then burned at the stake. Deprived of his antagonist, Aureliano seeks "the arduous limits of the Empire, the heavy swamps and the contemplative deserts so that solitude might help him understand his destiny." It is here, beyond power and self-interest, that the revelation comes to him that he and John are the same person in the eyes of God.

The dispute between John and Aureliano occurs at the center of the empire and serves its larger strategy, for which their knowledge is instrumental. Only on the frontier, physically removed from the demands of the state and without the stimulus of rivalry, does Aureliano experience a moment of intensity and of reflection: "In Hibernia, in one of the huts of a monastery surrounded by the forest, the sound of rain surprised him towards morning. He remembered a Roman night in which the same meticulous noise had surprised him." Thus, like Juan, Aureliano is burned to death when lightning strikes the trees around his hut and sets it on fire. But unlike John he has been allowed the godlike vision in which identities disappear, and the illusion that has produced them is laid bare.

The experience of the frontier necessarily involves distancing and this in turn permits change. The frontier is a place of reversal where the old values are transformed, where the civilized may become barbarian and the barbarian civilized, and where traditional moral categories acquire a quite different force. In "The Theologians," Aureliano's self-knowledge had involved destruction of the Other through treachery. By abstracting both the polemic of the theologians and the treachery from any current situation and relocating them in the remote past, Borges blocks conventional moral judgment and allows a "transvaluation" of values. Treachery and disloyalty can now become positive terms insofar as they are triggers of change. As such they may be grouped with the positive terms in other opposing pairs—nearness/distance, committed/free, state/individual, national/extranational, tradition/change—where the second term is the positive one.

These terms occur not only in the fictions but in the essays as well. Consider, for instance, Borges's often repeated statement that the Argentine like the Jew is not entrenched in any particular national tradition; he paraphrases Veblen to the effect that "though the Jew lives, let us say, in Western culture, he does not feel bound to it by any particular loyalty and thus he may invent, may change, may become a revolutionary, may be really important."[7] On this general plane where Jews and Argentines are equivalent, lack of tradition becomes positive and loyalty negative or, at the very least, uncreative. If we substitute *solidarity* and *commitment* for *loyalty*, we can see why Borges should be so ambiguous a figure for the left. On the one hand, he takes apart metropolitan knowledge production, which had imposed immaturity, backwardness, barbarism, underdevelopment, instability, and dependency on Latin America. In the face of the imbalance which gave Europe and then the United States an immense capacity for both material advance and technicopractical knowledge, Borges like other Third World intellectuals has unmasked the disinterested and apparently universal knowledge of the metropolis as an exercise of power, and has brought the destructive force of parody to bear on these knowledge effects. Yet, at the same time, the fictions hold out no possibility of solidarity. For, as allegories of reading and of writing, they equate these activities with *askesis;* in other words, they accentuate the process of privatization.

It should be understood, however, that for Borges the stakes are higher than they might at first appear. If he makes literature into an intensely privatized experience, it is because he believes that experience can only be individual: the more intense the experience the more it satisfies our immortal longings: "intensity" is thus what is at stake for Borges in literature. He differs from many of his predecessors in allowing this intensity to be readerly rather than reserving it to the poet or creator as representatives of the *communitas.* In this respect, he is obviously different from the committed or existentialist left in Latin America who have tried to envision a collective response to the enforced relegation of Latin America into the realm of the phenomenal. Consider two contrasting examples. In Neruda's *Canto General* [General Song], the poet's voice becomes the unproblematic voice of underground and hitherto suppressed history, responding to the oblivion into which the common people have been thrust. In the narratives of García Márquez, oblivion is turned into a creative force. Indeed, García Márquez used as the epigraph of his first novel, *The Leafstorm,* Creon's command that the bones of Polinices should be abandoned outside the city wall and left as the prey to the carrion birds, suggesting the power of metropolitan discourse which has the authority to draw the boundary between the memorable and the forgotten, between the honored and the unhonored. Not to mark Polinices's grave means not to commemorate, and not to commemorate means being condemned to the oblivion of the phenomenal.

The project of García Márquez and Neruda was to defy Creon's injunction. At the same time, both writers retain an identification of culture with community. Neruda creates a poetry that can be read aloud, thus reviving the power of the communal and orally transmitted culture which in Latin America has often afforded a strategy of resistance. García Márquez situates his narratives at the very moment when this traditional communal lore is on the point of disappearing and is about to be replaced by the privatized solitude of print culture. Both writers, emblematic of different kinds of relation to the idea of community, project utopian possibilities by inverting the values imposed by the metropolitan discourse of power. For Neruda and García Márquez, community (whether nation, class, or family) is productive of resistance to economic and to cultural domination. Liberation therefore must be national, social, and cultural. Borges, in contrast, attaches no value to community since, for him, "reality" belongs only to the level of individual perceptions. His social philosophy (if such it can be called) is purely pragmatic. Because of the "asiatic disorder" of the real world, it is better that "gentlemen" control politics. On this level, he acknowledges that there are nations with national characteristics but speaks as if international politics were conducted as duels to gain respect.[8]

Borges also stands in a curiously oblique relation to Argentina's historic debate between civilization and barbarism. The ur-text in this debate is an essay written by the post-Independence liberal politician, Domingo Sarmiento, *Facundo: Civilization and Barbarism* (1845). From his exile during the dictatorship of General Rosas, Sarmiento analyzed the dissolution of urban and civilized life that had resulted from the destructive onslaught of *gaucho caudillos* (exemplified by Facundo Quiroga); he demonstrated that this was the reason for Argentina's degeneration into barbarism and its eventual submission to dictatorship. For Sarmiento the classical parallel immediately came to mind. Argentina was like Thebes ravaged by a monster which had to be exterminated before the country could attain its age of glory. The argument for civilization would imply the repression and genocide of the nomadic peoples, now stigmatized as "barbarians."

General Rosas was overthrown in 1852. The labor of turning Buenos Aires into the Thebes of La Plata began with the conscription and integration of the nomadic *gauchos* into the army and the regular work force and continued with the war to exterminate the Indian tribes. The final step was the importation of hundreds of immigrants, mostly from southern and eastern Europe, and the transformation of Buenos Aires into a megalopolis. The familiar figures of nineteenth-century popular lore—the Indian, the *gaucho*, and the captive woman who lived in the Indian tents—would survive only as myths.

This policy did not, however, remove barbarism from within but merely transferred it from the nomadic *gaucho* to the new immigrants who would become a political force at the beginning of the twentieth century when a populist president, Hiplito Yrigoyen, came into power. In 1930, soon after he had been elected president for a second term, a military regime seized the government and succeeded for a decade in stemming the growing power of the masses who would eventually put Perón into the government.

The terms *civilization* and *barbarism* had by now shifted ground. The independent *gaucho* came to incarnate individual freedom of a kind that was certainly beyond the possibility of the struggling immigrant. The poem of *gaucho* life, *Martín Fierro* (first part, 1872, second part, 1879) was raised to the status of a national epic. It was no longer the *gaucho* who was stigmatized but "cabecitas negras" [the little black heads]—the new arrivals from southern Europe, with their uncertain Spanish, their violent gangs, and their vulgar lifestyle. Torn from communities and families, marginalized by poverty, the immigrant experience was privatized in the extreme. Education was the one means of social mobility for the middle class, which was itself ambivalent in its attitude to history and to its own social role. Irony was not just a literary style for such people, but a way of thinking and a gut fear of the spontaneous reaction that might betray their carefully acquired *persona*. Irony was, moreover, a manner of marking a distance from the *vulgo:* it was as if the very avowal of any loyalty or commitment constituted a social solecism. Cortázar's *Hopscotch* captures the style to perfection. Not surprisingly, Borges's early desire to express "the noble pathos of the creole"[9] was quickly eroded not only by the prevalent skepticism but also by his own distrust of the masses, a distrust intensified in the 1930s when he was obliged to live a "demeaning existence" working in a small library among people who only talked of football or exchanged smutty stories.[10] During this period, he collaborated on the journal *Sur,* whose role in Argentina—that of maintaining taste and discrimination—offers analogies with that of *Scrutiny* in England.[11] The full force of his irony and satire would, however, only become apparent during the Perón regime (1943–53) which, persecuting him, his family, and friends, exacerbated his already covert dislike of the masses and their charismatic leaders and representatives. In 1945, soon after Perón had taken power, he wrote a satirical parody, *A Model for Death*, in collaboration with his friend, Adolfo Bioy Casares, which ridicules in devastating fashion both populism and nationalism, the satire being directed against a mythical organization, the A.A.A. (Aboriginal Association of Argentina), whose aims were to protect the purity of the Argentine language and to catalog the lexicon of the tango, and whose members speak a graceless *argot*, drink national champagne, and refer to themselves as "Indians" to affirm their legitimate national sentiment.[12] With some impartiality the authors also parody the snobbish Europeanized Argentine, thus ridiculing both sides in the tired old argument between cultural nationalism and cosmopolitanism.

This "plague on both your houses" owes much to Borges's conviction that the aesthetic experience is individual and beyond social strategies, and that the social arena is best occupied by those who will defend order (*disorder* meaning mass participation). The Perón regime became the deterrent, the exemplary instance of what happens when the populace are given access to power. It was during this period of the Perón regime that Borges revised his own earlier inclination to consider the *gaucho* Martín Fierro a national hero and declared that had Argentina celebrated Sarmiento instead of Martín Fierro "another and better history would have been ours."[13] Perón was a hoodlum, outside the category of the civilized (but so was Robert Lowell, whom he met in the 1960s).[14] Gentlemen (i.e., those who maintained order) returned to power after the fall of Perón: General Videla is adjudged a gentleman.[15] Borges's support of Nixon and of the Americans during the Vietnam War, his celebration of the North American victory over the Mexicans at the Alamo, his support of the military *juntas* in the Argentine and Chile, his astonishment in Texas at hearing ditchdiggers speak English (a language he had thought reserved to the educated classes) not only denote an exacerbation of the snobbery which he once described as the sincerest passion of the Argentinian but also a tendency to equate the social good with keeping the masses and the Third World in a position of inferiority. In this sense, Borges's project is not comparable to the fascism of Céline and Wyndham Lewis. If it is akin to any political philosophy at all, it is to libertarianism—an extreme form of individualism—which privileges the freedom of the powerful and is not concerned with liberation from scarcity and economic oppression. Indeed, he has himself aptly written its motto: "Blessed are those who do not hunger for justice, because they know that our destiny whether adverse or benign is the result of chance and is inscrutable."[16]

THE BETRAYAL PARADIGM

I felt ashamed quite early to be a bookish kind of person, not a man of action.
—*Autobiographical Essay*

Borges has established control over his past by emphasizing certain moments in the development of his writing and displaying these with translucent though misleading candor. In his *Autobiographical Essay*, he appears enchanted with the symmetry of a lineage which, on both his father's and his mother's side, kept a balance between arms and letters. He has chosen not to give prominence to the mercantile members of the family, preferring the legend of his grandfather, Colonel Borges:

> In the complicated circumstances surrounding his defeat at La Verde, he rode slowly on horseback, wearing a white poncho and followed by ten or twelve of his men, towards the enemy lines, where he was struck by two Remington bullets. This was the first time Remington rifles were used in the Argentine, and it tickles my fancy to think that the firm that shaves me every morning bears the same name as the one that killed my grandfather.[17]

This "amusing" incident connects the Borges of the present with a Borges in the past; without knowledge of Argentine history the reader might miss the fact that the colonel was in reality committing suicide. The "complicated circumstances" are interesting enough. Colonel Borges, an Indian fighter and veteran of the war against Paraguay as well as civil war between Buenos Aires and the provinces, had, in 1874, become involved in an antigovernment plot against Sarmiento and his candidate for the Presidency. Challenged by Sarmiento, he promised loyalty until 12 October, the day the uprising was to take place. However, the date of the coup was advanced, and Colonel Borges, evidently a stickler for the letter of his promises, refused to participate. To his friends, he appeared to be a traitor. When October the twelfth came, he joined the rebel forces under Mitre and when these were forced to retreat, Borges rode out, arms across his chest, toward the enemy lines and was fatally wounded.

> In his epic world, riding on his horse.
> I leave him almost untouched by my verse.
> —"Allusion to the death of Colonel Francisco Borges"

What is so striking in this story is the literal power that Colonel Borges attached to pledging his word, even though it made him a traitor both in the eyes of his friends and of the government. What attracts Borges the writer is the abstract purity, the willingness to break with both state and loyalty to friends in order to preserve a personal pledge, however absurd. Colonel Borges's heroism and his faith in the word is not unlike that of the writer himself.

The son of bookish and cultivated parents, Jorge Luis Borges was educated in Switzerland during World War I and then spent some years in Spain. He returned to Buenos Aires in 1921 as an "Ultraist" (an avant-garde literary movement initiated in Spain) and during the twenties was actively involved in several avant-garde journals in Buenos Aires. In his autobiographical essay, he gives prominence to two decisive breaks in his career as a writer—the first stylistic, the second having to do with genre. The first he describes as a gradual process which made him abandon the mannered baroque style of his early writing. The second break was more drastic; indeed, it is described in religious terms as an entry into paradise. In 1938, he was working in a small provincial library, reading among other things, *The Divine Comedy*, when his father died. Shortly afterward he had a severe accident, lost the power of speech, and feared his mental integrity. On convalescing, "I decided I would try to write a story." The result was "Pierre Menard, Author of Don Quixote." As he gained confidence in his writing, he withdrew more and more from his colleagues, who "thought of me as a *traitor* for not sharing their boisterous fun" (italics mine). Though it is tempting to read this crisis in oedipal terms, the account is perhaps most interesting as Borges's own version of a vocation which announced itself when speech was lost; and of the treachery to family ties and loyalties that this vocation involved. He himself had asserted that both his father and mother, who had definite ideas about what constituted good literature, had at times voiced their disapproval of his subject matter (in particular, they thought his essay on a minor writer, Evaristo Carriego, to be a waste of time). His father's death may thus have given him a greater sense of artistic freedom. Yet to reduce the antagonistic struggle and betrayal of the stories to the oedipal conflict with the father ignores the social investment of the unconscious of which oedipal figures are representations; and, as René Girard has shown, concentration on the remote influence of the father may mask more immediate rivals.[18] Certainly, the theme of treachery occurs in Borges's writing long before the crucial date of 1938. One of his early poems, "General Quiroga rides in his carriage," records a famous historical case of treachery, while in 1927 he wrote the first outline of a never completed story which became the paradigm for his later works: "Pursued by the police, an outlaw is betrayed by a guitar player. He escapes prison one night and has a single night in which to avenge himself. By following the sound of a guitar, he finds the man who has betrayed him and kills him."

"This story," he confesses, "I have been retelling with small variations ever since."[19] It is, indeed, essentially the plot of the very first story he wrote, "Street-corner man," in which a young man kills the knife-fighter he admires because he cannot bear to think of him as a coward. In the canonical fictions, treachery, the theme of the pursuer and the pursued, recur again and again—in "Death and the Compass," in "The Garden of Forking Paths," in "The Form of the Sword," "The Theologians," "Deutsches Requiem," "Three Versions of Judas," "The End," and "The Waiting."

Such a repetitive pattern—the list is by no means exhaustive—suggests the reenactment of some primary obsession.[20] What is fascinating, however, is the way that this anachronistic theme (it is the theme of the Argentine classic, *Martín Fierro*) becomes displaced, first through a process of defamiliarization (in the exotic imaginary lives of *The Universal History of Infamy*[21]) and thereafter by a process of abstraction which turns violence and treachery into an allegory of writing and reading. Thus, for Borges the writer, treachery not only motivates the device but involves a necessary suspension of loyalty to all other commitments but that of writing. The power and effectiveness of the writing will now depend on the writer's ability to redeploy material, while readerly ability will depend on freedom from preconceptions. The reason Borges's paradigm story made it difficult for him to "begin" as a writer was perhaps its association with Argentine regionalist and popular literature. Hence, the necessary stage of *The Universal History of Infamy* in which anecdotes and tales of trickery and deceit were borrowed from obscure secondary sources in order to defamiliarize the theme and abstract it from its social context. The exotic and infamous characters of this book include Billy the Kid, Nat Turner, Monk Eastman, and the Tichbourne claimant; in these tales, Borges adopts the voice of the traditional storyteller who must secure the attention of his listeners by recounting marvelous events. By removing the paradigm of treachery to Japan, China, and the United States, Borges performs the displacement required to discourage the reader from placing the tales back into the concrete context of the Argentine situation. Even at this early stage, however, it is interesting that the fable of betrayal and loyalty is not simply a cloak for the oedipal but often involves the betrayal of public duties in favor of a private obsession and the adoption of a mask or *persona* in order to attain the required end. The story of the Tichbourne claimant who successfully posed as the heir to the Tichbourne name and fortune despite his lack of resemblance to a long-lost heir is one obvious example of this fable of betrayal. In "The Insulting Master of Etiquette Kotsuke no Suke," the master who is a representative of the state makes rule and insults those who do not obey them. The retainers of a lord who have been forced to commit *hara-kiri* because of his failure to observe the rules plot vengeance. Their leader adopts the persona of a debauchee to throw Kotsuke no Suke off his guard so that he can be cornered and killed (he is too cowardly to commit suicide). The forty-seven loyal retainers now commit *hara-kiri*, having achieved their vengeance. We note here that disloyalty to the state implies loyalty of a higher (and more personal) kind, for it is carried to the extreme test of death.

The difference between these early tales and the mature fables of *The Aleph* and *Fictions* is that in the later stories Borges secures the participation of the reader in the process of seduction, betrayal, and mastery. The "Garden of Forking Paths" affords a particularly good example of this since it deploys a complexity of epistemological procedures. It is, first of all, a story embedded in a framing device which appears to give high value to empirical evidence. Liddell Hart's *History of the War in Europe* serves as the undisputable authority that the historical event on which the story is based—a British offensive against the Germans in July 1916—really took place. The confession of the spy Yu Tsun thus supposedly fills a gap or space in Liddell Hart's text and therefore shows up the incompleteness of history, which can never know the personal and subjective factors operating at any given time.

Yu Tsun's story is, however, fragmentary. It begins *in medias res* with the discovery by Richard Madden, an agent on the British side, that Yu Tsun is spying for the Germans. The latter must now attempt to warn his German masters of the impending British offensive before his inevitable capture. This spy thriller quickly moves from the empirical reality of World War I to a more abstract level. The rivals, Madden and Yu Tsun, are both traitors to their national origins, since Madden is Irish and Yu Tsun Chinese; characteristically, this frees them for creative action. In his flight from Madden, Yu Tsun makes for the mysterious garden of forking paths and the house of a certain Albert whom he discovers to be a sinologist, the only person in the world to have unraveled the secret of the labyrinth constructed by his own grandfather, Ts'ui Pên. He is thus the one person really worthy of Yu Tsun's loyalty. Yu Tsun however must kill Albert because he is needed in another strategy—his name, Albert, is that of the artillery park which the British are to attack and hence the signal Yu Tsun needs to warn the Germans. Because Albert's murderer is Chinese, the code is easily deciphered by the Germans from the newspaper accounts of the murder. Yu Tsun's strategy, devised out of pride (to prove that a yellow man could save the German army), overcomes the loyalty to a brother: Albert has to be killed in order to become a sign. "The Garden of Forking Paths" thus operates the detachment of the sign (Albert) from its empirical matrix, exactly on the lines that Roland Barthes outlined in *Mythologies*.[22] As in the Barthesian definition of myth, the sign is defined by its intention (as a warning to the Germans) rather than by its literal sense (Albert the man). But this is not the end of Borges's story, for Yu Tsun's treachery also produces a vision of the labyrinth of possibilities which Albert's death forecloses as well as "innumerable contrition and fatigue" which anticipate his own death.

Yu Tsun's communicative strategy is paralleled by another epistemological procedure—the hermeneutic strategy which enables Albert to solve the riddle of the labyrinth. But where Yu Tsun's model is that of *instrumental* knowledge and technical control, Albert's decipherment of the labyrinth is a *hermeneutic* process: the object of knowledge (the labyrinth) being detached from any concrete historical situation and made available for study as a dehistoricized enigma. Albert's solution—that the labyrinth is a book—is elegant but also makes understanding seem absurd, since the labyrinthine text he envisages allows for all the unthematized possibilities in any situation, thus reproducing the vast, ungraspable variety of unactualized possibilities inherent in any act. The critic Pierre Macherey points out that this labyrinthine text reflects Borges's endeavor as a writer, for it "constitutes the possibilities of one text . . . and allows the importance of what has been lost to come to light." In this way, "through the insufficiencies of the story, Borges manages to show that we have lost nothing."[23] However, precisely the problem with Ts'ui Pên's text is that it is like a map so accurate and complete that it becomes equivalent to the actual geographical location and therefore redundant.

Rather than project Yu Tsun's text as a model for Borges's own, it would seem more fruitful to note the interplay between Albert's hermeneutic strategy and Yu Tsun's communicative strategy, for in each case, the author/solver appears to be in complete control, to be the subject of one particular process when, in fact, each is from another point of view also a victim. In one configuration, Albert is the emitter of the message (the secret of the labyrinth), while in another "plot," he is Yu Tsun's victim. And Yu Tsun, who appears to be the sender of the message to the Germans, is also a sign in the strategy of the German high command. The potentially fraternal bond between Yu Tsun and Albert is sacrificed to the strategic demands of the state. The failure and death of both protagonists are, however, necessary to achieve transcendence of illusion (in Schopenhauer's sense) and so permit access to a higher level of abstraction.

It is now possible to trace a recurrent process in the fictions by means of which a contemporary dispute or problem (rivalry, hatred, the position of the intellectual against the state) is defamiliarized by placing the conflict in an exotic setting. The subject position in the story, which in other writers provides stability to the meaning-making process while suggesting a continuous identity, is in Borges revealed to be a shifter to be filled, sometimes by an acting subject, sometimes by a passive victim. This instability of the subject is, in turn, not intended to produce a multiplicity of meanings. Rather, we are expected to view the characters as exchangeable positions and thus to convert our reading into a more abstract operation by means of which both "understanding" and "communication" can be shown to be misguided and bound to end in frustration.

Such processes are commonly celebrated by commentators as evidence of Borges's "universality," an attribute which for historical reasons is highly regarded by Latin Americans. Yet Borges's "universality" is different from the older humanistic cultural theory according to which literature appeals to universal human nature, universal emotions or taste. The Borges fiction is, instead, a context-free paradigm which can be reactivated through reading at any time and under any circumstances. This is exemplified in "The Search of (or for) Averroes."[24] Averroes, like all nonmetropolitan intellectuals, is forced to think out problems central to Western culture without having all the relevant data. In his particular case, he attempts to understand Aristotle's discussion of comedy and tragedy through living in a society (medieval Muslim Spain) which has no theater and no tradition of stage representation. Averroes's "solution" to the problem of the meaning of comedy and tragedy is erroneous if we are concerned with historical accuracy but felicitous in the context of Islamic belief. His quest is universal not because it originates a new discourse or arrives at a truth but because it can be re-actualized by Borges and the reader. Moreover, (perhaps like Borges) Averroes *appears* to be conservative in the eyes of his contemporaries because he sacrifices innovation and engages in an act of understanding which depends not on external factors but on reading and glossing texts. In his way, he is able to establish fraternal relationships with other readers across time:

> I felt that Averroes, trying to imagine what a drama is without having suspected what a theater is, was no more absurd than I, trying to imagine Averroes with no raw material but a few scraps of Renan, Lane and Asín Palacios. I felt, on the last page, that my narrative was the symbol of the man I was while I was writing and that, in order to write that narrative, I had to be that man, and that, in order to be that man, I had to write that narrative, and so on *ad infinitum* (at the moment I stop believing in him "Averroes" disappears).

Clearly this process of actualization is more akin to reading than what is normally recognized as "creation." Borges destroys the authorial position which assumes absolute knowledge and control in order to decenter the creative process and abstract it as an intention. The return of Averroes is enabled precisely because his intention is bonded to that of Borges.

MEMORY/INTENSITY/RETURN

Averroes attains a kind of immortality through Borges's actualization of his success (and failure). This intensity on the edge of oblivion is the heroism without heroes for which literature offers the exemplary practice. The hero is a figure of the past, linked to the age of conquest and felicitously commemorated in epic, which, unlike print, retained only the really memorable. Borges is undoubtedly nostalgic for this epic age and celebrates the fact that in the Argentine there is still "autobiographical memory" of it: "the conquest and colonization of these regions," he wrote, "was such an ephemeral operation that a grandfather of mine in 1872 could command the last important battle against the Indians, thus realizing in the latter half of the nineteenth century the conquering project of the sixteenth."[25] Characteristically, he lauds the heroism of his grandfather and forgets the pampa Indians who were virtually annihilated in those very battles. But his attempt to commemorate his heroic ancestors — Colonel Borges and Isidoro Suárez, the hero of the Independence battle of Junín — is, in effect, an act of personal piety, and owes much to his conviction that if we survive after death, it is only in the memories of others. In "Inscription on any Tomb," he glosses Sir Thomas Browne and writes, "Blindly the willful soul, / Asks for length of days / When its survival is assured by the lives of others / When you yourself are the embodied continuation / Of those who did not live into your time / And others will be (and are) your immortality on earth." It is a conviction which is reflected in this fondness for poetic epitaphs.[26]

In modern society, on the contrary, there is no epic celebration of the hero, only the inevitable trivialization of print. Individuals have, therefore, lost their power over posterity. Faced with a similar concern, the Japanese writer Yukio Mishima would adopt a deliberately anachronistic revival of personal heroism: "Just as Alexander the Great acquired heroic stature by modelling himself on Achilles, the condition necessary for being a hero must be both a ban on originality and a true faithfulness to a classical model; unlike the words of a genius the words of a hero must be selected as the most impressive and noble among ready-made concepts. And at the same time they, more than any other words, constitute a splendid language of the flesh."[27] Though Borges regretted not being a man of action, he could not himself be content with such heroic poses, even though in the early twenties, he did conceive a kind of literary heroism which might be achieved by those writers who exercised the "magic" of a "demi-god, the angel whose deeds change the world. To annex provinces to Being, to imagine cities and spaces of contiguous reality—that is a heroic venture."[28] But sometime during the late twenties and early thirties, he abandoned even this concept of heroism; in order to achieve the "immortality" of the hero, the modern writer must forego the very notion that it can be invested in an individual: modern heroism has no heroes.

He is, however, obsessed by eternity: and it was after reading the elegy of the sixteenth-century Spanish poet, Jorge Manrique, for the death of his father (an elegy which is also a meditation on the transitoriness of human life), that he conceived a response "intuited or indicated by this phrase: *what really was is not lost: intensity is a form of eternity.*"[29] What he meant by this would be illustrated by an experience so vivid that he described it on two separate occasions. It occurred when he was walking through a Buenos Aires suburb at nightfall, along "streets of unvanquished American clay penetrated by the pampa." There was a "rose-coloured wall in the moonlight," (significantly, the title of his first published story was "The Man on the Rose-Coloured Street-Corner") and on this frontier, between city and pampa, between day and night, he felt himself "to be an abstract perceiver of the world, an indefinite fear imbued with knowledge. That pure representation of homogenous facts—calm night, limpid park, a provincial scent of honeysuckle, basic clay—is not merely identical to what there was on this corner many years ago, it is without similarities or repetitions, the same." Among similar impersonal experiences of "return," he notes "those of physical pleasure and pain, those of drowsiness, those of listening to a single piece of music, those of great intensity and disillusion."[30]

It is significant that this experience occurs at a kind of frontier between city and pampa, for the frontier as the privileged place for return would never entirely disappear from the fictions. It is the desert of "The Theologians" and "The Immortal" and the pampa of "The South." And the cast of characters in the old civilization-and-barbarism debate could also be abstracted from national myth and marshalled as figures which convert repetition into intensity. For example, in "The Captive" (*Dreamtigers*), the old story of the child carried off by Indians and converted to barbarism becomes just such a fable of intensity. The boy captive, now an Indian, finds himself near his old home, goes straight into the kitchen, puts his hand into the chimney, and takes out a knife he had hidden there years before. The narrator comments: "I would like to know what he felt in the instant of dizziness in which past and present fused. I would like to know if the lost child was reborn and died in the ecstasy and if he recognized, if only as a child or as a dog might recognize, his parents and the house." What mediates the return in this particular instance is the symbolic knife. The captive had been brutally severed from his family, but this very separation permits the ecstasy of the return. Without the break (during which the family are forgotten), without the knife (the symbol of death and of castration), and the miraculous recovery of power, there would be no return. The captive, it will be noted, does not return in order to replace the father. Rather, the very symbol of absence, separation, and death becomes the device that produces a rebirth (or a conversion).

Memory provides Borges with an important analogy for the return since it too is discontinuous and activated against a background of oblivion. In "Funes the Memorious," the narrator remembers Funes because of the extraordinary circumstances of the meeting:

> We were running a kind of race with the storm. We entered an alley-way that sank down between two very high brick sidewalks. It had suddenly got dark; I heard some rapid and almost secret footsteps up above; I raised my eyes and saw a boy running along a narrow and broken path as if it were a narrow and broken wall. I *remember* his baggy gaucho trousers, his rope-soled shoes. I *remember* the cigarette in his hard face, against the now limitless storm cloud (italics mine).

The intensity of the experience (the contrast and differentiation) is what makes memory possible. Funes himself, on the other hand, cannot experience intensity because he cannot forget.

Memory of this intensified kind is not simply repetition, for it is both active and selective. Indeed, repetition, reproduction, and reflection are all anathema to Borges since they disperse or dilute intensity, while *novelty*, because it is not a return and is therefore unique, also fades into oblivion. Borges stresses this by choosing as the epigraph for "The Immortal" a quotation from Sir Francis Bacon: "Salomon saith: There is no new thing upon the earth so that as Plato hath an imagination that all knowledge is but remembrance, so Salomon giveth his sentence, that all novelty is but oblivion." It is precisely by transcending the oblivion of novelty and the oblivion of repetition that "The Immortal" illustrates the manner in which intensity can be reactivated.

"The Immortal" is supposedly the transcript of a manuscript found in the pages of pope's translation of the *Iliad*, and this very genealogy, alluding as it does to intertextuality, serves to distance the fable from empirical reality. The first-person and sometimes plural narrator, Marcus Flaminius, describes his search for the legendary river of the immortals, his discovery of the river and of the speechless but immortal troglodytes who, because they cannot die, have reached a state of total indifference. He drinks the waters of the river and, followed by one of the troglodytes, explores the monstrous and deserted city whose architecture is purposeless and incomprehensible. The city of the immortals is so horrible "that its mere existence, even though in the middle of a secret desert, contaminates the past and the future and in some way even endangers the stars. As long as it lasts no one in the world can be strong or happy." Approximate images for it are "a chaos of heterogeneous words, the body of a tiger or a bull in which teeth, organs and head monstrously pullulate in mutual conjunction and hatred." The city is the image of abstract and impersonal forces, now reified into unchanging structures which are both manmade and inhuman. Intensity cannot be experienced within its walls. Marcus Flaminius returns to the desert accompanied by the troglodyte to whom he has given the name of Ulysses's dog, Argos, and to whom he attempts to teach language. Like the dogs and cats in other Borges stories, Argos appears to live in a perpetual present.

> I thought that perhaps our perceptions were the same but that Argos combined them in another manner and constructed other objects with

them; I thought that perhaps there were no objects for him, but a ver-tiginous and continuous play of very brief impressions. I thought of a world without memory or time; considered the possibility of a lan-guage which ignored nouns, a language of impersonal verbs and of undeclinable epithets.

It is easy to recognize in "Argos" another embodiment of the captive who has forgotten civilization, but this forgetting, as Nietzsche pointed out, is also essential for the return: "Isn't forgetting the source and indispensible condition not only for the appearance of his Eternal Return but for trans-forming the very identity of the person to whom it appears? Forgetting thus raises eternal becoming and the absorption of all identity to the level of being." For Nietzsche as for Borges's narrator, the return brings about the relevation that "all names of history, finally, are me."[31] Forgetting, like the captive's knife severs the experience from all that has gone before so that the activation of intensity through differentiation can occur. In "The Immortal," it is a sudden shower of rain in the arid desert which moves Argos so much that he begins to speak and utters not original words but those of Homer's text: "Argos, Ulysses' dog abandoned in the heaps of dung." Argos is Homer who is also nobody and everybody (or all the names of history). Borges's aim is not simply to describe intensity but to produce it in the reader by first severing him or her from certainty and stability. Doubts are therefore cast on the authorship of Marcus Flaminius's text. A commentator points out that the manuscript must be the work of two men, one a man of action and the other a man of letters. A second commentator reveals that Marcus Flaminius's text is, in reality, a *collage* of many other texts. Such doubts cast on a unique authorship and on the coherence of the story then send the reader back to verify through a rereading, which is also a form of return since it is a reactivation rather than a repetition. The rereading is intended to convert the "rhetorical" text into a dialectical one. It is stimulated, moreover, by interruption and separation which disturbs the smooth surface of the narration and allows the reader to begin again, freed from the superstition of authorship and originality.

LANGUAGE

When the legionnaire in "The Immortal" imagines Argos as having a completely different perception of the world from himself, he is voicing Borges's view of what happens when any two people try to communicate.

"You who read me. Are you sure that you understand my language?" he asks in "The Library of Babel." The skeptical critique of language which is deeply embedded in the fictions has its origin in a precursor of Wittgenstein, Fritz Mauthner, whose *Philosophical Dictionary* Borges frequently mentions.[32] Curiously, although critics have often noted a wide range of philosophical references in Borges, from Berkeley and Hume to Schopenhauer, they have tended to overlook Mauthner, perhaps because his work was superseded in the history of philosophical inquiry by Wittgenstein's language games. For Borges, Mauthner's ideas were extremely productive, perhaps more directly so than those of Schopenhauer and Nietzsche whose "return" will prove to be significantly close to and significantly different from that of Argos.

Mauthner believed that all knowledge is based on the senses, which are contingent and which we can only experience as individuals.[33] What perceives cannot be regarded as a ghost in the machine for there is no stable and continuous ego or self. This means that only relative and not absolute truth is available to the perceiver. Perception occurs by means of the construction of an inner object. What the individual experiences as a separation between subject and object is illusory, and is in fact created by language itself: "It is language which splits the world into an observer and an object: into things in and for themselves and into things for me. But the world does not occur twice. The world occurs only once. I am nothing if I am not an object. But I have no object. The object is nothing if it is not in me. The object is not outside me. The object is subjective."[34] Language thus neither expresses an inner form as Humboldt would have it, nor does it directly refer to objects "out there." In Mauthner's view, language and thought are identical, and the critique of language becomes indispensable because we think in terms of reified substantives such as "race," "humanity," and "cause" which have to be deconstructed in order to reveal their emptiness. Yet he viewed even this task with skepticism, acknowledging his conviction that "man can never succeed in getting beyond a metaphorical description of the world, whether he uses everyday language or philosophical language."[35]

In Mauthner's system, *parole* (the individual act of speaking) and not *langue* assumes the greatest importance. Since each individual builds up a personal store of memories and associations based ultimately on sense impressions, each individual effectively has a private language. People communicate because they share common conventions but they can never arrive at a complete understanding of one another's meaning since their experiences can never be the same.

Multiple traces of this critique of language are to be found in Borges's writing. For instance, Mauthner argued that sentences and not words form the basic units of communication, that adjectives are more allusive than substantives, that powerful language (like that of poetry) alludes to but never tries to name reality, and that because each person inhabits a different linguistic territory there are no true synonyms—all these arguments appear in Borges's own writing. The invented languages in his fictions are often inspired by Mauthner, as, for instance, with the two languages of Tlön (in "Tlön, Uqbar, Orbis Tertius"), one of which is primarily verbal and the other adjectival (and therefore more capable, in Mauthner's view, of conveying sense impressions. Meanwhile, an early essay on "The Nothingness of Personality" also reflects Mauthner's thinking on the coherence and identity of the self. In it, Borges shows that there can be no continuous or overall "I" and illustrates this by describing the process of writing in which the "I" of the text can be described as writerly purpose. "This purpose and a few muscular sensations and the vision of the clear tracery of boughs which the trees place before my window construct my present 'I.'" The "I" of the reader is strategically positioned by discourse and has no more continuity or identity than the "I" of the writer. Thus, the reader is either an "indifference slipping over the argument which I indicated or a judgment about the opinions I demonstrate."[36] Early on, therefore, Borges is able to make a crucial distinction between the empirical I and the I of the enunciation, between the empirical and the virtual reader (as well as between the indifferent and the active reader). The model for literature is not, however, a communication model based on the circuit sender/message/receiver. Following Mauthner, Borges does not believe that any two people can read in precisely the same way. Communication is, rather, a strategic game, a purposeful activity which has its own conventions. "The more participants, the more compelling it will be," wrote Mauthner. "However, it is neither going to grasp nor alter the real world."[37] This strategic game of miscommunication is exemplified in Borges's story "The Other" (*Brodie's Report*) in which the older Borges confronts his younger self on a bench in the park. The older Borges finds he cannot comprehend a younger self who believes in the brotherhood of man and writes social poetry. The younger Borges, for his own part, cannot understand the older man's experience. Yet because they share the same body and mind, they are unable to deceive one another as people normally do and therefore the exhilaration of the game is missing from the encounter. "We were too different and too much the same. We could not deceive one another which makes dialogue difficult." Mauthner's world (and that of Borges) is a vertiginous one, fixed only by the temporary orders which are imposed by an act of will or by the reified and misleading substantives like "humanity" and "race" to which people attach meanings even though they are empty. Since language "came about from the memory of *Zufallsinne* (contingent senses) and was extended through metaphorical conquest to everything knowable," [38] it follows that a critique of language would deconstruct the empty substantives and emphasize the "verbal world" of process and time and the "adjectival world" of qualities, both of which are more faithful to our sensory reality.

One of the substantives that was most in need of deconstruction was, in Mauthner's view, causality: "The oldest belief of mankind, the belief in the world of reality coincides with another very old article of belief, which we are in the habit of parading as science, it coincides with the belief in causality, with the belief in the notion of cause and effect in nature." [39] For Mauthner, even laws of nature are metaphorical traces with no existence in reality: there are no such laws, only chance phenomena without any causes. In parallel fashion, Borges would describe natural causality as "the incessant result of endless, uncontrollable processes." [40] Now this denial of causality takes a crucial place in Borges's thinking and writing. To trace the "causes" of any particular event is equivalent to trying to speak of infinity; to ascribe causality to human events and invoke historical law seems doubly absurd, given the fact that even a meeting between two people depends on a properly infinite chain of accidents and coincidences. According to Borges, a single event such as Bartolomé de las Casas's proposal to introduce black slaves into the Americas to replace Indian labor, could result in a variety of consequences from Martín Fierro's assassination of a black man, the deplorable rhumba, "The Pea-nut Vendor" all the way to the "truncated and imprisoned Napoleonism of Toussaint l'Ouverture." [41]

Borges would also agree with Mauthner that "historical study is not an impersonal search for objective laws but a deed, always pursued from the point of view of the present and in the language of the present which is the only language we really understand." [42] In consequence, historiography is not a science but a matter of personal ideology. Thus "it does not matter whether we study history as a product of free will or of determinism and since nobody knows which system governs the world each one provides an equally valuable or contingent explanation."[43] In this way, Borges trivializes historical study, and this devaluation then becomes a necessary step in the freeing of the fictions from all external determinations.

Radical skepticism about the world, history, the laws of nature, and the self lead both Mauthner and Borges to renounce the ego and withdraw to the godlike abstraction from which individuation is seen to be illusory. Mauthner reaches this position by exercising his radical deconstructive techniques which he describes as if they were spiritual exercises.

> For a decade I have been teaching: the feeling of the Ego is a delusion. The unity of the individual is a delusion. If I am not me, yet exist, then I am entitled to believe of all others: they only appear to be individuals, they are not different from me, I am one with them, they and I are one. Are these mere philosophical word sequences? Games of language? No. What I can experience is no longer mere language. What I can experience is real. And I can experience, for short hours that I no longer know anything about the principle of individuation, that there ceases to be a difference between the world and myself. "That I become God." Why not?[44]

Borges, on the other hand, will attain this godless spiritual state through the writing of fictions which allow him to deploy at an abstract level the causality he had removed from history and the world. By introducing controllable causality into the short story, he can both create a well-made plot to seduce the reader and encourage the skeptical conviction that any order is a plotting and therefore contingent.

PLOT

The fact that certain mass cultural forms such as popular film and the detective novel have perfected the well-made plot has led some contemporary critics to deplore this device. According to their view, plot effects a closure of meaning, a subjection of all elements of the text to the final solution, thus making inevitable the priority of an authoritative authorial version. Borges takes a different view. In contrast to the formless psychological novel, he finds in well-plotted stories the essential element which differentiates fiction from the "asiatic disorder" of life. He therefore admires the ability to create well-made plots and this, in turn, accounts for his preference for Chesterton, Stevenson, and Kipling over Proust.[45] Just as Mauthner believed that causality, although nonexistent in nature and history, was necessary in language, so Borges believes causality to be necessary to narrative art. The term *magic* which he used in an early essay, "Narrative Art and Magic," however, also underlines the fact that he regards the causal as simply a device for combining unlikely elements into a narrative coherence. Magic is the "coronation or nightmare of the causal and not its contradiction." "This fear that a terrible event may be brought on by its mere mention is out of place or pointless in the asiatic disorder of the real world though not in the novel, which ought to be a precise play of attentions, echoes and affinities. Each episode in a careful story prefigures something still to come."[46] He would repeat this maxim in a discussion of Chesterton, in whose stories "everything is justified; the briefest and most fleeting episodes prefigure things to come."[47] It is important, however, to stress that his plots differ from those of Chesterton in one respect: whereas *The Man who was Thursday* has to be read as Christian allegory, Borges's fictions imply no such allegorical reference.[48] Rather, plot is important to Borges as a demonstration of control or mastery, the ability to produce what Alfonse Reyes described (with reference to Chesterton) as "an hallucination or a true nightmare."[49] Borges would similarly describe his stories as "controlled hallucinations" and "controlled dreams." Mauthner's view that "necessity is contingency" applies perfectly to the causality of the Borges plot, which is precisely the demonstration of the necessity which creates a certain coherence and verisimilitude at the same time that it unmasks this coherence as merely one possible ordering of the text. Mastery is also demonstrated by the use of oxymoron (a figure of speech which combines seemingly contradictory elements) since this allows extremes to be linked in an ingenious fashion. The manner in which Judas can become Christ, the traitor a hero, the detective a victim is the mark of the writer's skill in bringing together such unlikely extremes.[50] And this mastery is, in turn, deployed in order to seduce the reader. Like Japanese sword-play, plotting is a kind of archaic skill no longer socially significant, but which nevertheless can be turned into an exercise of individual control. The difference is that in the Borges story the reader position is needed to provide the fragile tension which will propel virtuosity toward self-mastery.

"The South" illustrates this process of control and contingency to perfection. The protagonist, Dahlmann, is of Germanic ancestry on his father's side and Argentine ancestry on his mother's. He is thus a living oxymoron, a Northern Latin or a Latin German. He has lived all his life as a Buenos Aires bureaucrat while longing for the mythic south of the *gauchos* and the cattle ranches. On his way home from buying a copy of

One Thousand and One Nights (the paradigm of the power of storytelling to stave off death), Dahlmann wounds himself on a broken window and soon afterward finds himself, or dreams he finds himself, on an operating table in the hospital. Either he is cured and goes south by train or he dreams on the operating table that he is going south. His first act on reaching the real (or illusory) south is to go into a bar where he is insulted by a *gaucho* and forced to fight. The unskilled Dahlmann prepares to fight to the death with a skilled opponent; but perhaps he simply dies on the operating table, dreaming of a heroic death. In the dream story, then, Dahlmann is converted from a patient/victim (or a passive reader) into an active though unskillful fighter who will be killed by someone more skillful than himself. If this were all the story was, however, it would be an allegory of reading which simply displayed the unequal power of a writer and reader. Yet despite appearances the dream version of the story and the "real" version are not offered as alternative readings in which the reader is supposed to exercise choice. What is produced, rather, is a necessary second reading in which elements which had once seemed to belong to a particular plot are now seen to be ambiguous and *disponible*. To try and integrate everything into one or other version produces inconsistency. We must either forego Dahlmann's coherence as a character or accept a coherence that allows him to be in two places at once. Thus the "causality" of one story has to be sacrificed to construct the coherence of another and vice versa. The causality that induces an "everyday" reading (accident, blood, hospital bed, feverish dream, operating table, death) can be redisposed to form another sequence (accident, operating table, feverish dream, journey, knife fight, death). There is no hierarchy to tell us that one should be preferred over the other. Both the desire to know what happened to Dahlmann (the empirical level) and the desire to be mastered by the author (in the dream version) lead to death. As in "The Captive," the knife is the symbol of a separation which severs the reader from the desire to know or the desire to be seduced, and the reader is then able to view the totality of devices, the false suggestion of coherence and causality, which have led him or her astray. The reader has, in a sense, been twice "mastered" by the plot—as a passive reader and as an active but less skillful participant—and only after this humiliation is permitted to become godlike by withdrawing from desire.

An even more obvious example of a story which provokes a second reading by tricking the reader is "Death and Compass," in which the detective Lönnrot becomes the victim of a murder. In this case, Lönnrot is not so much analogous to a passive reader as to a reader who arrives at the text with a decided preference for coherence which leads him or her to look for recurrent patterns. Lönnrot's single-minded obsession is to trap Red Scharlach (his own mirror image), and this very obsession together with his high regard for symmetry makes him overlook a veritable forest of symbols which might have warned him of the trap laid by his enemy who has the advantage of knowing the way his mind works. This parallels the writer's ability to forestall the reader. Thus Lönnrot takes a train at *night*fall, notices a railway car on a *dead* end of the track, treads on "generations of rigid broken eucalyptus leaves," passes "glacial statues of Diana and stagnant fountains." When he reaches the villa which is his destination and end he finds himself in a room with a dead rose which crumbles to his touch, much as the scenario he himself has constructed crumbles before the superior strategy of Red Scharlach. What is interesting in this case is the way the symbolic level becomes visible when the hermeneutic and proairetic codes have reached closure.[51]

Red Scharlach and Lönnrot are, in fact, very similar to Yu Tsun and Albert, for though the pursuers are successful and triumph on the strategic level the puzzle solvers suggest alternative versions of the plot which would, in a sense, destroy it. Albert's book of infinite ramifications reproduces the infinite ramifications of life; Lönnrot on the point of death suggests a better plot to Scharlach, one which consists of a single, incessant, and invisible straight line (in other words the irreversible labyrinth of human destiny). Now it is interesting that the writer/plotter seduces or entraps by deploying causality, the reader/solver seduces by suggesting meanings out of a desire for coherence. Both attempt to exercise control, yet neither can succeed. To kill the rival as Red Scharlach does destroys the game. To solve the problem satisfactorily, the solution must be as near as possible to life. The solution of the enigma and the completion of the action both destroy the story. However, it is at this point when the desire to know and control can be suppressed that the symbolic code becomes visible as the space where contraries and oppositions dissolve and reader and writer become interchangeable: Aureliano of Aquilea and John of Panonia are the same in the eyes of God. Similarly in Borges's fiction, the reader becomes writer and the writer becomes a reader.[52]

This superior register can only be attained after a sacrifice which kills desire. "The Intruder," a story from the late collection *Brodie's Report*, dramatizes a fraternal relationship (an allegory of the reader/writer relationship) fraught with rivalry, severed by desire, and finally bonded by murder.

A woman whom two brothers share interferes with their brotherly relationship. One of them kills her, and over the grave they feel themselves united "by the woman sadly sacrificed and the obligation to forget her." This story is unusually transparent and it is without the surprise ending which helps to activate a second reading. Yet precisely because of this transparency, it also preeminently reveals the didactic and allegorical thrust of the Borges fiction, for, though Borges deplores allegory in the traditional sense, his fictions can be described as allegories of reading and writing in which these two apparently opposing practices are brought together and, indeed, become identical.

DESTRUCTION OF THE RIVAL

The Borges fiction deploys a considerable amount of persuasion in order to activate this level of reader competency and in doing so caricatures, parodies, and otherwise discredits rival literary practices. The fiction thus becomes a more effective way of destroying rivals than the essay, in which some justice has to be done to the opposing position. In "The Aleph," Borges uses the simple device of setting up an absurd personage, Carlos Daneri, making him the proponent of realism (his hobby is photography). The protagonists, Borges and Daneri, constitute rival aesthetics and rival projects of immortality. At the beginning of the story, the death of the narrator's Beatriz, whose life had been dedicated to the oblivion of fashion, occurs on a February morning, and the changing of the tobacco advertisements in Constitution Square appears to hasten her voyage into the forgotten, "for I understood that the incessant and vast universe was already slipping away from her."

Indeed, the narrator's rival and Beatriz's cousin, Carlos Argentino Daneri, has set himself up as the Dante of the age of mass communications. Using telegraphs, phonographs, cinema, timetables, agendas, and bulletins, he is engaged in writing a vast poem, called *Earth*, in which the entire universe can be reflected without the poet having to leave his study. Daneri's project reflects the myth of technological progress of certain sectors of the avant garde (the Futurists, for instance) and the totalizing and cognitive project of a long tradition of Latin American poetry. From Andres Bello in the early nineteenth century to Leopoldo Lugones at the turn of the century and Neruda in modern times, a succession of Latin American poets have undertaken the Orphic task of creating the "great song of

America." Daneri, it should be noted, is an imperfect anagram of Neruda, and the story dates from 1943 when Neruda had already announced his intention of writing the *General Song* which would embrace the entire history of the Americas. But it is characteristic that Borges should use Daneri to score not only against the left-wing Neruda but against the conservative Leopoldo Lugones whose style he parodies in the extracts from *Earth*. The Orphic and mimetic fallacies (poetry as a mode of knowing the world, poetry as a reflection of the world) are symbolized in the Aleph, a mysterious object which Borges views in Carlos Daneri's cellar. It is a small aperture in which everything is simultaneously revealed and in which he sees the tiniest detail, down to pornographic letters that Beatriz had written to Carlos Argentino Daneri and the cancer in the breast of a woman living in the north of Scotland. Carlos's Aleph reveals everything that exists; it thus both duplicates the world and reveals its secrets. Following Dante's path, however, the narrator emerges from this cellar of condemned knowledge (condemned at least as far as Borges is concerned) into the light of revelation. He knows that he can destroy Daneri's Aleph simply by not mentioning it and thus consigning it to oblivion. In writing the story, however, he contradicts his own design, perhaps because ridicule is more effective a weapon of destruction than oblivion. But he also believes that a true Aleph exists and can be discovered through the tenuous allusions of written texts and hence through reading. This Aleph, he conjectures, is found in the pillar of a mosque and can be heard as an incessant humming. It is the murmur of the universe, the endless connotations and evocations of language which have been enclosed within the comparative permanence of form and which, alone, will allow Beatriz some measure of immortality. And though this Aleph has its origin on a frontier, it has also been enclosed though not rigidly ordered by a form constructed by settled peoples, for "in republics founded by nomads, the assistance of foreigners is indispensable in all that concerns masonry." Thus, in this elliptical way, Borges permits an allusion to the imposition of foreign cultures on the Americas while, in a more general sense, the pillar constructed in a mosque (i.e., in the service of a religion which does not allow representation) and by foreigners who are anti-Islamic marks the frontier between the "nomadic" oral tradition and the more fixed and permanent forms permitted by writing. Borges has thus destroyed both a rival and rival views of literature by ridicule in order to allusively project his own alternative.[53]

Borges does not always confine the rhetoric of persuasion to literary rivalry, however. In "Brodie's Report," an even more savage ridicule destroys any possibility that a tribe of Yahoos should be considered human beings.

"Brodie's Report" is an account by a puritanical Scottish missionary of the disgusting customs of a tribe of Yahoos who live in the region of Brazil and Argentina. The story parodies cross-cultural studies and is made all the funnier by Brodie's determination to redeem a tribe whose customs violate all his standards of civilization and decency. They blind and mutilate their king, delight in filth, and, from Brodie's point of view, engage in completely irrational customs. Yet, at the same time, his arguments for trying to redeem them are based on their humanity—much like the arguments of some of the earlier missionaries to the Americas:

> They have institutions, they have a king, they speak a language based on generic concepts, they believe like the Hebrews and the Greeks in the divine origin of poetry and conjecture that the soul outlives the death of the body. They affirm the truth of punishments and rewards. They represent, in short, culture, just as much as we do, despite our numerous sins.

Thus Brodie manages to discover in the welter of disgusting practices those which the Yahoos hold in common with the "highest" civilizations.

On one level, therefore, the story satirically exposes the imperialistic hubris of "higher" cultures seeking to bring civilization to the "primitive." But the story also strikes at some targets nearer home. For the Yahoos are not natural men who have not yet known civilization but have *fallen* into savagery. The branch of the tribe who live near Buenos Aires, for instance, are described as cunning traders even though they cannot even count, suggesting that Borges is settling a score with his fellow countrymen. Moreover, on returning to Glasgow, Brodie feels that he is surrounded by Yahoos on the streets, which suggests that degenerate mass man hides under the disguise of the Yahoo. Though the story satirizes Brodie's persistent desire to find good qualities in people it is best not to meddle with, it also confirms the "otherness" of the masses of the people and their perverse enjoyment of ignorance and filth.

The satire is much broader in the stories that Borges wrote in collaboration with Adolfo Bioy Casares. In one of the chronicles of Bustos Domecq, for instance, "On the Brotherhood Movement," it is directed against "unionism." The protagonist invents a theory of "unions" composed of any people who, at any time, have analogous desires (for the scent of jasmine, for example) or who are performing analogous activities.

Perfectly structured and steered by an expert helmsman, the brother-hood movement would constitute the bedrock of resistance against the lava-like torrent of anarchy. Let us, however, not shut our eyes to the inevitable offshoots of strife that the well-meaning doctrine may awaken: the man getting off a train will pull a switchblade on the man who boards: the incognizant buyer of gumdrops will try to strangle the master hand who dispenses them.

Treachery is thus the rule of human interaction and entropy is the most powerful law of Borges's world; solidarity, on the other hand, becomes an absurd and idealist illusion.

CONSPIRACY

Sociability is thus not a quality which particularly interests Borges ex-cept as a target for satire. The one social activity which he is willing to entertain in his fictions is, however, conspiracy. Yet his conspiracies are somewhat different from the great conspiracy novels—Dostoyevsky's *The Possessed*, Conrad's *The Secret Agent*, Chesterton's *The Man Who Was Thurs-day*, and the two Argentine conspiracy novels, Ernesto Sábatos's *Of Heroes and Tombs* and Robert Arlt's *The Seven Madmen*—all of which, in different ways, reveal the dark and somber fears behind the liberal facade. Borges's conspiracies, in contrast, are benign and have much in common with the avant-garde hoaxes that he himself had enjoyed perpetrating in the twen-ties. Yet they also reflect the hubris of authorship, the desire of the con-spirators to become authors in the true sense, even though in order to con-spire effectively they must also conceal their identities. In "The Theme of the Hero and the Traitor," for instance, a certain Nolan stages an elaborate deception based on Caesar's assassination in order to represent the murder of a traitor as if it were the assassination of a hero. The plan is so bril-liantly successful that it is only years later that someone guesses the truth; by that time, it is irrelevant. For time is the true conspirator, and with time the passions that had originally motivated the events disappear, render-ing them indifferent. Human intervention, however successful, eventually comes to seem futile, a single wave in a sea of accidents. Yet the urge to play God (and to become an author) is irresistible.

The analogy between a conspiracy against posterity and authorship itself was already implicit in Mauthner's discussion of the term *encyclopedia* in his *Philosophical Dictionary*. He considered that the eighteenth-century encyclopedists and Diderot in particular had attempted to shape the minds of generations to come, notwithstanding the fact that the order of the encyclopedia (an alphabetical order) is particularly absurd and arbitrary.[54] In "Tlön, Uqbar, Orbis Tertius," Borges turns this suggestion into a fable of authorship. At the beginning of the story, Bioy Casares is attempting to trace a quotation about mirrors which he remembers having seen attributed to one of the heresiarchs of Uqbar. A search of encyclopedias takes place and this eventually leads him and Borges away from their original quest and sets them searching for the mysterious planet Tlön mentioned in one of the entries they consult. The discovery of part of an encyclopedia of Tlön appears to give credence to the existence of the planet. However, the encyclopedia turns out to be an elaborate hoax planted by a group of idealist philosophers and an eccentric millionaire, Ezra Buckley, who did not believe in God but nevertheless wished to demonstrate for this nonexistent entity that mortal men were capable of inventing a world. What Buckley desired, therefore, was power; he wished to be an author in the true sense. But Tlön, because it was invented by human beings, is simply the mirror opposite of our world in which everything is seen in reverse, so that instead of being governed according to a realist illusion, its entire system of knowledge assumes an idealist interpretation.

The encyclopedia itself, however, strongly reinforces the realist illusion by lending authority to the planet's existence, and the narrator then furthers this illusion by describing heavy objects which have appeared on the earth and which he attributes to Tlön. By attempting to persuade the reader (in a printed text) of the existence of these objects which defy our physical laws, Borges himself joins the conspiracy, which soon takes on Orwellian proportions:

> The conjectural primitive language of Tlön has already penetrated the schools: the teaching of its harmonious history (full of harmonious episodes) has obliterated the history that dominated my childhood, already a fictitious past occupies the place of the other in our memories, of which we know nothing with certitude, not even that it is false. A scattered dynasty of solitary men have changed the face of the world. The task goes on.

The reader, by now, is aware that Tlön is analogous to discourse in Foucault's sense. It is authored by human beings out of a will to order but eventually takes on a trajectory of its own, making humanity "forget that its rigor is of chess players and not of angels." Its authors aspire to be godlike but their intervention is trivial, since the discursive practices inculcated by schools, families, professions, and prisons ingest the willed activities of individuals, which are merely fuel to the system.

Where Borges differs from Foucault is in seeing this conspiracy of discourse in purely abstract terms, utterly disconnected from domination, class struggle, biology, or economics. Better still, he distances himself from such conspiracies in such a way that (as in "The Theme of the Traitor and the Hero"), the passions of the movement are burned away and the interplay of forces can be seen on a more abstract level.

"The Lottery in Babylon" exemplifies such distantiation with its Borges-like narrator who has retired from the scene, yet attempts to chronicle the history of the lottery with some impartiality, even though he himself has participated in it. The narrator would like to believe that the lottery has been invented by a controlling company, but the system of rewards and punishments that has come into being is so complex as to force him to admit that many people no longer believe in the company but have become agnostics. There has thereby sprung up the vilest of beliefs "that to affirm or deny the reality of the tenebrous corporations is a matter of indifference since Babylon is nothing more than the infinite game of chance." The narrator, on the other hand, is himself a "theist" because the only way he can rationalize the constant redeployment and reinvestment of power among individuals is by attributing the activity to an institution of conspiracy: the mysterious company itself. He has been given the letter Beth to wear as an emblem: "This letter on nights of full moon gives me power over men whose mark is Ghimel but subordinates me to those of Aleph, who, on moonless nights owe obedience to those of Ghimel." According to this account, power circulates among people owing to the "natural" influence of the moon; there is no such thing as a dominant group who attempt to maintain power and, indeed, control its distribution and reproduction.[55] Those who distance themselves from the system are in the position to uncover rules and speculate on them but are powerless to intervene in the regulation and quantification. Conspiracy, like plotting, conducts us irrevocably toward disillusion and encourages the *askesis* or withdrawal which Harold Bloom has noted in much contemporary writing. The retirement or withdrawal of the narrator at the end of the story (the renunciation of authorship) is meant on the level of plot to be exemplary. At the end of "Tlön, Uqbar, Orbis Tertius," in much the same way, Borges had resigned himself to the triumph of the illusory Tlön, withdrawing to his house in Adrogué to work on a translation of one stoic writer, Sir Thomas Browne, into the style of another, Quevedo. The stoics are perfect models for a writer for whom power is an illusion and time the destroyer of historical order. As one commentator has pointed out, stoicism has traditionally provided a consoling doctrine "for private citizens of large impersonal states." [56] Borges, in his poems, likes to evoke embattled situations and the lives of lonely survivors during hostile periods—the end of the Roman Empire, Anglo-Saxon England, Medieval Ireland.[57] At such times, withdrawal from public affairs allows the stoic to disregard "those differences between men which are merely the consequence of externals." The supreme heroism at such moments is renunciation (the paradigmatic suicide of his grandfather) rather than control. The conquering hero is transcended by the hero who withdraws from battle, as Simón Bolívar was eclipsed by the greater heroism of San Martín, the great Independence leader of Latin America who, at the very moment of triumph, left Bolívar in sole command of the armies. This kind of heroism, a commentator in *Sur* noted, is unlikely to appeal to the masses, but "to govern a passion, an ambition, an instinct is, at times, more terrible than to lead an army." [58]

Indeed, Borges specifically relates the renunciation of power by San Martín to the renunciation of authorship in his story "Guayaquil" (*Brodie's Report*). The narrator is a bookish Argentine whose genealogy bears some resemblance to that of Borges; his ancestors have fought in the country's greatest battles and have, traditionally, been supporters of San Martín. He is now about to depart for Sulaco (named after the mythical country of Conrad's *Nostromo*) in order to be the official historian and the first to read and transcribe a newly discovered letter by Bolívar which is thought to hold the answer to the enigma of San Martín's renunciation. The letter, it should be noted, has been discovered among the papers of Dr. Avellanos (a character from *Nostromo*). This plan is spoiled by the appearance of a rival, a certain Zimmerman who is a refugee from Germany. Unlike the privileged narrator, Zimmerman by inclination and by race (he is Jewish) has concerned himself with persecuted and silent minorities. His major work is a study of the Carthaginians whom posterity knows only through the Roman versions of their history. He himself was forced to flee from Nazi Germany primarily because of the hostility and the denunciation of a powerful rival, Heidegger, with whom he had engaged in a polemic. This Heidegger-Zimmerman polemic had concerned the nature of representation. Heidegger believed that the leader should represent the people. Zimmerman, like Borges, opposes representation. Yet he now, in another context, becomes the ambitious and unscrupulous rival whose ingenious arguments force the narrator to withdraw from his project by showing him that his partisan involvement in the outcome makes him unfit for the task. The narrator's renunciation of the opportunity to make a name for himself thus parallels San Martín's renunciation. He also shows his moral superiority to his rival by overcoming his resentment through the writing of a story which he promises to burn. The real Borges has to betray the promise of his own virtual narrator.

It is significant that the only utopia in Borges is the bleak "Utopia of a Tired Man" (*The Book of Sand*)[59] and that this should be set in the cold wastes of North America on the eve of the narrator's departure for self-immolation in a crematorium. Yet it is very much a Borges world which the story depicts, one in which people develop only the arts and sciences they personally need, in which empty collective nouns such as "Canada" and "The Common Market" have disappeared, and in which the newspapers that commemorated the trivial have been abolished. It is a world in which each person produces one child: a lonely and isolated utopia, yet one which marks his distance from the hedonism of many contemporary critics as well as from critics such as Foucault or Deleuze and Guattari— whose deconstructions of philosophy and psychology are not accompanied by withdrawal from the world but are the preliminary steps to new kinds of social action. Borges assumes social action and solidarity to be futile and kills desire. And though it may be inferred that the interest in the reader is a model of brotherhood, this is misleading. Like the smile of the Cheshire cat, the reader/writer relationship is all that remains of the *corps plein* of the phalanstery, once the ideal of humanistic Latin American intellectuals. Reader and writer are coupled only to show that they are interchangeable, once the reader has been divested of hopes and loyalties. Though Borges undoubtedly values the immediacy of orally transmitted culture and of direct speech which can reply to the questions asked of it, the speech act or interpersonal action is not his model for writing, which has to be liberated from its material base. The dialogue is reinvented as a more shadowy encounter which allows the born-again reader to be interchangeable with the writer.

As I have argued in this essay, a good deal of persuasion is exercised to produce this interchange. Once liberated from the "retarding" effect of custom and prior knowledge, the fictions can become an efficient machine which, like modern technology, needs not life experience but only know-how. In this sense, they properly take their place with all those other pleasure machines at our disposal under advanced capitalism. They suppose that all dependency or loyalty to a community are obstacles to the release of energy for the experience of intensity. The exposition of mastery and the powerful weapon of ridicule have to be brought to bear so that the reader can be separated from empirical experience and historical knowledge. This violent separation permits the conversion from the social to the private, "freeing" the reader from the expectations derived from experience and conditioning him or her into enjoyment of literature as a uniquely privatized experience.[60] Little wonder that Borges has become the guru of university circles, since his stories both flatter the reader's smartness while diverting skills into the harmless zone of a game of solitaire. In achieving this, they are didactic, though in a manner different from traditional didactic narrative. They function not by example but by conditioning. In this sense too they are indeed modern, for they school the reader into that free-floating adaptability which has become the very requisite of modernization under advanced capitalism.[61] Thus it seems that the Latin American writer must not only make a sacrifice in order to be invited to the banquet of civilization (to use Alfonso Reyes's term) but must persuade himself and others that no sacrifice has been made.[62]

NOTES

1 Jorge Luis Borges "El idioma analítico de John Wilkes," in *Otras Inquisiciones* (Buenos Aires: Emecé Editores, 1960), 142.

2 Michel Foucault, *The Order of Things: An Archaeology of the Human Sciences* (New York: Vintage Books, 1975), xv.

3 See, for instance, the special issue of *Revista Iberoamericana* 42 (June–Dec., 1977): 100-1.

4 Paul Fussell, review of Paul Theroux's *The Old Patagonian Express* in the book supplement of the *New York Times* (26 August 1979).

5 See, for instance, Juan Fló, *Contra Borges* (Buenos Aires: Galerna, 1978), and Pedro Orgambide, *Borges y su pensamiento político* (Mexico: Casa Argentina, 1978). For reception in the Argentine, see María Luisa Bastos, *Borges ante la crítica argentina, 1923-60* (Buenos Aires: Hispamérica, 1974).

6 Harold Bloom, *The Anxiety of Influence* (New York: Oxford University Press, 1975), 116, terms *askesis* "a way of purgation, intending a state of solitude as its proximate goal."

7 Jorge Luis Borges "The Spanish Language in South America: A Literary Problem," in *Diamente* 15 (London: Canning House, 1964), 6. He has frequently made this comparison. See also, Jorge Luis Borges "El escritor argentino y la tradición," in *Discusión* (Buenos Aires: Emecé Editores, 1957).

8 See, for example, Richard Burgin, *Conversation with Jorge Luis Borges* (New York:

Avon Books, 1970), 46–47, and Paul Theroux, *The Old Patagonian Express* (Boston: Houghton Mifflin, 1979), 362–77.

9   This is particularly evident in a series of essays which he now repudiates, *El tamaño de mi esperanza* (Buenos Aires: Proa, 1926).

10 Jorge Luis Borges, "An Autobiographical Essay," in *The Aleph and Other Stories, 1933–69*, trans. Norman Thomas Di Giovanni (New York: Dutton, 1970), 240–42.

11 Frances Mulhern, *The Moment of Scrutiny* (London: New Left Books, 1979).

12 Jorge Luis Borges and Adolfo Bioy Casares, *Un modelo para la muerte* (Buenos Aires: Edicom, 1970). The first edition was privately printed. Other parodies written under their joint pseudonym, Bustos Domecq, include *Crónicas de Bustos Domecq* (Buenos Aires: Losada, 1967) and *Seis problemas para Isidoro Parodi* (Buenos Aires: Sur, 1942).

13 Prologue to Domingo Sarmiento, *Facundo* (Buenos Aires: Librería El Afenco, 1974), included in Jorge Luis Borges, *Prólogos* (Buenos Aires: Torres Aguero, 1975), 139. For an account of the changes in Borges's position, see Humberto N. Rasi, "The Final Creole: Borges's View of Argentine History," *Triquarterly*, no. 25 (fall 1972): 149–71.

14 Burgin, *Conversation*, 129–30; Ronald Christ, "Borges at NYU," *Triquarterly*, no. 25 (fall 1972): 458. On Lowell, see Enrique Hank Lopez, "An Audience with Borges," *San Francisco Sunday Examiner and Chronicle* (23 Sept. 1979). Borges has, of late, revised his attitude to the *junta* and expressed criticism.

15 Theroux, *The Old Patagonian Express*, 373.

16 Jorge Luis Borges, "Fragmentos de un evangelio apócrifo," in *Elogio de la sombra* (Buenos Aires: Emecé Editores, 1969). See also Borges, "An Autobiographical Essay," 233.

17 Borges, "An Autobiographical Essay," 233. For relations with the family see E. Rodríguez Monegal, *Jorge Luis Borges* (New York: Dutton, 1979).

18 René Girard, *To Double Business Bound: Essays on Literature, Mimesis and Anthropology* (Baltimore: The Johns Hopkins University Press, 1978), esp. chap. 5.

19 Borges, "An Autobiographical Essay," 231–32. A translation of the story, which was written in 1927, appears in *Triquarterly*, no. 25 (fall 1972): 182.

20 For an oedipal reading, see Mary H. Lusky, "Pierre Menard Autor," *The Texas Quarterly* 47 (spring 1975): 104–16.

21 Jorge Luis Borges, *A Universal History of Infamy*, trans. Norman Thomas di Giovanni (New York: Dutton and Co., 1972), 11–12.

22 Roland Barthes, "Myth Today," in *Mythologies*, trans. Annette Lavers (New York: Hill and Wang, 1975), 109–59.

23 Pierre Macherey, *Pour une théorie de la production littéraire* (Paris: Francois Maspéro, 1966), 285.

24 "The Search for Averroes" appears to have been inspired by the entry "Fatalismus" in Mauthner's *Philosophical Dictionary* (see note 33).

25 Jorge Luis Borges, *Evaristo Carriego* (Buenos Aires: Gleizer, 1930), 88 (see also p. 27).

26 See especially the poems of "Fervor of Buenos Aires" in Jorge Luis Borges, *Selected Poems, 1923-1967*, ed. Norman Thomas de Giovanni (New York: Delta, 1973).

27 Yukio Mishima, *Sun and Steel* (New York: Grove Press, 1978), 81.

28 See the title essay of Borges, *El tamaño de mi esperanza.*

29 "Las coplas de Jorge Manrique," in *El idioma de los argentinos* (Buenos Aires: Emecé Editores, 1928), 99.

30 The same description appears in Borges, "Dos esquinas," in *El idioma de los argentinos*, 150, and Jorge Luis Borges, *Historia de la eternidad* (Buenos Aires: Emecé Editores, 1969), 38-40. See also *Otras Inquisiciones* (Buenos Aires: Sur, 1952), 179-80.

31 Pierre Klossowski, "Nietzsche's Experience of the Eternal Return," in *The New Nietzsche*, ed. David B. Allison (New York: Delta, 1977), 108. For some sources of the story, see Ronald Christ, *The Narrow Act* (New York: New York University Press, 1969), 192-225.

32 See, for instance, the interview with James Irby, in James Irby, Napoleón Murat, Carlos Peralta, *Encuentro con Borges* (Buenos Aires: Galerna, 1968), 43-44.

33 Fritz Mauthner, *Wörterbuch der Philosophie*, 2 vols. (München and Leipzig: George Muller, 1910), 370-71. See also Gershon Weiler, *Mauthner's Critique of Language* (Cambridge: Cambridge University Press, 1970), 182. For Mauthner's relation to Wittgenstein, see Allan Janik and Stephen Toulmin, *Wittgenstein's Vienna* (New York: Simon and Schuster, 1973), 121-32. On the relation of Borges's theory to the Cabbala, see Saúl Sosnowski, *Borges y la Cabala: La búsqueda del verbo* (Buenos Aires: Hispámerica, 1976).

34 Mauthner, *Wörterbuch*, 1: xi.

35 I am indebted to Peter Biergen for help with translating Mauthner.

36 Jorge Luis Borges "La nadería de la personalidad," in *Inquisiciones* (Buenos Aires: Proa, 1925), 85.

37 Quoted by Janik and Toulmin, *Wittgenstein's Vienna*, 126. For Mauthner's view of poetic language, see entries under "Kunst" and "Poesie" in *Wörterbuch*.

38 Weiler, *Mauthner's Critique*, 158-59. See also Mauthner, *Wörterbuch*, 2: 603.

39 Weiler, *Mauthner's Critique*, 199.

40 Ibid., 185-95.

41 Jorge Luis Borges, "The Dread Redeemer Lazarus Morell," in *A Universal History of Infamy*, 19-20. For an extensive discussion of Borges's philosophical concerns, see the pioneer work of Ana María Barrenechea, *La expresión de la irrealidad en la obra de Jorge Luis Borges* (Mexico: Colegio de Mexico, 1957).

42 Weiler, *Mauthner's Critique*, 311.

43 Jorge Luis Borges, "Un método curioso," *Ficción*, no. 6 (March–April 1957).

44 Weiler, *Mauthner's Critique*, 295; Mauthner, *Wörterbuch*, 2: 132.

45 See for instance, Borges's prologue to Adolfo Bioy Casares, *La invención de Morel* in *Prólogos*, 22–24.
46 "Narrative Art and Magic," *Triquarterly*, no. 25 (fall 1972). I have offered a more literal translation than this version.
47 Jorge Luis Borges, "Modos de G. K. Chesterton," *Sur* (July 1936): 50.
48 In "The Search for Almotasim" (*Ficciones*), Borges goes out of his way to show his difference from Chesterton. Almotasim reaches no goal; there is no fixed meaning or set of beliefs which would explain the search.
49 G. K. Chesterton, *El hombre que fue jueves*, trans. Alfonso Reyes (Buenos Aires: Losada, 1938), 13.
50 For a discussion of this figure in Borges, see Jaime Alazraki, *La prosa narrativa de Jorge Luis Borges* (Madrid: Gredos, 1968) and *Jorge Luis Borges* (New York: Columbia University Press, 1971).
51 I have used the codes described by Roland Barthes in *S/Z* (New York: Hill and Wang, 1974). The difference between the coding of a Borges story and that of a classical realist text is that the solution of the enigma often suggests that it could have been reached by other means. It is therefore both necessary and contingent. For a more extended discussion of Borges's procedures, see Silvia Molloy, *Las letras de Borges* (Buenos Aires: Sudamericana, 1979), and John Sturrock, *Paper Tigers* (New York: Oxford University Press, 1977); Roland Christ, *The Narrow Act: Borges' Art of Allusion* (New York: New York University Press, 1969).
52 Gérard Genette, "La littérature selon Borges," *L'Herne* (1964): 323–37, pointed out the importance of the reader in Borges's writing. In a more general sense, see Paul de Man's *Allegories of Reading* (New Haven, Conn.: Yale University Press, 1979).
53 Roberto Paoli, *Borges: Percorsi de Significanti* (Firenze: D'Anna, 1977), deals with the Dante paradigm.
54 Mauthner, *Wörterbuch*, 1: 250–66.
55 For Foucault's views on this, see his conversation with Gilles Deleuze, "Intellectuals and Power," in *Language, Counter-Memory, Practice*, trans. Donald E. Bouchard and Sherry Simon (Ithaca, N.Y.: Cornell University Press, 1977), 205–17.
56 Stoicism thus becomes the ultimate posture in the repudiation of all concrete forms of collective experience.
57 One of Borges's projects for a movie plot was called *Invasion*. It was a paranoic nightmare in which a few defenders, "perhaps not heroes," fight to the end "without suspecting that the battle is infinite." Eduardo Cozarinsky, *Borges y el cine* (Buenos Aires: Sur, 1974), 83.
58 Carlos Alberto Erro, "Un filósofo americano: Waldo Frank," *Sur* 2 (April 1933): 45–95.
59 Jorge Luis Borges, *El libro de arena* (Buenos Aires: Emecé Editores, 1975).
60 In this respect, Borges's debt to Mauthner leads to a concern with language paralleled by that of another Mauthner disciple, Samuel Beckett; see Linda Ben

Zvi, "Fritz Mauthner and the Limits of Language," *PMLA* 95, no. 2 (March 1980).

61 Richard J. Barnet and Ronald E. Miller, *Global Reach* (New York: Simon and Schuster, 1974), 58. I am at present preparing a study of "modernization" and Latin American culture.

62 On the question of "didacticism" in apparently "open" texts, see an unpublished dissertation on Macedonio Fernández, one of Borges's mentors, by Aurea Sotomayor (Stanford University, 1980).

SELF-DESTRUCTING HEROINES

*T*o describe someone as a "public woman" in Latin America is simply not the same as describing someone as a public man—and therein hangs a tale. The public woman is a prostitute, the public man a prominent citizen. When a woman goes public, she leaves the protected spaces of home and convent and exposes her body on the street or in the promiscuity of the brothel.

> Blacks, mulattoes, mixtures of all kinds, drunks, somnolent or frightened half-breeds, skinny Chinese, old men, small groups of young Spaniards and Italians walked through the patios out of curiosity. They walked to and fro passing the open doors of the bedrooms, stopping to look in from time to time. The prostitutes, dressed in cotton clothes, were sitting at the back of the rooms on low boxes. Most of them sat with their legs apart, showing their sex, the "fox" which sometimes they had shaved and sometimes they hadn't.[1]

You have only to look at the gridiron plan of a traditional Hispanic town to know how important the distribution of space is and how completely public space—the cafés, the park benches, the civic buildings—are male preserves, places where they make speeches, run businesses, and argue about literature. Women's space is far more privatized—the enclosed world of the home or the convent, both of which are turned away from the street to look inward into a series of patios. Women and men meet in church or at the market but seldom casually. This division of the traditional city into public (male) spaces and private space where women's power derives from motherhood or virginity has deeply affected both political life and the imaginary repertoire on which literature draws. The Latin American novel came into being as a national endeavor programmed by masculine phalansteries and feminine marginality. More than poetry (which

Originally published in *The Minnesota Review* 22 (1984): 105-15.

allowed for male erotic fantasy and hence "feeling"), the novel is centered on the drama of male enterprise or impotence, the search for male identity that depends on the allegorization of women characters in their virtually invariant positions of mother, prostitute, or love object. Even the great historical novels of contemporary Latin America—*Terra Nostra* by Carlos Fuentes, *La guerra del fin del mundo* [The War of the End of the World] by Mario Vargas Llosa, *Yo el Supremo* [I the Supreme] by Roa Bastos, *El otoño del patriarca* [The Autumn of the Patriarch] by Gabriel García Márquez, novels which are extraordinarily detailed models of societies with their histories, their social classes, their art and literature, their battles and deaths —take as given the contrast between male (activity and enterprise) and female (passivity and reproduction). These novels are such efficient machines that we forget that there isn't an intelligent woman in any of them or that the most common form of male and female intercourse is rape.

Obviously these are giant generalizations which do not take into account a certain "feminization of discourse" (notably in the novels of Manuel Puig). But exceptions do not alter the fact that women in reality as well as in literature are overwhelmingly identified with fixed territories. In one of his poems, for instance, Vallejo turns his mother's body into a building which is both house and temple. Father and son pass

> Between the colonnade of your bones
> that cannot be brought down even with lamentations
> and into whose side not even Destiny
> can place a single finger.[2]

In this poem, reproduction is valued; the mother takes the place of Christ who is invulnerable to the gesture of doubting Thomas. Yet her body does not speak. It is a mute vessel whose role is to offer the transient male his only security in life. The mother does not *say*. She *is* a place, a house, and a temple. The mother's body offers a return to childhood before the entry into the symbolic order of language. Women are prior to language and therefore to literary creation. To sanctify motherhood, even ironically, as Vallejo does, only reinforces the taboo on creation, a creation that seems to involve risk, mobility, and the male's alienation from the female, and from the motherly qualities of connectedness and caring.

In Vargas Llosa's novel *La casa verde* [The Green House], there is an even more powerful and devastating form of female silence—the silence of the woman who has been mutilated as a direct result of violence. A brothel owner, Anselmo, conceives a passion for an adolescent girl, Antonia, who had once been abandoned in the desert after a robbery and murder and whose eyes and tongue had been pecked out by vultures. Blind and mute, she is apparently docile and at the same time mysterious. Anselmo kidnaps her and hides her in a tower in the brothel, supplying her with his voice and his sexual fantasy to which she eagerly responds. Long after Antonia's death in childbirth, her memory continues to haunt Anselmo. Yet Antonia epitomizes female mutilation rather than romantic love. Her mute blindness graphically illustrates the fact that the virtuoso male fantasy depends on women being the blank page on which male writers can write their own story. In Vallejo's poem, women are ineluctably associated with reproduction; in Vargas Llosa's novel, they are the docile performers of a male script which they may interrupt but in which they play no creative part.

These narrative fantasies and resolutions are obviously fueled by myths of creativity like those described by Sandra Gilbert and Susan Gubar in *The Madwoman in the Attic.* As long as women's creativity can be reduced to reproduction, men can freely usurp intellectual and literary creation, presenting it either as the virile activity of the father or, with equal audacity, as a form of male birthing. Latin American writers are astonishingly blatant in their usurpation of creative power. In a recent play by Mario Vargas Llosa, *La señorita de Tacna* [The Señorita from Tacna], the protagonist Mamaé is an incontinent old woman who pees all over the stage. Women's bodies are unreliable (the same author's *La tía Julia y el escribidor* [Aunt Julia and the Scriptwriter] has another incontinent female letting her husband down in public) and thus provide a comic form of subversion of respectability, a kind of latter-day carnavalesque. Further, the uncontrollable body is linked to Mamaé's unbridled romantic memory which flows as freely as her bodily liquids. But far from subverting the traditional subordination of female creativity, the play reaffirms it. The real protagonist turns out to be Mamaé's great-nephew who boasts the all-conquering name Belisario, and who sits at the side of the stage agonizing over his writing and his decision to give up a law career. What bothers him most, however, is that he is inexplicably drawn to writing about his great-aunt and using her "women's material" in his own writing. It is as if the old, public "male" themes of death and heroism have been played out so that the writer is now forced to incorporate formerly despised material. The play is unusually blatant in revealing a yearning for feminine feeling although the author can only present this in comic form.

Latin American women, like their counterparts in Europe and North

America, have thus been faced with powerful taboos on literary creativity while their own cultural forms—gossip, romantic narrative, lullaby—have been devalued or usurped. It is not surprising that the poet Gabriela Mistral, writing half a century ago, should come to sense that poetic creation was abnormal, a monstrous substitute for the "real" creation of human life. In the last decade, though, this situation has radically changed, not only because of the emergence of many women writers in Latin America but also because women have been thrust into the public sphere. The politics of death, fear, and disappearance, the destruction of the immunity formerly accorded to the Church and to middle-class women, the transformation of popular culture by a ruthless "modernizing" capitalism using the mass media as its instrument—all these have radically changed the older structures of everyday life. In the vacuum left by the outlawing of political parties, new movements have come to the fore, many of them under the aegis of women and the clergy. In Argentina, the mothers of the disappeared began to hold demonstrations in the Plaza de Mayo in Buenos Aires, inaugurating a symbolic action that has been adopted in Chile and in El Salvador. These women took over public space, their only weapons being white headscarves and photographs of disappeared children. They refused to stay in the privatized space of the home, nursing their grief behind four walls and were not afraid to display their sorrow, to show the mutilation of loss. In Chile, families of the disappeared chained themselves to public buildings; in Mexico, they held fasts and vigils.³ In countries in which women's public behavior has been carefully circumscribed, they made spectacles of themselves.

There are many parallels in literature to this occupation of public space. But what interests me here are not so much the novels that deal with torture, violence, and political themes,⁴ but rather the emergence of certain *topoi*—in particular, the *topoi* of the stigmatized female body and that of the liberated artist or performer. Both *topoi* respond to a system of representations found in works by male authors; in the first case to the representation of sadomasochistic relations and in the second case to the "immobile" and fixed spaces of femininity (house, brothel, convent) which the actress alone transgresses. Yet performance is also a problematic metaphor for liberation. In *Ways of Seeing*,⁵ John Berger pointed out that women are always performing, always self-conscious because they are subject to the judging male look. Women can never forget their looks as males can. Thus, for women writers to depict creativity in terms of a performance inevitably exposes the painful contradiction that, to be creative, she must become a public woman, a public woman whose shame and failure are exposed to ridicule.

In Griselda Gambaro's play *El campo* [The Camp][6] first published in 1967, the female fantasy of performance is subjected to devastating exposure. Obviously, that fantasy is not peculiar to Latin America. Doris Lessing's Anna in *The Golden Notebook* (to mention only one example) has a similar fantasy. But in *The Camp*, all structures are at the point of breakdown and madness. The setting of the play is "Auschwitz." Its title, *The Camp*, is ambiguous since in Spanish *camp* means both "countryside" and "concentration camp." The play uses both meanings simultaneously. Both concentration camp and countryside are offstage, heard by the audience through offstage sounds—singing peasants and playing children to suggest country pastoral; screams, sirens, and dogs to suggest inhuman oppression. Characters refer to the outside either as nature (fox hunting) or to comment on the barbed wire and the smell of burning flesh (people or animals). Onstage, some characters wear ss uniforms and one of them is said to resemble Mengele, the notorious operator of the Auschwitz ovens. However, the set always suggests a certain "normal" everyday life, for it is by turns an office, a dining room, a concert hall or a private house.

Briefly summarized, the plot is about the incorporation of a liberal individual, Martin, into the authoritarian state through his "seduction" by a prison inmate, Emma, and by the force and persuasion of a camp commandant, Franco. At the end of the play, Franco has apparently freed Martín from the camp, but he is branded by officials who thus incorporate him into the totalitarian society. And the play can be taken as an allegory of "man's eternal inhumanity to man" or as an allegory of the subjection of the individual to the totalitarian state, in which case Martín can be considered the protagonist. But it is the figure of Emma which is most interesting. She is, from the first, presented as totally subjugated by the camp commander, Franco, who barks orders, manipulates her, wheedles, promises, and threatens by turn but always orchestrates the situation. He incarnates the Subject with a capital S, the system itself, which by turns appears benign, homely, authoritarian, and savage (e.g., Franco takes off his jacket, puts his feet on the table, kisses Emma's hand, or appears with a hunting rifle). His only consistency is that like the state his actions are never predictable. Emma, on the other hand, bears the visible signs of her subjection. She is barefooted, wears camp uniform, has a shaved head, a wounded hand, and is branded. Her body is totally out of gear with her words. She has an itch she cannot control. Ordered by Franco to behave seductively to Martín, she can only arouse his pity and disgust—which, however, are as potent a method of seduction as the erotic.

Now quite clearly in this play, Franco attempts to use desire in order to captivate Martín; yet desire cannot be enjoyable. Relations of authority and power encourage sadomasochistic positions: hence Emma's abjection, her insistence that Franco is really a friend of the family and that she has been branded because she was always getting lost. Outwardly Emma connives with the system but her body signals its rebellion through the constant itching which also prevents her from being made into a love object. Body and speech have no natural connection. Emma sometimes speaks as if she were a society lady or an ambitious concert pianist or a seductress. But her appearance and her body do not cooperate in this masquerade. Gambaro thus presents us with a dysfunctional system in which subjects like Emma are forced to adopt contradictory positions, in which there is no fixed identity except the permanent identity of abjection. This is brilliantly illustrated by the stage directions. For instance, when Franco kisses Emma's hand in order to suggest his conventional respect for a lady, the directions read, "the gesture should slowly lose its genteel character and should become a gesture of domination." Ordered to seduce Martín, Emma halfheartedly attempts to do so while Franco, at the other side of the stage, beats the ground with a whip. With every blow, Emma cries out as if the whip had been laid across her body. It is "as if" Emma had been beaten, for she has an imaginary relationship with real repression.

The climax of the first part of the play is Emma's concert, which is attended by ss guards, camp inmates, and by Martín and Franco. However, Franco sabotages the performance. There are no programs, Emma wears a wig which falls off, Franco tears her dress, and the piano tuner hastily called in at the last moment untunes the piano. When Martín protests, the ss guards rough him up and he is forced, out of compassion for Emma, to admit that he had "enjoyed" the concert. In the second act, Martín and Emma are thrown together in a room from which they can hear the sound of hunting. Again the ambiguity of camp/countryside affects our understanding of events: Franco appears in hunting clothes and orders Emma to go and see the animals that he has killed though, plainly, the animals could also be people. Inexplicably, he also orders Martín to take Emma home and the stage is immediately converted into a private house. Though there is nothing to suggest domesticity, Emma begins to act in a different way; her memories are no longer the Franco-inspired memories of friendship and childhood but "real" memories of her arrival at the camp, of the dogs that bit her in a certain place — "guess where . . . It was a bit of luck because there is not much flesh there . . . all the same it hurt." Clearly this is a reference to her symbolic castration by the state. Yet even though she fragmentarily grasps the fact that she has been subjugated, she cannot form an alliance or relationship with Martín and cannot even remember his name. She is still hooked on the sadomasochistic relationship with Franco. Even so, she tries to lay claim to some semblance of normal life. She unpacks her suitcase and takes out a change of clothes only to find that it is a prison uniform identical to the one she is wearing. Finally, when the camp employees come to brand Martín, she tries to account for her stigmatized body and to rationalize her abjection: "I had to bear some kind of mark. We have to know who we are — a little mark." It is in this final desperate moment, when the liberal Martín is about to be marked by the state, that she finally remembers his name.

Gambaro's plays are not written as feminist works; but they are important because they allow us to understand that the social construction of the feminine position within the overall sexual politics of sadomasochism is symptomatic of the state's manipulation of the erotic in order to secure obedient subjects. Female sexuality is a lure. Further, women incline to perform this script written by the state because their creativity is often a desire for performance. Indeed, the concert performance in *The Camp* is one of the most powerful and pitiless representations of women's desire to liberate itself from sadomasochistic performance only to find all other forms of expression closed. The performance is, after all, the state's gift to Emma for seducing Martín (which she cannot really accomplish because of her unpleasant, subjected appearance). Emma herself desires neither love nor motherhood, though she obediently performs Franco's script; rather she aspires to the kind of power known as art. She does not aspire to create in the true sense but rather to perform on a public stage. But Emma not only has to perform in a prison camp atmosphere to an audience of drilled prisoners but is also the butt of their jokes, so that the performance becomes a ritual of humiliation. Nothing is genuine except the disharmony produced by the piano. Worst of all, her body betrays her and she cannot play for itching, an itching that is made worse by the lotion that Franco provides. Because the piano does not work she is forced to *pretend* to play on soundless keys; to supply the want of sound, she hums a Chopin polonaise.

The audience of prisoners demands an encore. In Gambaro's stage directions,

Emma sits down and repeats the same performance. At a given moment, the ss guard gives a signal and the prisoners begin to hum, softly
at first, but gradually they increase the volume with the obvious intention of drowning Emma's voice. She sings more loudly but despite
her increasingly desperate efforts, the chorus of prisoners drowns her
voice. At another signal from the ss officer, the prisoners abruptly stop
singing. Emma goes on pretending to play but though she tries to
open her mouth, only a hoarse murmur can be heard. Franco begins
to applaud. The audience mechanically demands an encore.

Following this fiasco, Franco kisses her hand, thanks her, forces a bunch of
flowers on her, but when she mutely tries to shake Martín's hand, Franco
brutally reminds her that her own hand is wounded. Meanwhile, Franco
also comments on the smell of burning bodies that now penetrates the
auditorium. As Emma throws herself to the ground, unable to bear her
itching body any longer, Franco hysterically forces Martín to admit that
he had indeed enjoyed the performance.

Emma is caught in the double bind that harnesses women to repressive
social orders. Yet there is a way in which she also seems to be the author's
scapegoat, a figure of shame and self-hatred. Similarly, that woman as creator easily turns to self-parody can also be observed in some of the short
novels and stories by the Puerto Rican writer, Rosario Ferré. In "La bella
durmiente" [Sleeping Beauty],[7] Ferré's heroine is a dancer, María de los
Angeles, who has a tragicomic fixation on the film *The Red Shoes*. Using letters, newspapers reports, interior monologue, Ferré parodies the language
and limitations of Puerto Rico's Beautiful People (the BPs). Like Emma,
María de los Angeles wants to perform but finds herself up against the
state—in this case, her own industrialist father, the convent in which she
has been educated, and her own social class. But dancing is also a metaphor
for the bodily freedom which has been denied women. This can best be
understood in the light of another of Ferré's stories, "La muñeca menor"
[The Youngest Doll], which, under an apparently comic surface, presents
a ferocious satire on women's immobility. The protagonist of the story is
a maiden aunt who as a young woman had been bathing in a flooded river
with her hair streaming toward the sea when a chigger entered her body,
lodged in her thigh, and caused it to swell to immense proportions. To
compensate for her unmarried state and her immobility, the aunt makes
life-sized dolls and presents one to each of her nine nieces when they
marry. The youngest niece marries an ambitious doctor whose father had

made a fortune out of the aunt's leg and on her marriage she receives a special doll with diamonds for eyes. The greedy doctor takes out the eyes and ants crawl inside the doll, which had been stuffed with honey. But as the years pass, the doctor's wife comes more and more to resemble the doll; on the day that she appears to relapse into porcelain-like immobility, the doctor applies his stethoscope to her chest as the angry chiggers reach out to attack him from the empty eye sockets.

The dolls are clearly like upper-class women who are made of honey and spice and all things nice, but who are both deprived of movement and inwardly resentful. Because their only function is to reproduce, these women are identified with nature; but the chiggers are also part of nature. So nature is double-edged—honey and devouring ants, the river and the chiggers. Women are forced to be like nature, but also to be narcissistic, because they are evaluated by the male look. Even their self-expression is a form of narcissism. Thus it is particularly appropriate that the aunt should pay attention to the doll's eyes which (except in the case of the youngest doll) she has imported from Europe. The eyes are then soaked in the river "so that they could learn to recognize the slightest movement of the chigger's antennae." Men deprive women of eyes. They rob them of the look that is power, and reduce their knowledge to the instinctual. To be "blind" in a society where eyes are the most important source of knowledge means to be shut off from positive knowledge and hence from the symbolic order. It means that women are thrust back into nature, but a nature that is not simply good motherhood but also a furiously angry chigger.

"The Youngest Doll" with its angry immobile woman helps us to account for María de los Angeles's fascination with dance in "The Sleeping Beauty." In this *nouvelle*, Ferré constructs a collage out of letters, newspaper reports, wedding invitations, the announcement of a birth, the captions written under wedding photographs, and all the other minor documents of everyday life. The action of the story covers a brief period of two years when María de los Angeles, an aspiring dancer, leaves convent school, attempts to dance in defiance of her family, marries because she thinks her husband will encourage her dancing, but finds herself pregnant when the husband rapes her in order to consummate the marriage. María de los Angeles gives birth to a son but plots revenge. Her alter ideal is the daring circus performer and her father's former mistress, Carmen Merengue. María de los Angeles's fantasy relationship with Carmen acknowledges a suppressed part of her father's life and valorizes a marginalized class. Since María de los Angeles is forbidden to dance, she hires a hotel room and practices Carmen Merengue's high-wire act there. At the same time, she fabricates her own death by writing anonymous letters to her husband in which she encourages him to believe that she is being unfaithful. The husband bursts into the hotel room, finds María de los Angeles with a man she has picked up from the street and kills himself and his wife. The son and heir will be taken in by the grandparents to continue the true line.

"The Sleeping Beauty" is written as farce, yet the joke consists of the twist it gives to the usual love triangle. María de los Angeles fabricates the triangle because she is unfaithful not with a man, but with art. Dancing is her husband's rival because it is taboo for a woman. It is thus interesting that "adultery" and illicit love, once a favorite theme of women writers, should have become a pretext that enables women writers to deal with the forbidden passion for creativity: yet more than individual creativity is involved. In two works written about Argentina, the woman artist and performer finds herself participating in a different kind of public performance. In Luisa Valenzuela's "Cuarta versión" [Fourth Version],[8] an actress called Bella (another Beautiful Person) negotiates her way from party to party and into an ambassador's bed. The embassy is a haven in the midst of political turmoil, but a haven that is soon invaded by political refugees. Valenzuela's story is the "fourth version" of a narrative about Bella that the author is trying to write, one in which the true story, the story of the disappeared, of terror and political exile, cannot be told. By pretending to write Bella's love story, the narrator is aware that she is *not* telling this other story, the story in which Bella is *not* a protagonist but "one more pawn in the game." In the course of the overt narration which eventually fuses with the censored and clandestine narration, Bella becomes the ambassador's lover: she stars as the only performer in a dramatic monologue, is offered a tour in the ambassador's native country (somewhere in Central America), and during the tour her apartment in Buenos Aires is ransacked by the police. When she returns home, she again takes up her affair with the ambassador, whose wife has now left him, and moves in to the embassy. But the affair comes to an abrupt end as the ambassador is recalled because of his policy of offering exile to political prisoners. He and Bella throw one final party in which Bella invites families who are seeking diplomatic immunity in order to escape the terror. But before the party ends, the police enter the embassy and Bella is killed. In this way, the story registers the breakdown of sanctuary which had once protected embassies and churches in Latin America and which the killing of nuns, priests, the bombing of cathedrals and embassies has brought to an end.

Beneath the telling of Bella's story, however, there is a subtext. Whenever the ambassador wants to communicate something that cannot be communicated in ordinary speech, he tells a story about his mythical Uncle Ramón. Bella's story is part of a similar device. What cannot be "narrated" because it is fear, terror, and oppression has to be displaced onto a love story which demands a certain kind of protagonist, a protagonist who can hook the reader because she is beautiful, seductive, and independent. But of course this is also a feminine fantasy, a fantasy of a heroic "free" woman who, like Emma in *The Camp*, projects female fantasy as performance. The actress is able to cross boundaries; in traditional terms, she uses the influence of the "bottom sheet"—that is, the influence of the courtesan. But in Valenzuela's story, such seduction is both parodied and finally undermined by "real" events.

The ambivalence of the performance metaphor is also starkly exposed in Marta Traba's novel *Conversación al sur* [Mothers and Shadows].[9] One of the women who participates in this conversation is an actress, an older woman whose son is missing in Chile. She confronts a younger friend, Dolores, who had participated in underground movements, had been arrested, and had aborted a child under torture. The novel is, however, less a conversation and more of a meeting of memories on the eve of death. The memories of the actress include one particular traumatic moment during a visit to Buenos Aires. Her friend Elena had lost a daughter, Victoria, who is now numbered among the "disappeared." Elena takes the actress to the demonstration of the "madwomen" of the Plaza de Mayo, a demonstration that horrifies the actress and shows her a different kind of performance. Here the women wear white handkerchiefs and perform their grief to a silent city square. They hold up photographs which no one will see and shout questions that no one will answer. Naked grief has abolished distinctions of social class and all feeling of shame or respectability. To her horror, the actress also finds herself screaming; but hers is a different script.

Clearly the figure of the performer provides these women writers with a device for referring to both sexual and public politics. In contrast to some male writers like Gabriel García Márquez, who wishes to keep the masculine and feminine sphere strictly separated and who recently declared in a *Playboy* interview that women make toffee animals so that men can go off to the wars (even as a joke this is dubious), these women writers have had to find ways of overcoming the limitations imposed by restricted female territories. By "territories" I mean both the privatized spaces (convent and home), and the feminine connotations that have accrued to their immobility and passivity because of this restriction. The "deterritorialization" of the feminine and of the indigenous has occurred not only in recent literature but also in society at large. There has been massive migration into cities, the uprooting of entire populations, the removal of indigenous peoples from their traditional territories, as well as the destruction of hitherto "sacred" territories such as embassies, churches, and middle-class homes and hence the dismantling of the imaginary repertoire on which writers draw. Once the state invades homes, converts mothers into madwomen, and bombards cathedrals and embassies, we know that the hegemonic discourse has undergone a change. "Home," "family," "church" can no longer underpin regimes which attack these territories. What authoritarian discourse attempts to do is to displace the meaning of these spaces, to make them both more abstract and more restricted in meaning. Thus they qualify them so that church implies "loyal and traditional church" and family means "disciplined and obedient" family. But by qualifying these terms, they wrest universality from the hegemonic discourse. They also create exclusions, forcing the excluded to regroup themselves in spaces which the military ignores or leaves open. Literature registers such changes as shifts in the imaginary repertoire or as stereotyped gestures which are now only available as traces of the past. Whereas many male writers tend to conceal the stereotype by veiling it as history (this is the way things *really* were), women writers are forced to parody the stereotype for otherwise they would have to deny the possibility of any breakthrough. The figuration of woman as performer thus becomes a device that permits them to explore the traditional limitations on creativity even though, as I have shown, it also opens up ambiguities that invite parody. In trying to influence the public as performers, Emma, Bella, and María de los Angeles become "public" women. Their desire to create is at once passionate but grotesquely distorted, for they are still besieged by the negative eros of death and destruction that tears apart Latin American political life and has its roots in *machismo*. The sadomasochism that underpins *machismo* allows space to performers because it is itself highly theatrical. By liberating themselves from the fixed spaces to which Latin American women have traditionally been condemned, Emma, María de los Angeles, and Bella find themselves performing a sadomasochistic script in which their originality can only take the form of abjection or death. They are self-destructing heroines, but their failed performance should not deter us from envisioning a society that would give them room.

NOTES

1 José María Arguedas, *El zorro de arriba y el zorro de abajo* (Buenos Aires: Losada, 1971). Translation mine.

2 Poem LXV from the collection *Trilce* (1922). The translation is my own.

3 See, for instance, Hernán Vidal, *Dar la vida por la vida: La agrupación chilena de familares de detenidos desaparecidos* (Minneapolis: Institute for the Study of Ideologies and Literature, 1982).

4 These have been constant preoccupations in women's writing over the last few years. See, for instance, Elena Poniatowska, *La noche de Tlatelolco*, Elvira Orphée, *La última conquista de el Ángel*, and Luisa Valenzuela, *Donde viven las águilas*.

5 John Berger, *Ways of Seeing* (New York: Penguin, 1972).

6 Griselda Camparo, *El Campo* (Buenos Aires: Ediciones Insurrexit, 1967).

7 Both of the stories I discuss, "La bella durmiente" and "La muñeca menor," are included in Rosario Ferré, *Papeles de Pandora* (Mexico: Joaquín Mortíz, 1976).

8 Included in Luisa Valenzuela, *Cambio de armas* (Ediciones de Norte, 1982).

9 Marta Traba, *Conversación al sur* (Mexico: Siglo XXI, 1981).

SATIRE AND THE DIALOGUES OF THE DEAD

Diachronic Discourses in I the Supreme

*I*n his essay "The Ontology of the Photographic Image," André Bazin describes the artistic obsession with the "preservation of life by representing life," and he traces this trend back to the ancient practices of embalming the body and recreating its figure in funeral statues. This aspect of the plastic arts—the necessity "of having the last word in the polemic with death via the use of lasting forms"—finds its natural culmination, according to Bazin, in the photograph.[1]

This "pathos" of mortality has also been one of the most intense obsessions of literature, and it has been particularly important in Latin America, where individuals not only confront death in very personal terms, but the whole continent seems to be enthralled by this universal consciousness.

Thus, the well known *topos* of the dispute between *armas* [weapons] and *letras* [letters] (action and writing) acquires an ironic twist in its attempt to articulate opposing claims for future generations. If writing seems to have won the battle in the modern world, the reader cannot help noticing the kamikaze nature of this victory. This textual feature is especially prominent in contemporary Latin American literature—the theme of the final holocaust or self-immolation, where the triumph of writing is also its destruction.

At the end of Borges's "Guayaquil," the triumphant "author" burns his manuscript. In Onetti's *Dejemos hablar al viento* [Let the Wind Speak] and García Márquez's *Cien años de soledad* [One Hundred Years of Solitude], fictional societies are created in order to be destroyed. We could also refer to the collapse of the pyramid and the madness of the person who is theoretically the narrator at the end of Fuentes's *Cambio de piel* [Change of Skin] or the immolation of the narrator that the author describes at the end of *Aura*.

Originally published as "El pasquín y los diálogos de los muertos: discursos discrónicos en *Yo el supremo*" in *Augusto Roa Bastos y la producción cultural americana*, trans. Mario Toer, ed. Saul Sosnowski (Buenos Aires: Ediciones de la Flor, 1986), 179-196. Translated by Carla Faini.

This fictional destruction must be examined in contrast to the obsession to honor the remains of public figures as they appear from time to time, such as the discovery of Cuauhtemoc's bones, or the return of Eva Perón's and Rosas's bodies to their country.[2] It is as if the fetishistic preservation of the body guarantees honor and immortality. Inversely, a dishonorable burial guarantees that one will be forgotten. It was not merely capriciousness that led García Márquez to include a citation from Antigone as an epigraph to his first novel, *La hojarasca* [Leaf Storm]:

> But Polynices, just as unhappily fallen—the order
> says he is not to be buried, not to be mourned; to be left unburied,
>   unwept, a feast of flesh
> for keen-eyed carrion birds. The noble Creon
> It is against you and me he has made this order.
> Yes against me.
> . . . This is no idle threat;
> the punishment for disobedience is death by stoning.[3]

These words are an antecedent to the anonymous, satirical text with which *Yo el supremo* [I the Supreme] begins, and they also reveal the enigma that is the central point of the entire novel. An honorable funeral implies the possibility of a resurrection, either in social memory or in history, which contrasts with the absence of memory outside the city walls.

I the Supreme adds a significant new dimension to this preoccupation with rotting corpses and eternal glory. It is not only burial "without a cross or a marker" which horrifies Dr. Francia but rather an even worse fate— burial in the tomb of writing. In the final pages of the novel *Tenebrus Obscurus*, the true image of Francia, is devoured as if by a giant fly, leaving not a single trace of his actions. The innumerable eyes of posterity are not focused on the "true reality," but, rather, like the images found in the fly's line of sight, they see his petrified images, eternally cemented in the descriptions of Francia written by his enemies. In the last paragraph of the novel, those eyes "devour my image, until it is impossible to distinguish their image wrapped in a black cape with a scarlet lining" (p. 453).[4] This "other" image that disappears from the dying Francia's point of view is the "immortalized" image created by the Robertson brothers and his other detractors; it is the final image of the novel, given that the rest of the documents that follow are petrified ("the next ten folios were petrified"). As it had been foretold at the beginning, "the chimera has replaced me" (p. 15).

Almost a century ago Thomas Carlyle commented on this strange dupli-

cation of Francia as both an enigmatic personality and a public image created by hostile critics.[5] Carlyle was suspicious of modern democracy: in
his opinion, a nation was only as good as its heroes. Therefore, he had very
little sympathy for the Robertson brothers' screams of horror concerning Francia's dictatorship. On the contrary, he decided to include Francia
on the list of Latin American heroes whose many feats were unknown
in Europe. Latin America found its Washington in Bolívar; its Hanni-
bal in San Martín; its Napoleon in Iturbide. However, Carlyle cannot
explain Latin America's disastrous absence from the universal Parnassus.
This is due to Carlyle's inability to recognize the hegemonic urban centers'
power to construct and disseminate their view of history and their version of universal memory. In any case, Francia was seen as different from
the aforementioned emancipators because of the "black legend" that surrounded him, which was encouraged by the "missionaries of capitalism,"[6]
who firmly believed that democracy was indisputably linked to industrial
development and who were outraged by the autarchic and despotic nature
of Francia's regime. Carlyle's antidemocratic preconceptions allowed him
to read the Robertson brothers' protests in such a manner that he salvaged Francia's heroic potential as the person who kept the sacred flame
of knowledge alive in the Paraguayan deserts and swamps, without any
other resources than second-hand French books by Volny and Rousseau.
Although this flame was weak, malnourished, flickering, and nearly dead, it
was still considered "sacred." All that was needed to reveal this remote and
courageous heroism to the world was the "genius of Paraguayan writing."
"If the creative genius which produces writing is alive and well in Paraguay, it is invited to participate in the current project. Surely, everywhere
that the spirit of writing exists, it should be encouraged by the spirit of
action when it is inverted and joins with the former to say: 'Now or never,
writing is the thing for me'" (p. 273–74).

When Roa Bastos, as Dr. Francia's "spirit of writing," finally emerges in
1970, he does not try to act like the Siamese twin of the "spirit of action,"
or like a "body without organs" (the Siamese twin of *I the Supreme* lives in
the body of his sister). In the era of the decline of capitalism, the ambiguity
surrounding Francia's image grows. From the twentieth-century perspective, it is clear now that democracy and capitalism are not necessarily
linked, and that authoritarian states are more common than participatory
ones. Furthermore, we now recognize that writing is not simply the neutral technology of the state's knowledge, but rather constitutes one of its
power bases. The Francia of *I the Supreme* cannot be described in terms of

fictitious or historical features, but rather as the product of the intersection of different discourses, located at the site where the despotic state (that literally dictates its own existence) comes face to face with an entirely new phenomenon—the capitalist state whose power is derived from writing and which creates an alliance of writing with other more subtle power bases.

The confrontation between these different types of states, including those which never communicate with each other, can be understood in the light of Nicos Poulantzas's analysis of the discourse of the precapitalist and capitalist state. In the former, "discourse takes the form of a revelation, based on the Prince's statements, which expresses once again the inscription of the Sovereign's person on the Social Body" (p. 58).[7]

> The capitalist State is not dependent upon revelation, but rather upon writing. Nothing exists in the capitalist state unless it is written, whether it takes the form of a signature, a note, a report or a complete archive. The capitalist State's anonymous writing does not repeat its discourse, but it does outline a certain path, making note of the positions and bureaucratic mechanisms and presenting the hierarchical space of the centralized State. The massive accumulation of paper that accompanies the organization of the modern State is not related to picturesque detail, but rather it is necessary for its very existence, and functions as the internal cement of the State's intellectual function, which delineates the relationship between the State and intellectual labor (p. 59).

Seen in the light of this explanation, the different speech genres in *I the Supreme*—edicts, "infinite circulars," speeches, dialogues, and polemics—are not simply allegories of reading or of the author, independent of the state's apparati. Rather, the novel is a compilation of the different discourses of power, whose characteristics have been analyzed exhaustively.[8] It is also important to point out that the text is located at the historical conjuncture where new types of power, articulated with different technologies of knowledge, confront each other. The novel develops the confrontation between Dr. Francia's despotic state, which relies on visual communication (written texts and drawings) and verbal messages, and the bureaucratic state, which is enunciated in anonymous texts, which are perpetuated by repetitive documentation. Both types of state are based on the silencing of popular power and the prevention of participation, given that all of their embodiments are dead, silenced, or reduced to the murmurs of parody.

In any case, the novel incorporates a third level, the utopian position from which it is possible to imagine a society in which manual labor is not subordinated to intellectual work, and the masses are not subordinated by a leader or the state.

LEGITIMIZING DESPOTIC STATES

As Poulantzas argues, the precapitalist state legitimizes itself through the discourse of the prince. It is communicated "by means of the narrative, to fill the space between the principles of sovereign power and the world" (p. 58). Deleuze and Guattari also describe the despotic state as "immobile, monumental, incapable of change; . . . it acts with the most elevated and transcendental unity, depending on dictates and decrees."[9] The voice of the state is "written down on tablets, stones and books." The subordination of written speech to the voice inspires "a fictitious voice from on high which, inversely, no longer expresses itself except through the writing signs it emits (revelation)" (p. 204). The edict is the privileged mode of communication for despotic power. The state that Dr. Francia conceived differs from traditional despotism only in its origins. Since Francia did not inherit his power by divine right, he has to provide a variety of miraculous legitimations. Most important, Francia's own origins have to be rewritten in order to erase his natural father and establish his birth as a self-creation. Francia proclaims that his power is natural, unique, and indivisible. "The Supreme is that person who is Supreme naturally. He never reminds us of another, only the image of the State, the Nation, the People, the Country" (p. 64).

The Supreme is the abstraction of the nation; he is not human, yet he is incarnated in the person of Dr. Francia, whose solitary unique power is undermined by paranoid fears of impostors, such as the Marqués de Guaraní, and by copiers, usurpers, sycophants, imitators, and doubles.

The integrity of the state is thus maintained by paranoia.

Given that Francia is the supreme power and a living person, and thus subject to mortality, there are always gaps in his legitimizing discourse. One of these gaps appears when he rejects his father and his sister so that it is necessary to invent a magical legend of his birth, according to which his father, Don Engracia, is killed by a tiger; Francia then emerges from the tiger: "I closed my eyes and felt that I was being born." This allows him to imagine his own birth as purely an act of self-fashioning. "I drank my own questions. I nursed on my own milk, which I got from my breasts" (p. 309). In fact a number of myths of autogenesis appear during the course of the narration. On one occasion, Francia takes the story of Hero, the viceroy's dog, who had begun to tell the myth of the origin of the world, and converts it into a new myth in which a pair of twins of divine birth give birth to each other, thus creating their own origin:

> They conceived, or rediscovered the possibility, not only of two, but of many, of innumerable sexes. Though the man is the reasonable sex. Only he is capable of reflection. Hence, too, only he is called upon, destined, condemned to render an account of his unreason. How is it possible that we should have a single progenitor and a single mother? Can one not perhaps be born of oneself?[10]

At the bottom of the page, Francia adds, "I have no family; if indeed I was really born, which has yet to be proved, since only what has been born can die. I was born of myself and I alone have made myself Double."[11]

Given this transcendental reason, he could not have human origins. Reason is masculine; because of its claims to universality, it must monitor errors and nonsense. Francia not only identifies thinking with being, but also, given that he is the only supreme being, he becomes aware that he is the only "organic intellectual" in his own state, despite the fact that he has been condemned to live and die in a body whose mortality he denies.

Given this nonextensive aspect of the state and the person of the dictator, power is basically exercised through paranoia; not only the paranoid fear of the impostors of the dictator himself, but also the fear that is disseminated through his subjects, who are constituted as such by being constantly spied upon. Deleuze and Guattari's description of the despotic state, based on earlier forms of alliance and kinship, is pertinent in this case.

The despot "has installed himself at the limit, at the horizon, in the desert, the subject of a deterritorialized knowledge that connects him directly to God and connects him to the people. For the first time, something has been withdrawn from life and the earth, that will make it possible to judge life, and to survey the earth *from above:* a first principle of paranoic knowledge" (p. 194, italics mine).

In *I the Supreme*, this deterritorialized knowledge takes the form of science, particularly astronomy. Francia's passion for the "star of the North" and his relationship with his subjects is mediated by the vigilant eye of the telescope. This distance is rationalized as science: "my race is the constellation that I should locate, measure, and know in its smallest secrets, in order to be able to guide her. I am part of her. But I also need to remain outside. Observe her at a distance" (p. 109). The cosmological view is essential for this perception of power, according to which everything is seen from above. There is no communication between popular traditions and the Supreme, who scorns the populist pretensions of intellectuals and who would like to live in "a world composed of elements that are different from them, with whom they would like to become intermingled. They think that they are the guiding light of an imaginary people. With the help of random luck, they sometimes take pride in the stupidity of this mob, turning it into an even more imaginary creation" (p. 23). Francia does not represent the people. He is the state in its dual representation in the living body of the despot, and in writing (lists, edicts, letters, and perpetual circulars) that disseminates his paranoid power. The fetishistic objects of this knowledge-power include a meteorite that was dragged through Paraguay by his subjects and installed in his study as a symbol of his control over fate; the amaranth flower, which symbolizes immortality; the skull, the empty receptacle of absolute knowledge that symbolizes the death desired by the Supreme after he found out that he could only be immortalized after death: "death is the only remedy for this desire to be immortal for the person whose path is blocked by the sepulchre" (p. 166).

Francia's singular concept of immortality is that his memory should be perpetuated through actions, although his resistance to popular power means that his monument will be a solitary and grotesque experiment, and not the vital development of the society. This paradox is illustrated by a fantasy encounter with Belgrano in which their horses soar above the crowd. Francia comments: "those real people, those possible beings would interrogate us, clamor for us, give us their innocent mandate, given that we are beings without fathers or mothers, proudly mounted on our ideas, which are dead ideas, unless one carries them out" (p. 228). This distance makes his last statement a paradox and leads him to try to invent or imagine all kinds of discourses or thoughts and actions that would allow him to communicate directly with posterity and avoid the ambiguity of writing and the inevitable implications of the death of the author, who is survived by the text.

Francia's power is, paradoxically, incorporeal (transcendental) and also incarnated in a mortal human being, who treats Paraguay as if it were an extension of his own person; for this reason, he always confronts foreigners —Argentines, Brazilians, British, and French—as threats to his bodily integrity. When his thoughts turn toward the arms trafficker Andaluza, for example, it is in order to remember the "red handkerchief" of her menstrual blood; he associates her attempt to enter Paraguay with the fetid smell of death and seduction. The "Catalan-Frenchy" Legard, nicknamed the "seducer," is said to have planned a seduction of the dictator which would involve telling him pornographic stories based on the novels of the Marquis de Sade, whom he had encountered in the Bastille. Even the Robertsons defend the pleasure principle in their conversations with the dictator. Francia counters these seductive foreigners with his version of the organic state. Paraguay "has in me its material body" which is governed by a pentagon of powers: "Head, Heart, Belly, Will Power, Memory" (p. 128). Any invasion of Paraguay would imply an invasion of Francia's body; similarly, a concern with bodily functions runs through all of his meditations.

The "invaders" are frequently physically punished. He makes the Robertsons drink fermented beer: "They will urinate my beer until the end of time, because they are dull and greedy" (p. 140). He has the Brazilian representative, Correia de la Cámara, wait on the frontiers in a house that has been invaded by a plague of flies and whose roof is the scene of a public copulation.

When Francia considers the state to be an organism, he cannot relegate it to the tomb of writing, since his plans call for the direct transmission of voice and image. Based on this premise, he comes up with the introduction of artifacts like the "pen-carrier of memories" that anticipates the cinema in its capacity to reproduce iconographic images (p. 214), or the "listening barrel butts" that anticipate the tape recorder. These artifacts register the gap in the despotic system, which has been conceived of as an organic society but lacks the means to incorporate popular power unless it is by and through the dictator. The incorporation of popular power into the state would imply, in fact, the breakdown of the separation of intellectual work from manual labor, which forms the base of Francia's power, as well as that of the capitalist state.

THE LAMPOON

Francia's plan to convert himself into a single machine which operates by means of both written and verbal communication, which addresses the people through edicts and circulars, has certain consequences. Paraguay becomes an autarchy symbolized by an immobile ark which is anchored in the river. It is the immobility of the defensive, despotic state that confronts the always mobile and versatile invasion, not only of armies but, even worse, of money, goods, agents, traditions, and symbols that accompany capital wealth. The text of the ambiguous lampoon cited at the beginning of the novel confronts this new bodiless power and acts as the intermediate stage between Francia's writing and a one-person bureaucratic state that can reproduce itself in anonymous writing. The anonymous lampoon not only constitutes the beginning of a hermeneutic code, but also marks the limits of Francia's organic state. Furthermore, except for a letter written by Pueyrredón (concerning the conquest of Entrerríos, Corrientes, and Paraguay) the lampoon is the only document in the novel that is reproduced as if it were an original manuscript, that is, as a historical document—the irony being that it is not original at all since it is an imitation. It is written as if it were an edict and could have been considered one, except for the parodic manner in which Francia refers to it.

Historically, lampoons were defamatory, calumnious attacks (often written in verse). They expressed public opinion before it became institutionalized by the press. The document which begins the novel is thus very different from the traditional lampoon, given that its voice is apparently that of the state, and it confirms the perpetuation of its power beyond the life of any individual. The author of the lampoon must be a power (the "he"), or someone parodying that power—in which case it would indicate the emergence of a type of writing that would have the dangerous capacity to simulate personal authority (I the Supreme) and exact obedience in an abstract manner. We can compare this edict-lampoon with the interpellation of ideology that constitutes the people as subjects, thus locating them in a specific manner.

The lampoon orders the decapitation of the dictator's body, the humiliating public display of his head (the location of knowledge)—a punishment usually given to traitors, and the execution of his civil servants and military troops, whose bodies should be buried in "unmarked graves outside the city walls, in fields, without a cross or a headstone to identify them" (p. 7). Since only the Supreme (the organic state) has the power to carry out this order, the "I" of the edict is clearly an impostor, the temporary maintenance of perpetual power that cannot be embodied in a person.

The introduction of this incorporeal subject could lead us to believe that the novel will address some contemporary problems that are linked to writing—problems like the rupture of intentional continuity between the writer and the text, the separation of history as narration from discourse, as a narrative strategy. What prevents the novel from being read as an allegory of writing and reading is that the play of enunciation is not

simply related to literary authorship, but rather to the state's interpellation of society. Dr. Francia's obsession with a document that suggests that
he could be replaced by an anonymous power that will continue exercising
its authority after his death is justified. If Francia is clearly the originator of the majority of the discourses of the novel—the edicts, the dictates
of the "perpetual circular," the legends about his origin, the discourses on
science, history, commerce, law, charity, and even the "progressive" discourses on indigenous peoples and the inhabitants of his country—then
they are compromised by the mystery of the anonymous satire that haunts
the Supreme: "Let us return to the pamphlet that was found this morning on the door of the cathedral" (p. 19); "We will begin the cycle again.
Where is the anonymous satire? This scrap of paper puzzles me" (p. 31); "I
think that I recognize the handwriting, this paper" (p. 52); "What is going
on with the investigation of the anonymous satire found at the cathedral?
Have you identified the handwriting?" (p. 425).

    The lampoon indicates a gap in Francia's own discourse, his failure to
recognize the potential power of the disembodied signifier. Indeed, it is
striking that among the signs that foreshadow Francia's own death (at least
as they are told by the unreliable narrator Patiño) is the birth of twins, one
of whom is a "creature without organs," without a head, who is capable of
living off the organs of the other. Francia immediately recognizes that this
headless parasite could be a potentially useful addition to the machinery of
his own state. However, Francia's ideal state is always a hybrid of the completely disembodied signifier and signifiers that act like writing but are still
"natural" signifieds. For this reason, he constantly consults "oracles," the
stars, spirits, petroglyphs, skulls, meteorites, and even the stagnant pool of
water where his secretary washes his dirty feet while taking dictation. He
also consults with an Indian "witch doctor" in order to determine whether
it will be possible for him to die and then reproduce himself: "in such a
manner that although he was dead, he wouldn't really be dead, it would
be my repetition. Only the shell of my first soul would be broken or dead
after having hatched the others" (p. 183). The egg becomes an important
metaphor for regeneration, one quite different from the abstract game of
differentiating between the "white and the black" of writing, which seems
to fascinate the dictator up to the moment of his death.

DIALOGUES OF THE DEAD

Sultán, the dictator's dog, predicts the bureacracy's usurpation of power when he returns from the dead to defend "Black Pilar," a servant whom the dictator had erased as if he were a bad word: "The Black. Suppressed. In the same manner that one suppresses a bad word. No risk. Defective. Erased. Abolished. Forgotten" (p. 416). Thus, in spite of his rejection of the disembodied signifier during the course of the novel, Francia inevitably anticipates an incestuous state based on writing and the production of signs. "In the style of the man who slept with three girls who were actually his daughters; one of the girls had married his son; thus, he slept with her, her sister, his daughter and his daughter-in-law, and forced his son to sleep with his sister and his mother-in-law" (p. 416).

But this, of course, seems to reflect the writing of the novel itself and the paradox which neither *I the Supreme* nor Roa Bastos can escape. The novel implicitly raises the question of the subversive character of the signifier, given that although the anonymous lampoon is subversive, it is also the precursor of a more efficient state, just as the aesthetic vanguard (which is based on the subversion of the sign) can be seen, from a certain point of view, as the teachers who will instruct the reader in the techniques that are needed to produce the signifiers of advanced capitalism. In any case, given that the novel is not written as a traditional narrative but rather consists of documentation and a series of speech genres (mandates, reminiscences, dialogues), Francia, as a person or as the state, can assume a position that is openly polemical and that would seem excessive or too direct in a traditional novel. Latin American novels from the nineteenth and the beginning of the twentieth century are full of episodes in which characters make pronouncements that would be more appropriate in an essay, commentary, or educational exposition than in dialogic narrative. Roa Bastos, however, has written a novel that is closer to dramatic monologue or to certain types of dialogue that were popular during the Enlightenment.

The "dialogue of the dead" is the most interesting of these; its literary antecedents stretch back to Plato, Homer, and Dante. In the nineteenth century, dialogues between historical characters such as Catón and Caesar, Demosthenes and Heraclitus, became popular through the influence of Fénélon's "dialogues des morts," in which the dead did not speak as if they belonged to another era of history but rather as if they were directly linked to the present. The dead spoke dramatically and dialectically, in defense of their own lives and principles. They adhered to the formal standards of debate and oratory. In any case, what is of interest to us here is that the relationship between the present and the past appears to be radically different from that which the Enlightenment and the positivist theory of human progress imagined, in which the past is inevitably relegated to a subordinate position as the seed from which the present era has grown, a barbarous horror which has thankfully been left behind, or an inferior moment against which progress can be measured.

The historical novel, which was imbued with this sense of retrospective knowledge, tended to organize and frame the narratives of past events from the "superior" point of view of the present.

The dialogues of the dead, in spite of being openly didactic, enjoyed a certain advantage over the historical novel because they established a live connection, a direct exchange between different historical periods, from the point of view of outlining not the difference, but rather the similarities of the human predicament at different historical conjunctions. One of the most interesting examples of this genre in Latin America are the dialogues of Fernández de Lizardi, in which some of the deceased participants of the uprisings of 1810—Hidalgo, Allende, Matamoros, Morelos, Bravo, Galeano, and Mina—speak about current events.

The self-criticism of Hidalgo, for example, is an antecedent of the self-evaluations of Francia in his private notebook:

> I would like to have avoided these outrages; but I had neither the force nor the eloquence to hold back or to persuade a barbarous and enraged people that I needed and in whom I trusted the safety of my person and the fulfillment of my projects. When I confess the hatefulness of these crimes, I am far from wishing to justify myself. I ought to have died rather than to have agreed to a single murder. Natural and divine law decrees this; still I would like to have seen whether in my place, any of my accusers would have let themselves be humbly slaughtered, scorning the chance to save themselves as happened to me.[12]

Despite Lizardi's typical moralizing tone, the dialogue allows Hidalgo to explain his conduct to the living, who may then, in this case, identify with his dilemma. Since, in this case, Lizardi is referring to the recent past, it does not require a huge stretch of the imagination.

Addressing the living from the point of view of the dead shows how one can establish a shared universe of mutual comprehension between the voices of the past and the future. The diachronic is thus incorporated in the interior of the dialogue, and at the same time it synchronizes the moral parameters of the past and the present.

Many of the discourses of *I the Supreme* acquire the form of replies or dialogues with a silent partner—the silence of posterity, the silence of the dead (Belgrano), or the silence of the absent (the Robertsons). Given that the novel includes all the discourses of the state and those of "rational subjects" which are constituted by ideological interpellations,[13] these discourses are not self-sufficient or decontextualized texts, but rather they represent responses, as much to specific historical conjunctures, rather than to contemporary interrogators of Francia, such as Patiño.

Roa Bastos's novel reopens the debate that liberal discourse had closed: it is a debate in which Francia's autarchic state and the liberal state (although they correspond to different historical moments and different geographical centers) find themselves locked in a common universe, which they share in a subliminal fashion—the universe that is shackled by writing.

There is, nevertheless, a third dimension, a history which has not been finished (or perhaps it has been repressed) whose actors have not yet been able to contend with each other. This history is implicit in the dialectic of the novel, and it requires that the reader conceive of at least the possibility of a transcendence which can only take the form of a state based on popular power. If the possibility of this utopian transcendence is suggested in the passages of different discourses (which cannot be privileged or taken out of context, however), it can only be understood in a negative fashion, as that which cannot be thematized in these discourses, and which is lived in the ephemeral activities of daily life.

This lived experience can only communicate with the future through its silences or through the interweaving with other daily lives that reproduce the human condition.

But this is located beyond the novel's boundaries; as Dr. Francia himself would discover, it has never been and never will be expressed in writing.

NOTES

1 André Bazin, "The Ontology of the Photographic Image," in *What Is Cinema?* vol. 1 (Berkeley: University of California Press, 1967–1971), 9–16.
2 The most recent event in the debate about the bones of the deceased appeared in "The Polemic in Nicaragua concerning Rubén Darío's Brain," *Ultima Hora*, Lima, 7 March 1979.

3 Sophocles, "Antigone," in *The Theban Plays*, trans. E. P. Watling (London: Penguin Classics, 1947), 127.

4 Augusto Roa Bastos, *Yo el supremo* (Buenos Aires: Siglo Veintiuno, 1974). All page numbers in the text, unless otherwise noted, correspond to the original Spanish edition.

5 Thomas Carlyle, *Critical and Miscellaneous Essays*, vol. 4 (New York: n.p., 1899), 261–321.

6 Jean Franco, "Un viaje poco romántico: viajeros británicos hacia Sudamérica: 1818–1828," *Escritura* 4, no. 7 (1979): 129–42; this volume, pp. 132–46.

7 The references to page numbers are taken from Nicos Poulantzas, *State, Power, Socialism* (London: Verso, 1978).

8 Seminar, "*Yo el supremo* de Augusto Roa Bastos" (Poitiers: Centre de Recherches Latino, Americaines de Université de Poitiers, 1976).

9 Gilles Deleuze and Félix Guattari, *Anti-Oedipus: Capitalism and Schizophrenia* (New York: Viking Press, 1977).

10 Augusto Roa Bastos, *I the Supreme*, trans. Helen Lane (New York: Alfred A. Knopf, 1986), 132–33.

11 Ibid., 133.

12 Luis González Obregón, ed., *Diálogos sobre cosas de su tiempo, sacado del olvido* [Dialogues about Things from Their Time, Retrieved from Oblivion] (Mexico: Tip. Murgia, 1918), 38–39.

13 For a clear analysis of the ideology and the formation of the position of the subject, see Goran Therborn, *The Ideology of Power and the Power of Ideology* (London: NLB, 1980).

PASTICHE IN CONTEMPORARY

LATIN AMERICAN LITERATURE

*M*any novels published in Latin America over the last few years can be described as pastiche novels. They include Roa Bastos's *Yo el supremo* [I the Supreme] (1893), Elena Poniatowska's *Querido Diego* [Dear Diego] (1987), Juan José Saer's *El entenado* [The Trapped] (1988) Edgardo Rodríguez Juliá's *Las aventuras del héroe Baltasar* [The Adventures of the Hero Baltasar] (1989) and *La noche oscura del niño Avilés* [The Dark Night of the Boy Avilés] (1989), Mario Vargas Llosa's *El hablador* [The Storyteller] (1987) and Silviano Santiago's *Em Liberdade* [In Liberty] (1981). Many other novels—including *El otoño del patriarca* [The Autumn of the Patriarch] (1975) by García Márquez and the novels of Manuel Puig incorporate imitations of other styles without this necessarily being parody.

The dictionary defines *pastiche* as both imitation and a melange of styles. Unlike the older term *parody*, the word *pastiche* only entered the vocabulary in the eighteenth century even though nonsatiric imitation was common before this. *Pastiche* is a relatively modern term and needs the notion of originality as its counterpoint. Preromantic culture more easily accommodated mimicry and, indeed, regarded it as a form of homage. Sor Juana's "imitation" of Góngora (which was also a subtle form of differentiation) was considered an achievement rather than a defect.[1] When the "new" became the absolute criterion for great art (and especially with Modernism imitation was the sign of lack of originality) as Theodor Adorno has pointed out, the Modernists' emphasis on originality quickly came up against limits.[2] As a result of the exhaustion of high culture's search for originality, there occurs, according to Fredric Jameson, "the moment of pastiche in which energetic artists who now lack both forms and content cannibalize the museum and wear the masks of extinct mannerisms."[3]

Yet critics are far from agreeing on the usefulness of the term *pastiche*,

Originally published in *Studies in Twentieth Century Literature* 14 no. 1 (winter 1990): 95–107.

and many disregard it altogether. Gérard Genette, who attempted to systematize all forms of palimpsest or "second degree" literature, described it as "non-satiric imitation" thus distinguishing it from parody.[4] On the other hand, Linda Hutcheon has used the term "modern parody" to describe novels such as James Joyce's *Ulysses*, which incorporate that very nonsatiric imitation that Genette attributes to pastiche.[5]

Meanwhile, Bakhtin, who is centrally concerned with all forms of imitation, ironic inversion, and parody, hardly uses the term *pastiche* at all, preferring *stylization* or, more generally, *double-voicing*. *Stylization* is, however, not a substitute for *pastiche*, for it refers rather to the conflation of certain conventions into a recognizable epochal style. Nevertheless, Bakhtin's theory of double-voicing is also applicable to pastiche. As is well known, this theory is based on everyday speech situations from which literary language is often derived. For Bakhtin, the repetition of words can never be reduced to mere parroting (imitation). When two people say, "beautiful weather," these are two utterances belonging to different voices, though they may be "linked by dialogic relations of agreement."[6] Not only literature but also everyday speech is, for Bakhtin, full of other people's words: "with some of them we completely merge our own voice, forgetting whose they are; others, which we take as authoritative, we use to reinforce our own words; still others, finally, we populate with our own aspirations, alien or hostile to them."[7] The "stylizer" works with "someone else's point of view." When the author uses "someone else's discourse for his or her own purposes by inserting a new semantic intention into a discourse which already has (and which retains) an intention of its own" then "two semantic intentions appear, two voices."[8] In parody, in contrast to stylization, opposing intentions come into conflict; a second voice, "that having lodged in the other speech, clashes antagonistically with the original, host voice and forces it to serve directly opposite aims."[9]

Even though Bakhtin does not use the term *pastiche*, he, however, clearly differentiates between an antagonistic relationship to a "host voice" and other kinds of double-voicing. Yet, as I propose to argue and as Bakhtin suggests, an echo of the voice of the other is inevitably a displacement or a substitution. There is no innocent relationship between discourses.

Bakhtin was of course primarily interested in the eruption of popular voices into the literary languages. But there are forms of double-voicing that shade into mimicry and that acquire deep significance within a colonial or "peripheral" context such as obtains in Latin America. The implications go beyond the literary. One has only to think of a society such as

Japan, which for so long was defined as a mere imitation of the West. In the context of the struggle for national autonomy in Latin America, *originality* and *emancipation* were key words, while *imitation, copying,* and *repetition* were slurs.[10] This explains the gleeful force that avant-garde movements like *Ultraísmo* in Argentina or Modernism in Brazil brought to their parodies of prior traditions, their insistence on the originality of America and its art. Yet, significantly, parody existed alongside pastiche; both functioned as declarations of cultural affinities by introducing new sets of canonical texts. Since pastiche does not set out to satirize prior texts, however, it can constitute a sympathetic relation with the past which may act as a pointed critique of the present. When Juan Montalvo wrote *Capítulos que se olvidaron a Cervantes* [Chapters that Cervantes Forgot] (1892), he was attempting to introduce the humanistic values represented by Cervantes into an atmosphere of authoritarianism and terror. In the poetry of Rubén Darío, nostalgia for the gracious aristocratic style of eighteenth-century France (itself a pastiche of classical style) is an implied judgment on the vulgarity of the times. Clearly this "non-satiric" imitation includes all manner of appropriation, expropriation, "cannibalization," and celebration, and requires more extensive exploration than is possible here. For the purpose of this essay, I shall limit my discussion to those texts in which pastiche marks a subtle displacement of hierarchy, especially the hierarchy that privileges the present over the past, the near over the remote.

The ur-text of contemporary Latin American pastiche is Borges's story, "Pierre Menard, autor del Quijote" [Pierre Menard, Author of Quixote], which was written in the thirties.[11] It is not without significance that this is the story crucial to Borges's own career as a writer, one which exorcised the ghosts of his own past.[12] In describing the efforts of the twentieth-century author, Pierre Menard, to create an exact replica of Cervantes's text, Borges introduces a protagonist who is indifferent to originality and yet can never reproduce the seventeenth-century novel even though he uses the same words, since four centuries of history inevitably intervene. Words change their meanings and become loaded in ways that Cervantes would never have dreamed of. Because all that is archaic in Cervantes's text leaps to the reader's notice, pastiche draws attention to changes in meaning, to what Bakhtin calls the speech of the other.[13]

There is an interesting example of the double-voicing that occurs through historical change in Gabriel García Márquez's novel, *El otoño del patriarca* [The Autumn of the Patriarch]. This is an episode in which the Papal Nuncio, while riding over the mountains on his mule to investigate claims that the dictator's mother is a saint, is shot by the dictator's men and falls down a deep ravine. The description of the fall is composed of citations from school geography textbooks, travel books, and nineteenth-century fiction:

> One heard the endless wail of fright of the tumbling mule as it went on falling dizzily and endlessly from *the peaks of perpetual snow* through *successive and instantaneous climes* out of natural-history prints of the precipice and the birth trickle of *great navigable waters* and the high cornices up to which the learned doctors of the botanical expedition had climbed on Indian backs with their herbal secrets, and the steppes of wild magnolias where warm-wooled sheep grazed the ones *who give us generous sustenance and cover and good example* and the mansions of the coffee plantations with their paper wreaths on solitary balconies and their endless invalids and the perpetual roar of the turbulent rivers of the great natural boundary lines where the heat began (p. 142).

The italicized lines clearly belong to the discourse of the other, to a discourse that belongs, in fact, to a secular and positivistic culture that was introduced in the nineteenth century, replacing the hitherto hegemonic Catholic culture. What is particularly interesting is the intersection of two different literary planes—that of action, the movement of characters, what Barthes refers to as the proairetic code and, on the other hand, the geography (and the cultural code) into which this protagonist falls, thus suggesting both the fall of the Church to the secular order and the fact that this order is constructed out of a bricolage of imported clichés.[14] The significance of the pastiche here is precisely to underline the imitation and copying which, in nineteenth-century Latin America, passed for progress. Although it could be argued that in this episode the line between parody and pastiche is a fine one, nevertheless the skillfully interwoven melange foregrounds not only textual citation but also a reference to a larger text— that of "Latin America" itself, as a pastiche.

I shall now turn to two different and more extended examples—Mario Vargas Llosa's *El hablador* [The Storyteller] and Silviano Santiago's *Em liberdade* [At Liberty], both of which could be described as pastiche novels.[15]

In the first of these, *The Storyteller*, pastiche of indigenous lore and legend are interwoven with chapters that relate several journeys made by a narrator (Mario Vargas Llosa) to the Amazon rain forest. The novel thus juxtaposes modern and primitive, the individualized subjectivity of the contemporary writer in contrast to the community-based storyteller, the jet-age global view (from Florence, to Lima, to the jungle) and the circumscribed view of a man whose territory is covered by walking.

The novel is both the story of a search and the story of the elusive object of that search, but the search itself is a dual one. While living in Florence, Vargas Llosa comes across an exhibition of photographs of Machiguenga Indians who inhabit the Amazon basin and whom the author had visited under the auspices of the Summer Institute of Linguistics. One of the photographs captures a shadowy figure who Vargas Llosa believes is the legendary Machiguenga storyteller whom outsiders rarely if ever see. The photographs trigger Vargas Llosa's recollections of his visit to the Machiguengas and also his memories of a school and college friend and member of a Jewish family, Saúl Zuratas, who had first spoken to him of the Machiguenga tribes and of his intention to become an ethnographer. The time frame of the story covers a period of some thirty years, from the period when the young Vargas Llosa befriends Saúl to the story's present in Florence. Vargas Llosa's own reminiscences are told in chronological order, but these are interrupted from time to time by the voice of the storyteller whose narrative is a pastiche without any apparent chronological order and who weaves together autobiography, history, story, and myth. Clearly Vargas Llosa wishes to bring out the differences between traditional storytelling and the modern author though, as I will show, it is by no means clear that he is necessarily valorizing the latter. One of the ways in which this difference becomes apparent is in the constant recourse to referentiality in the telling of the autobiographical story, for not only are there references to well-known Peruvian historians and ethnographers, to his own visits to the Amazonian jungle when doing research for his novel, *La casa verde* [The Green House]—there are references as well to his work on a television show for which he interviewed missionaries of the controversial Summer Institute of Linguistics. The autobiography is not only a foil for the pastiche; it is also written in a style that suggests an engaging frankness, that persuades us that Vargas Llosa is a reasonable man who is just going about his work like everybody else. Yet this reasonable air is something of a smokescreen, allowing the author to pass off dubious political positions as if they were common sense. The most egregious example of this is his references to the missionaries of the Summer Institute of Linguistics. While Vargas Llosa does not disguise the fact that the Summer Institute is controversial, he portrays the missionaries as essentially benign and carefully skirts the murkier aspects of the Institute's relationship to both national governments and indigenous groups. Yet, in the fifties (more or less the time that the novel begins) the Institute was gathering data on about thirty tribes. What appeared to be a worthy scholarly activity, writing down indigenous languages, was also a form of information retrieval, the aim of which was conversion. Ever since the time when the founder of the Summer Institute was first invited to Mexico by Lázaro Cárdenas, it has been a constant source of controversy. It was expelled from Peru in the early seventies and later from Ecuador. The missions thus come into conflict with national policies and have been criticized for destroying the delicate balance of life in the region. A Venezuelan filmmaker, Carlos Azpurúa, who did work on the New Tribes Mission in Venezuela, commented that conversion destroys the tribes' belief system: "And when you destroy that, material aspects are affected. When material aspects are affected, it affects patterns and ways of life. . . . It is no coincidence that they (the indigenous) have lived and survived in this region, ecologists by nature, for 30,000 years." [16] Thus, as is often the case in Vargas Llosa's novels, the insertion of autobiographical "fact" authenticates ideological positions and, indeed, disguises them.

The intercalated chapters, on the other hand, are told by a second storyteller who can gradually be identified as Saúl Zuratas, the student who had disappeared from Lima apparently to go back to Israel but who (it turns out) has become the storyteller of the Machiguenga tribe. References to a parrot (Saúl had a pet parrot) and to a birthmark make this identification of Saúl with the storyteller possible. These personal references, in contrast to the Vargas Llosa chapters, are buried in mythic stories recounted in the formulaic style of the traditional storyteller. Thus, for instance, a new episode often begins with formulae such as "this was the story of Kachiborerine. That was in olden times." It is, perhaps, no accident that the man who becomes the storyteller of the vanishing tribe is Jewish. He is nicknamed "Little Mask" (Mascarita) because of the giant birthmark that disfigures his face and makes him an outcast. By disappearing into the forest and becoming the tribal storyteller, he buries his name, his ethnic origin, and his ambition in the anonymity of oral tradition. Yet the stories he tells are not only reproductions of Machiguenga lore—for instance stories of outwitting the devils, the story of the primal pair, the story of Pareni, and the transformation of Kachiborerine into a comet (all Machiguenga foundation myths)—they are also tales of his own induction into shamanism and historical episodes that refer to the rubber boom, to the influence of the white fathers (the Dominicans) who pass on their sickness to the Indians, and the constant flight of the Machiguenga from civilization. Although it is possible to read Vargas Llosa's pastiche as a response to the movement known as "indigenismo" and the representation of the Indian by urban and nonindigenous writers, the novel does not register the contemporary indigenous movements in any way. There is no reference to contemporary battles and antagonisms, the political protests, or the international network of indigenous organizations which have sprung up over the last few years.

The function of pastiche in the novel is to present a contrast not between the primitive and the modern but between the contemporary writer's search for material and the tribal storyteller's relation to tradition. In this case, it should be added, however, that the tradition on which Vargas Llosa draws is not an oral tradition as such, but the documentation of that tradition by both Protestant and Catholic missionaries.[17]

It is likely, therefore, that Vargas Llosa was not primarily interested in the Machiguenga but rather in the motif of the "storyteller." For the pastiche clearly betrays nostalgia—not for tribal life, but for the storyteller's relation to a community. Hence too, the significance of those autobiographical episodes, in which Vargas Llosa represents himself as a novelist engaged in a lonely struggle with his material or researching his novel, *The Green House*, and as a television producer struggling with the technological complexities of putting on a show. In contrast to print culture, television reporting involves team work; yet, as described by Vargas Llosa, it is more a question of management than of creation. His program is called "The Tower of Babel" and it consists mainly of interviews. The novel is thus centrally concerned with the different technologies that transpose "reality" into fiction and it also describes the different forms of reception—the small family group listening to the storyteller in the jungle and bonded through him with other family groups, the separation of the modern novel writer from a public (Vargas Llosa's isolation in Florence), and finally the global reach of the television team which, however, meets the public only through technology. In other words, Vargas Llosa's novel puts Benjamin's "storyteller" into the age of mechanical reproduction. In his well-known essay on Leskov, Walter Benjamin describes storytelling as a dying art and points out that the secular productive force of history has been removing narrative "from the realm of living speech and at the same time is making it possible to see a new beauty in what is vanishing."[18] In this light, it is possible to read *The Storyteller* as a desire not to return to primitive storytelling, but only to capture the moment of its disappearance and its replacement with the "magic" of television.

Read in this way, pastiche is what allows the contemporary author to appropriate indigenous culture for his or her own use, rather as the photographs of the Machiguenga are decontextualized and put on display in an art gallery in Florence. In *The Storyteller*, the photographs of the Machiguenga and the shadowy figure of the storyteller are disturbing only to the narrator and only because he has direct knowledge of the tribe. What makes him tell the story to others is his curiosity about Saúl's regression into primitive life, which is transposed into his curiosity for a form of storytelling that is disappearing from the modern world. Pastiche is therefore a form of nostalgia, but one which hardly subverts the experience of the novelist or reader. In addition, there is the important fact that the storytelling tradition is kept alive by the universal outsider, the Jew, a device that drains all particularity from the American indigenous experience.

A completely different use of pastiche is illustrated by *At Liberty*, a Brazilian novel by Silviano Santiago, in which recent history is used to interrogate the present. *At Liberty* appropriates the name and style of a well-known Brazilian writer, Graciliano Ramos, who, in March 1936, was imprisoned by the government of Getulio Vargas as a political detainee. Before his detention, Ramos had worked in the office of Public Education in the provincial town of Alagoas and had been somewhat marginalized from the cultural centers of Brazilian life in Rio de Janeiro, São Paulo, and Bahia. He was released in January 1937, but it took him ten years before he could undertake the writing of his prison memoirs. It was, in fact, after completing a translation of Camus's *L'Etranger* [The Stranger] that he began what turned out to be a long and somewhat truculent narrative.[19] It is possible that one reason for the delay was his reluctance to use the first person singular, though (possibly with Camus's example in mind) he eventually conquered his distaste and wrote what is now considered a classic of Brazilian letters. *At Liberty* purports to be written by Graciliano Ramos immediately after his release from prison, that is, during the period when he felt unable to compose his prison memoirs. It is also supposedly a text that Ramos had ordered destroyed.

What induced Santiago to write a pastiche of this well-known text? In the first place, as he himself explains in his essays, he believes that the notions of purity and coherence have always been challenged by Latin American writing, that Latin American writing is always "speaking against" or "responding to" other writing.[20] Barthes once asked what he should read in order to write (and rewrite). Santiago points out that reading in order to write has long been a practice among authors in dependent cultures where "reading is understood as a search for a writable text, a text that can stimulate them to work and serve as a model in the organization of their own writing." Santiago argues that "The Latin American writer plays with the signs of another writer and another text. The words of the other present themselves as objects that fascinate his eyes, his fingers, and the writing of a second text is in part the story of his sensual experience with the alien sign."[21] Santiago thus dispenses with any notion of originality and regards all Latin American literature as pastiche, parody, or translation, as always a deliberate meditation on other texts rather than a spontaneous production.

This situation is common to writers in all colonial and dependent cultures. Commenting on Borges's story, "Pierre Menard," Santiago points out that freedom for Pierre Menard "is controlled by the original text [i.e., *Don Quixote*], just as the freedom of citizens in colonized societies is monitored by metropolitan forces."[22] At the same time, he values pastiche over parody, for "pastiche does not reject the past in a gesture of mockery, contempt or irony. Pastiche accepts the past as it is and the work of art is nothing more than a supplement. . . . I would not say that pastiche is reverence towards the past, but I would say that it assumes [*endossa*] the past, contrary to parody which always ridicules it."[23]

Santiago's own description of *At Liberty* is that it is "a false diary of the moment in which he left prison, a diary that he never had the courage to write, for the prison experience is the experience of martyrdom, the experience of suffering and pain. There is no criticism of this. But exactly what I wanted was to write a supplement to this, to supplement what is already complete. . . . Notice that I was appropriating the voice and style and even the life, of another."[24] The mention of "supplement," of course, immediately evokes the Derridian supplement, that is the power of substitution that undermines all essentialisms. We must assume then that Santiago's "supplement" is intended to unsettle Ramos's text, which is itself an account of disorientation.[25] From familiar surroundings, he is taken as a prisoner by train to a prison in which he is no longer a middle-class bureaucrat but part of an undifferentiated mass. From now on he has to try and preserve a distance not only from the seductions of the powerful within the prison society, but also from the seductions of the Communist party organization within the jail. *At Liberty* reverses this situation, by depicting the estrangement of freedom, his difficult relationship with his wife and other writers, and with a reading public whose expectations threaten to close "successive doors to freedom." For Santiago's Ramos, "the real mark of courage is to refuse the medal"—that is to refuse the role of martyr, or heroic example.

Out of prison, Ramos can only earn his living by journalism, which for him is the equivalent of silence as a writer. The journalist simply produces according to fixed conventions: "I shall become a professional able to do a job whose place and function is already predetermined before my entry onto the stage. I shall perform as a great actor. My knowledge of the Portuguese language (my 'direct and dry style' as they say), resembles the way in which the builder of the cathedrals used the artisan who could work in stone. I do anonymous service. We are all artisans constructing the cathedral of Vargas' authoritarian government."

Now Ramos's dilemma speaks not to the thirties—the age of the personality cult and of martyrdom for a cause (antifascism, the Spanish Civil War)—but rather to the seventies and eighties, to generations that had to reconcile everyday life and its small pleasures, with authoritarian government. For this generation self-sacrifice in the name of a cause cannot achieve anything. In Ramos's words, "If I could believe in self-sacrifice as an ethical salvation, half of my problems would be solved. I would attain the tranquility of a whole man, prisoner of an unjust legal system, persecuted by an authoritarian society." But this is precisely what is unacceptable to him, and why he chooses to "err": "I err in order to attain my authenticity. I would be right if I denied my will to live. I err to negate my slow suicide. I would be right if I pleased other people. I err to stop the opposition from falling into the panacea of martyrdom. I err in order to affirm that the condition of persecuted and massacred cannot serve as an example."

Such comments on the position of the writer in the thirties caught between his love of life and the externally imposed duty to risk his life for a cause cannot but be read in the light of the military regimes of the late sixties and the early seventies and the literature of heroic guerrilla resistance.[26] For the ethics of the Brazilian opposition to military government was based on the mystique of sacrifice. Survival, on the other hand, inevitably was seen as a form of silent collaboration.

This problem is familiar to readers of contemporary Latin American literature. Manuel Puig's *The Kiss of the Spider Woman* formulates it as a dialogue between a homosexual dedicated to survival within the prison system and a guerrilla bent on sacrifice. Santiago's pastiche is, in contrast, a dialogue in which the past speaks, as it were, to the present, to a generation for whom the memoirs of guerrillas such as Fernando Gabeira became best-sellers. By concentrating not on heroism and martyrdom, but on the problems of freedom—on modest pleasures, on personal frictions and on problematic relationships—*At Liberty* both provides a supplement to Ramos's prison memoirs and allows the silences of the prior text to speak.

As these two novels demonstrate, pastiche goes far beyond copy or imitation for it involves the appropriation of another's style in order to make it say something else. It is a differentiation that emphasizes the interval between two narrative instances, between the individual writer and the communal storyteller whose language he borrows in *The Storyteller*, and between the writer living under authoritarianism in the eighties and the writer living in the thirties. The second voice indeed foregrounds the act of mimicry itself.

NOTES

1 See chapter 2 of Jean Franco, *Plotting Women: Gender and Representation in Mexico* (New York: Columbia University Press, 1989), 23–54.

2 Theodor Adorno, "Arnold Schoenberg, 1874–1951," in *Prisms: Cultural Criticism and Society*, trans. Samuel and Shierry Weber (London: Neville Spearman, 1967), 147–72.

3 Fredric Jameson, "The Shining," *Social Text* 4 (fall 1981): 114.

4 Gérard Genette, *Palimpsestes: La littérature du seconde degré* (Paris: Seuil, 1982).

5 Linda Hutcheon, "Modern Parody and Bakhtin," in Gary Saul Morson and Caryle Emerson, eds., *Rethinking Bakhtin: Extensions and Challenges* (Evanston, Ill.: Northwestern University Press, 1989), 87–103.

6 Mikhail Bakhtin, *Speech Genres and Other Essays*, trans. Vern W. McGee (Austin: University of Texas Press, 1986), 125.

7 Mikhail Bakhtin, *Problems of Dostoevsky's Poetics*, trans. Caryl Emerson (Minneapolis: University of Minnesota Press, 1984), 195.

8 Ibid., 189.

9 Ibid., 193.

10 Homi Bhabha, "Of Mimicry and Man: The Ambivalence of Colonial Discourse," *October* 28 (spring 1984): 125–33.

11 Jorge Luis Borges, "Pierre Menard, autor del Quijote," included in the collection *Ficciones*, first published in Buenos Aires in 1944.

12 Jorge Luis Borges, "An Autobiographical Essay," in *The Aleph and Other Stories*, trans. Norman Thomas Di Giovanni (New York: Dutton, 1970), 240–42.

13 Mikhail Bakhtin, "Discourse in Dostoevsky," in *Problems of Dostoevsky's Poetics*, 181–269.

14 The quotation is from *The Autumn Of the Patriarch*, trans. Gregory Rabassa

(New York: Avon, 1977). Barthes sets out his theory of narrative codes in his *S/Z*, trans. Richard Miller (New York: Hill and Wang, 1970), 142.

15 Page references are to Mario Vargas Llosa, *El hablador* (Barcelona: Seix Barral, 1987) and Silviano Santiago, *Em Liberdade* (Rio de Janeiro: Paz e Terra, 1981).

16 "In crusade against outside interference," Azpurúa documents Amazonian cultures," *The Daily Journal* (Caracas) (17 June 1987): 18.

17 Mario Vargas Llosa mentions some of these readings in the course of the novel, the works of Padre Vicente Cenitagoya (1943) "y algunos articulos de otros misioneros sobre su folklore y su lengua, aparecidos en las revistas de la Orden Dominica" (p. 80). He also mentions the travels of Charles Wiener and some Summer Institute missionaries named Schniel, who were possibly based on the Snells who studied the Machiguenga language and whose studies have been published in *Studies in Peruvian Languages I*, Summer Institute of Linguistics (Mexico, 1963). See also P. Andrés Ferrero, *Los Machiguengas. Tribu selvática del sur-oriente peruano* (Peru: Instituto de Estudios Tropicales, 1966).

18 Walter Benjamin, "The Storyteller. Reflection on the Works of Nikolai Leskov," in *Illuminations*, trans. Harry Zohn (London: Jonathan Cape, 1970), 83–109.

19 Graciliano Ramos, *Memórias do Cárcere*, 4 vols. (Rio de Janeiro: José Olympio, 1956).

20 Silviano Santiago, "O Entre-lugar do discurso latino-americano," in *Uma literatura nos trópicos. Ensaios sobre dependencia cultural* (São Paulo: Editora Perspectiva, 1976).

21 Ibid., 23.

22 Ibid., 26.

23 Silviano Santiago, "A permanência do discurso da tradição no modernismo," in *Nas Malhas da letra. Ensaios* (São Paulo: Editora Schwarcz, 1989), 94–123, esp. 115; my translation.

24 Ibid., 116.

25 George Yúdice discusses Santiago's use of the Derridian term *supplement* in *On Edge: The Crisis of Contemporary Latin American Culture*, ed. George Yúdice, Juan Flores, and Jean Franco (Minneapolis: University of Minnesota Press, 1992). Quotations from Santiago's text are taken from this essay. Derrida discusses supplement in several places of his writing, but in particular in his discussion of Rousseau in *Of Grammatology*, trans. Gayatri Chakravorty Spivak (Baltimore: Johns Hopkins Press, 1974), 242–55.

26 Fernando Gabeira, *O crepúsculo do macho: depoimento* (Rio de Janeiro: Codecor, 1980).

COMIC STRIPPING

Cortázar in the Age of Mechanical Reproduction

icardo Piglia's *La Argentina en pedazos* [Argentina in Fragments] is a compilation of essays and comic strips originally published in the mid-eighties in *Fierro*, a magazine aimed at young readers. The format was a brief critical digest followed by comic strip versions of well-known Argentine literary texts by Esteban Echeverría (*El matadero* [The Slaughterhouse]), David Viñas, Discépolo, Lugones ("Las fuerzas extrañas" [Strange Forces]), Borges, and Cortázar.[1] Although there is a long tradition of comic book classics, this is the first comic book literary criticism, as far as I know, to have been written and edited by a well-known Latin American novelist. García Márquez, Vargas Llosa, Luis Rafael Sánchez, and Manuel Puig have all, in their different ways, made their overtures to mass culture—García Márquez in his *telenovelas*, Vargas Llosa in *La tía Julia y el escribidor* [Aunt Julia and the Scriptwriter], Manuel Puig beginning with his first novel, *La traición de Rita Hayworth* [The Betrayal of Rita Hayworth]. It was not only the prospect of reaching bigger audiences as well as the need to hold onto the slipping hegemony of the intelligentsia that induced García Márquez to write *telenovelas* and Vargas Llosa, Octavio Paz, and Juan José Arreola to anchor cultural programs on television.[2] Piglia's comic strip criticism marks a more advanced stage in the long and complex two-step, the moment when the book itself has become an adaptable and transient commodity and the author a brand name.

I am here using the term *mass culture* not to refer to the imagined degradation that sullies the purity of "true" or "authentic culture," but to refer to the "assembly-line" culture targeted through market techniques to particular consumers. So-called pulp literature, cinema, animation, and comic strips provided new media for narrative, altering, by the very method of production, received notions of author (there is often no single author),

Julio Cortázar: New Readings, ed. Carlos Alonso (Cambridge: Cambridge University Press, 1998). Reprinted by permission of Cambridge University Press.

reception, and originality. The violent rejection of mass culture as anti-art by many modernists was, in fact, only the initial stage in a long and intricate relationship marked by denunciation, appropriation, and, finally, celebration. "Mechanical reproduction" opened up the possibility of destroying the hierarchical structures underpinning artistic institutions. Not only did new media allow the intensification of shock effects by means of collage, photomontage, cinematic montage, and mixed media, but they also encouraged the persistence and resurrection of older forms of narrative such as melodrama and romance; indeed, in some contemporary writing, mass culture is associated with nostalgia for affect at a time when romantic love and passion seem anachronistic.[3] Older subgenres revitalized through pastiche act as reminders of the time when emotional expression (exiled from literature by irony) was still believed to be the common currency in the "low" sphere of popular urban culture.

Walter Benjamin was, as is well known, one of the first to understand the revolutionary potential of the new technologies. His essay "The Work of Art in the Age of Mechanical Reproduction" first appeared in 1936 in the *Zeitschrift fur Sozialforschung*. The now familiar argument on which Benjamin's essay is based is that "the technique of reproduction detaches the reproduced object from the domain of tradition. By making many reproductions it substitutes a plurality of copies for a unique existence. And in permitting the reproduction to meet the beholder or listener in his own particular situation, it reactivates the object reproduced."[4] One consequence of this is that what will now be considered to be "culture" spills out of the confines of the concert hall, the museum, the theater, and the book. The modest range of mechanical reproduction Benjamin takes into account—primarily photography and cinema—must now be extended to include photocopying, electronic mail, the screening of film "versions" of novels before the printer's ink is even dry, the travels of genres such as melodrama from stage to screen to *telenovela* and back to "real life," the universal use of pastiche and even virtual reality. Yet what was and remains innovative in Benjamin's essay is that, while arguing that mechanical production would result in the tarnishing of that uniqueness or aura of the work of art, he embraced the liberatory possibilities opened up by that very loss. The artwork potentially comes to inhabit new and unsanctified environments rubbing shoulders with the commodity, while appropriating technology in order to create dialectic images.

Benjamin foresaw that techniques of reproduction that bypassed hierarchy and tradition had explosive and revolutionary possibilities and thus inevitably annihilated older cultural institutions. Writing of the filmmaker Abel Gance, whose methods imply a "liquidation of the traditional value of the cultural heritage," he quotes the latter's belief that "all legends, all mythologies and all myths, all founders of religion, and the very religions . . . await their exposed resurrection" (p. 224). Benjamin believed that this was an invitation to the funeral of what had formerly been considered high art and, while shedding no tears, he saw that the changes in reception and sensibility were irrevocable.[5]

There are analogies between the German situation which motivated Benjamin's essays and Peronist Argentina. Mass consensus was achieved in Peronist Argentina as in fascist Germany through ritual — Benjamin would call it the aestheticization of politics — and also through the ruling elite's speedy grasp of the importance of the media in securing consent. Although in his own personal mythology, Cortázar liked to attribute his politicization to the Cuban Revolution, his rejection of nationalism, his assertion of solidarities based on personal sympathies were attitudes shaped by Peronist Argentina. This helps to explain why, even when Cuba was embracing "patria o muerte" [fatherland or death] politics and when the director of Casa de las Américas was arguing that writers could not write effectively outside their own national boundaries,[6] Cortázar would refuse to be drawn into this particular guilt trip.

> The fact that my books have been available for years in Latin America does not invalidate the deliberate and irreversible fact that I left Argentina in 1951, and that I continue to reside in a European country that I chose for no other reason than my sovereign will to live and write in the form that seemed the fullest and most satisfying to me.[7]

He goes on to argue that not only does his engagement with Latin American politics spring from "a much more European than Latin American and a more ethical than intellectual perspective (p. 30)," but also that writing outside a national context gains in breadth what it loses in local detail: "it becomes so to speak more global, it operates by means of assemblages and synthesis, and loses the energy that is concentrated in an immediate context; on other hand, it achieves a lucidity that is sometimes unbearable but always enlightening" (p. 31).

National identity was never a priority for Cortázar: "I am very much of a mimic. I am sure that if I were to live for five years in the United States, I would feel identified with what I like in the United States which is less than what I don't like. But I would identify myself deeply with what I liked."[8] The final phrase epitomizes what will afterward constitute, for Cortázar, the grounds for sociability and identity—namely, taste.

Because, in the contemporary world, taste can no longer be grounded in firmly established values or universal criteria, it becomes a matter either of market classification or of elective affinities. The arbitrariness of these affinities in Cortázar's work—the bond may be forged just as effectively through the mediation of Louis Armstrong, or of Gesualdo, or by a shared project such as traveling slowly along the freeway from Paris to Marseille—destroys "distinctions" on the grounds of nationality, class, gender (let's overlook for the moment the notorious "lector hembra" [female reader].[9]) These social groups may form short-lived heterotopias like the motorists in "Weekend" (Autopista del sur).

However, group cohesion also depends on the exclusion of those who do not understand, of those who are bound by routine, lacking in imagination and emotionally crippled.

Considered in this light, Piglia seems to have hit the target when he calls Cortázar's writing "an epic of consumption," "The adventure of a seasoned and cunning explorer who tries to leave his footprint in the indiscriminate jungle of the capitalist marketplace" (p. 40).

For Piglia, this epic of consumption encompasses two seemingly incompatible regimes:

> on the one hand there is the search for some exclusive and secret object whose value derives from its scarcity and originality: on the other hand, it is a question of discovering and salvaging certain popular artifacts that are selected for their authenticity and for the dignity that derives from a slight anachronism: Xenakis and Rosita Quiroga, Hermann Broch and Cesar Bruto, gulash and bitter mate, hashish and a touch of eccentricity. Whereas one series is private and refined and is constituted by collecting, the other series is mass-mediated, "natural" and is constituted by means of selection and exclusion (p. 40).[10]

The implications of this are far-reaching. Since Cortázar repeatedly constitutes ephemeral groups on the basis of arbitrary and unmarketable taste, it follows that value, once thought to be intrinsic in the work of art, has migrated to the aesthetic experience itself. Cortázar's focus on reception (which critics too often identify *only* with the reader), involves far more than literature in the conventional sense, for the "conjuntos y síntesis" [assemblages and syntheses] which produce profane illumination are unpredictable, unclassifiable, and can be motivated by almost any change in a pattern.

As I suggested above, Peronist Buenos Aires was instrumental in the shaping of this aesthetic. The novel, *El examen* [The Examination], written in 1950 and published in 1986, already sketches in the recurring incidents and characters of his later writing—the apocalyptic cityscape shrouded in fog, a routinized populace, traces of a decayed high culture (books rotting in the humidity, the concert in which the protagonist fails to perform as planned), a small group of students, and a "chronicler" wandering through this city and united by affect and by taste. Groups are bonded by a shared or idiosyncratic repertoire of cultural references drawn from popular music, literature, painting, or simply everyday objects.[11]

It is not only the political circumstances of the writing that makes *The Examination* interesting, however, but the fact that the art object already seems to have been contaminated; one of the characters has the following confrontation with a recording of Beethoven's Seventh: "I entered my darkened room and picked up an album of the Seventh Symphony, subtitled "the apotheosis of the dance." As I picked it up in pitch darkness, I felt it moving in my hand. You can imagine my reaction; The Seventh flew to the other end of the room with me groping like a madman for the lightswitch. Then I saw on my hand the hairs of a still-wriggling centipede" (p. 197). The contact with the insect obviously ends any prospect of aesthetic pleasure but, in any case, this has already been sullied by the commercial renaming of the symphony as "the apotheosis of the dance." The auratic work seems to have undergone an unpleasant metamorphosis as well as having been turned into a commodity—the novel is replete with reference to *Reader's Digest*, the yellow press, and Peronist rhetoric. Still there remains the possibility of redemption; music *can* be resacralized— for instance, the chronicler of *The Examination* treats the corny "London calling" by Eric Coates with religious respect. The group in *The Examina- tion* anticipates the Serpent Club of *Rayuela* [Hopscotch] and La Joda of *El libro de Manuel* [A Manual for Manuel] whose members are bonded by private codes and references that often depend on a ritualistic object. But if *any* object can be resacralized then there is no basis, other than a volun- taristic one, for discrimination. It also follows that traditional class strati- fication or "distinction" no longer coincides with the distinction between high and mass culture.[12] The implications of this are explored in "Las puertas del cielo" [The Gates of Heaven], the story originally included in *Bestiario* [Bestiary] (1951) and comic-stripped in Piglia's *La Argentina en pedazos* [Argentina in Fragments].

In his later years, "The Gates of Heaven" would embarrass Cortázar because of its grotesque and racist portrayal of the masses. It is the story of the narrator Hardoy's fascination with the "low" Mauro and his girlfriend Celina. From the vantage point of the early seventies and the revived if transient hopes in left-wing Peronism, Cortázar would feel called on to apologize for the political implications of the narrative. It expressed, he said, "a lot of friction, a lot of tension for political reasons, in Argentina, between ourselves, the petty bourgeoisie and those we called 'little black-heads,' the low-class Peronists who, according to us, had invaded Buenos Aires."[13]

Looking back on this period of his life, he describes his anti-Peronism as a political mistake but argues, "I was exasperated by this type of invasion of the lower classes of the population of the capital and of what I call the monsters who were called at that time the 'little black heads' " (p. 97).

His attempt to immerse himself in the underclass was initially inspired by literature, by reading Roberto Arlt, and wanting to see "what we called 'el bajo.' " "El bajo" in Buenos Aires was the waterfront but it also means the low life of the brothel and prostitution. The dance hall gave him entry into this world:

> So I was at this dancehall, I saw the women and men, saw them danc-ing. I saw that scene in which one of them slapped his woman around, because she was dancing with someone else and he didn't like it and he gave her a blow that knocked her sideways. And no-one stepped be-tween them, because if anyone had done so it would have been a fight to the death and nobody thought it was worth the trouble. If he wanted to hit her, let him hit her. Nobody interfered. And I think that at that moment at that dance, I was Hardoy? What was his name? (p. 97).

"I was Hardoy" is not a surprising admission given that Hardoy is the avatar of a whole series of Cortázar narrators and protagonists from Bruno of "The Pursuer," Oliveira of *Hopscotch*, and Michel of "Blow-up." What is surprising is Cortázar's apparent attribution of Hardoy's views to himself when, in the narrative, irony seems to intervene to prevent such an iden-tification. (In this respect, it is significant that in the interview he cannot remember Hardoy's first name.)

His opinion of the Peronists had undergone a radical change by the early seventies so that he came to believe that "The Gates of Heaven" reflected a mistaken view of things, forgetting perhaps that the viewpoint in the story is supposedly Hardoy's. However it can also be argued that the caricaturesque descriptions of "the monsters," as seen by the fastidious chronicler, Hardoy, are functional to the narrative since the resolution of the story depends on maintaining this very distinction between intellectual and mass. It is, after all, not Hardoy who enters the gates of heaven but the vulgar Celina. Aesthetic rapture is not the exclusive domain of the lettered but can be experienced just as well in the dance hall as in the private reading. That the representation is grotesque hardly needs emphasis. Hardoy confesses:

> It seems right for me to say here that I come to this dance hall to see the monsters, I know of no other place where you get so many of them at one time. They heave into sight around eleven in the evening, coming down from obscure sections of the city, deliberate and sure, by ones and by twos, the women almost dwarves and very dark, the guys like Javanese or Indians from the north bound into tight black suits or suits with checks, the hard hair painfully plastered down, little drops of brillantine catching blue and pink reflections, the women with enormously high hairdos which make them look even more like dwarves, tough, laborious hairdos of the sort that let you know there's nothing left but weariness and pride (p. 129).[14]

"The Gates of Heaven" faithfully (perhaps too faithfully for an older Cortázar) translates the official discourse of the thirties and early forties which had associated the immigrant population with contamination. Celina dies of tuberculosis at the beginning of the story. Puig's *Boquitas pintadas* [Heartbreak Tango] set in the 1940s would pick up this same association between immigration and sickness. However, Celina is contaminated not only because of her disease but because of her association with the dance halls. With the closing of the Buenos Aires brothels in the 1930s the dance halls had become marketplaces for prostitutes and pimps[15] and in Cortázar's narrative, they metonymically link Celina to the degeneration of society as a whole. In fact, Perón's attempts to reopen the brothels met with opposition precisely because this discourse of degeneration and contamination was so deeply rooted among the "gente decente."[16]

In Piglia's version of "The Gates of Heaven," the comic strip drawn by Carlos Nine exaggerates the grotesque features of the lower classes. The drawings of Mauro often focus on one facial feature—his aggressively curly black hair, his uneven teeth, his large, thick-lipped mouth. In one close-up there is only a protruding eye shedding giant tears over a huge hooked nose. Celina has thick lips, bushy hair, and a wide mouth. The sweating masses are shown cheering on fighters in the boxing ring and slurping their drinks. In contrast, Marcelo's face is never fragmented. His features conform to the conventions of comic strip handsomeness but reveal nothing of his feelings. The comic strip also reaffirms the "Hardoy soy yo" [I am Hardoy] theme though in ironic fashion, since at the end, Cortázar is seen beside a microscope, holding a cigarette whose smoke roughly reproduces Latin America as a monster being tweaked by Donald Duck. The concluding sentence of the comic and the story are almost identical: "he knew that he was wasting his time, that he would come back, tired and thirsty, not having found the gates of heaven among all that smoke and all those people" (p. 51).

What the comic "digests" to the point of disappearance, however, is the subtler aspect of the dénouement, in other words the difference that Hardoy establishes between his own experience of the sublime and Mauro's inferior search for Celina's copy. A reference in "Gates of Heaven" to Ortega y Gasset provides the clue to this difference. Ortega's dissection of "el hombre masa" [the mass man] in *La rebelión de las masas* [The Rebellion of the Masses] (1924) was of course part of the intellectual baggage of the period.[17] Thus it is not surprising that one of Hardoy's "fichas" [filecards] specifically identifies Mauro with Ortega y Gasset's scathing description of those who use technology without contributing to its invention or understanding of the underlying scientific principles. Echoing Ortega, Hardoy comments:

> Exactly where one would imagine a cultural shock, there is, on the contrary, a violent assimilation and enjoyment of the progress. Mauro talks about refrigeration units and audio-frequency amplification with the self-sufficiency of the Buenos Aires inhabitant who firmly believes he has everything coming to him.

Yet if Mauro represents Ortega's mass man, Hardoy himself reminds us of the "disinterested" artist in *La deshumanización del arte* [The Dehumanization of Art] (1925).[18] It will be recalled that, at the beginning of his essay, Ortega had described the different attitudes toward death experienced by the dying man's wife, the doctor, a reporter (who feigns emotional involvement while keeping a professional distance), and the artist, the latter being the most detached from emotional or intellectual involvement and concerned primarily with the visual scene. Cortázar's story includes the same cast of characters—the emotionally involved family, the doctor, and Hardoy who doubles as artist and reporter/recorder with his card file, absorbed in registering reality and distanced from the emotional scenes at the wake and the funeral—"I hardly heard the old women crying and the commotion in the courtyard, but on the other hand I remember that the taxi cost two pesos sixty, and that the driver had a shiny cap" (p. 118). Hardoy is transformed into the artist when at the end of the story Celina's face, in his imagination, becomes dehumanized, "all her face changed and muddied by the yellow light of the smoke"[19] (p. 136).

Piglia argues that the fascination with the low and the feminine, and for those who "incarnate the elemental and monstrous world of passion and feeling" is a recurrent feature of Cortázar's writing: "That world of the others, of the monsters who invade and destroy order, contaminates all reality; the fascination with this contamination is one of the great themes of Julio Cortázar's fiction" (p. 40).

But there is another aspect to this fascination. Andreas Huyssen has shown that modernist writing tended to exclude women and mass culture from the aesthetic on similar grounds. Both were identified with the indiscriminate, with the chaotic, with unbridled emotion, with loss of boundaries.[20] "The Gates of Heaven" is interesting because, although it seems to exaggerate this modernist position (Celina is identified not only with mass culture but also with sexuality and contamination), the conclusion nevertheless suggests, in the manner of certain poststructuralists, that feminine "jouissance" is beyond the limits of patriarchal discourse. Cortázar would seem to be taking both an ironic stance against older modernist notions that excluded mass culture and woman from the aesthetic as well as against Adorno's negative dialectic that places mass culture entirely on the side of the routinized and the systemic.[21] His "gates of heaven" (and of course the references to Dante in the story) rather evoke the profane illumination of Walter Benjamin and the surrealists.[22]

Only Celina can enter the gates of heaven (albeit in Hardoy's vision), for woman embodies what is unrepresentable. Yet the story is perhaps less about Celina who is the pre-text than about the difference between the two men. For whereas Mauro goes to the Santa Fe palace in search of a copy of Celina (he is, after all, mass man), Marcelo experiences the "sublime" through the impossible and visionary resurrection of the dehumanized original. As Lyotard suggests, there is a distinction in Kantian aesthetics between the sublime and taste, for the sublime is the idea "of which no presentation is possible" and "modern aesthetics is an aesthetic of the sublime, though a nostalgic one. It allows the unpresentable to be put forward only as the missing contents; but the form, because of its recognizable consistency, continues to offer to the reader or viewer matter for solace and pleasure" (p. 81). The postmodern, in this account is

> that which, in the modern, puts forward the unpresentable in presentation itself; that which denies itself the solace of good forms, the consensus of a taste which would make it possible to share collectively the nostalgia for the unattainable; that which searches for new presentations, not in order to enjoy them but in order to impart a stronger sense of the unpresentable.[23]

What is significant in Cortázar's story is that the difference between Mauro and Hardoy has now (ironically) become a difference between the secondary and unsatisfactory but perhaps attainable copy and the unrepeatable and unpresentable sublime. As for Celina, like the Lacanian mystic she experiences *jouissance* "but doesn't know anything about it."[24]

Benjamin wrote that "The reader, the thinker, the loiterer, the flaneur, are types of iluminati just as much as the opium eater, the dreamer, the ecstatic. And more profane."[25] Interestingly, however, Hardoy is not quite redeemed in "The Gates of Heaven." Starting out as Ortega's "disinterested" artist, his voyeuristic experience of sublimity is, in reality, no more authentic or satisfying than Mauro's search for the copy.

Cortázar's description of a different experience of the sublime — "Louis, enormísimo cronopio" [Louis, the enormous *cronopio*] (see n. 28) — included in *La vuelta al día en ochenta mundos* [Around the Day in Eighty Worlds][26] — was written shortly after Louis Armstrong's Paris concert of 9 November 1952 and thus belongs roughly to the same period as *The Examination* and "The Gates of Heaven."

Jazz is, of course, not to be equated with mass culture; its roots are popular and collective, the antithesis of commodification. Nevertheless by becoming the first great solo performer, Armstrong "moved jazz into another era: the ascendancy of the soloist began."[27] Collective improvisation was replaced by "individual expressiveness." And jazz recordings subverted the one-time-only improvisation that is crucial to the very essence of jazz. When Armstrong visited Paris in 1952 his style was already considered passé for those for whom jazz had become identified with the cool and "highbrow" style of Miles Davis.

Although Cortázar's essay describes a moment when the boundaries between self and other erode, in this essay, the erosion has strong connections to male sexuality. The male musicians get their high by playing on female instruments. "Arvel Shaw who plays bass as if holding a naked shadowy woman in his arms and Cozy Cole who arches over the drums like the Marquis de Sade over the backsides of eight whipped and naked women" (p. 122). Louis, on the other hand, is described in terms that remind us of the mystics:

> From Louis's trumpet the music emerges like the ribbons of speech from the mouths of primitive saints, a hot yellow writing is inscribed on the air, and after this first signal *Muskrat Ramble* is unleashed and those of us in the stalls, hanging on to anything that can be hung on to, and our neighbours do the same, so that the auditorium seems like a vast gathering of crazed octopus and in the midst of everything is Louis with the whites of his eyes behind the trumpet, with his handkerchief waving in a continuous farewell to something that we can't identify, as if Louis had to continually say goodbye to that music that creates and disintegrates in the instant, as if he knew the terrible cost of that marvelous liberty of his (p. 123).

The turned-up whites of the eyes recall those of the (female) mystic ("elle" jouit). But the *jouissance* is transmitted to an audience and bonds those who are participants. As for those members of the audience who are not *cronopios*, "naturally they didn't understand anything."[28]

To follow the thread of this particular discrimination between those who are "in" and those who are "out" as it runs through Cortázar's work would be an interminable and probably a superfluous exercise. One has only to recall the reiteration in Cortázar's work of different forms of discrimination (the separation between "cronopios" and "famas," for instance). From *Los premios* [The Winners] to his final *Los autonautas de la cosmopista; un viaje atemporal Paris-Marsella* [Autonauts of the Cosmoway; An Atemporal Trip from Paris to Marseilles][29] there are constantly shifting boundaries, separating those who are "in" from those who are "out"— for instance, the levels of complicity that divides the readers of *Hopscotch* into "complices" [accomplices] and "hembras" [females], the "insider's" vision of Latin America experienced by the narrator of "Apocalypse in Solentiname" and the outsider and surface vision of his girlfriend Claudine and so on and so forth. What I am emphasizing here is not only the drawing of boundaries, but rather an aspect of Cortázar's writing that made it so exemplary of the zeitgeist of the sixties when the "advanced" position included both a liberation from the tyranny of proletarian consciousness (and realism) and from the political ascesis of high modernism. Put, in another way, "us" and "them" were now configured by new social actors—on the one hand classless, uprooted visionaries, and on the other the entire body of those who had bought into consumer society ranging from workers to the haute bourgeoisie.

Interestingly two films inspired by Cortázar stories—Antonioni's *Blow-up* (1966), described as a "hypnotic pop-culture parable of a photographer caught in passive life-style" and Godard's *Weekend* (1967), "an essential sixties time-capsule"[30]—register this new divide. Neither film is, in reality, a true adaptation; indeed, Godard's film is, in many ways its antithesis but they reflect the "holy madness" of the time.

Antonioni's *Blow-up* was "inspired" (according to the credits) by Cortázar's story, "Las babas del diablo" [also translated as "Blow-Up"].[31] However, in the film, Cortázar's amateur photographer and translator is transformed into a trendy narcissist living in swinging London. Antonioni's film is based on a fairly conventional contrast between imagination and routine, between a "real" woman, Vanessa Redgrave, and the conveyor-belt women who work as models for the photographer. The "blow-up" becomes a lesson in imagination ("l'imagination au pouvoir") that culminates in the famous finale—a tennis game played by carnavalesque figures without rackets or balls. There are, of course, huge differences between film and story. For one thing, Antonioni allows the Vanessa Redgrave character to be a participant rather than simply an object focused by the camera lens ("l'objectif") and the boy of Cortázar's story has become an older man. Yet the topics of the film—consumer culture, loss of affect, simulation, and redemption through imagination—belong to a shared zeitgeist. The carnavalesque crowd in Antonioni's film resemble one of Cortázar's "clubs" formed without any reference to anterior ties of class identity.

Weekend on the other hand, is closer to Buñuel than to Cortázar. Godard would say, about his film *One plus One* that featured the Rolling Stones and was made just after *Weekend*, "What I want above all is to destroy the idea of culture. Culture is an alibi of imperialism. There is a Ministry of War. There is also a Ministry of Culture. Therefore, culture is war."[32]

Apart from the prolonged tracking shot of cars jammed on a highway, *Weekend*, which Godard described as "a film adrift in the cosmos" and "found on the scrap heap" has only a tenuous link to Cortázar's "La autopista del sur" [Highway to the South].[33] If anything, the film resembles the end of the orgy as described by Baudrillard: "We live amid the interminable reproduction of ideals, phantasies, images and dreams which are now behind us, yet which we must continue to reproduce in a sort of ines-capable indifference."[34] Godard's and Antonioni's films both identify the common enemy as a "consumer culture" that provokes violence and en-courages conspiracy. This Cold War zeitgeist was shared by Cortázar who began to explore the possibility of political intervention through litera-ture, notably in *Libro de Manuel* [A Manual for Manuel] and *Fantomas*. It is clear that in these two texts the air of the *faux naif* which had served Cortázar well in much of his fiction becomes strained under the pressure of documentation on torture and disappearance.

The attempt in *A Manual for Manuel* to bridge the political and the liter-ary caused him a great deal of anguish. The novel marks the moment when he (like his alter ego, Andrés) connects the avant-garde and vanguard.[35] The effectiveness of the move, however, depends on the reader's accep-tance of conspiracy and violence as overriding political realities which can only be opposed by conspiracy and violence. In other words, such an analy-sis presupposes the nonexistence or the fragility of the public sphere of democratic debate. This is reflected in the entangled codes, puzzles, and private languages of the novel. At the same time, the reappearance in dif-ferent forms of the "club," "la Joda," the telephone community suggests that Cortázar needs to envisage these heterotopias as substitutes for a pub-lic sphere which as yet no longer has any material existence.[36] It is in this light that I wish to examine Cortázar's anachronistic choice of *Fantomas* as a bridge between the intelligentsia and mass culture which he saw as having coopted the public sphere.

Anachronism is hardly an innocent word in dealing with Cortázar. In *A Manual for Manuel* he introduces a long meditation on the archaic piano that Stockhausen uses in his music along with electronic and aleatory de-vices. Even though (following the logic of the avant garde), the piano should be destroyed, Andrés suggests that these anachronistic references are needed as bridges that extend toward the unknown. The familiar sound of the piano may well induce automatic responses, thus interfering with the creation of the new; however Andrés "understands" why Stockhausen feels the need to retain this instrument: "You've got the bridge problem too, you have to find the way of speaking intelligibly" (p. 27).

In *Around the Day in Eighty Worlds*, on the other hand, anachronism is clearly nostalgic, for the Pannemaker engravings from the first edition of Verne's collected works not only refer the reader back to "innocent" adven-ture stories, but also to a moment when there was a shared popular culture.

Fantomás y los vampiros multinacionales [Fantomas and the Multinational

Vampires] (1975) bridges high and popular culture in a different way for it takes us back not to childhood but to a more sinister and violent world that heralded modernity. The first *Fantomas* novel published in 1911 and coauthored by Pierre Souvestre and Marcel Allain ushered in a new stage of mass culture, new, at least, in France. The novels were read, writes John Ashbery, by "Countesses and concierges: poets and proletarians; cubists, nascent Dadaists, soon-to-be-surrealists. Everyone who could read, and even those who could not, shivered at posters of a masked man in impeccable evening clothes, dagger in hand, looming over Paris like a somber Gulliver, contemplating hideous misdeeds from which no citizen was safe."[37] This popularity, however, reflected a social imaginary of urban violence and conspiracy.

The authors were journalists who drew on the popularity of the yellow press and possibly on the sensational accounts of anarchist groups active around 1911 and 1912 whose deeds were not very different from those of "la Joda" in *A Manual for Manuel*.[38] The popularity of the series was secured both by slick advertising and by the five Fantomas films which were screened between 1913 and 1915 and directed by Louis Feuillade. Allain, in particular, had carefully calculated consumer needs: "The public of popular fiction is essentially a public that wants to know 'how it ends.' If the author allows their curiosity to be aroused between one book and the next, the series is assured of a growing success."[39] Allain, who survived Souvestre and continued the series as sole author, was quick to grasp the importance of adapting *Fantomas* for radio, the comic strip, and even eventually for television.[40]

The first Fantomas adventure modestly priced at sixty-five centimes was so popular that there were thirty-one sequels, each sequel being motivated by the villain's miraculous escape from imminent capture by the police chief, Juve, and his increasingly violent and improbable escapades that often involved the destruction of sacred Paris monuments. Fantomas robs the gold from the dome of the Invalides, brings about the crash of the Simplon-Paris express, robs the Banque de France, and blows up the Montmartre reservoirs. In the cat-and-mouse game of the novels, the police chief Juve is often outwitted. His sidekick, Bertram/Fayard, who comes from an aristocratic family, works as a police informer and journalist on a newspaper appropriately named *La Capitale*. The capital city, Paris (*la capitale*), is not only the preferred scene of the Fantomas adventure but also provides productive capital (*le capitale*) on which the novels can draw.

Although these popular novels have antecedents in the nineteenth-century master criminal novels (of which Balzac's *Comédie humaine* surely holds pride of place), they ushered in a new era of mass-marketed fiction. Image and legend rapidly outstripped the confines of the book. The covers of Fantomas novels illustrated by Gino Starace were luridly gripping and designed to glamorize the villain. It was this, no doubt that inspired the interest of the avant-garde. Soon after the publication of the first *Fantomas* Guillaume Apollinaire founded the Society of the Friends of Fantomas. The mystery man inspired poems by Max Jacob and verses by Neruda and he was admired by Aragon, Colette, Raymond Queneau, and Cocteau;[41] in 1933, Robert Desnos wrote a Fantomas "Complainte" or lament that was set to music by Kurt Weil and sung by a chorus conducted by Antonin Artaud.[42] The Belgian poet, Ernst Moerman, referred to him as a "world lost in space" and invited him to "save poetry," long before Cortázar invited him to save books.[43]

The avant garde and the Surrealists were drawn to Fantomas novels because of their antisocial violence. As an enemy of the established order, and especially of the police, he was compared to Maldoror for he blatantly defied the moral code as it was defined by bourgeois society. More significantly Fantomas was a symptom of the dark side of modernity. Like their predecessors (Eugène Sue and Balzac), Allain and Souvestre depicted an urban world in which "identity" has become a matter of performance and acting a significant trope. In the first *Fantomas*, Gant (Fantomas) is caught and condemned to the guillotine. When the blade falls, however, it is not on Fantomas but on an actor who unknowingly has been trapped into impersonating him. In these novels nobody retains his or her original identity for very long. Fantomas's mistress, Lady Bertram, doubles as head of a convent, Juve appears in many disguises: as a man in a wheelchair, as a "pale man with a greenish complexion," and as a "mysterious tramp." In *The Secret Executioner*, Fantomas is both a doctor and a low-life thief.[44] Anticipating the stake-outs of the drug era, the police themselves engage in elaborate charades, constantly appearing in disguise as gang members and criminals. In the world in which Fantomas has the power of ubiquity (just as in Conan Doyle's Sherlock Holmes mysteries, this is helped by railway time tables), nobody is safe, locked doors are no protection, and the most innocent-looking bystander is either a criminal or a police spy.

For Cortázar, Fantomas as popular villain and avant-garde hero provided a useful bridge. In an earlier story, "The Other Heaven," he had explored the ominous urban cityscape conflating the arcades of nineteenth-century Paris with Peronist Buenos Aires.[45] *Fantomas*, on the other hand, was published in 1975,[46] at a time when the "conspiracy" of the multi-national corporations in Chile was still on people's minds, and he gave it the subtitle, *Una Utopía realizable* [A Realizable Utopia].

Cortázar's *Fantomas* was published by *Excelsior*, the Mexican newspaper which, at the time, under Julio Scherer was showing some independence from government control; the royalties went to the Russell Tribunal which was investigating torture in Latin America. In Cortázar's text, the Fantomas comic is a Mexican adaptation.[47] The narrative begins with Cortázar-as-narrator picking up a Mexican comic at the railway station. In the opening episode, Fantomas, disguised as a young theatergoer emerges from *The Threepenny Opera* and is shown explaining to his female companion that Brecht uses criminals to parody the customs of the bourgeoisie since he realized that there was hardly any difference between the gangster and the financier.

Cortázar's *Fantomas* combines the comic strip with the narrative of Cortázar's train journey from Brussels to Paris after a session of the Russell Tribunal.[48] It also includes serial views of Wall Street, of Washington, of the IBM logo, of the Paris police, and of automatic weapons as well as nineteenth-century illustrations from popular literature, a photo montage of a knife cutting an eye (a reference to Buñuel, it goes without saying), newspaper reports, and an appendix that includes the Russell Tribunal report. "Mechanical reproduction" (the multiple photographs of Capitol Hill) like the "hormigas" [ants—a term that refers to the enemy] in *A Manual for Manuel*, illustrates the reproduction of U.S. hegemony, while the multiple disguises of Fantomas (even as a lone ranger his tactics are anachronistic) anticipate the heterogeneity of "the people" whose cause is taken up, among others, by that cult figure Susan Sontag (seemingly the only woman intellectual whose word counted for anything). The story culminates in a communication miracle when the silent masses are heard on the telephone, a feat apparently accomplished by Fantomas who, as it were, creates a network of solidarity. The text thus pits the monumentalism of the hegemonic power against a civil society that is truly heterogeneous and seems to prefigure the as yet nonexistent global public sphere.

Toward the end of his life, Cortázar tended to explore literature as a form of political intervention and came to see mass culture as a bridge which would have to be seized by "la avanzada" [the advance column]. Indeed, he often speaks in apparently contradictory ways, sometimes using the traditional language of class struggle (the bourgeoisie and the petit bourgeois), while at the same time he also evokes a culture in which such class terms no longer seem relevant. After his visit to Sandinista Nicaragua, he would refer to cultural workers[49] and urge his colleagues not only to become actively engaged in alternative politics but also to use video, cartoons, photonovels, and comic strips, citing Luis Britto García on the need to gain access to the mass media. His goal is still the utopian one of liberating the creative potential of Latin America which he now envisages as "that immense book that we can write all together and for us all" (p. 97). But Cortázar never repeated the *Fantomas* experiment. When, in the eighties, Piglia followed Cortázar's injunction to use mass culture in order to reach new publics, the latter were already way ahead of the intelligentsia in their reading of images and their speedy adoption of new music styles. Is it high culture's representation of Argentina that has left it in fragments? Piglia's comic-stripping of Argentine literature seems to underscore the fact that "the immense book" (whether of the nation or of Latin America as a whole) can no longer be bodied forth from high culture and that, since the wall between high and mass culture has come down, the former may now simply have become the repertoire for the latter.

NOTES

1 Ricardo Piglia, *La Argentina en pedazos* (Buenos Aires: Ediciones Urraca, 1993).

2 Nestor García Canclini, "De las Utopías al mercado," in *Culturas híbridas. Estrategias para entrar y salir de la modernidad* (Jalapa, Mexico: Grijalbo, 1989), 31–63.

3 A good example of this is Luis Rafael Sánchez's deployment of *bolero* lyrics in *La importancia de llamarse Daniel Sánchez* (Hanover: Ediciones del Norte, 1988), and in a rather different mode, Manuel Puig's use of melodrama and sentimental radio novel in *Boquitas pintadas* (Buenos Aires: Sudamericana, 1969).

4 Walter Benjamin, "The Work of Art in the Age of Mechanical Reproduction," in *Illuminations: Essays and Reflections* (London: Jonathan Cape, 1970), 233.

5 In the epigramatic conclusion of the essay, Benjamin sets Communism's "politicization of art" against fascism's "aestheticization of politics." What he could not foresee was the virtual disappearance of politics in a global culture.

6 This was the position advanced by Haydée Santamaria to the jury of the Casa de los Américas prize in 1969 and it was reiterated by Oscar Collazos in his essay, included in *Literatura y revolución*, to which both Cortázar and Vargas Llosa wrote replies.

7 Julio Cortázar, "Acerca de la situación del intelectual latinoamericano." The essay was published in *Revista de la Casa de las Américas* (Havana, Cuba, 1967) and is included in the collection, *Textos políticos* (Barcelona: Plaza y Janes, 1984), 27–44. See esp. 29.

8 Evelyn Picon Garfield, *Cortázar por Cortázar* (Jalapa, Mexico: Universidad Vera-

cruzana, 1978), 50. Cortázar would maintain this position until the end of his life. In a speech, "El escritor y su quehacer en America Latina," in *Nicaragua tan violentamente dulce* (Managua: Editorial Nueva Nicaragua, 1983), 86–98, he would reaffirm that exile was an enrichment.

9   In a personal conversation in 1981, Cortázar once told me that was a phrase he came to regret. Even so, I don't think his perceptions of gender difference underwent any radical change. This is evident from his replies to Evelyn Picon Garfield in *Cortázar por Cortázar* and in his articles on Nicaragua, *Nicaragua tan violentamente dulce*, in one of which he says he has no information on the sandinistas' policy on birth control—something that would hardly have been difficult to discover. In fact, Church pressure prevented any measures on abortion from being passed.

10 Rosita Quiroga was a popular singer, César Bruto a comic strip artist. Thanks to Josefina Ludmer for clarifying these references.

11 Julio Cortázar, *El examen* (Madrid: Alfaguara, 1986). Nicolás Rosa discusses aspects of Cortázar's groups in the preface to "El perseguidor y otros cuentos," in *Antología* (Buenos Aires: Capítulos, Centro Editor de América Latina, 1981).

12 The thesis of "distinction" or social stratification that is constituted by "habitus" and as taste was advanced by Pierre Bourdieu, *Distinction. Critique of the Social Judgement of Taste* (Cambridge, Mass.: Harvard University Press, 1986).

13 Garfield, *Cortázar por Cortázar*, 17.

14 Donna Guy, "Tango, Gender, and Politics," in *Sex and Danger in Buenos Aires. Prostitution, Family, and Nation in Argentina* (Lincoln: University of Nebraska Press, 1990), 144–74.

15 Donna Guy, "Patriotic Prostitutes and Dangerous Men," in *Sex and Danger*, 180–204.

16 Julio Cortázar, "Las puertas del cielo," *Bestiario* (Buenos Aires: Sudamericana, 1978), 117–37.

17 For the intellectual atmosphere of this period, see John King, *Sur: A Study of the Argentine Literary Journal and its Role in the Development of a Culture, 1931–1970* (Cambridge: Cambridge University Press, 1986).

18 José Ortega y Gasset, *La deshumanización del arte*, 11th ed. (Madrid: Ediciones Revista del Occidente, 1976).

19 "Desdecía" is here translated as "muddied" but though the Spanish word means "degenerated" it is formed from *decir* (to speak) and so vividly suggests a discursive construct that is dissolving into smoke.

20 Andreas Huyssen, "Mass Culture as Woman, Modernism's Other," in *Beyond the Great Divide: Modernism, Mass Culture, Postmodernism* (Bloomington: Indiana University Press, 1986), 44–62.

21 Theodor Adorno, *Aesthetic Theory*, trans. C. Lenhardt (London: Routledge, 1984). See esp. 336–37 for the dilemma of art as commodity.

22 Walter Benjamin, "Surrealism," in *Reflections: Essays, Aphorisms, Autobiographi-*

cal Writings, trans. Edmund Jephcott (New York: Harcourt Brace Jovanovich, 1978), 177–92.

23 Jean-François Lyotard, *The Postmodern Condition: A Report on Knowledge*, trans. Geoff Bennington and Brian Massumi (Minneapolis: University of Minnesota Press, 1984).

24 For a discussion of woman as unrepresented in discourse, see Alice A. Jardine, *Gynesis: Configurations of Woman and Modernity* (Ithaca: Cornell University Press, 1985), esp. 167.

25 Benjamin, "Surrealism," 90.

26 Julio Cortázar, "Louis enormísimo cronopio," in *La vuelta al día en ochenta mundos* (Mexico: Siglo Ventiuno, 1967), 121–25.

27 Leroi Jones, *Blues People: Negro Music in White America* (London: MacGibbon and Kee, 1965), 155.

28 Julio Cortázar, *Historia de cronopios y de famas*, trans. P. Blackburn (New York: Pantheon, 1969) introduces a classification based not so much on taste as on attitudes to life. The *cronopios* are spontaneous enthusiasts who are not quite synchronized with "real life."

29 Carol Dunlop and Julio Cortázar, *Los autonautas de la cosmopista. Un viaje atemporal Paris-Marsella* (Mexico: Nueva Imagen, 1984). This book, written in collaboration and completed just before the death of his companion, Carol Dunlop, constitutes a heterotopia within the freeway system.

30 The digests are from the updated edition of Leonard Maltin, *TV Movies and Video Guide* (New York: New American Library, 1989).

31 The literal translation would be "devil's spit," which apparently refers to a kind of wispy cloud formation.

32 Quoted by James Miller in *The New York Times* (25 July 1989), 20.

33 Julio Cortázar, "La autopista del sur," in *Todos los fuegos el fuego* (Buenos Aires: Sudamericana, 1966).

34 Jean Baudrillard, *The Transparency of Evil*, trans. James Benedict (London: Verso, 1993), 4.

35 Garfield, *Cortázar por Cortázar*, 61.

36 Julio Cortázar, *Libro de Manuel* (Buenos Aires: Sudamericana, 1973). *Heterotopia* is a word used by Foucault to account for the existence of antisystemic groups within the system though he never really develops this concept. Emily Hicks has a Deleuzian interpretation of *Libro de Manuel* which interprets the book as "border writing." See her *Border Writing The Multidimensional Text* (Minneapolis: University of Minnesota Press, 1991). She also tries to read the structure of the novel in terms of Stockhausen's music.

37 Marcel Allain and Pierre Souvestre, *Fantomas*, introduction by John Ashbery (New York: William Morrow, 1986), 1.

38 Louis Chavance notes the coincidence of the publication of the first volume and the first reported activities of the anarchist Bonnot gang. See "La morale

de Fantomas" in the special issue on Fantomas of *Europe* 590–592 (juin–juillet 1978): 64–68, esp. 67.

39 Marcel Allain, "Du roman populaire et de ses possibilités commerciales," *Europe* 590–592: 23. My translation.

40 The *Europe* bibliography includes the novels, plays, comic strips, and photo-novels. See "Bibliographie de Fantomas," *Europe* 590–592: 141–61.

41 Fantomas is mentioned in Neruda's poem, "Las Pacheco," in *Memorial de Isla Negra, Obras completas*, 3rd ed. (Buenos Aires: Losada, 1968), 2:510. For the various avant-garde admirers of Fantomas, see Roland Stragliati, " 'Fantomas'? Oui, mais . . ." *Europe* 590–592: 72–78.

42 Hubert Juin, "Pour éveiller nos joies un beau crime est bien fort," *Europe* 590–592: 11.

43 Cited in ibid., 14–16.

44 Marcel Allain and Pierre Souvestre, *The Silent Executioner* (New York: William Morrow and Company 1987).

45 "The Other Heaven" (El otro cielo) with its allusions to Lautreaumont, and possibly to Benjamin of the *Passagenwerk* includes a guillotining episode which could well have been lifted out of a *Fantomas* novel. "El otro cielo" is included in the collection *Todos los fuegos el fuego* (Buenos Aires: Sudamericana, 1966).

46 Julio Cortázar, *Fantomas contra los vampiros multinacionales: Una Utopía realizable* (México: Excelsior, 1975). See Ellen M. McCracken, "*Libro de Manuel* and *Fantomas contra los vampiros multinacionales*," in *Literature and Popular Culture in the Hispanic World* (Gathersburg: Hispamérica, 1981), 69–77. It is interesting that it was written before Cortázar came up against the wilder claims of certain guerrilla movements to be initiating a nationwide revolution. See note 48.

47 Fantomas comics began to be published in Mexico in the 1930s by Paquín comics. In the 1970s they were published by Editorial Novaro. See Irene Herner's exhaustive history of the comic strip in Mexico in Irene Herner and Maria Eugenia Chellet, *Mitos y monitos: Historietas y fotonovelas en Mexico* (Mexico: Nueva Imagen, 1979), esp. 22, 172.

48 The Russell Tribunal was initiated by the Bertrand Russell foundation during the Vietnam War. The Russell Tribunal II dealt with Latin America and met twice—in Rome (1974) and Brussels (1975). It has to be remembered that in the early seventies, "human rights" were not yet incorporated into the U.S. official policy. Because it had no government backing either in Europe or the United States, the tribunal was not able to put into effect recommendations or even effectively publicize its work which is why its recommendations were included in *Fantomas*.

  For a comment on Cortázar's position vis-à-vis the ERP guerrilla movement and his activity in the tribunal, it is interesting to read Maria Seoane, *Todo o nada. La historia secreta y la historia pública del jefe guerrillero Mario Roberto Santucho* 3rd ed. (Buenos Aires: Planeta, 1992). Santucho, who interviewed Cortázar and Jaime Petras, wanted the tribunal to make a public declaration in favor of the guerrilla movement. Both Cortázar and Petras doubted the realism of their war tactics and argued that their request was not within the tribunal's competence. But reportedly Cortázar was deeply disturbed by the hostility of the guerrilla to this response.

49 "El escritor y su quehacer en América Latina," in *Nicaragua tan violentamente dulce* (Managua: Editorial Nueva Nicaragua, 1983), esp. 95.

4 $\mathscr{M}$EXICO

JOURNEY TO THE LAND OF THE DEAD

Rulfo's Pedro Páramo

And now the souls of the dead who had gone below came swarming up from Erebus—fresh brides, unmarried youths, old men with life's long suffering behind them, tender young girls still nursing this first anguish in their hearts, and a great throng of warriors killed in battle, their spear wounds gaping yet and their armour stained with blood. From this multitude of souls, as they fluttered to and fro by the trench, there came a moaning that was horrible to hear.

—HOMER, *The Odyssey*

he anguish of the dead when confronted by the living is one of the tragic themes of literature. Deprived of a future, the shades turn toward the past like the inhabitants of Amos Tutuola's "Dead's Town," who can only go backward, while the living are drawn onward into a future that multiplies with possibilities. The lesson alike of the classical texts and of Dante's *Divine Comedy* is the deadness of the dead, for they are forever halted, stilled. Theirs is the tragedy of completion.[1] No wonder, then, that Charon finds it so easy to detect the living Dante as he tries to cross the river among the dead souls, ordering him onto another boat:

> Per altra via, per altri porti
> verrai a piaggia, non qui, per passare
> piú leve legno convien che ti porti.

> [Away with thee! for by another road
> and other ferries thou shalt make the shore
> Not here, a lighter skiff must bear thy lead.][2]

Originally published as "Viaje al país de los muertos" in *La narrativa de Juan Rulfo: Interpretaciones críticas*, ed. Joseph Sommers (Mexico: SepSetentas, 1974), 117–40. Translations by Soledad Gelles.

Yet, as the North American writer LeRoi Jones perceives, to the modern world "Dante's hell is heaven" for its values are stable and its punishments are predictable, whereas, in contemporary literature, while the living continue to make Dante's journey into the underworld the frontiers have become blurred, ghostliness has invaded this side of the Styx, and the living seem to lack substance—to have been turned into shadows.

The topography of Dante's hell—the walled cities, the deep precipices, and the plains aflame—reflects the rigid destiny of the damned and the diversity of the sins to be punished. Although Dante always refers to large masses and categories of sinners, the voices that interpellate the traveler belong to specific individuals condemned for *specific* sins. Dante's hell is a hell for individuals.

We think it a paradox that the Middle Ages, a time of categories and estates, would produce a poem so concerned with individual human destiny, while in the seventeenth century, at the time of the beginning of bourgeois individualism, Quevedo's hell is a hell for the masses, dehumanized and bureaucratic. In "Las Zahurdas de Plutón" [The Hovels of Pluto],[3] the nuances and pathetism that came along with individual destiny disappear. Cataloged by devil officials at the entrance of hell, sinners walk in hundreds, and they are condemned not individually but rather as members of certain social classes. This amounts to a considerable change since Dante's times. Now, the damned belong to particular professional groups or to artisan guilds (doctors, lawyers, pharmacists) who do not at all resemble the members of the feudal estates and whose work is valued in terms of money. Quevedo explains that "Las Zahurdas de Platón" are inspired in a dream that he had after reading Dante, but his "Sueño" [Dream] is a grotesque parody of the original. Salvation and sin do not appear to be individual conscious choices, but are rather inexplicably linked to the work that is being sold (and selling is synonymous with cheating). It is only by implication that we can perceive the positive values of honesty, authenticity, and seriousness in this landscape of human vanity, and these positive values are already considered as something archaic. They are values and attitudes on the brink of disappearance in a society that still preserves feudal characteristics but that also includes new social groups motivated by the necessities of money. However, sin can still be identified. The real moral confusion only occurs with the degeneration of Christianity.

It is obvious that a radical change in the sense of self has come about since Dante's time. Devoid of the hope for eternal salvation, the contemporary writer contemplates the journey to the land of the dead with some of the elegiac pathos of the pagan world. It is interesting, however, that three contemporary works dealing with the topic were written by men from marginal cultures: *The Palm-Wine Drinkard* by the Nigerian Amos Tutuola, *The System of Dante's Hell* by the African American LeRoi Jones, and *Pedro Páramo* by the Mexican Juan Rulfo.[4] Tutuola's book is close to folk tale[5] and shows us a tribal culture invaded and distorted by contact with the outside world. His hero is a culture hero whose journey takes place in a mythic past when "towns and villages were not so near each other as nowadays" (p. 9), when the narrator was "father of the gods who could do anything in the world" (p. 10). Yet the magical power of this "father of the gods" coexists uneasily with the marvels of the technological era. When he turns himself into a big bird, this is "like an airplane." He is burdened with a "half-bodied" child who talks in a low tone "like a telephone." People laugh "as if bombs explode." While the bush is full of weird bush creatures who imprison, torment, and put obstacles in the narrator's way, there also lurks beneath the surface all kinds of new and equally incomprehensible forces which seem to have been introduced from outside. Thus, although *The Palm-Wine Drinkard* is a "naïve work," for this very reason it presents the clash of culture almost at the subliminal level.

The hero/narrator is a superhuman figure, a consumer of vast quantities of palm wine, a man who does not need to work only consume, and thus symbolizes the plentitude of tribal society whose aim is abundance for everybody (not surplus profit)—and hence, liberation from work. When death comes to the palm wine tapster, who is the indispensable creator of this surplus, the drunkard sets out to the dead's town and, on his way there, performs a number of magic feats. He rescues a lady from a "complete Gentleman" (p. 18), the parts of whose body are all rented and have to be returned, leaving only a rolling skull. The drunkard marries this lady and they bear a monster child who has to be burned to death. Their journey in search of the dead tapster takes them to "wraith-island," to "the unreturnable heaven's town" (p. 57), to a tree inhabited by "faithful mother" (p. 68), and to the "red-town" which they rescue from a curse. The bush they travel through is inhabited by marvelous and supernatural creatures, including Drum, Song, and Dance who have the power to raise the dead. But into this marvelous world there has crept another and an extraneous force—foreign money. On his way to the dead's town, the narrator works as a ferryman and earns £7.5.3 in one day. He and his wife sell their "death" for £70.18.6 and their fear for £3.10.0. And in a new town where they become wealthy, they are approached by an "invisible pawn" who tells them that he "was always hearing the word—POOR, but he did not *know* it. He said that he wanted to borrow some amount and he would be working for me in return as a pawn or as permanent hired labourer" (pp. 85–86). The pawn who turns out to be a destructive bush creature is hired for 2,000 cowries or sixpence in British money. So poverty is associated with the sale of labor and the magic of tribal society appears to be undermined by the new fetish—money, which devalues traditional native money (cowries) as against the British sixpence.

The goal of the journey in *The Palm-Wine Drinkard* is the Dead's Town in which men walk backward and which the palm wine tapster had only reached after "two years in training and after he had qualified as a full dead man." The town is multiracial and totally reverses the world of the living: "both white and black deads were living in the Dead's Town, not a single alive was there at all. Because everything that they were doing there was incorrect to alives and everything that all alives were doing was incorrect to the deads too" (p. 100). The goal of the search—the palm-wine tapster—symbol of the old abundance, has been reached, but he cannot be restored to the land of the living. All that the narrator takes back from the Dead's Town is a magic egg which brings discord to the family. *The Palm-Wine Drinkard*, then, is an elegy for the old magic world and an announcement of a new era which comes with the reconciliation of heaven and earth (and the recognition of earth's subordinate position). The ghosts and bush creatures disappear before a purely natural order. Unlike Macondo, in which the long rainstorm brings ruin, the three months of rain that close the Nigerian novel are a step toward a new order in which man reconciles himself to nature. But the ending is also enigmatic. Though the search for the magic abundance of the past forms the thread of the novel, the ending suggests that there is also a future (heaven) which puts fear into men and thus induces them to conform to what is given.

In *The System of Dante's Hell*, the tribe has been replaced by the street gang and the model is not folktale but Dante's *Commedia*, with the inferno transferred to North American cities and the moral categories (whether broad categories such as the Incontinents, the Violent, the Simply Fraudulent, and the Treacherous or the subcategories of the Lascivious, the Gluttonous, the Avaricious, the Violent against others, against self and God, nature, and art) are simply labels, random appendages in an environment in which men have no relations that are solid enough for sin.

The System of Dante's Hell is a decentered novel; there is a narrator but his perspective is always likely to merge with that of another or with one

of the narrator's former selves. His journey to the world of the dead is
a visit to his own immediate past in New York and other places, with its
population of dead men and memories. "The place is filled with shades . . .
Ghosts. And the huge ugly hands of actual spooks. Standing around the
bar, spilling wine on greasy shirts" (p. 9). Even the present so transient, so
rapidly forgotten, is ghostly. The mobility of city life erases identity, produces those terrible opening words: "But Dante's hell is heaven" (p. 9)—
heaven because it is fixed, eternal, the place of no change. In contrast, in
the modern hell, the streets and residences can be identified more readily
than the people whose memories they hold. So when numbered army men
(46 and 64—possibly two former selves of the narrator) talk, their points
of reference are streets and buildings:

> I cd walk out of yr life as simply as I tossed newspapers down the sewer.
> It was Nassau St., mostly, and later the street where Skippy lived. Also
> Johnny Holmes. But that was cross town so I don't know if you know.
> I used to live in the insurance projects, right across from Tolchinskies
> pickle works. I almost killed myself twice around there. But we moved
> a couple of times since then. Even back here. Dey St. is where I live
> now and I control the Secret Seven (p. 81).

Changes of place involve total changes of relationship, of personality—"I
almost killed myself twice around there. But we moved a couple of times
since then" (p. 95). Moving erases the previous selves, or makes them
memory ghosts. Being across town involves differences so great as to be
incommunicable. "I talk like Morton Street, Newark, where I live now"
(p. 85), says number 64. Crime and punishment are arbitrary. A woman is
flung out of a moving car and the car speeds on too quickly for those inside
to know more than that she is left squatting on the pavement. On the other
hand, one can go to jail for "having the sleeves of the shirt rolled up." This
arbitrary, identityless world is above all for that of the black man one in
which he is "focused as object not as subject," helplessly tossed about by a
destiny on which he has no shaping influence. Whereas in Tutuola's world
man is still trying to live according to nature, having lost any pretense of
controlling nature magically, in LeRoi Jones's world, he is controlled and
limited, not by nature but by unseen forces who manipulate and determine
him. So, "Hell is actual and people with hell in their heads," and the journey to the past takes the narrator not simply to a land of ghosts but also
to the realization of black consciousness: "And we remember w/ love those
things bathed in soft black light" (p. 154).

Disparate as they are, Tutuola and Jones are both writing from situations in which the moral order and their beliefs are out of key with "what they feel." It is this dichotomy that is also central to *Pedro Páramo*, which, like the two other novels, is structured around a search for origins.[6] The narrator here is the young man Juan Preciado, who sets out to Comala in search of his father, Pedro Páramo, but quickly finds himself trapped by the dead who have now invaded the spaces of this world. Dante's and Quevedo's hells were divided geographically from the living world. In Jones's New York and Rulfo's Comala, the boundaries have been broken down, the dead have invaded the territory inhabited by the living and have ousted them.[7] The same topography serves as both heaven, hell, and this world. So Comala is "la mera boca del infierno" [the very mouth of hell] and "una llanura verde" [a green plain], a land flowing with milk and honey of which Juan Preciado's mother speaks in memory, and "un horizonte gris" [a gray horizon] in which "todo parecía estar como en espera de algo" [everything looked as if it were waiting for something] (p. 10). It is a place of abundance and of poverty, an oasis of brilliance "blanqueando la tierra, iluminándola durante la noche" [whitening the earth, lightening it up at night] (p. 10) but empty and abandoned: "The windows of the houses opened up to the sky, letting the weeds peer out of them. The walls were peeling, showing their rotted adobes" (p. 54). Comala as paradise exists on the auditory level. It is what Juan Preciado *hears* transmitted by the mother's voice (unlike the Christian paradise which is a goal in the future, Comala-paradise is situated in the past). What he *sees* is the ruined village which is the creation of the father. Eyes and ears do not register the same truth, nor the same sector in the time continuum.

Unlike Dante, whose entry into the afterworld is only achieved by special grace, Juan Preciado has no difficulty in entering the world of the dead. The "casa del puente" [house at the bridge] (p. 14) inhabited by Doña Eduviges, a woman who committed suicide, is the threshold between the two worlds. When Juan Preciado tries to knock on the door, "mi mano se sacudió en el aire como si el aire la hubiera abierto" [my hand knocked on empty air, as if the wind had opened the door] (p. 14). No doors bar his passage through the house and he sleeps in a room which he later learns had been impenetrable, sealed off because Toribio Aldrete had been murdered there. His third guide, Damiana, is surprised at the fact that he had managed to get in at all: "I don't know how you got in, when there isn't any key to open this door" (p. 43). But Juan Preciado is always able to cross the threshold between life and death. Besides, the dead invade the world of the living, suck dry its abundance, and now inhabit the empty structures. The house at the bridge is full of bundles, *tiliches*, which people have left behind and never returned for, so that these objects appear to have displaced living people:

> I could see shadows on both sides and I felt we were walking through a narrow passageway between piles of bundles.
> "What have you got in here?" I asked.
> "Junk," she said. "The whole house is full of junk. All those that went away picked this house to keep their furniture and belongings in, and nobody has come back for them" (p. 15).

This displacement of the living by furniture foreshadows the retrospective history of Comala, which is a place where human relationships have become reified. Because of the bundles, there is only "un angosto pasillo" [a narrow passageway] through which Eduviges and Juan Preciado pass. But it is not only the furniture which crowds out the living but the ghosts themselves, whose accumulated guilt is too much for the intercession of those who are left behind and who exhaust the air until Juan Preciado suffocates: "There's so many of them, and so few of us, we don't even try to pray for them so their souls can rest. Our prayers wouldn't be enough for all of them. Perhaps a bit of the paternoster might reach them, but it wouldn't do them any good" (p. 65). The streets of the village are filled with the dead silently clamoring for intercession. Their numbers and their murmurings kill Juan Preciado: "I began to sense that muttering coming nearer and circling round me like a swarm of bees, till finally I could make out a few words, almost devoid of noise: 'Pray to God for us.' That's what they were saying to me. Then my soul froze" (p. 74). In Comala, then, there has been a breakdown between a moral and social order to which these ghosts are still attached, and a present which regards this moral and social order as a dead one. The dead social order was paternalistic, based on relationships or feudal service with power invested in the father/chieftain, Pedro Páramo, whose children they all are. To this social order corresponds a Catholic moral order which stresses the power of a father and obedience. But the father that Juan Preciado eventually finds in Comala is *not* this kind of father. For this reason, he would like to complain to his dead mother, "You gave me a wrong address. You didn't give me the right directions. You sent me to 'the-where-is-this and the-where-is-that?' To a dead village. Looking for somebody who doesn't exist" (pp. 13–14). Instead of finding the roots he seeks, he has found only vestiges of the past and moral confusion, the "¿dónde es esto y dónde es aquello?" [the-where-is-this and the-where-is-that].

The dead social and moral orders are totally divorced from conduct and the pursuit of happiness or fulfillment. The Heavenly Paradise is in *Pedro Páramo*—and traditionally—a reward for right conduct on earth, but men dream of an earthly paradise which is a prize that comes to them without regard to the way they behave. The earthly paradise is associated in the novel with the mother image and fulfillment which the mother symbolizes. But confusion arises because of the fact that the earthly paradise has existed only in an ideal past and the present always stands against it as a poor shadow.

Within the novel, there is one passage which is a micromodel of this relationship between past and present. Juan Preciado is in the village street, watching ox carts pass on a journey which resembles man's journey through life: "I saw the carts passing. The oxen slowly moving. The sound of the stones under the wheels. The men as if they were asleep" (p. 58). Here there is nothing more than the *sounds* of passage as if time were audible. The time/noise appears to have lulled the man into a somnambulistic state. And then there is the mother's voice which turns those same carts into a cornucopia and fills the empty passage of time with meaning:

> Every morning at dawn the village trembles with the passing of the carts. They come in from everywhere, loaded with saltpeter, with corn, with hay. Their wheels creak, rattling the windows and waking up the village. That's the hour when the ovens are opened and the air smells of fresh-baked bread. And it may thunder. Rain may fall. Spring may come. You'll learn there what "perhaps" means, my son (pp. 58–59).

Here the carts do not only creak over the stones but awaken people to life; they are filled with food and fertilizers and they come at the hour of bread-making, of communion. Gone is the even monotony of a time which is empty. Instead there is springtime and rain which suggest promise of change and transformation. "Los derrepentes" [the perhaps] are like miracles which can change lives. But in contrast to what Juan Preciado *hears*, there is the emptiness of what he *sees*: "Empty carts, grinding the silence of the streets. Vanishing down the dark road of the night. And the shadows. The echo of the shadows" (p. 59). Here there is emptiness, negation (the shadows), and repetition, a repetition that is emphasized by the gerund, "remoliendo" [grinding]. There are no carts filled with corn, only a grinding of shades. But we only *know* the emptiness of the present through evocation of fulfillment in the past.

The passing of the ox carts is the prelude to one of the key incidents of the novel, an incident that illuminates the break between the dead moral and social order and the empty present. Juan Preciado is on the point of turning back:

> Then somebody touched me on the shoulder.
> "What are you doing here?"
> "I came here to look for . . ." I was about to tell him, but I caught myself. "I came to look for my father."
> "And why don't you come in?"
> I went in. It was a house with half of the roof fallen in. Roof-tiles were scattered over the floor. The roof was on the floor. And in the other half there were a man and a woman.
> "Are you dead?" I asked them.
> And the woman smiled. The man looked at me solemnly.
> "He's drunk," the man said (p. 59).

This enigmatic, haunting pair with whom Juan Preciado seeks shelter are themselves defenseless and vulnerable. They believe themselves to be alive but describe their existence as "desviviéndose" [unliving], they appear to be married and are later discovered to be brother and sister. Their shelter has a broken roof, an obvious symbol for a broken identity, for a radical break in their vision of the world. They know vaguely that a road leads through this broken roof but have no notion of where it may go, just as they have no experience of the other roads around the house:

> There's lots of roads. One of them goes to Contla; another one comes in from there. There's another one that goes straight to the sierra. The one you can see from here I don't know where it goes,"—and she pointed out the gap in the tiles where the roof was broken. This one over there goes through Media Luna. And there's still another, that crosses the whole place, and it is the one that goes farther than any of them (p. 63).

"Los Confines" appears to be a goal but is merely a pathway to an unknown destination, and although the couple has some function or task connected with the salvation and intercession for souls, they have forgotten its purpose and perform it halfheartedly. The critic Julio Ortega sees them as "los primeros padres condenados a lamentar su culpa en el infierno" [the first/original parents, condemned to pay for their guilt in hell] and the roads suggest to him "el espacio del infierno" [the space of hell], but this couple is an Adam and Eve in reverse. Adam and Eve were cast out of paradise after clothing themselves, whereas this man and woman have put away their clothes and were waiting naked: "There was an oil lamp. There was a crude bed, and a chair with the woman's clothes on it. Because she was as naked as when God sent her into the world. So was he" (p. 59). Even the logic of the passage is in reverse. The clothes have been put away *because* they are naked. There is a suggestion almost of renunciation of worldly goods. Their nakedness is not the nakedness of the newborn and the innocent, but that of a man and woman on the threshold of death, ready to enter the afterworld. *But there is nowhere for them to go.* The road through the roof leads nowhere. What had been a shelter is now open to the elements without being an *opening*, an exit. It is simply a hole made by the breakdown of the house. Furthermore, their relationship is sterile, incestuous. The couple *should* bear children, *should* represent harmony and fulfillment. Instead they are disunited, for the husband only wants to sleep while the wife is kept awake by guilt. This pair who cannot help themselves is expected to shelter and help others; yet they are uneasy and suspicious of Juan Preciado and show him little sympathy. They are supposed to feed the hungry but they have no food; and although the man goes off to search for "un becerro cimarrón" [a stray calf] his wife believes that he has run away, not that he is a good shepherd. The pair is too human itself to save others: "There isn't one of us still living who's in the grace of God. No one can raise his eyes without feeling them right away dirty with shame. And shame doesn't cure anything" (p. 65). Moral precepts appear to be out of reach to humanity. There is an unbridgeable gap between the moral ideal and behavior. "So that's why this is full of spirits, a whole throng of wandering souls that died in sin and can't find any way of getting pardon, least of all with our help" (p. 66). This means, according to the direct and childlike logic of the novel, that the number of guilty souls increases and soon outnumbers the living. Guilt, accumulated over the past, chokes out any other sentiment.

The moral standards which the couple find impossible to obey are abstract ones, totally alien to the human condition. The bishop, for example, had ordered the pair to separate, when the natural inclination is for people to crowd together in their likeness. The human condition is one of isolation and solitude that can only be broken down by love, so the woman tries to explain to the bishop, "I wanted to tell him that life had brought us together, had captured us and placed us next to each other. We were so alone here that we were the only ones. And the village had to be populated somehow" (p. 66). What life demands is very different from what the bishop expects them to do. And it is not only the moral precepts which are out of key. The heavenly paradise promised by Christianity, the one which Padre Rentería tries and fails to communicate to Susana San Juan ("El gozo de los querubines y el canto de los serafines" [The joy of the cherubim and the songs of the seraphim]) (p. 140), has nothing to do with the earthly paradises which fill people's imaginations. Juan Preciado's mother, Pedro Páramo, Susana, Dorotea, dream of private paradises of self-fulfillment, divorced from their conduct in the present and not connected to it by any systems of rewards and punishments. There is no connection in Comala between man's vision of the good life and his actions, between accepted moral precepts and social behavior.

The enigmatic couple in the broken house represent the complete *stasis* to which these conflicts lead. They are enclosed in an incestuous circle but represent sterility, not fulfillment, the reduction of experience to the level of impoverishment. "And we're so alone here. Dying to know at least a little something of life" (p. 64). They inhabit the limbo of "desvivir" [unliving], neither whole-heartedly living, which would mean going out into the world, nor wholly dedicated to the life hereafter. For Juan Preciado, they are the foreshadowing of a death without peace, and although the woman offers him her bed he finds it a stifling, airless place: "I had to swallow the same air I breathed out, holding it back with my hands so it wouldn't escape" (p. 71). The brother/husband's name is Donis, which suggests the "Dona nobis pacem" of the Agnus Dei, but instead of peace there is insomnia. Instead of purity regained there is the same stale air breathed in over and over again, a stale repetition without salvation. Contrast Dante's journey, which opens the possibility not only of salvation in heaven but of the transformation of life on this earth:

> But as my sight by seeing learned to see,
> The transformation which in me took place
> Transformed the single changeless form in me.[8]

Not only this sterile couple but the priest himself in *Pedro Páramo* is incapable of opening the door to salvation, for he has lost all notion of what heaven and hell might mean: "What did he know about heaven and hell? And nevertheless, he, who was lost in a nameless village, knew who had deserved to go to heaven" (p. 41). As he recites the names of saints, he reflects that it is like counting goats before going to sleep. The heaven and hell he promises to Susana are mere fairy tales, unimaginable, "The marrow of our bones turned to light, and the veins of our blood to threads of fire, causing us to stop and think due to its incredible pain; a pain that never lessens; a pain kindled forever by the Lord's wrath" (p. 140). But this description of the terrors of hell is literary, abstract, and pales by the side of the real agony of Susana. To Padre Rentería, the Christian heaven and hell are mere formulae because his actions are based on quite a different code, one which is actually linked to the social stratification of the community in which he lives. The rewards and punishments he promised bear no relation to moral conduct but rather are dictated by the wealth and social status of the sinner. The kindly suicide, Eduviges, cannot be saved, and Pedro Páramo's wicked son, Miguel, can. Divine providence can thus be commuted into cash. Padre Rentería's rewards simply crown the inequalities of the social system and seek to prolong them into eternity.

After his death, Juan Preciado shares a grave with Dorotea, one of the inhabitants of Comala who has suffered the most frustration in her lifetime, since she has not even been able to bear a child. A vision she has of heaven (not of the earthly paradise) reveals the unsavory nature of this place, the dull uniformity of the angels among whom she cannot recognize her child. A saint shows her that she cannot have a child by taking a nutshell out of her stomach. "I wanted to tell them that it was only my stomach, all shriveled up from never having enough to eat, but one of those saints pushed me by the shoulder and took me to the door: 'Go back to earth and rest a little longer, my daughter, and try to be good so you won't stay so long in purgatory'" (pp. 75–76). Not only does heaven *not* compensate for the frustrations of earth but it is an alien place, and the vague precept—"procura ser buena" [try to be good] (p. 76)—will only earn a shorter purgatory and nothing more positive than this. Unfulfilled in this world, Dorotea can only find in the next the confirmation of its injustices, the poverty she has suffered being no passport for future happiness. There remains for such people only the private paradises which are projections of frustrations and these private paradises—Dolores Preciado's memory of her husband Florencio—are all in the past. The earthly paradise is over and done with, the heavenly paradise is unreal.

Meanwhile, actual human relationships invariably follow a pattern of exploitation and self-interest in which the weaker are crushed by the stronger. This cruelty and injustice are, however, mystified or glossed over because people still apply, to their own situation, the ideal codes of conduct which the heavenly paradise demands. An odd and isolated incident in the novel illustrates this. Two voices are heard in conversation—those of a man and a girl. The man asks the girl to run away with him, to which she replies that she must stay to look after her aged father. The man is too impatient to wait any longer and announces that if she will not run away with him he will transfer his affections to Juliana "que se desvive por mí" [who's dying for me] (p. 58). He makes one last attempt, however, to persuade her with the following words: "He'll find some old woman to take care of him. There's plenty of compassionate souls around here" (p. 58). This last phrase, "Aquí sobran almas caritativas" [There's plenty of compassionate souls around here], does not correspond to the reader's experience of Comala. It is sheer rhetoric. The girl has the choice of staying with the father, in which case she will not be fulfilled as a woman although she will have done her duty, or of escaping with a man who, in reality, offers her nothing except an opportunity to escape from the father. The choices are safety or risk and, in either case, the girl will probably suffer. Actual moral situations are of this kind, although their real nature is usually concealed by words which are tied to the dead social and moral order.

Pedro Páramo can be seen as a novel that reproduces not a coherent worldview but the actual fragmentation and breakdown of a social and moral order, the survival within a new social order of remnants of previous codes and the conflicts and confusions which arise from this mingling of the new and the old. The intense solitude of the character, so often mentioned by critics, the intense but isolated scenes which make up the novels are functional, related to the fragmentation of an order, the break-up of the tribe, and its replacement with an individualistic code. Instead of the universal vision of Catholicism, there are small private heavens and hells inhabited by people who can no longer make themselves heard. Characters are constantly calling without people hearing them, speaking without receiving any answer:

> "Pedro," they called after him, "Pedro."
> But he did not hear anymore. He was far off (p. 12).

Juan Preciado calls Damiana and finds himself "sólo en aquellas calles vacías" [alone in those empty streets] (p. 122), answered only by an echo. People are deafened by bell-ringing when Susana San Juan dies. Abundio feigns deafness, partly because speech appears useless to him: "He used to say it didn't make any sense to say things he didn't hear, things that sounded empty to him. It all started when one of those skyrockets we use around here to frighten away the watersnakes, exploded right next to his head. From that moment on, he stopped talking, even though he was not mute" (pp. 22–23). Although a physical explanation is given for Abundio's "dumbness," he is not really dumb. His silence is rather the fruit of a physical assault—the noise made to frighten away the watersnakes. There is perhaps a parallel here with speech and words that like the rockets ineffectually drive away fears. Abundio's reaction is to deny speech and so recognize its futility.

At the center of this total breakdown, there is, of course, Pedro Páramo himself. A feudal overlord, chieftain of the tribe, father of the village, and sole owner of the estates of Media Luna, he is, like the Christian moral order, an anachronism. The nature of feudal or tribal society is that men give service in exchange for protection. The chief has duties and obligations toward his kin and servants. But here again there is a dislocation between the ideal and reality. Villagers and employees give Pedro Páramo the obedience, respect, and devotion due to the feudal chief. They go to him in trouble, ask him for money. But just as the Christian heaven is no longer there as a reward or compensation for the good life, so the feudal chief has abdicated his obligations. Force and money are the basis of his power; the cash nexus determines all relationships—the marriage with Dolores, the seizure of Toribio's land and his murder, the buying off of the revolutionaries. Money is the great corrupting force that has subverted both the social and the moral order: "what would have been the cost for Don Pedro if these things had gotten all the way there, to the authorities? And what about the rapes? How many times did he have to take money out of his own pocket so that the women would keep quiet?" (p. 128). These are the words of Gerardo Trujillo, whose faithfulness to Pedro Páramo will never be rewarded because the new, money-dominated order has made personal obligations useless. As Marx has pointed out, money is the fetishistic element which introduces a new kind of relationship between man and society.[9] In *Pedro Páramo*, money dispenses the overlord from any personal confrontation, absolves him from the moral consequences of his actions. And because, as Blanco Aguinaga has pointed out, he is a "historical presence, pointing outward" who "dominates the world of Comala, in life and in the rumors of death. Everything is born from him, everybody lives (and dies) from him and under him."[10] The change of values that he introduces affects the lives of the inhabitants. But precisely because the "dead" moral code still persists, there is also a perpetual conflict between people's expectations and their fulfillment. Fulgencio, Gerardo Trujillo, Abundio, each in turn go to Pedro Páramo in expectation of reward or charity, and in each case it is refused. The social structure of feudalism *appears* to be preserved in *Pedro Páramo* but it has been demolished from within by money, which imposes a new kind of relationship, one based on value. Pedro Páramo no longer feels any obligation to pay Gerardo Trujillo when his services are no longer useful. But human suffering can never be dealt with wholly in this way. His overseer, Fulgencio, has already discovered that there is no price for grief: "I know how to measure grief, Don Pedro. And that woman carried it by the basketful. I offered her a fifty hectolitres of corn if she'd forget the affair, but she didn't want them" (pp. 80-81). The priest to whom Padre Rentería goes for confession recognizes that "Ese hombre de quien no quieres mencionar su nombre ha despedazado tu Iglesia y tú se lo has consentido" [That man whose name you won't utter has destroyed your Church, and you've let him do it] (p. 88). Pedro, the rock on which the church has been built, is the demonic force of destruction.

On her deathbed, Pedro Páramo's last wife and his childhood sweetheart, Susana San Juan, recalls the distant past when her father, Bartolomé, sent her down an excavation in search of gold.

> She had entered through a little hole among the slabs. She had walked across old rotten planks, all splintered, and covered with sticky earth:
> "Go lower, Susana, and you'll find what I told you."
> And she went down and went down swaying and rocking in the depths, with her feet searching for a hold (p. 111).

Susana's descent is another visit to the land of the dead, but a very different one from that of Juan Preciado. Her father, like Pedro Páramo, has abdicated his function as father, preferring gold to his daughter's safety. Susana swings in the darkness with no place to rest her feet until finally they touch a skeleton:

> The skeleton crumbled into fragments. The jawbone came loose as if it were made out of sugar. She passed on to him piece after piece until she reached the little bones of the toes, and she gave him joint after joint. And the skull first; and that round ball that fell to pieces in her hands.
> "Look for something else, Susana. Money. Round wheels of gold. Look for them, Susana" (p. 112).

In this journey to the land of the dead, Susana finds no ghosts, only the skull like a *memento mori* which comes to pieces as if it were a sugar skull. In the

Catholic moral order, the *memento mori* reminded men and women of the fact that they were beings for death and hence shocked them into a recognition of the true values of life—but in this new and desolate world, the skeleton cannot remind Bartolomé of his errors. All that he can see is the gold.

Miguel, Pedro, and San Juan are saints of the Catholic pantheon, transformed by Juan Rulfo into the demonic forces of a new order which has destroyed the old without substituting a new moral code. The sterile personal dreams which have replaced the universal, collective vision are translated into the sterile social and economic order. The lands are laid waste and the inhabitants abandon Comala.

The world of *Pedro Páramo* is not unlike that of Europe in the seventeenth century. The elements of feudal society were still noticeable in the social order, for the chief, the clan, and priest were still in positions of authority although their functions had been transformed. But in European society, there was a new element—the bourgeoisie—who was transforming society through work and enterprise and was anxious to move into positions of power. In contrast, the Mexican society of *Pedro Páramo* is a feudal and tribal structure onto which has been grafted a money economy which is connected with the existence of a bourgeoisie. This means that the work and effort at the core of the puritan ideology that characterized the nascent European bourgeoisie are absent from Comala. The fetish of bourgeois society exists (i.e., money) without the substance. That is why Comala is a land of ghosts, tormented by a moral order which is no longer applicable and which haunts the empty shells of communal life. Cut off from heaven, their private dreams are retrospective, reminiscences of communal plenty and fulfillment, but they are not dreams which are capable of transforming society. In consequence, they can only be changed in the direction of degradation, not of growth. At the end of the novel, Pedro Páramo is left staring at a road (the road of life) which goes through sterile fields: "La tierra en ruinas estaba frente a él, vacía" [The ruined fields were in front of him, empty]. "Vaciedad" [emptiness] is the impression which remains, emptiness the product of these lives.

Unlike Dante, Juan Preciado does not emerge alive from his visit to the land of the dead. He is stifled and not transformed. His three guides—Abundio, Dorotea, and Eduviges—have, through experience, come to take a more realistic attitude to life but are powerless to change it, unless we except Abundio's solitary gesture of killing a Pedro Páramo who is, in reality, already dead. Hence, like the roads that go through the roof of the broken house, the gestures of the novel point to emptiness.

Despite the difference in the cultural context that gave rise to them, the three novels dealing with the journey to the land of the dead have interesting similarities. In all three, natural relationships are broken up by urbanization or by the introduction of a money economy. In all three, the relation between the living and the dead has changed. In *The Palm-Wine Drinkard*, the domination of heaven over earth strikes fear in the hearts of men and replaces tribal wisdom; in *The System of Dante's Hell*, urban mobility has destroyed Dante's stable categories; in *Pedro Páramo*, the Christian heaven cannot coexist with the earthly paradise which fills men's imagination. All three novels place this earthly paradise in the past, in a period where man's relation to nature was direct. Original sin is the sin of separation from nature and, in two of the novels at least, it is money which operates as an agent of separation.

But money is only the symbol of an even graver breakdown. In these contemporary novels, the additional factor, and one which lay outside Quevedo's universe, is the factor of colonialism and slavery. It is that which introduces a money economy; that which changes social relations, breaking down family and tribal structures. Precisely because people cannot form new and meaningful relationships, precisely because of the mediation of money, they find themselves deprived of a future, cut off from utopia, and hence are haunted by memories of a more perfect past before the fall.

NOTES

1 E. Auerbach, "Farinata y Cavalcante," in *Mimesis* (Mexico: Fondo de Cultura Económica, 1950), pp. 166–92.

2 Alighieri Dante, *The Divine Comedy*, vol. 1, trans. Dorothy L. Sayers (London: Penguin, 1949) 87.

3 Francisco Gómez de Quevedo, *Los sueños*, vol. 1 (Madrid: Clásicos Castellanos, 1953), 93ff.

4 Page references are taken from the following editions: Amos Tutuola, *The Palm-Wine Drinkard* (New York: Grove Press, 1953); LeRoi Jones, *The System of Dante's Hell* (New York: Grove Press, 1965); and Juan Rulfo, *Pedro Páramo* 3rd ed. (Mexico: Fondo de Cultura Económica, 1961), English translation by Lysander Kemp (New York: Grove, 1959). In his *A History of Neo-African Literature* (London: Faber, 1968), Janheinz Jahn points out Tutuola's debt to Yoruba oral tradition and in particular to the work of Fagunwa.

5 Roman Jakobson, "On Russian Fairy Tales," in *Structuralism A Reader* (London: Cape, 1970), 184–201, declares "A fairy tale fulfills the role of a social Utopia. It is a dream about the conquest of nature—about a magic world where 'at the

pike's command, at my own request,' all the pails will go up the hill by themselves" and he notes the ease with which technical and social innovations are
incorporated into the story. In this respect, Tutuola's novel is close to fairy tale.

6 See, for instance Julio Ortega's "Pedro Páramo," in *La contemplación y la fiesta*
(Lima: Editorial Universitaria, 1968), 17–30. Other critical works include Luis
Harss, "Juan Rulfo o la pena sin nombre" in *Los nuestros*. (Buenos Aires: Edi-
torial Sudamericana, 1968), 301–37. The structure of the novel is discussed by
Margit Frank in "Pedro Páramo," an essay included in the anthology of criti-
cism, *Juan Rulfo* (La Habana: 1969), 84–96. See also J. Sommers, *After the Storm*
(Albuquerque: University of New Mexico Press, 1968), 69–94 and C. Blanco
Aguinaga, "Realidad y estilo de Juan Rulfo," in J. Lafforgue, *Nueva novela latino-
americana* (Buenos Aires: Editorial Paidós, 1969).

7 The emphasis in this article does not exclude a considerable use of Mexican
folklore, a use which has frequently been noted by critics. See, for instance,
Sommers, *After the Storm*.

8 Dante, *The Divine Comedy*, vol. 3, 346.

9 Karl Marx, "Money as a symbol of alienation in capitalist society," in *Marx's
Grundrisse* (London: 1971), 59–64.

10 Aguinaga, "Realidad y estilo de Juan Rulfo," 106.

DOMINANT IDEOLOGY AND LITERATURE

The Case of Post-Revolutionary Mexico

*I*n this essay I shall examine some of the formal aspects of texts that make the dominant ideology of post-revolutionary Mexico "visible." In order to focus the discussion, I will refer to texts written between 1915 and 1953—that is, during the period in which a foundation was laid for the development of dependent capitalism, and in which an ideology was formulated that offers a utopian vision for the people as well as legitimizes the State. This ideology is reproduced by the practices of daily life, by formal education, and by public institutions, and it creates the impression that Mexico is an autonomous nation in which the classes live in harmony. Nevertheless, as revealed by the concessions made by President Calles in the 1920s to the American and English oil interests (to cite only one example), Mexico functioned as just one more dependent country within the larger global capitalist framework.

When we talk about the dominant ideology in Mexico, therefore, we are talking first of all about the nationalist and populist ideology of the successive post-revolutionary governments, which included versions as different as those of presidents Calles, Cárdenas, and Ávila Camacho—versions that were, in reality, displaced images of the ideology of the metropolis. On the other hand, there existed a dependent relationship with the metropolis that had produced throughout all of Latin America an ideology of modernization—an ideology of progress (by exploiting mineral resources and using foreign capital to construct railroads) and, at the same time, tended to attribute the backwardness of Latin America to factors that concealed the dependent relationship. It seemed natural, for example, for the products of the metropolis to monopolize the marketplace, and the reason for this seemed to be their superior quality. It also seemed natural for countries

Originally published as "Ideología dominante y literatura: el caso de México posrevolucionario" in *Cultura y dependencia*, ed. Carlos Blanco et al. (Guadalajara: Departamento de Bellas Artes, Gobierno de Jalisco, 1976), 9–34. Translated by Patricia Heid.

dependent on the metropolis to be unable (because of the racial inferiority of their people, because of their inherent character, etc.) of producing more than raw materials. In general, this was the ideology of the groups most successfully integrated into the global system. It is evident that for the lower classes and marginal groups either repression or the influence of the church were intended to keep them docile.

The situation of intellectuals in this scenario is ambiguous. On one hand, because they were generally marginalized from power they criticized the repression of the people; on the other hand, in their reading, they were exposed to the ideology of the metropolis, expressed in the most subtle and refined forms. As in today's media, the printed book led to new forms of transnational perception and communication. At the end of the nineteenth century, Gutiérrez Nájera accurately described what this meant for the intellectual: "The writer travels, the writer is in close communication with ancient civilizations and with the entire modern world."[1] Thus, the intellectual felt that he existed on the most advanced cultural plane, and that he was the most active participant in a universal tradition. It is worth emphasizing, nevertheless, the profound difference between what this technology meant for the young European bourgeoisie of the seventeenth and eighteenth centuries, and what this same technology meant for a dependent economy such as Mexico's.

In Europe, printing helped to liberate the bourgeoisie from the authority and monopoly that limited the growth of knowledge within a feudal system. It stimulated the development of literature as a type of individual production contrasting with oral tradition, which had been oriented toward the preservation, ritualization, and adaptation of the collective patrimony. The oral tradition began to lose ground in the seventeenth century and eroded rapidly with the expansion of industrialized cities and the spread of universal public education in the nineteenth century. In contrast with the festive and communitarian spirit that characterized much oral culture, print literature implied a solitary creator who wrote for a solitary reader. Reading aloud, which frequently was practiced in the eighteenth and nineteenth centuries, was a type of transition between oral culture and the printed word read in private. The advantage of the printed book was that it permitted the accumulation of knowledge. Nevertheless, the universal diffusion of this knowledge, which made accumulation possible was, in reality, a double-edged sword. The bourgeoisie had fought and won the freedom of press as an absolute freedom, and therefore they could do no less than make its products available to all the social classes. In France and

England the general level of education in the middle of the nineteenth century made necessary new ideological instruments, such as the popular press, in order to counteract the formation of subversive ideologies.

It is important to understand the process by which the press was utilized not only as a weapon for liberation but also as a means of structuring information and systematizing knowledge. It is a common tendency for us to consider a certain technology as neutral or free when in reality it functions within a class system. In a liberal society, however, the power of manipulation is limited, although the level of communicative freedom notably diminishes and direct repression tends to increase as soon as we begin to focus on the lower social strata of the population. In peripheral countries, these "lower social strata" include the large majority of the population, and the freedom to read, to express oneself, and to criticize was, in reality, enjoyed by very few people (and perhaps by almost none in some dictatorships, such as that of Somoza in Nicaragua, for example). Alejo Carpentier's novel, *El recurso del método* [Reasons of State] precisely reveals that for a small group of the dependent elite, to enjoy the freedom and refinement of the metropolis meant paying for the privilege with the repression of their very own nation.

This is one of the differences between the press as an instrument of the European bourgeoisie and the press in peripheral countries, where it tended to create a gap between those who were considered "civilized," and those considered "barbaric," or, rather, between those who were assimilated and those who were marginalized. This difference helps us to explain why nineteenth-century Hispanic American intellectuals and writers, although marginalized, nevertheless rejected the oral culture with all its vitality, powers of adaptation, and inventiveness—because it differed too greatly from the culture of the metropolis. One of the paradigmatic works of that century, Domingo Faustino Sarmiento's *Facundo*, dismisses the "originality" of the gaucho's life by considering it to be primitive and backward and belonging to an age that was destined to disappear as it ceded to the superior advantages of the printed book. Sarmiento, of course, did not notice that the cost of the modernity disseminated in European and North American books would be neocolonialism. Sarmiento associated the concept of civilization with literacy and the concept of culture with the printed word to such a degree that it was disconcerting to discover that Facundo, "the tiger of the plain," had issued written documents. In his preface to the second edition of *Facundo*, Sarmiento emphasizes the fact that these documents do not affect his portrayal of the barbarian because they reveal an "incorrect language-use" and since "the incoherence of their ideas and the usage of words that either signify only what they are intended to express, or else show the confusion and embryonic state of the ideas, reveal in these proclamations the uncultivated soul, the arrogant instincts of the common man, and the candor of one who, inexperienced in letters and learning, does not even suspect that he lacks the capacity to express his ideas in writing."[2]

Although José Martí is an exception—he warns of the deforming influence of the imported book in "Nuestra América" [Our America]—the great majority of writers believed in the magical power of the printed word. Thus it is not surprising that so many generations regarded literacy as a panacea and the schoolteacher as a savior. There is no better example of this kind of idealization than the letter directed to the teachers of Peru written by Guillermo Mercado for the first issue of *Amauta* (1926), in which he declares that "the happiness of future generations will depend on their work of absolute love and pure reason." The idealized teacher inspired generations, beginning with the publication of Rodó's *Ariel* (1900), and culminating in Rómulo Gallegos's *Doña Bárbara*, whose protagonist, Santos Luzardo, civilizes his pupil and future wife by teaching her how to read. We could cite many other examples—the rural schoolteacher in Gabriela Mistral's poems, or the teacher in one of the first works by José María Arguedas, *Runa Yupay* (1939), who shows the indigenous peoples the importance of an organized census taken by the government. However, wider diffusion of Latin American authors was impeded not solely by a lack of infrastructure or weak efforts to promote books, not by a lack of talent, as writers like Machado de Assis demonstrate. Rather the Hispanic American author considered "modern" or "advanced" in his own country, was considered anachronistic or irrelevant in comparison to the metropolis.

Post-revolutionary Mexico promised to change this situation by bringing literacy to the masses. In the political arena the post-revolutionary governments were forced to take the rural and urban population into account. They discovered new means of ideological diffusion, such as the rural school, the labor unions, and the political party, which led them into a struggle with the church, which defended more traditional interests, and which came to a head in the War of the Cristeros. The Revolution had recast the traditional relationship between the advanced intellectual and the "backward" people because initially it was the people who had overthrown Porfirio Díaz and Huerta by using new methods of combat. Thus the muralist movement emerged as one response to the problems of how to address the people. The poets, who perhaps could have followed the same strategy as the Spanish Civil War poets—that is, approaching the people through popular poetry and public readings—opted for another alternative: they valued individual expression as the greatest human activity, and they pursued a subjectivity that, dispensing with all regional references, could be assimilated to a universal culture.

The need to take the people into account had a more direct resonance in the essay and narrative than in poetry. The problem inherent in the essay is that of reconciling this new element in national life with the universal humanism of the metropolis. The cosmic race of José Vasconcelos and the theories of "mestizaje" had this totalizing function. We must emphasize that the essay, as civilized discourse *par excellence*, implies both a nonspecialized point of view and a humanist educational background, which permits the author to judge his generation from the more purified heights of high culture. There is no better example of this than the essays of Alfonso Reyes. In these, the humanist tradition based on the classics and on Hispanic culture represents an abstract ethical ideal that is associated, although not explicitly, with a political and economic ideal—that is, the ownership of a small piece of property as the "Utopia of philosophers," "the dream of all free men."

In the "Discurso por Virgilio" [Homage to Virgil] (1931), Alfonso Reyes represents the classical man as the highest expression of humanity. He declares that "the Latin world returns man to his place in the tranquil harmony of nature, and restores the rational will to its ancient throne within the over-excited heart of man." [3] We also discover that this ideal is not only a moral one but is based as well on an economic order—Reyes considers Virgil the poet "of the common workers, of the humble rural landowners, of the small parcel of land which his father owned and on which he had watched him labor when he was a boy" (p. 175). This allows Reyes to draw a parallel with President Calles, who was himself a cultivator of grapes and a defender of private property.

In Europe, classical culture was used in this same way to legitimize groups in power. Napoleon was named consul; the first iron piers constructed by industrialists in Liverpool in the nineteenth century had a "classical" style. The future imperial bureaucracy of Great Britain was taught the works of Caesar and Cicero in order to better govern the colonials. The classical humanist ideal had never included the common people. On the contrary, it opened a cultural gap between social classes.

Perhaps this explains the contradictions we find in Reyes's essay. First, he favors the study of Latin in post-revolutionary Mexico, declaring, "I want those on the left to learn Latin, since there is no sense in them losing what they have already accomplished. And I see the Humanities as the natural vehicle for autochthonous culture" (p. 160–161). Then he concedes that he does not intend Latin for those people who need only "the plow, basic literacy and soap" (p. 162), since this would be to ignore completely "the natural hierarchy of studies, which is a necessary feature of national education, and the flexibility required of any system to be applied to a heterogeneous population; indeed, this would be to grossly ignore the changes that only time can produce on the cultural level of a country which is following a sensible educational policy" (p. 162).

According to this viewpoint the common people, as a natural resource, will be assimilated by the superior culture, whose power of abstraction (and of universalization) is much greater. "The autochthonous culture," he asserts, is "an enormous reserve of raw material, of objects, shapes, colors and sounds, which need to be incorporated and dissolved in the fluidity of the broader culture, to which it lends its condiment of mixed, tasty spices" (p. 161). Elsewhere, he compares the autochthonous culture with "red clay" (p. 161), destined to be washed in Latin waters, which implies that the energy comes from Western culture and the raw material from the people. Reyes does not see popular culture as dynamic enough to produce more than "delightful ornaments for culture to pin on its chest" (p. 170). It is clear that in this conceptual scheme, the people are not producers of culture, since this is a role that can only be assumed by the metropolis.

And what about the Latin American intellectual? His only alternative is to take the role of consumer or mediator between the metropolis and the "native." It is not surprising that in Reyes a whole series of metaphors derives from food because he belonged to a generation brought up on Plato's *Symposium*—and also a generation that delighted in opulent banquets. Using the metaphor of the banquet Reyes can dismiss the backwardness of Mexico as something accidental. The Latin American at the banquet has the role of the guest, who contributes good conversation to a social function prepared and hosted by others. "The Latin American people," he says, "have arrived at the banquet just as the meal is being served—and this allows us to arrive in a better mood and better rested" (p. 174). We should not forget that at this banquet, the autochthonous culture is only a condiment that makes food more easily digested.

The "Discurso por Virgilio" demonstrates, perhaps only too explicitly, that humanism based on the classical model ends up reproducing the hierarchy of values associated with social class and consecrated by the metropolis, while at the same time reducing the autochthonous culture to a passive state. In *Perfil del hombre y de la cultura de México* [Profile of the Man and Culture of Mexico] (1934) by Samuel Ramos, this passive element is associated with the Indian. Once Mexico has overcome its inferiority complex, which, for Ramos, explains its backwardness, it must "transcend" the Indian as a precondition for its economic development.

In the work of Ramos and later in that of Leopoldo Zea, humanism has not only a totalizing function but also serves as a means of defense against technology. Ramos mentions "establishing humanism in education in order to counteract the effects of a deceptive civilization that secretly possesses, like a modern-day Circe, the magical potential for changing men into the machines they admire, the machines that seduce men with their beauty." In *El Occidente y la conciencia de México* [The Western World and the Consciousness of Mexico], Leopoldo Zea seems to believe that the Mexicans could somehow "humanize" technology. It is clear, however, that because it was outside the reigning pragmatism liberal humanism had already been limited in its scope by the technocrats of the metropolis, though it survives into the 40s and 50s. In this situation the essayists, who had no other skill beyond general culture, were anachronistic voices, irrelevant beings like those we find parodied by Carlos Fuentes in *La región más transparente* [Where the Air Is Clear].

In contrast to the essay, which attempts to dissolve the condition of "backwardness" in abstract humanism, the revolutionary novel had to be based on history; it represented characters and events that could be judged and appreciated by readers on the basis of their referentiality. Mariano Azuela's *Los de abajo* [The Underdogs] is paradigmatic in this respect, because the novel seems to be modeled, albeit in a condensed form, in the historical process of the Revolution—it follows the uprising from the isolated outbreaks of individual rebellion through the crucial battle of Zacatecas in which the united revolutionary forces fought together, and describes the struggle between the followers of Carranza and those of Villa, with the eventual defeat of the latter. What makes the events seem "realistic" is the historical background as well as the social division of characters between those who are naïve and spontaneous (and come from a rural environment) and those who are corrupt and opportunistic (and come from an urban environment). In spite of this historical-social structuring, Azuela has another reference point, which contradicts the first one: he uses nature as a way to represent the forces that underlie the historical events and ultimately determine the failure of the struggle. Beneath its appearance of historicity Azuela's design is based, in reality, on a naturalistic vision.

The Revolution as a natural force becomes a commonplace of many narratives written during the time President Calles was in power. In many of these narratives, historical events act as signifiers in a mythical system, the essence of which can be summarized in Azuela's own words: "A country without a leader, a country of tyrants." This accounts for the episodes of violence that occur in many of these novels. In Martín Luis Guzmán's *El águila y la serpiente* [The Eagle and the Serpent], the narrator (Guzmán himself) serves as a screen onto which the author paints episodes rich in visual detail, as if this screen/consciousness could only register events *from which he was far removed*. One episode is especially significant in this respect—a crazy military officer, under the cloak of night and the revolution, commits a series of senseless murders. Thus Guzmán shows that war makes visible the "other world" normally hidden from view to the "civilized" man. It should not surprise us that this other world relies more on the sense of touch for communication than on words. The first time Guzmán meets with Pancho Villa, he sits down on the leader's bed and describes how "the warmth of the bedding penetrated his clothes down to his skin."[4] Later, while reflecting on the meeting, he refers to the sense of touch to describe his reaction to the hot-tempered Pancho Villa, "whom we touched all over with our caressing hands, fearing that otherwise he would break our necks" (p. 229).

This "other world" produces in the "civilized" man a fear of drowning in the masses. Guzmán clearly expresses this in many parts of the novel. On one night, for example, he finds himself dragged along by a revolutionary crowd to a secret night meeting:

> Paddling in the mud, lost in the shadows of the night and consciousness these men seemed to renounce their humanity as soon as they got together. They were like the soul of a monstrous reptile, with hundreds of heads and thousands of feet, dragging themselves along, in an alcoholic stupor, between the walls of a dark street in a city left deserted by its inhabitants. (p. 219)

For Guzmán the masses represent backwardness, a loss of identity rather than a new state of consciousness. Not surprisingly much of *El águila y la serpiente* takes place at night in an atmosphere of irrationality. A train trip at night turns into a mad race, during which the narrator asks, "What was I doing there?" (p. 305). The same question is asked implicitly throughout Mariano Azuela's *Los de abajo* by the intellectual Solís, who watches the battle of Zacatecas from a point above it. What was Solís doing there observing and not acting, marginalized and not participating? In order to justify his actions, he had to interpret events not as part of a historical process that would lead to revolutionary change but rather as an irrational and inexplicable aberration of normality. This is clearly revealed in the structure of *El águila y la serpiente*. There is one moment in this narrative that is especially significant because it constitutes a break in the narrative style itself. This moment occurs in "La fiesta de las balas [The Shooting Party]," where Guzmán describes how Rodolfo Fierro, Villa's lieutenant, personally kills in cold blood three hundred followers of Huerta, who had been taken prisoner. The way in which Guzmán presents this episode is important because of its mode of representation:

> Keeping in mind all that was said about Villa and his political program, as well as everything I saw around me, I would often ask myself when in Ciudad Juárez which heroic deeds were most representative of the Northern Division: those strictly considered historical, or those considered legendary: those considered to be witnessed within the strictest reality, or those which, with the help of poetic adornment, gave us the essential facts. And it was always this latter type of heroic deed that seemed most truthful to me, which, in my opinion, seemed most worthy of making History. (pp. 323-324)

The episode following this passage not only represents Fierro as the mirror of Pancho Villa's political agenda but is also the only episode of the book that is not told in the first person but rather is narrated in the third person. This is not simply a small detail that holds interest only for literary critics. It means that in this episode Guzmán crosses the barrier that once separated him from the other world: he is no longer a detached observer. Not only does he describe Fierro's horse and clothing in great detail, he also interprets his feelings. "Fierro feels happy . . ." (p. 324), "his inner happiness revealed itself in physical sensations that made him welcome the whipping of the wind and the horse's gallop. . . ." (pp. 324-325). Guzmán delves into the most intimate thoughts of Fierro, who was looking at the prisoners "of the fine race of Chihuahua" (p. 325), "when he felt a strange sensation, a shiver that went from his heart, or maybe from his forehead, toward the index finger of his right hand. Without consciously deciding it or even feeling it, he rested the palm of his hand on the revolver handle. 'This is a strange kind of battle,' he thought" (p. 325).

The entire episode of the massacre is narrated in this way: Fierro goes on shooting until the last prisoner is killed and finally lies down to sleep in the very same bloody corral—which does not prevent Guzmán from ending the chapter with a cosmic vision: "The moon seemed to sail upon the limitless waters of its own blue light. Beneath the covering of the stable, Fierro slept" (p. 332). It is clear that the author, in order to increase the drama of the scene, uses a technique that eliminates distance. This lack of critical distance, combined with the way he presents the episode as "worthy of making History" and Fierro as a mirror of Villa, indicates the key significance of the narrative. It is clear that for Guzmán the Revolution did not mean a change in social structure but rather a concept of violence as a heroic deed. Given this perspective it is understandable why the author considers this massacre of prisoners a representative occurrence and why he interprets Fierro's decision personally to assassinate them as a result of his desire for greatness. I do not need to emphasize the Nietzschean antecedents here (or, at least, the distortion of Nietzsche), nor the fact that this vision of the Superman contrasts with the failure of Villa's political agenda, which is made clear at the end of the book.

In *Mythologies* Roland Barthes demonstrates that modern myths are formed by abstracting certain signs from their context and making them into signifiers within a new system of signs. In Guzmán the abstraction of violence from any context that could serve to explain it obscures an important relationship between violence and the human exploitation that gave rise to it. Guzmán mythifies Villa and Fierro by presenting their "extravagant" sides in the same tone as that used by the old epic poets. The anachronism then underscores the inevitable failure of Villa and Fierro in the modern world.

The admiration for the barbarous/heroic side of the Revolution was not shared by most of the intelligentsia. One year before the publication of *El águila y la serpiente*, upon getting word of the assassination of General Serrano and his followers (which is the theme of Guzmán's novel *La sombra del caudillo* [The Caudillo's Shadow]) Gómez Marín writes from London: "From here, Mexico is something dark and bloody." And he continues: "Today all of London knows what happened in Mexico, and in the hotel and out on the street, we are aware that everyone knows we are Mexicans, and they look at us with horror and disgust."[5] Gómez Marín does not mention that in this same year the Europeans were also conducting themselves in a barbarous manner in Morocco, because for him, as for the Europeans, barbarism was an attribute of marginalized peoples. Guzmán, by contrast, had tried to delve into this other world, but with ambiguous results as we have already noted.

To encounter a new perspective on this kind of "irrational" barbarism, we have to wait for a new generation of writers—that of Juan Rulfo and José Revueltas. In *El llano en llamas* [The Burning Plain] (published in 1953) by Rulfo, and *El luto humano* [Human Mourning] (1943) by Revueltas, this change of perspective results in part from a new historical configuration, that of the Cristero war. Moreover, in both cases it is possible to speak of a *literary praxis* that no longer duplicates the values of the metropolis but rather inverts them.

In Rulfo's story *El llano en llamas* there is one episode that seems to imitate "La fiesta de las balas" and is worthy of notice. It involves a scene in which the caudillo, Pedro Zamora, stages a bullfight (in which he participates as the bull) with some imprisoned soldiers, and kills all of them with the razors that he wears as horns. What makes this episode especially unique is the euphemistic language adopted by the narrator. For example, a corporal who had been mortally wounded "didn't seem to realize what had happened, because he kept on waving the blanket up and down for a was scaring off wasps."[6] It is this last phrase, "as if he was scaring off wasps," that lends the action a kind of naturalness, such that it almost seems domestic. And because there is such a wide gap between the words and the event they represent, our attention remains fixed on the narrator, for whom words serve to disguise the horror of what he himself is writing. This gap between words and action foregrounds the process of "naturalization," which is the way in which ideology also functions. The protagonist of *El llano en llamas* is not aware of the reason for his actions nor their purpose. As in Guzmán's narrative, violence *is* the Revolution, but in contrast to Guzmán Rulfo does not simply mythologize but rather shows how language can make us accept and even approve of the most inhuman occurrences. Another example, taken from the story "La Cuesta de las Comadres" [The Hill of the Comadres], demonstrates in an even more exaggerated fashion how language serves as a means of self-justification. The narrator kills the bully, Remigio, with a large needle:

> Then I saw him looking sad, as if he was beginning to feel sick. It'd been a long time since I'd seen such a sad look and I felt sorry for him.

>That's why I pulled out the needle from his belly and stuck it higher
>up, where I thought his heart must be. And, yes, that's where it was,
>because he just gave two or three jerks like a chicken with its head
>chopped off and then he was still. (p. 27)

The familiar comparison, "like a chicken with its head chopped off," and
the use of the diminutive "a little higher up" [más arribita] gives an intimate and tender tone to the description, which allows the author to describe the process of finishing off the victim as if it were an act of charity.
Also worth noticing is the use of the causal conjunction "because" that
seemingly *explains* the murder and, therefore, makes it seem like a *reasonable* action.

Especially notable is the contrast with Guzmán, who represents the
massacre as a heroic deed by utilizing the third-person narrative voice to
give it dramatic relief and presents the actors as belonging to another
world, from which the intellectual remains separated (because fundamentally he is superior to that world). Rulfo, on the contrary, does not represent his narrators in this way. As his novel *Pedro Páramo* clearly reveals,
the priest and the people, the men and the women, the landowners and the
peasants are all in the same situation; the gap between words and actions
does not result from a personal decision or a certain existential configuration, but rather from the disruption of an order. In *Pedro Páramo*, this
disruption is the consequence of money that has transformed the ethical
relationship between people into a relationship mediated by this abstraction. Here I am most concerned with emphasizing the difference between
a structure that reproduces the ideology of the metropolis and that which
opens a space for criticism of it.

In *El luto humano* by José Revueltas, we find a very different kind of
disruption in the order. In contrast to Alfonso Reyes's humanism, which
requires an adjustment upward before it can incorporate the masses in
the humanist scheme, Revueltas views the problem of the human situation
from a borderline perspective. Liberal humanism had been based on an
abstract idea of the person. By contrast, Revueltas's characters are "nailed
to" or "anchored to" the earth, or "enchained" by the corpse of a child
whose wake they are attending. Writing in the 1940s after many years
of leftist militancy, Revueltas was opposed to both liberal and socialist
humanism—neither of which seemed to explain adequately the violence of
the Revolution or the continued violence of the rural areas. Set in a period
just following the defeat of the Cristeros[7] and the festering resentment of

the defeated, Revueltas seems unable to free himself completely from the notion of primordial or natural violence which was apparent in both *Los de abajo* and *El águila y la serpiente*. The novel focuses on a group of workers involved in a dam construction project on a river in a rural area. The dam project fails, the river is in flood, and the group is resigned to the inevitability of their death in the floodwaters. The river comes to represent continuity, the force of nature, the anonymity of death, and the violence of the past for the Cristero war is also described as a river—a dirty, blind river.

Thus Revueltas, like Azuela, seems to dissolve the problem of ideology by resorting to the primordial force of nature—but this does not prove to be exactly the case. *El luto humano* is a flawed work that cannot maintain the allegory around which it is constructed, but its failure is not without interest. For what defeats the community project is not class struggle but rather the divisions among the underdogs in whom religious belief, hope of salvation and redemption, and ancestral feelings of possession and revenge come into conflict with the secular belief in the possibility of a just society.

In *El luto humano* the only character to represent the new man, the appropriately named Natividad, is killed before the action of the novel and survives only as an idealized figure. Revueltas himself had experienced during his own lifetime the crushing of the left, the outlawing of the Communist party, and the assassination of rural leaders. By 1943, the hope of a socialist Mexico was fast receding as President Ávila Camacho pursued a policy of developmentalism. But Revueltas represents this defeat not as a historical defeat but as a mythic event related not simply through the narrative but in essay-like interventions in which the author pronounces on the national problem:

> As long as the tragic symbol of the serpent and the eagle, the tragic symbol of venom and rapacity, persisted, there would be no hope. This most atrocious symbol had been chosen to represent so perfectly and so pathetically this absurd nation, where the prickly pear with its bloody flowers was loyal and sad, its arms extended out over the water, a strange cross, timid, Indian and resigned.[9]

Revueltas inexplicably displaces the political battle onto this mythical ground in which the symbol of the eagle and the serpent represents deeply rooted evil in the human soul. There is a contradiction between the socialist realist aspects of the novel—the assassination of the rural leader—and this metaphysical level.

How can we account for this? In both Rulfo and Revueltas the narrative of progress is undermined by *ressentiment*. At the time they were writing, this "pessimism" seemed out of tune, quite contrary to the general optimism and the belief in progress. With hindsight, it is perhaps easier to see that they were grappling with a more intractable problem.

In this essay I have attempted to explore some of the representations of revolutionary violence. The process of mythologizing begins with Azuela who subordinates history to nature. In Guzmán's novelized memoirs the author immerses himself in the events only at the moment of supremely irrational violence, a moment when he enters into, and vicariously lives, the slaughter of the prisoners. In Rulfo and Revueltas the narratives are more complex and violence seems to become all the more atrocious because it stems from the *ressentiment* of centuries of defeat. Rulfo handles this by depicting characters whose language conceals the horror of their actions. Revueltas is forced to supplement his narrative in order to explain. Nevertheless, their preoccupation with "inexplicable" violence, far from being anachronistic, acquires ever greater resonance toward the fin de siècle.

NOTES

All notes herewith were created for the English version of this essay.

1   Manuel Gutiérrez Nájera, *Obras*, vol. 1 (Mexico: Centro de Estudios Literarios, Universidad Nacional Autónoma de México, 1959), 84–86.

2   Domingo Faustino Sarmiento, *El Facundo*, Preface to 2nd edition, 1851.

3   Alfonso Reyes, "Discurso por Virgilio," in *Obras completas*, vol. 11 (México, Fondo de Cultura Económica, 1955), 163 (page numbers for subsequent quotes appear in parentheses in the text).

4   Martín Luis Guzmán, "El águila y la serpiente," in *Obras completas*, vol. 1 (Mexico City: Fondo de Cultura Económica, 1992), 228 (page numbers for subsequent quotes appear in parentheses in the text).

5   Quoted in Enrique Krauze, *Los caudillos culturales en la Revolución Mexicana* (Mexico City: Siglo Veintiuno Editores, 1976).

6   Juan Rulfo, *The Burning Plain and Other Stories*, trans. George D. Schade (Austin: University of Texas Press, 1973), 90.

7   The Mexican church outlawed Catholic rites during the twenties, which led to a Catholic rebellion especially in Jalisco and Tabasco.

8   José Revueltas, *Human Mourning* trans. Roberto Crespi (Minneapolis: University of Minnesota Press, 1990), 32.

WOMEN, FASHION, AND THE MORALISTS IN
EARLY-NINETEENTH-CENTURY MEXICO

The denunciations of fashion and luxury common in French eighteenth-century writing often associated these with women's change-
able character, their superficiality. Similar diatribes began to appear in
Diario de México in early-nineteenth-century Mexico despite the fact that
the periodical press catered to some extent to the thirst for novelty.[1] But
though the press and *Diario de México*, in particular, responded to a world
newly opened up by commerce, many of its correspondents were deeply
disturbed by what they perceived as the dangerous seduction of consumer
culture. The tunic or Empire style which had replaced the more cum-
bersome clothes of the eighteenth century caused special alarm and was
described by one writer as a "horroroso trastorno de lo más natural" [hor-
rifying upheaval of what is most natural] for which he blamed the luxury
and corruption of the times:

> Aquella dama del túnico estrecho semejante a una mortaja, de los bra-
> zos enormes, largos, rollizos y desnudos, diáfana como cristal, y a quien
> V vio tal cual puede verla su marido mismo, esa Señora, cuyo pecho
> está tan a la vista como su mismo rostro, a nadie quiere, de nadie se
> acuerda, y sólo piensa en cierto túnico de mil pesos, que ayer se le ha
> presentado de venta. Comprarlo es lo que desea, y sólo amaría la talega
> de pesos que le satisficiese su voluntad.

> [That woman in the tight tunic looks like someone in a funeral shroud,
> with her big arms, big, round, and naked, diaphanous like cristal, and
> anyone in the world can see her like that, even her husband, that
> woman, whose chest is on display just as much as her face, does not
> love anyone, does not think of anyone; she only thinks of that thou-

Originally published in *Homenaje a Ana María Barrenechea*, eds. Lia Schwartz Lerner and Isaías
Lerner (Madrid: Castalia, 1984), 421–30.

sand peso tunic, which was offered for sale yesterday. She wants to buy it, and she will only love the sack of pesos that can satisfy her wishes.] [2]

Fashion, immorality, the cash nexus have now become Trojan horses within society and the "espíritu de superficialidad e indiferencia" [spirit of superficiality and indifference] common among women make them ready allies in the subversion of social stability. Under these circumstances, it is hardly surprising that one contributor to *Diario de México* suggested putting women into uniform according to their social class, a suggestion that clearly indicates that the differentiation between the dress of the upper class, the *gente decente* [decent people] and the underclasses no longer operated. The writer was, however, more concerned with women spending excessive amounts on clothes which was clearly against nature since women had fewer needs than men.[3]

Fashion as a symptom of modernity thus began to appear in the staid world of colonial Mexico and, with modernization, came the danger that the relative standard of taste might nudge out the stable values of Christian asceticism symbolized by the nun's habit. It is, indeed, interesting to remind ourselves that the feminine *la moda* was a comparatively recent loan word from the French, unlike the older *modo* (manner, originally *measure* and *moderation* or *limit*). However, it was not until the beginning of the nineteenth century in Mexico that fashion or *la moda* came to be seen as a social problem which affected values in general. Fernández de Lizardi, always quick to comment on changes of manners, called one of his journals *La alacena de frioleras* [The Closet of Baubles], compared his articles to different types of imported cloth, and even held sales of his ideas, thus commodifying literature and appealing to a public of buyers.[4]

Yet it was also in response to the relative values of taste that Fernández de Lizardi offered his treatise on the education of women, *La educación de las mujeres o la Quijotita y su prima* [the Education of Women or the Little Quijote and her Cousin] since a new kind of society made a new kind of secular education necessary.[5] Lizardi's "historia muy cierta con apariencias de novela" [true story which resembles a novel] was a blueprint for a secularized family, one in which children would be socialized by discipline and work, in which women were to find their one true career, and in which individual happiness could be achieved. Much of his material, as he acknowledged, came from seventeenth- and eighteenth-century treatises on the education of women, most of them first published in France where the emergence of the bourgeois family had drawn attention to the importance of early childhood and hence to the role of the mother. This literature, though commonly associated with Rousseau was not initiated by him. His *Émile* popularized many ideas—breast-feeding children, their physical education, the education of girls for their roles as mothers—which were already familiar topics. The literature goes back to Fénélon's *Traité de l'éducation des filles* (1687) which, though written in the seventeenth century, was still used as a manual in nineteenth-century France and was popular in Mexico in the early nineteenth century. Rousseau was, however, a more interesting writer which explains why *Émile* has become more familiar than the works of the Abbé Blanchard, Mme. de Lambert, Antoine Léonard Thomas, and Holbach, who had similarly argued that because women were physically weaker than men, their main contribution to social life must be the upbringing of children for which they had to be carefully educated.[6] All these writers (including Rousseau in the chapters of *Émile* devoted to women's education) belonged to a tradition of conservative thought that used the argument of women's physical weakness to subordinate them to the more active male and to circumscribe their lives in a way that was quite contrary to the more egalitarian and radical thinking of *philosophes* such as Diderot, Laclos, and Helvetius.[7] It is the former rather than the latter who influenced Lizardi's writing.

Thus it is not at all in a radical spirit that Lizardi undertook to write on the education of women though it must be stressed that *La Quijotita* [The Little Quijote] is intended partly as a satire on particular female defects, partly as the blueprint of an ideal family. Lizardi had given a foretaste of his utopian view of matrimony in the Arcadian marriage scene that marks the entry of his *pícaro* [rogue], Periquillo, into the world of respectability. The exemplary family described in *La Quijotita* is, if anything, even more utopian when compared with actual social practices in early-nineteenth-century Mexico. As Silvia Arrom (working on data from the 1811 census) has pointed out, a great many women lived outside the family structure at this time—nuns, domestic servants, and other unmarried working women as well as widows who were often heads of households and solely responsible for the upkeep of their children. Married women living with their husbands and children were thus not in the majority at the time when Lizardi was writing his novel.[8]

Lizardi's project was, however, twofold—to prepare women for their role in a new kind of family which was to become the secular agent for the reproduction of social values and at the same time to satirize the "madness" of women who tried to emancipate themselves from male authority.

His aim was to provide a model for the future rather than to reflect the present. The novel was, however, not a particularly suitable genre for such doctrinaire substance. However, it was probably because novels were commonly thought to be a female genre that Lizardi chose it over the more overtly didactic genres such as the dialogue and the homily. Thus he purportedly wrote *La Quijotita* in response to a letter from one of the women readers of *El Periquillo* [The Itching Parrot] who signs herself La Curiosa and asks for a novel that would avoid the heavy sermonizing of erudite tracts "porque las niñas, que algún día han de ser madres, por lo común no son aficionadas a esta clase de lecturas serias, que *parece no hablan con ellas*" [because girls, who will be mothers someday, usually are not fans of this type of serious reading, which doesn't seem to speak to them] (p. 8; italics mine). Whether this letter was real or invented by Lizardi himself is immaterial; in either case, he shows his sensitivity, at least in theory (and as he had done in *The Itching Parrot*) to a new class of reader whose culture did not run very deep. In practice, he was unable to produce a pleasurable text, however, because he assumed his readers lacked discrimination and judgment, nor could he liberate his novel from the influence of the rational genres such as the sermon, homily, and dialogue. That Lizardi himself was not completely happy with the novel form seems to be indicated by the fact that he described *La Quijotita* as a "historia muy cierta con apariencias de novela" [true story which resembles a novel], stressing that its characters were real people and known to La Curiosa. He attempted to reinforce this appearance of reporting a true history by introducing a first-person narrator who, like a fly on the wall, was able to overhear women's gossip which he reported back, as if he were a spy, to the paternalistic father of the text, Don Rodrigo.

Despite such obvious defects, *La Quijotita* is not without interest as long as we treat it primarily as the exposition of a new paternalism promoted from an advanced liberal position. This new paternalism which I have described elsewhere,[9] involved converting the family into a relatively autonomous unit which could, of itself, reproduce the values necessary for a stable society. Paternalism was no longer to be invested in the Viceroy or head of state but was internalized in every citizen.

The French *philosophes* had also made a distinction between the absolute power of the old order and this new paternal power defined as a "droit de superiorité et de correction" [right of superiority and correction] yet considered as a duty rather than a right.[10]

In *La Quijotita*, Lizardi would contrast the harmony and order of this new paternalism with the disorder of a "Dionysian" family given over to pleasure and dominated by women. The names of these two contrasting families indicate the functional nature of each member who, rather than characters, appear as the theses and antitheses of a dialogue. The good family is headed by a retired colonel with the good *castizo* [blueblood] name of Don Rodrigo; his wife has the plain unpretentious name, Matilde. Pudenciana epitomizes the modesty and reserve proper to the daughter's role. The family of Matilde's sister is quite the reverse. The father, Don Dionisio is, of course, lackadaisical, unable to manage his affairs and given over to pleasure. His wife is Eufrosina whose name symbolizes pagan frivolity,[11] and his daughter Pomposa (the Quijotita of the title) is all vanity and froth, pomp and bubble.

What is striking is that in this liberal tract, the ideal of domestic life has become, if anything, more circumscribed than that described by Fray Luis de León in *La perfecta casada* [The Perfect Wife]. Fray Luis de León had conceived of the family as the center of artisan activity, with the good wife supervising what was virtually a small factory:

> Y verá que, estándose sentada con sus mujeres, volteando el huso en la mano, y contado consejas (como la nave, que, sin parecer que se muda, va navegando y pasando un dia y sucediendo otro, y viniendo las noches y amaneciendo las mañanas, y corriendo, como sin menearse, la obra), se teje la tela y se labra el paño y se acaban las ricas labores; y, cuando menos pensamos, llenas las velas de prosperidad, entra esta nuestra nave en el puerto, y comienza desplegar sus riquezas, y sale de allí el abrigo para los criados, y el vestido para los hijos, y las galas suyas y los arreos para su marido, y las camas ricamente labradas, y los atavíos para las paredes y salas, y los labrados hermosos, y el abastecimiento de todas las alhajas de casa, que es un tesoro sin suelo.

> [And you will see her, seated with her women, whirling the spindle in her hand, and telling stories (like the ship, that, without appearing to move, steers its course and one day follows the next, and night falls, and morning dawns, and the work flows smoothly, as if it did not move at all), the cloth is woven, and the material is embroidered and the rich labors are finished; and, when we least expect it, the sails fill with prosperity, our ship enters the port, and begins to display its treasures, and from it comes the coats for the servants, the clothing for the children, and finery for her and trappings for him, and the richly embroidered beds, and the finery for the walls and the rooms, and the beautiful

carvings, and the provision of all of the furniture of the house, which is a treasure without comparison.] [12]

The perfect wife is able to justify her lesser estate (inferior to that of the religious orders) by this busy productivity. In contrast, in *La Quijotita*, Matilde no longer has any role in productive labor; she is first and foremost a mother who once her child enters school occupies herself in religious devotions, in the religious instruction of her child and her maids and in making her husband's life comfortable.

> Acabada la comida reposamos un rato hasta las tres o poco más; él suele irse y yo me pongo en el estrado rodeada de mi familia, o con el bastidor y con la almohadilla hasta las cuatro y media que van por mi hija; luego que ésta viene rezamos el rosario y les leo algo del catecismo a mi hija, a Tulitas y a las mozas, pues, porque ya sabes es obligación precisa de los amos el enseñar la doctrina a sus criados. En esto dan las oraciones, se van a sus quehaceres, las niñas a jugar y yo a guardar mi ropa. A esta hora viene Linarte, tomamos chocolate y unas veces nos ponemos a platicar, otras a tocar mi clave, o me voy a tu casa y alguna vez al coliseo (pp. 103–4).

> [When the meal is finished we rest a little while until three or a bit later; he tends to go out and I retire to the drawing room, surrounded by my family, or with my embroidery frame and sewing cushion until half past four when the servants go to pick my daughter up from school; after she has arrived we pray the rosary and I read something from the catechism to my daughter, and Tulitas and the maids, because, as you already know, it is the specific obligation of the masters to teach doctrine to their servants. We pray together, then they go back to their chores, the girls play, and I arrange my clothing. At this time Linarte arrives, we drink hot chocolate and sometimes we chat, other times I play the piano, or I go to your house and sometimes to the coliseum.]

The good wife passes most of her days indoors; in one of his lengthy homilies, Don Rodrigo Linarte (who, it is worth stressing, is a retired colonel although he spends much of his day outdoors on unspecified business) justifies the restriction of women to these domestic tasks on the grounds of their physical weakness. For this reason, women cannot participate in more active male pursuits. A woman with a child in her arms could scarcely be expected to carry a gun nor could she wield a chisel or pen or push a plough. Woman's subjection is thus due entirely to her physical condition:

> La inferioridad de la mujer respecto al hombre . . . no consiste en otra cosa que en la debilidad de su constitución física, es decir, en cuanto al cuerpo; pero en cuanto al espíritu, en nada son inferiores a los hombres, pues no siendo el alma hombre ni mujer, se sigue que en la porción espiritual sois en todo iguales a nosotros (pp. 72–73).

> [The inferiority of women with respect to men . . . doesn't consist of anything other than the weakness in their physical constitution, in other words, in terms of the female body; but in terms of the spirit they are in no way inferior to men, because the soul is neither masculine or feminine, it follows that in the spiritual realm, you are in all ways equal to us.]

However, this supposed equality is neutralized since in women, the body influences the spirit. In adolescence, they are prone to "furor uterino, el cual es un delirio o frenesí que las hace cometer, por obra o por palabra, mil excesos vergonzosos y repugnantes a toda persona honesta y recatada" [uterine fury, which is a delirium or frenzy that causes them to commit, by word and by deed, a thousand excesses that are shameful and repulsive to honest and virtuous people] (p. 75). Women are thus made responsible for sexual disorder so that their careful disciplining is all the more necessary.[13] Yet, even Rodrigo's obedient wife protests that spiritual equality has not prevented their being held in contempt. The colonel has thus to assure her that uncivilized behavior toward women is prevalent only among savages in the countryside and amongst the "pícaros" [rogues] of the city. If civilized men have kept women out of public affairs "no es un efecto de desprecio, sino de respeto a su débil constitución, y por reservarlas para aquellos objetos a cuya conservación la naturaleza privativamente las destina" [it is not a sign of contempt, but rather one of respect for your weak constitution, and in order to save you for those tasks for which nature has privately destined you] (p. 79).

Mothering as a gift of nature thus becomes the main reason for confining women to the home. Since the colonel does not argue that they are intellectually inferior, he can only explain the fact that the majority of women may not aspire to serious and abstract study, nor to careers in the university and the Church on the grounds that these are outside their true sphere of motherhood.

Lizardi has the colonel send his daughter to school at an early age but insists that even in early childhood she should be segregated from boys. Her father, however, takes an active part in her education, even counseling her on courtship and the evils of adultery as soon as she reaches marriageable age. Though allowed to dance, Pudenciana's father allows her to participate only in dances such as the minuet and the *bolero* and not in the lascivious waltz. Except for the fact that she learns to repair watches (in case widowhood should ever leave her without any means of sustenance) and also learns to ride astride a horse instead of sidesaddle, her education does not differ much from that advocated in Fénélon's seventeenth-century manual on the education of girls.[14] Yet though the restrictions on Pudenciana make her home life resemble that of a convent, Lizardi makes it clear that he regards marriage as preferable to convent life. One of the tales inserted in the novel, after the manner of Cervantes, tells of a tyrannical father who wants to force his daughter to take vows against her wishes in order to prevent her from marrying the man she loves. The religious life goes against women's true function as a mother responsible for the nurturing of children. The stress on the mothering role also accounts for the colonel's delight at seeing his wife breast-feeding his daughter and his statement that neglect of domestic duties amounts to social heresy.

Since the novel is primarily a polemic which juxtaposes two ways of life, Lizardi structures his novel around two girls of totally different character. They are the only children of their respective families—in Eufrosina's case because she loses two sons after putting them out to nurse, in Matilde's case, we are told of a mysterious disease caused by her first pregnancy which leaves her sterile. These explanations are obviously intended as concessions to verisimilitude, yet it is also evident that the colonel's small family, isolated from other relatives and centered in on itself reflects a bourgeois ideal. "In the eighteenth century, the family began to hold society at a distance, to push it back beyond a steadily extending zone of a private life."[15] Lizardi's "good" family thus is also the utopian representation of a new privatized space in which husband and wife were bound not simply by interest and inheritance but also by intimacy and affection. In this respect, Lizardi upholds a more humanitarian ideal, not only with regard to the relations between husband and wife but also in the humane treatment and parental affection shown by father to daughter. This humane treatment of children, however, as well as the colonel's control of discipline and correction is authorized by a rejection of older forms of knowledge and experience now stigmatized as superstition. In other words, some skills which had seemed to be passed on from one generation of women to another are now equated with the "ignorance and superstition" of servants and low-class women:

> Por desgracia, ordinariamente, los niños no se ven rodeados sino de un enjambre de mujeres ignorantes, que con muy buena intención conspiran a hacerlos malcriados e insufribles. Las madres, las nodrizas o *chichiguas*, las ayas o pilmamas, las maestras, las parientas, las amigas y hasta las criadas de las casas, ¿qué hacen sino pervertir el espíritu del niño desde los principios, fomentar sus caprichos, inspirarles errores, apoyar sus falsas ideas, defender sus extravagancias y adular sus inclinaciones a diestra y a sinestra? (p. 174).

> [Unfortunately, ordinarily, children are surrounded by nothing but a horde of ignorant women, who with very good intentions conspire to make them spoiled and insufferable. The mothers, the wet nurses, the governesses, the teachers, the relatives, the friends and even the maids of the house, do nothing but pervert the spirit of the child from the very beginning, encouraging his capriciousness, instilling errors, supporting his false ideas, defending his extravagances and flattering his whims left and right.]

Since men have become the authorities responsible for rational discourse, since education and child welfare are on the verge of becoming sciences, women are gradually deprived of all intellectual input into mothering which is to be confined to the "natural" connection between breast and hunger, desire and food.

Pudenciana triumphantly justifies the colonel's careful upbringing. She marries Don Modesto, a man without a family of his own, "absolutamente solo" [absolutely alone] the Mexican equivalent of a self-made man "que se ejercitaba en el comercio y aunque su capital era corto, bastaba para sostener a una niña decente" [who worked in commerce and although he had limited resources, he had enough money to maintain a decent girl]; in accordance with this ideal of the small, self-sufficient family, the couple immediately separate themselves from the father's household and set up their own home.[16]

Lizardi's "utopian" family brings into being, therefore, a new kind of female social subject, ideologically positioned as an instrument of nature. Her education is intended both as a disciplining of the passions and as a supplement to the "mothering" function, the discipline being made necessary by the seductions of social living. Matilde's sister, Eufrosina, represents the "alter" ideal of a life devoted to pleasure and consumption. Lizardi cannot, of course, give her a fair hearing and her absurd arguments in favor of the superiority of women are easily countered by the colonel. Since we are dealing with an exemplary tract inspired by religious literature, rather than a novel in the true sense, Eufrosina and "La Quijotita" cannot even be allowed to take over as comic characters. There is thus a vast gulf between Lizardi's work and that of his Cervantine paradigm; for it is not only that Lizardi is a less skillful narrator but also that the pleasure text, the "deleitar" [delight] has become positively dangerous. The colonel who, as Eufrosina notes, acts as if he were a missionary or priest, intercedes whenever the "dionysian" discourse seems in danger of seducing the reader. Yet, in many ways, the "evil" family's lack of verisimilitude is more interesting than that of the ideal family since they have to incarnate the varied practices which, in the eyes of the liberal ideologues, had become a threat to the social order.

However, because Eufrosina and Pomposa have to play out all the roles that make women a threat to the social order, this also works against them becoming "characters" in the full sense of the realist novel. Eufrosina is indeed more like a debating opponent who upholds not only the superiority of women but their right to pursue pleasure and their liberation from male control. She describes her life as a constant round of socializing and entertainment. Like her daughter, however, she is obliged (as the surface realization of different actants) to uphold blatantly contradictory positions, being both a snob and too intimate with the lower classes. Pomposa, for her part, has to incarnate the contradictory roles of extreme religiosity and extreme licentiousness, of luxury and austerity, of snobbery which makes her only want to marry a marquis and a lack of discrimination which makes her unable to distinguish between people according to their social status. Lizardi attempts to give verisimilitude to these wild contradictions by attributing them to the general capriciousness and propensity to excess, inherent in the female character. Pomposa's nickname, "La Quijotita," given her by a certain "Sansón Carrasco" underlines the "locura" [madness] which, in women, takes the form of excess. She learns the catechism too rapidly without understanding it, parrots pedantic speech (thus aspiring imperfectly to male discourse), refuses to marry anyone from a class lower than the nobility, dances wildly, goes out onto the streets without proper chaperones, toys with male affection, has a vision of the devil, holds a funeral ceremony for her pet dog, and runs away in order to become a hermit. When her father loses his fortune and leaves home, she makes an imprudent marriage and is then forced into prostitution by her mother who becomes the real villain of the novel, responsible for her daughter's disgrace and death. Such severe fictional punishment was certainly intended to serve as a harsh warning against female mobility and individuality since it is hardly warranted on the narrative level by Pomposa's mild escapades.

As in many later novels of the century, both European and Hispanic, fashion, overspending, sexuality, and financial disaster are closely allied. We recall the long moralistic discourse on fashion that links *La Cousine Bette* to *Mme. Bovary*, *La de Bringas* to *Os Maias*. In Lizardi's more primitive tract, the verisimilitude of character and social context take second place to the preaching of a clear and unequivocal message. Having no concept of the "unconscious," moreover, there is not even the possibility of a slippage or ironic disarticulation between a character's thoughts and his or her actions. Instead, the two match perfectly. Hence the colonel's rational arguments as well as Eufrosina's and Pomposa's "locuras" [follies] are expounded verbally and illustrated by actions. Though potentially comic figures, Eufrosina and her daughter are never allowed the freedom of comic action allowed to Don Quijote since in the nineteenth century comedy has, itself, become dangerous because of its association with pleasure. Hence the author takes considerable care not only to follow the comic escapades with moralizing sermons but also makes Pomposa and Eufrosina into exemplary warnings of the danger of a world turned upside down by childish caprice. In Rousseau, we recall that childhood perversion had consisted in moving others in accordance with their caprices and thus bringing dangerous disorders into the world.[17] These caprices are associated with the "emancipated" females of *La Quijotita*, since their very mobility constitutes a threat. When Pomposa runs off to be a hermit, for instance, she is forced to take shelter in the hut of an "indio carbonero" [Indian coal-burner], thus irreparably demeaning herself. Furthermore, in Lizardi's view, the virtues demanded by the new society—thrift, hard work, obedience, self-discipline—though supposedly rational and hence given by nature, need the supplement of education if untutored nature is not to be seduced by pleasure. Even the lowly Indian would be better off, therefore, simply by forgoing pleasure and spending money on the education of his children rather than "en fiestas, loas y otras frioleras inútiles cuando no perniciosas a ellos mismos" [on feasts, plays and other trifles that are useless if not pernicious to them]. Similarly among the urban lower classes there has to be both the discipline provided by education but also some active discour-

agement of pleasurable activities. Theater falls into this category for spectacles provided a constant allurement, particularly those offering "hechos
maravillosos y que están fuera del orden natural" [fantastic things that are
outside of the natural order] (thus encouraging superstition). Fantasy and
imagination have also to be discouraged in favor of didacticism. That is
why Lizardi's novel logically includes guidance as to proper reading matter
for women and why he makes a distinction between spectacle and a rational theater that would appeal to the mind rather than simply to the taste
for pleasure (p. 345). Further, many of those spaces which even in the colonial period had been used by women for the expression of creativity—for
instance, fashion, gossip, story-telling, seeing visions of saints or the devil,
dancing, and music—were now hedged in with taboos and restrictions.

What *La Quijotita* demonstrates, therefore is that the liberal project
involved both the establishment of a new intellectual authority (that of
the secular ideologue) and at the same time, the subordination of women,
children, and the uneducated according to a rationale somewhat different
from that used by the Church. As work became a form of discipline, those
sectors who appeared particularly susceptible to pleasure and vice began
to come under special care and supervision.

Lizardi's novel is thus as much a treatise on the dangers of pleasure as
on the substance of education. This becomes clear when it is compared
to writing by early nineteenth-century women, some of whom had read
the same educational treatises as Lizardi but were more concerned with
the practical questions of how to earn a living when widowed than with the
dangerous seductions that Lizardi saw on every side. Perhaps the most
interesting document of this kind is a letter written by a "widow of Que-
rétaro" to *Diario de México* in 1808.[18] This young widow who supported
five children and a mother used Fénélon to good effect in order to devise a
plan for the training of women teachers who, in turn, would school other
women in skills more practical than dancing, music, and French. Women
would still be taught sewing and domestic skills since these "tocan privativamente a las mugeres, como que es lo único que nos han dexado los
hombres para buscar nuestra subsistencia o para perfeccionar la economía" [are privately assigned to women, since they are the only avenues left
open to us by men so that we may earn our subsistence or augment our
income]. The widow argues that, in addition, women should be taught to
think clearly and precisely in order to "saber rectificar los juicios, arreglar
el discurso, saber distinguir lo verdadero de lo falso" [know how to rectify

judgments, to speak correctly, and to distinguish true from false]. With proper education

> ni serán tantas las preocupaciones, que nos envilecen, ni seremos tratadas como unas muñecas, tal vez como unas esclavas, y sabremos dar a nuestros hijos, si Dios nos tiene para ser madres, la leche del espíritu, junto con la de nuestro corazón, distinguiendo el verdadero amor maternal de los mimos, y ternezas mal entendidas, que tanto daño hacen a la educación.

> [there will not be so many worries to vex us, nor will we be treated like dolls, nor as slaves, and we will know how to give to our children, if God intends for us to be mothers, the milk of our heart and our spirit, differentiating true maternal love from indulgence, and misguided tendernesses, that are so damaging to children's upbringing.]

The widow was not an isolated case. Even male correspondents sometimes urged that women should be allowed to acquire skills that would allow them to earn their living.[19] And there was a vigorous protest as early as 1805 from a woman who realized that the denunciations of fashion and luxury were in danger of reducing women's lives to an intolerably narrow space. "No podíamos estar siempre encerradas en nuestras casas. Huir de las concurrencias, nos acabaría de secar el corazón. Véanos V muy estéricas, y luego condenársenos a clausura, que bien quedaríamos" [We could not always be locked up in our houses. Forbidding us from attending gatherings would turn our hearts into dust. You view us as very hysterical, and then you condemn us to confinement, which is bound to make us so].[20]

Yet what *La Quijotita* clearly demonstrates is that rationalizing discourse underpinned by writing implied both the establishment of a new kind of intellectual authority (that of the secular ideologue) and, at the same time, the subordination of women, children, and the uneducated on the grounds of their immaturity. What was thus excluded or disqualified by this discourse of reason (which would prevail because institutionalized) later reentered the liberal program in a different guise as populism or sensibility. Popular culture, for instance, would be integrated into literature and painting through "costumbrismo" which initiated a discourse that described the popular while relegating it to anachronism. One area of women's creativity — fashion and taste — would become associated with criterion of sensibility and discrimination, the implied rules of which would be dictated by a predominantly male avant-garde and their aesthetics.

NOTES

1 See Jean Franco, "La heterogenidad peligrosa: la prensa y el escritor en México en vísperas de la Independencia," *Hispamérica* 12, no. 34–35 (1983): 3–34.

2 "Espíritu de superficialidad de las mugeres," *Diario de México* 2, no. 191 (9 April 1806). See also "Lujo en las mugeres," *Diario de México* 3, no. 219 (7 May 1806).

3 "Uniformes de mugeres," *Diario de México* 8, no. 914 (31 March 1808).

4 "La gran barata de frioleras," introduction to *Alacena de Frioleras*, included in José Joaquín Fernández de Lizardi, *Obras* 4 (Mexico: UNAM, 1968), 99. Lizardi did not initiate the metaphor. It is also to be found in the *Diario de México*'s first editorial, 1, no. 1 (1 October 1805).

5 Page references refer to the edition published by the Cámara Mexicana del Libro (Mexico, 1942).

6 For a study of French ideas on the family, see Dianne Lynn Alstad, *The Ideology of the Family in Eighteenth-Century France* (University Microfilms, Ann Arbor, Michigan, 1972); for the early nineteenth century in France, see Jacques Donzelot, *The Policing of Families* (New York: Pantheon Books, 1979).

7 Alstad, *Ideology of the Family*, 152–53.

8 Silvia Marina Arrom, *Women in the Family in Mexico City: 1800–1857* (Ph.D. diss., Stanford University, December 1977).

9 Franco, "La heterogeneidad peligrosa."

10 Alstad, *Ideology of the Family*, 98.

11 Eufrosina is one of the three graces according to the *Diccionario Enciclopédico Hispano-Americano* (Barcelona, 1890). It was also the name of a depraved twelfth-century Greek empress.

12 Fray Luis de León, *La perfecta casada*, 4th ed. (Madrid: Espasa Calpe, 1944), 57.

13 Part of the colonel's statement is a quotation from Antoine Léonard Thomas, author of a series of "éloges" of great men and an "Essai sur le caractére, les moeurs et l'esprit des femmes dans les differents siècles" [Essay on the character, custom, and spirit of women in different centuries], published in *Oeuvres, l'ère partie* (Paris, 1819). He separates the sphere of male and female on the well-known grounds that "Au milieu des travaux et parmi tous les arts, l'homme deployant sa force, et commandant à la nature, trouve des plaisirs, dans son industrie, dans ses succès, dans ses efforts même. La femme plus solitaire a bien moins de ressources. Ses plaisirs doivent naître de ses vertus: ses spectacles sont sa famille" [By using his strength and by dominating nature, in work and in all the arts, man finds pleasure in industry, success, and in his very effort. More solitary, woman has less resources. Her pleasures must come from her virtues: Her entertainment is her family] (p. 593).

14 Even in France, this work was still being reprinted in the early nineteenth century. I consulted *De l'Education des Filles*, by Messire François de Salignac de la Mothe-Fénélon, Archevèque-Duc de Cambray (Lyon, 1811).

15 Philippe Ariès, *Centuries of Childhood*, trans. Robert Baldik (New York: Knopf,

1961), 399. For changes in private houses which reflected changes in the family see the work done on Buenos Aires by Diana Hernando, *Casa y Familia: Spatial Biographies in Nineteenth-Century Buenos Aires* (Ann Arbor Microfilms, 1979).

16 For the limits on paternal power over adult offspring, see Alstad, *Ideology of the Family*, 98–99.

17 See Derrida's now classic discussion of the relationship in Rousseau's thought between the deficiencies of childhood (and nature), education, language, and writing (and masturbation) in ". . . That Dangerous Supplement . . . ," in *Of Grammatology*, trans. Gayatri Chakravorty Spivak (Baltimore: Johns Hopkins University Press, 1976), esp. 146–48.

18 The letter appeared in the following issues of the *Diario de México* 8, no. 954 (10 May 1808); no. 955 (11 May 1808); no. 972 (28 May 1808); no. 973 (29 May 1808), no. 974 (30 May 1808).

19 "Ocupaciones de mujeres," *Diario de México* 3, no. 247 (4 May 1806).

20 Letter signed by Antonio Pozelo Mosto, *Diario de México* 1 (11 November 1805).

WAITING FOR A BOURGEOISIE

The Formation of the Mexican Intelligentsia
in the Age of Independence

The first decades of the nineteenth century in Mexico tend to confuse literary critics. Colonial culture had not entirely disappeared but the new culture had not yet come into being. Nevertheless, it is in many ways a key period—a period that witnessed the formation of an intellectual terrain different from that of the colonial period and observed the development of a lay intelligentsia with a vision of a new culture and a new society.

This lay intelligentsia emerged in societies where great importance was attached to the spoken word; where the very act of giving one's word, or betraying the word of another, sealed alliances or caused wars; where the rich popular culture—organized around holiday celebrations, music, dance, and *tertulia* [salon]—counted for much more than the abstract and meager culture of books. Nevertheless, it was precisely this exuberant diversity of popular culture which, for the intelligentsia, educated in the rationalistic spirit of the Enlightenment, came to represent the incurable backwardness of the entire continent. Hostile to racial mixing, local customs, traditions, and holiday celebrations, the intelligentsia longed for a more disciplined society; such a society would be based on the work ethic and on a vision of a society bonded by books and guided by "ideological teachers" whose authority derived from their access to print culture. The ideal of a disciplined society not only implied a radical break with the past, but also it embodied a program for the secularization of knowledge, as well as of daily life and ethics. This program included linguistic standardization, the organization of urban life, and the imposition of new codes of dress and social conduct.[1]

This kind of radical break with colonial practice and discourse was made possible by new spaces and institutions, among which the press was of pri-

Originally published as "En espera de una burguesía: La formación de la inteligencia mexicana en la época de la Independencia" in *Actas del VIII Congreso de la Asociación Internacional de Hispanistas*, eds. David Kosoff, et al. (Madrid: Istmo, 1986), 21–36. Translated by Patricia Heid.

mary importance. The press (whose diverse output ranged from partisan political tracts to scandalous pamphlets) introduced a discourse in the first decades of the nineteenth century that was very different in form from the type of hierarchical address used in the colonial period. The *Diario de México* [The Mexican Daily], founded in 1805 and edited for a time by Carlos María Bustamante, can be considered representative of this new form of expression: its novelty consisted precisely in the juxtaposition of heterogeneous types of discourse that included sermons, essays, news, and commercial advertisements. As might be expected, this discourse reached only a small group of subscribers and their friends. Nevertheless, the *Diario de México* reflected a level of public opinion which, as Jürgen Habermas has indicated, depended on the existence of "a public capable of reflection."[2]

As in Europe, where newspapers countered official authority while remaining within the general norms of civility,[3] the daily newspaper in Latin America instituted a public platform for the intelligentsia. The structure and style of the contributions to the newspaper were as important as their content. In contrast with the monolithic discourse of the Church, a newspaper like the *Diario de México* offered a selection of heterogeneous topics, from which its readers could freely choose according to their personal tastes; thus, it implied a different reader from the reader of religious discourse. The implied reader of the secular press was ideally conceived as a reasoning participant in a dialogue, from which all "irrational" elements had been removed. Therefore, the *Diario de México* ignored or criticized (and even parodied) popular imagination and culture, colloquial speech, and all similar "irrationality." Within these limits, it offered a variety of didactic genres—poetry, moral fables in verse and prose, sermons, letters, homilies, news, advice, and satire.

The lay ideologues owed their intellectual formation to the new space opened by the press—ideologues like José María Luis Mora, Carlos María Bustamante, and José Joaquín Fernández de Lizardi, the "first" novelist of Latin America.[4] Lizardi, in particular, exemplified a new type of independent thinker whose authority was based on his activities as a public writer, and not on traditional wisdom. In spite of being sporadically persecuted by the Church, Lizardi managed to work with remarkable success as an independent writer. He was also fully conscious of belonging to a new generation whose intellectual formation presupposed access to a body of secular knowledge (of European origin), which offered, in a rational language, new criteria for public conduct and private life.

In 1812, the imprisonment of Lizardi, who had been accused of insulting the viceroy in the ninetieth issue of his newspaper, *El pensador mexicano* [The Mexican Thinker], not only underscores the revolutionary character of his discourse but also indicates a difference between the new intelligentsia and the clergy (including the rebellious clergy, such as Fray Servando Teresa de Mier), whose point of reference continued to be theology. In contrast, Lizardi based his authority on the new knowledge he had acquired in the works of lay authors.

The ninetieth issue of *El pensador mexicano* had appeared immediately after the declaration of freedom of the press in Mexico, by the Congress of Cádiz. Lizardi wrote an article, in which he used some aggressive language, to criticize the sentencing of a small group of rebellious priests by the military courts.[5] Citing a series of treatises on education and the conduct of princes, Lizardi not only criticized the viceroy but also addressed him as an equal, as a mere human being: "Today in my writing, you will see a wretched mortal, a man like all other men, a contemptible atom on the face of the Almighty."[6] Although the viceregal government did not enjoy the same prestige as it did in earlier times, Lizardi's words signify more than an act of boldness—they imply a radical change in the writer's position with respect to authority. Comparing his pen to a telescope, Lizardi focuses on the viceroy from a perspective that diminishes his importance. Lizardi's pen reduces the viceroy, and thus it is analogous to the eye of the "Almighty," who sees all human beings as mere atoms. Writing, which in the viceregal court was considered either an instrument of bureaucracy or a means of flattering those in power, now becomes a way of seeing, godlike in its power. Writing allows the writer to distance himself from events and to write objectively, thus giving him independent authority, removed from the ups and downs of the state. It is worth examining the wording of Lizardi's "insult" more closely. It begins with the deictic "today," thus situating Lizardi in the present, which for the viceroy is a future, when he will be seen as a mere human being. Writing implies a spatial and temporal distance between the referent (the viceroy) and the sign, which produces a dramatic change of perspective, thus allowing the writer to adopt a prophetic position.

When Lizardi is later interrogated by the prosecutors, their questioning of him testifies to both the uniqueness and the novelty of his position. When the prosecutors discovered that Lizardi possessed only the rudiments of Latin grammar, philosophy, ethics, and literature, they expressed their surprise that someone of so "little enlightenment" could make such serious arguments. Rather than calling attention to his originality, Lizardi defended himself by claiming he had plagiarized: "I have copied the depiction of his Excellency as a mortal man exposed to all the weaknesses of his species, partly from the *Empresas* [Enterprises] of Zaavedra, and partly from the works of Macana, inserted almost directly into the *Seminario erudito* [Erudite Seminarian], as well as from Macana's untitled work, the *Amigo de Príncipe* [The Prince's Friend], from which I have also copied a good part of what he says about flatterers." The prosecutors came to the conclusion that the article did not contain a single original idea by Lizardi, and that he had "copied all of it from a passage here, a passage there, contained in the variety of reading he had done."[7] In an age which did not place much value on originality, Lizardi was not ashamed of having plagiarized. On the contrary, he proudly displayed his discovery of such an abundance of wisdom in popular manuals and miscellanies.

Fernández de Lizardi's conception of writing was not traditional for his epoch. In his pieces, he addressed the subscribers directly; he took into consideration the varied and heterogeneous tastes of the readers who were buying his newspapers and novels. Although his friends accused him of writing for profit, it did not bother him in the least to be earning his living in that manner.[8] On several occasions, he compared selling ideas to selling merchandise. In one of his newspapers, *La alacena de frioleras* [The Closet of Baubles] (1815–16), he went so far as to put his own ideas on sale: "Well, sir, whoever may have stuff, let him sell them cheaply; since I do not have anything in my cabinet except trifles, trifles and more trifles, I must sell them cheaply, very cheaply."[9] For Lizardi there existed a direct relation between commerce and the writing that liberated the writer from the system of colonial patronage, by making him respond to the varied and variable tastes of his readers; it is the "true merits" of these readers that Lizardi celebrates in the introduction to his novel *El periquillo sarniento* [The Itching Parrot].[10]

The recognition of a marketplace for writing made it impossible for Lizardi to address his writing to a noble or idealized reader. The social or ethical position of the buyer could not be known ahead of time; and because among all the possible readers there were rogues, prostitutes, and thieves, it was not possible to compose a "noble" literature for them. Although no other writers from the period speak so openly about the transformation of literature by the marketplace, this practical aspect does not conflict with the importance Lizardi attributed to the writer as a representative of public opinion. For this reason, Lizardi described himself as a "thinker" or "public writer," whose skills were repeatedly put to the test in debates in which he argued against the ignorance of the masses.[11]

The concept of egalitarian discourse, which was supported at first by the *Diario de México* and strengthened by the liberal dogma of "equality before the law," did not, however, prevent the acceptance of a certain kind of hierarchy—that of the teacher and the student. This relationship of teacher/student not only influenced written modes of enunciation (in didactic writing), but also it was reflected in the philosophy of education. The Latin American intelligentsia (heirs of the Enlightenment) privileged direct experience, and the clear and distinct ideas which could be communicated without error from one mind to another; thus, it privileged the pedagogical situation in which both interlocutors are present, but not as equals. The senses were considered the most reliable source of knowledge, followed by the dialogue held between two people. Writing was less effective than both the spoken word and physical discipline. Guillermo Prieto, for example, lauded one of his teachers, who could move his students with the power of the spoken word: "It was, without my realizing it, the great oral lesson, spoken unto a child: its wisdom penetrated my soul with the enchantment of a story, with the magic of the fairy tale."[12] This acknowledged superiority of spoken over written language explains why the intellectual elite feared the effects of "fairy tales" and the "legends" of popular fantasy, which had the power of seduction only possible in oral communication.

Because writers could not acquire knowledge within traditional institutions, they educated themselves in reading groups and they were self-taught. They had access to contemporary thought through friends who were booksellers and through wealthy friends who traveled often. The author of one of the greatest poems of Mexican Romanticism, "La profecía de Cuautémoc" [The Prophecy of Cuautémoc], Rodríguez Galván, worked in his uncle's bookstore where a literary *tertulia* was held weekly. During the thirties, these *tertulias* and reading groups had turned into informal schools that encouraged people with literary talent and stimulated programs of reform. In this respect, Mexico's situation was not that different from the situation of other Latin American countries during the nineteenth century. Undoubtedly, this monopoly of "modern" thought is what enabled the intelligentsia to aspire to political power: at the height of the nineteenth century they saw themselves as the only persons capable of guiding the people and introducing reforms. These *tertulias* and meetings, which were held in private homes or in institutions like the Hidalgo Institute and the Academy of San Juan de Letrán in Mexico, compensated for the lack of formally structured institutions.[13] Although the participants in these meetings were few in number, they had lofty ambitions and they formulated long-term programs that took into account the politics as well as the culture of the new nations. Women, however, remained marginalized from this activity: their confinement to the private sphere made it difficult for them to participate in the project of forming national cultures.

The eclectic character of the literary production of this period resulted, in part, from the informal scholarship acquired in the *tertulia*, from borrowed books, and newspaper articles. As critics have observed, the intellectual elite acted as critics, poets, novelists, politicians, and sociologists up until the end of the nineteenth century.[14] There was no such thing as areas of specialization, and genres were rigidly defined. Science was discussed in the essay, as well as in poetry or in the novel. Religion was criticized in poetry, theater, oratory, and the essay. It is this flexibility of genres which leads some modern critics to describe nineteenth-century letters as anachronistic. In order to arrive at a more precise notion of what literature was like in that period, we need to revise our theory of literary genres.[15] First of all, the distinction between imaginative and scientific works, and between poetry and narrative, did not correspond to modern categories. For the intellectual elite at the beginning of the nineteenth century, the distinction between the rational (which included all writing, as well as spoken language that was rational) and the irrational (stories and poems from oral tradition, legends, and superstitions) was the most significant. Moreover, what was considered "rational" (that is, all writing) included genres which are no longer recognized as "literary"—for example, the dialogue, the allegory, and the sermon were all commonly used genres, and all of them could be represented in poetry as well as in prose. It is true, as Bakhtin observes, that the novel tends to absorb all the other genres; thus, in *The Itching Parrot* one finds the genres of debate, sermon, utopia, and dialogue. However, the quality that is valued most is not originality, or the writer's imagination, but his ability to express himself rationally—that is, by means of an unequivocal language composed of clear and distinct ideas. In sum, "literature" was the responsibility of small groups of educated persons, mostly self-taught, who considered it in its broadest sense as the foundation of good government. In the face of the heterogeneity of popular cultures, which were viewed as a threat to social order and good government, the intellectual elite proposed a more homogeneous, more disciplined, and more uniform society—in sum, a "civilized" society.[16]

The intellectual elite began to appropriate the idea of civilization at the same time that it began to formulate the concept of the nation. Civilization was a concept that had already achieved a certain prominence in Europe, and above all in France, where, as Norbert Elias indicates, the bourgeoisie had used it as an ideological weapon in its internal conflicts against the aristocracy.[17] When the bourgeoisie came to power after the French Revolution, the concept of civilization was gradually fused to the concept of nationality. And when the French nation began to develop a colonial ideology after the conquest of Egypt, civilization served as a justification for domination and control. Moreover, the concept of civilization not only embraced culture, but also the rules of daily life, which were imposed by the dominant countries and included correct behavior, manners, and mode of dress.

Civilization also implied the idea that life should be ordered according to the rhythm of capitalist labor, and not according to the calendar of religious rites or the cycles of the harvest, which still predominated in rural areas. During the eighteenth century, the conspicuous consumption practiced by the aristocracy had transformed their lives into a kind of theater or dance of perpetual masks. The progressive imposition of a more austere manner of dress and models of bourgeois behavior announced the beginning of the industrial era and the work ethic. This ethic was undoubtedly fostered by the terrible lesson of the French Revolution, in which the guillotine had put an end to the aristocracy's conspicuous consumption.

We must not forget, however, that in this period the word *civilization* possessed an emotive force and an emphasis that pointed toward a kind of well-ordered daily life. Of course, in Latin America the intellectual elite was continually confronting a heterogeneous society in terms of both regional and racial characteristics, and the fear of a war between castes was widespread—particularly after the events that occurred in Haiti. In this context, civilization was equated with the discipline that was to be imposed on the lower classes by means of education and good manners. In this "civilizing" project, a lot of attention was focused on clothing as a symbol of modern attitudes. Thus Sarmiento declared that "if Lavalle had fought his 1840 campaign on an English saddle and wearing a French frock-coat, today we would be on the banks of the Plata River, regulating steam navigation and distributing plots of land to European immigrants."[18] "Modern" customs—English and French, in this case—are directly related to European military discipline. In contrast, traditional clothing is perceived as a sign of barbarism. By adopting the manner of dress of the *gaucho* and the plainsman, General Rosas of Argentina and General Páez of Venezuela showed solidarity with their troops; but such clothing horrified the intellectual elite, who saw in it the visible display of backwardness.

Not surprisingly, travel books written by Europeans who had visited the New World after independence reinforced the attitude of the intellectual elite, who saw reflected in these books the barbarity of their own customs. These European travelers thought and acted like official missionaries of capitalism: they considered the natives to be unsuited for modern labor.[19] These travel books, which were widely read, did not limit themselves to creating stereotypes of America in Europe, but they also encouraged the paranoia of the Latin American intelligentsia, who always felt the "civilized" gaze of Europe fixed on them. Fernández de Lizardi, for example, was outraged by the murder of a North American traveler, primarily because of its repercussions in the foreign press.[20] The past was engraved on the faces, clothing, and customs of the Indians, *gauchos*, underclasses, and blacks. From this perspective, it was impossible for the intellectual elite to appreciate the culture of this anachronistic humanity, which it wanted either to reform or eradicate.

The most dangerous classes of people included not only the "savage" Indians and the rural workers, but also the "lumpen" inhabitants of the cities—for example, the underclasses of Mexico City. However, in order to achieve a disciplined society, these layers of the population had to be reformed. It was not only necessary to educate them, but also to control spontaneous expressions of emotion and their street celebrations. The disapproval of the relaxed customs of the masses is evident in Fernández's description of a visit to a church in Xochimilco, where he sees "candies on the benches, the *shrieking* of small children throwing stones, the *shouting* of older boys running to catch them, the constant *talking* and *laughing* of the people, the *scratchy-sounding* music and the nonsense being *murmured* in the chorus of the indians, who were possibly drunk" (emphasis mine).[21] The behavior and religious rites of the lower classes were seen as chaos and disorder, which did not coincide with Fernández de Lizardi's ideal of social behavior.

Because the intellectual elite could not put their social project into practice in the years immediately following independence, literature became the utopian space for envisaging the model society. Civil wars, and the lack of state and institutional apparatus that could potentially have transformed society, gave literature special importance in the newly developing civil society, in spite of the illiteracy of those groups toward whom the literature ostensibly was directed. The possibility of teaching the masses under the guise of entertainment was the motive that inspired Lizardi to write *The Itching Parrot*. Some decades later, José María Luis Mora, for example, would declare in an optimistic tone that this goal had been achieved and that "stories and anecdotes . . . have not only ennobled and refined all the passions of the Mexican soul, but they have also publicized innumerable observations about all branches of learning related to them, and they stimulate the curiosity of their readers. Our knowledge, our imagination, our souls and our language have all been enriched by reading them."[22] In 1851, in his acceptance speech for the presidency of the Hidalgo Institute, Francisco Zarco specifically emphasizes that literature gives us access to the sphere of the universal, that is, to civilization.[23]

This concept of literature as a model for social conduct is not restricted to Latin America. However, while European authors could count on a public which was already disciplined and integrated into the daily routine of working life (the *habitus* of the city, to use Bourdieu's expression[24]), in Latin America there persisted either a criticism of barbarism (*Amalia*, *El matadero* [The slaughterhouse], historical novels) or a utopian vision of a society that had not yet been achieved. Let us keep in mind that writers did not have an imaginative repertory or a novelistic tradition which would facilitate the representation of this new society. Writers attempted to resolve the problem of representability in two ways: first, by utilizing genres such as the dialogue, which implies the possibility of directly communicating ideas to a public capable of rationally understanding them and putting them into practice, and, second, by resorting to the Hispanic tradition of the picaresque novel, the story, and the theater. What is obvious is that the "rational," because it tended to devalue the fantastic, limited playful utopian representations. Thus, the utopian tends to be projected not in futuristic fantasies but in dialogues, as models of rational communication.

Latin American dialogues from the period of independence attempt to create a space for public opinion and a model for language. However, since dialogue excluded irrational elements it could not accurately depict the real extremes of society. In Argentina, for example, the gauchesque dialogues of Bartolomé Hidalgo represent the attempt to create public opinion by giving voice to an individual who comes from a world far removed from official circles—such as the *gaucho*—and by means of the invention of a rustic language that purposefully differs from official prose. Yet, it is interesting to observe that in one of the dialogues between "Joaquín Chano, the overseer of a farm on the Tordillo Islands, and the gaucho of the Mountain Guards," Chano is described as "the old singer," or as a "man of reason" and a "man of letters"—in other words, he is not an illiterate laborer. The rustic dialect connotes the authenticity and the solid virtues of the rural provinces, still unaffected by the egoism and factionalism of contemporary politics, which Chano criticizes in the dialogue.[25]

Fernández de Lizardi, the author of numerous dialogues in prose about themes as diverse as the bullfight and the constitution, also utilized the dialogue as a didactic genre. The points of view of the participants in the dialogue rarely represent ideological oppositions, but rather generational differences (for example, between Don Toribio and his nephew) or regional ones (the girl from the country and the girl from Mexico City). When different ideologies are put into play, as in the case of the "tertulia of the dead," it is with the intention of bringing the opposing positions into agreement. "The tertulia of the dead," although modeled after "the dialogues of the dead" by Fenélon (who derived moral lessons from the lives of men in antiquity), differs greatly from this model. Written in 1821, the year of the Plan of Iguala, which guaranteed religion, independence, and the union of Mexico, the dialogue clearly illustrates how those considered "irrational" are excluded from the social project. The *tertulia* includes various historical personalities, ranging from the Spanish Colonel Concha to the rebels—Hidalgo, Matamoros, and so on. For Concha, the rebels were a "wretched bunch and an impenetrable mob," "an undisciplined rabble," "uncultured and immoral men" who have converted the rebellion into "a riot and a frightening Babylon."[26] The rebels defend themselves, and even Concha admits that Morelos died without renouncing the Catholic faith. On his own behalf, Hidalgo is willing to admit having made some mistakes, and he confesses his excessive confidence in the "barbarous citizenry":

> I wish I would have avoided these excesses; but I had neither sufficient energy nor eloquence to restrain or persuade a barbarous and enraged citizenry, whom I needed, and to whom I entrusted the security of my person and the realization of my projects. . . . When I confess the detestable nature of these crimes, I am in no way trying to justify my actions. I would rather have died before consenting to a single murder. This is what the natural and divine laws required of me; but I would like to have seen what any of my accusers would have done in my place,

if they would have let themselves be destroyed by giving up the chance to save themselves, a chance which fell straight into my lap.[27]

It is perfectly conceivable that these lines reflect Lizardi's own sense of guilt: some years before he was accused of having helped the rebels in Taxco. However, what stands out here is not the autobiographical element, but rather the distinction which Lizardi makes between the heroes and the masses. Hidalgo and Morelos are turned into exemplary figures by separating their discourse and their intentions from the actions of the *rabble*, which had filled all *decent people* with terror-stricken panic.

What also stands out in the "tertulia of the dead" is the profound difference between the intellectual elite of Latin America and their contemporaries in France. The latter had fought against the aristocracy by fighting for the cause of universal emancipation; after they had established their power the problem of social discipline began to make itself felt. In contrast, in Latin America the first goal had to be establishing order and discipline; the new generation of Latin American intelligentsia confronted first their own fellow citizens whose culture they despised. Lizardi's *Tertulia of the Dead*, a text which attempts to heal the wounds caused by the civil war, places in relief the enormous distance between the project of the *men of reason*, and those they considered to be *irrational*.

The intellectual elite, in effect, could only speak in the future tense, thus their need for utopian discourse. The case of Fernández de Lizardi is again particularly instructive because his career as a writer spans the period which extends from the rebellion of 1810 to the declaration of the constitution of 1824. Lizardi died in 1827, and the majority of his oeuvre was written before independence, when censorship made it difficult to openly analyze certain facets of society. Perhaps it is for this reason that on two separate occasions he mentions the need for a utopian discourse. In 1814 he publishes in *El pensador mexicano* a fictional letter received from an alleged brother who was the victim of a shipwreck. This brother, Manuel, finds himself on the island of Ricamea, where he has married the daughter of the president. When the father dies, Manuel, although a foreigner, comes to occupy the office of governor. He writes to his brother, El Pensador, asking him for advice on how to govern and explaining to him that the problems of Ricamea are very similar to those of Mexico. The population of Ricamea is a mix of races — blacks, mulattoes, creoles, Europeans, and Indians, the latter characterized as "half-savage, stupid by nature, ignorant, superstitious and cowardly; however, the citizens of the island use them for work in the fields, the transport of goods, and other insignificant tasks." And in order to emphasize Ricamea's similarity to Mexico, in case this had not been made sufficiently clear, he adds: "Since these Indians are exactly like those over there in America, you can surely imagine what their manners are like."[28] The new governor is a *merchant*, which suggests Lizardi's confidence in this class to bridge the transition between the colonial epoch and the independent state. Unfortunately, we do not have a more precise vision of that new society because Lizardi never published a response to his brother's request. The letter reveals the need to define the ideal role of the intelligentsia: the brother summarizes this function when he tells Lizardi to "picture in your mind a kingdom, and imagine yourself as the king or prime minister of that kingdom, and in this way you announce your laws, confident that as bad or preposterous as they may be, since they are merely part of a dream, they could not do harm to anyone."[29] The letter to Lizardi clearly points to the merchant as the "new prince" of an independent Mexico and to the writer as the prince's guide.

Utopian elements are present throughout Fernández de Lizardi's novel, *The Itching Parrot*, even though, at first glance, such elements may seem to be a late manifestation of the Spanish picaresque tradition. The picaresque novel, as a genre which emerges during a period of decadence in Spain, does not seem to be the most adequate instrument for projecting a vision of utopia. However, Fernández de Lizardi attempts to adapt the genre to the objective which interests him most, and he even includes a utopian episode. Even more important, he sees in the novel a way of reading which ideally might transform the reader into the "new man" of the bourgeois society. This didactic purpose detracts from the novel's most attractive quality, which is its ability to entertain its audience. Because the audience of that period justified fiction for its usefulness, and reading for pleasure was considered frivolous, the novel in this period was written not so much for enjoyment as for instruction. This results in the moral digressions and homilies that interrupt the plot. It was necessary to save the readers, as it was Periquillo himself, from the potential dangers of pleasure and idleness.

Who are these readers? As the prologue makes clear, at least in theory they included thieves, vagrants, and rogues. Lizardi claimed to be addressing the underclasses of Mexico City, and his protagonist is an individual who comes from a family of "decent people," but who has fallen into "honest vagrancy." This group included decent and wayward young boys who, with their cloaks, caps and even perfume will be idle the rest of their lives, perpetual members of all the tertulias, lovers of every coquette they meet, seducers of as many married women as possible, gamblers, cheats and gamesters whenever possible: troublemakers at dances, the nightmare of parties, intrusive parasites, shameless and impudent men, fools from the time they are born, incessant talkers, and dressed-up, scandalous and harmful machines in the unfortunate society in which they live.

By attempting to reform the taste of readers that could identify with these vagabonds, Lizardi converts the novel into an exercise in discipline. The plot focuses on the story of the old and dying Don Pedro—the reformed Periquillo—who, as a now inactive but moralizing old man, analyzes the adventures of his youth.[30] The old Pedro Sarmiento who narrates is one of the many "fathers" who, in various moments of the novel, try to guide the young Periquillo. These "fathers"—a teacher, a priest, a merchant, an army colonel, an innkeeper—represent different aspects of the paternal character: erudition, honesty, respect for the law, and generosity. Obviously, Lizardi was attempting to introduce a secular morality that would be based on the work ethic, but he also wanted to indicate that this kind of discourse could only be enunciated from a paternal position: the father represented both the law and the social experience that needed to be transmitted to the next generation. The "natural" hierarchy of the family, in which the father's word is the law, offers the perfect model because, as one of the characters of *The Itching Parrot* indicates, "in what nation, however barbarous, is the father not recognized as the highest authority for directing the child?" On the other hand, in the case of weak or absent parents, paternalism does not need to be limited to the family. In effect, the discourse of the "fathers" suggests that Lizardi was thinking of a new type of state where, if necessary, paternalistic discourse—related to the family, but separated from it—could override the voice of the natural father.

The situation of writing in the new society is demonstrated most clearly in the utopian chapters of the novel. In these chapters, Periquillo is the victim of a shipwreck on an island where he makes friends with a prominent citizen—a wealthy Chinese man who explains to him the island's social structure and customs. Although the social structure largely resembles that of the viceroyalty of Mexico, insofar as it is based on an inflexible system of castes identified by different manners of dress, the utopian society is free of the defects of colonial society, such as idleness, poor education, and the system of primogeniture. There are two basic causes for the superiority of the island society: the presence of merchants who govern the island, and the use of writing, by means of which the citizens learn the laws. The law is inscribed in tablets of marble, from which the citizens obligatorily copy in order to learn it. Writing is, therefore, a way of inculcating discipline, and by being inscribed in marble it is more permanent than the ephemeral human being. The law is the discourse of an absent paternalistic authority, the power of which is exercised by means of the written word. By copying down the laws, obedient citizens inscribe themselves, in a very real sense, within the paternalistic order.

Lizardi expresses in his own unique way a concept that will later be demonstrated by Poulantzas—that the state depends on writing for transmitting, maintaining, and reproducing power and authority. However, as we have explained, Lizardi always firmly believed that writing was inferior to direct example. For this reason, those who govern his utopia do not restrict themselves to teaching the laws, but they also insist on draconian punishment for those who transgress these laws. They engage in the practice of bodily mutilation because, in this way, the body of the criminal becomes a living lesson to others. When they cut off the criminal's hand, "he is left punished and necessarily reformed, yet still able to enjoy the greatest good of all, which is life itself. Citizens can feel secure with his behavior, and the example of his punishment is lasting and effective." Mutilation, according to Lizardi, is particularly convincing in influencing children, since the criminal

> stays among the good and the bad, and for this very reason, his example endures, and it is not isolated to a single city or a town, but rather it extends to wherever these unfortunate souls may go, and children are filled with a terror against committing robbery and a fear of punishment, because they see with their very own eyes the most eloquent lesson of all.[31]

Lizardi's utopia emphasizes the author's problem in trying to project a new social order without an agent—the bourgeoisie—which in Europe had already established a new society and a new social subject. The importance which Fernández de Lizardi attributes to punishment responds to the threat represented by the "wretched bunch" who had participated in the first movement for independence, and it proves that there did not yet exist a state apparatus capable of disciplining the lower classes. Fernández de Lizardi demonstrates his originality as a thinker in foreseeing that a legal subject would have to be constituted in a different way; on the other hand, by privileging concrete example over that of the written word, he also betrays his lack of confidence in the power of writing—that would become the most powerful instrument of the new state.

It is possible to attribute too much importance to the experience of a single writer such as Fernández de Lizardi; nevertheless, I believe that his "revolutionary" position in the intellectual arena as well as his "disciplinary" discourse are symptomatic of the time. Just like Sarmiento, Echeverría, and Bello, Lizardi frees himself from Spain in order to confront the problem of a heterogeneous society. Thus, he had to direct his writings not only against the old ideological apparatus represented by the Church, but also against the underclasses—the most "irrational" sectors of society. It was in the limited terrain between the authoritarianism of the past and the dissolution of society in which he formulated his utopia, a utopia in which discipline prevailed over democratic participation.[32]

NOTES

1 The most important book about intellectuals is that of Angel Rama, *La ciudad letrada* (Hanover, N.H.: Ediciones del Norte, 1984) [the English edition, *The Lettered City*, edited and translated by John Charles Chasteen, was published in 1996 by Duke University Press]. However, Rama sees a continuity between "the learned city" of the colonial period and that of the nineteenth century during the time of the *caudillos*. In contrast, I want to call attention to new factors which come into play with independence.

2 Jürgen Habermas, "The Public Sphere: An Encyclopedia Article," trans. Sara Lennox and Frank Lennox, *New German Critique* 32 (1964): 49–55.

3 Ibid., 52.

4 Noël Salomon, "Introducción a José Joaquín Fernández de Lizardi," *Casa de Tiempo* 2, no. 16 (December 1981): i–xvi.

5 The *Obras* of José Joaquín Fernández de Lizardi have been published by the Universidad Nacional Autónoma de México. The articles published in *El Pensador Mexicano* can be found in *Obras III—Periódicos* (Mexico: UNAM, 1968). The articles have been compiled, edited, and annotated by María Rosa Palazón and Jacobo Chencinsky, and the latter also wrote the introduction to the collection.

6 Lizardi, *Obras*, 3: 83–84.

7 To consult the prosecutors' report, see Genaro García, ed., *Documentos históricos mexicanos* (Mexico: Museo Nacional de Arqueología Historia y Etnologia, 1910), 459–62.

8 The summary of these criticisms of Lizardi is found in the preliminary notes of Jacobo Chencinsky, *Obras*, 1: 37.

9 José Joaquín Fernández de Lizardi, "La gran barata de frioleras," *La alacena de frioleras* 17 (Thursday, 13 July 1815), included in *Obras* 4: 99.

10 Lizardi, *Obras*, 8 and 9 (Mexico, UNAM, 1982).

11 Paul Radin, "The Opponents and Friends of Lizardi," *Occasional Papers*, Mexican History Series, no. 2, part 2 (San Francisco: Sutro Library, 1939).

12 Guillermo Prieto, *Memoria de mis tiempos* (Mexico: Editorial José M. Cajica Jr., S. A., 1970), 57.

13 Ibid., 181–82.

14 See, for example, Angel Rama, *Rubén Darío y el modernismo: circunstancias socioeconómicas de un arte americano* (Caracas: Universidad Central de Venezuela, 1970), 45.

15 Bernard Duffey makes a similar revision with respect to the United States in his book, *Poetry in America: Expression and its Values in the Times of Bryant, Whitman and Pound* (Durham, N.C.: Duke University Press, 1978).

16 On this point, see the article of George Reid Andrews, "Spanish American Independence. Structural Analysis," *Latin American Perspectives* 12, no. 1 (winter 1985): 105–30. See also Charles A. Hale, *El liberalismo en México en la época de Mora, 1821–53* (Mexico: Siglo XXI, 1978).

17 Norbert Elias, *The History of Manners* (New York: Pantheon Books, 1978), 49.

18 Domingo Sarmiento, *Facundo: Civilización y Barbarie*, 4th ed. (Buenos Aires: Espasa Calpe, 1958), 133.

19 Jean Franco, "Un viaje poco romántico. Viajeros británicos hacia Sudamérica, 1818–28," *Escritura* 4, no. 7 (January-June 1979): 129–42; Mary Louise Pratt, *Imperial Eyes: Travel Writing and Transculturation.* (London: Routledge, 1992).

20 Lizardi, "Tercera Conversación del Payo y el Sacristán," in *Obras* (Mexico: UNAM, 1973), 5: 97.

21 Ibid., 96.

22 José María Mora, *México y sus revoluciones* (Mexico: Porrúa, 1950), 1: 122.

23 Francisco Zarco, "Discurso sobre el objeto de la literatura, pronunciado el día 10 de junio de 1851, por Francisco Zarco al tomar posesión de la presidencia del Liceo Hidalgo," *La Ilustración Mexicana* 1 (1851): viii.

24 Pierre Bourdieu, *Outline of a Theory of Practice* (Cambridge: Cambridge University Press, 1977), esp. 77–78.

25 Bartolomé Hidalgo, *Cielitos y diálogos patrióticos*, vol. 7 of the collection *Capítulos* (Buenos Aires: Centro Editor de América Latina, 1967), 39–51. See also Angel Rama, *Los gauchipolíticos rioplatenses* (Buenos Aires: Calicanto, 1976).

26 José Joaquín Fernández de Lizardi, "Las tertulias de los muertos antiguos y modernos," in *El Pensador Mexicano: Diálogos sobre cosas de su tiempo, sacados del olvido por Luis González Obregón* (Mexico: Typ. Murgia, 1918), 36.

27 Ibid., 39.

28 *El Pensador Mexicano*, nos. 2, 3, and 4, corresponding to Thursday, 20 January 1814; Thursday, 27 January 1814; and Thursday, 3 February 1814, included in *Obras*, 3: 386–99. The quote is found on 397.

29 *Obras*, 3: 398.

30 See John M. Fein, "Inconsistencies of Characterization in the *Periquillo*," *Modern Language Notes* 73 (1958): 428–31. See also Noël Salomon, "La crítica del sistema colonial de la Nueva España en *El Periquillo Sarniento*," *Cuadernos Americanos* 138 (January–February 1965): 166–79.

31 José Joaquín Fernández de Lizardi, *El Periquillo Sarniento*, 7th ed. (Mexico: Porrúa, 1965), 348–49.

32 Torcuato di Tella, "Las clases peligrosas a comienzos del siglo XIX en México," *Desarrollo económico* 12, no. 49 (January–March 1973): 761–91.

DELUDED WOMEN

*W*riting in the *Boletín del Archivo General de la Nación* [Bulletin of the National Archive], Julio Jiménez Rueda notes that between the year 1649 and 1659 the secret prisons of the Holy Office housed some strange bedfellows—people, he says, that nowadays would be classified as unbalanced or mad. In this period the tribunal passed judgment on cases such as that of Don Guillén de Lampart, "who wished to free New from Old Spain"; the astrologer Melchor Pérez de Soto, a cathedral teacher and distinguished bibliophile, who was "too melancholy and suffering from some defect in his imaginative capacity"; Don José Bruñón de Vertiz, "the so-called knight of the Miracle"; the four Romero sisters, who had claimed to have experienced revelations, raptures, and other experiences common at this time; and an Aponte who seemed not to feel physical pain.[1]

Rueda was writing before Foucault, otherwise he might have observed in more detail the transgressive behavior of this diverse group of people who threatened the purity of boundaries of the Church—to bring it to the low "other" of demon-inspired "fictionality." What many of these madmen and madwomen have in common is that they have blurred the boundaries and at times have stepped over into the devil's domain of fiction and mimesis.[2] As one Inquisition witness in an eighteenth-century trial put it:

> el demonio puede fingir éxtasis, arrobamientos, locuciones espirituales, palabras de la escritura, coloquios entre Dios y el alma, profecías falsas de cosas naturales, resplandores exteriores, efusiones exteriores y apariencia de sangre, falsa obediencia en lo que él quiere que obedezca la persona que domina para engañar con más seguridad, fingir enfermedades que parezca que agoniza la persona, hacer volver en sí, cuando él lo quiere los impedimentos que él mismo pone.

This heretofore unpublished essay was written in 1996.

[the devil can feign ecstasy, rapture, spiritual pronouncements, words from the scriptures, consultations between God and the soul, false prophecies in nature, earthly splendor, external effusions and manifestations of blood, false obedience to his will by the person he controls to deceive more fully, he can feign illness so a person appears to be dying then return them to life when he chooses.][3]

Thus did the devil own mimesis (he is the great monkey), performance, and the weaving of fictions.

In this respect the interconnection between what De Certeau calls the mystical fable and the category of transgressor known as the *ilusa* [deluded woman] is particularly interesting. The mystic and the *ilusa* handle the same material, use similar language, and engage in similar practices. In his book *La fable mystique*, Michel de Certeau observes that the great age of mysticism occurs when religion becomes more professionalized so that the spirit cannot "speak" spontaneously: mystical language now tends to resemble that of the marginalized—the child, the woman, the illiterate, the mad, the angels, and the body.[4] But the Inquisition cases of *ilusas* in New Spain also reveal that the mystical fable embraces something much broader than what we commonly understand by mysticism.[5] It is a language that refers to the senses at a time when sensuality could not be spoken otherwise, it is language that does not always need speech but can be read in bodily signs, it is a knowledge that does not require books, it is a story whose only verification is inner experience, of losing one's senses, of losing one's sense of self. Luce Irigaray, in her essay, "The Mystérique," calls it the only place in the West where women were able to speak and act so publicly.[6] This being so, and given that in colonial society fiction and imagination were suspect unless guided in the direction of allegory, is it surprising that the mystical fable should become a form of women's popular culture?

Mysticism provided women with an imaginary repertoire, a language and a structure of behavior much as the Romantic or Gothic novel did in Protestant Europe, but it was the Church that monitored the boundaries between what could and what could not be said and done. The mystical repertoire allowed women who were not written as protagonists into the epic narrative of the Conquest to imagine themselves as heroines of the faith. They enjoyed escape fantasies, which nearly always involved getting away from their families to live as hermits or die as martyrs. Such narratives and images belong, of course, to an ancient and recurrent repertoire. Yet, it is precisely the recurrence that is interesting. Sucking, imbibing directly from the Holy Body, flight from the narrow confines of the cell, most of all the rebellious body, the legs that refuse to walk, the mouth that refuses to speak or speaks what ought not to be spoken, or the heart migrating into Christ's body suggest an extraordinary concentration on the very body that had to be transcended.

The problem was that as soon as the mystical fable passed beyond the walls of the convent it seemed to cause delusion, especially among women. Indeed, it has been argued that the Inquisition was forced to invent the category of *ilusa* because of the freelance practices of those they considered pseudomystics or even dangerous *alumbradas* [enlightened ones]. These *ilusas* are not to be confused with witches: they did not boast of having made pacts with the devil—rather, they claimed that they had a special relationship with our Lord and the Saints, that their bodies bore the marks of these encounters, and that they had the gift of prophecy and could be transported in dream from one place to another. Whereas the mystic's experience was closely controlled and watched over by the confessor to whom she professed obedience, the *ilusa* often defied the confessor and tried to change the rules of the game. Claire Guilhem, who studied cases of heretical women accused of being *alumbradas* in Spain, attributes the emergence of the *ilusa* to the fact that women, in the words of Saint Teresa, "soñaba con tener la libertad de predicar, de confesar y de llevar las almas a Dios" [dreamt of being free to preach, confess, deliver souls to God]. She declares that "las ilusas que van ante la Inquisición rechazan el control de los confesores porque se niegan a practicar la autorepresión. Se niegan a ser definidas y limitadas por un saber que les dice quienes son, que son sus visiones y sus revelaciones" [the *ilusas* who appear before the Inquisition reject the control of the confessors because they refuse to practice self-repression. They refuse to be defined and limited by a system of knowledge that dictates their identity, their visions and their revelations.][7] In New Spain, where the *ilusas* often attracted a public who paid in kind to witness the performance, they were considered politically dangerous—the source of possible disturbances among the marginalized urban classes. In these women we see the forerunners of García Márquez's Blacaman the Bad, who attracted a public by resuscitating from death—a feat that was performed by many *ilusas*. The most famous seventeenth-century *ilusa* was the Peruvian Angela de la Carranza, who preached on the steps of Lima cathedral in an Augustian friar's gown and who ran a veritable industry of religious articles. But the case I want to discuss is that of Teresa de Romero, who was arrested by the Inquisition in Mexico in 1649 and appeared ten years later stripped to the waist in the *auto de fe* where she was publicly whipped.

Like Don Quijote, Teresa de Romero had her head turned by books — though by lives of saints rather than novels of chivalry. Teresa was eighteen when she was arrested and twenty-eight by the time she was sentenced. Although accused of belonging to the heretical sect of the *alumbrados*, it is clear that both she and the three sisters arrested with her had invented their own performance, which they had put together from reading the lives of saints and the mystics. Teresa belonged to the lower rungs of the *criollo* class and was raised by an aunt married to a farmer. She had lived in Puebla before arriving in Mexico City with her family three years before her arrest. Her father was described by the Inquisition as "un hombre satírico" [a satyr] who had been run out of town in the area of Texcoco by angry Indians and who, before his death, seems to have encouraged the girls in their strange manner of earning a living. When arrested, Teresa was found to be pregnant and later gave birth to a child whose father was said to be an Indian or a *mestizo*. During the ten years before she was sentenced, the child was with her in the prison and she constantly petitioned the Inquisitors on his behalf.

Teresa was self-taught and an avid consumer of stories about the lives of saints. She told the Inquisitors that she knew how to "leer en libro" [read in books], that she had taught herself and did not know anything else. On the recommendation of her confessor, she read of Marina de Cruz whose virtue was so great that she spoke directly to God and no longer spoke to men, for as her confessor explained, "de aquella manera se servía a Nuestro Señor, y que aquella santa ni comía ni bebía, porque toda su voluntad y entendimiento tenía en Nuestro Señor" [in that way she served Our Lord, and this holy woman neither ate nor drank, because all her will and understanding were with Our Lord]. Unfortunately, according to the Inquisitors these good counsels had the wrong effect, "pues tomando de memoria esto, por acreditarse de santa fingió después de algunos días un rapto" [for recalling this statement, to make herself a credible saint, she later feigned a trance]. In her confessions, Teresa was to reveal herself to have been an impressionable reader who had imitated actions that she had read or heard read. For instance, when the priest read her a story about the sighs of Saint Augustine, she feigned a rapture. And readings of Santa Teresa and Sor Ana María de San José caused her to imagine she was followed by a faceless hulk that took on different forms, sometimes that of a toad, sometimes that of a handsome young man who provoked her to carnal acts. She told people that she wanted to go to China and be martyred, a tale that obviously was inspired by Santa Teresa. And many of her other actions were inspired by stories that had been read to her by priests. In this manner, Teresa had learned the life of San Juan de la Cruz by heart and knew how to distinguish between the *vía activa y contemplativa*

> y que en los raptos en que fingió la visión de dichas moradas, y de dichas peñas, fingió asimesmo otras visiones para confirmación de lo que en dichos raptos decía, y que se les explicaba Nuestro Señor preguntándoselo ella; como son la de una sala con mucha luz, donde oía música sin ver los que cantaban: que significaba la música callada y la soledad sonora, de que gozaban los espirituales que ejercitaban la oración, palabras que oyó leer a dicho religioso en dicho libro.

> [and in the trances where she feigned the vision of these places and sufferings, she feigned other visions as well to confirm what she said in the trances, in which God explained them to her at her request; such as a vision of a room full of light where she heard music without seeing those who sang, which meant silent music and loud silence, enjoyed by the spiritual ones who prayed, words she heard this religious read in the above-mentioned book.]

Among other saintly writers she quoted were Santa Juana de la Cruz and Santa Catalina de Siena. And she also claimed she spoke intimately with San Pedro of Alcántara, and that her actions, deeds, and words were guided from heaven and directed by Santa Teresa.

What the case of Teresa de Romero reveals is that in a society in which the novels of chivalry were forbidden, the mystical fable became a kind of popular fiction for women. In turn, this interest was paradoxically encouraged by the view of women as only partly rational and therefore incapable of aspiring to the highest levels of theological wisdom. It was commonly argued that, in the words of one doctor of mysticism, "women are not suitable for the priesthood or for apostolic preaching, therefore God honors them in this manner with visions, raptures and revelations."[8] Nevertheless in ceding this space to women, the clergy found that they also had given women a space for self-expression that was difficult to control. In the case of nuns, the clergy exercised vigilance by having the women write down any unusual experiences, which were then carefully examined in order to distinguish them from demonic fictions and imitations. Moreover, there were sets of rules for determining what constituted a genuine vision: the vision must not contain anything contrary to the Scriptures nor intrinsically evil, frenetic, or furious, and they must not include novelties never preached by the Church. Those who had visions should be in good bodily shape, should be silent rather than talkative, and should not be old in the event that the visions might be attributed to senility. In addition, any revelations by women were to be treated with more suspicion than those of men because "women are not only weaker and more susceptible, but are humid crass and viscous by nature and because of this temperament are not only subject to lunatic impressions, but are easily overcome by passions of hatred, love, happiness and sadness."[9]

Thus the mystical experience of women was always subject to special control, even when the mystic was a nun. The confessor was the mediator and judge of the raw material of experience which, when tested and found true, was transformed into exemplary life stories which were often laundered versions of the *beata*'s own words.

The threat posed by the *ilusa* was that she was usually outside this system of control. Drawing on a repertoire, on *topoi* relayed through lives of saints, she shared with the mystic the gift of prophecy and an imaginary dominated by the female symbolism of lactation, bleeding, and *jouissance*. The difference was in her use of the fable, which she transposed from the safe domain of the religious institution into the turbulent street world. The *ilusa* was a practitioner of the marvelous, who used the mysterious power of the female body as her one economic resource—her one source of status. The *ilusas* of New Spain usually came from the lower rungs of the *criollo* classes, among whom neither marriage nor the convent were viable alternatives and therefore were left to fend for themselves. They did so by putting on freelance performances of marvels. In the trials of the Romero sisters, it was repeatedly emphasized that they earned money by their mystical raptures. Teresa was said to eat very well and her sister Josefa Romero was even more successful—she dressed in fine clothes and pearls and traveled in her own coach. The sisters arranged banquets and invited people to see them in ecstasies "as if they were in the theater," according to one witness. Josefa even had a disciple, a Spanish priest named Bruñón de Vertiz, who wrote two volumes based on the sayings of Josefa. He also wrote a manuscript, now lost, that describes the

> Favores del cielo comunicados en raptos vocales a su regalada sierva Jusepa de Jesus y de San Luis Beltrán, con un discurso sobre el estado que dicen de simpleza y propiamente raptos continuados sobre su beneficio

divino o ilusión fantástica del enemigo, como algunos los presumen. Dedicado a la Sacratísima Reina de los Angeles y Vírgen Santísima del Pilar de Zaragoza por un devoto esclavo suyo, natural de España.

[Favors from heaven told in vocal rapture to your loyal servant Jusepa de Jesus y de San Luís Beltrán, with a discourse on the so-called state of simpleness, and continuous raptures about his holy goodness or the fantastic delusion of the enemy, as some presume. Dedicated to the Holy Queen of Angels and the Holy Virgin of Pilar de Zaragoza, by a devoted slave, citizen of Spain.] [10]

The state of "simpleza" [simpleness] seems to have been the speciality of the *ilusas*—by becoming holy idiots they could act out their fantasies. Teresa, for instance, pretended to suckle an image of the child Jesus, and relapsed into baby talk:

Y para acreditar más su enajenación de sentidos y potencias, fingiá decir todo lo referido con notable sencillez y alegría; y hacía los chiqueos, quejidos, pucheritos y lágrimas de una criatura de dos años, llamando a este grandísimo embuste rapto continuado: y que a nadie conocía de vista, ni oídas, si no era a cierto clérigo presbítero, su confesor; de todos se enfadaba y huía, y daba a entender que solo conocía por el tacto; y así, tocando al rostro y las manos, nombraba luego las personas, como si fuera gran maravilla, estándolas viendo y conociéndolas.

[And to make her trance more credible, she pretended to say everything with great simplicity and glee . . . and she whined, pouted, and cried like a two-year-old, calling this fakery rapture; and she recognized no one by sight or sound except a certain priest, her confessor, whom she knew only by touch; and so, touching people's faces and hands, she named people as if this were a great marvel even though she was looking right at them.]

The Inquisition record itself takes on a ludic tone in referring to Teresa's *embustes* [fakery] Describing the lamoness that came and went at will, they write,

Y que estando en estos tullimientos, que ella llamaba raptos amorosos, y arrobada, si le daba alguna cosa, luego al instante se destullía, y si la cosa para recibirla requería una mano, aquella sola se destullía y si requería ambas a dos manos se destullían, y acabado de recibir lo que le daban, se volvían al instante a tullir.

[and in these bouts of paralysis, which she called amorous raptures, entranced, if anything was given to her she uncrippled immediately, and if she needed a hand to receive what was offered, it alone would move, and if two hands were needed, both would move, and on receiving what was offered, they became paralyzed again.]

What is interesting is that similar incidents can be found in the lives of *beatas* (María de Jesús Tomelin, for instance, had no less than three clerical biographers); if there is a difference it is one of epithets — one is termed "venerable virgin," the other is called a fraud.

It is precisely the public performance of the *ilusa* that was considered subversive and condemned as a comedy or a farce. Teresa de Romero, dressed in

galas con profanidad, paseando en carrozas, asistida y regalada a título de Santa, de muchas personas, llevandola a sus casas y teniéndola por muchos días y meses consigo, donde se arrobaba y aun robaba, pues a título de santa pedía lo que no le daban, haciéndola banquetes y convocando gente para verla arrobada, como si fuera una comedia . . . besando los rostros a los hombres, llamándolo de tatas fingiéndose simple y diciendo gracias, solo a fin de estafarlos, de llevar adelante la emulación de la dicha su hermana Josefa, y de encubrir sus muchas desdichas en materia de sensualidad.

[profane finery, going around in coaches, regaled and attended like a saint, [was] received by many in their homes for days and months at a time, where she both raved and robbed. . . . In the name of sainthood she asked for what was not offered, and they held banquets for her, inviting people to see her entranced, as if to a play. . . . And she kissed men's faces, calling them Papa, pretending to be a simpleton and telling jokes just to swindle people, to follow the footsteps of her sister Josefa, and to disguise her many miseries in sensuality.]

Teresa changed her story many times as she tried to minimize her faults and claim that she had acted "without malice." To the Inquisitors it was clear that she was a villain, a willing participant in a con game whose principle instigator had been her father (who died before the Inquisition hearings). The Inquisition record is like horrified running commentary on her devilish ingenuity. She invented a second purgatory known as the *penaculario.* She claimed to have seen the child Jesus sitting on the cushion that she was embroidering, "as if," the Inquisitors commented, "this famous trickster knew what work was: for surely had she really any regard and friendship for her cushion, she would not have ended up as a false saint and trickster." Of course she overdid it. When Saint Paul appeared to her, she asked him for a cigar as if using the saint as an alibi for her indulgence in "the infernal vice of smoking tobacco." But there was more horror to come: the Inquisitors also accused her of trying to abort a child that she had by a *mestizo* "who looked more like an Indian" and when she did not succeed, of abandoning it outside a house. Bearing a child out of wedlock could not itself have been a problem. After all, it was precisely at this time that the mother of Sor Juana was doing just that, without apparently being treated as a pariah. In Teresa's case it is the putative father's ethnic characteristics that support the accusations of licentiousness.

Teresa's story can be read against the grain of the Inquisition record, as inventiveness born out of familial and personal crisis. A virtuoso performer in her own right, she was so skillful that it seemed that she actually saw what she represented. But it was also an imagination that had nowhere to go. What Teresa did rapidly transcended the boundaries of what was permissible, and that she was again pregnant when arrested and gave birth in the prisons of the Inquisition was one more proof of her "dangerously licentious" nature.

Yet Teresa's sad petitions for release sent to the administration reveal the desperate loneliness of her life in that isolated and dark cell, as well as her struggle to bring up a child there. Teresa the trickster may also have been Teresa the good mother. The child was initially given to a wet nurse since she did not have enough milk to feed it. In her petitions, she asks for small favors such as chocolate to drink, tobacco, a shirt, shoes, sewing thread, ointment, and a smock for her child. At one time she describes the two of them as "naked." Perhaps the most pathetic request is for a piece of paper so that she can teach her child to read, because the piece that she had had been eaten by mice.

After 1656 no more is heard from her. Did she die from one of her frequent illnesses or was she released? We can only be sure of one thing: during the years in prison her fantasy had been tamed.

In *From the Beast to the Blonde*, a book on European fairy tales, author Marina Warner argues against psychological interpretations of fairy tales. She states that they offer a case "where the very contempt for women opened an opportunity for them to exercise their wit and communicate their ideas: women's care for children, the prevailing disregard for both groups and their presumed identity with the simple folk, the common people, handed them fairy tales as a different kind of nursery, where they might set their own seedlings and plant their own flowers."[11] The mystical fable offered material similar to the imagination, with the difference that the penalties for giving the imagination free rein were deadly. And this makes the practices of the *ilusas* all the more extraordinary. There is a case for considering the *ilusa* the true nonconformist, but one whose only activities necessarily passed through the fictional.

NOTES

1 The trial which I would like to research in more detail has been partially transcribed by Julio Jiménez Rueda, "El proceso de una seuda iluminada—1649" [The trial of a *pseudo-iluminada*] tomo xvii 1–3, *Boletín del archivo general de la Nación*, México, Secretaría de Gobernación, México 1946. The essay was begun several years ago when I was working on another Inquisition case.

2 For a fuller treatment, see Jean Franco, *Plotting Women: Gender and Representation in Mexico* (New York: Columbia University Press, 1989), esp. chap. 3 on the trial of Ana de Aramburú.

3 *Ana Rodríguez de Castro y Arambbhuru, Ilusa, Afectadora de Santos, Falsos Milagros y Revelaciones Divinas: Proceso Inquisitorial de la Nueva España (Siglos xviii y xix)*, with an introduction by Dolores Bravo, transcribed by de Alejandra Herrera. (Mexico City: Universidad Autónoma Metropolitana, 1984), 29.

4 Michel de Certeau, *La fable mystique, xvi–xvii siecle* (Paris: Gallimard, 1982).

5 Claire Guilhem, "La Inquisición y la devalución del verbo femenino," in Bartolomé Benasar, ed., *Inquisición española*, 2nd ed. (Barcelona: Editorial Crítica, 1984). On the Mexican Inquisition the most important work to date is Solange Alberro, *Inquisición y sociedad en México 1571–1700* (Mexico: Fondo de Cultura, 1988). However, Alberro is primarily interested in the workings of the Inquisition and in cases of heresy and witchcraft, and pays no particular attention to the *ilusa*.

6 Luce Irigaray, "La Mystérique," in *Speculum of the Other Woman*, trans. Gillian C. Gill (Ithaca, N.Y.: Cornell University Press, 1985), 181.

7 Guilhem, "La Inquisición y la devaluación del verbo femenino."

8 Father Luis Martin, *Daughters of the Conquistadores* (Albuquerque: University of New Mexico Press, 1983).

9 Ibid.

10 Miguel Godínez, *Práctica de la Theologia Mystica* (Seville, 1682).

11 Marina Warner, *From the Beast to the Blonde: On Fairy Tales and Their Tellers* (New York, Farrar, Straus and Giroux, 1994), xxiii.

AFTERWORD: THE TWILIGHT OF THE VANGUARD
AND THE RISE OF CRITICISM

*I*n the early 1960s, a group of Latin American writers devoted themselves to revolutionizing the reading of literary texts. Some belonged
to the generation formed in the avant-garde movements of the 1920s
and 1930s. Other, younger members of the group had come together in
support of the recently triumphant Cuban Revolution. None of these critics, of course, were academics. Their names were Borges, Fuentes, Cortázar, Vargas Llosa, Onetti, Lezama Lima, García Márquez. The majority of
them — Vargas Llosa is an exception — had not passed through departments
of literature. Like many of his generation, Carlos Fuentes, for example, had
studied law. Along with Sergio Pitol and Marco Antonio Montes de Oca,
he attended classes given by Manuel Pedroso who, according to Fuentes
himself, "led us to an understanding of bourgeois law by means of the
social energy of Balzac, the private sensibility of Rousseau, or the bureaucratic melancholy of Galdós."[1] Fuentes also attended the gatherings of
Alfonso Reyes's literary circle in the latter's home and library, following a
tradition of literary apprenticeship which dates back to the literary acade-
mies of the nineteenth century.[2]

In Latin America, small groups of intellectuals formed around journals. These were the years of *Amaru* in Peru, of the *Corno Emplumado*, of
Casa de las Américas in Cuba, of *Siempre* and *Novedades* in Mexico, of *Marcha* in Uruguay. These groups and other isolated individuals like Clarice
Lispector, for example, comprised not only the aesthetic vanguard but
also the most advanced criticism of the period. Representing a diversity of
perspectives, they all nonetheless agreed on the necessity of transforming
reading and changing readers. The principal instruments of this transformation would be the novel and the short story. It is interesting that the
literary and cultural critics most closely associated with the new literature

Originally published as "El ocaso de la vanguardia y el auge de la crítica" in *Nuevo Texto Crítico*
7, nos. 14–15 (1994–95): 11–21. Translated by Milos Kokotovic.

were not full-time academics. Emir Rodríguez Monegal and Angel Rama managed and edited journals during the 1960s.[3] Carlos Monsiváis never taught at a university.[4]

It is important to emphasize the spaces that permitted the development of an essayistic criticism which did not necessarily conform to academically imposed models and was written in a language intelligible to nonspecialist readers. Apart from the truly exceptional cases of Antonio Cándido, Noé Jitrik, and Ana María Barrenechea, established critics within the university kept their distance from the new literature.

It comes as no surprise, therefore, that it was the writers themselves who took on the task of importing, disseminating, and inventing theory. It was Octavio Paz who produced a book on Lévi-Strauss in 1967.[5] And in *Historia de un deicidio* [History of a Deicide], Vargas Llosa attempted to combine an autobiographical study with an analysis of the diegetic and symbolic structures of García Márquez's narrative. It was Carlos Fuentes who launched an attack on provincialism in numerous essays, citing the most illustrious names in contemporary literature as well as critics and philosophers from Paul Ricoeur to Michel Foucault, from hippies to happenings. It was Cortázar who used the novel to propose a new poetics of narrative,[6] while Borges and Cortázar both subverted the separation between high and mass culture, taking seriously genres like the detective novel and jazz.[7] For both these authors, however, popular culture was of course not the common variety, but rather an exotic and imported culture accessible only to a sophisticated minority. Nonetheless, their gesture may be seen as a challenge to academic norms, a challenge which came to be fundamental in the novels of Cabrera Infante and Manuel Puig. Meanwhile, in the community of Solentiname, Ernesto Cardenal was putting into practice one of the avant-garde's old projects, that of making an artist out of every worker.

This generation carried out a significant revision of the literary canon. Although Carlos Fuentes's proposals in *La nueva novela hispanoamericana* [The New Spanish American Novel] were often sloganistic, the innovation of including Brazilians (Guimarães Rosa) and Spaniards (Goytisolo) should be noted. Mario Vargas Llosa's defiant celebration of the chivalric novels which many critics knew only as precursors of *Don Quijote* was another significant change in the literary canon, above all because it placed fantastic literature at the origins of the modern novel.[8] Vargas Llosa's book on Flaubert (*La orgía perpetua* [The Perpetual Orgy], 1975), Carlos Fuentes's reading of Cervantes (*Cervantes o la crítica de la lectura* [Cervantes, or the Critique of Reading], 1976) and the recovery of the baroque by Lezama

Lima and Severo Sarduy[9] inverted the metropolis-periphery relationship in which it had traditionally been the metropolis which read, researched, observed, and recovered information about the periphery. These essays affirmed the rights of Latin Americans to interpret, appropriate, and transform European culture. Finally, although they privileged literature, this generation of writers did not ignore new information technologies. I have in mind, for example, the way Cortázar experimented with the form of the book, or the essays and poems of Octavio Paz,[10] or the hibridization of genres practiced by Manuel Puig (in *Kiss of the Spider Woman*, 1976) and Luis Rafael Sánchez (in *Macho Camacho's Beat*), among others.

Readers' expectations were changed by the "boom" authors. The writers were aided in this by a small group of allied critics such as Angel Rama, who in the pages of *Marcha* reflected on modernity, pop art, and the Cold War phenomenon of subsidized editions of North American books. Edited by Emir Rodríguez Monegal and published in Paris, *Mundo Nuevo* actively promoted the avant-garde, experimental literature, and the counterculture. In Mexico, at Radio Universidad and in the cultural supplement of *Siempre*, Carlos Monsiváis engaged in a cultural criticism which ridiculed academic discourse. His style of writing was closer to Thomas Wolfe and the North American counterculture than to Leo Spitzer. In Buenos Aires, Tomás Eloy Martínez at *Primera Plana* and Enrique Pezzoni and José Bianco at the journal *Sur* enthusiastically supported the new novelists.

My aim is not to present an idyllic vision of the 1960s and the post-1960s period, but rather to highlight the fact that at that moment cultural criticism and theoretical reflection on culture were more developed in literary works and essays than in academic texts, and that a notion of an "avant-garde" or a "vanguard" still existed. This situation changed in the 1970s, after which writers could no longer (as Carlos Fuentes wanted) announce the future.[11] Quite the contrary, and virtually without exception, writers expressed an uneasiness with the political, cultural, and social transformations taking place. An apocalyptic tone predominated, and it was due less to the military governments which took power and were of course an easy target for criticism than to a new pluralism which permitted everything and valued nothing. Writers had for some time viewed the "metanarratives" of the past with skepticism—Marxism, nationalism, and teleological versions of history. But with pluralism, value and judgments of value were no longer necessarily the province of high culture. For some, domestic rock music was worth just as much as a five-hundred-page novel. And, in any case, postmodernism cannot rely on fixed positions. It is more a question of tactics than of a qualitative separation between high culture and consumer culture.[12]

Faced with this situation, some "traditional" intellectuals opted for the defense of an abstract freedom which for them took priority over social justice. This group does not represent an avant-garde but rather a kind of self-generating "common sense." Vargas Llosa is the clearest example, although one could consider Octavio Paz the pioneer of this position.[13]

According to the conservative line, socialism is a dinosaur and all guerrilla or revolutionary movements a mistake. The attack launched against the Salvadoran guerrilla movement and the Sandinistas in the pages of *Vuelta* is symptomatic of this.[14] More surprising is the ferocity of the attack against liberal positions like that of Carlos Fuentes. It is significant that Enrique Krauze published an essay in a conservative magazine from the United States in which he tries to ridicule Fuentes, who has maintained a critical, "Latin" position toward an interventionist U.S. foreign policy.[15]

The gap has widened between the "conservatives" and a group which includes García Márquez and Carlos Fuentes, who, although they no longer talk of socialism, nonetheless maintain some notion of alternatives to neoliberalism, regional alternatives different from the economic policy which now dominates the continent. What definitely seems to have disappeared is the notion of writers' political commitment and responsibility, a favorite topic at the round table discussions of the 1960s. If something remains of this tradition it is to be found perhaps in certain forms of women's writing, such as the works of Elena Poniatowska, for example.[16]

The rise of conservatism is of course not the only reason for the currently anachronistic status of words like *commitment* and *responsibility*. The problem also has to do with the exhaustion of the words themselves at a moment when poststructuralist criticism, among other factors, has cast doubt on intellectuals' role as the "voice" of the voiceless, or, more radically, as those who "allow" others to speak.[17]

The retreat from vanguard positions also means that there is no longer any resistance to the consumerism which has effectively erased the separation between high and mass culture. In contemporary societies, consumers (and readers) are distinguished less by their nationality and social class than by their tastes and preferences. And many authors now frankly address their works to a transnational reading public.[18] One notes, for example, the change of style between Fuentes's *Terra Nostra* (1975) and *La campaña* [The Campaign] (1991); or between García Márquez's *Autumn of the Patriarch* (1975) and *The General in His Labyrinth* (1989); or between

Vargas Llosa's *Conversation in the Cathedral* (1969) and *In Praise of the Step-mother* (1988). And it is not only a matter of style. Novels like *Conversation in the Cathedral* and *Terra Nostra* responded to concerns about Hispanic, Latino, Peruvian, and *mestizo* identity—issues with a long history in Latin America. They are, therefore, novels which demand a degree of effort from non–Latin American readers. This is not the case with the more recent novels—there is a price to be paid for "universality."

As far as the literary work is concerned, the skepticism toward terms like *originality* leads to pastiche and a concern for historical themes.[19] But there are also more radical changes which affect the very structure of a literary institution once based on the author as the only source of the text, on the autonomy of the literary text itself, and on the cooperation of the complicit reader. The proliferation of translations, the adaptations of novels to other media, and the transnationalization of literature have cast doubt on the notion of a single, solitary author, on the autonomy and stability of the text, and on the complicit reader. Today it is possible to find radio listeners or television viewers of García Márquez's stories who have never seen them in print, or movie fans who have never read Manuel Puig's *Kiss of the Spider Woman* but know it through the film version. For its part, the best-seller crosses national borders and thus tends to sacrifice a certain specificity—references shared by the imagined community of the nation or of Spanish America. What Juan Goytisolo had to say about post-Franco literature in Spain can be applied to much Latin American literature today. In an interview with the magazine *Babel*, he explains, "Today the most common aspiration is to write this year's best-seller or become a million-aire by winning the Planeta [literary prize]." He then adds, "In a country where everything has changed in recent years, only the ceremonies, attitudes, and habits of the intelligentsia remain the same."[20]

The boom writers have registered the rise of mass culture in different ways and sometimes schizophrenically. In a 1981 essay, Vargas Llosa had expressed his pessimism regarding what he called pseudo-cultural products, saying that "the vulgarity and conformism, the intellectual poverty and artistic indigence, the formal and moral misery of these pseudo-cultural products profoundly affect the spiritual life of a nation." The responsibility of the writer is, therefore, "to conquer them for real culture, elevating the level of the public through education and training, returning to the public, ever more rigorous, unsettled, and critical."[21] But this 1981 declaration is no longer valid. Like many other authors he uses the media, and his novels refer to them more frequently.

One of the first Latin American writers to realize the importance of mass culture was Manuel Puig. For Puig, narrative and poetry are not to be found only in the novel or the lyric poem. On the contrary, the social imaginary of our time is disseminated through movies, romance and detective novels, and the lyrics of the *bolero* and the tango. García Márquez has gone even further. He founded the Cinematographic Institute in Cuba and writes soap operas which reach an even bigger audience than do his novels. In Chile Antonio Skármeta has inaugurated a television program, "The Book Show," whose purpose is to stimulate readers.

Those without the global "visibility" which provides access to the media are more uneasy. The old values have disappeared and the new ones have not yet taken shape. In 1985, Héctor Libertella noted a shock "which puts in parenthesis our forms of thought from two decades ago. It is as if our discussions, our passions, our style of wanting to construct or to dissent have fallen into a kind of abyss. And as if we had not prepared the safety net which could protect us from the impact of that fall."[22] At the same roundtable discussion organized by the Noble Foundation, J. C. Martini spoke of an inexplicable "lack" in his country's literature, a lack which goes beyond "the economic crisis, the political transition, the inefficiency of cultural policies, Argentina's cultural isolation, the bewildering nature of the communications media, the disappearance of the cultural figure of the editor, the growing hegemony of other cultural forms and products and literature's specific transition toward other forms and materials."[23]

What these writers register is the loss of prestige suffered by literature and the suspicion that the power writers once possessed has flowed elsewhere. Moreover, literature tends to lose its critical capacity when it passes through the media or through the mass-market book industry. For this reason, some young poets and writers try to preserve a marginal position. The clearest example is poetry, which only survives today thanks to the artificial respiration provided by the community of poets. But one can also point to a considerable number of young writers (many of them women) who have rejected the temptation of the best-seller in order to write from outside international circuits.[24]

Cultural criticism has taken advantage of this situation and is no longer a delayed reflection of literary movements. Indeed, poststructuralism, sociocriticism, and deconstruction have contributed to a questioning of literature as an institution and of literature's hegemony over other cultural practices. At the same time, the divisions between high, popular, and mass culture are no longer so solid. It is not only a matter of the appropriation of popular culture by authors such as Luis Rafael Sánchez and Manuel Puig but, rather, as William Rowe and Vivian Schelling indicate, of the flexible nature of popular cultures which defy all attempts at totalization or institutionalization.[25] Contemporary criticism must therefore be an open criticism, constantly on guard against attempts at institutionalization.

Before celebrating the vitality of the new critical attitude evident in the number and diversity of books and journals, I think it is necessary to make a few observations. For although criticism is skeptical of institutionalization, the majority of critics today occupy academic positions. Another observation: although the contribution of Latin American and European universities is important, the growing number of Latin American students "processed" by North American universities must be noted because these institutions inevitably impose their own concept of professionalization, which may have little to do with Latin American needs.

The editing and publication of critical texts, however, may be considered a true achievement. In the past, the lack of such texts prevented in-depth study of certain areas, particularly the colonial period and the nineteenth century. While in Mexico, for example, there are facsimile editions of the most important literary magazines, these are not available in many other countries. More surprising is the lack of an adequately annotated edition of the works of Rubén Darío and Gabriela Mistral. When I wrote my book on Vallejo in the 1970s, I had to admit that my study of the *Poemas humanos* was provisional. A critical edition by Américo Ferrari did not come out until just two years ago. The Biblioteca Ayacucho, with Angel Rama's participation, engaged in a truly heroic effort to provide scholars with correct editions of the most basic books. But access to non-canonical texts was still difficult—for example, the writings of nuns from the colonial period and indigenous manuscripts—many of them in North American and European libraries (thanks to the looting and sale of Latin American collections). With the help of foundations and universities, the preparation of reliable texts is just beginning in Latin America, while in Europe this task was for the most part completed in the nineteenth century or at the beginning of the twentieth. The new translations and transcriptions of indigenous texts and the transcriptions of colonial ones—for example the lives of nuns or the trials of the Inquisition (which are of considerable interest)—will surely change the writing of Latin American literary history. The publication of previously unavailable texts will permit a revision of literary history, which is currently conceived much more as a history of texts and their reception—for example the history of texts such as the *Popul Vuh* or pre-Columbian codices—than a "development" or a "current" which leads to emancipation or maturity.

The new cultural scene requires a new criticism because what has ended is not just a literary cycle but also a particular way of looking at literary history. The privilege conceded to the evolutionary view of "national" literatures with distinctive characteristics, or, on the other hand, the broader view of Latin America's evolution as a whole, suppressed many cultural areas not encompassed by these versions of history. The demand for national coherence excluded the subaltern and the heterogenous, and the obsession with the novel precluded the appreciation of a variety of narrative forms, from oral tradition[26] through radio and soap operas to cinematographic narrative. Terms once used in histories of literature—*maturity, generation, literary currents*—are no longer considered valid.

It is not merely a question of changing intellectual fashions, but rather something much deeper. For instance, feminist criticism, research on "otherness," and postnationalism have emphasized everything which the literary institution had formerly marginalized or excluded—noncanonical genres, vernacular languages, languages other than Spanish or Portuguese. Once the nation ceases to be the essential framework for literary history it becomes possible to examine problems which had always exceeded its limits.[27] Perhaps indigenous culture is the most obvious example because it never fit very easily within a national framework. A book such as Gordon Brotherson's *The Fourth World*, for example, starts from the premise that a continental "American" culture cannot be subsumed under the term "Latin America."[28]

Poststructuralist criticism also pays attention to rhetoric, to translation, to the history of the text. Unlike the "close reading" of North American New Criticism, poststructuralism does not confine itself to the study of just one genre or even to the broader category of literary texts. This contribution has been truly revolutionary. Discourse analysis, semiotics, and reception theory are today considered essential for the study of history and anthropology. At the same time, literary works enter into dialogue with, contest, and allude to other discourses—legal, ethnographic, theological—and to other discursive genres—the sermon, the travelogue, the trial.[29] For this reason, researchers from different disciplines frequently study the same documents—the chronicles of the discovery, oral tradition, essays on the nation, the trials of the Inquisition—and often share similar theoretical perspectives.

All this implies that the boundaries between disciplines are no longer so clear. Therefore, in some cases research is defined less by disciplinary criteria than by the research topic—the conquest and colonization, cultural hibridization, nation and state formation, the struggles for interpretive power by indigenous peoples, blacks, or women. This tendency is most evident in studies of the colonial period. Tzvetan Todorov's book *The Conquest of America* (1982) provoked a more general interest in the discovery and the conquest, but it had two fundamental defects: first, the author made no reference to the considerable contributions of previous researchers, especially Latin Americans; and, second, its argument was too rudimentary, too constrained by contemporary concerns to encompass a process as complex as the conquest. Nonetheless, Todorov's book demonstrated a kind of research no longer defined by a discipline but rather by its object of study, in this case the colonial social imaginary. The relation between writing and the social imaginary of a period became a principal concern of historians (such as Alberto Flores Galindo and Sergio Gruzinski) as well as literary critics (Beatriz Pastor, for example).[30] Discourse analysis and semiotics—the books and essays of Rolena Adorno and Walter Mignolo, for example—have opened new lines of inquiry for the study of discourse during the colonial period.[31] The book which is perhaps most representative of this interdisciplinary approach is Regina Harrison's *Signs, Songs and Memory in the Andes*. It includes studies of oral tradition, colonial documents, analysis of literary texts, and a discussion of how to translate certain concepts from Quechua into Spanish.[32]

The tendency toward examining diverse sources, documents, and testimonials which formerly "belonged" to different disciplines is already being institutionalized under the banner of "cultural studies." It is interesting that in Latin America the impetus for this movement comes out of social science departments and institutes while in England and the United States departments of literature are generally the ones which have taken the initiative. The explanation for this difference lies, in part, in recent history. During the military regimes of the Southern Cone, the military took control of the universities. Research survived in independent institutions such as FLACSO and CENECA (Chile), CEBRAP (Brazil), and CEDES (Argentina). Researchers in these institutions began to realize the importance of studying culture—particularly popular culture—for understanding the roots of authoritarianism. The research of José Joaquín Brunner and Bernardo Subercaseaux in Chile, Josefina Ludmer and Beatriz Sarlo in Argentina, and Renato Ortiz in Brazil[33] continued throughout the period of the military dictatorships and often represented a heroic and silent effort under difficult circumstances. At the same time in Mexico, Néstor García Canclini and Jesús Martín Barbero (who would later return to Colombia to continue his work) launched innovative research projects on popular culture and the reception of the mass communication media.[34] And, in Peru, Mirko Lauer undertook a study of folk art.[35]

It is impossible to summarize the work of all these researchers in a few words, but a couple of recent tendencies can be highlighted: the exciting concern with democratization and the attempt to understand processes of modernization and modernity. One found much more perceptive analyses of contemporary culture in journals such as *David y Goliath* (the FLACSO journal), *Diálogos de Comunicación*, the organ of the Latin American Federation of Social Communication Faculties and Associations, and *La Revista de Crítica Cultural* (Chile), than in literary magazines. The study of culture in the era of globalization can be undertaken today in large part thanks to the work of these critics.

The experience of this group of researchers has been instructive. It is clear to me that traditional literary criticism provides us with neither the language nor the method for addressing contemporary realities. This is why it has been necessary to open new spaces. Perhaps for the first time, Latin American researchers are observing, studying, and analyzing metropolitan culture. Beatriz Sarlo's analysis of the use of information technology during the Gulf War comes to mind. While in the past information moved exclusively from the metropolis to the periphery, today there is a "two-way traffic."[36]

In the United States, cultural studies have developed in a different manner, largely as a response to demographic changes. A growing number of women and minority groups have demanded to study subject matters which go beyond the old disciplines. Feminism in the United States has clearly had a pioneering role in this respect. It was a question of studying not so much women as the constitution of "gender," which then implies tackling questions of representation, subjectivity, history, law, psychoanalysis, and culture. This kind of interdisciplinarity also characterized Chicano, Puerto Rican, and African American studies.[37] The curriculum changes which these new studies implied were not achieved without opposition. The defenders of Western culture took their polemic to the pages of newspapers and magazines and attacked multicultural texts in a particularly aggressive manner.

Despite the different approaches and objectives of Latin American and North American researchers (for obvious reasons I cannot speak of European research), it seems to me that cultural studies are an important zone of contact which will permit the examination of theoretical problems, which in my view have not yet been adequately addressed. One of these problems is the status of exception still accorded to Latin America in almost all areas of contemporary debate—postmodernity, for example, and postcolonialism and feminism. In spite of postmodernity, in spite of the dissolution of the center and the dissemination of power, there is still a tendency to continue debating in terms determined by French or Anglo-Saxon criticism when in fact there exist more fruitful approaches to contemporary realities.[38] The challenge is to find ways to account for more and more complex relationships between the reception and circulation of symbolic goods at transnational, national, and regional levels, and to take in a culture which today is not only transnational or national but also regional and local. The fluidity of demographic currents confers an ethical responsibility on all those able to translate not only from one language to another but from one cultural environment to another. All this implies rethinking the question of identity. It is not a question of defending supposedly pure identities but, rather, on the contrary, researching the new forms of culture which constitute the multiple identities of our time.

As Beatriz Sarlo has noted with respect to the modernization of the 1920s: "The new elements which are the lived form of modernization and for this reason appear as a cultural cutting edge, could not be present with the same productive intensity in all material and symbolic manifestations of the popular imagination. They are emergent features which do not yet form a continuum, but are rather conglomerations of meaning with a high mythical content which make possible the processing of technological changes. But they are islands, often unsystematic groupings of motifs which never lose their fragmentary character."[39] The observation remains valid in the contemporary world and clearly requires a criticism capable of capturing the immediate.

Exemplary in this respect is Carlos Monsiváis's book *Escenas de pudor y liviandad* [Scenes of Modesty and License], a veritable treatise on taste and the formation of cultural identities in the flux of the transnational scene.[40] The labyrinth of solitude has become the labyrinth of the city, where cultures collide, defend, and invent themselves. What Monsiváis's book demonstrates is the distance between academic criticism and the emerging culture. He implicitly proposes another form of criticism which requires a cultural immersion difficult to engage in within existing academic institutions. For this reason the renewal of criticism must lead to self-reflection and to the transformation of institutions too archaic to adapt themselves to a culture which eludes their grasp.

NOTES

1 Carlos Fuentes, *Tiempo Mexicano* (Mexico: Editorial Joaquín Mortíz, 1971), 57.
2 Ibid.
3 Both edited *Marcha*. Rama continued teaching at the university, but Rodríguez Monegal left the university for a period in order to edit *Mundo Nuevo* from Paris.
4 Carlos Monsiváis edited the literary pages of *Siempre* and worked as a researcher in the Mexican Institute for Anthropology and History.
5 Octavio Paz, *Claude Lévi-Strauss: An Introduction* (Ithaca: Cornell University Press, 1970).
6 Carlos Fuentes, *La nueva novela hispanoamericana* (Mexico: Editorial Joaquín Mortíz, 1969); Julio Cortázar, *Rayuela* (Buenos Aires: Editorial Sudamericana, 1963).
7 For example Borges's obsession with the books of G. K. Chesterton, inventor of Father Brown, an author virtually forgotten today in the world of English letters; in Cortázar's case, jazz is not only an important theme in *Rayuela* and in "El Perseguidor." Cortázar in fact devoted several essays to jazz; see for example "Louis enormísimo cronopio" and "La vuelta al piano de Thelonius Monk" in *La vuelta al día en ochenta mundos* (Buenos Aires: Siglo Veintiuno, 1967).
8 Mario Vargas Llosa, foreword to *Tirant lo Blanc*.
9 José Lezama Lima, *La expresión americana* (Madrid: Alianza Editorial, 1969); Severo Sarduy, *Escrito sobre un cuerpo* (Buenos Aires: Editorial Sudamericana, 1969).
10 For example, "la planta baja" of Cortázar's *Ultimo Round* or Octavio Paz's *Blanco*, which subvert conventional notions of the book.
11 Fuentes, *La nueva novela*, 96.
12 Nelly Richard, "Postmodernism and Periphery," *Third Text* 2 (winter 1987/88): 5–12.
13 Mario Vargas Llosa, *Contra viento y marea (1962–1982)* (Barcelona: Editorial Seix Barral, 1983). The essays included in this book clearly indicate the transformation in Vargas Llosa's thinking during the 1970s.
14 Gabriel Zaid wrote an article on El Salvador for *Vuelta* 56 (July 1981).
15 Krauze's attack was rapidly exported from Mexico to conservative North American magazines. See Enrique Krauze, "Guerilla Dandy. The Life and Easy Times of Carlos Fuentes," *The New Republic* 27 June 1988: 28–38.
16 See especially *La noche de Tlatelolco* (Mexico: Ediciones Era, 1971); *Fuerte es el silencio* (Mexico: Ediciones Era, 1980); *Nada, nadie. Las voces del temblor* (Mexico: Ediciones Era, 1988).
17 Gayatri Chakravorty Spivak's essay is key in this debate. See "Can the Subaltern Speak?" in her *In Other Worlds* (New York: Methuen, 1987).

18 According to Néstor García Canclini (*Culturas híbridas. Estrategias para entrar y salir de la modernidad* [Mexico: Grijalbo, 1991]) book sales and reading have increased considerably in the age of mass culture.

19 See Jean Franco, "Pastiche in Contemporary Latin American Literature," *Studies in 20th Century Literature* 14, no. 1 (winter 1990): 95–107 and this volume pp. 393–404.

20 Juan Goytisolo, cited in *Narrativa Argentina, Segundo Encuentro de Escritores Dr. Roberto Noble* Cuaderno 4 de *Clarín* (September 1987): 15.

21 Vargas Llosa, "El elefante y la cultura," in *Contra viento y marea*, 445.

22 Héctor Libertella, interview in "La Razón," cited in *Segundo Encuentro de Escritores Dr. Roberto Noble*, 45.

23 J. C. Martini, contribution to the debate in *Segundo Encuentro de Escritores Dr. Roberto Noble*, 45.

24 The clearest case is the Chilean author Diamela Eltit whose work does not lend itself to easy reading. See, for example, her novels *Lumpérica* (Santiago: Ediciones del Ornitorrinco, 1983) and *Por la patria* (Santiago: Ediciones del Ornitorrinco, 1986).

25 William Rowe and Vivian Schelling, *Memory and Modernity: Popular Culture in Latin America* (London: Verso, 1991).

26 Martin Lienhard, *La voz y su huella* (Havana: Casa de las Américas, 1990).

27 There is also a revalorization of how the nation has been narrated. See Doris Sommer, *Foundational Fictions: The National Romances of Latin America* (Berkeley: University of California Press, 1991); Beatriz González Stephan, *La historiografía literaria del liberalismo hispanoamericano del siglo XIX* (Havana: Casa de las Américas, 1987).

28 G. Brotherston, *The Book of the Fourth World: Reading the Native Americas through their Literature* (New York: Cambridge University Press, 1992). Regarding the problem of Latin American criticism's object of study, see Antonio Cornejo Polar, "Los sistemas literarios como categoría histórica," *Revista de Crítica Literaria Latinoamericana* 15, no. 29 (1989): 19–24.

29 See Mary Louise Pratt's book on travel writing and exploration, *Imperial Eyes: Travel Writing and Transculturation* (London: Routledge, 1992); Roberto González Echeverría, *Myth and Archive: A Theory of Latin American Narrative* (New York: Cambridge University Press, 1990).

30 Beatriz Pastor, *Discursos narrativos de la conquista: mitificación y emergencia* (Hanover, N.H.: Ediciones del Norte, 1993); Alberto Flores Galindo, *Buscando un Inca: identidad y utopía en los Andes* (Havana: Casa de las Américas, 1986).

31 Rolena Adorno, *Guamán Poma: Writing and Resistance in Colonial Peru* (Austin: University of Texas Press, 1986); Walter Mignolo, "Teorizar a través de fronteras culturales," *Revista de Crítica Literaria Latinoamericana* 17, no. 33 (1991): 103–12. See also Elizabeth Hill Boone and Walter Mignolo, eds. *Writing Without Words: Alternative Literacies in Mesoamerica and the Andes* (Durham, N.C.: Duke University Press, 1994).

32 Regina Harrison, *Signs, Songs and Memory in the Andes: Translating Quechua Language and Culture* (Austin: University of Texas Press, 1989).

33 José Joaquín Brunner, *Un espejo trizado. Ensayos sobre cultura y políticas culturales* (Santiago: Facultad Latinoamericana de Ciencias Sociales, 1988); Beatriz Sarlo, *Una modernidad periférica: Buenos Aires 1920–1930* (Buenos Aires: Ediciones Nueva Visíon, 1988). Though published after the fall of the military government, this book reflects the methodology and concerns developed earlier in *Punto de Vista*. Renato Ortiz, *A Moderna Tradição Brasileira. Cultura Brasileira e Industria Cultural* (São Paolo: Editora Brasilense, 1988).

34 Néstor García Canclini, *Culturas populares en el capitalismo* (Havana: Casa de las Américas, 1982); *Culturas híbridas. Estrategias para entrar y salir de la modernidad* (Mexico: Grijalbo, 1989); Jesús Martín Barbero, *De los medios a las mediaciones* (Mexico: Grijalbo, 1987).

35 Mirko Lauer, *Crítica de la artesanía. Plástica y sociedad en los Andes peruanos* (Lima: DESCO, 1982).

36 Beatriz Sarlo, *La imaginación técnica. Sueños modernos de la cultura argentina* Buenos Aires: Ediciones Nueva Visión 1992); Ortiz, *A Moderna Tradição Brasileira*.

37 For examples, see Marc Zimmerman, *U.S. Latino Literature: An Essay and Annotated Bibliography* (Chicago: MARCH/Abrazo Press, 1992).

38 Carlos Rincón, "Modernidad periférica y el desafío de lo posmoderno. Perspectivas del arte narrativo latinoamericano," *Revista de Crítica Literaria Latinoamericana* 15, no. 29 (1989): 61–104; George Yúdice, "¿Puede hablarse de posmodernidad en América Latina?", *Revista de Crítica Literaria Latinoamericana* 15, no. 29 (1989): 105–28.

39 Sarlo, *La imaginación técnica*, 12.

40 Carlos Monsiváis, *Escenas de pudor y liviandad* (Mexico: Grijalbo, 1981).

Jean Franco was born into a working-class family in Dukinfield, England, in 1924. She holds a B.A. with First Class Honors in History from the University of Manchester (1944) and a B.A. with First Class Honors in Spanish from the University of London (1960). In the years following college, Franco's longstanding interest in art and politics—as well as fate—took her to Italy, France, Guatemala, and Mexico, with a brief stop in Santiago de Cuba when the transatlantic liner on which she was traveling put in to port there after the attack on the Moncada. Franco spent 1950-1952 in Florence on a British Council Research Fellowship studying art history (her son, Alexis Parke, was born in Italy). Franco and her husband, Guatemalan painter Juan Antonio Franco, experienced the Guatemalan coup of 1954 and went into exile in Mexico City, where Franco became a part of the vibrant artistic and intellectual community of the time. Returning to London after a divorce, she pursued a doctorate degree in Spanish (King's College, 1964), and wrote a dissertation on the Spanish writer Angel Ganivet, because at that time it was not possible to specialize in Latin American literature.

Franco became a key figure in the reorientation of the study of Hispanic letters. Her book *The Modern Culture of Latin America* (1967) set the stage in the English-speaking world for the emergence of Latin American literary studies as separate from Peninsular studies, helped promote and contextualize the literature of the boom, and became part of a critical canon which looks at literary texts as simultaneously aesthetic and political documents. Franco helped found the Society of Latin American Studies of Great Britain, and, when she moved from the University of Essex where she had been Chair of the Department of Literature to Stanford University, she carried this activism into the Latin American Studies Association and later served as its president from 1989 to 1991.

During her years teaching at Stanford University (1972-1982), where she was the Olive H. Palmer Chair of the Humanities (1979-1982), and

Columbia University (1982-1994), where she was Director of the Institute of Latin American Studies (1984-86), Franco trained several generations of scholars in the United States in not only the letters and history of Latin America but also in the debates of literary and continental theory, feminism, mass and popular culture, and that which came to be called cultural studies. She was a founding member of the editorial board of *Tabloid: A Review of Mass Culture and Everyday Life* (1981-1984). Her books since *The Modern Culture of Latin America* include *An Introduction to Spanish American Literature* (1969), *A Literary History of Spain and Spanish American, Volume IV* (1972), *César Vallejo: The Dialectics of Poetry and Silence* (1976), *Plotting Women: Gender and Representation in Mexico* (1989), and *Marcar diferencias, cruzar fronteras* (1996).

Currently, Franco serves as a general editor of the Library of Latin America of the Oxford University Press (1993-present). In 1996, she received the PEN award for her contributions to the dissemination of Latin American literature in English, as well as the Gabriela Mistral medal from the Chilean government, and the Andrés Bello medal from the Venezuelan government. Now Professor Emerita, Franco is working on a book on the problematic relation of culture and politics in the Americas during and since the cold war.

INDEX

Abjection, 113, 115, 117–18

Abortion, 124, 125, 127–28

Academe, 169, 509, 511–12

Accomplice readers, 98

Adoption stories, 217

Adorno, Rolena, 511

Adorno, Theodor, 170, 259, 393

Adventures of Robinson Crusoe, 191

Aesthetic: eighteenth-century, 135–36, 142–43; Modernist, 413–14; value and, 204–5

Affect, 107, 117, 210

Agency, 54, 113, 224–26

Aguer, Hector (Bishop), 123

Agüero, Pedro de, 87

El águila y la serpiente (The Eagle and the Serpent), 454–56, 459

Aguirre, the Wrath of God, 182

Agustín, José, 200, 296

AIDS, 110

Alarcón, Norma, 79

Albó, Xavier, 224

Alcántara, San Pedro de, 497

Aleph, El (The Aleph), 328–29, 338

Alfonsín, Raúl, 101

Alienation, 135–36, 138–40

Allain, Marcel, 418–19

Allegory, 151–53, 161, 165, 243–45, 256, 268–71, 318, 353

Allende, Isabel, 55, 57, 97–98, 100

Allende, Salvador, 10, 22, 174

Alumbradas, 495

Alvarez Bravo, Armando, 243

Amadís de Gaula, 73

Amalia, 484

Ambiguity, 312–13

Amerika Terra Incógnita, 192

Amor es más laberinto (Love is the Greater Labyrinth), 84, 86–87, 93–94

Amor perdido (Lost Love), 199

Anachronism, 149, 152, 162, 166, 183, 264, 287, 417, 456

Andrews, Joseph, 134–44

Angel, Albalucía, 57

Anthropology, 215

Anti-Oedipus, 226

Antonioni, Michelangelo, 416–17

Anzaldúa, Gloria, 111, 225, 228

El apando (The Womb), 288

Apollinaire, Guillaume, 419

Appropriation, 191–92

Aragon, Luis, 419

Archetypes, 242, 257

El arco y la lira (The Bow and the Lyre), 285

Arenas, Reinaldo, 292, 305

La argentina en pedazos (Argentina in fragments), 405, 410

Arguedas, José María, 172, 191, 285, 288, 290, 450

Ariel, 450

Arlt, Roberto, 356, 410

Las armas secretas (Secret Weapons), 262, 272, 302

Armstrong, Louis, 408, 414

Arráncame la vida (Mexican Bolero), 98, 100–101

Arreola, Juan José, 201, 405

Art: innocence and, 273–75. *See also* Revolutionary art
Artaud, Antonin, 419
Art criticism, 109
Art exhibitions, 40–41, 198
Art romance, 98–101
Ashbery, John, 418
El astillero (The Shipyard), 153, 157, 295–96, 311–25
Asturias, Miguel Angel, 191
Aura, 262, 268–69, 272, 282, 379
Austerity, 135, 142, 144–45
Authenticity, 201
Author, 147, 149–50, 164, 345, 356, 357; as founder, 153–59; popular culture and, 159–60; storyteller and, 151–53. *See also* Narrator/storyteller; Superstar
Authoritarianism, 3–4, 49, 50–51, 177
Authority, 478, 489
Los autonautas de la cosmopista (Autonauts of the Cosmoway), 415
Autonomy, 295, 296
Avant-garde, 165, 203–4, 302–4, 503; as cultural ghetto, 304–6; neo-avant-garde, 97, 101–2, 117–18
Las aventuras del héroe Baltasar (The Adventures of Hero Baltasar), 393
Averroes (Ibn Rushd), 340–41
Avila, Teresa de (Santa), 496–97
Avila Camacho, Manuel, 447, 459
Azcárraga, Emilio, 197
Azpurúa, Carlos, 398
Azuela, Mariano, 453–55, 459–60

Bachelard, Gaston, 12
Bacon, Francis (Sir), 344
Bakhtin, Mikhail, 394–95, 481
Balzac, Honoré de, 149–50, 163, 311, 419
Banality, 166, 250, 254, 255, 256
Barbarism, 332–33, 449–50, 456–58, 483–86
Barnet, Miguel, 172, 304
Baroque, 277–78, 279
Barrenechea, Ana María, 504
Barrios de Chungara, Domitila, 54

Barthes, Roland, 20, 266, 276–77, 281, 300, 327, 401, 456
Bartolovich, Cristal, 224
Bartra, Roger, 75, 205
Bataille, Georges, 60, 266
Baudot, Georges, 76–77
Bazin, André, 379
Beaumont, J. A. B., 134–45
Beckett, Samuel, 327
Bello, Andrés, 490
Benedetti, Mario, 292
Benítez Rojo, Antonio, 205, 211, 228–29
Benjamin, Walter, 148, 286, 399, 406–7, 413–14
Berger, John, 369
Berrigan, Daniel, 185, 187
El beso de la mujer araña (Kiss of the Spider Woman), 402, 505, 507
Bestiario (Bestiary), 410
Betrayal, 335–41
Bhabha, Homi, 74, 208
Bianco, José, 505
Bilbao, Josefina, 127
Billy the Kid, 337
Binary polarities, 18, 27, 28, 42, 330
Biografía de un cimarrón (Autobiography of a Runaway Slave), 304
Bioy Casares, Adolfo, 333, 355, 357
Blades, Rubén, 200–201, 212–13
Blank, Les, 186–88
Bloom, Harold, 358
Blow-up, 416
Boal, Augusto, 304
Bodies That Matter, 113
Body, 45, 59–60, 106, 107, 368; flow and, 222–23; individual and, 20–21; organ transplant rumors, 216–17; private and, 59–60
Bolero, 211
Bolívar, Simón, 117–18, 200, 213, 359, 381
Bonafini, Hebe de, 32, 34–35
Book industry, 202–3
Boom writers, 159, 260–61, 285, 294–97, 505, 507
Boorman, John, 182, 188–90

Boorstin, Daniel, 150
Boquitas pintadas (Heartbreak Tango), 199, 211, 411
Borderlands, 225, 228
Borderlands/La frontera, 111
Borges, Jorge Luis, 98, 328-61, 379, 395, 405, 408, 416-17, 503-4
Boullosa, Carmen, 57
Bourdieu, Pierre, 179, 216, 484
Bourgeoisie. *See* Intellectuals
Brecht, Bertolt, 286, 305
A Bridge Called My Back, 112
La de Bringas, 471
Britto García, Luis, 421
Brothels, 14-15, 116, 367, 410, 411
Brotherston, Gordon, 510
Browne, Thomas, 341, 359
Brunner, José Joaquín, 511
Bruñon de Vertiz, José, 493
Buddenbrooks, 11, 311, 325
Buñuel, Luis, 191, 416
Bunyan, John, 241
Burdens of Dreams, 186-89
Bureaucratization, 23, 28
Bustamante, Carlos María, 477
Butler, Judith, 110, 112-13
Butor, Michel, 269

La cabeza de la hidra (Hydra Head), 164
The Cabinet of Dr. Caligari, 163, 164
Cabrera Infante, Guillermo, 151, 159, 239-40, 504
Caesar, Julius, 389, 451
Calibán, 292
Calles, Plutarco Elías, 447, 451, 454
Cambio de piel (Change of Skin), 151, 162-64, 268, 272, 285, 293, 299, 379
Camoes, Luís Vas de, 137
La campaña (The Campaign), 506
El campo (The Camp), 370, 376
Camus, Albert, 233, 400
Cándido, Antonio, 504
Cannibalism, 191
Cánon de alcoba (Canon of the Boudoir), 105

Canto general (General Song), 287, 307, 331, 354
Capitalism, 49, 117, 119, 144-45, 189, 215, 324; deterritorialization and, 10-11, 226-27; ethic within, 189; film and, 187-88; goals, 137-38; writing and, 381-82
Capítulos que se le olvidaron a Cervantes (Chapters that Cervantes Forgot), 395
Cardenal, Ernesto, 191, 304, 504
Cárdenas, Lázaro, 398, 447
Carlyle, Thomas, 380-81
Carpentier, Alejo, 153, 166, 190-91, 292, 306, 449
Carranza, Angela de la, 495
Carranza, Venustiano, 453
Carriego, Evaristo, 336
La casa de los espíritu (House of the Spirits), 100
Carta Atenagórica, 83, 94
La casa verde (The Green House), 14, 153, 157, 295-96, 367, 397, 399
Castañeda, Jorge, 196
Castellanos, Rosario, 78
Castillo, Adelaide R. del, 78
Castillo, Otto René, 291
Castillo Armas, Carlos, 16
Catholic Church, 9-10, 50-51; *fineza* and, 85-86; gender debate and, 123-29; marriage and, 87-88; Protestant view of, 140; symbolism, 42, 75-76, 314-15, 367; United Nations and, 125-26
Causality, 348-52
Censorship, 202
Center, 214-15, 222
Certeau, Michel de, 192, 194
Cervantes o la crítica de la lectura (Cervantes, or the Critique of Reading), 504
Cervantes y Saavedra, Miguel de, 395, 504
Chaos theory, 228
Character, 157, 159, 260, 296
La chartreuse de Parme (The Charterhouse of Parma), 100
Chateaubriand, François René de, 184

Chessler, Melissa, 44

Chesterton, Gilbert Keith, 349–50, 356

Chicano movement, 78

Chodorow, Nancy, 27

Chopin, Frederic, 372

Christian symbolism, 42, 75–76, 314–15, 367

Chronicler/storyteller. *See* Narrator

Chronopolitics, 222

Cien años de soledad (One Hundred Years of Solitude), 12, 100, 152–53, 158, 293, 295–96, 325, 379

Cisneros, Antonio, 291

La ciudad y los perros (The Time of the Hero), 27, 196, 295

Civilization, 86, 332–33, 482–83

Civil society, 214, 483–84

Cixous, Hélène, 57, 277, 281

Class issues, 410–11; dominant ideology and, 447–49; marriage and, 87–90; pleasure and, 471–72; women's writing and, 52–53

Cobra, 262–82

Cochones, 114–15

Cocteau, Jean, 419

Coleridge, Samuel Taylor, 137

Colette, 419

Collazos, Oscar, 265, 293, 303

Collor de Mello, Fernando, 200

Colonization, 133–34, 186. *See also* Capitalism

Comédie Humaine, 150

Comedy, 471

Comic strips, 405, 411–12, 420–21

Communication, 171, 345–47, 383, 385

Community, 148, 152, 154–55, 157, 172–73, 211, 329–34, 360–61

Les confessions (Confessions), 86

Confesiones de un agente de seguridad (Confessions of a security agent), 25

Conjunciones y disjunciones (Conjunctions and Disjunctions), 280

La conquête d'Amerique (The Conquest of America), 6, 511

Conrad, Joseph, 133, 159, 356, 359

Conspiracy, 356–61

Constructionism, 112, 113, 114

Consumerism, 140, 236–39, 452, 482, 506–7; novel and, 266–68; popular culture and, 150, 162, 174, 408, 416–17; women and, 461–62

Convents, 11, 14

Conversación al sur (Mothers and Shadows), 376

Conversación en la Catedral (Conversation in the Cathedral), 98, 203, 233–34, 325, 507

El coronel no tiene quien le escriba (No One Writes to the Colonel), 295

Cortázar, Julio, 98, 135, 151, 153, 159, 164, 165, 191, 197, 242–43, 266–85, 291–95, 300–303, 405–21, 503–5

Cortés, Hernán, 42, 66–76

Cortijo, 201

Costa, Olga, 43

Costa Gavras, Constantin, 25

Costumbrismo, 171–72, 473

Counterhegemony, 214

Counterinsurgency movement, 11–12

Courtly love. See *Fineza*

La Cousine Bette (Cousin Betty), 471

Creativity, 165, 368–69

Crisis of the popular, 208, 209, 214, 217–18

Critical reading, 97–98

Criticism, 109, 503–4, 508–11; humanistic, 259–60; literary history and, 510; research topics, 511–13

Cruz, Celia, 200, 212–13, 227

Cruz, Juana de la (Sor), 83–95, 393, 497, 501

Cruz, Marina de, 496

El cuarto mundo (The Fourth World), 105, 119

Cuauhtémoc, 380

Cultural capital, 98

Cultural imperialism, 174–76, 199

Cultural populism, 200, 204

Cultural specificity, 192–93

Cultural studies, 3, 512–13

Culture, national, 39–40, 197–98

Culture of poverty, 174
Cultures of fear, 22-24, 49-50, 202
Cumpleaños (Birthday), 268

Dalton, Roque, 291
Dante Alighieri, 389, 429-45
Danzón, 199, 211
Darío, Rubén, 99, 197, 228, 395, 509
Dávila, Juan, 117, 214
Davis, Miles, 414
Death, 18, 22, 252-53; ethics and, 20-21,
    35, 215-16; postmodern age and, 18-19;
    space of, 31-32
Death camps, 24-25, 28, 31
The Death of the Family, 59
Death without Weeping, 215
Decline and Fall of the Roman Empire, 144
Deconstruction, 260, 276-77
Defoe, Daniel, 191
Dejemos hablar al viento (Let the Wind
    Speak), 379
de Kock, Paul, 99
de Lauretis, Teresa, 67
Deleuze, Gilles, 10-11, 158, 210, 225-29,
    327, 360, 383
De Niro, Robert, 184, 186
Dependency, 144, 157, 158, 268, 272, 295,
    401; metropolis and, 447-48, 452-53
Depoliticization, 19, 61
Derrida, Jacques, 327, 401
La deshumanización del arte (The De-
    humanization of Art), 412
Desmasiado amor (Too much Love), 98
Desnos, Robert, 419
Deterritorialization, 10-11, 117, 210,
    226-27, 384
The Devil and Commodity Fetishism, 176
Devil beliefs, 176-77
Dialectic of Sex, 123
Dialogue of the dead, 389-91
Dialogues, 484-85
Diary of a Chilean Concentration Camp, 28
Dias de guardar (Holy Days), 304
Díaz, Porfirio, 450
Díaz del Castillo, Bernal, 67-75

Diderot, Denis, 357, 463
Didion, Joan, 19, 22
Disappearance, 12, 15, 19, 34
Discépolo, Armando, 405
Discourse, 357-58, 510, 511
Dittborn, Eugenio, 214
The Divine Comedy, 336, 429
El dock (Dock), 103
Dominant ideology, 447-60
Doña Bárbara, 450
Donoso, Claudio, 116
Donoso, José, 14, 115
Dorfman, Ariel, 55, 174
Double Day, 62
Double-voicing, 394, 395-96
Dreaming in Cuban, 98
Dreiser, Theodor, 149
The Dunciad, 249

Eagleton, Terry, 56
Eastman, Monk, 337
East/West dichotomy, 280
Echeverría, Esteban, 145, 490
Echeverría Alvarez, Luis, 264
Eco, Umberto, 171, 178
Ecological concerns, 183, 188-90
Écriture, 259, 260, 278, 285-86, 307(n8),
    327
*La educación de las mujeres o la Quijotita y su
    prima* (The Education of Women or the
    Quijotita and her Cousin), 462-73
Education, women and, 462-63, 468,
    472-73
Electroshock, 21, 23
Elias, Norbert, 86, 482
Elizondo, Salvador, 300-301
Elogio a la madrasta (In Praise of the
    Stepmother), 507
Elshtain, Jean Bethke, 27
Eltit, Diamela, 52, 103-7, 119-20, 202, 205,
    214
The Emerald Forest, 4, 182, 189
Émile, 463
Em liberdade (In Liberty), 393, 400-401,
    403

Los empeños de una casa, 83, 86, 88–89, 93
Emptiness, 311–12
Endangered species, 189–90
El entenado (The Witness), 393
El entierro de Cortijo (Cortijo's Burial), 223
Entrada libre (Free Entry), 214
Entrepreneurs, 134–35, 138, 140, 144–45, 155–58, 295–96
Errázuriz, Paz, 107, 116, 214
Escenas de pudor y liviandad (Scenes of Modesty and License), 513
Escritos sin futuro (Writings without a Future), 225
Esquivel, Laura, 97–98, 100, 203
Essay, 451
Essentialism, 112
En estado de memoria (In a State of Memory), 60, 104
Ethics, 3–4, 20–21, 226; capitalism and, 189; death and, 20–21, 35, 215–16
Ethnocentricity, 192
L'Etranger (The Stranger), 400
El examen (The Examination), 409, 414
Exchange, 75
Exile, 60–61
Existentialism, 163

Fabian, Johannes, 215
La fable mystique (The Mythic Fable), 494
Facundo: Civilización y Barbarie (Facundo: Civilization and Barbarism), 332, 449
Fairy tales, 501–2
The Fall, 233
Family, 11, 462–65, 470, 488; authoritarianism and, 50–51; homosexual, 127–28
Family values, 124, 125, 127
Fantomás contra los vampiros multinacionales (Fantomás against the Multinational Vampires), 165, 276, 303, 417, 420
Faraboeuf, 300
Fashion, 461–62, 471, 473
Faulkner, William, 310
Fear, cultures of, 22–24, 49–50, 202
Feminine, as destabilizing, 102, 117–19

Feminism, 27, 48, 124, 512; light literature and, 100, 102, 106
Fénélon, François de Salignac de la Mothe, 389, 485
Fernández de Lizardi, José Joaquín, 390, 462–90
Fernández Retamar, Roberto, 292
Ferrari, Américo, 509
Ferré, Rosario, 55, 57, 373–74
Ficciones (Fictions), 328, 338
Fictionality, 493–94
Film, 165–66, 173; nature films, 4, 182–90
Fineza, 83–85, 88–90; free will and, 93, 94–95; violence and, 89–90; women's behavior and, 93–94
Firestone, Shulamit, 123
Fitzcarraldo, 187–88
Fitzcarraldo, 4, 182–91
Flaubert, Gustave, 160, 504
Flores, Juan, 201
Flores Galindo, Alberto, 511
La "Flor de lis," 52
Flow, 222–24; self and, 226
Folklore, 170
Folk tale, 431–32
Foppa de Solórzano, Alaíde, 9, 16–17
Foucault, Michel, 20, 149, 327, 329, 357–58, 360, 493, 504
Fournier, Alain, 100
Fourth world, 119–20
The Fourth World, 510
Francia, José Gaspar Rodríguez de, 191, 305, 381
Fraser, Nancy, 48
The French Connection, 221
Freudianism, 76, 110
Frida, el pincel de la angustia (Frida, the Brush of Anguish), 99
Frida (Herrera), 99
From Beast to Blonde, 501
From Caligari to Hitler, 164
Frye, Northrop, 100
Fuentes, Carlos, 149–65, 191, 197–98, 201, 262–99, 305, 367, 379, 453, 503–6
Fuera del juego (Out of the Game), 292

Fujimori, Alberto, 124, 128
Los fundadores del alba (The Founders of Dawn), 291

Gabeira, Fernando, 403
Galdós, Benito Pérez, 503
Galeano, Eduardo, 55
Gallegos, Rómulo, 450
Gambaro, Griselda, 57, 370–72
Gance, Abel, 407
Garber, Marjorie, 111
García, Cristina, 98
García Canclini, Nestor, 198–99, 208, 213, 512
García Cubas, 171
García Márquez, Gabriel, 12, 55, 97, 147–59, 197, 201, 203, 243, 295, 304–5, 325, 331–32, 367, 376, 379–80, 393, 395, 405, 495, 503–8
García Márquez: Historia de un deicidio (History of a Deicide), 295, 504
Garro, Elena, 78
Gauchos, 143–44, 319, 332–33, 334, 449
Gender: abjectness and, 117–18; authoritarianism and, 3–4; Catholic Church and, 123–29; signification and, 27, 29; social construction of, 26–27, 34–36, 124; as term, 112, 124; torture and, 26–30; transvestism and, 111–12
Gender Trouble, 113
El general en su laberinto (The General in His Labyrinth), 203, 506
Genette, Gérard, 327, 394
Geuna, Graciela Susana, 29
Gheerbrant, Alain, 190
Ghettoization, 105
Gibbon, Edward, 144
Gift exchange, 74, 76
Gilbert, Sandra, 368
Glantz, Margo, 78
Globalization, 264, 506–7; body exploitation, 216–17; hybridity and, 208, 209, 210, 217; individualism and, 281–82; international division of labor, 215, 297. *See also* Popular culture

Godard, Jean-Luc, 416–17
The Golden Notebook, 370
El Golem, 164
Góngora y Argote, Luis de, 393
González de León, Adriano, 291
Gothic novel, 269
Goytisolo, Juan, 504, 507
Graham, Robert Cunningham, 144
Gramsci, Antonio, 177, 214
Le Grand Meaulnes, 100
Greenblatt, Stephen, 4, 66–68, 77
Grotesque, 138–39, 245, 255–56, 410, 411
Gruzinski, Sergio, 511
La guaracha del Macho Camacho (Macho Camacho's Beat), 505
Guattari, Félix, 10–11, 158, 210, 225–29, 360, 383
Gubar, Susan, 368
Guerra, Juan Luis, 200–201, 212
La guerra del fin del mundo (The War of the End of the World), 367
Guerrilla warfare, 291
Guevara, Che, 290–91
Guido, Beatri, 98
Guilhem, Claire, 495
Guimaraes Rosa, Jo, 504
Gutiérrez Nájera, Manuel, 448
Guzmán, Martín Luis, 454–60

Habermas, Jürgen, 20, 329
El hablador (The Storyteller), 4, 393, 396, 400, 403
Hall, Stuart, 178
Haraway, Donna, 112, 225
Hardy, Thomas, 99, 159
Harris, Wilson, 311
Harrison, Regina, 511
Hart, Liddell, 338
Hartsock, Nancy, 27, 34
Harvey, David, 226
Hasta no verte Jesús mío (Until I see you, Jesus), 100
Head, Frances Bond, 134–44
Hegel, G. W. F., 61, 104, 147, 149
Hegemony, 70–71, 191, 214; homosexu-

Hegemony (*continued*)
ality and, 114-15; popular culture and, 177-78; writing and, 381-82
Helvetius, 463
Henríquez Ureña, Pedro, 2
Heraclitus, 389
Heraud, Javier, 291
Heroism, 248-50, 342, 359, 401-2
Herrera, Hayden, 44, 99
Herz, Robert, 31
Herzog, Werner, 4, 182-89
Hicks, Emily, 228
Hidalgo, Bartolomé, 390, 484-86
High culture, 170
El hipogeo secreto (The Secret Hypogeum), 300
Historia de Mayta (The True Story of Alejandro Mayta), 196
Historia de un naúfrago (Story of a Shipwreck), 304
La historia univeral de la infamia (A Universal History of Infamy), 337
La historia verdadera de la conquista de la Nueva España (The True History of the Conquest of Mexico), 69
Historical novel, 390
Historicity, 241-42, 251, 257
Historiography, 348-49
History, 149, 156-58, 166, 305-6, 391, 501; narrative and, 185-86; realism and, 286-90
The History of Manners, 86
History of the Conquest of Mexico, 68-69
La hojarasca (Leaf Storm), 158, 331, 380
Homenaje a los indios americanos (Homage to the American Indian), 305
Homogeneity, 209
Homosexuality, 114-15, 127-28
Hopenhayn, Martín, 225-26
Horkheimer, Max, 11, 70
The Hour of the Star, 58
Howells, William Dean, 149
How Tasty Was My Little Frenchman, 191
Hudson, William Henry, 144
Huerta, Victoriano, 450, 455

Humanism, 259-60, 451-53, 458
Human rights, 424(n48)
Hume, David, 348
Hutcheon, Linda, 394
Huyssen, Andreas, 99, 413
Hybridity, 208, 209, 210, 217

Identity, 111-12, 347-48; destruction of, 20-21, 24-25; national identity, 66, 209, 407-8; space and, 222-23, 229
Identity politics, 113-14
Ideology, dominant, 447-60
Ilusas, 494-502
The Image, 150
Imagination, 243, 244, 262, 265, 296, 300
Immigrants, 332-33, 410-11
Imperialism, cultural, 174-76, 199
The Importance of Being Earnest, 99
La importancia de llamarse Daniel Santos (The Importance of Being Daniel Santos), 199, 211
Improvisation, 213-14
Indigenismo, 178-79, 190-91, 399
Indigenous peoples: mimesis and, 74; otherness of, 71-72, 181-82, 190; pastiche and, 396-400; popular culture and, 172-73; resistance and, 188
Individual, 150, 296-97, 320, 430; desacralization of, 20-21, 24-25; globalization and, 281-82; novel and, 153, 156-57, 263, 281
Industrialization, 144, 160, 172, 173, 297, 301, 313
El infarto del alma (Soul Attack), 105, 106, 107
El informe de Brodie (Brodie's Report), 359
El ingenioso hidalgo Don Quijote de la Mancha (Don Quixote), 504
El inmortal (The Immortal), 161
Innocence, 273-75
Intellectuals: as consumers, 452; dominant ideology and, 447-49; revolution and, 290-92, 453; women, 48-49, 51-53
Intelligentsia: agency and, 224, 225-26; clergy and, 477-78; nation-state and,

224–25; oral culture and, 476, 480;
    utopia and, 196–97, 223, 486
Intensity, 331, 341–43
Intercession, 435
Internalization, 74
Interpretation, 3, 4–5, 67–71
Irigaray, Luce, 27, 73, 494
Irony, 235, 247–48, 333
Iturbide, Graciela, 54

Jacob, Max, 419
James, Henry, 99
Jameson, Fredric, 100, 156, 159, 226, 393
Jaramillo, Juan, 61
La jaula de la melancolía (The Cage of
    Melancholy), 205
Jazz, 165, 414–15
Jesuits, 183–85, 187
Jiménez Rueda, Julio, 493
Jitrik, Noé, 504
Joffe, Roland, 182, 184, 189
Jones, LeRoi (Amiri Baraka), 430–34
Jouissance, 413, 414, 415
Journey from Buenos Aires, 134
Journey to the Far Amazon, 190
Joyce, James, 159, 394
Juntacadávares (Body Snatcher), 153, 321,
    322

Kahlo, Frida, 42–46, 109–10
Kent, Mary, 212
The Killing Fields, 182
Kinski, Klaus, 187
Kipling, Rudyard, 27, 349
Kirkwood, Julieta, 50–51
Knowledge, 331, 346, 361
Kracauer, Siegfried, 164
Krauze, Enrique, 506
Kristeva, Julia, 117
Kubrick, Stanley, 221–22

Lacan, Jacques, 27
Lamarck, Jean Baptiste Pierre Antoine de
    Monet, 123
Lampoons, 386–88

Lancaster, Roger, 114–15
Landi, Oscar, 202
Landscapes, 135–37, 142–43
Language, 66–67, 263–64, 267–68, 277–
    79, 345–49; communication, 171,
    345–47; dialogues, 484–85; empire and,
    67–68, 70–71; of mysticism, 494–97;
    of torture, 23–24, 25, 28; word play,
    279–81. *See also* Literature; Writing
Lara, Augustín, 199
Larraín Fernández, Hernán, 127
Las Casas, Bartolomé de, 348
Latin American studies, 5
Lauer, Mirko, 512
Lawrence of Arabia, 185
Leavis, F. R., 170
Lector hembra, 408
La Légende des Siècles (Legend of the
    Centuries), 187
Leira, Zulema, 35
Leiris, Michel, 60
Lemebel, Pedro, 110, 205
Leñero, Vicente, 159
León, Luis de (Fray), 465
León Caride, Susana, 26
Lesbianism, 78, 110
Lessing, Doris, 370
Letters on Paraguay, 135, 138
Lévi-Strauss, Claude, 162, 190, 504
Lewis, Oscar, 174
Lezama Lima, José, 239–57, 503–5
The Liberal Imagination, 259
Libertarianism, 334
Libertella, Héctor, 298, 508
El libro de arena (The Book of Sand), 360
El libro de Manuel (A Manual for Manuel),
    165, 275–76, 291, 302–3, 409, 417–18,
    420
Life is Hard, 114
The Life of Perón, 105
Lifton, Robert J., 19, 24
Light literature, 97–100
Like Water for Chocolate, 98, 100, 203
Limpieza de sangre, 75
Lispector, Clarice, 57–58, 98, 503

173–74; in peripheral countries, 449; television, 59, 201–2, 399–400, 405. *See also* Popular culture

Melancholy, 105

Memory, 103, 117, 148, 341–45

Menchú, Rigoberta, 54, 193

Mendes, Chico, 182

Menem, Carlos, 126

Mengele, Josef, 370

Mercado, Guillermo, 450

Mercado, Tununa, 59–61, 101–7

Merengue, 212

Mesa Bains, Amalia, 211

Messinger Cypess, Sandra, 74

Mestizaje, 75, 76–77, 451

Metropolis, 4, 19–20, 22, 149, 154, 209, 293; dependency and, 447–48, 452–53; popular culture and, 215; print culture and, 448–50; privatization and, 197, 331–32

A Midsummer Night's Dream, 89

Mier, Servando Teresa de (Fray), 478

Miers, John, 134–44

Mignolo, Walter, 511

Migration, 172–73

Militancy, 29

Mille plateaux (A Thousand Plateaus), 227, 228

Mimesis, 73–74, 299–300, 354, 393, 403, 493–94

Mind control, 20–21, 23–24

Minimalism, 103, 104

Mishima, Yukio, 342

The Mission, 182–91

Missionaries, 183–85

Mistral, Gabriela, 369, 450, 509

Mitchell, Juliet, 27

Moby Dick, 313

Mock heroic, 248–50

Moctezuma, 67, 71, 74

Modernism, 18, 159, 191, 203–4, 286, 307(n6); aesthetics, 58, 413–14; originality and, 395

Modernization, 11–12, 128, 513; fashion

and, 462; media and, 173–74; novel and, 260–62

Money, 430, 431–32, 442–43, 445

Monsiváis, Carlos, 2, 55, 172, 198–203, 214, 304, 504–5, 513

Montalvo, Juan, 395

Montemayor, Jorge de, 241

Montes de Oca, Marco Antonio, 503

Mora, José María Luis, 477, 484

Moraga, Cherríe, 78, 111–12

Moral order, 433–36, 438–39, 441–43

Moral right, 11

Moravia, Alberto, 165, 303

Moreiras, Alberto, 105, 209

Morley, David, 179

Morris, Meaghan, 189, 191

Mothers, 31–36, 49–50, 215–16, 369; outcast status, 31–33; paternalistic view of, 462–63, 466–69; space and, 12–14, 50. *See also* Women

La muerte de Artemio Cruz (The Death of Artemio Cruz), 153, 269, 295

El mundo alucinante (Hallucinations), 292, 305

Muralist movement, 450–51

Music, 183–84, 187, 192, 200, 211–13, 417

Musil, Robert, 27

Mysticism, 494–98

Mythological references, 161–62, 244–46, 248–54, 262

Mythologies, 456

Nada, nadie (Nothing, Nobody), 54

Nahuiolin: La mujer del sol (Nahuiolin: The Woman of the Sun), 99, 109

Napoleon I, 381

Narcissism, 192

Narrative, 59, 61–62, 102–3, 147, 269, crisis of, 259–60, 285; history and, 185–86; mimesis and, 73–74; patriarchal, 98; self-consciousness and, 159; tense and, 269, 272–73, 289, 455–56. *See also* Travel books

Narrator/storyteller, 147, 148, 210–11, 337,

Narrator/storyteller (*continued*)
398–400, 454–55; author and, 151–53.
See also Author; Superstar
Nascimiento, Milton, 180
National culture, 39–40, 172, 190, 197–98
National identity, 66, 209, 407–8
Nationalism, 77–78, 172
National popular, 214
Nation-over-the-state, 224
Nation-state, 52, 224
Nature, 320–22, 374, 453–54, 457–59
Navarro-Vals, Joaquín, 126
Neo-avant-garde, 97, 101–2, 117–18
Neo-indigenismo, 178–79, 190, 399
Neoliberalism, 101–2, 115, 116, 197
Neruda, Pablo, 56, 282, 293, 306, 331–32, 353–54, 419
Neutrality, 20–21, 301
Newspapers, 477
Nietzsche, Friedrich, 345–46
Nixon, Richard, 334
No, mi general (No Sir General), 304
La noche de Tlatelolco (The Night of Tlatelolco), 54, 304
La noche oscura del niño Avilés (The Dark Night of the Boy Avilés), 393
Noches, de Adrenalina (Nights of Adrenaline), 59, 60
Nosferatu, 164
Nostalgia, 211–12, 217, 399, 400
Nostromo, 359
Novaro, María, 199
Novel: consumerism and, 266–68; Gothic novel, 269; historical novel, 390; individual and, 153, 156–57, 263, 281; as masculine, 366–67; modernization and, 260–62; picaresque novel, 487–88; popular culture and, 150–51; rationality and, 481–82; as revolutionary, 265–67, 453
La nueva novela hispanoamericana (The New Spanish American Novel), 262, 285, 299, 504

Objective world, 316–19, 323

Objects, 346, 409
El obsceno pájaro de la noche (The Obscene Bird of the Night), 14
Ocampo, Silvina, 98
El occidente y la conciencia de México (The Western World and the Consciousness of Mexico), 453
Odría, Manuel, 233, 235
Oedipus myth, 76, 189, 336
Olalquiaga, María Celeste, 214
Olivares, Cecilia, 126
Ollé, Carmen, 59–60
One plus One, 416
Onetti, Juan Carlos, 98, 153, 294–95, 314, 321–42, 379, 503
Operación masacre (Operation Massacre), 304
Oral culture, 99, 147–48, 151, 398–99: indigenous peoples and, 172–73; intelligentsia and, 476, 480; transition to print culture, 448–49
Organ transplants, 216–17
La orgía perpetua (The Perpetual Orgy), 504
Originality, 393, 395, 507
Orozco, José Clemente, 44
Ortega, Julio, 106, 247, 437–38
Ortega y Gasset, José, 97, 170, 412
Ortiz, Renato, 511
Os Maias (The Maias), 471
Osorio, Pepón, 211
Otherness, 58, 355: of indigenous peoples, 71–72, 181–82, 190; macho ritual and, 27–28
El otoño del patriarca (Autumn of the Patriarch), 203, 305, 367, 393, 395, 506

Padilla, Heberto, 197, 292–93
El padre mío (My Father), 105–6, 119
Páez, José Antonio, 483
País portátil (Portable Country), 291
The Palm-Wine Drinkard, 430–32, 445
Pampa, 135–36, 343
Paradiso, 239–57, 292
Paranoia, 383–84

Paredes, Américo, 172

Paris Is Burning, 113

Parody, 377, 393-95, 401

Los pasos perdidos (The Lost Steps), 153, 166, 190

Pasquali, Antonio, 175

The Passion According to G.H., 58

Pastiche, 393-96, 406, 507; indigenous peoples and, 396-400; nostalgia and, 399, 400

Pastor, Beatriz, 511

Paternalism, 115-16, 183, 462-69, 488

Paula, 98

Paz, Octavio, 40-43, 56, 66, 77, 84, 94, 165, 198, 201, 213, 266, 279-80, 285, 287, 297-98, 301, 303, 405, 504-6

Pedro Páramo, 434-45

Pedroso, Manuel, 503

Pereira dos Santos, Nelson, 191

Pérez de Soto, Melchor, 493

La perfecta casada (The Perfect Wife), 465

Perfil del hombre y de la cultura de México (Profile of the Man and Culture of Mexico), 453

Performance, 110, 111, 113; by *ilusas*, 499-501; state and, 372, 373; women and, 369-70, 372-77

Performativity, 113, 114

Periphery, 214-15, 218, 394

El periquillo sarniento (The Itching Parrot), 464, 479, 481, 484, 487-88

Peri Rossi, Cristina, 57

Perón, Eva, 166, 380

Perón, Juan, 334

El perro del hortelano (The Gardener's Dog), 88

El persiguidor (The Pursuer), 165

El pez en el agua (A Fish in the Water), 203

The Phenomenology of Mind, 61, 104

Philosophical Dictionary, 346, 356

Philosophical references, 346

Photography, 379

Picaresque novel, 487-88

Picasso, Pablo, 181

Piccini, Mabel, 178

Piglia, Ricardo, 405, 408, 410-11, 421

Pilgrim's Progess, 241

Pinochet, Augusto, 10, 22, 119, 205

Pitol, Sergio, 503

Plato, 148, 271, 389, 452

Pleasure, 471-72

Plot, 103, 349-53

Pluralism, 52, 61-62, 101-2, 115, 202, 205, 263, 505

Poemas humanos (Human Poems), 509

The Poetics of Space, 12

Poetry, 59-60, 102, 239-41, 244, 298, 481; history and, 305; popular culture and, 203, 450-51

The Political Unconscious, 100

Poniatowska, Elena, 54-55, 78, 99-100, 109, 198, 265, 304, 393, 506

Pope, Alexander, 249

Popol Vuh, 510

Popular, crisis of, 208, 209, 214, 217-18

Popular agency, 54

Popular culture, 2, 99, 159-62, 405-6; author and, 159-60; capitalism and, 150, 162, 174, 408, 416-17; definitions, 170-71; Fantomas stories, 417-20; hegemony and, 177-78; improvisation, 213-14; indigenous peoples and, 172-73; marginalization and, 214-15, 218; mass media and, 304-5, 506-8; poetry and, 450-51; privatization and, 173-74, 176-77, 197-99; repetition and, 150-51, 159, 162; resistance and, 171, 172, 213, 214, 304; terminology, 169-71. *See also* Media

Population control, 128-29

Populism, 200, 204

Por la patria (For the Fatherland), 105, 119

Por la vida (For life), 52

The Possessed, 356

Postmodern age, 18-19

Postmodernism, 198-99, 513

Poststructuralism, 510

Poulantzas, Nicos, 382-83, 489

Prado Oropesa, Renato, 291

Praxis, 290-93, 297

Los premios (The Winners), 415

Prescott, William, 66

Price, Vincent, 269

Prieto, Guillermo, 480

Print culture, 148–49, 175, 201–2, 448–50

Private, 45, 50; body and, 59–60; women's reinhabiting of, 56–57; writing and, 103

Privatization, 222, 282, 468; metropolis and, 197, 331–32; national culture and, 39–40, 197–98; popular culture and, 173–74, 176–77, 197–99

Protestantism, 10, 140

Proust, Marcel, 349

Public space, 223–24, 466; brothels, 14–15, 116, 367; women's appropriation of, 53–55, 376–77

Puig, Manuel, 56, 151, 159, 164–65, 199, 211, 367, 393, 402, 405, 411, 504–9

Queerness, 110, 114

Queneau, Raymond, 419

Querido Diego, te abraza Quiela (Dear Diego), 393

Quevedo y Villegas, Francisco de, 359, 430, 434

Quiroga, Facundo, 332

Radway, Janice, 101

Rama, Angel, 2, 203, 504–5, 509

Ramos, Graciliano, 400–401

Ramos, Samuel, 453

Rape, 12

Rationality, 481–82, 484, 485–86

Rayuela (Hopscotch), 98, 153, 275, 295, 302, 333, 409, 411, 415

Reading, 178–79, 347, 351–52, 360, 400–401, 477, 503–4

Reading groups, 480–81

Reagan, Ronald, 47

Realism, 156, 260, 265, 281, 285; history and, 286–90; magical realism, 55, 100, 204

La rebelión de las masas (The Rebellion of the Masses), 412

Reception theory, 178–79

Reconversion, 198

El recurso del método (Reasons of State), 306, 449

Redemocratization, 49, 61, 104, 117, 202

The Red Shoes, 373

Referentiality, 4–5, 53, 286–89, 297–98, 300, 302–3

La región más transparente (Where the Air is Clear), 453

The Repeating Island, 205, 211, 228

Repetition, 150–51, 159, 162

Representation, 379, 455, 484

Reproduction, 406–7

Reproductive rights, 124, 129–30. *See also* Abortion

Residencia en la tierra (Residence on Earth), 56

Resistance, 420–21; family and, 11; mothers and, 31–36; popular culture and, 171, 172, 213, 214, 304; rock music and, 200–201; space and, 223

Respuesta a Sor Filotea de la Cruz (Response to Sor Filotea de la Cruz), 85

Ressentiment, 460

Resurrection, 243–44

Reterritorialization, 227–28

Return, 343, 345

Revolutionary art, 286, 290–93, 300–301, 420–21; Baroque and, 277–78, 279; novel, 265–67, 453

Revueltas, José, 149, 265, 287–90, 457–60

Reyes, Alfonso, 292, 350, 361, 451–52, 458, 503

Ribeyro, Julio Ramón, 247

Richard, Nelly, 102, 117–19, 202, 214, 228

Ricoeur, Paul, 504

Ríos Montt, Efraín, 10

Rísquez, Diego, 192

Ritual, 162

Rivadavia, Bernardino, 134

Rivalry, 329–30, 353–56

Rivera, Diego, 44, 109

Riviere, Joan, 110

Roa Bastos, Augusto, 133, 151, 158, 172, 288, 305–6, 381, 389, 391, 393

Robertson, J. P., 135–45, 381
Robertson, W. P., 135–45, 381
Rockefeller, Nelson, 166
Rock music, 200–201
Rodó, José Enrique, 200, 213, 292, 450
Rodrígues de Ocaña, Gonzalo, 70–71
Rodríguez, Jesusa, 46, 79, 202, 205
Rodríguez, Oscar (Archbishop), 126
Rodríguez Galván, Ignacio, 480
Rodríguez Juliá, Edgardo, 201, 210–11, 223, 393
Rodríguez Monegal, Emir, 504–5
Roffé, Reina, 57
Romance, 100–101
Romanticism, 186–87
Romero, Oscar (Archbishop), 9, 33
Romero, Teresa de, 495–501
Rosas, Juan Manuel de, 332, 380, 483
Rosencof, Mauricio, 30
Rough Notes, 142
Rousseau, Jean Jacques, 86, 135, 183, 242, 381, 463, 503
Rowe, William, 509
Rulfo, Juan, 56, 431–60
Runa Yupay, 450

Sábato, Ernesto, 356
Saer, Juan José, 393
Sainz, Gustavo, 296
Salceda, Alberto G., 84
Salinas de Gottari, Carlos, 41
Salsa, 200–201
Salvador, 19
Sánchez, Luis Rafael, 151, 199, 211, 405, 505, 509
Sánchez, Matilde, 103
Sánchez, Nestor, 300
San José, Ana María de (Sor), 496
San Martín, José de, 359–60, 381
Santiago, Silviano, 393, 396, 400–402
Sarduy, Severo, 120, 262, 266–67, 276–81, 287, 300–301, 505
Sarlo, Beatriz, 202, 204, 224–25, 511–13
Sarmiento, Domingo, 332, 335, 449, 482, 490

Sartre, Jean Paul, 267, 292
Schelling, Vivian, 509
Scheper-Hughes, Nancy, 215–16
Scherer, Julio, 420
Schiller, Herbert, 174
Schjeldahl, Peter, 44
Schopenhauer, Arthur, 322–23, 346
Science, 384–85
The Secret Agent, 356
The Secret Executioner, 419
Seduction, 101
Seed, Patricia, 87
Sefchovich, Sara, 97–100
Self, flow and, 226
La señora de los sueños (The Lady of Dreams), 98
La señorita de Tacna (The Señorita from Tacna), 368
Serialization, 211
Sexual contract, 49, 57, 74–79
Sexuality, 112–13, 203
Shakespeare, William, 139, 149, 239
Siena, Catalina de, 497
Los siete locos (Seven Madmen), 356
El siglo de las luces (Explosion in the Cathedral), 292
Signs, Songs, and Memory in the Andes, 511
Singers, 212–13
Siqueiros, David Alfaro, 44
62 Modelo para armar (62: A Model Kit), 300
Skármeta, Antonio, 201, 508
Soap operas, 148, 151, 160–61, 213, 508
Sobre héroes y tumbas (Of Heroes and Tumbs), 356
Socialization, 74
Social movements, 48–51
Social order, 435, 440, 441, 442–44
Socius, 10
Solanas, Fernando, 199
Solers, Phillipe, 266
La sombra del caudillo (The Caudillo's Shadow), 456
Sommers, Armonía, 98
Somoza, Anastasio, 449

Sonatas, 248, 249

Sontag, Susan, 165, 303, 421

Souvestre, Pierre, 419

Space: of death, 31–32; feminine, 12–15, 50; identity and, 222–23, 229; public space, 14–15, 53–55, 116, 223–24, 366–67; sanctuary, 9–10, 12–17

Speech, 346–47, 441–42

Speech act theory, 113

Speech genres, 382, 389

Spencer, Herbert, 263

Spirit of Cristianity, 184

Spitzer, Leo, 505

Spivak, Gayatri Chakravorty, 215, 225

Spota, Luis, 99

Stalky and Co., 27

Stasis, 439

State, 49, 51, 52, 224, 382–83, 391; legitimization of, 383–86; performance and, 372, 373

State of Siege, 25

Steiner, George, 276

Storyteller. *See* Narrator/storyteller

Strategies of containment, 155–56, 178

Strawberry and Chocolate, 114

Student demonstrations, 264–65, 296–97

Stylization, 394

Subaltern, 215, 219–20(n24)

Subercaseaux, Bernardo, 511

Sue, Eugène, 419

Suffering, 44–45, 109–10

Superbarrio, 199

Superstar, 147, 150, 159–67, 212–13

Supplement, 401, 403

Surrealism, 278, 279, 285, 419

Survival, 3–4, 34, 35, 51, 189, 193

Symbolism, 240, 247, 254–55, 312–13

Symposium, 452

The System of Dante's Hell, 431, 432, 445

Taboos, 152, 161

Tango argentino, 211

Tangos: El exilio de Gardel, 199

Taste, 408, 462, 513

Taussig, Michael, 31, 118, 176

Teacher/student relationship, 480

Technique, 287, 288–89, 294

Technology, 262–64, 412; class issues and, 449; as neutral, 20–21, 297–98, 299; social action and, 198–99

Television, 59, 201–2, 399–400, 405; telenovelas, 99, 201–2, 405

Tellado, Corín, 99

Temporality, 436–37

Terra Nostra, 98, 164, 270, 301, 305, 367, 506–7

Tertulia, 480–81

La tertulia de los muertos (Tertulia of the Dead), 486

Testimonial, 3, 4, 53–54, 106, 204

Texts, 178, 509–10

Theater, 304–5

Third degree, 21

Third World, 215, 292–93

Thompson, E. P., 3, 11

Thorndyke, Guillermo, 304

La tía Julia y el escribidor (Aunt Julia and the Scriptwriter), 151, 160–61, 368, 405

Timerman, Jacobo, 24, 30

Tinísima, 99, 109

Todorov, Tvetzan, 4, 66–68, 77, 511

Tolstoi, Leo, 149

Torture, 21–24, 116; gender issues and, 26–30; language of, 23–24, 25, 28; macho ritual and, 24–30, 34

Torture in the Eighties, 21

Totalitarianism, 164

Tourism, 41

Traba, Marta, 376

Traditional institutions, 9–10

Tragedy, 252–53, 429

La traición de Rita Hayworth (Betrayed by Rita Hayworth), 165–66, 405

Traité de l'éducation des filles (Fenelon on Education), 463

Las trampas de la fe (The Traps of Faith), 94

Transgression, 267–68, 300, 494

Trans-state nation, 224

Transvestism, 102, 110–12, 117–19

Travel books, 134–38, 483; alienation and, 138–40; perils of luxury and, 142, 144; progress and, 141–42; temporality in, 140–41

Travels in Chile and la Plata, 134, 139

Tres tristes tigres, 98, 239

Tribal culture, 431–32

Trilce, 56

Trilling, Lionel, 189

Trinh, T. Minh-Ha, 259

Tristes tropiques, 19

Trotsky, Leon, 61

Turner, Nat, 337

Tutuola, Amos, 429, 431, 434

2001: A Space Odyssey, 221–22

Ulysses, 159

Under Fire, 18

United Nations, 125–26

Universality, 340–41

Un modelo para la muerte (A Model for Death), 333

Utopia, 54–55, 152–53, 165, 214, 303, 360; intelligentsia and, 196–97, 223, 486; writing as, 257, 259, 276, 277, 280

Vaca sagrada (Sacred Cow), 105, 119

Valdés, Hernán, 28

Valenzuela, Luisa, 57, 103, 203, 375

Valle-Inclán, Ramón María del, 248–49, 255

Vallejo, César, 13–14, 56, 59, 243, 367–68, 509

Values, 204–5, 239, 316–18

Vargas, Getulio, 400

Vargas Llosa, Mario, 4, 14, 27, 41, 55, 151–60, 196–203, 213, 242–43, 262–63, 285–95, 325, 367–68, 393–99, 405, 503–4, 507

Vargas Vila, José María, 99

Vasconcelos, José, 197, 451

Vega, Ana Lydia, 57

Velásquez, Diego, 192

Veloso, Caetano, 201, 212–13

Verne, Jules, 417

Vested Interest, 111

Vidal, Hernán, 24, 28

Los vigilantes (The Vigilantes), 105, 106

Villa, Pancho, 161, 453–56

Villaflor, Azuzcena de Vicenti, 33

Viñas, David, 405

Virgin, 42, 75–76

Virilio, Paul, 221

La vuelta al día en ochenta mundos (Around the Day in Eighty Worlds), 414

Wallerstein, Immanuel, 196

Walsh, Rodolfo, 15, 304

Warner, Marina, 501

Wast, Hugo, 99

Watteau, Antoine, 222

Ways of Seeing, 369

Weekend, 416

Weil, Kurt, 419

Where Green Ants Dream, 182

Wilde, Oscar, 99

Williams, Raymond, 3, 173, 210

Williams, William Carlos, 66

Wittgenstein, Ludwig, 346

Wolfe, Thomas, 505

Woman, as mediator, 39–44, 62, 66–70

Women: consumerism and, 461–62; creativity and, 368–69; education and, 462–63, 468, 472–73; *fineza* and, 93–94; intellectuals, 48–49, 51–53; literary genres and, 52–55, 59; Modernist view of, 413; performance and, 369–70, 372–77; physical condition, 466–67; in politics, 49; public space and, 53–55, 376–77; subaltern writers, 53–54; subjugation of, 29, 50–51, 370–72; writers, 48–62, 98–108. *See also* Mothers

Writing, 103–5, 148–49, 293; art romance, 98–101; authority and, 478, 489; commerce and, 479; écriture, 259, 260, 278, 285–86, 307(n8), 327; feminist, 100, 102, 106; as hegemonic, 381–82; as self-discovery, 266, 268; women's, 48–62, 98–108. *See also* Language; Literature; Revolutionary art

The Year 2000, 20

Yo el Supremo (I the Supreme), 98, 158–59, 305, 367, 380–91, 393

Young, Arthur, 135

Young Törless, 27

Yrigoyen, Hipólito, 333

Yúdice, George, 113

Zabludosky, Jacobo, 178

Zamora, Martha, 99

Zapata Olivella, Manuel, 172

Zarco, Francisco, 484

Zea, Leopoldo, 452

Zeitschrift fur Sozialforschung, 406

Zola, Emil, 149

Zona sagrada (Holy Place), 161, 162, 268

El zorro de arriba y el zorro de abajo (The Fox Above and the Fox Below), 205, 288

Zurita, Raúl, 223–24

*J*EAN FRANCO is Professor Emerita of English and Comparative Literature at Columbia University. She is the winner of the 1996 PEN award for lifetime contribution to disseminating Latin American literature in English, and has been recognized by both the Chilean and Venezuelan governments with the Gabriela Mistral medal and the Andres Bello medal for advancing literary scholarship on Latin American literature in the United States. Her previous books include *On Edge: The Crisis of Contemporary Latin American Culture, Plotting Women: Gender and Representation in Mexico,* and *A Literary History of Spain and Spanish America.*

MARY LOUISE PRATT is the Olive H. Palmer Chair of the Humanities at Stanford University. She is the author of a number of books, including *Imperial Eyes: Travel Writing and Transculturation.*

KATHLEEN NEWMAN is Associate Professor in the Department of Spanish and Portuguese at the University of Iowa. She is the author of *La violencia del discurso: estado autoritario y la novela politica argentina.*

Library of Congress Cataloging-in-Publication Data
Franco, Jean.
Critical passions : selected essays / Jean Franco ; edited with an introduction
by Mary Louise Pratt and Kathleen Newman.
p. cm.
Includes bibliographical references and index.
ISBN 0-8223-2231-5 (cloth : alk. paper) — ISBN 0-8223-2248-X (pbk. : alk. paper)
1. Latin America—Civilization.   2. Politics and culture—Latin America.   3. Women
and literature—Latin America—History.   4. Popular culture—Latin America.
5. Spanish American literature—History and criticism.   I. Pratt, Mary Louise,
1948-.   II. Newman, Kathleen E. (Kathleen Elizabeth)   III. Title.
F1408.3 .F85   1999
306'.098—dc21   98-20723   CIP

Literary praxis, 457
Literature: art romance, 98–101; boom
    writers, 159, 260–61, 285, 294–97, 505,
    507; destruction and, 379–80; func-
    tions, 148–49; genres, 52–55, 59, 203,
    481; humanistic criticism, 259–60; light
    literature, 97–100, 102, 106; market
    and, 55–56, 202–3, 266–67, 479–80;
    popular culture and, 202–6, 304–5,
    506–8; private and, 56–57; rivalry and,
    353–56; social conduct and, 484; trans-
    national, 506–7; by women, 48–49,
    51–53, 98–101. *See also* Language; Novel;
    Revolutionary art; Writing
Livingstone, Jenny, 113
El llano en llamas (The Burning Plain),
    457
The Location of Culture, 209
Lomas Garza, Carmen, 211
Lope de Vega y Carpio, Félix, 88
López de Gómara, Francisco, 68–69
Lore, 170
Los de abajo (The Underdogs), 455, 459
Love, 106–7. See also *Fineza*
Loyalty, 71–72, 74
Ludmer, Josefina, 511
El lugar sin límites (Hell Has No Limits),
    115
Lugones, Leopoldo, 353–54, 405
Lúmperica (E. Luminata), 105, 119
El luto humano (Human Mourning),
    457–59
Lyotard, Jean-François, 226, 413

Machado, Gerardo, 242
Macherey, Pierre, 329
Macho ritual, 24–30, 34; machismo, 377
Madame Bovary, 471
Madonna, 44–45
The Madwoman in the Attic, 368
Magical realism, 55, 100, 204
Malinche, La (Doña Marina, Malinalli,
    Malintzin), 4, 42, 66–78
Malinchismo, 77–78

Malvido, Adriana, 99, 109
Mann, Thomas, 11
Manrique, Jorge, 342
The Man Who Was Thursday, 356
La manzana de Adán (Adam's Apple), 116
Marcuse, Herbert, 16, 224
Marginalization, 60–62, 102–3, 106–8,
    510; of author, 164; popular culture and,
    214–15, 218; transvestism and, 112, 113,
    116, 119
Market, 55–56, 101–2, 202–3, 213, 266–67,
    479–80
Marquis de Sade, 140
Marriage, 87–90
Martí, José, 196, 253, 450
Martin, Mary-Anne, 45
Martín-Barbero, Jesús, 213, 512
Martín Fierro, 337
Martínez, Tomás Eloy, 505
Martínez de Hoz, José A., 22
Martini, J. C., 508
Martorell, Antonio, 211
Martyrdom, 401–2
Marvelous Possessions, 66
Marx, Karl, 170, 221, 226
Marxism, 241, 298
Masculinity, 26–27, 377
Masculino/Femenino (Masculine/Femi-
    nine), 102, 118
Massera, Emilio, 24
Mastery, 328–29
Mastretta, Angeles, 97–101
El matadero (The Slaughterhouse), 138,
    405, 484
Matisse, Henri, 181
Mattelart, Armand, 174–75
Mattelart, Michèle, 170, 178
Mauriac, François, 267
Mauthner, Fritz, 346–56
McDonald, Dwight, 170
McLuhan, Marshall, 162
Media, 2, 148, 171, 353, 476–77; cultural
    imperialism and, 174–76; literature
    and, 202–6, 304–5; modernization and,